The Myth of the 'Islamic' headscarf

By Omar Hussein Ibrahim

The Myth of the ‘Islamic’ headscarf

ISBN: 978-0-244-51768-7

Dedicated to the memory of Sir Zaki Badawi,
former senior imam at the Central London Mosque,
Regent's Park and dean of the Muslim College.

Preface

A book containing the fullest coverage as to why Islam does ***not*** oblige Muslim women to cover their hair.

Compiled by Omar Hussein Ibrahim, based in London, using the best academic material and press commentary available today.

Contents

Page

Chapter 1

Treat your women well and be kind to them: Prophet Mohammad 1
Muslim women advised to abandon hijab to avoid attack 2
Will dropping the hijab make women safer? 3
The headscarf martyr 4
A target for hate 6
The Freedom to Go Topless, by Amir Taheri 8
This is not Islam, by Amir Taheri 10
Will Chirac fight fascism? by Amir Taheri 12
Koranic Law Does not Impose the Headscarf, by Khaled Fouad Allam 14
Should Muslims cast aside hijabs and beards? 16

Chapter 2

The Muslim Magazine, *Q-News*, headscarf debate 1997 – 1998 17
Branson firm 'sacked Muslim in row over beard' 25
Muhammad Asad's '*The Message of* THE QURAN' detailing verses 30
and 31 of Surah 24, The Light (An-Nur) 28
Quranic extracts from Surah 53, The Confederates (Al-Ahzab)
- from Muhammad Asad's '*The Message of* THE QURAN' 38
Karen Armstrong in her acclaimed biography of the Prophet,
- *Muhammad* - details the fact that it was only Muhammad's wives
that were to be secluded 40
The Concise Encyclopedia of Islam: definition of the Veil 43
Q-News, February 2003 - Zaki Badawi: Pioneer of a British Islam 44

Chapter 3

The miracle that was Zaki Badawi: 1922 – 2006 49

Chapter 4

Muslim women's struggle to wear what they like 59
French school bars girls for wearing headscarves 60
Muslim girls face scarf ban at French schools 62
Belgium next in line as Europe's veil ban spreads 63
Why should we defend the veil? 65
France votes for hijab ban 66
Cleared in minutes 67
Jurors clear teacher over Muslim girl's assault claim 68
The Concise Encyclopedia of Islam: definition of Fundamentalism 69
Muslim dress ban thwarts extremists 72
Is it a human right to make girls wear Islamic dress? 74
Revealed: radicals who backed girl in dress fight 75
As a Muslim, I say no to the cover-up 77
Lifting the veil on women's suffering 79
School bans all skirts 80
Trousers only ...school bans skirts after girls refuse to cover up 81
Headmaster's ban on bellies and bottoms 82
Why it's right to ban the hijab in schools 84
Muslim pupils bow to scarf ban 85
First girls expelled over headscarf ban 86
Schoolgirl banned from wearing Muslim dress wins appeal 87
Muslim girl had been denied right to manifest religion 88
The Queen on the application of
Shabina Begum v. Headteacher and Governors of Denbigh High School.
Court of Appeal judgment 2nd March 2005 90
Religion and school rules must both be respected 106
Revealed: the brutal truth that hides inside the burqa 107
House of Lords overturn Court of Appeal decision:
House of Lords Regina (Shabina Begum) v Denbigh High School, March 2006 110

Chapter 5

The Legacy of Mrs Ataturk 113
European Court of Human Rights judgements regarding the headscarf:
29th June 2004 and 10th November 2005 116
Arab women 125

Chapter 6

Muslims are right about Britain 131
Our 'decadent' society 133
Yes we DO need drastic measures -
because Labour has engineered a collapse in morality 133

Chapter 7

Octoberfest 2006

Take off the veil, says Straw, to immediate anger from Muslims 137
One glance took away my freedom 139
I would prefer women not to wear the veil at all, says Straw 140
Why Muslim women should thank Straw 142
We don't yet live in an Islamic republic so I will say it - I find the veil offensive 144
Niqab nonsense 145
BAN IT! 146
Islamic leaders in Sarajevo, Bosnia in 1947 promote abandonment of the veil 148

Chapter 8

The Christian Veiling, by Leland M. Haines 149
The Biblical Practice of Headcovering, by Dr. Brian Allison 162
The Concise Encyclopedia of Islam: definition of Christianity 171
The Concise Encyclopedia of Islam: definition of Jesus 172

Chapter 9

Perverse interpretations

The Concise Encyclopedia of Islam: definition of Abortion 175
The Association of Lawyers for the Defence of the Unborn 176
Female circumcision 179
Minister warns over in-breeding in Asians 181
Storm over Muslim cousin marriages 182
It is one of the great taboos of multi-cultural Britain - and one of the most heart-breaking:
children born with cruel genetic defects because their parents are cousins 185
Muslim pupils kept out of music lessons 189

Chapter 10

Hijabi robots

The Quran does not require the headscarf 190
The so-called 'Islamic' headscarf helps destroy Muslim hopes 193
Islamic State and the headscarf 195
The fanatics have even infected Wales 196
Hijabi clones 197
Children forced to wear headscarf in Iran 198

Chapter 11

Saudi Madness

From Chapter 15 'Women' in Ed Husain's book 'The House of Islam - A Global History' 200

Chapter 12

Zaki Badawi

The Reformers of Egypt, - A Critique of Al-Afghani, 'Adbuh and Ridha 201
Preface 202
Introduction 204
Chapter 1 - Jamal Al-Din Al-Afghani 209
Chapter 2 - Muhammad 'Abduh 219
Chapter 3 - Muhammad Rashid Ridha 255

Chapter 1

We begin by looking at an extract from Jan Goodwin's book *Price of Honour* first published in 1994 by Little, Brown and then published by Warner Books in 1995. *Price Of Honour* sub-titled 'Muslim Women Lift the Veil of Silence on the Islamic World' is a fascinating work which makes easy, uncomplicated and precise reading.

The eminent Islamic scholar, the late Dr. Zaki Badawi, former director of the Central London Mosque in Regent's Park and later Principal of the Muslim College in London gives his opinion regarding the issue of the veil in Islam, in Chapter 2 of *Price Of Honour*, as follows:

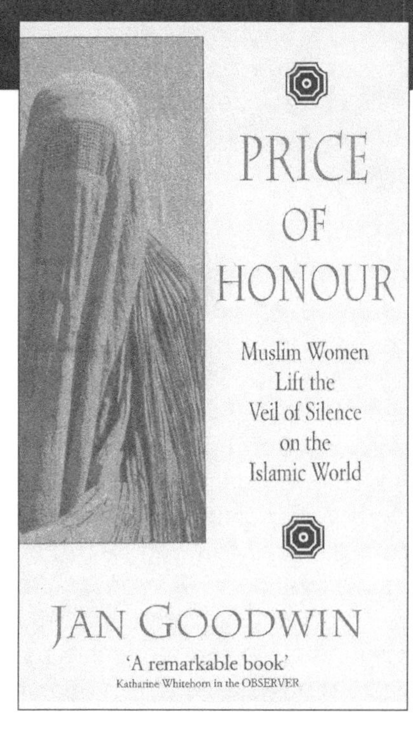

Muslims, the first Feminists

***Treat your women well, and be kind to them.* Prophet Mohammad**

DESPITE ITS RAPID SPREAD, Islam is not a religion for those who are casual about such things; adhering to its five pillars takes effort and discipline. One must rise before dawn to observe the first of five ritual prayers required daily, none of which can take place without first ritually cleansing oneself. Sleep, work, and recreational activities take second place to prayer. Fasting for the month of Ramadan, undertaking the Hajj pilgrimage to Mecca at least once in a lifetime, paying Zakat tax for relief of the Muslim poor, in addition to accepting Islam's creed, which begins, "There is no God but Allah, and Mohammad is his messenger," require a serious and energetic commitment. And the vast majority of Muslims worldwide do observe those tenets.

[and later]:

So it is ironic that the most outstanding contradiction regarding the inequities suffered by Muslim women is that Mohammad, the founder of Islam, was among the world's greatest reformers on behalf of women. He abolished such sex-discriminating practices as female infanticide, slavery and levirate (marriage between a man and his brother's widow), while introducing concepts guaranteeing women the right to inherit and bequeath property, and the right to exercise full possession and control over their own wealth. Islam, in fact, may be the only religion that formally specified women's rights and sought ways to protect them. Today's Islamic spokesmen frequently extol the Prophet's revolutionary innovations, but usually fail to note that they are rarely honored in reality. They fail to observe, for example, that it is not the Koran that's compels Islamic women to be enshrouded from head to toe or confined to their home while men feel free to pester women who do venture out. Mohammad's directives on this issue were addressed to both sexes and could not be clearer:

**Say to the believing men that they should
Lower their gaze and guard their modesty...
And say to believing women that they should
Lower their gaze and guard heir modesty...**

Said Islamic scholar Dr. Zaki Badawi, "This section of the Koran also states that women should not show 'their adornment except what normally appears.' This means it is left to custom. There has never been an Islamic obligation for women to cover at any time. In fact, veiling the face is an innovation that has no foundation whatsoever in Islam. Even in Saudi Arabia the covering of women from head to toe is recent; it was not required before the discovery of oil.

"The *hijab* veil (which covers all of a Muslim woman's hair) is also not obligatory. And in Europe, for example, it should be prohibited because it creates a lot of problems for women. If women are attacked because they are wearing the hijab, as happened in France not so long ago, then they should not wear it. I have spoken out on this issue on a number of occasions, and since I began doing so, a lot of Muslim women in Europe have started leaving off the head covering."

The veil originated as a Persian elitist fashion to distinguish aristocracy from the common masses, and has moved in and out of fashion ever since. Early Islamic scholars, for example, tried to enforce veiling by declaring "all of women is pudendal." Islamic studies specialist Nancy Dupree, of Duke University, explained its more recent use. "At the time of national movements against colonial powers, it became a symbol of resistance against alien politics that were generally viewed as a move to encourage female over permissiveness. After independence was won and governments embarked on their indigenous Western–oriented paths, the veil was discredited as an emblem of enforced orthodoxy and suffocating social control, an archaic social institution similar to slavery."

Like Pakistan's first female Prime Minister, Benazir Bhutto, many Muslim women who grew up in the less-restrictive era wore Western dress. Bhutto took to Islamizing her wardrobe only when she began her election campaign. Throughout her time in office she has had great difficulty keeping her head modestly covered simply because she is unused to wearing the *chador* intended for that purpose, and it keeps sliding off.

As Islamic radicalism rose at the beginning of the last decade, the pendulum for Muslim women swung the other way again. Once more they were to be hidden behind veils, a development that now seemed to legitimize and institutionalize inequality for women. In fact, calls by Islamic organizations in recent years for Muslim women to veil themselves have been followed shortly thereafter by demands that women stop working, stay home, limit their educations, and resign positions of authority. Insists Dr Badawi, however, "This is not required by Islam. According to our religion, women have a perfect right to take part in society."

[And later on page 293 of *Price of Honour*]:

Palestinian women have long participated in their nationalist movement, and many removed their hijabs for he first time in demonstrations against the creation of Israel in 1948. Despite this, in the first year of the Intifada, Hamas zealots, many mere teenage boys, forced women in Gaza, where the extremists then had more control, to wear the Islamic head covering again. Having achieved that goal, Hamas then insisted that women wear the fill length Islamic coat or *abaya*, and more recently women have been bullied into wearing face veils and gloves. In Gaza today it is rare to find a woman who does not dress like her counterpart in Saudi Arabia. In East Jerusalem and the West Bank, an estimated 50 percent of women are now veiled, and the number is steadily growing even in towns like Ramallah. *(Copyright © Jan Goodwin 1994).*

Muslim women advised to abandon hijab to avoid attack

The Guardian, August 4th 2005

6 The Guardian Thursday August 4 2005

Call to faith Muslim women advised to abandon hijab to avoid attack

Vikram Dodd

A leading British Islamic scholar has advised Muslim women not to wear the traditional hijab head scarf to protect themselves from attack after the July 7 bombings.

Professor Zaki Badawi, head of the Muslim College in London and chairman of the Council of Mosques and Imams, made his call amid fears that wearing the hijab would make women more vulnerable to attack or abuse.

On Tuesday, the Metropolitan police released figures showing a 600% rise in faith-hate crimes in London directed at Muslims since the bombings.

In his fatwa, or religious ruling, Professor Badawi wrote: "In the present tense situation, with the rise of attacks on Muslims, we advise Muslim women who fear being attacked physically or verbally to remove their hijab so as not to be identified by those who are hostile to Muslims.

"A woman wearing the hijab in the present circumstances could suffer aggression from irresponsible elements. Therefore, she ought not to wear it. Dress is meant to protect from harm not to invite it."

According to some with knowledge of police intelligence, the backlash since the bombings has not led to a noticeable rise in attacks on Muslim women wearing the hijab.

But since the attacks on the US on September 11 2001 — and particularly since the London bombings — Muslims have reported greater fear of Islamophobic attacks.

Dr Badawi's ruling provoked a mixed reaction among British Islamic groups.

Inayat Bunglawala, of the Muslim Council of Britain, said: "It is not Muslim women who need to change their behaviour, it is those thugs and the far right who may target them who need to change."

Massoud Shadjareh, of the Islamic Human Rights Commission, said: "Muslim women are being attacked without wearing the hijab, non-Muslim Asians are being attacked. We need to address the issue of Islamophobia."

A Guardian poll last week found that one in five Muslims said they or a family member had suffered hostility or abuse since July 7.

Ameem Bint Amir, of Hayes, Middlesex, sings a prayer for peace in memory of the victims of the July 7 bombings at King's Cross last month Photograph: Dan Chung

A leading British Islamic scholar has advised Muslim women not to wear the traditional hijab head scarf to protect themselves from attack after the July 7 bombings.

Professor Zaki Badawi head of the Muslim College in London and chairman of the Council of Mosques and Imams, made his call amid fears that wearing the hijab would make women more vulnerable to attack or abuse.

On Tuesday, the Metropolitan Police released figures showing a 600% rise in faith-hate crimes in London directed at Muslims since the bombings.

In his fatwa, or religious ruling, Professor Badawi wrote: "In the present tense situation, with the rise of attacks on Muslims, we advise Muslim women who fear being attacked physically or verbally to remove their hijab so as not to be identified by those who are hostile to Muslims. A woman wearing the hijab in the present circumstances could suffer aggression from irresponsible elements. Therefore, she ought not to wear it. Dress is meant to protect from harm not to invite it."

According to some with knowledge of police intelligence, the backlash since the bombings has not led to a noticeable rise in attacks on Muslim women wearing the hijab.

But since the attacks on the US on September 11 2001 – and particularly since the London bombings – Muslims have reported greater fear of Islamophobic attacks.

Dr Badawi's ruling provoking a mixed reaction among British Islamic groups.

Inayat Bunglawala, of the Muslim Council of Britain, said: "It is not Muslim women who need to change their behaviour, it is those thugs and the far right who may target them who need to change."

Massoud Shadjarah, of the Islamic Human Rights Commission, said: "Muslim women are being attacked without wearing the hijab, non-Muslim Asians are being attacked. We need to address the issue of Islamophobia."

A Guardian poll last week found that one in five Muslims said they or a family member had suffered hostility or abuse since July 7.

From The Times newspaper website:

Will dropping the hijab make women safer?

TIMESONLINE, August 04, 2005

Sheikh Dr Zaki Badawi, one of the most senior Muslims in Britain, has advised women to stop wearing the hijab because of an increase in hate attacks since the July 7 London bombings. Other leaders urged women not to surrender to intimidation by thugs. Send us your view using the form below:

Dr Badawi has made a practical suggestion. He is not asking anyone to give up their faith. After all, a Muslim who does not wear a hijab is no less a Muslim. ***Vinay Mehra, Purley, Surrey.***

People who dress in an unusual manner are perceived as being "different" and tend to be trusted less. None of the dress codes for the worlds religions were handed down on clay tablets - the wearing of turbans, skullcaps, hijabs, etc, is due to dress code guidelines introduced by religious leaders. It might be better if religious people just wore something less conspicuous in the future, like a small badge. ***Tony Lawrence, Bournemouth.***

I lived the first 25 years of my life in India - the country with the second highest Muslim population in the world, after Indonesia. Yet I had never heard of the hijab, and Muslim women there never wore one. The garment is purely an Arab interpretation of the Koran, and women of Pakistani or Bangladeshi origin have never traditionally worn it. It is a symbol of man's domination over women and progressive British Muslim women should reject it as something alien to their culture. ***Maran Vish, London.***

The fact is Dr Zaki Badawi, in principle, was against the wearing of the headscarf, but he knew many of his less enlightened female constituents would have trouble coming to terms with his view and so he tried to coax them, at times through the back door, into not wearing it. He allowed his students and staff at the Muslim College to wear the garment if they wanted to. Badawi was the consummate PR man. His fears for the safety of hijabi women were well illustrated by the brutal murder of an Egyptian woman in Germany in 2009, described in the article overleaf.

The headscarf martyr: murder in German court sparks Egyptian fury at west's 'Islamophobia'

Woman was stabbed 18 times during hijab trial

Outrage at lack of media coverage fuels protests

Kate Connolly, Berlin
Jack Shenker, Cairo

The Guardian, 8th July 2009.

It was while Marwa el-Sherbini was in the dock recalling how the accused had insulted her for wearing the hijab after she asked him to let her son sit on a swing last summer, that the very same man strode across the Dresden courtroom and plunged a knife into her 18 times.

Her three-year-old son Mustafa was forced to watch as his mother slumped to the courtroom floor.

Even her husband Elvi Ali Okaz could do nothing as the 28-year-old Russian stock controller who was being sued for insult and abuse took the life of his pregnant wife. As Okaz ran to save her, he too was brought down, shot by a police officer who mistook him for the attacker. He is now in intensive care in a Dresden hospital.

While the horrific incident that took place a week ago today has attracted little publicity in Europe, and in Germany has focused more on issues of court security than the racist motivation behind the attack, 2,000 miles away in her native Egypt, the 32-year-old pharmacist has been named the "headscarf martyr".

She has become a national symbol of persecution for a growing number of demonstrators, who have taken to the streets in protest at the perceived growth in Islamophobia in the west. Sherbini's funeral took place in her native Alexandria on Monday in the presence of thousands of mourners and leading government figures. There are plans to name a street after her.

Sherbini, a former national handball champion, and Okaz, a genetic engineer who was just about to submit his PhD, had reportedly lived in Germany since 2003, and were believed to be planning to return to Egypt at the end of the year. They were expecting a second child in January.

Unemployed Alex W. from Perm in Russia was found guilty last November of insulting and abusing Sherbini, screaming "terrorist" and "Islamist whore" at her, during the Dresden park encounter. He was fined €780 but had appealed the verdict, which is why he and Sherbini appeared face to face in court again.

Even though he had made his anti-Muslim sentiments clear, there was no heightened security and questions remain as to why he was allowed to bring a knife into the courtroom.

Angry mourners at the funeral in Alexandria accused Germany of racism, shouting slogans such as "Germans are the enemies of God" and Egypt's head mufti Muhammad Sayyid Tantawy called on the German judiciary to severely punish AlexW.

"Anger is high", said Joseph Mayton, editor of the English-language news website Bikya Masr. "Not since Egypt won the African [football] Cup have Egyptians come together under a common banner."

In Germany the government of Angela Merkel has been sharply criticised for its sluggish response to the country's first murderous anti-Islamic attack. The general secretaries of both the Central Council of Jews and the Central Council of Muslims, Stephen Kramer and Aiman Mazyek, who on Monday made a joint visit to the bedside of Sherbini's husband, spoke of the "inexplicably sparse" reactions from both media and politicians.

They said that although there was no question that the attack was racially motivated, the debate in Germany had concentrated more on the issue of the lack of courtroom security. "I think the facts speak for themselves," Kramer said.

The government's vice spokesman Thomas Steg rebuffed the criticism, saying not enough was yet known about the details of the incident.

"In this concrete case we've held back from making a statement because the circumstances are not sufficiently clear enough to allow a broad political response," he said, adding: "Should it be the case that this was anti-foreigner [and] racially motivated [the government] would condemn it in the strongest possible terms".

As hundreds of Arab and Muslim protesters demonstrated in Germany, and observers drew comparisons with the Danish cartoon row, Egyptian government representatives in Berlin said it was important to keep the incident in perspective.

"It was a criminal incident, and doesn't mean that a popular persecution of Muslims is taking place," Magdi el-Sayed, the spokesman for the Egyptian embassy in Berlin said.

But because it occurred just days after Nicolas Sarkozy gave a major policy speech denouncing the burka, many Egyptians believe the death of Sherbini is part of a broader trend of European intolerance towards Muslims.

The Guardian | Wednesday 8 July 2009

International

Comment is free...
Do you have to wear orange robes to be a real Buddhist? guardian.co.uk/commentisfree

Racism row

The headscarf martyr: murder in German court sparks Egyptian fury at west's 'Islamophobia'

Woman was stabbed 18 times during hijab trial

Outrage at lack of media coverage fuels protests

Kate Connolly Berlin
Jack Shenker Cairo

The murder of Marwa el-Sherbini, whose funeral is pictured below, and the shooting of her husband Elvi Ali Okaz made them a symbol of Islamophobia Photograph: EPA

It was while Marwa el-Sherbini was in the dock recalling how the accused had insulted her for wearing the hijab after she asked him to let her son sit on a swing last summer, that the very same man strode across the Dresden courtroom and plunged a knife into her 18 times.

Her three-year-old son Mustafa was forced to watch as his mother slumped to the courtroom floor.

Even her husband Elvi Ali Okaz could do nothing as the 28-year-old Russian stock controller who was being sued for insult and abuse took the life of his pregnant wife. As Okaz ran to save her, he too was brought down, shot by a police officer who mistook him for the attacker. He is now in intensive care in a Dresden hospital.

While the horrific incident that took place a week ago today has attracted little publicity in Europe, and in Germany has focused more on issues of court security than the racist motivation behind the attack, 2,000 miles away in her native Egypt, the 32-year-old pharmacist has been named the "headscarf martyr".

She has become a national symbol of persecution for a growing number of demonstrators, who have taken to the streets in protest at the perceived growth in Islamophobia in the west. Sherbini's funeral took place in her native Alexandria on Monday in the presence of thousands of mourners and leading government figures. There are plans to name a street after her.

Sherbini, a former national handball champion, and Okaz, a genetic engineer who was just about to submit his PhD, had reportedly lived in Germany since 2003, and were believed to be planning to return to Egypt at the end of the year. They were expecting a second child in January.

Unemployed Alex W. from Perm in Russia was found guilty last November of insulting and abusing Sherbini, screaming "terrorist" and "Islamist whore" at her, during the Dresden park encounter. He was fined €780 but had appealed the verdict, which is why he and Sherbini appeared face to face in court again.

Even though he had made his anti-Muslim sentiments clear, there was no heightened security and questions remain as to why he was allowed to bring a knife into the courtroom.

Angry mourners at the funeral in Alexandria accused Germany of racism, shouting slogans such as "Germans are the enemies of God" and Egypt's head mufti Muhammad Sayyid Tantawy called on the German judiciary to severely punish Alex W.

"Anger is high", said Joseph Mayton, editor of the English-language news website Bikya Masr. "Not since Egypt won the African [football] Cup have Egyptians come together under a common banner."

In Germany the government of Angela Merkel has been sharply criticised for its sluggish response to the country's first murderous anti-Islamic attack. The general secretaries of both the Central Council

'The tragedy is real, but her death has been recruited to channel resentment of the west'
The Arabist blog

of Jews and the Central Council of Muslims, Stephen Kramer and Aiman Mazyek, who on Monday made a joint visit to the bedside of Sherbini's husband, spoke of the "inexplicably sparse" reactions from both media and politicians.

They said that although there was no question that the attack was racially motivated, the debate in Germany had concentrated more on the issue of the lack of courtroom security. "I think the facts speak for themselves," Kramer said.

The government's vice spokesman Thomas Steg rebuffed the criticism, saying not enough was yet known about the details of the incident.

"In this concrete case we've held back from making a statement because the circumstances are not sufficiently clear enough to allow a broad political response," he said, adding: "Should it be the case that this was anti-foreigner [and] racially motivated [the government] would condemn it in the strongest possible terms".

As hundreds of Arab and Muslim protesters demonstrated in Germany, and observers drew comparisons with the Danish cartoon row, Egyptian government representatives in Berlin said it was important to keep the incident in perspective.

"It was a criminal incident, and doesn't mean that a popular persecution of Muslims is taking place," Magdi el-Sayed, the spokesman for the Egyptian embassy in Berlin said.

But because it occurred just days after Nicolas Sarkozy gave a major policy speech denouncing the burka, many Egyptians believe the death of Sherbini is part of a broader trend of European intolerance towards Muslims.

The German embassy in Cairo has sought to calm the situation, organising a visit of condolence by the ambassador to the victim's family and issuing a statement insisting that the attack did not reflect general German sentiment towards Egyptians.

There have been repeated calls by protesters for the German embassy to be picketed. The Egyptian pharmacists' syndicate said it is considering a week-long boycott of German medicines.

The victim's brother, Tarek el-Sherbini, labelled Germany as a "cold" country when interviewed by a popular talk show host. Media pundits such as Abdel Azeem Hamad, editor of the daily al-Shorouk newspaper, have attributed the western media's disinterest in the story to racism, arguing that if Sherbini had been Jewish the incident would have received much greater attention.

Politicians in Egypt have been scrambling to ride the groundswell of popular feeling. But some commentators have criticised reaction to the murder as a convenient distraction for the unpopular regime of President Hosni Mubarak, which is currently being challenged by a nationwide series of strikes and sit-ins.

"The tragedy of Marwa el-Sherbini is real, as is anti-Arab racism in Europe and elsewhere, but ... her death has been recruited to channel resentment of the west, Danish-cartoon style," the popular blogger The Arabist said.

The German embassy in Cairo has sought to calm the situation, organising a visit of condolence by the ambassador to the victim's family and issuing a statement insisting that the attack did not reflect general German sentiment towards Egyptians.

There have been repeated calls by protesters for the German embassy to be picketed. The Egyptian pharmacists' syndicate said it is considering a week-long boycott of German medicines.

The victim's brother, Tarek el-Sherbini, labelled Germany as a "cold" country when interviewed by a popular talk show host. Media pundits such as Abdel Azeem Hamad, editor of the daily al-Shorouk newspaper, have attributed the western media's disinterest in the story to racism, arguing that if Sherbini had been Jewish the incident would have received much greater attention.

Politicians in Egypt have been scrambling to ride the groundswell of popular feeling. But some commentators have criticised reaction to the murder as a convenient distraction for the unpopular regime of President Hosni Mubarak, which is currently being challenged by a nationwide series of strikes and sit-ins.

"The tragedy of Marwa el-Sherbini is real, as is anti-Arab racism in Europe and elsewhere, but... her death has been recruited to channel resentment of the west, Danish-cartoon style," the popular blogger The Arabist said.

A target for hate

Tarek Fatah, National Post (Toronto, Canada).

Published Wednesday, 8th July 2009

Marwa Sherbini, a 32-year-old Egyptian mother, was murdered in a German courtroom in Dresden this week. She was killed as she waited to give evidence against a German man of Russian descent who had been convicted for calling her a "terrorist" because she wore the hijab (a Muslim headscarf concealing the head and neck).

Sherbini, who was three months pregnant with her second child, was stabbed 18 times by a man identified only as Axel W. The woman's husband, Elvi Ali Okaz, was also critically injured as he tried to protect her.

Last year, when Axel W. claimed Sherbini was a "terrorist," he was fined 780 [euros]. It was during the appeal proceeding, on July 1, that Axel W. and Sherbini found themselves again in the same room. Before she could give evidence, the man lunged at her and stabbed her to death.

The alleged murderer, if convicted, should spend the rest of his life behind bars. The murder of Marwa Sherbini is a blot on the face of Germany, but it should also be cause for concern for Muslims everywhere in the West.

Two years ago, when the hijab controversy erupted in Quebec, I had warned that sooner or later there was bound to be a backlash against Muslims if Islamists continued to push the hijab and the niqab (which covers the entire body, except the eyes) as political symbols of Islamism, and thereby thumb their noses at non-Muslim North American and European society. However, I could never have imagined that the backlash would take such a bloody turn as this.

The question we Muslims have to ask is this: what do we gain by using our daughters, sisters and wives to carry the false burden of the hijab as if it were the flag of Islam?

While I am totally opposed to the ban on the Hijab in France and Turkey, and would defend the right of a Muslim woman to wear one, I am also unwilling to give up my right to expose the political symbolism that hides behind the banner of religiosity.

Most Muslims know that the Koran does not ask Muslim women explicitly to cover their heads or their faces as a fundamental practice of Islam. Yet Islamists inspired by Iran and Saudi Arabia continue to push for this attire.

What are we gaining by thumbing our noses at the host societies of the West that have allowed us to be fellow citizens? Why have we told our young women that not wearing such garments is somehow tantamount to nakedness?

On one hand, we have the rise of the racist right in Europe. On the other, we have a gleeful Islamist left, for whom this murder will prove to be manna from heaven. Sherbini's murder will be portrayed as the ultimate symbol of the West's "War against Islam," and fuel the propaganda that Muslims are victims. Never mind the murder of Neda Agha-Soltan in Tehran, killed by fellow Muslims. Already, there are protests in Egypt asking for revenge.

I have been to Europe six times in the last year and I can see the rise of racism against visible Muslims that parallels a suicidal effort by jihadis to flaunt their contempt for Western civilization and its values. Things are getting worse because two other segments of society that can help cool the situation are either silent or paralyzed by political correctness.

The first is secular and liberal Muslims, who form the vast majority of Europe's Islamic community. They need to organize and confront the jihadis. Not for the sake of government grants and NGO funding, but for the sake of our future as equal citizens in the Western world.

The other group is the European and North American left, wiiich has become a collective apologist for all things Islamist. This group is so consumed by its knee-jerk anti-Americanism that it finds parallels between Mahmoud Ahmadinejad and Osama bin Laden on one hand and Che Guevara and Simon Bolivar on the other. They are so obsessed by their hatred of Washington that they have missed the news; it is their man in the White House, not Dubya.

Now is the time for these two groups to stand up and be counted. The racists and the Islamists have to be challenged. Otherwise, more Marwa Sherbinis and Neda Agha-Soltans will die.

-Tarek Fatah is author of Chasing a Mirage: The Tragic Illusion of an Islamic State. Currently, he is working on his second book on the roots of Jewish-Muslim friction, to be published by McClelland & Stewart in the fall of 2010. Fatah is also co-host of Strong Opinions, an afternoon talk show on CFRB 1010 in Toronto.

canada.com Network | nationalpost.com | financialpost.com | Today's Paper & Archive | Delivery | Digital Paper

NATIONAL POST

A target for hate

Tarek Fatah, National Post
Published: Wednesday, July 08, 2009

Cris Bouroncle, AFP, Getty Images

The father of Marwa Sherbini, an Egyptian woman stabbed to death in a courtroom in Dresden, Germany, on July 1, prays next to her casket in the Ibrahim Mosque in Alexandria on Monday.

Marwa Sherbini, a 32-year-old Egyptian mother, was murdered in a German courtroom in Dresden this week. She was killed as she waited to give evidence against a German man of Russian descent who had been convicted for calling her a "terrorist" because she wore the hijab (a Muslim headscarf concealing the head and neck).

Sherbini, who was three months pregnant with her second child, was stabbed 18 times by a man identified only as Axel W. The woman's husband, Elwi Ali Okaz, was also critically injured as he tried to protect her.

Last year, when Axel W. claimed Sherbini was a "terrorist," he was fined 750. It was during the appeal proceeding, on July 1, that Axel W. and Sherbini found themselves again in the same room. Before she could give evidence, the man lunged at her and stabbed her to death.

The alleged murderer, if convicted, should spend the rest of his life behind bars. The murder of Marwa Sherbini is a blot on the face of Germany, but it should also be cause for concern for Muslims everywhere in the West.

Two years ago, when the hijab controversy erupted in Quebec, I had warned that sooner or later there was bound to be a backlash against Muslims if Islamists continued to push the hijab and the niqab (which covers the entire body, except the eyes) as political symbols of Islamism, and thereby thumb their noses at non-Muslim North American and European society. However, I could never have imagined that the backlash would take such a bloody turn as this.

The question we Muslims have to ask is this: What do we gain by using our daughters, sisters and wives to carry the false burden of the hijab as if it were the flag of Islam?

While I am totally opposed to the ban on the Hijab in France and Turkey, and would defend the right of a Muslim woman to wear one, I am also unwilling to give up my right to expose the political symbolism that hides behind the banner of religiosity.

Most Muslims know that the Koran does not ask Muslim women explicitly to cover their heads or their faces as a fundamental practice of Islam. Yet Islamists inspired by Iran and Saudi Arabia continue to push for this attire.

What are we gaining by thumbing our noses at the host societies of the West that have allowed us to be fellow citizens? Why have we told our young women that not wearing such garments is somehow tantamount to nakedness?

On one hand, we have the rise of the racist right in Europe. On the other, we have a gleeful Islamist left, for whom this murder will prove to be manna from heaven. Sherbini's murder will be portrayed as the ultimate symbol of the West's "war against Islam," and fuel the propaganda that Muslims are victims. Never mind the murder of Neda Agha-Soltan in Tehran, killed by fellow Muslims. Already, there are protests in Egypt asking for revenge.

I have been to Europe six times in the last year and I can see the rise of racism against visible Muslims that parallels a suicidal effort by jihadis to flaunt their contempt for Western civilization and its values. Things are getting worse because two other segments of society that can help cool the situation are either silent or paralyzed by political correctness.

The first is secular and liberal Muslims, who form the vast majority of Europe's Islamic community. They need to organize and confront the jihadis. Not for the sake of government grants and NGO funding, but for the sake of our future as equal citizens in the Western world.

The other group is the European and North American left, which has become a collective apologist for all things Islamist. This group is so consumed by its knee-jerk anti-Americanism that it finds parallels between Mahmoud Ahmadinejad and Osama bin Laden on one hand and Che Guevara and Simon Bolivar on the other. They are so obsessed by their hatred of Washington that they have missed the news; it is their man in the White House, not Dubya.

Now is the time for these two groups to stand up and be counted. The racists and the Islamists have to be challenged. Otherwise, more Marwa Sherbinis and Neda Agha-Soltans will die.

-Tarek Fatah is author of Chasing a Mirage: The Tragic Illusion of an Islamic State. Currently, he is working on his second book on the roots of Jewish-Muslim friction, to be published by McClelland & Stewart in the fall of 2010. Fatah is also co-host of Strong Opinions, an afternoon talk show on CFRB 1010 in Toronto.

The Freedom to Go Topless

by Amir Taheri.
Wall Street Journal
December 6, 2002

"The girls are ecstatic and the teachers feel liberated," says Zohreh Shamloo, headmistress in a south Tehran school. "It is as if the sun is shining again." Ms. Shamloo's school is one of 12 in the Iranian capital where girls, aged between six and 17, and the all-female staff, have been allowed to remove the officially imposed headgear (hijab) while inside the building.

The permission to cast off the hijab inside the schools is part of an experiment launched by the education ministry in September. To make sure that the girls and their teachers are not exposed to "stolen gazes" from men, six-foot high plastic extensions have been added to the walls of the buildings of the schools concerned.

Inside, the girls are also allowed to cast off the long black overcoats that all females aged six or above must wear in the Islamic Republic. "With the new walls the school looks like a prison," comments Ms. Shamloo. "But inside it we feel free!"

The experiment, to be reviewed in three months, was approved after a nationwide study showed that the imposition of hijab on young girls caused "serious depression and, in some cases, suicide." But it has drawn the wrath of Khomeinists.

The newspaper Jumhuri Islami (Islamic Republic), owned by Iran's "Supreme Guide" Ali Khamenehi, has lashed out against "this slippery slope towards scandal." "Casting off the hijab encourages the culture of nudity and weakens the sacred values of Islam," the paper warned on Nov. 20. Former President Hashemi Rafsanjani has gone even further.

"A strand of woman's hair emerging from under the hijab is a dagger drawn towards the heart of Islam," he told a recent Friday prayer gathering in Tehran.

Perhaps it is worth recalling at this point that radical Islam's obsession with women's hair is a new phenomenon. Mussa Sadr, an Iranian mullah who won the leadership of the Shiite community in Lebanon, invented this form of hijab in the early 1970s. The first neo-hijabs appeared in Iran in 1977 as a symbol of Islamist opposition to the Shah.

By 1979 when the mullahs seized power the number of women wearing it had multiplied by the thousands, recalling sequences from Hitchcock's thriller "The Birds."

In 1981, Abol-Hassan Bani-Sadr, the first president of the Islamic Republic, announced that scientific research had shown that women's hair emitted rays that drove men insane. To protect the public, the new regime passed special legislation in 1982 making the new form of hijab mandatory for all females aged above six, regardless of religious faith. Violating the hijab code is punishable by 100 lashes of the cane and six months imprisonment.

So by the mid-1980s a form of hijab never seen in Islam before the 1970s had become standard headgear for millions of Muslim women all over the world, including Europe and North America. Many younger Muslim women, especially Western converts, were duped into believing that the neo-hijab was an essential part of the Islamic faith.

Muslim women, like women in all societies, had covered their head with a variety of gears over the centuries. These had such names as rusari, ruband, chaqchur, maqne'a, and picheh among others. All had tribal, ethnic and generally folkloric origins and were never specifically associated with religion. In Senegal, Muslim women wore a colorful headgear but went topless.

Muslim women anywhere in the world could easily check the fraudulent nature of the neo-Islamist hijab by leafing through their own family albums. They will not find the picture of a single female ancestor of theirs who wore the cursed headgear now imposed upon them as an absolute "must" of Islam.

This fake Islamic hijab is thus nothing but a political prop, a weapon of visual terrorism. It is the symbol of a totalitarian ideology inspired more by Nazism and Communism than by Islam.

The garb, moreover, is designed to promote gender Apartheid. It covers the woman's ears so that she does not hear things properly. Styled like a hood, it prevents the woman from having full vision of her surroundings.

But the harm that Islamism is doing to Muslim women is not limited to the evil headgear. In every Muslim country the number of women out of work is at least twice that of men. Women's wages are less than a quarter of what men get.

The Pakistani fundamentalist coalition that won almost a quarter of the seats in last month's parliamentary elections campaigned for "kicking women out of offices and giving the jobs they have stolen to men."

Barbarous traditions such as the so-called "honor-killing" are widespread. In the year 2000 alone, over 6,000 women were murdered in Pakistan by their fathers or brothers for having "dishonored" the family. In Jordan over 700 women fell victims to "honor killing" in the same year. In Egypt and the Sudan an estimated 150,000 girls, aged four or above, suffer genital mutilation in the name of Islam each year.

Almost everywhere in the Muslim world, rape, including the most horrible cases of incest, end up with the punishment of the victim. In most Muslim countries women cannot travel without the written permission of a male guardian. And in Saudi Arabia women are not allowed to drive cars. Against such a background two recent highly publicized seminars on women in the Muslim world appear rather tame, if not actually insulting, exercises.

The first, funded by the World Bank and held in Amman, Jordan, gave a standing ovation to a Tunisian lady who, having managed to get a divorce from a cousin, persuaded an Englishman to convert to Islam so that they could marry. Not a bad story, except that the message was that if Muslim women could divorce husbands they did not love, they might attract new converts to the faith!

The second event, also held in Amman, attracted a number of Arab first ladies. It ended with a spineless appeal for "educational opportunities for girls."

The fact is that Muslim girls have already kept their end of the bargain as far as education is concerned. They have all the degrees they need but are still not allowed to leave home without a chaperon or wear the kind of clothes they like. They cannot get the jobs they merit or choose whom to marry.

The two Amman events were a far cry from the first congress of Muslim women held in Kazan, then part of the Russian Empire, in 1875, in which over 800 women delegates unanimously voted for "full equality of sexes, and the abolition of all discrimination." Sadly, the Western powers have done little to help Muslim women in their struggle for freedom and equality.

Leading Western ladies, including former Irish president Mary Robinson and the ubiquitous Danielle Mitterrand, wife of the late French President Francois Mitterrand, have frequently visited Tehran and other Islamic capitals wearing the evil neo-hijab. The list of topics that the European Union wants to raise in its "critical dialogue" with Iran has 22 items. Yet not one is concerned with the gender Apartheid imposed by the Islamists. Some French, German and British leftists have even praised the fascist neo-hijab in the name of "cultural diversity."

Many courageous women are fighting against the age of darkness that Islamism is trying to impose on the whole world. Democrats everywhere have a duty to support that fight so that the sun will shine for Ms. Shamloo's girls all the time and everywhere, not just for three months inside a school-cum-prison.

THIS IS NOT ISLAM

by Amir Taheri.
New York Post
August 15, 2003

August 15, 2003 -- FRANCE'S Prime Minister Jean-Pierre Raffarin has just appointed a committee to draft a law to ban the Islamist hijab (headgear) in state-owned establishments, including schools and hospitals. The decision has drawn fire from the French "church" of Islam, an organization created by Raffarin's government last spring. Germany is facing its hijab problem, with a number of Islamist organizations suing federal and state authorities for "religious discrimination" because of bans imposed on the controversial headgear. In the United States, several Muslim women are suing airport-security firms for having violated their First Amendment rights by asking them to take off their hijab during routine searches of passengers.

All these and other cases are based on the claim that the controversial headgear is an essential part of the Muslim faith and that attempts at banning it constitute an attack on Islam.

That claim is totally false. The headgear in question has nothing to do with Islam as a religion. It is not sanctioned anywhere in the Koran, the fundamental text of Islam, or the hadith (traditions) attributed to the Prophet.

This headgear was invented in the early 1970s by Mussa Sadr, an Iranian mullah who had won the leadership of the Lebanese Shi'ite community.

In an interview in 1975 in Beirut, Sadr told this writer that the hijab he had invented was inspired by the headgear of Lebanese Catholic nuns, itself inspired by that of Christian women in classical Western paintings. (A casual visit to the Metropolitan Museum in New York, or the Louvre in Paris, would reveal the original of the neo-Islamist hijab in numerous paintings depicting Virgin Mary and other female figures from the Old and New Testament.)

Sadr's idea was that, by wearing the headgear, Shi'ite women would be clearly marked out, and thus spared sexual harassment, and rape, by Yasser Arafat's Palestinian gunmen who at the time controlled southern Lebanon.

Sadr's neo-hijab made its first appearance in Iran in 1977 as a symbol of Islamist-Marxist opposition to the Shah's regime. When the mullahs seized power in Tehran in 1979, the number of women wearing the hijab exploded into tens of thousands.

In 1981, Abol-Hassan Bani-Sadr, the first president of the Islamic Republic, announced that "scientific research had shown that women's hair emitted rays that drove men insane." To protect the public, the new Islamist regime passed a law in 1982 making the hijab mandatory for females aged above six, regardless of religious faith. Violating the hijab code was made punishable by 100 lashes of the cane and six months imprisonment.

By the mid 1980s, a form of hijab never seen in Islam before the 1970s had become standard gear for millions of women all over the world, including Europe and America.

Some younger Muslim women, especially Western converts, were duped into believing that the neo-hijab was an essential part of the faith. (Katherine Bullock, a Canadian, so loved the idea of covering her hair that she converted to Islam while studying the hijab.)

The garb is designed to promote gender apartheid. It covers the woman's ears so that she does not hear things properly. Styled like a hood, it prevents the woman from having full vision of her surroundings. It also underlines the concept of woman as object, all wrapped up and marked out.

Muslim women, like women in all societies, had covered their head with a variety of gears over the centuries. These had such names as lachak, chador, rusari, rubandeh, chaqchur, maqne'a and picheh, among others.

All had tribal, ethnic and generally folkloric origins and were never associated with religion. (In Senegal, Muslim women wear a colorful headgear against the sun, while working in the fields, but go topless.)

Muslim women could easily check the fraudulent nature of the neo-Islamist hijab by leafing through their family albums. They will not find the picture of a single female ancestor of theirs who wore the cursed headgear now marketed as an absolute "must" of Islam.

This fake Islamic hijab is nothing but a political prop, a weapon of visual terrorism. It is the symbol of a totalitarian ideology inspired more by Nazism and Communism than by Islam. It is as symbolic of Islam as the Mao uniform was of Chinese civilization.

It is used as a means of exerting pressure on Muslim women who do not wear it because they do not share the sick ideology behind it. It is a sign of support for extremists who wish to impose their creed, first on Muslims, and then on the world through psychological pressure, violence, terror, and, ultimately, war.

The tragedy is that many of those who wear it are not aware of its implications. They do so because they have been brainwashed into believing that a woman cannot be a "good Muslim" without covering her head with the Sadr-designed hijab.

Even today, less than 1 percent of Muslim women wear the hijab that has bewitched some Western liberals as a symbol of multicultural diversity. The hijab debate in Europe and the United States comes at a time when the controversial headgear is seriously questioned in Iran, the only country to impose it by law.

Last year, the Islamist regime authorized a number of girl colleges in Tehran to allow students to discard the hijab while inside school buildings. The experiment was launched after a government study identified the hijab as the cause of "widespread depression and falling academic standards" and even suicide among teenage girls.

The Ministry of Education in Tehran has just announced that the experiment will be extended to other girls schools next month when the new academic year begins. Schools where the hijab was discarded have shown "real improvements" in academic standards reflected in a 30 percent rise in the number of students obtaining the highest grades.

Meanwhile, several woman members of the Iranian Islamic Majlis (parliament) are preparing a draft to raise the legal age for wearing the hijab from six to 12, thus sparing millions of children the trauma of having their heads covered.

Another sign that the Islamic Republic may be softening its position on hijab is a recent decision to allow the employees of state-owned companies outside Iran to discard the hijab. (The new rule has enabled hundreds of women, working for Iran-owned companies in Paris, London, and other European capitals, for example, to go to work without the cursed hijab.)

The delicious irony of militant Islamists asking "Zionist-Crusader" courts in France, Germany and the United States to decide what is "Islamic" and what is not will not be missed. The judges and the juries who will be asked to decide the cases should know that they are dealing not with Islam, which is a religious faith, but with Islamism, which is a political doctrine.

The hijab-wearing militants have a right to promote their political ideology. But they have no right to speak in the name of Islam.

WILL CHIRAC FIGHT FASCISM?

by Amir Taheri.
New York Post
December 14, 2003

December 14, 2003 -- ANYONE following the French media these days might get the impression that we are heading for "a war of values" and a "clash of civilizations" over what is known as "le foulard islamique."

The controversial foulard is a special headgear, inspired by the hood worn by Capuchin monks, and designed to cover a woman's head, leaving only her face exposed.

The issue has divided French society across religious and cultural fault-lines that few would have acknowledged a decade ago: Should the government forbid girls from wearing the foulard at state schools?

A special committee, set up by President Jacques Chirac last summer, has just submitted its report on the subject, suggesting that the foulard be banned from public schools along with other "ostensible signs of religion" such as Jewish skullcaps and large crosses. The president is scheduled to unveil his conclusions in a televised address this week.

Some secularists insist that the foulard should be banned from schools, hospitals and other public institutions by a special law because it represents "an ostentatious religious sign" in spaces that should remain neutral as far as religion is concerned. Others believe that an outright ban could be seen as an attack on individual beliefs, and force girls who wish to wear the foulard to switch to private Koranic schools.

All this may well be a result of a misunderstanding. To start with, the term "foulard islamique" is inaccurate because it assumes that the controversial headscarf is an article of Islamic faith, which it emphatically is not. It is a political symbol shared by several radical movements that, each in its own way, tries to transform Islam from a religion into a political ideology.

One could describe these movements as Islamist, but not Islamic. A new word has been coined in Arabic to describe them: Mutuasslim. Its equivalent in Persian is Islamgara.

The foulard should be seen as a political symbol in the same way as Nazi casquettes, Mao Zedong caps and Che Guevara berets were in their times. It has never been sanctioned by any Islamic religious authority and is worn by a tiny minority of Muslim women.

It was first created in Lebanon in 1975 by Imam Mussa Sadr, an Iranian mullah who had become leader of the Shi'ite community there. Sadr wanted the foulard to mark out Shi'ite girls so that they would not be molested by the Palestinians who controlled southern Lebanon at the time.

In 1982, the Lebanese-designed headgear was imposed by law on all Iranian girls and women, including non-Muslims, aged six years and above. Thus, Iranian Christian, Jewish and Zoroastrian women are also forced to wear a headgear that is supposed to be an Islamic symbol. The Khomeinist claim is that women's hair has to be covered because it emits rays that turn men "wild with sex."

From the mid 1980s, the foulard appeared in North Africa and Egypt before moving east to the Persian Gulf, the Indo-Pakistani Subcontinent and Southeast Asia. It made its first appearance in France in 1984, brought in by Iranian Mujahedin asylum seekers. Today, thousands of women, especially new converts, wear it in Europe and North America.

That the foulard did not exist before 1975 is easy to verify. Muslim women could refer to their family albums to see that none of their female parents and ancestors ever wore it.

Megawati Sukarnoputri, President of Indonesia, the world's largest Muslim nation, does not wear it. Nor does Khalidah Zia, prime minister of Bangladesh, the world's second most populous country. Shirin Ebadi, the first Muslim woman to win the Nobel Peace Prize, does not wear it, except inside Iran - where she would go to jail if she did not.

That the foulard is a political invention can be ascertained in two other ways. First, there is the Iranian law of 1982 that specifies the shape, size and even the "authorized" colors of the headscarf.

Second, the various Islamist movements have developed specific color schemes to assert their identity. The Khomeinists wear dark blue or brown. The Sunni Salafis, who sympathize with al Qaeda and the Taliban, prefer black. Supporters of Abu-Sayyaf and other Southeast Asian radical groups wear white or yellow. Supporters of

Palestinian radical groups don checkered foulards.

Islamism is a totalitarian ideology like Communism and Fascism. And like them it loves uniforms. While it forces, or brainwashes, women into wearing the foulard, it also presses men to grow beards as an advertisement of piety.

Like people of other faiths and cultures, Muslim men and women often covered their heads. But the headgear used had no political significance and reflected local cultural, tribal and folkloric traditions. No one ever claimed that donning any particular headgear, whether for men or women, was a religious duty.

In any case Islam, with its rich tradition of iconoclasm, is not a religion of symbols. It also abhors any advertisement of piety which, known as tajallow (showing off), is regarded as a sin.

By trying to turn the issue of the foulard into a duel between Islam and secularism, the French may be missing the point. The real problem is posed by organized and well-funded efforts of Fascist groups to develop a form of apartheid in which Muslims in France, now numbering almost 6 million, will not be protected by the French political system and the laws that sustain it.

As things are, the foulard concerns a small number of Muslim women in France. The French Interior Ministry's latest report says that only an estimated 11,200, out of some 1.8 million Muslim schoolgirls, wore the "foulard" at schools last year.

The same report says that only 1,253 of those who wore the foulard were involved in incidents provoked by their attempts to force other girls to cover their heads.

A survey by a group of Muslim women in the Paris suburb of Courneuve last May shows that 77 per cent of the girls who wore the foulard did so because they feared that if they did not they would be beaten up or even disfigured by Islamist vigilantes. Girls refusing the foulard are often followed by gangs of youth shouting "putain" (whore) at them.

In some suburbs, the Islamist Fascists have appointed an Emir al-Momeneen (Commander of the Faithful) and set up armed units that the French state fears to confront. These groups tell Muslims not to allow their womenfolk to be examined by male doctors, not to donate blood or receive blood from Jews or Christians, and to prevent girls from studying science, swimming or taking part in group sports.

What the French state needs to do is to protect Muslims on its territory, especially women, against the Fascists who are setting up "emirates" around major French cities, notably Paris.

What France is witnessing is not a clash of civilization between Islam and the West. It is a clash between a new form of fascism and democracy. Islamism must be exposed and opposed politically. To give it any religious credentials is not only unjust but also bad politics.

Koranic Law Does not Impose the Headscarf

by Khaled Fouad Allam
(appearing in 22nd January 2004 edition of 'La Repubblica' in Italy)

Historically speaking, the "hijab" (or Islamic headscarf) has never represented any form of Islamic dogma, legal obligation or religious symbol, even if today the impression is such.

Jurists during the classical period of Islam – who when Muslim law was first formulated for the four great legal schools of Islam – never presented any theories on the headscarf. The celebrated jurist and founder of the Theological University of Fez in Morocco, Qayrawin (died in 996), spoke about the headscarf only in reference to prayer rituals, when women enter mosques to pray on Fridays. And the word he used was "khimar", a veil covering women from head to toe. He never used the term "hijab". It is the same with other authors of the period.

There is indeed an explanation for all this. Classical Islam jurists warned of the need to formulate legal theory concerning the headscarf or veil, simply because a woman's medieval world was that of a cloister, where she didn't leave home, leading her life within the borders of private property. And when she did venture out, which was rare, she had to do so with the authorization of a male figure – whether it be her father, husband or brother – and only under exceptional circumstances, as for some formal ceremony or pilgrimage.

The hijab is an invention of the 14th century, and it has no real basis in the Koran. In the Koran, "hijab" comes from the root "hjb", which refers not to an object, but an action: wearing a headscarf, pulling down a curtain or screen or reducing light so as to prevent others from prying or looking in.

The change to the word "hijab", from signifying an action to meaning an object, comes in the 14th century. The jurist, Ibn Taymiyya, was the first to use the word "hijab" to mean "headscarf". It was a headscarf that distinguished Muslim from non-Muslim women. It came to distinguish a woman's identity and religious association.

Ibn Taymiyya stated that a free woman has the obligation to cover herself with a headscarf, while a slave is not obliged as such. He justified this based on a maximalist interpretation (cf. Koran, verse 31, sura 24), transforming the words of a generic statement into a principle, by giving it a binding or legal sense. Yet all this – and we do well to point it out – was still an interpretation, an interpretation which gave rise to a rule.

This change in language and social interpretation is a sign of crisis within the 14th century Muslim world: the end of the great Islamic empires and the invasion of Baghdad by a foreign power – the Mongols of Genghis Khan. The "ummah" (the community of believers) had to therefore face and struggle with what nowadays we call the principle of "otherness". This posed the same problem then as it does nowadays: today's Muslims now must cope with how to be themselves in a society dominated by non-Muslims. The headscarf is a sign of the Muslim community's defensive reactions and focuses on legal norms not to create leeway for freedom of expression, but rather to establish a form of control – on Islam itself.

Therefore it is no coincidence that Ibn Taymiyya (died 1328) is a daily point of reference in neo-fundamentalist language.

However the decisive change for the "hijab" in terms of meaning and law occurs in the 20th century, especially in its last fifty years. In Muslim countries, following the period of decolonization, the processes of modernization created great difficulties for traditional societal structures and institutions. Two unprecedented phenomena occured: literacy of the masses and women going to school, work and out from their homes. The outside world was added to their main world of reference.

In the face of such social changes, many exegetes in Islam have reacted in neo-conservative ways, creating a legal system legitimizing and prescribing the use of the hijab. The headscarf thus becomes a distinct symbol of Islamic identity and separation between sexes. The headscarf's introduction and use into public areas indeed favors the creation of a gender barrier, which today is not limited to the headscarf itself, but in some other countries has given rise to an actual division of space, even in public transport vehicles (e.g. some neo-fundamentalist-minded architects have drawn up ideas for separate elevators for men and women). Thus public space, instead of sanctioning a principle of equality, focuses on sexual discrimination.

However, all these changes in the headscarf's use and practice is joined to that which is a constant in the customs and norms of Muslim society: the dichotomy between the pure and impure, and prohibition as a basis for Islamic law.

The frequent emphasis in sacred texts – that women mustn't do anything to look at other men and draw attention to themselves, hence covering up their figures – has indeed led the collective Muslim unconscious to associate femininity with lust. In this way women have become synonymous with the chaos and disorder attributed to vice. Hence with women there is always the imminent risk of committing acts of impurity. Due to their reproductive role, women are invested with a certain sacred nature. Therefore, breaking the rule – that is to say, showing themselves off – means contaminating their original purity.

This taboo spells for a puritan society and articulates a legal system of control. Muslim societies are obsessed by issues of impurity; and the headscarf tends to symbolically preserve the bounds between the pure and impure.

Today the headscarf takes on the meaning of an identity crisis. In addition to expressing the widespread malaise found in Islamic society, the headscarf conceals its changes and exacerbates people's fears. Whoever wears it, especially in the West, does so because they are coerced or conditioned to do so or are claiming their rights and asserting free choices. There are many opinions, but they all defer to a series of unsolved conflicts: between Islam and the West, with Islam itself and between law and culture.

From The Times newspaper website:

Should Muslims cast aside hijabs and beards?

TIMESONLINE, July 27, 2005

Amir Taheri urges Muslims to stop "using their bodies as advertising space for al-Qaeda" by wearing hijabs, beards and Taleban-style clothes which, he says, have nothing to do with Islam: "Muslims who wear such clothes in the belief that it shows their piety, in most cases, are unwittingly giving succour to a brand of Islamist extremism." Send us your view using the form below:

I came to England in 1972 from Uganda. There were Muslims living in Leicester, and it was rare to see women wearing hijabs or seeing lots of men with beards and white robes. Then all of a sudden, there were lots of women wearing hijabs and men wearing beards and white robes. It seems to me that this sudden change was caused by some ideological change in the outlook of these people. This questions the oft-quoted argument about "freedom". If it was a quesion of freedom, then we would expect the law of averages to apply; however, here there is something more going on. ***Ashok Dattani, London***

I am a Saudi woman living in London and I am so happy to live and work without wearing hijabs or yashmaqs. I can never understand Muslim women in this country who feel the need to wear medieval dress. Women who wear traditional dress in a country like Saudi Arabia have no choice; women who wear it by choice can be nothing more than fanatics in my opinion. You can be Muslim and you do not have to dress like a circus tent. ***Amina Al-Gahtani, London***

In the five years that I lived in the Middle East, young Saudis, to avoid referring to anyone directly by name, would mime stroking imaginary long beards when talking about someone whom they considered a fundamentalist. In the very heartland of Islam the way you dress and present yourself physically is a crucial sign of your political and religious allegiences. I think that it is impossible to dismiss wearing a hijab or long beard and short gown as having no other significance than showing yourself to be extra pious. In my experience, those Muslims who did not make such a fuss about their external appearances were usually the more genuinely devout. ***Dene Croxford, Southall, Middx***

Many Muslims living in Britain and elsewhere in the World who do not wear hijabs or beards, including me, lead perfectly peaceful and God-fearing lives and they do not feel lesser Muslims because of that. I think people who think wearing a hijab or beard makes them good or better Muslims are, to put it mildly, simply wrong. ***Khalid Abbas, London.***

Chapter 2

In the late 1990's the Muslim Magazine, *Q-News*, based in London tried to persuade us that the headscarf was obligatory or at least that the wearing of the headscarf was a part of the original ideal prescribed for Muslim women.

What follows is the itemisation of the detailed debate that took place from 1997 to 1998 in the letters section of *Q-News*, interspersed with articles on the headscarf.

Q-News

news

Body Shop in hijab sacking row

A teenager who was laid off from her post with the global cosmetics chain, The Body Shop, after she adopted the hijab has filed a case of discrimination against the company.

17 year-old Amna Mahmood was told that she was surplus to requirements just one week after wearing the head-dress to the store in Hounslow, Middlesex where she had worked for over a year.

Miss Mahmood began working for Anita Roddick's celebrated company in September 1995 as a Saturday Sales Assistant and retained a spotless employment record.

However, Miss Mahmood's relationship with management deteriorated after she decided to take up the hijab as an expression of Islamic modesty. Although the Body Shop has no policy on headscarves, Miss Mahmood said she felt the atmosphere

"I felt humiliated and devastated," said Miss Mahmood. "I cried because I felt I had been let down by people I trusted and a company I had invested a lot of energy in. I found it difficult to eat and sleep and suffered from a migraine after many years."

Miss Mahmood, whose parents are Pakistani, has taken her grievance to the Commission for Racial Equality who will decide whether to back her case. A victory over The Body Shop would represent a prestigious scalp for the CRE not least because it would send a clear warning to the new breed of 'ethical' companies that pious policy statements do not exempt them from scrutiny.

Owned by Anita Roddick, The Body Shop prides itself on moral business practices with diverse peoples from all over the world. Accusations of religious intolerance would severely dent

Amna Mahmood: Claims she was the victim of workplace hijabophobia

Body Shop in hijab sacking row

Q-News 7 February 1997 (No. 251-254)

A teenager who was laid off from her post with the global cosmetics chain, The Body Shop, after she adopted the hijab has filed a case of discrimination against the company.

17 year-old Amna Mahmood was told that she was surplus to requirements just one week after wearing the head-dress to the store in Hounslow, Middlesex where she had worked for over a year.

Miss Mahmood began working for Anita Roddick's celebrated company in September 1995 as a Saturday Sales Assistant and retained a spotless employment record.

However, Miss Mahmood's relationship with management deteriorated after she decided to take up the hijab as an expression of Islamic modesty. Although The Body Shop has no policy on headscarves, Miss Mahmood said she felt the atmosphere change when colleagues saw her new attire.

"When I walked into the staffroom, I felt ignored and to some extent disrespected," she said.

"Later on that day my manageress suddenly became aware of my scarf. This was the first time she had mentioned it and we had a conversation about why as a Muslim I should be wearing it."

The following week Miss Mahmood's deputy manager accosted her as she walked home from college. "I was called upstairs without the faintest idea I was going to be sacked," she recounted. Miss Mahmood was told that Saturday staff reductions were in order and that she would have to be relieved of her duties. At the time, The Body Shop was recruiting more part-time workers for the Christmas period. Miss Mahmood was also the longer serving and more experienced of two Saturday staff employed at the branch.

"I felt humiliated and devastated," said Miss Mahmood. "I cried because I felt I had been let down by people I trusted and a company I had invested a lot of energy in. I found it difficult to eat and sleep and suffered from a migraine after many years."

Miss Mahmood, whose parents are Pakistani, has taken her grievance to the Commission for Racial Equality who will decide whether to back her case. A victory over The Body Shop would represent a prestigious scalp for the CRE not least because it would send a clear warning to the new breed of 'ethical' companies that pious policy statements do not exempt them from scrutiny.

Owned by Anita Roddick, The Body Shop prides itself on moral business practices with diverse peoples from all over the world. Accusations of religious intolerance would severely dent its carefully cultivated reputation.

However, for the moment, The Body Shop in Hounslow, which trades as a franchise, is denying the allegations claiming that Miss Mahmood was the unfortunate but unavoidable victim of staff cutbacks. Miss Mahmood's is the latest in a series of religious discrimination complaints to surface of late. In December 21 year-old Farida Khanum lost an internal appeal after being dismissed from her job as an engineer by Luton car manufacturer, IPC, weeks after returning from a pilgrimage and adopting the hijab. She is also taking her case to an industrial tribunal.

The case adds to a growing dossier of evidence being compiled by Muslim organisations and minority relations groups in support of demands for laws prohibiting religious discrimination; at present there is no such legislation on the statue books.

BT operating tacit anti-Muslim policy

Q-News June 1997 (No. 268-269)

One of the country's largest employers is operating an unwritten policy of discrimination against and actively discouraging Muslim women from taking up job opportunities.

Inquiries by *Q-News* have corroborated the observations of BT staff that the telecommunications giant has a tacit code of placing Muslim women in non customer-facing roles. The few who may choose to wear the obligatory hijab later into their employment face being penalised for not adhering to the official uniform.

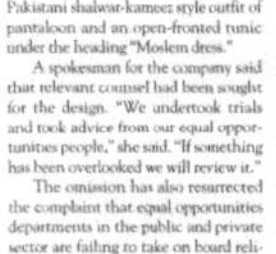

home news

BT operating tacit anti-Muslim policy

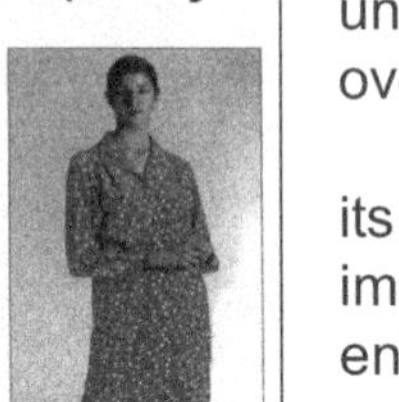

BT's "Moslem dress"

Q-News June 1997

Although BT's self-vaunted equal opportunities policy extends to cover religious dress, it fails to incorporate the hijab. The company's Corporate Wear Catalogue features only a Pakistani shalwar-kameez style outfit of pantaloon and an open-fronted tunic under the heading "Moslem dress."

A spokesman for the company said that relevant counsel had been sought for the design. "We undertook trials and took advice from our equal opportunities people," she said. "If something has been overlooked we will review it."

The omission has also resurrected the complaint that equal opportunities departments in the public and private sector are failing to take on board religious concerns.

"In our experience these offices are usually manned by non-Muslims with a poor understanding of the community's sensibilities or with prejudices about the faith," said Khalida Khan of the an-Nisa Society. "It seems inconceivable that any uniform for Muslim women should overlook the hijab - it is so obvious."

BT's dress catalogue says that its policy is necessary to promote an image of professionalism and to enhance the corporate identity but part of the code may be operating to exclude Muslim women.

Former and current employees have confided to *Q-News* that they had noticed a marked absence of Muslim women on the shop floor, a key customer-facing position. This has led them to suspect that a tacit exclusion policy is at work.

Shameem Patel, a directory enquiries operator in east Lancashire, said that proportionately more Muslim women worked in non-customer contact jobs. "I've never seen anybody around here wearing a headscarf, definitely not in the BT shop."

Calls to BT shops in areas of high Muslim density confirmed the findings. In Blackburn, home to 35,000 Muslims, a member of staff politely replied that "we've never had an Asian girl working here."

The same response came from Bradford where the central business district is ringed by poor Muslim areas suffering from endemic unemployment. BT's Birmingham city centre store stated that they knew of no Muslim girl worker wearing a headscarf. In London's Oxford Street, there was not a hijab in sight and in Harrow, a female employee scoffed at the idea that somebody of that description might be working alongside.

BT failed to disclose how many "Moslem dresses" had been ordered since they became available in 1992.

Hijab: mind over matter

I am surprised at the rigid stance you adopt against British Telecom's dress code for not including the hijab as part of the "Moslem dress" (Q-News 268-269).
Having researched this area quite thoroughly I fail to find anywhere in the Quran which obligates women to wear a scarf, let alone the hideous veil which has become fashionable since the Iranian revolution.
As a man of reason, I cannot see anything sexual in exposing the hair. Muslims appear to be blaming the victim and failing to acknowledge their own shortcomings. Surely, if men cannot get along without being turned on at the first sight of a loose frond, then it says more about their own spiritual weakness than about the moral standing of a woman.
I understand that Zaki Badawi of the Muslim College is one of those scholars who upholds the view that the hijab is a cultural accoutrement which takes varying forms in different societies. For example, in India and Pakistan, women do not cover all their hair but in Saudi Arabi many cover their entire face. In European Muslim societies like Bosnia, women do not wear scarves at all.
However, in the West that we know, the scarf has never been an accepted item of clothing and these days is all to readily identified with Islamic extremism and backwardness. I find the the current popularity of the hijab to be a somewhat reflex action. Most Muslim women I know wear it as a statement of anti-Western defiance.
Modesty is a state of mind, the disposition of a pure heart, which cannot be substituted by any amount of external attire.

Umar Tomkinson
Devon

Q-News July 1997

Hijab: mind over matter

Q-News July 1997 (No. 270-271)

I am surprised at the rigid stance you adopt against British Telecom's dress code for not including the hijab as part of the "Moslem dress" (Q-News 268-269). Having researched this area quite thoroughly I fail to find anywhere in the Quran which obligates women to wear a scarf, let alone the hideous veil which has become fashionable since the Iranian revolution. As a man of reason, I cannot see anything sexual in exposing the hair. Muslims appear to be blaming the victim and failing to acknowledge their own shortcomings. Surely, if men cannot get along without being turned on at the first sight of a loose frond, then it says more about their own spiritual weakness than about the moral standing of a woman.

I understand that Zaki Badawi of the Muslim College is one of those scholars who upholds the view that the hijab is a cultural accoutrement which takes varying forms in different societies. For example, in India and Pakistan, women do not cover all their hair but in Saudi Arabia many cover their entire face. In European Muslim societies like Bosnia, women do not wear scarves at all. However, in the West that we know, the scarf has never been an accepted item of clothing and these days is all to readily identified with Islamic extremism and backwardness. I find the the current popularity of the hijab to be a somewhat reflex action. Most Muslim women I know wear it as a statement of anti-Western defiance. Modesty is a state of mind, the disposition of a pure heart, which cannot be substituted by any amount of external attire.

Umar Tomkinson
Devon

More of the scarf

Q-News July 1997 (No. 272-273)

It is erroneous to believe that women are not required to cover their hair in Islam (Q-News, July 1997). Is brother Umar Tomkinson suggesting that the great believing women of the past, the mothers of the faithful, did not cover thus? The brother may notice the Quranic injunction where Allah instructs believeing women to cover themselves, viz - their hair, neck and body, in the following verse:

"...And tell the believing men and women to lower their gaze and to guard their modesty, and not to display their adornments, except what ordinarily appears thereof, and to draw their head-veils over their necks and bosoms..." (al-Noor, 30-31) For argument's sake, let us say that the translation of the meaning of this verse may differ slightly with scholars, and the order to cover may not be so explicit. But there are authentic ahadith that enjoin and support covering hair with a scarf. For example, a Companion of the Prophet (pbuh) reported him as saying: "If a woman reaches the age of menstruation, it is not allowed that any of her should be seen except this - and he pointed to his face and two hands" (al-Bayhaqi). Hijab requires that women physically cover the specified parts in an attitude of modesty and purity. This is reconciled in Allah's words: "And let not the womenfolk appear in the manner of the times of ignorance." (al-Ahzab, 33)

Ayesha bint Mahmood, *London*

Q News no. 272 - 273 July 1997

More of the scarf

It is erroneous to believe that women are not required to cover their hair in Islam (Q-News, July 1997). Is brother Umar Tomkinson suggesting that the great believing women of the past, the mothers of the faithful, did not cover thus? The brother may notice the Quranic injunction where Allah instructs believeing women to cover themselves, viz - their hair, neck and body, in the following verse:
"...And tell the believing men and women to lower their gaze and to guard their modesty, and not to display their adornments, except what ordinarily appears thereof, and to draw their head-veils over their necks and bosoms..." (al-Noor, 30-31)
For argument's sake, let us say that the translation of the meaning of this verse may differ slightly with scholars, and the order to cover may not be so explicit. But there are authentic *ahadith* that enjoin and support covering hair with a scarf. For example, a Companion of the Prophet (pbuh) reported him as saying: "If a woman reaches the age of menstruation, it is not allowed that any of her should be seen except this - and he pointed to his face and two hands" (al-Bayhaqi).Hijab requires that women physically cover the specified parts in an attitude of modesty and purity. This is reconciled in Allah's words: "And let not the womenfolk appear in the manner of the times of ignorance." (al-Ahzab, 33)

Ayesha bint Mahmood
London

This particular hadith (i.e reported saying of the Prophet Mohammad), by Al-Bayhaqi, quoted by Ayesha bint Mahmood is *definitely not* of proven authenticity as confirmed by Dr. Zaki Badawi to me personally and he added that his former colleague, the late Dr. S. M. Darsh and Islamic scholars in general concurred. And that this hadith should not therefore be relied upon.

Hijab: For and against

Q-News August 1997 (No. 274)

I would like to congratulate Umar Tomkinson on a truly excellent letter (Q-News 270). I agree with his views entirely that the hijab is not a part of true Islam. I regard the hijab as a perversion of Islam and accordingly I condemn anyone who wears it. If one reads Mohammed Asad's translation of the Quran and in the footnote to verse 31 of Surah 24 it is obvious that the hijab was indeed only a cultural accoutrement at the time of the Prophet Mohammed.

However, I also condemn the way most young European women dress, especially in the summer. Their semi-nakedness is a disgrace. Too many young girls tend to be exhibitionist in nature and this is evident from the parallel explosion in pornographic literature and videos. I myself am a solicitor who has been officially reprimanded at work by the company secretary for criticising a female employee wearing a see-through blouse to work. Fortunately, one week later the Daily Mail supported my view that such attire was unsuitable for work and published a photograph of the offending garment.

We Muslims are trying to bring non-Muslims to Islam but associating the hijab with Islam will drive them away altogether. Only those converts who are brainwashed seem to wear the hijab. If Muslim women want to protest against western decadence, they can take up the Mary Whitehouse example and begin for instance by going to newsagents (largely owned by Asians now) and persuade them to remove the vast stocks of pornography that line their top shelves. The poor Asian shopkeepers need to make money, but this way is pure hypocrisy, as such exhibitionism and titillation is against the cultural and moral teachings of the Asian community, be they Hindu, Sikh or Muslim, I have told British Telecom and the Body Shop not to allow women to wear the hijab on the grounds that these women should not be following a corruption of our great religion.

Farid el-Diwany
Brentwood, Essex

Q News no. 274 August 1997

letters to the **editor**

Send letters to Q-News, Dexion House, 2-4 Empire Way, Wembley, Middx HA1 4ET or fax on 0181- 903 0820

Hijab: For and against

I would like to congratulate Umar Tomkinson on a truly excellent letter (Q-*News 270*). I agree with his views entirely that the *hijab* is not a part of true Islam. I regard the *hijab* as a perversion of Islam and accordingly I condemn anyone who wears it. If one reads Mohammed Asad's translation of the Quran and in the footnote to verse 31 of Surah 24 it is obvious that the *hijab* was indeed only a cultural accoutrement at the time of the Prophet Mohammed.

However, I also condemn the way most young European women dress, especially in the summer. Their semi-nakedness is a disgrace. Too many young girls tend to be exhibitionist in nature and this is evident from the parallel explosion in pornographic literature and videos. I myself am a solicitor who has been officially reprimanded at work by the company secretary for criticising a female employee wearing a see-through blouse to work. Fortunately, one week later the Daily Mail supported my view that such attire was unsuitable for work and published a photograph of the offending garment.

We Muslims are trying to bring non-Muslims to Islam but associating the *hijab* with Islam will drive them away altogether. Only those converts who are brainwashed seem to wear the *hijab*. If Muslim women want to protest against western decadence, they can take up the Mary Whitehouse example and begin for instance by going to newsagents (largely owned by Asians now) and persuade them to remove the vast stocks of pornography that line their top shelves. The poor Asian shopkeepers need to make money, but this way is pure hypocrisy, as such exhibitionism and titillation is against the cultural and moral teachings of the Asian community, be they Hindu, Sikh or Muslim.

I have told British Telecom and the Body Shop not to allow women to wear the *hijab* on the grounds that these women should not be following a corruption of our great religion.

Farid el-Diwany
Brentwood, Essex

4

More on the scarf

Q-News September 1997 (No. 275)

Three 'well dones'! to *Q-News*. Firstly, to Farid el-Diwany for pointing out the embarrassment of Muslim newsagents stocking pornography. Secondly, to Imad el-Guyoushi for highlighting the off-putting atmosphere at Regent's Park Mosque; and thirdly to Suhail Malik for underlining the difference, as regards the Muslims of USA, between the so-called 'Nation of Islam' and the six million real Muslims there (I have just returned from lecturing at the New Mexico Dar al-Islam). The only good thing I can say about the 'Nation of Islam' is that hopefully if they are allowed to keep the name 'Islam' without being sued for misappropriation, they should start to read the Quran and discover the truth for themselves. As regards Regent's park Mosque I am at a loss to add to the comments of others that there are far more welcoming mosques elsewhere. During my last visit I could not take a photograph until I has signed a form and recorded all my details. During the previous visit I had felt so much a stranger that I went and prayed in the park opposite. I felt awful about it. It is something that really needs tackling, because I'm sure the congregation there does not mean to give this hostile impression. Maybe they could all take a trip to Dar al-Islam or perhaps to the wonderful mosque in Zagreb, Croatia which welcomes the general public to a decent restaurant and a pleasant garden and fountains.

Ruqayyah Waris Maqsood
Hull

I am writing in response to Farid el-Diwany's letter (Q-News 274) declaring the hijab as not being part of Islam.
I strongly object to the brother's letter. The requirements of dress in Islam is written very clearly in the Quran and Hadith. Furthermore, it is wrong of Mr El-Diwany to assume that he has the authority to speak on behalf of all Muslims. His instruction to BT and the Body Shop to ban headscarves is totally out of order. Wearing the hijab willingly does no harm to anyone while not allowing someone to wear the hijab violates a fundamental right.

Nasar ul-Haq
Huddersfield

It seems strange that *Q-News* chose to publish the letter by Farid el-Diwany (No 274). After all, wasn't it *Q-News* who championed the rights of Farida Khanum. Amna Mahmood and Safiah Abbasi, some brave Muslimahs to wear the hijab to work? And yet we have Mr Farid el-Diwany ringing up the same organisations that discriminate against our sisters telling them that it is okay to do so. I am sure that Mr Farid's fatwa comes as a relief to your own Dr Darsh who has written a whole book on the subject. Maybe the title of the book should be changed from 'Hijab or Niqab' to 'Hijab or Niqab or Mr Farid's Alternative'. After all, who needs our great intellectual heritage of the past when we have Mr Farid pass fatwas allowing Muslim women to walk around with their 'wash and go' counterparts. It saddens me that after all your work campaigning for the rights of Muslimahs to wear the hijab, somebody like Mr el-Diwany is undoing all the good work. By the way I'm sure our sisters in Europe would be delighted to hear Mr el-Diwany's fatwa. Do *Q-News* deliver to France?

Muzammil Syed
Willesden Green, London

More on the scarf

Three 'well dones'! to *Q-News*. Firstly, to Farid el-Diwany for pointing out the embarrassment of Muslim newsagents stocking pornography. Secondly, to Imad el-Guyoushi for highlighting the off-putting atmosphere at Regent's Park Mosque; and thirdly to Suhail Malik for underlining the difference, as regards the Muslims of USA, between the so-called 'Nation of Islam' and the six million real Muslims there (I have just returned from lecturing at the New Mexico Dar al-Islam). The only good thing I can say about the 'Nation of Islam' is that hopefully if they are allowed to keep the name 'Islam' without being sued for misappropriation, they should start to read the Quran and discover the truth for themselves. As regards Regent's park Mosque I am at a loss to add to the comments of others that there are far more welcoming mosques elsewhere. During my last visit I could not take a photograph until I has signed a form and recorded all my details. During the previous visit I had felt so much a stranger that I went and prayed in the park opposite. I felt awful about it. It is something that really needs tackling, because I'm sure the congregation there does not mean to give this hostile impression. Maybe they could all take a trip to Dar al-Islam or perhaps to the wonderful mosque in Zagreb, Croatia which welcomes the general public to a decent restaurant and a pleasant garden and fountains.
Ruqayyah Waris Maqsood
Hull

I am writing in response to Farid el-Diwany's letter (*Q-News* 274) declaring the hijab as not being part of Islam.
I strongly object to the brother's letter. The requirements of dress in Islam is written very clearly in the Quran and Hadith. Furthermore, it is wrong of Mr El-Diwany to assume that he has the authority to speak on behalf of all Muslims. His instruction to BT and the Body Shop to ban headscarves is totally out of order. Wearing the hijab willingly does no harm to anyone while not allowing someone to wear the hijab violates a fundamental right.
Nasar ul-Haq
Huddersfield

It seems strange that *Q-News* chose to publish the letter by Farid el-Diwany (*No 274*). After all, wasn't it *Q-News* who championed the rights of Farida Khanum. Amna Mahmood and Safiah Abbasi, some brave Muslimahs to wear the hijab to work? And yet we have Mr Farid el-Diwany ringing up the same organisations that discriminate against our sisters telling them that it is okay to do so.
I am sure that Mr Farid's fatwa comes as a relief to your own Dr Darsh who has written a whole book on the subject. Maybe the title of the book should be changed from Hijab or Niqab to Hijab or Niqab or Mr Farid's Alternative'. After all, who needs our great intellectual heritage of the past when we have Mr Farid pass fatwas allowing Muslim women to walk around with their 'wash and go' counterparts.
It saddens me that after all your work campaigning for the rights of Muslimahs to wear the hijab, somebody like Mr el-Diwany is undoing all the good work. By the way I'm sure our sisters in Europe would be delighted to hear Mr el-Diwany's fatwa. Do *Q-News* deliver to France?
Muzammil Syed
Willesden Green, London

Hijab again

Q-News September 1997 (No. 276)

I must respond to the letters published in the Issue 275 criticising my stance and by association that of Umar Tomkinson in issue 270-271. I have based my objections to the hijab on solid ground:-

1. The Qur'an itself does not oblige women to cover their hair and the fact that many do has arisen out of a customary practice being mischievously adopted as a religious one.
2. As far as I am aware none of the hadith on the subject of the hijab are of proven authenticity and should not therefore be relied upon.

As attractive as a woman's hair can be, a woman must be allowed to appear in public as a woman and be visually identifiable as such by showing her hair and her face, provided the general Quranic injunctions as to modesty in dress and behaviour are followed. It is God that gave men their very powerful sex instinct which should be restrained by the practice of sexual relations within marriage.

In effect the supporters of the hijab are saying that the mere sight of a woman, i.e. meaning the combination of her hair and face only in public, is a sin as they claim that it directly provokes thoughts or acts of lewd conduct by both men and women. This is an insult to God's gift of sex. Thoughts of sex and the desire to have sex will exist even without being able to see a woman's hair because men are born with the sex instinct. On the other hand, the sight of woman's cleavage and thighs in public is certainly provocative. It would be safe to say that it is good Islam for a woman to cover below the knee and up to the neck. The Qur'an does not provide an exhaustive list of prohibitions on dress but leaves a lot to our own good sense of decency based on the desire to please God.

I believe the hijab and the mentality of its practitioners and supporters encourages fear of social contact between men and women on a purely decent basis. This social vacuum for Muslim men often induces depression, loneliness and the use of ludicrously impersonal medium of advertising for a spouse. It also encourages the widespread use of prostitutes, blue movies and pornography as a substitute for (being unable to find) a wife. Further in the Middle East it results in many weak men resorting to homosexual acts,

letters
to the **editor**

Send letters to Q-News, Dezion House, 2-4 Empire Way, Wembley, Middx HA1 4ET or fax on 0181- 903 0820 E-mail q-news@aapi.co.uk

Hijab again

I must respond to the letters published in the Issue 275 criticising my stance and by association that of Umar Tomkinson in issue 270-271. I have based my objections to the hijab on solid ground:-
1. The Qur'an itself does not oblige women to cover their hair and the fact that many do has arisen out of a customary practice being mischievously adopted as a religious one.
2. As far as I am aware none of the hadith on the subject of the hijab are of proven authenticity and should not therefore be relied upon.
As attractive as a woman's hair can be, a woman must be allowed to appear in public as a woman and be visually identifiable as such by showing her hair and her face, provided the general Quranic injunctions as to modesty in dress and behaviour are followed. It is God that gave men their very powerful sex instinct which should be restrained by the practice of sexual relations within marriage.
In effect the supporters of the hijab are saying that the mere sight of a woman, i.e. meaning the combination of her hair and face only in public, is a sin as they claim that it directly provokes thoughts or acts of lewd conduct by both men and women. This is an insult to God's gift of sex. Thoughts of sex and the desire to have sex will exist even without being able to see a woman's hair because men are born with the sex instinct. On the other hand, the sight of a woman's cleavage and thighs in public is certainly provocative. It would be safe to say that it is good Islam for a woman to cover below the knee and up to the neck. The Qur'an does not provide an exhaustive list of prohibitions on dress but leaves a lot to our own good sense of decency based on the desire to please God.
I believe the hijab and the mentality of its practitioners and supporters encourages fear of social contact between men and women on a purely decent basis. This social vacuum for Muslim men often induces depression, loneliness and the use of ludicrously impersonal medium of advertising for a spouse. It also encourages the widespread use of prostitutes, blue movies and pornography as a substitute for (being unable to find) a wife. Further in the Middle East it results in many weak men resorting to homosexual acts, an abomination in Islam. The practice of Islam today is far removed from the ideal as promoted in the Qur'an. It is a case of one step forward and ten steps back. In this regard, I must recommend Jan Goodwin's book "Price of Honour" published by Warner Books, which tells how 'Muslim Women lift the Veil of Silence on the Islamic World'.
I am certainly not discriminating against our sisters by telling bewildered and confused employers that the hijab is not a part of true Islam. My campaign will continue in this respect. I am doing our sisters a favour by trying to prevent their justifiable ridicule and inevitable isolation.
Today the hijab is not just a protest against western decadence; it is also a protest against the betrayal of real Islamic values by many governments in the Islamic world. The women who cover are either doing it against their will or are erroneously convinced that the scarf represents the pinnacle of Islamic virtue which if followed by all women will return their people to an Islamic way of life not seen since the time of the Prophet Mohammed (peace be upon him).
No, the cult of the scarf is a periodic and fanatical overreaction by men who try and control and robotise women. We Muslims are in a pitiful state the world over. When it really mattered we couldn't even use God's gift of petrodollars to prevent our Bosnian brothers and sisters being slaughtered. On a day to day level, let us not continue to alienate our religion and our women by insisting that the hijab is a fundamental right or principle of Islam when clearly, its use achieves nothing.
Farid el-Diwany
Brentwood, Essex

4 Q-News September 1997

an abomination in Islam. The practice of Islam today is far removed from the ideal as promoted in the Qur'an. It is a case of one step forward and ten steps back. In this regard, I must recommend Jan Goodwin's book 'Price of Honour' published by Warner Books, which tells how 'Muslim Women Lift the Veil of Silence on the Islamic World'. I am certainly not discriminating against our sisters by telling bewildered and confused employers that the hijab is not a part of true Islam. My campaign will continue in this respect. I am doing our sisters a favour by trying to prevent their justifiable ridicule and inevitable isolation.

Today the hijab is not just a protest against western decadence; it is also a protest against the betrayal of real Islamic values by many governments in the Islamic world. The women who cover are either doing it against their will or are erroneously convinced that the scarf represents the pinnacle of Islamic virtue which if followed by all women will return their people to an Islamic way of life not seen since the time of the Prophet Mohammed (peace be upon him).

No, the cult of the scarf is a periodic and fanatical overreaction by men who try and control and robotise women. We Muslims are in a pitiful state the world over. When it really mattered we couldn't even use God's gift of petrodollars to prevent our Bosnian brothers and sisters being slaughtered. On a day to day level, let us not continue to alienate our religion and our women by insisting that the hijab is a fundamental right or principle of Islam when clearly, its use achieves nothing.

Farid el-Diwany
Brentwood, Essex

More hijab (please)

Q-News September 1997 (No. 278)

letters to the **editor**

Send letters to **Q-News**, Dexion House, 2-4 Empire Way, Wembley, Middx HA1 4ET or fax on **0181- 903 0820** E-mail **q-news@aapi.co.uk**

More hijab (please)

Aya 31 of Sura An-Nur (The Light) instructs Muslim women to pull their head-coverings over their chests. Were Farid el-Diwany to discuss how far this ayah can be applied or not applied in the context of our contemporary world, we could enter into a dialogue with him, but to deny the existence of the ayah is outright dishonest.
What is worse, he then tries to argue that wearing hijab is in fact against Islam without being able to support his argument with a single ayah of the Quran nor even the most obscure hadith (and I doubt whether he is capable of judging the proven authenticity otherwise of the hadith which do make mention of women covering their hair).
So he wants to stop Muslim women, the majority of whom still insist on wearing hijab, from continuing this practice merely on the evidence of his own concocted opinion or, as the Quran puts his, following his own desires. And then he has the cheek of talking about men controlling women through the cult of the scarf. What else is he, a man, doing but to dictate to women, whose wish to wear the scarf he cannot comprehend, his own ideas based on his own farfetched philosophy of sexual relations in true male chauvinistic fashion.
Doing them a favour? Come off it!
Sahib Mustaqim Bleher
General Secretary
Islamic Party of Britain

I thank Mr Farid el-Diwany for his letter [*Q-News* issue 276]. I agree with him in everything he wrote. I have noticed that most of us Muslims follow the rule of logic backward. You notice this particularly when it comes to justifying the wearing of the hijab "in order to stop *fitna*": hijab is to be by women to stop men being "turned on" by seeing a bit of the woman's hair.
Don't you think the obligation should lie on the men to respect women and harness their (the men's) desires even if the woman is attractive? If they can't do this such men don't deserve the degree they have been given over women in the first place.
Let us give a parallel example. If someone carried a ten pound note in his hand and waved it above his head should that give the right for people around him to snatch it away from him? I don't think so. If anybody did that it will be considered as robbery and the appropriate punishment meted out.
For the only people who would stretch their hands and steal the money would be thieves. Honest people would never even consider taking away what doesn't belong to them because they normally respect other people's property and freedom. But in the hijab case we want to put the blame on the victim rather than punishing the thief.
The woman should unveil if she wants to. The man should have enough will to harness his desire and to treat her as an equal human being regardless of her sex. We should treat woman as partners not as sex object. It will be easy for true Muslims to respect a woman and not to succumb to his animal desire.
A hadith mentions that Muslims should look away from a woman, not stare at her and check if she has covered or uncovered her hair.
May God bless us all.
Ahmed Dabbagh
Wickford

4 Q-News September 1997

Aya 31 of Sura An-Nur (The Light) instructs Muslim women to pull their head-coverings over their chests. Were Farid el-Diwany to discuss how far this ayah can be applied or not applied in the context of our contemporary world, we could enter into a dialogue with him, but to deny the existence of the ayah is outright dishonest. What is worse, he then tries to argue that wearing hijab is in fact against Islam without being able to support his argument with a single ayah of the Quran nor even the most obscure hadith (and I doubt whether he is capable of judging the proven authenticity otherwise of the hadith which do make mention of women covering their hair). So he wants to stop Muslim women, the majority of whom still insist on wearing hijab, from continuing this practice merely on the evidence of his own concocted opinion or, as the Quran puts [it], following his own desires. And then he has the cheek of talking about men controlling women through the cult of the scarf. What else is he, a man, doing but to dictate to women, whose wish to wear the scarf he cannot comprehend, his own ideas based on his own farfetched philosophy of sexual relations in true male chauvinistic fashion.
Doing them a favour? Come off it!

Sahib Mustaqim Bleher
General Secretary
Islamic Party of Britain

I thank Mr Farid el-Diwany for his letter [Q-News issue 276]. I agree with him in everything he wrote. I have noticed that most of us Muslims follow the rule of logic backward. You notice this particularly when it comes to justifying the wearing of the hijab "in order to stop fitna": hijab is to be [worn] by women to stop men being "turned on" by seeing a bit of the woman's hair. Don't you think the obligation should lie on the men to respect women and harness their (the men's) desires even if the woman is attractive? If they can't do this such men don't deserve the degree they have been given over women in the first place. Let us give a parallel example. If someone carried a ten pound note in his hand and waved it above his head should that give the right for people around him to snatch it away from him? I don't think so. If anybody did that it will be considered as robbery and the appropriate punishment meted out. For the only people who would stretch their hands and steal the money would be thieves. Honest people would never even consider taking away what doesn't belong to them because they normally respect other people's property and freedom. But in the hijab case we want to put the blame on the victim rather than punishing the thief.

The woman should unveil if she wants to. The man should have enough will to harness his desire and to treat her as an equal human being regardless of her sex. We should treat woman as partners not as sex object. It will be easy for true Muslims to respect a woman and not to succumb to his animal desire. A hadith mentions that Muslims should look away from a woman, not stare at her and check if she has covered or uncovered her hair. May God bless us all.

Ahmed Dabbagh
Wickford

Sahib Mustaqim Bleher is a German convert to Islam and founded the Islamic Party of Britain. The Prophet Mohammad was reputed to have worn a beard. So in order to be 'closer' to the Prophet Mohammad Mr Bleher sports a beard: a kind of badge of honour as Muslims are told to follow the example of the Prophet.

I consulted Dr. Zaki Badawi on the subject of the beard. He told me that there are many hadith on the topic but they have to be read in their totality and seen in context. That the Prophet's command was for Muslim men to make themselves look different from the Jews and the Christians. And that this instruction from the Prophet came at a time when society was illiterate and was meant for a specific purpose: to make Muslim men distinctive so they could be identified in their new religion. And recognised by their fellow Muslims to enable a community of the faithful to establish themselves and spread the faith. So the Muslim men grew beards. But the purpose behind the instruction - to be distinctive so as to foster the establishment of Islam - no longer applies, said Badawi, as Islam is now well established and has millions of adherents world wide.

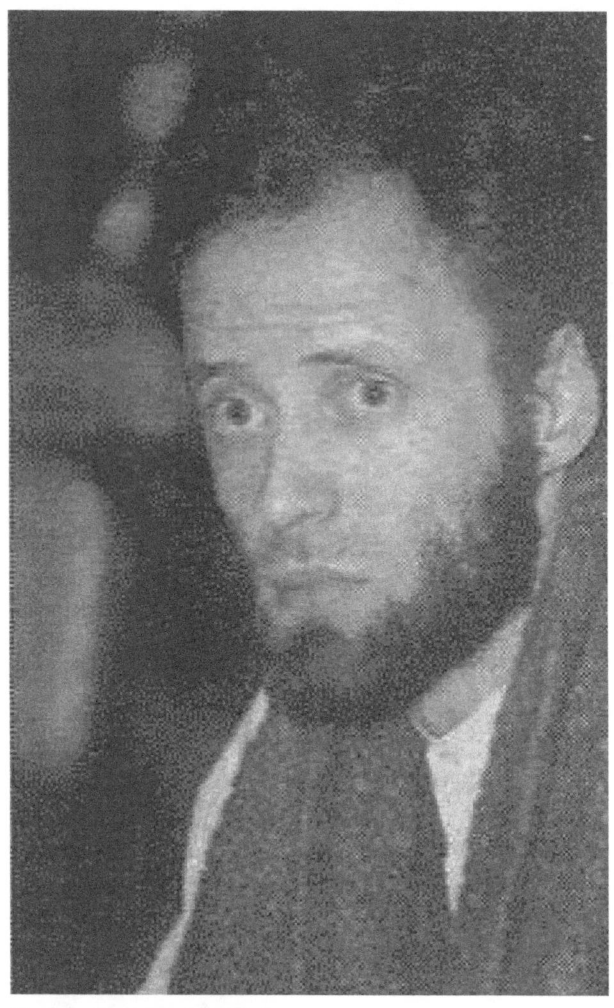
Sahib Mustaqim Bleher

But many Muslim men still believe that this now ostentatious identification with Islam - the beard in its various forms - has to be practised as an obligatory element of their faith. They get lost in arguments over how long the beard should be: whether it should ever be trimmed; whether a moustache should be grown; whether it is effeminate not to have a beard etc. etc.

The wearing of a beard by so many Muslim men has additionally almost become a form of idolatory of the Prophet. Some Muslim men would not be seen without it. The Prophet Mohammad was also reputed to have had long hair but today those Muslims who insist it is their religious duty to wear a beard do not grow long hair. They have short haircuts, because long hair is associated with Western decadance. Logically however, if the Prophet Mohammad wore long hair then his bearded followers of today should also grow long hair.

Mr Bleher, you can see, is very keen to condemn Mr El Diwany but if Mr Bleher had bothered to read previous issues of *Q-News* he would have seen that Mr El Diwany did make reference to Aya 31 of Surah An-Nur (Issue no. 274). *Q-News* themselves should have pointed this out but their objective was to humiliate Mr El Diwany. But more of this later.

THE INDEPENDENT
Wednesday 11 August 2004

HOME NEWS 17

Branson firm 'sacked Muslim in row over beard'

BY JAMES STURCKE

HE HAS one of the most famous beards in the country and, as a flamboyant entrepreneur who's not frightened of a bit of publicity, has no qualms about showing it off.

As boss of a plane and train empire who also has a penchant for daring boat and ballooning adventures, Virgin's Sir Richard Branson probably has some of the most travelled whiskers around.

But now one of his workers is claiming he was told to shave off his beard and has accused his bosses of religious discrimination.

Mohsin Mohmed, 22, from Ilford, east London, is taking Virgin Trains to an employment tribunal after losing his job as a customer services assistant at Euston station in London.

Virgin denies the claim of discrimination and claims that Mr Mohmed was dismissed after his probationary period for poor performance.

Mr Mohmed, who is Muslim, is said to have told rail bosses his faith required him to have a beard at least one fist's length, about four inches.

According to his claim, he had been told to crop the beard in September last year by his manager David Adams, a month after starting his £17,000-a-year job. Mr Mohmed alleges that Mr Adams regularly harassed him and that he had explained how he trimmed his beard on a number of occasions to the minimum required by his religion.

He said: "Nobody tells Richard Branson to shave his beard off. Why should I have to get rid of mine?"

A Virgin spokesman said that the company would not comment as the case was continuing.

A full hearing is expected to take place at Woburn Place employment tribunal in October.

Sir Richard's beard is believed to have played a role in his business success. The former British Airways chairman, Lord King, is reputed to have said he would have taken the threat from Virgin Atlantic more seriously if the entrepreneur had worn a suit and shaved off his beard. The Virgin boss did, however, shave off his beard and moustache on one occasion – to publicise Virgin Brides, when he also wore a wedding dress.

Mohsin Mohmed says he lost his Virgin Trains job because he refused to cut his beard, a fate unlikely to be shared by his former boss, Sir Richard Branson

Branson firm 'sacked Muslim in row over beard'

The Independent, 11th August 2004

HE HAS one of the most famous beards in the country and, as a flamboyant entrepreneur who's not frightened of a bit of publicity, has no qualms about showing it off.

As boss of a plane and train empire who also has a penchant for daring boat and ballooning adventures, Virgin's Sir Richard Branson probably has some of the most travelled whiskers around.

But now one of his workers is claiming he was told to shave off his beard and has accused his bosses of religious discrimination.

Mohsin Mohmed, 22, from Ilford, east London, is taking Virgin Trains to an employment tribunal after losing his job as a customer services assistant at Euston station in London. Virgin denies the claim of discrimination and claims that Mr Mohmed was dismissed after his probationary period for poor performance.

Mr Mohmed, who is Muslim, is said to have told rail bosses his faith required him to have a beard at least one fist's length, about four inches.

According to his claim, he had been told to crop the beard in September last year by his manager David Adams, a month after starting his £17,000-a-year job. Mr Mohmed alleges that Mr Adams regularly harassed him and that he had explained how he trimmed his beard on a number of occasions to the minimum required by his religion.

He said: "Nobody tells Richard Branson to shave his beard off. Why should I have to get rid of mine?"

A Virgin spokesman said that the company would not comment as the case was continuing.

A full hearing is expected to take place at Woburn Place employment tribunal in October.

Sir Richard's beard is believed to have played a role in his business success. The former British Airways chairman, Lord King, is reputed to have said he would have taken the threat from Virgin Atlantic more seriously if the entrepreneur had worn a suit and shaved off his beard. The Virgin boss did, however, shave off his beard and moustache on one occasion - to publicise Virgin Brides, when he also wore a wedding dress.

Sacked bearded Muslim loses case

Industrial Tribunal 7th January, 2005

Case Number: 2201814/04

LB

RESERVED JUDGMENT

THE EMPLOYMENT TRIBUNALS

BETWEEN

Claimant		*Respondents*
Mr M Mohmed	**AND**	West Coast Trains Limited (1) Mr David Adams (2)

JUDGMENT OF THE EMPLOYMENT TRIBUNAL

HELD AT: London Central

ON: 12 – 14 October 2004
In chambers 15 & 27 October 2004

CHAIRMAN: Mr C A Carstairs

MEMBERS: Mrs F I A Mansfield
Mr C J Storr

Appearances

For Claimant: Miss C McCann of counsel

For Respondents: Miss J Eady of counsel

JUDGMENT

The unanimous judgment of the Tribunal is that

(1) by consent the second Respondent is dismissed from the proceedings; and

(2) the Claimant's claims fail and are dismissed.

CHAIRMAN

JUDGMENT SENT TO THE PARTIES ON

7 Jan 05

AND ENTERED IN THE REGISTER

FOR SECRETARY OF THE TRIBUNALS

"Do you wear that in bed?" boss torments hijabd woman

Q-News October 1997 (No. 278)

"Do you wear that in bed?" boss torments hijabd woman

A woman engineer, who was referred to as "Yasser Arafat" by her colleagues when she started wearing a headscarf and eventually sacked, has taken her former employers to court.

Farida Khanum, 22, told Bedford Industrial Tribunal Court how she was asked by the men at the Luton car firm where she worked whether her hijab was a "new type of hard hat" or a "motorcycle helmet". Her foreman even inquired whether she liked to wear it in bed.

During a three day hearing from 17 to 19 September, the tribunal heard how Miss Khanum's employers and colleagues at IBC changed their attitude towards her when she started wearing the head-dress after coming back from performing umrah (lesser pilgrimage) in Saudi Arabia.

Miss Khanum, who had been working as a robot technician at the car giant owned by General Motors for four years had, until her dismissal, an "exemplary record". She had received a written commendation and had been promoted rapidly.

But things changed overnight when Khanum returned to the 2000-worker plant wearing a hijab after visiting the holy city of Mecca in September 1996.

The court heard how Miss Khanum's foreman removed her from the shop floor claiming it was for her own safety until the Health and Safety Department had assessed the dangers of wearing a headscarf on the production line. Khanum was told the hijab impaired her vision and that it could get caught in machinery, even though IBC, manufacturers of Vauxhall cars, allows its Sikh employees to wear turbans while working under moving parts.

Bosses also started to question Khanum's work performance for the first time. She was kept away from duties for a whole month while her superiors decided what to do with her. "I spent my time in the workshop just twiddling my fingers," she said.

During her time in the industrial wilderness, Miss Khanum claims she was subjected to a stream of interrogation and abuse. On one occasion her immediate foreman, who had ignored her for over a week since his return from holiday, took her into the control room and demanded an explanation for why she was "wearing the chador". When Miss Khanum replied that the headscarf was obligatory for her, he queried: "Do you wear that in bed?"

"I was gobsmacked," said Khanum. "There was only one way he could have meant it. I felt deeply hurt and humiliated."

Soon after, she was suspended and then sacked for gross misconduct. Her employer said the reason was she had taken half a day off without permission a month earlier when she attended a university open day. She vehemently denies the charges.

"They've used the charge as a pretext to fire me from the company because they can't deal with a woman wearing a hijab," she said. "I had permission from my foreman for the three hours that I took off."

Her barrister described how an employee who had missed work for a whole week whilst on a drinking-spree kept his job at the firm. And, in a twist to the proceedings, it came to light that two of the senior staff at IBC who had testified against Khanum, Miss Coony and Mr Thorburn, had been having an affair without anybody's knowledge. "Everybody at the firm knows they hadn't been doing their work properly for ages - their mind was on other things. Why weren't they disciplined?" asked Khanum's barrister.

The trial was due to be completed in the three days, but due to the complexity of the case it will now continue on 27 and 28 October.

Below are the relevant pages of the Quran obtained from Muhammad Asad's *'The Message of* THE QURAN' detailing verses 30 and 31 of the 24th Surah An-Nur (the Light) in English and Arabic. The footnotes: 36, 37, 38, 39, 40 and 41 provide much clarity.

[enjoined upon you] for your own good, so that you might bear [your mutual rights] in mind.[33]

(28) Hence, [even] if you find no one within [the house], do not enter it until you are given leave;[34] and if you are told, "Turn back," then turn back. This will be most conducive to your purity; and God has full knowledge of all that you do.

(29) [On the other hand,] you will incur no sin if you [freely] enter houses not intended for living in but serving a purpose useful to you:[35] but [always remember that] God knows all that you do openly, and all that you would conceal.

(30) TELL the believing men to lower their gaze and to be mindful of their chastity:[36] this will be most conducive to their purity – [and,] verily, God is aware of all that they do.

(31) And tell the believing women to lower their gaze and to be mindful of their chastity, and not to display their charms [in public] beyond what may [decently] be apparent thereof;[37] hence, let them draw their head-coverings over their bosoms.[38] And let

تذكرون ﴿٢٧﴾ فإن لم تجدوا فيها أحدا فلا تدخلوها حتى
يؤذن لكم وإن قيل لكم ارجعوا فارجعوا هو أزكى
لكم والله بما تعملون عليم ﴿٢٨﴾ ليس عليكم جناح
أن تدخلوا بيوتا غير مسكونة فيها متاع لكم والله يعلم
ما تبدون وما تكتمون ﴿٢٩﴾ قل للمؤمنين يغضوا من
أبصارهم ويحفظوا فروجهم ذلك أزكى لهم إن الله
خبير بما يصنعون ﴿٣٠﴾ وقل للمؤمنات يغضضن
من أبصارهن ويحفظن فروجهن ولا يبدين زينتهن إلا
ما ظهر منها وليضربن بخمرهن على جيوبهن ولا يبدين

33 This categorical prohibition connects with the preceding passages inasmuch as it serves as an additional protection of individuals against possible slander. In its wider purport, it postulates the inviolability of each person's home and private life. (For the socio-political implications of this principle, see *State and Government in Islam*, pp. 84 ff.)

34 I.e., by the rightful owner or caretaker.

35 Lit., "uninhabited houses wherein there are things of use (*matāᶜ*) for you". In the consensus of all the authorities, including the Companions of the Prophet, this relates to buildings or premises of a more or less public nature, like inns, shops, administrative offices, public baths, etc., as well as to ancient ruins.

36 Lit., "to restrain [something] of their gaze and to guard their private parts". The latter expression may be understood both in the literal sense of "covering one's private parts" – i.e., modesty in dress – as well as in the metonymical sense of "restraining one's sexual urges", i.e., restricting them to what is lawful, namely, marital intercourse (cf. 23 : 5–6). The rendering adopted by me in this instance allows for both interpretations. The "lowering of one's gaze", too, relates both to physical and to emotional modesty (Rāzī).

37 My interpolation of the word "decently" reflects the interpretation of the phrase *illā mā ẓahara minhā* by several of the earliest Islamic scholars, and particularly by Al-Qiffāl (quoted by Rāzī), as "that which a human being may openly show in accordance with prevailing custom (*al-ᶜādah al-jāriyah*)". Although the traditional exponents of Islamic Law have for centuries been inclined to restrict the definition of "what may [decently] be apparent" to a woman's face, hands and feet – and sometimes even less than that – we may safely assume that the meaning of *illā mā ẓahara minhā* is much wider, and that the deliberate vagueness of this phrase is meant to allow for all the time-bound changes that are necessary for man's moral and social growth. The pivotal clause in the above injunction is the demand, addressed in identical terms to men as well as to women, to "lower their gaze and be mindful of their chastity": and this determines the extent of what, at any given time, may legitimately – i.e., in consonance with the Qurʾanic principles of social morality – be considered "decent" or "indecent" in a person's outward appearance.

38 The noun *khimār* (of which *khumur* is the plural) denotes the head-covering customarily used by Arabian women before and after the advent of Islam. According to most of the classical commentators, it was worn in pre-Islamic times more or less as an ornament and was let down

them not display [more of] their charms to any but their husbands, or their fathers, or their husbands' fathers, or their sons, or their husbands' sons, or their brothers, or their brothers' sons, or their sisters' sons, or their womenfolk, or those whom they rightfully possess, or such male attendants as are beyond all sexual desire,[39] or children that are as yet unaware of women's nakedness; and let them not swing their legs [in walking] so as to draw attention to their hidden charms.[40]

And [always], O you believers – all of you – turn unto God in repentance, so that you might attain to a happy state![41]

(32) AND [you ought to] marry the single from among you[42] as well as such of your male and female slaves as are fit [for marriage].[43]

If they [whom you intend to marry] are poor, [let this not deter you;] God will grant them sufficiency out of His bounty – for God is infinite [in His mercy], all-knowing. (33) And as for those who are unable to marry,[44] let them live in continence until God grants

زِينَتَهُنَّ إِلَّا لِبُعُولَتِهِنَّ أَوْ ءَابَآئِهِنَّ أَوْ ءَابَآءِ بُعُولَتِهِنَّ
أَوْ أَبْنَآئِهِنَّ أَوْ أَبْنَآءِ بُعُولَتِهِنَّ أَوْ إِخْوَٰنِهِنَّ أَوْ بَنِىٓ إِخْوَٰنِهِنَّ
أَوْ بَنِىٓ أَخَوَٰتِهِنَّ أَوْ نِسَآئِهِنَّ أَوْ مَا مَلَكَتْ أَيْمَٰنُهُنَّ أَوِ
ٱلتَّٰبِعِينَ غَيْرِ أُو۟لِى ٱلْإِرْبَةِ مِنَ ٱلرِّجَالِ أَوِ ٱلطِّفْلِ ٱلَّذِينَ
لَمْ يَظْهَرُوا۟ عَلَىٰ عَوْرَٰتِ ٱلنِّسَآءِ ۖ وَلَا يَضْرِبْنَ بِأَرْجُلِهِنَّ
لِيُعْلَمَ مَا يُخْفِينَ مِن زِينَتِهِنَّ ۚ وَتُوبُوٓا۟ إِلَى ٱللَّهِ جَمِيعًا أَيُّهَ
ٱلْمُؤْمِنُونَ لَعَلَّكُمْ تُفْلِحُونَ ﴿٣١﴾ وَأَنكِحُوا۟ ٱلْأَيَٰمَىٰ مِنكُمْ
وَٱلصَّٰلِحِينَ مِنْ عِبَادِكُمْ وَإِمَآئِكُمْ ۚ إِن يَكُونُوا۟ فُقَرَآءَ
يُغْنِهِمُ ٱللَّهُ مِن فَضْلِهِۦ ۗ وَٱللَّهُ وَٰسِعٌ عَلِيمٌ ﴿٣٢﴾ وَلْيَسْتَعْفِفِ
ٱلَّذِينَ لَا يَجِدُونَ نِكَاحًا حَتَّىٰ يُغْنِيَهُمُ ٱللَّهُ مِن فَضْلِهِۦ ۗ

---

loosely over the wearer's back; and since, in accordance with the fashion prevalent at the time, the upper part of a woman's tunic had a wide opening in the front, her breasts were left bare. Hence, the injunction to cover the bosom by means of a *khimār* (a term so familiar to the contemporaries of the Prophet) does not necessarily relate to the use of a *khimār* as such but is, rather, meant to make it clear that a woman's breasts are *not* included in the concept of "what may decently be apparent" of her body and should not, therefore, be displayed.

39 I.e., very old men. The preceding phrase "those whom they rightfully possess" (lit., "whom their right hands possess") denotes slaves; but see also note 78.

40 Lit., "so that those of their charms which they keep hidden may become known". The phrase *yaḍribna bi-arjulihinna* is idiomatically similar to the phrase *ḍaraba bi-yadayhi fī mishyatihi*, "he swung his arms in walking" (quoted in this context in *Tāj al-ʿArūs*), and alludes to a deliberately provocative gait.

41 The implication of this general call to repentance is that since "man has been created weak" (4 : 28), no one is ever free of faults and temptations – so much so that even the Prophet used to say, "Verily, I turn unto Him in repentance a hundred times every day" (Ibn Ḥanbal, Bukhārī and Bayhaqī, all of them on the authority of ʿAbd Allāh ibn ʿUmar).

42 I.e., from among the free members of the community, as is evident from the subsequent juxtaposition with slaves. (As most of the classical commentators point out, this is not an injunction but a *recommendation* to the community as a whole: hence my interpolation of the words "you ought to".) The term *ayyim* – of which *ayāmā* is the plural – signifies a person of either sex who has no spouse, irrespective of whether he or she has never been married or is divorced or widowed. Thus, the above verse expresses the idea – reiterated in many authentic sayings of the Prophet – that, from both the ethical and the social points of view, the married state is infinitely preferable to celibacy.

43 The term *aṣ-ṣāliḥīn* connotes here both moral and physical fitness for marriage: i.e., the attainment of bodily and mental maturity as well as mutual affection between the man and the woman concerned. As in 4 : 25, the above verse rules out all forms of concubinage and postulates *marriage* as the only basis of lawful sexual relations between a man and his female slave.

44 I.e., because of poverty, or because they cannot find a suitable mate, or for any other personal reason.

The value of the veil

Q-News October 1997

I fully agree with Mr Dabbagh (issue 278) for turning the attention away from the much-debated issue of women's clothing for once and actually emphasising the duty of Muslim men to lower the gaze. But using his example of waving a ten pound note and then seeing who snatches it and who refrains, I think he is far too simplistic in making a distinction between people who are "inherently honest" and "inherently thieves". Just as it is not right to blame just women it is not right to blame men.

letters to the **editor**

Send letters to **Q-News**, Doxion House, 2-4 Empire Way, Wembley, Middx HA1 4ET

The value of the veil

I fully agree with Mr Dabbagh (issue 278) for turning the attention away from the much-debated issue of women's clothing for once and actually emphasising the duty of Muslim men to lower the gaze. But using his example of waving a ten pound note and then seeing who snatches it and who refrains, I think he is far too simplistic in making a distinction between people who are "inherently honest" and "inherently thieves". Just as it is not right to blame just women it is not right to blame men.

As someone who has recently adopted the veil I completely disagree with the idea that it achieves nothing. I truly believe that Islam requires women to wear the hijab but were this requirement ever to come into serious question, for many Muslim women the mere social gains of wearing the hijab are enough to keep it on.

Contrary to what Mr el-Diwany may believe, many women are wearing the hijab out of choice and if anything other than Islamic doctrine has driven them to it it is the experience and consequences of the very "social contact between men and women" that Mr el-Diwany is out to promote. Furthermore, Allah has given us the gift of reasoning and if in toady's immoral age we are witnessing the extreme and upsetting outcomes of liberated sexual expression, then surely it is our duty to adopt more rigorous measures to control the conditions which spread evil.

As for the idea that hijab equals male depression equals pornography/prostitution/homosexuality I really cannot see the logic in this. For surely sexually frustrated men do not make a conscious attempt to be among the minority of hijabed women and then get themselves depressed over the fact that they see no hair. And even if this were the case then why should women start unveiling just to satisfy male desire? If veiling is a symbol of male oppression then surely the act of unveiling equally reflects domination by men. Does Mr el-Diwany really believe that in a hijab-less society there would be less adultery and fornication? Surely, the example of the West has taught us otherwise.

Please Mr el-Diwany, spare us hijabi sisters your pity and shower it on those 'free and liberated' women who have become victims of their own liberation.

Shagufta Yaqub
London

It looks as though the preoccupation with the hijab is going to rumble on and divert us from the things that really matter if we are going to make Islam our complete way of life - things like courage, compassion, tolerance, honesty, generosity, etc.

At no stage did the Prophet (peace be upon him) ever lay down any kind of 'school uniform' regulation for women. The revelation of the Quran is totally silent on the subject except for the proviso that no human being has the right to declare anything haram that Allah has actually allowed. Nowhere are women asked to cover their heads at all; men and women both have to 'veil their gaze' and women were required to cover their bosoms. Arab costume at the time of the Prophet (peace be upon him) was apparently rather free in this respect, with women making easy access for breastfeeding , sometimes feeding their babies in public, and traditionally baring their breasts completely when they led their armies into battle.

Muslim women were expected to be different - to completely cover their bodies. Those who wore head-veils, usually hanging down the back in a decorative manner held on with an *agal*, showing most of their hair, were asked to draw this veil across their bosoms - and if the veil was transparent (as it usually was), to make it of thicker material.

It is well known that the Prophet (peace be upon him) unfortunately made an ambiguous attempt when he said that adult women should show no more than 'this and this'. He pointed at his hands, and his face. The problem is, the face is stuck on to the front of the head, and whereas many men have interpreted 'this' as simply 'face', it might actually have meant nose or chin.

The minimum requirement for Muslim women is not to cover the head and the neck. Those were the two bits not demanded, but left to individual women to decide. The minimum requirement is to cover the entire body from the neck down, as is the normal female practice. There is no ruling whatsoever about colours - the favourites of Aishah were scarlet and golden yellow. There is nothing wrong with bright materials. Muslim women are not required to make themselves look dowdy or ugly, only modest.

However, natural modesty suggests that too much ostentation with expensive decoration, jewellry and fabrics is not the correct spirit when one is mixing with women of modest means. Allah does ask women not to display their ornaments; some scholars make tortuous interpretations of this meaning hair and so on, (even a woman's voice!), when it most obviously refers to the highly glamorous and expensive jewellry worn by women in the Arab world, especially when the phrase is linked to the jangling of ankle-bracelets.

Ruqaiyyah Waris Maqsood
Hull

I read the article entitled 'Muslim Pub Owner Threatened' in your last issue.

Quite a few Muslims drink in my local area. In fact most off-licences are owned by Muslims who also participate in selling Scratchcards and National Lottery tickets.

It amazes me how Islam survives here with so many, sometimes illegal substances.

I know that only Allah is perfect but the local Muslims seem to be straying from the straight path. I am learning about Islam and hoping to embrace it. This behaviour does not give me a good impression of Islam and it seems as if the local scholars are turning a blind eye to the activities.

Is there anyway forward or are we all going backwards? Islam has a lot going for it but the Muslims themselves seem to be undermining it. No wonder Islamophobia is beginning to take a grip.

G Grant
Accrington, Lancs.

Q-News October 1997

As someone who has recently adopted the veil I completely disagree with the idea that it achieves nothing. I truly believe that Islam requires women to wear the hijab but were this requirement ever to come into serious question, for many Muslim women the mere social gains of wearing the hijab are enough to keep it on. Contrary to what Mr el-Diwany may believe, many women are wearing the hijab out of choice and if anything other than Islamic doctrine has driven them to it it is the experience and consequences of the very "social contact between men and women" that Mr el-Diwany is out to promote. Furthermore, Allah has given us the gift of reasoning and if in today's immoral age we are witnessing the extreme and upsetting outcomes of liberated sexual expression, then surely it is our duty to adopt more rigorous measures to control the conditions which spread evil. As for the idea that hijab equals male depression equals pornography/prostitution/ homosexuality I really cannot see the logic in this. For surely sexually frustrated men do not make a conscious attempt to be among the minority of hijabed women and then get themselves depressed over the fact that they see no hair. And even if this were the case then why should women start unveiling just to satisfy male desire? If veiling is a symbol of male oppression then surely the act of unveiling equally reflects domination by men. Does Mr el-Diwany really believe that in a hijab-less society there would be less adultery and fornication?

Surely, the example of the West has taught us otherwise. Please Mr el-Diwany, spare us hijabi sisters your pity and shower it on those 'free and liberated' women who have become victims of their own liberation.

Shagufta Yaqub, *London*

It looks as though the preoccupation with the hijab is going to rumble on and divert us from the things that really matter if we are going to make Islam our complete way of life - things like courage, compassion, tolerance, honesty, generosity, etc.

At no stage did the Prophet (peace be upon him) ever lay down any kind of 'school uniform' regulation for women. The revelation of the Quran is totally silent on the subject except for the proviso that no human being has the right to declare anything haram that Allah has actually allowed. Nowhere are women asked to cover their heads at all; men and women both have to 'veil their gaze' and women were required to cover their bosoms. Arab costume at the time of the Prophet (peace be upon him) was apparently rather free in this respect, with women making easy access for breastfeeding, sometimes feeding their babies in public, and traditionally baring their breasts completely when they led their armies into battle.

Muslim women were expected to be different - to completely cover their bodies. Those who wore head-veils, usually hanging down the back in a decorative manner held on with an agal, showing most of their hair, were asked to draw this veil across their bosoms - and if the veil was transparent (as it usually was), to make it of thicker material.

It is well known that the Prophet (peace be upon him) unfortunately made an ambiguous attempt when he said that adult women should show no more than 'this and this'. He pointed at his hands, and his face. The problem is, the face is stuck on to the front of the head, and whereas many men have interpreted 'this' as simply 'face', it might actually have meant nose or chin. The minimum requirement for Muslim women is not to cover the head and the neck. Those were the two bits not demanded, but left to individual women to decide. The minimum requirement is to cover the entire body from the neck down, as is the normal female practice. There is no ruling whatsoever about colours - the favourites of Aishah were scarlet and golden yellow. There is nothing wrong with bright materials. Muslim women are not required to make themselves look dowdy or ugly, only modest.

However, natural modesty suggests that too much ostentation with expensive decoration, jewellry and fabrics is not the correct spirit when one is mixing with women of modest means. Allah does ask women not to display their ornaments; some scholars make tortuous interpretations of this meaning hair and so on, (even a woman's voice!), when it most obviously refers to the highly glamorous and expensive jewellry worn by women in the Arab world, especially when the phrase is linked to the jangling of ankle-bracelets.

Ruqaiyyah Waris Maqsood, *Hull*

Mr El Diwany is reprimanded by Ms Yaqub for equating the hijab with sexual repression. However, all of the weddings where the hijabi women get married are marked by the strict separation of the men and women guests at the celebrations. The men are in one room and the women in another. They can't even say hello to each other, thus preventing, say, prospective partners from meeting one another with a view to eventual marriage. How cruel and repressive a practice, so in keeping with the fanatical Asian element imported in to Great Britain. Many of the hijabi women adamantly refuse even to shake the hand of a man that is not within their immediate family on the grounds that it is immoral.

The letter written by Hull schoolteacher Ruqaiyyah Waris Maqsood is much more in touch with reality. See however the vitriol that is poured upon her in the next issue of *Q-News*.

Shagufta Yaqub went on to become the editor of *Q-News*.

Last of the veil

Q-News November 1997 (No. 279-280)

I feel I must respond to the 'Hijab Again' letter to clear this matter up. First of all, many of the issues brought up about hijab were false. Mr. Farid el-Diwany totally misinterpreted the Quran and upset a lot of my sisters as well as myself. I would advise him to go and read the Quran and sunnah all over again, this time with his glasses on. I also advise him to find himself some male friends for companionship to prevent so called depression from loneliness and to prevent this 'cotton social vacuum for men' from sucking him up.

Secondly I would like to inform dear brother Farid, that I and a lot of other sisters are disappointed that such statements could come out of a Muslim brother's mouth. People these days need any excuse to get out of this so called 'isolation' of hijab and by stating this false information, you are just giving Shaytan a chance to put doubts in people's minds. There is a verse in Surah Nisa which tells us specifically about hijab and the Prophet (saw) also said that women should cover all but their face and hands. Then I ask, why can't you accept this? Why the big issue? Allah told us to wear hijab so we wear it. I am so sick of people trying to find something wrong with hijab. You also say that the Quran leaves a lot to our own sense of decency, well I'd like to inform you that people have different levels of what they consider decent. If Allah left things like that, then a lot of people would simply say that wearing mini skirts and short dresses was what they considered to be decent.

You say that women should be visually identified as women, and showing the hair tells you if someone is a woman. A lot of men these days have women's haircuts and a lot of women have men's haircuts, so you often cannot tell which is which anyway. Life is a test, I do know that it is hard and everybody wants to make it just a little bit easier but what you have to understand is, that by disobeying Allah, you are making life harder for many people who believe you and for yourself. It may not be your intention but you are asking it happen. So I ask you, brother Farid, one last time, to read the Quran and get your answers from there.

Sonia Malik, aged 14, *Manchester*

A huge shame on you, Ruqaiyya Waris Maqsood for your contribution to the ludicrous debate about the validity of the hijab. It is ludicrous because it is akin to Muslims debating the validity of the five daily prayers or the pilgrimage to Makkah. Despite the overwhelming evidence for the hijab contained in the Quran and the sunnah of the female companions and family members [of] our Messenger, some Muslims persist in denying the existence of all such evidence. What do these people hope to achieve by chipping away at the basic foundations of Islam? Do they hope to destroy the entire edifice of Allah's religion? And what next? Will they call on Muslims to stop fasting in Ramadan, perhaps even cease studying the Quran? Allah alone knows the hidden agendas of such people but I would advise them to consult the instructions of the Almighty as contained in the Quran and implemented by his Messenger and not to consult the devilish inclinations of their own hearts.

Ms Khola Hasan
Al-Quran Society, Tottenham

letters to the editor

Send letters to **Q-News**, Dexion House, 2-4 Empire Way, Wembley, Middx HA1 4ET or fax on **0181- 903 0820** E-mail **q-news@aapi.co.uk**

Administration: Zeeshan Khan

MANCHESTER
Bureau Chief
Qasim Afzal
Tel/fax:
0161 205 2885

Thank you to all our subscribers and readers.

Subscriptions:
Annual subscription rates
UK £35;
Europe £54;
overseas £60.

Call 0181-903 0819 for more details and special offers.

Last of the veil

I feel I must respond to the 'Hijab Again' letter to clear this matter up. First of all, many of the issues brought up about hijab were false. Mr. Farid el-Diwany totally misinterpreted the Quran and upset a lot of my sisters as well as myself. I would advise him to go and read the Quran and sunnah all over again, this time with his glasses on. I also advise him to find himself some male friends for companionship to prevent so called depression from loneliness and to prevent this 'cotton social vacuum for men' from sucking him up.

Secondly I would like to inform dear brother Farid, that I and a lot of other sisters are disappointed that such statements could come out of a Muslim brother's mouth. People these days need any excuse to get out of this so called 'isolation' of hijab and by stating this false information, you are just giving Shaytan a chance to put doubts in people's minds. There is a verse in Surah Nisa which tells us specifically about hijab and the Prophet (saw) also said that women should cover all but their face and hands. Then I ask, why can't you accept this? Why the big issue? Allah told us to wear hijab so we wear it. I am so sick of people trying to find something wrong with hijab. You also say that the Quran leaves a lot to our own sense of decency, well I'd like to inform you that people have different levels of what they consider decent. If Allah left things like that, then a lot of people would simply say that wearing mini skirts and short dresses was what they considered to be decent. You say that women should be visually identified as women, and showing the hair tells you if someone is a woman. A lot of men these days have women's haircuts and a lot of women have men's haircuts, so you often cannot tell which is which anyway. Life is a test, I do know that it is hard and everybody wants to make it just a little bit easier but what you have to understand is, that by disobeying Allah, you are making life harder for many people who believe you and for yourself. It may not be your intention but you are asking it happen. So I ask you, brother Farid, one last time, to read the Quran and get your answers from there.

Sonia Malik, *aged 14*
Manchester

A huge shame on you, Ruqaiyya Waris Maqsood for your contribution to the ludicrous debate about the validity of the hijab. It is ludicrous because it is akin to Muslims debating the validity of the five daily prayers or the pilgrimage to Makkah.

Despite the overwhelming evidence for the hijab contained in the Quran and the sunnah of the female companions and family members our Messenger, some Muslims persist in denying the existence of all such evidence. What do these people hope to achieve by chipping away at the basic foundations of Islam? Do they hope to destroy the entire edifice of Allah's religion? And what next? Will they call on Muslims to stop fasting in Ramadan, perhaps even cease studying the Quran?

Allah alone knows the hidden agendas of such people but I would advise them to consult the instructions of the Almighty as contained in the Quran and implemented by his Messenger and not to consult the devilish inclinations of their own hearts?

Ms Khola Hasan
Al-Quran Society
Tottenham

Please stop this long running 'soap opera' of letters regarding 'hijab'. It has now ceased to serve any purpose except to further undermine what little unity Muslims profess to having. Instead of highlighting our unity it seems we Muslims take a pleasure in actively seeking to destroy it. As second generation Muslims we must share a new sense of compassion and use this to work towards a common goal.

The only useful thing left to be said about the issue of 'hijab' is that the truth is clearly laid down, not in personal opinions, but in the three accepted sources of Islamic jurisprudence - the Quran, the *Ahadith*, and the writings of the Ulema. It is for each Muslim to seek knowledge and guidance and Allah will make the path easy for those who strive towards the Truth (Insha'Allah). So please put an end to publishing counter-productive letters which have failed for some time to be of any informative value, and instead advise your readers to search out the truth about 'hijab' for themselves.

S. El-Darsh,
North London

4 — **Q-News** November 1997

Please stop this long running 'soap opera' of letters regarding 'hijab'. It has now ceased to serve any purpose except to further undermine what little unity Muslims profess to having. Instead of highlighting our unity it seems we Muslims take a pleasure in actively seeking to destroy it. As second generation Muslims we must share a new sense of compassion and use this to work towards a common goal. The only useful thing left to be said about the issue of 'hijab' is that the truth is clearly laid down, not in personal opinions, but in the three accepted sources of Islamic jurisprudence - the Quran, the Ahadith, and the writings of the Ulema. It is for each Muslim to seek knowledge and guidance and Allah will make the path easy for those who strive towards the Truth (Insha'Allah). So please put an end to publishing counter-productive letters which have failed for some time to be of any informative value, and instead advise your readers to search out the truth about 'hijab' for themselves.

S. El-Darsh
North London

Issue no. 279-280 of November 1997 sees *Q-News* go out of their way to further humiliate Mr El Diwany by printing a letter from a 14 year old, Sonia Malik from Manchester. The extreme reaction of Ms Khola Hasan of the Al-Quran Society, Tottenham, further illustrates just how backward and aggresive some of the 'sisters' can be.

Hijab, again

Q-News January 1998

As someone who values the work and personality of Sister Ruqaiyyah Waris Maqsood, I must leap to her defence regarding the 'shame on you' letter from Khola Hassan (Q-News 279). Ms Hassan is certainly aware of the different interpretations of Islamic practice on most matters and the many schools of thought with which she may not personally agree.

Hijab, again
As someone who values the work and personality of Sister Ruqaiyyah Waris Maqsood, I must leap to her defence regarding the 'shame on you' letter from Khola Hassan (*Q-News 279*).
Ms Hassan is certainly aware of the different interpretations of Islamic practice on most matters and the many schools of thought with which she may not personally agree.
In today's over-zealous climate, the badge of loyalty to Islam appears, for some, to be a piece of cloth covering the hair ! This is put above kindheartedness, mercy, spirituality and other virtues.
Anyone who reads Ms Maqsood's books will literally feel her love for her faith. To accuse her of deliberately seeking to destroy Islam is both ludicrous and cruel and unbecoming of a fellow sister-in-faith.
A famous writer once wrote of Catholicism: "The Church knows all the rules but it does not know what goes on in a single human heart". Is this what we want our beloved faith to be?
Name supplied
Essex

In today's over-zealous climate, the badge of loyalty to Islam appears, for some, to be a piece of cloth covering the hair ! This is put above kindheartedness, mercy, spirituality and other virtues.

Anyone who reads Ms Maqsood's books will literally feel her love for her faith. To accuse her of deliberately seeking to destroy Islam is both ludicrous and cruel and unbecoming of a fellow sister-in-faith. A famous writer once wrote of Catholicism: "The Church knows all the rules but it does not know what goes on in a single human heart". Is this what we want our beloved faith to be?

Name supplied
Essex

Ameena Mohammed

Boxing and kicking a habit

Q-News August 1998
(No. 293)

Mix a pair of boxing gloves and hijab and what do you get? Ameena Mohammed, Britain's first female Muslim Thai boxer. Explosive stuff - but then so is the challenge of self defence. **Shagufta Yaqub** meets a martial warrior intent on terminating stereotypes.

Every training session for the country's first female Muslim Thai boxer is a relentless war against prejudice and ignorance. Whenever Ameena Mohammed gets into a boxing ring she has more than the sparring partner in front of her to deal with: sexism and confusion on what a Muslim woman can do in life.

But the 24 year old has learnt to take it all in her increasingly lethal stride. "All women, including Muslims, have to be able to defend themselves," says Ameena, while Mohammed, her 16-month old baby, plays on her lap. "We can't be completely dependent on our husbands for everything" she points out. "When all the men are at war, who will protect the children?" she adds in a soft voice.

In Page Hall, Sheffield, where Ameena has lived all her life, nobody questions her guts. Six years ago she made the courageous decision to

SPORTS
Ameena Mohammed
Boxing and kicking a habit
Mix a pair of boxing gloves and hijab and what do you get? Ameena Mohammed, Britain's first female Muslim Thai boxer. Explosive stuff - but then so is the challenge of self defence. **Shagufta Yaqub** meets a martial warrior intent on terminating stereotypes.
30 Q-News August 1998

embrace Islam. "It wasn't easy, but it was the best thing for me: Islam gives me all the relevant answers to my life," she says.

Ameena took up Thai boxing 18 months ago after a nasty experience convinced her that she has to acquire the ability to defend herself. "I used to be a taxi driver and then became a bus driver," she says. "A nasty threatening incident on the bus made me realise how defenceless and vulnerable I was." The incident made it clear to her that she needed some skills of "self preservation". Next thing she did was walk into the Sheffield Thai Boxing Club and the rest is history.

Her martial arts training has, among other things, convinced Ameena of the need for Muslim women to take up some form of physical exercise. Ameena believes that the majority of Muslim women today are dangerously lazy and unhealthy. "If the women of the time of the Prophet were here today they would laugh at us" she says. "Those women were active: they fought in jihads alongside men and they knew how to protect themselves and their children. How many of us can do that today?" she asks.

Being physically fit, she points out, is part and parcel of the Islamic way of life. "A mother who is physically well is better to deal more ably with her other responsibilities including the spiritual ones."

But Ameena's healthy call has not been positively welcomed by everyone in her predominantly Muslim neighbourhood. "Some very cultured Muslim brothers tell me it's not an acceptable sport for a Muslim woman. They say it's haraam [prohibited] but I challenge them to produce one verse from the Holy Quran as evidence. If they do that I promise to stop going to classes," she says.

Ameena's husband, a kickboxer himself, is however fully supportive of his wife's martial training. "He's absolutely brilliant about it, in fact if I ever feel lazy about going he's the one who forces me to go" she claims. Ameena feels that it is the Muslims who carry a heavy burden of culture and tradition that are the most negative about women's activities. "It's the husbands who need to be educated and to realise that sports and particularly training in self-defence is not haraam" she says.

Ameena trains with women most of the time but her trainer is male and she often has to train with other men. "It is more realistic to be training with men" she says. "It is harder and it makes me a lot tougher". Ameena seems undisturbed by her mixed training sessions. "I am totally comfotrtable with it and if I got any bad vibes I would be out of there" she says.

"Personally, I believe it's the intentions that matter" she says. "For me Thai boxing is a form of daw'a. I always get non-Muslims asking me if Muslim women are allowed to keep fit, just like they used to ask me if Muslim women are allowed to drive when I used to be a bus driver. It is important they can see that the hijab is supposed to protect women but not to oppress them" she says.

"Non-Muslims are now very accepting of it and the questions they ask are only out of curiosity, like 'Don't you get hot in that!?'"

Ameena, however, continues to hope that she can convince more Muslim women to take up some form of sports or martial arts. "Maintaining your body is part of your diin and you will be accountable to Allah for looking after it," she says. "Somebody has to encourage Muslim women to look after themselves and their bodies and and if I can do that and get rewards for it then that's great," she says. "I do eventually want to use my skills to teach other sisters but I have six bands to get through yet" she says.

So far, however, Ameena has not managed to influence the other Muslim women in her community to take up the sport. "It's unfortunate that there are no places where women can learn from other women in Sheffield" she says. "I completely understand that some women are not comfortable training with men" she says, "and nor do other sisters have to do something as rigorous as Thai boxing, as long as its something to do with keeping fit and self-defence."

But Thai boxing is no longer just about fitness and self-defence for Ameena. It is also a sport that she immensely enjoys and her trainer, Mick Mullaney is looking forward to the day she is ready to fight a competitive match. "I'm not doing it for fame or money" says Ameena, "I couldn't get rich from Thai boxing even if I wanted to, and my first competition is still a long way away yet."

Her first competiting might be a long way off but Ameena Mohammed is most probably a great champion in the eyes of thousands of young British Muslim women who will surely follow her progress with a tinge of both envy and admiration.

[The article continued under a second sub-title, ' Women, sports and fatwas']:

Women, sports and fatwas

Q-News October 1997

Women, sports and fatwas

Ameena's decision to pursue her training in Thai boxing has provoked a strong response from Muslim scholars contacted by *Q-News*. "Tell her to stop immediately," said Dr Zaki Badawi of The Muslim College, London. "She will make the hijab look ridiculous."

But Ameena begs to differ with the scholar claiming that it is more a gender issue than an impartial fiqh verdict. "When it comes to women it is always a 'no' or a question mark. Nobody complains about Muslim male footballers, swimmers, wrestlers, etc. not being dressed appropriately," she says. "But yet they are the first to shout and rave as soon as a woman decides to do something."

"Personally, I think a large extent of the objection to my doing Thai boxing has its roots in the restrictive attitude of many cultured Muslims who have a more narrow and restricted stereotype of a Muslim woman than even many non-Muslims. If mixed training sessions were not the problem they still would come up with something else."

However Dr Badawi, considered 'liberal' in some quarters, made it clear that there is nothing intrinsically wrong with self defence or sports for women but insisted that "where it involves fighting in a ring with spectators cheering you on, that is clearly not accpetable in Islam." Referring to Muslim women fighting battles in the history of Islam, he pointed out that "those women fought only for defence and out of neccessity, and they did not parade for money, fashion or prowess."

"We are not talking about competitive training - we are simply talking about basic self preservation skills and overall physical well-being. Yes, mixed training sessions might not be the ideal situation but the responsibility of creating this ideal situation remains with the men," says Ameena.

"The Prophet encouraged archery, swimming and horse-riding in an undisputed hadith. Yet tell me of one Muslim organisation that has made the facilitation of any of these possible to our community? At the end of the day Muslim women up and down the country have to make daily decisions between lesser evils. We will only get better if our choices are made more varied and relevant. And this only the men can do for they have the 'power'," points out Ameena.

"In conclusion, to be honest, in the matter of martial arts and physical fitness Muslim women would always have problems because our men cannot appreciate the matter. If they did, how can one explain their state of health?"

French Islamophobia still thriving

Q-News August 1998 (No. 294)

Barely have the curtains come down on one of the greatest global celebrations of human diversity than the spectre of Francophone xenophobia has reasserted itself with a postscript that would have even Jean-Marie Le Pen beaming with glee.

Obviously resistant to the atmosphere of unity left behind by the recent World Cup, French border police sent a British munaqqaba packing because she insisted on having her identity verified by a female official.

Thirty-four year-old Mrs Farrukh Shaikh was travelling with her husband and four children from Dover to Calais when her ordeal began. Having disembarked in the French port she was confronted by immigration officials who refused her request to have the routine identity check

NEWS

French Islamophobia still thriving

Barely have the curtains come down on one of the greatest global celebrations of human diversity than the spectre of Francophone xenophobia has reasserted itself with a postscript that would have even Jean-Marie Le Pen beaming with glee.

Obviously resistant to the atmosphere of unity left behind by the recent World Cup, French border police sent a British *munaqqaba* packing because she insisted on having her identity verified by a female official.

Thirty-four year-old Mrs Farrukh Shaikh was travelling with her husband and four children from Dover to Calais when her ordeal began. Having disembarked in the French port she was confronted by immigration officials who refused her request to have the routine identity check performed by a female.

Speaking no English, the guards repeatedly motioned Mrs Shaikh to raise her veil. When it become clear she would not they frogmarched her to the police station where they held her for two hours before ordering her to reveal her face or be returned home on the next sailing.

"I'm quite strict about this so I stood by my principles", said Mrs Shaikh, a part-time children's worker with Leicester City Council.

On board the ferry French officials demanded she fill out a disembarkation form - not normally required for European Community residents. They also withheld Mrs Shaikh's passport until she arrived back in Dover - where however a female attendant was on hand to carry out a check.

Back at home in Leicester Mrs Shaikh told *Q-News*: "The whole thing made me feel like I was being discriminated against because I am a Muslim. It was humiliating being escorted by the police like we were criminals to the station and then the ferry."

A well-travelled person, Mrs Shaikh said it was the first time she has seen her request treated so contemptibly. "I went to Canada last year and there was no problem. Before that I went by road for *Umrah* and everywhere I went I could rely on female officials to perform the checks."

Asked if there were guidelines for staff dealing with veiled women, the French Interior Ministry responded with characteristic disdain: "There is no guideline. We are in a secular republic which doesn't treat people differently on the basis of race or custom or belief", said press counsellor Anne Cublier. "Women don't need to be veiled. In fact I am very shocked that a woman should refuse to be examined like that."

She added: "Everyone is treated in the same way. If people want to come to France they have to respect our beliefs."

Meanwhile Mrs Shaikh has had to make new arrangements: "We took the kids to Drayton Manor Park and we've got plans to visit Woburn for the day."

Mrs Shaikh's experience follows another last year in Bradford in which Yorkshire Buses issued an apology after one of its drivers declined to let a veiled Muslimah board his bus unless she showed her face.

While some organisations employ procedures which clearly reduce the risk of such incidents others have looked to draw up special guidelines on how to deal with the *munaqqaba*.

British Customs and Excise South East said that they operated under strict rules which required frisking and body searches to be performed by staff of the same sex. "While there hasn't been a specific complaint that anyone can recall we do have guidelines asking our staff to be sensitive to the headgear of certain ethnic groups," said spokesman Mike Thompson. "Where there may be sensitivities, and this applies to Sikh men too, they must proceed with tact."

Robin Pulford of London Underground said: "The simple answer to that is that people who wear covering masks simply do not use those of our services which require ID. We discussed this issue in detail when we issued photocards some years ago but nothing was resolved. Strictly speaking, our passes require a full face photo but the policy vis-a-vis veiled women has never been put to the test."

Suhail Malik

8 Q-News August 1998

performed by a female.

Speaking no English, the guards repeatedly motioned Mrs Shaikh to raise her veil. When it became clear she would not they frogmarched her to the police station where they held her for two hours before ordering her to reveal her face or be returned home on the next sailing.

"I'm quite strict about this so I stood by my principles", said Mrs Shaikh, a part-time children's worker with Leicester City Council.

On board the ferry French officials demanded she fill out a disembarkation form - not normally required for European Community residents. They also withheld Mrs Shaikh's passport until she arrived back in Dover - where however a female attendant was on hand to carry out a check.

Back at home in Leicester Mrs Shaikh told *Q-News*: "The whole thing made me feel like I was being discriminated against because I am a Muslim. It was humiliating being escorted by the police like we were criminals to the station and then the ferry."

A well-travelled person, Mrs Shaikh said it was the first time she has seen her request treated so contemptibly. "I went to Canada last year and there was no problem. Before that I went by road for Umrah and everywhere I went I could rely on female officials to perform the checks."

Asked if there were guidelines for staff dealing with veiled women, the French Interior Ministry responded with characteristic disdain: "There is no guideline. We are in a secular republic which doesn't treat people differently on the basis of race or custom or belief", said press counsellor Anne Cublier. "Women don't need to be veiled. In fact I am very shocked that a woman should refuse to be examined like that."

She added: "Everyone is treated in the same way. If people want to come to France they have to respect our beliefs."

Meanwhile Mrs Shaikh has had to make new arrangements: "We took the kids to Drayton Manor Park and we've got plans to visit Woburn for the day."

Mrs Shaikh's experience follows another last year in Bradford in which Yorkshire Buses issued an apology after one of its drivers declined to let a veiled Muslimah board his bus unless she showed her face.

While some organisations employ procedures which clearly reduce the risk of such incidents others have looked to draw up special guidelines on how to deal with the munaqqaba.

British Customs and Excise South East said that they operated under strict rules which required frisking and body searches to be performed by staff of the same sex. "While there hasn't been a specific complaint that anyone can recall we do have guidelines asking our staff to be sensitive to the headgear of certain ethnic groups," said spokesman Mike Thompson. "Where there may be sensitivities, and this applies to Sikh men too, they must proceed with tact."

Robin Pulford of London Underground said: "The simple answer to that is that people who wear covering masks simply do not use those of our services which require ID. We discussed this issue in detail when we issued photocards some years ago but nothing was resolved. Strictly speaking, our passes require a full face photo but the policy vis-a-vis veiled women has never been put to the test."

Suhail Malik

French Islamophobia

Q-News September 1998 (No. 295)

I refer to Suhail Malik's article in Issue No. 294, August 98, of *Q-News*. The question of Algeria aside, I think the French are quite right to object to the wearing of the veil and hijab by "exhibitionist" Muslim women. The French are naturally bewildered by this sociophobic form of dress. As a Muslim I will be encouraging the French authorities at the highest level to maintain their stance relating to the perversion of Islam by misguided Muslims who support the wearing of the hijab and also the veil.

When one reads the enlightened footnotes numbered 37 and 38 of Muhammad Asad's translation of the Quran in connection with verse 31 of Surat-al-Noor, it is quite clear that the purpose behind the revelation of verse 31 refers merely to the form of dress that women wore at the time of the Prophet Muhammad and was not in any way related to a head-covering that permanently covered the hair.

Non-Muslims will never appreciate the beauty of Islam as long as certain brain-washed Muslim women, supported by their ignorant men, pervert the founding values of Islam by telling the world that either the head-scarf or the veil is a principle of Islam. The hysterical panic of these Muslim women when merely being seen "uncovered" by male members of the public has to be seen to be believed. It is nauseous and defies common sense which is what Islam is based on.

Farid El Diwany
London

French Islamophobia
I refer to Suhail Malik's article in Issue No. 294, August 98, of *Q-News*. The question of Algeria aside, I think the French are quite right to object to the wearing of the veil and hijab by "exhibitionist" Muslim women. The French are naturally bewildered by this sociophobic form of dress. As a Muslim I will be encouraging the French authorities at the highest level to maintain their stance relating to the perversion of Islam by misguided Muslims who support the wearing of the hijab and also the veil.
When one reads the enlightened footnotes numbered 37 and 38 of Muhammad Asad's translation of the Quran in connection with verse 31 of Surat-al-Noor, it is quite clear that the purpose behind the revelation of verse 31 refers merely to the form of dress that women wore at the time of the Prophet Muhammad and was not in any way related to a head-covering that permanently covered the hair.
Non-Muslims will never appreciate the beauty of Islam as long as certain brain-washed Muslim women, supported by their ignorant men, pervert the founding values of Islam by telling the world that either the head-scarf or the veil is a principle of Islam. The hysterical panic of these Muslim women when merely being seen "uncovered" by male members of the public has to be seen to be believed. It is nauseous and defies common sense which is what Islam is based on.
Farid El Diwany
London
Q-News September 1998

Q News no. 296 October 1998
More on Hijabs
I know Mr Farid El Diwany is notoriously known for filling up your letters page with his extreme anti-hijab views but his last letter was completely outrageous. I hate to prolong this ongoing debate but I just had to point a few things out. He criticises veiled women for taking the hijab too seriously and yet he seems to be the only one who is really obsessed with this whole hijab thing. Wearing it is one thing, but writing letters left right and centre to all sorts of organisations protesting against it is what I call 'taking it too seriously'. At the end of the day, nobody's asking him to wear it, and I doubt if he can claim to have suffered any personal loss as a result of others wearing it, so what's his problem? And who does he think he is to call our veiled Muslim sisters 'exhibitionists'? Is he including the Prophets wives (peace be upon them) among these exhibitionists?
Mr Diwany wants non-Muslims to appreciate the beauty of Islam. Maybe he means rather he wants them to appreciate the physical beauty of Muslim women. If only he knew where the true beauty lies in a believing woman.
Daud Johnson
Reading

More on Hijabs

Q-News October 1998 (No. 296)

I know Mr Farid El Diwany is notoriously known for filling up your letters page with his extreme anti-hijab views but his last letter was completely outrageous. I hate to prolong this ongoing debate but I just had to point a few things out. He criticises veiled women for taking the hijab too seriously and yet he seems to be the only one who is really obsessed with this whole hijab thing. Wearing it is one thing, but writing letters left right and centre to all sorts of organisations protesting against it is what I call 'taking it too seriously'. At the end of the day, nobody's asking him to wear it, and I doubt if he can claim to have suffered any personal loss as a result of others wearing it, so what's his problem? And who does he think he is to call our veiled Muslim sisters 'exhibitionists'? Is he including the Prophets wives (peace be upon them) among these exhibitionists?

Mr Diwany wants non-Muslims to appreciate the beauty of Islam. Maybe he means rather he wants them to appreciate the physical beauty of Muslim women. If only he knew where the true beauty lies in a believing woman.

Daud Johnson
Reading

Daud Johnson, a convert to Islam, is barking up the wrong tree. He mentions the Prophet's wives who, it is true, were asked by the Prophet himself to be accorded special reverence, due to their elevated status. Below are the Quranic extracts from Surah 53 - The Confederates (Al-Ahzab) - from Muhammad Asad's '*The Message of* THE QURAN', dealing with the veil vis a vis the Prophet's wives only. Footnotes 68, 69 and 75 are most instructive.

(53) O YOU who have attained to faith! Do not enter the Prophet's dwellings unless you are given leave; [and when invited] to a meal, do not come [so early as] to wait for it to be readied: but whenever you are invited, enter [at the proper time]; and when you have partaken of the meal, disperse without lingering for the sake of mere talk: that, behold, might give offence to the Prophet, and yet he might feel shy of [asking] you [to leave]: but God is not shy of [teaching you] what is right.[68]

And [as for the Prophet's wives,] whenever you ask them for anything that you need, ask them from behind a screen:[69] this will but deepen the purity of your hearts and theirs. Moreover, it does not behove you to give offence to God's Apostle – just as it would not behove you ever to marry his widows after he has passed away:[70] that, verily, would be an enormity in the sight of God.

(54) Whether you do anything openly or in secret, [remember that,] verily, God has full knowledge of everything.

(55) [However,] it is no sin for them[71] [to appear freely] before their fathers, or their sons, or their brothers, or their brothers' sons, or their sisters' sons, or their womenfolk, or such [male slaves] as their right hands may possess.

But [always, O wives of the Prophet,[72]] remain conscious of God – for, behold, God is witness unto everything.

(56) Verily, God and His angels bless the Prophet:

لَا تَدْخُلُوا بُيُوتَ النَّبِيِّ إِلَّا أَن يُؤْذَنَ لَكُمْ إِلَىٰ طَعَامٍ
غَيْرَ نَاظِرِينَ إِنَاهُ وَلَٰكِنْ إِذَا دُعِيتُمْ فَادْخُلُوا فَإِذَا طَعِمْتُمْ
فَانتَشِرُوا وَلَا مُسْتَأْنِسِينَ لِحَدِيثٍ إِنَّ ذَٰلِكُمْ كَانَ
يُؤْذِي النَّبِيَّ فَيَسْتَحْيِي مِنكُمْ وَاللَّهُ لَا يَسْتَحْيِي مِنَ
الْحَقِّ وَإِذَا سَأَلْتُمُوهُنَّ مَتَاعًا فَاسْأَلُوهُنَّ مِن وَرَاءِ حِجَابٍ
ذَٰلِكُمْ أَطْهَرُ لِقُلُوبِكُمْ وَقُلُوبِهِنَّ وَمَا كَانَ لَكُمْ أَن تُؤْذُوا
رَسُولَ اللَّهِ وَلَا أَن تَنكِحُوا أَزْوَاجَهُ مِن بَعْدِهِ أَبَدًا إِنَّ
ذَٰلِكُمْ كَانَ عِندَ اللَّهِ عَظِيمًا ﴿٥٣﴾ إِن تُبْدُوا شَيْئًا أَوْ تُخْفُوهُ
فَإِنَّ اللَّهَ كَانَ بِكُلِّ شَيْءٍ عَلِيمًا ﴿٥٤﴾ لَّا جُنَاحَ عَلَيْهِنَّ فِي
آبَائِهِنَّ وَلَا أَبْنَائِهِنَّ وَلَا إِخْوَانِهِنَّ وَلَا أَبْنَاءِ إِخْوَانِهِنَّ
وَلَا أَبْنَاءِ أَخَوَاتِهِنَّ وَلَا نِسَائِهِنَّ وَلَا مَا مَلَكَتْ أَيْمَانُهُنَّ
وَاتَّقِينَ اللَّهَ إِنَّ اللَّهَ كَانَ عَلَىٰ كُلِّ شَيْءٍ شَهِيدًا ﴿٥٥﴾ إِنَّ اللَّهَ
وَمَلَائِكَتَهُ يُصَلُّونَ عَلَى النَّبِيِّ يَا أَيُّهَا الَّذِينَ آمَنُوا صَلُّوا

68 Connecting with the reference, in verses 45–48, to the Prophet's mission, the above passage is meant to stress his unique position among his contemporaries; but as is so often the case with Qurʾanic references to historical events and situations, the ethical principle enunciated here is not restricted to a particular time or environment. By exhorting the Prophet's Companions to revere his person, the Qurʾān reminds all believers, at all times, of his exalted status (cf. note 85 on 2 : 104); beyond that, it teaches them certain rules of behaviour bearing on the life of the community as such: rules which, however insignificant they may appear at first glance, are of psychological value in a society that is to be governed by a genuine feeling of brotherhood, mutual consideration, and respect for the sanctity of each other's personality and privacy.

69 The term *ḥijāb* denotes anything that intervenes between two things, or conceals, shelters or protects the one from the other; it may be rendered, according to the context, as "barrier", "obstacle", "partition", "screen", "curtain", "veil", etc., in both the concrete and abstract connotations of these words. The prohibition to approach the Prophet's wives otherwise than "from behind a screen" or "curtain" may be taken literally – as indeed it was taken by most of the Companions of the Prophet – or metaphorically, indicating the exceptional reverence due to these "mothers of the faithful".

70 Lit., "to marry his wives after him".

71 I.e., the wives of the Prophet (connecting with the injunction, in verse 53 above, that they should be spoken to "from behind a screen").

72 This interpolation is conditioned by the feminine gender of the subsequent plural imperative *ittaqīna*.

650

[hence,] O you who have attained to faith, bless him and give yourselves up [to his guidance] in utter self-surrender!

(57) Verily, as for those who [knowingly] affront God and His Apostle – God will reject them[73] in this world and in the life to come; and shameful suffering will He ready for them.

(58) And as for those who malign believing men and believing women without their having done any wrong – they surely burden themselves with the guilt of calumny, and [thus] with a flagrant sin!

(59) O Prophet! Tell thy wives and thy daughters, as well as all [other] believing women, that they should draw over themselves some of their outer garments [when in public]: this will be more conducive to their being recognized [as decent women] and not annoyed.[74] But [withal,] God is indeed much-forgiving, a dispenser of grace![75]

(60) THUS IT IS: if[76] the hypocrites, and they in whose hearts is disease,[77] and they who, by spreading false rumours, would cause disturbances[78] in the City [of the Prophet] desist not [from their hostile doings], We shall indeed give thee mastery over them, [O Muḥammad] – and then they will not remain thy neighbours in this [city] for more than a little while:[79] (61) bereft of God's grace, they shall be seized wherever they may be found, and slain one and all.[80]

عَلَيْهِ وَسَلِّمُوا۟ تَسْلِيمًا ﴿٥٦﴾ إِنَّ ٱلَّذِينَ يُؤْذُونَ ٱللَّهَ وَرَسُولَهُۥ
لَعَنَهُمُ ٱللَّهُ فِى ٱلدُّنْيَا وَٱلْـَٔاخِرَةِ وَأَعَدَّ لَهُمْ عَذَابًا مُّهِينًا ﴿٥٧﴾
وَٱلَّذِينَ يُؤْذُونَ ٱلْمُؤْمِنِينَ وَٱلْمُؤْمِنَٰتِ بِغَيْرِ مَا ٱكْتَسَبُوا۟
فَقَدِ ٱحْتَمَلُوا۟ بُهْتَٰنًا وَإِثْمًا مُّبِينًا ﴿٥٨﴾ يَٰٓأَيُّهَا ٱلنَّبِىُّ قُل
لِّأَزْوَٰجِكَ وَبَنَاتِكَ وَنِسَآءِ ٱلْمُؤْمِنِينَ يُدْنِينَ عَلَيْهِنَّ مِن
جَلَٰبِيبِهِنَّ ذَٰلِكَ أَدْنَىٰٓ أَن يُعْرَفْنَ فَلَا يُؤْذَيْنَ وَكَانَ ٱللَّهُ
غَفُورًا رَّحِيمًا ﴿٥٩﴾ ۞ لَّئِن لَّمْ يَنتَهِ ٱلْمُنَٰفِقُونَ وَٱلَّذِينَ
فِى قُلُوبِهِم مَّرَضٌ وَٱلْمُرْجِفُونَ فِى ٱلْمَدِينَةِ لَنُغْرِيَنَّكَ بِهِمْ
ثُمَّ لَا يُجَاوِرُونَكَ فِيهَآ إِلَّا قَلِيلًا ﴿٦٠﴾ مَّلْعُونِينَ أَيْنَمَا ثُقِفُوٓا۟

73 In classical Arabic, the term *laᶜnah* is more or less synonymous with *ibᶜād* ("removal into distance" or "banishment"); hence, God's *laᶜnah* denotes "His rejection of a sinner from all that is good" (*Lisān al-ᶜArab*) or "exclusion from His grace" (*Manār* II, 50). The term *malᶜūn* which occurs in verse 61 below signifies, therefore, "one who is bereft of God's grace".

74 Cf. the first two sentences of 24 : 31 and the corresponding notes 37 and 38.

75 The specific, time-bound formulation of the above verse (evident in the reference to the wives and daughters of the Prophet), as well as the deliberate vagueness of the recommendation that women "should draw upon themselves some of their outer garments (*min jalābībihinna*)" when in public, makes it clear that this verse was not meant to be an injunction (*ḥukm*) in the general, timeless sense of this term but, rather, a moral guideline to be observed against the ever-changing background of time and social environment. This finding is reinforced by the concluding reference to God's forgiveness and grace.

76 For my above rendering of *laᵓin*, see *sūrah* 30, note 45. With this passage, the discourse returns to the theme touched upon in verse 1 and more fully dealt with in verses 9–27: namely, the opposition with which the Prophet and his followers were faced in their early years at Yathrib (which by that time had come to be known as *Madīnat an-Nabī*, "the City of the Prophet").

77 See note 16 above.

78 Thus Zamakhsharī, explaining the term *al-murjifūn* in the above context.

79 I.e., "there will be open warfare between thee and them", which will result in their expulsion from Medina: a prediction which was fulfilled in the course of time.

80 Lit., "slain with [a great] slaying". See in this connection note 168 on 2 : 191. For my rendering of *malᶜūnīn* as "bereft of God's grace", see note 73 above.

Verse 53 of the Confederates has been used to support the belief that the Prophet's wives covered their hair and even their faces. Verse 59 of the Confederates has been used (some would say, twisted) to support the belief that all Muslim women should cover their hair and faces in public. But Verse 53 is specific to the Prophet's wives. And just as the Prophet wore a beard which many Muslim men copy, then many Muslim women think that by wearing the "seperating curtain" of the face veil/hijab/jilbab in public they will emulate the Prophet's wives and thus be 'better' Muslims. Given that Muslims accept that the Prophet's wives were addressed from behind a screen in the home by the Prophet's companions, there is no evidence however to suggest that any of the Prophet's wives, when outside the home, wore the "seperating curtain" of a veil covering their faces. Karen Armstrong in her acclaimed biography of the Prophet, - *Muhammad* - published by Phoenix Press (Copyright © 1991 by Karen Armstrong) details the fact that it was only Muhammad's wives that were to be secluded. I reproduce Karen Armstrong's text from pages 197 to 199:

'Shortly after Zaynab's wedding celebrations and possibly connected with it, came the revelation known as the Verses of the Curtain, which decreed that Muhammad's wives must be secluded from the rest of the umma. Muslim traditions explain the introduction of the hijab, which is usually translated as 'the Veil', in various ways. Some say that it was Umar, who had aggressively chauvinist views, who urged Muhammad to seclude his wives from view by means of a curtain. There had recently been unpleasant incidents when the Hypocrites had insulted Muhammad's wives as they went out at night to relieve themselves. Others say that as Muhammad became more important and more aware of life in the civilised countries, he wanted to adopt the Persian and Byzantine custom of secluding women of the upper classes as a mark of his wives' new dignity. All, however, point out that sexual morality was lax in Arabia during the pre-Islamic period. There tended to be a great deal of indecent talk and innuendo and a great deal of flirting and propositioning. In traditional society, a sexual scandal can be extremely serious and arouse strong emotions in a community. Muhammad was probably well aware that Ibn Ubbay and his supporters would be delighted to damage the Muslim cause by pointing to a disgrace in his own family.

It is said that at Zaynab's wedding feast, some of the guests stayed too long and made a nuisance of themselves. This prompted a revelation which put some distance between Muhammad's family and the rest of the umma:

Believers, do not enter the houses of the Prophet for a meal without waiting for the proper time, unless you are given leave. But if you are invited, enter; and when you have eaten, disperse. Do not engage in familiar talk, for this would annoy the Prophet and he would be ashamed to bid you go; but of the truth, al-Llah is not ashamed. If you ask his wives for anything, Speak to them from behind a curtain [hijab]. This is more chaste for your hearts and their hearts.

Muhammad, it will be remembered, had no room of his own at the mosque; he simply slept in the apartments of his wives. But as he became more important in Medina his home inevitably became a public place, as more and more people came to consult him about their personal or religious problems or asked him to arbitrate in a dispute. Some Muslims liked to approach him through his wives, in the hope of getting his ear. Aisha, for example, was known to have had several friendly chats with a particular young man, which people remembered later when a scandal broke out that threatened to split the umma down the middle. The hijab or curtain was not intended to be an oppressive measure. It was designed to prevent a scandalous situation developing which Muhammad's enemies could use to discredit him.

We should pause to consider the question of the hijab, and the Muslim institution of the veil. It is often seen in the West as a symbol of male oppression, but in the Quran it was simply a piece of protocol that applied only to the Prophet's wives. Muslim women are required, like men, to dress modestly, but women are not told to veil themselves from view, nor to seclude themselves from men in a separate part of the house. These were later developments and did not become widespread in the Islamic empire until three or four generations after the death of Muhammad. It appears that the custom of veiling and secluding women came into the Muslim world from Persia and Byzantium, where women had long been treated in this way.

In fact the veil or curtain was not designed to degrade Muhammad's wives but was a symbol of their superior status. After Muhammad's death, his wives became very powerful people: they were respected authorities on religious matters and were frequently consulted about Muhammad's practice (sunnah) or opinions. Aisha became extremely important politically and in 656 led a revolution against Ali, the Fourth Caliph. It seems that later other women became jealous of the status of Muhammad's wives and demanded that they should be allowed to wear the veil too. Islamic culture was strongly egalitarian and it seemed incongruous that the Prophet's wives should be distinguished and honoured in this way. Thus many of the Muslim women who first took the veil saw it as a symbol of power and influence, not as a badge of male oppression. Certainly when the wives of the Crusaders saw the respect in which Muslim women were held, they took to wearing the veil in the hope of teaching their own menfolk to treat them better. It is always difficult to understand the symbols and practices of another culture. In Europe we are beginning to realise that we have often misinterpreted and undermined other traditional cultures in our former colonies and protectorates, and many Muslim women today, even those who have been brought up in the West, find it extremely offensive when Western feminists condemn their culture as misogynist. Most religions have been male affairs and have a patriarchal bias, but it is a mistake to see Islam as more at fault in this respect than any other tradition. In the Middle Ages the position was reversed: then the Muslims were horrified to see the way Western Christians treated their women in the Crusader states, and Christian scholars denounced Islam for giving too much power to menials like slaves and women. Today when some Muslim women resume traditional dress, it is not always because they have been brainwashed by a chauvinist religion, but because they find that a return to their own cultural roots is profoundly satisfing. It is often a rejection of the Western imperialist attitude which claims to understand their traditions better than they do themselves.'

Regarding Karen Armstrong's work - *Muhammad* - the magazine *Muslim News* gives the following accolade: 'Not just a sympathetic book that would dispell the misconceptions and misgivings of its western readers, but also a book that is of considerable importance to Muslims.'

Just what constitutes a woman's 'charms' that may be legitimately displayed in public, from an Islamic perspective? Whilst well conditioned hair or indeed hair that is in any way presentable may be attractive is it not also the case that the face of (many) a woman is also attractive and very much part of her beauty? This is the reason that in some quarters Muslim women cover their faces altogether or at least the whole of the face save for the eyes. After all, men are attracted by a pretty face. And those sleek, elegant hands are also very attractive. That is why similarly some Muslim women put on gloves when they go out. The Hanafi and Maliki schools of thought believe that the face and hands are not to be covered, while Shafii and Hanbali schools of thought believe that a woman has to be completely covered (as ordered by the Taliban). Nothing but nothing must be shown in public to induce the slightest temptation in a man.

The reality is that, in an orderly society, if Muslim women permanently removed their headscarves the vast majority will find no difference in the behaviour of the male population that pass them by. To put the issue into perspective, in 1970's Britain the phenomenon of the headscarf was then unknown. One rarely saw anyone wear the garment in public. It never occured to anyone that in seeing a woman's hair one was looking at a sexual appendage. Everyone regarded it as completely normal for a woman to show her hair in public. The proportion of women whose appearance (exposing hair and face) risked unduly inflaming the passions of men was always insignificant. Many women, in any case, are not so attractive that they need to cover their hair (or their faces). For pretty Muslim girls who fear that the allure of their luxuriant hair in public will excite men to such an extent that the men may be left broken-hearted (love at first sight!) in not being able to make their acquaintance, then by all means cover up.

At the turn of the millenium, with a sizeable Muslim population in place, the hijab explosion occurred in Britain and western Europe. Most of these covered women were economic migrants (or their offspring), having fled with their menfolk from the chaos of their third world 'Muslim' homelands. Somali women, for instance, started covering up en masse as a penance for their perception that God had punished them through famine and prolonged and brutal civil war (which ended for the most part in 1997 but continues in the southern and other regions to this day) for being lapsed Muslims. Greatly encouraged by their menfolk Somali women thought that in covering up, God would forgive the Somalis for going astray. The fact is that Somalia, a Sunni Muslim country, had destroyed itself by tribal/clan based rivalries - the precise iniquity that the Prophet Mohammad had tried so hard to repair by supplanting such divisions with the unifying concept of the brotherhood of Islam. For Somali women the headscarf had filled the vacuum of their failed state: by following the recurrent trend of the 'visible Muslim' they hoped to recover their sense of purpose.

But as Muhammad Asad has stressed in his above commentary on verse 31 of Surah 24 and verses 53 and 59 of Surah 33 the Prophet Mohammad's words were left *deliberately* vague, the result of which excluded any injunction that a Muslim woman must cover her hair. The Quran, in verse 31 of Surah 24 - The Light - does however specifically command women to cover their bosoms.

CYRIL GLASSÉ, a Muslim, in his work *The Concise Encyclopaedia of Islam* (published in 2001 by Stacey International, London) comments on the Veil as follows -

Veil (Ar. *hijab*, "cover", "drape", "partition"; *khimar*, "veil covering the head and face"; *litham*, "veil covering lower face up to the eyes"). The covering of the face by women is usually referred to by the general term *hijab* in the present day; it is called *purdah* in the Indo-Persian countries, and Iran has furnished the use of the word *chador* for the tent-like black cloak and veil worn by many women in the Middle East. The Koran advises the Prophet's wives to go veiled (33:59).

Koran 24:31 speaks of covering women's adornments from strangers outside the family. In traditional Arab societies, even up into the present day, women at home dressed in surprising contrast to their covered appearance in the street. This latter verse of the Koran is the institution of a new public modesty rather than veiling the face; when the pre-Islamic Arabs went to battle, Arab women seeing the men off to war would bare their breasts to encourage them to fight; or they would do so at the battle itself, as in the case of the Meccan women led by Hind at the Battle of Uhud.

This changed with Islam, but the general use of the veil to cover the face did not appear until 'Abbasid times. Nor was it entirely unknown in Europe, for the veil permitted women the freedom of anonymity. None of the legal systems actually prescribe that women must wear a veil, although they do prescribe covering the body in public. The prescription that a woman's body must be covered in public to the neck, the ankles, and below the elbow is not in the Koran, which, for its part, enjoins modesty. Covering to the neck, wrist, etc. is simply the interpretation of one particular society in the Middle Ages as to what modesty is. In many Muslim societies, for example in traditional South East Asia, or in Beduin lands a face veil for women is either rare or non-existent; paradoxically, modern fundamentalism is introducing it. In others, the veil may be used at one time and European dress another. While modesty is a religious prescription, the wearing of a veil is not a religious requirement of Islam, but a matter of cultural milieu.

In India the introduction of the use of the veil among Muslims, which happened comparatively recently, amounted to a great liberation. *Purdah*, the separation of women from men, meant that women of the classes that could afford to practice purdah could not leave their homes. The introduction of the veil amounted to a portable *purdah* and allowed women a mobility they had not previously enjoyed. This aspect of mobility granted by the use of the veil, a freedom to come and go, is an unsuspected advantage in those societies; there are some Muslim societies where women go sometimes veiled and sometimes unveiled according to their desire to be seen or unnoticed, as the case may be. *See* HIJAB; WOMEN.

VALIDE — VIZIER

V

Valide, *see* UMM al-WALAD.

Veil (Ar. *hijāb*, "cover", "drape", "partition"; *khimār*, "veil covering the head and face"; *lithām*, "veil covering lower face up to the eyes"). The covering of the face by women is usually referred to by the general term *ḥijab* in the present day; it is called *purdah* in the Indo-Persian countries, and Iran has furnished the use of the word *chador* for the tent-like black cloak and veil worn by many women in the Middle East. The Koran advises the Prophet's wives to go veiled (33:59).

Koran 24:31 speaks of covering women's adornments from strangers outside the family. In traditional Arab societies, even up into the present day, women at home dressed in surprising contrast to their covered appearance in the street. This latter verse of the Koran is the institution of a new public modesty rather than veiling the face; when the pre-Islamic Arabs went to battle, Arab women seeing the men off to war would bare their breasts to encourage them to fight; or they would do so at the battle itself, as in the case of the Meccan women led by Hind at the Battle of Uḥud.

This changed with Islam, but the general use of the veil to cover the face did not appear until 'Abbāsid times. Nor was it entirely unknown in Europe, for the veil permitted women the freedom of anonymity. None of the legal systems actually prescribe that women must wear a veil, although they do prescribe covering the body in public. The prescription that a woman's body must be covered in public to the neck, the ankles, and below the elbow is not in the Koran, which, for its part, enjoins modesty. Covering to the neck, wrist, etc. is simply the interpretation of one particular society in the Middle Ages as to what modesty is. In many Muslim societies, for example in traditional South East Asia, or in Beduin lands a face veil for women is either rare or non-existent; paradoxically, modern fundamentalism is introducing it. In others, the veil may be used at one time and European dress another. While modesty is a religious prescription, the wearing of a veil is not a religious requirement of Islam, but a matter of cultural milieu.

In India the introduction of the use of the veil among Muslims, which happened comparatively recently, amounted to a great liberation. *Purdah*, the separation of women from men, meant that women of the classes that could afford to practice *purdah* could not leave their homes. The introduction of the veil amounted to a portable purdah and allowed women a mobility they had not previously enjoyed. This aspect of mobility granted by the use of the veil, a freedom to come and go, is an unsuspected advantage in those societies; there are some Muslim societies where women go sometimes veiled and sometimes unveiled according to their desire to be seen or unnoticed, as the case may be. *See* ḤIJĀB; WOMEN.

"Verse of the throne", *see* ĀYAT al-KURSĪ.

Vilayat-i al-Faqih, *see* WILĀYAT al-FAQĪH.

Vizier, *see* WAZĪR.

468

Zaki Badawi:

Pioneer of a British Islam

Q-News February 2003 (No. 348) (Taken from The Guardian of 15th January 2003)

In another age, Zaki Badawi would probably have held the title "Grand Mufti of Islam in Britain." Then everyone would know that, on matters of faith, his word ranks alongside that of the Archbishop of Canterbury, the Chief Rabbi and the Roman Catholic Archbishop of Westminster. But with the collapse of the Ottoman Empire, that post died in the nineteenth century with Abdullah Quilliam, the last incumbent. So despite his religious expertise, unrivalled in Britain, Dr Badawi competes with a melee of Muslim politicians, local imams plus any hot heads an eager media happens to chance upon. Imagine a Roman Catholic cardinal battling for attention with Gerry Adams, the odd turbulent parish priest and the comedian Dave Allen on matters of Catholic doctrine and you get the picture.

On January 14 2003, however, a party marking the Egyptian-born leader's 80th birthday celebrated his attempts to establish a modern Islam that can fit comfortably with British values. It was attended by senior figures from the major faiths alongside representatives of Prince Charles and the Prime Minister. Amid looming war and fears of British Islamic support for al-Qaida, Dr Badawi's views matter.

His message, combined with his seniority, explains the uniqueness of Badawi, chair of the Council of Imams and Mosques and founding Principal of the Muslim College, which trains imams for British mosques. Far from portraying Islam as at odds with modernity, he sees it as the immigrant's route to being a contented Briton. "Islam is a universal religion with many cultural manifestations," he argues. "There is no theological problem in Islam taking on a great deal of Western culture and values and incorporating them."

Thus he has waged scholarly war against, for example, forced marriages and female circumcision, practices he sees as having cultural rather than Islamic bases. He first coined the term "British Islam," much to the annoyance of those preferring ethnic terms such as British

profile

Zaki Badawi

Pioneer of a British Islam

Q-News Oct 02 - Feb 03 45

Asian or Black Briton. "Within a couple of generations," he says, "Muslims will lose their cultural baggage. Indian and Pakistani ways will disappear. They will adopt Western cultural values and the whole community will be brought together as British Muslims." His vision recalls how the children of the Irish who took the boat to England were deracinated and absorbed as British Catholics, educated in state-sponsored Catholic schools.

Many Home Secretaries have realised the success of the Irish absorption policy - the Troubles produced virtually no IRA recruits from England's loyal second generation Irish community. Badawi's message is, however, once more likely to have won support in the nineteenth century when religious practice was intrinsic to citizenship. Today it is difficult to win sympathy from the natural allies of immigrants: liberals who are deeply suspicious of all religion, particularly Islam, and more comfortable promoting ethnic diversity. Dr Badawi is however, more than the acceptable voice of Islamic learned scholarship. As a pioneering figure behind Islamic mortgages and insurance, his schemes, now backed by the Treasury, could soon transform the lives of British Muslims. Free from religious problems around paying interest, many more may soon be able, with a free conscience, to purchase a property here. Zaki Badawi has likewise revolutionised the

profile

Dr Zaki Badawi with Yousif Al-Khoei and Khalida Khan at his 80th birthday reception

Jack O'Sullivan

An edited version of this article was published in the Guardian on 15 January 2003. © Guardian Unlimited 2003

46 Q-News Oct 02 - Feb 03

training of Islamic thinkers in Britain, challenging the traditional inward-looking, rule-based education of most British imams with a broad, multi-faith training grounded in Western philosophical study. It will not be easy for Osama bin Laden to hijack these updated, westernised Islamic scholars.

We meet at the Muslim College, which he founded. It is an unassuming building squeezed within an Edwardian terrace in a west London suburb. Opening the door is his wife, Mavis, a child psychologist born into a middle class Buckinghamshire family. Her scarf and modest clothing veil a life very different from her contemporaries. They met in 1950s when both studied psychology at London University. She could speak French to the Egyptian Islamicist with poor English and they soon married.

He is small but confident, with curmudgeonly qualities that come with hitting 80. His vitality recalls two leaders. First Basil Hume who, like Badawi, set out to rescue his community from being marginalised as below-stairs outsiders apparently at odds with modernity. There is the same determination not to let old age get in the way of the vision: Hume stayed on beyond retirement age, desperate though unsuccessful in his desire to outlive the Pope, to avoid being replaced by a conservative. Likewise, Badawi recalls the late Michael Young, Labour peer and founder of the Open University and Consumer Association. Lord Young's indefatigable appetite for social innovation lasted, like Zaki Badawi's, well into his ninth decade.

Dr Badawi carries a few battle scars: the Rushdie affair, Osama bin Laden, the war in Afghanistan and the Iraq conflict have all threatened to put British Islam beyond the boundaries of respectability. Yet at each turn he brandishes his Qur'an to rally his community around non-violence, tolerance and loyal British citizenship.

The atrocity of September 11 was "a violation of Islamic laws and ethics," he declared immediately about the attack. He has urged Muslim British soldiers to obey their commanders against Saddam Hussein, warning his faithful that "citizenship is not a la carte." He ridicules claims that 7,000 British Muslims would fight alongside the Taliban. "I said that if they could find seven, I would give them a medal. In fact, not a single British Muslim fought against the British forces - the only ones who went there were on humanitarian work." When Bin Laden issued a fatwa on Americans, he dismissed it as without religious authority and declared in typically acerbic tone: "Fatwas have become a cheap business. Since Ayatollah Khomeini issued it against Salman Rushdie, everyone has opened a fatwa shop."

Ironically, today's celebration for the Muslim leader takes place 14 years to the day since Bradford's Muslims publicly burned Salman Rushdie's novel, *The Satanic Verses*. It set their community on a collision course with liberal Britain and brought Dr Badawi to public prominence as he called on Muslims to spurn the book but save the man. He broke ranks - leading him to fear for his own life at times - and declared on television that if Rushdie was being chased and knocked at his door, he would give him refuge. He would shut out the mob, just as he had hidden Christian Ibos, threatened by Muslims during the Nigerian civil war. Bold, and arguably brave, he told Ayatollah Khomeini that in sentencing the author to death, he was inciting a crime against Islam.

Indeed, he was involved in securing an apology from Rushdie that might have resolved the dispute. But Rushdie recanted. "I tried so hard to keep him on side. If he had, I knew we could divide him from the liberal establishment that was sympathetic to us before it all blew up.

But you can't trust what Salman says."

He goes on to discuss his heroes. There is Prince Charles, "the leader most admired and respected by the Muslim world." Cardinal Hume is his model religious leader: "It was so clever the way he inserted Catholicism into the Establishment without compromise." He sees Tony Blair as Britain's most successful politician. "He actually leads his party, which is very unusual in a politician. Even Margaret Thatcher never controlled her party in the same way."

These are not the sentiments normally voiced by the radicals of the Finsbury Park mosque, I suggest. "I've been called 'an Uncle Tom'," he laughs. "Some people even said that I was working for the British government. I have never received a penny from the British government. I am naturally a rebel. I have always refused to be deferential, even to heads of state. I won't tell you the names of some who now regret not listening to me in the past. Irreverence is part of my Islamic culture, of my training at Al Azhar."

He is referring to Al Azhar university in Egypt, Islam's Oxford, where he spent 23 years, going on to teach and lead communities in Malaysia, Nigeria and Singapore, before he came to Britain and was appointed the first Chief Imam at London's newly built Regent's Park Mosque in 1978.

Discussing this appointment, his uncompromising attitude, even to his own community is clear. "I was horrified that none of the other imams could speak English. I was amazed that they didn't understand anything about other religions and were so unfamiliar with Western culture. In some cases, even their knowledge of Islam was very limited."

Such statements occasionally leave Badawi looking isolated in his ivory minaret, an arrogant, elitist Arab, disparaging followers who come largely from a rural community rooted in the Indian subcontinent. Why does he attack his own people? "I blame my community because I consider that they have the ability to remedy the things I am asking them to do." He believes them often ill served by their representatives. "Muslim politicians have misled the community. They have taken upon themselves tasks that are beyond them. For too long, we have had Muslim chemists or businessmen represent us in a religious function. Because they lack knowledge they are often rigid whereas a scholar can be more flexible."

So how will he establish clear religious leadership? He does not want a title like the old one of Grand Mufti. "I don't want the Muslim position focused on an individual but on the concept of Islamic scholarship." He explains plans to establish in the spring a council of British Muslim scholars, whose authority will exceed rival voices and prevent Islam being hijacked. He also wants to raise salaries for imams, so that cheaper imams imported from the Indian sub-continent with little knowledge of English or British culture cease to predominate.

"I want the Government to help me in training better imams," he says, mindful though he is of ministers being unwilling to give money for religion. "Governments plead poverty. That is their mantra. But my argument is that it is cheaper than having to combat the effect of bad imams. If you have good Islamic leadership, it would save the Government an enormous amount of money."

Are ministers listening to him? "Under the present Government, things are moving in this direction," he contends. "They are pragmatic. The Government has appointed Muslims to the House of Lords. There are three MPs in Parliament and we now have four or five Islamic schools funded by the Government. It is through this process that we are coming to dig our roots here."

And are they listening to his warnings against war with Iraq? "If I were a British Prime Minister I would find it difficult not to see my interests being served by joining the Americans," he declares diplomatically. "I see the Americans as a brute force tempered by wisdom from Britain. But Bush's economy needs to capture some free oil. I don't think the people of Iraq will oppose the invasion. After all the inspectors are there to make sure that everything is OK, that the Iraqis have no weapons to oppose with. But if the Americans think a lawless world favours the strong, they are wrong. In the long run it destroys the powerful. Anyone reading the history of Rome should know that."

Jack O'Sullivan

An edited version of this article was published in the Guardian on 15 January 2003.

The AMSS Lifetime Achievement Award

Q-News, February 2003

profile

The AMSS Lifetime Achievement Award

Few contemporaries have touched and inspired so many people as Dr Zaki has done. His pioneering methodology in dealing with issues, especially those related to Muslim communities in the West, has been dominated by an approach which has sought to intelligently combine two essential readings, the reading of the Revelation and the reading of reality and the natural universe. He has used the Qur'an as a guide to the real-existential and the real-existential as a guide to the Qur'an, and in doing so has demonstrated fully his ability to act creatively not only as a Shari'ah scholar but also as a social scientist with good knowledge of many its various disciplines. By combining and integrating these two readings, and by not hesitating to voice his views boldly, Dr Zaki has helped to provide not only a theoretical but also a practical basis for a much needed Fiqh for Minorities. The elements of time and space have always been clear in his mind when debating issues or issuing a fatwa. Initially, many people naturally objected—some strongly—to this approach but when it proved its worthiness by overcoming the rigidity and inflexibility hampering discourse in a dynamic world, the majority came to admit—rather bravely—that his approach had been correct and far-sighted.

Shaikh Zaki's contribution to the Media, especially after 11th September, was not only impressive but provided one of the very few sane, sober, intelligent and balanced views. Dr Zaki also takes credit for the establishment of Muslim schools. I have worked closely with Dr Zaki during the last six years, especially on two very successful projects: The Association of Muslim Social Scientists (UK) and The Forum Against Islamophobia and Racism. All of us who worked with him were indeed impressed and rather surprised by his strong team spirit, because the Azharites, at least in my experience, are not known to be team workers. They mainly expect you to listen to them, all the time. He is an exception.

It is truly my pleasure and privilege to present to Shaikh Zaki today, on behalf of the AMSS Executive Committee and Advisory Board the 2002 AMSS Life Achievement Award. He follows in the footsteps of two distinguished recipients, the 2000 award having been presented to Professor Ali Mazrui and the 2001 award to President Alija Izetbegovic. We take this opportunity today to present Dr Zaki with this award as a token of our appreciation and an acknowledgement of his service to Islam and the Muslim community in this country. It is richly deserved. We wish him many years of the same success.

Dr Anas Shaikh Ali

"Both traditional and contemporary"

The Azharees (Azhar graduates) who lived in the West and mastered its languages culture and thought are very few.

Fewer than these are those who added to this a knowledge of Islam and its contemporary methodologies through which Islam can contribute to the West and to bring about the desired change in values and thought.

Professor Zaki Badawi is one of the most prominent of those. He had attained both the traditional and contemporary knowledge of Islam. He also attained the purest of Islamic thought and the best and most useful of Western Knowledge. Indeed, he is a model for contemporary Azharees, just as was Imam Muhammad Abdu in his time. Imam Muhammad Abdu then established a new school of thought which started its first steps towards reinforcing civilizational and cultural exchange, or what is referred to today as "interfaith." This definitely enhanced the bright image of Islam and its potential in civilisational and cultural dialogue as long as they recognise and respect the values that man was created to emulate.

I do hope that Al-Azhar and other Islamic universities and schools will consider Professor Zaki Badawi, and the few like him, as models to be emulated. In so doing we will, insha'Allah, revitalise the role of those Grand Imams who led the civilisational and cultural exchange movement in our history, such as Al-Qadi Al-Baqillani, Ibn-Rushd, Ibn-Khaldoon and others.

May Allah Almighty bless our Brother Professor Zaki Badawi with health and continued intellectual contribution. And may He bless him with a long fruitful life and reward him plentifully. May Allah bless our Ummah with more scholars of his calibre.

Dr Taha Jabir al-Alwani

"A great defender of mainstream Islam"

I am sorry that I cannot attend the reception to celebrate the 80th birthday of Shaikh Dr Zaki Badawi. I am, however, delighted to send my very best wishes for this important occasion.

Shaikh Badawi's contribution to British Islam has been invaluable. During the last three decades he has provided crucial leadership as an Imam, teacher and social commentator. Learned, articulate and bold he has been a great defender of mainstream Islam and its message of tolerance, compassion and justice. Over the years he has taken many initiatives aimed at establishing Islam in Britain, including setting up the Muslim College, the Council of Imams and chairing the Shariah Council.

I am pleased to send best wishes to Zaki on his 80th birthday and look forward to many more years of partnership in our efforts to make Britain a better society for all.

Rt Hon Prime Minister Tony Blair

Q-News Oct 02 - Feb 03 47

Few contemporaries have touched and inspired so many people as Dr Zaki has done. His pioneering methodology in dealing with issues, especially those related to Muslim communities in the West, has been dominated by an approach which has sought to intelligently combine two essential readings, the reading of the Revelation and the reading of reality and the natural universe. He has used the Qur'an as a guide to the real-existential and the real-existential as a guide to the Qur'an, and in doing so has demonstrated fully his ability to act creatively not only as a Shari'ah scholar but also as a social scientist with good knowledge of many of its various disciplines. By combining and integrating these two readings, and by not hesitating to voice his views boldly, Dr Zaki has helped to provide not only a theoretical but also a practical basis for a much needed Fiqh for Minorities. The elements of time and space have always been clear in his mind when debating issues or issuing a fatwa. Initially, many people naturally objected— some strongly—to this approach but when it proved its worthiness by overcoming the rigidity and inflexibility hampering discourse in a dynamic world, the majority came to admit—rather bravely—that his approach had been correct and far-sighted.

Shaikh Zaki's contribution to the Media, especially after 11th September, was not only impressive but provided one of the very few sane, sober, intelligent and balanced views. Dr Zaki also takes credit for the establishment of Muslim schools. I have worked closely with Dr Zaki during the last six years, especially on two very successful projects: The Association of Muslim Social Scientists (UK) and The Forum Against Islamophobia and Racism. All of us who worked with him were indeed impressed and rather surprised by his strong team spirit, because the Azharites, at least in my experience, are not known to be team workers. They mainly expect you to listen to them, all the time. He is an exception.

It is truly my pleasure and privilege to present to Shaikh Zaki today, on behalf of the AMSS Executive Committee and Advisory Board the 2002 AMSS Life Achievement Award. He follows in the footsteps of two distinguished recipients, the 2000 award having been presented to Professor Ali Mazrui and the 2001 award to President Alija Izetbegovic. We take this opportunity today to present Dr Zaki with this award as a token of our appreciation and an acknowledgement of his service to Islam and the Muslim community in this country. It is richly deserved. We wish him many years of the same success.

Dr Anas Shaikh Ali

"Both traditional and contemporary"

Q-News, February 2003

The Azharees (Azhar graduates) who lived in the West and mastered its languages culture and thought are very few.

Fewer than these are those who added to this a knowledge of Islam and its contemporary methodologies through which Islam can contribute to the West and to bring about the desired change in values and thought.

Professor Zaki Badawi is one of the most prominent of those. He had attained both the traditional and contemporary knowledge of Islam. He also attained the purest of Islamic thought and the best and most useful of Western Knowledge. Indeed, he is a model for contemporary Azharees, just as was Imam Muhammad Abdu in his time. Imam Muhammad Abdu then established a new school of thought which started its first steps towards reinforcing civilizational and cultural exchange, or what is referred to today as "interfaith." This definitely enhanced the bright image of Islam and its potential in civilisational and cultural dialogue as long as they recognise and respect the values that man was created to emulate.

I do hope that Al-Azhar and other Islamic universities and schools will consider Professor Zaki Badawi, and the few like him, as models to be emulated. In so doing we will, insha'Allah, revitalise the role of those Grand Imams who led the civilisational and cultural exchange movement in our history, such as Al-Qadi Al-Baqillani, Ibn-Rushd, Ibn-Khaldoon and others.

May Allah Almighty bless our Brother Professor Zaki Badawi with health and continued intellectual contribution. And may He bless him with a long fruitful life and reward him plentifully. May Allah bless our Ummah with more scholars of his calibre.

Dr Taha Jabir al-Alwani

"A great defender of mainstream Islam"

Q-News, February 2003

I am sorry that I cannot attend the reception to celebrate the 80th birthday of Shaikh Dr Zaki Badawi. I am, however, delighted to send my very best wishes for this important occasion.

Shaikh Badawi's contribution to British Islam has been invaluable. During the last three decades he has provided crucial leadership as an Imam, teacher and social commentator. Learned, articulate and bold he has been a great defender of mainstream Islam and its message of tolerance, compassion and justice. Over the years he has taken many initiatives aimed at establishing Islam in Britain, including setting up the Muslim College, the Council of Imams and chairing the Shariah Council.

I am pleased to send best wishes to Zaki on his 80th birthday and look forward to many more years of partnership in our efforts to make Britain a better society for all.

Rt Hon Prime Minister Tony Blair

Issue no. 348 of *Q-News* for October 2002 to Febuary 2003, with Shagufta Yaqub as editor, sees a three page tribute to Dr. Zaki Badawi who you will recall declared that the headscarf is not obligatory in Islam. A statement that in the mid 1990's caused fanatic Muslims to brand Dr. Badawi "a criminal", and "a forger" after he had gone on television in Holland to tell Muslim women that it is not necessary to wear the hijab as it is not required in Islam.

Chapter 3

The miracle that was Zaki Badawi: 1922 - 2006

Prince leads tribute to Badawi, Muslim voice of moderation

The Guardian, January 25th 2006

Egyptian-born academic Zaki Badawi, who died yesterday at 83, became a personal friend of Prince Charles.

Prince Charles last night led tributes to Zaki Badawi, the Egyptian-born academic who became Britain's best known Islamic spokesman and a forceful voice for moderation and tolerance. Dr Badawi died suddenly yesterday. The 83-year-old principal of the Muslim College had been due to attend a reception marking the Archbishop of Canterbury's inauguration of the Christian Muslim Forum at Lambeth Palace later in the day.

The prince, who had become a personal friend of Dr Badawi's through his interest in Islam, said in a statement: "'The sudden loss of Zaki Badawi is a devastating blow to this country and to me personally. His brand of wisdom, scholarship, far-sightedness and above all humour has ensured that Zaki played an extraordinarily important role in the life of this country and amongst the Muslim community.

"'His presence will be sorely missed but his hard won legacy will, I hope, provide a fitting tribute to a truly remarkable and warm-hearted man. For me, it was an immense privilege and joy to have known someone so special for whom I had the greatest possible admiration and whose advice and friendship I valued most highly."

Dr Badawi was a regular spokesman on Islamic issues seeking to build bridges with other faiths and explain his religion to fellow Muslims and the wider community. He was an outspoken critic of fundamentalist violence and a defender of women's rights. He served on several religious organisations and had been due to become an adviser to the new forum. Often used as the voice of British Muslims by the media, he may have been seen by some younger and more radical Muslims as too moderate and too close to the establishment, but he was the nearest the community had to a religious as opposed to a political spokesman.

Ghayasuddin Siddiqui, leader of the Muslim Parliament, said Muslims had lost a "great scholar, teacher and a man of peace and harmony", always opposed to fundamentalism and extremism.

Sir Iqbal Sacranie, secretary-general of the Muslim Council of Britain, said: "'We are deeply shocked and saddened by his sudden demise [which is] a major loss for British Muslims. We pray that God Almighty grants him a place in his paradise with the martyrs, the prophets and the righteous."

Shami Chakrabarti, director of Liberty, said: "People of all faiths, as well as those without faith, will mourn the loss of Dr Badawi, who provided unique leadership in a world gone mad. A younger generation of Muslims must now take on the sheikh's work - the promotion of faith built more on tolerance than judgment."

Stephen Bates
Religious affairs correspondent

The Guardian | Wednesday January 25 2006

Prince leads tributes to Badawi, Muslim voice of moderation

Stephen Bates
Religious affairs correspondent

Prince Charles last night led tributes to Zaki Badawi, the Egyptian-born academic who became Britain's best known Islamic spokesman and a forceful voice for moderation and tolerance. Dr Badawi died suddenly yesterday. The 83-year-old principal of the Muslim College had been due to be attend a reception marking the Archbishop of Canterbury's inauguration of the Christian Muslim Forum at Lambeth Palace later in the day.

The prince, who had become a personal

Egyptian-born academic Zaki Badawi, who died yesterday at 83, became a personal friend of Prince Charles

friend of Dr Badawi's through his interest in Islam, said in a statement: "The sudden loss of Zaki Badawi is a devastating blow to this country and to me personally. His brand of wisdom, scholarship, far-sightedness and above all humour has ensured that Zaki played an extraordinarily important role in the life of this country and amongst the Muslim community.

"His presence will be sorely missed but his hard-won legacy will, I hope, provide a fitting tribute to a truly remarkable and warm-hearted man. For me, it was an immense privilege and joy to have known someone so special for whom I had the greatest possible admiration and whose advice and friendship I valued most highly."

Dr Badawi was a regular spokesman on Islamic issues, seeking to build bridges with other faiths and explain his religion to fellow Muslims and the wider community. He was an outspoken critic of fundamentalist violence and a defender of women's rights. He served on several religious organisations and had been due to become an adviser to the new forum. Often used as the voice of British Muslims by the media, he may have been seen by some younger and more radical Muslims as too moderate and too close to the establishment, but he was the nearest the community had to a religious as opposed to a political spokesman.

Ghayasuddin Siddiqui, leader of the Muslim Parliament, said Muslims had lost a "great scholar, teacher and a man of peace and harmony", always opposed to fundamentalism and extremism.

Sir Iqbal Sacranie, secretary-general of the Muslim Council of Britain, said: "We are deeply shocked and saddened by his sudden demise [which is] a major loss for British Muslims. We pray that God Almighty grants him a place in his paradise with the martyrs, the prophets and the righteous."

Shami Chakrabarti, director of Liberty, said: "People of all faiths, as well as those without faith, will mourn the loss of Dr Badawi, who provided unique leadership in a world gone mad. A younger generation of Muslims must now take on the sheikh's work – the promotion of faith built more on tolerance than judgment."

Obituary, page 31 »

OBITUARY:
ZAKI BADAWI

The Times, January 25th 2006

Leading voice of moderate Islam who believed passionately in interfaith dialogue and the idea of the British Muslim

TIMES REGISTER | LAW REPORT Asylum tribunal jurisdiction limited by new Act PAGE 61 | WEATHER Overheated media melt new ice age PAGE 64

OBITUARIES — The Times Wednesday January 25 2006

ZAKI BADAWI

Leading voice of moderate Islam who believed passionately in interfaith dialogue and the idea of the British Muslim

Badawi, second from left, making a joint statement on September 12, 2001, with Sir Jonathan Sacks, the Chief Rabbi, Lord Carey of Clifton, then the Archbishop of Canterbury, and Cardinal Cormac Murphy-O'Connor, the Archbishop of Westminster

FEW MEN have done as much to reconcile Islam with modernity as Zaki Badawi, the founder and principal of the Muslim College in London. And few men have played such a crucial role in attempting to find a harmonious balance between the beliefs, culture and values of Islam and secular British society. Indeed, that almost two million British Muslims are today able to define themselves as such owes much to the vision of the Egyptian-born scholar who saw, early on, that the many Muslims who settled in Britain from different parts of the Islamic world would, one day, form a significant strand of British society — which happened to be Muslim.

For years, Badawi was the unofficial — and almost lone — spokesman for Muslims in Britain who had no visible figurehead or institutional structure. Appointed in 1978 as chief imam of the London Central Mosque as well as director of the Islamic Cultural Centre, he used these influential positions in the capital to call for an Islam that fitted comfortably with British values, so that younger generations, brought up and educated in this country, would find no conflict between their faith and their civic identity as British citizens.

To him, this meant an Islam that was inclusive, moderate, tolerant and without the rancour or hostility that marked attitudes to Western values prevalent in some of the more zealous sects of Arabia and the Middle East. He therefore devoted his life in Britain to building bridges - of faith, of dialogue and of scholarship. It is thanks largely to his pioneering work in the 1990s in helping to establish a forum for the three Abrahamic faiths — Christianity, Judaism and Islam — and his tireless, behind-the-scenes work in reaching out to British society and institutions that Britain has fared so much better than other European nations with Muslim minorities in integrating its Muslim citizens. But for Badawi, Britain might have fared far less well in avoiding the social alienation that has marked relations between Muslims and the rest of society in France.

Equally, however, Badawi was an outspoken voice in upholding Muslim dignity and the true values of his faith when these came under attack. This was never more crucial than in the aftermath of the September 11 atrocities in America. And when many other leading Muslim scholars were reluctant to speak out to condemn violence or denounce terrorism, he wrote an article for The Times in which he insisted that taking revenge on the innocent was abhorrent to Islam. He gave a warning that no society was immune from violence, and the worst was one which donned the garb of religion. But he said the Koran emphasised that those who disturbed the peace of society and spread fear and disorder deserved the severest punishment that could be imposed.

His denunciation of violence and extremism was forcefully repeated again last year, when he joined religious leaders in commemorating the victims of the London bombings and in calling for tolerance and calm. Again, his words, among others, may have helped Britain to avoid any widespread and violent backlash against Muslims across the country.

Born in Cairo in 1922, Badawi studied at al-Azhar University, where he claimed to have gained his rebellious streak. "I have always refused to be deferential, even to heads of state," he told a journalist in January 2003. "Irreverence is part of my Islamic culture, of my training at al-Azhar."

It did nothing to harm his studies: after an undergraduate degree in theology, Badawi gained a master's degree in Arabic language and literature and the King Faruq First Prize for best postgraduate student. After gaining his doctorate, he returned to teach at al-Azhar before coming to Britain for the first time in 1951. He gained a degree in psychology from University College London, followed by a doctorate from London University in modern Muslim thought.

He then spent several years in South-East Asia, setting up the Muslim College of Malaya and taking teaching posts in Singapore and Kuala Lumpur. He took up professorships in Kano and Zaria, Nigeria, and in Jeddah. He returned to London as a research professor for the Haj Research Centre of the King Abdul Aziz University in Saudi Arabia.

Badawi first came to grips with the British way of life, and the challenges it held for Muslims, in 1978 when he took the post of director of the Islamic Cultural Centre (ICC), while also serving as chief imam of the London Central Mosque in Regent's Park. He helped to establish the Shariah Council, to reconcile conflicts between Islamic and British law. He found it incredible that most imams would not — and could not — preach in the language of their adopted country, and he was the first Muslim to make this criticism clear.

He doubted, too, that priests or teachers could reach out to young British Muslims as if they were on home soil in Pakistan or Bangladesh, and was quite sure they should not try. As British Muslims became third and fourth-generation citizens, he felt certain that the cross-pollination of ideas needed a new, Westernised approach, and an awareness and respect of all faiths, in order to make sense of it.

The prospectus of the Muslim College, which he established in 1986 to train imams in the new approach, and where he served as principal, states that the training of "traditional" imams "is not always sufficient to deal with the cultural environment of modern Western Europe and the USA, nor with problems arising from interaction with Western societies".

Perhaps most infuriating to fundamentalists was Badawi's firm belief in the idea of British Muslims, with British as a badge of honour, a social and cultural designation, not a mere branch of one contiguous caliphate. "Within a couple of generations Muslims will lose their cultural baggage. Indian and Pakistani ways will disappear. They will adopt Western cultural values, and the whole community will be brought together as British Muslims," he said.

A dislike of "cultural baggage" was at the heart of Badawi's rebellious streak. He campaigned against female genital mutilation, insisting that it was an outmoded cultural, not religious, practice with no causal link to Islam. He stated that the fatwa had become overused, and that those who proclaimed them usually had no divine sanction. "Since Ayatollah Khomeini issued his against Salman Rushdie, everyone has opened a fatwa shop," he said.

Badawi incurred the wrath of Britain's imams in 1989 when he stated that, much as he disliked his book, should Rushdie knock at his door with the youth of Bradford at his heels, he would certainly give him sanctuary. He wished to restore the idea, lost in the Iranian Revolution, of loving the sinner, hating the sin.

Naturally, Badawi's belief in a type of Islam both acceptable to and supportive of Western society made him an "Uncle Tom" character to many imams. He seemed to represent the face of Islam that liberal, middle-class Britain hoped to do business with.

He was certainly an antidote to the gloom of 9/11 and the London bombings. Badawi, in explaining the religion's ability to adapt, would often refer to its golden age, its absorption of other faiths and its role in preserving the Classics. Such reasoned Islam, between mosque and minaret, he hoped would come to prominence in Britain.

Badawi prepared 38 articles on financial management with respect to Muslim law. In Britain, where most people maintain an enduring faith in the property market, Badawi's work in establishing sharia-compliant or "halal" mortgages may prove the most binding part of his work to bring the next generation into the fold. At the Islamic Real Estate Finance conference in London in July 2003, Badawi explained how Muslims could take advantage of his schemes, backed by the Treasury, to own property in Britain or overseas.

In 1997 Badawi established, with Sir Sigmund Sternberg and the Rev Marcus Braybrooke, the Three Faiths Forum -— "To encourage friendship, goodwill and understanding amongst people of the three

Abrahamic monotheistic faiths in the UK and elsewhere". He was vice-chairman of the World Congress of Faiths and director/trustee of the Forum Against Islamophobia and Racism (Fair). He was a founder-trustee of the Festival of Muslim Cultures, and it was his vision for UK Muslims to take a more prominent role that inspired the festival, which was launched this month.

Yet Badawi, given to the celebration of compatible faiths rather than a grudging cognisance of "people of the book", remained a maverick — albeit an increasingly important one.

Turned back from JFK Airport by US authorities in July last year, Badawi showed pity rather than anger. "They were very, very embarrassed and I felt sorry for them." He said, adding: "America is a lovely country. There is no reason why it should behave like that." Badawi had joined Iqbal Sacrani and other leaders of the faith to denounce the perpetrators of the London bombings eight days earlier. Their points of agreement were relatively few, however. Sacrani's recent statement that homosexuality is "not acceptable" and the Muslim Council of Britain (MCB) boycott last year of the Holocaust remembrance ceremony will give many cause to miss a peacemaker who would, wherever possible, give words of support and, where not, keep his own counsel.

In private, Badawi was jovial, warm and hospitable. He enjoyed nothing more than a friendly, reasonable debate on the values of Muslims in Britain today and the challenges of reconciling Islam and modernity in Britain and across the wider Muslim world.

He was, however, saddened by the growth of extremist sects and their appeal for many young, disillusioned Muslims. And he blamed the Government and press for listening to the self-publicists who, he believed, were trying to impose their leadership on the Muslim community in Britain.

Partly this was because he found that his own moderation was increasingly under attack from younger, more assertive leaders, and partly it was the natural resentment of an older man for those who, he believed, had, elbowed him out of the limelight.

But he relished his own acceptance into British society (he was a member of the Athenaeum) and the recognition he was accorded by other scholars and academics. Even in old age — which was certainly not visible in his face — he was active in writing, lecturing and preaching. He was glad that many of his causes, especially the demand that imams should be properly trained and speak good English, were finally recognised by the Government. The MCB, which now represents the main umbrella group of British Muslim organisations, was planning a ceremony to honour his scholarship, faith and role as a pioneer in British-Muslim relations. But he died before any such proposal could be advanced.

He was appointed OBE (hon) in 1998 and KBE in 2004. He is survived by his wife, Maryam, and by a son and a daughter.

Zaki Badawi, Muslim community leader, teacher and theologian, was born on August 11,1922. He died on January 24, 2006, aged 83.

OBITUARY:
ZAKI BADAWI

The Daily Telegraph, January 25th 2006

Islamic scholar who condemned the fatwa against Salman Rushdie and terrorist attacks in New York and London

ZAKI BADAWI, who has died aged 83, was the Principal of the Muslim College in London, which he established in 1986, and also chairman of the Imams and Mosques Council of the United Kingdom.

Badawi, who was generally regarded as the most senior and respected Islamic scholar in Britain, worked towards evolving what he described as a "European and even British form of Islam". Although he joked that some militant Muslims dismissed him as an "Uncle Tom", his formidable scholarship meant he came to be treated as the final authority on many issues of Sharia law.

On numerous occasions since the Salman Rushdie affair first erupted in 1989, Badawi spoke out against terrorism by Muslims. He was particularly vocal after the attacks on the Twin Towers in New York on September 11 2001 - "a violation of Islamic laws and ethics - I just felt utter disgust and really very, very great anger". Most recently, he condemned the suicide bombings in London in July last year.

Badawi opposed the Iraq war but said that Muslim soldiers in the British Army had a duty to fight for Queen and country - and their country was Britain. This was a stinging rebuke to Muslim hardliners who insisted their duty to Islam took precedence over loyalty to the Queen.

Zaki Badawi

The Daily Telegraph Wednesday, January 25 2006

Islamic scholar who condemned the fatwa against Salman Rushdie and terrorist attacks in New York and London

ZAKI BADAWI, who has died aged 83, was the Principal of the Muslim College in London, which he established in 1986, and also chairman of the Imams and Mosques Council of the United Kingdom.

Badawi, who was generally regarded as the most senior and respected Islamic scholar in Britain, worked towards evolving what he described as a "European and even British form of Islam". Although he joked that some militant Muslims dismissed him as an "Uncle Tom", his formidable scholarship meant he came to be treated as the final authority on many issues of Sharia law.

On numerous occasions since the Salman Rushdie affair first erupted in 1989, Badawi spoke out against terrorism by Muslims. He was particularly vocal after the attacks on the Twin Towers in New York on September 11 2001 – "a violation of Islamic laws and ethics – I just felt utter disgust and really very, very great anger". Most recently, he condemned the suicide bombings in London in July last year.

Badawi opposed the Iraq war but said that Muslim soldiers in the British Army had a duty to fight for Queen and country – and their country was Britain. This was a stinging rebuke to Muslim hardliners who insisted their duty to Islam took precedence over loyalty to the Queen.

While terrorists have used the Koran to justify suicide bombings and other acts of violence, Badawi, immensely more knowledgeable, used the same book to pinpoint why terrorism was a "declaration of war on God and on His Messenger".

He argued: "It is a negation of every rule of the Sharia which decrees that innocent life is sacred, property is inviolate and that the peace of mind of the public must be safeguarded. Those who preach the message of hate serve no religious cause and those who incite the ill-informed, maladjusted and alienated to commit criminal acts do so not as servants of a noble faith or a legitimate cause but operators for base ambitions disguised as pious and religious."

While continuing to speak on behalf of 1.6 million Muslims in Britain, Badawi's message remained the same – that the true teachings of the Koran were incompatible with terrorism. From his earliest days in Britain, he set out, through his writings, speeches, newspaper interviews, appearances on Radio 4 and on television, to advocate co-existence and the development of British Islam.

His philosophy could be summed up in a single sentence: "There is Egyptian Islam, there is Indian Islam, there is Saudi Wahhabi Islam, there is Iranian Shia Islam, so why can't there be British Islam?" It was perhaps a measure of the success of his long campaign that his primary belief – "people can be British *and* Muslim" – has recently received more widespread acceptance.

Outside Britain, Badawi was not always accorded the respect and courtesy that he received here. Last summer he was refused entry by US immigration at JFK airport, New York, despite landing with a visa. He was sent back to Britain. Though the Americans later apologised after realising they had expelled Britain's leading Muslim moderate, Badawi was deeply offended and did not return. The American insult's chief effect, however, was to reinforce his sense of Britishness.

Last November he gave a speech, aimed partly at British-born young Muslims, praising Britain for trying to find a sense of national cohesion through diversity.

"In Great Britain," he said, "we are lucky to have a society that is endeavouring to achieve the ideals accommodating differences, not simply with tolerant indifference, but with an interest in engagement with each other. This celebration of diversity sends a message to our people, and especially our youth, and the whole world that here is an example to emulate to build trust, harmony and peace in a modern society. There are elements who are misfits and who are disloyal to the basic values of our society. They do not reflect on the citizens of the country nor should they shame their particular community, nor should their crimes degrade the faith they claim to belong to... The strength of our common unity in diversity will help us through any difficulty."

Zaki Badawi came to Britain in 1951 from his native Egypt, where he was born just outside Cairo on August 11 1922. He was educated at al-Azhar University in Cairo, the leading Islamic academic institution in the world for Sunni Muslims. He obtained al-Aliyah, the equivalent of a Bachelor of Arts degree, from the College of Theology at the university, and al-Alimiyah degree (Masters) from the Faculty of Arabic Language and Literature in 1947. In the same year he received the King Farouk First Prize for the best postgraduate student.

He had been a member of the Muslim Brotherhood, which later attempted to assassinate Nasser, but left the organisation the previous year when it first advocated violence.

After teaching at al-Azhar for a short while, Badawi moved to the United Kingdom in 1951 to study Psychology at University College London, where he obtained his BA in 1954. He was later awarded a doctorate from London University in Modern Muslim Thought.

He married an Englishwoman, Mavis, in 1956, before returning to al-Azhar University to teach Muslim Thought and Scientific Research Methods. He was then sent as a representative of the university to Malaya to establish a Muslim college there. After teaching Arabic and Islamic Studies at the University of Malaya in Singapore, he lectured in the same course at the University of Malaya in Kuala Lumpur.

In 1964 Badawi was appointed Professor of Islamic Education at Ahmadu Bello University in Northern Nigeria and later Professor of Islamic Education and Dean of Arts at Bayero College, Nigeria. In 1976 he was appointed research professor at the Hajj Research Centre of King Abdul Aziz University in Saudi Arabia, stationed in London.

In 1978 he became director of the Islamic Cultural Centre (ICC) and Chief Imam of London Central Mosque in Regent's Park. He was elected chairman of the Imams and Mosques Council by the National Conference of Imams and Mosque Officials of the UK in 1984. Badawi subsequently held high office in many of the most important Islamic organisations in Britain and came to be considered possibly the "sanest and most moderate" Muslim voice in the country.

He was given an honorary knighthood in 2003 and took great pride in being a member of the Athenaeum.

He was an adviser to British financial institutions on such issues as Islamic mortgages. He was attending the fifth annual Islamic Finance Summit in London yesterday when he collapsed; he died shortly afterwards.

The Muslim College he founded was aimed at producing homegrown imams, which he felt would get round the problem of importing preachers who spoke little or no English and whose loyalties were sometimes a little suspect.

Badawi is survived by his wife, a son and a daughter.

Badawi: the "sanest and most moderate" Muslim voice

While terrorists have used the Koran to justify suicide bombings and other acts of violence, Badawi, immensely more knowledgeable, used the same book to pinpoint why terrorism was a "declaration of war on God and on His Messenger".

He argued: "It is a negation of every rule of the Sharia which decrees that innocent life is sacred, property is inviolate and that the peace of mind of the public must be safeguarded. Those who preach the message of hate serve no religious cause and those who incite the ill-informed, maladjusted and alienated to commit criminal acts do so not as servants of a noble faith or a legitimate cause but operators for base ambitions disguised as pious and religious."

While continuing to speak on behalf of 1.6 million Muslims in Britain, Badawi's message remained the same - that the true teachings of the Koran were incompatible with terrorism. From his earliest days in Britain, he set out, through his writings, speeches, newspaper interviews, appearances on Radio 4 and on television, to advocate co-existence and the development of British Islam.

His philosophy could be summed up in a single sentence: "There is Egyptian Islam, there is Indian Islam, there is Saudi Wahhabi Islam, there is Iranian Shia Islam, so why can't there be British Islam?" It was perhaps a measure of the success of his long campaign that his primary belief - "people can be British *and* Muslim" - has recently received more widespread acceptance.

Outside Britain, Badawi was not always accorded the respect and courtesy that he received here. Last summer he was refused entry by US immigration at JFK airport, New York, despite landing with a visa. He was sent back to Britain. Though the Americans later apologised after realising they had expelled Britain's leading Muslim moderate, Badawi was deeply offended and did not return. The American insult's chief effect, however, was to reinforce his sense of Britishness.

Last November he gave a speech, aimed partly at British-born young Muslims, praising Britain for trying to find a sense of national cohesion through diversity.

"In Great Britain," he said, "we are lucky to have a society that is endeavouring to achieve the ideals accommodating differences, not simply with tolerant indifference, but with an interest in engagement with each other. This celebration of diversity sends a message to our people, and especially our youth, and the whole world that here is an example to emulate to build trust, harmony and peace in a modern society. There are elements who are misfits and who are disloyal to the basic values of our society. They do not reflect on the citizens of the country nor should they shame their particular community, nor should their crimes degrade the faith they claim to belong to... The strength of our common unity in diversity will help us through any difficulty."

Zaki Badawi came to Britain in 1951 from his native Egypt, where he was born just outside Cairo on August 11 1922. He was educated at al-Azhar University in Cairo, the leading Islamic academic institution in the world for Sunni Muslims. He obtained al-Aliyah, the equivalent of a Bachelor of Arts degree, from the College of Theology at the university, and al-Alimiyah degree (Masters) from the Faculty of Arabic Language and Literature in 1947. In the same year he received the King Farouk First Prize for the best postgraduate student.

He had been a member of the Muslim Brotherhood, which later attempted to assassinate Nasser, but left the organisation the previous year when it first advocated violence.

After teaching at al-Azhar for a short while, Badawi moved to the United Kingdom in 1951 to study Psychology at University College London, where he obtained his BA in 1954. He was later awarded a doctorate from London University in Modern Muslim Thought.

He married an Englishwoman, Mavis, in 1956, before returning to al-Azhar University to teach Muslim Thought and Scientific Research Methods. He was then sent as a representative of the university to Malaya to establish a Muslim college there. After teaching Arabic and Islamic Studies at the University of Malaya in Singapore, he lectured in the same course at the University of Malaya in Kuala Lumpur.

In 1964 Badawi was appointed Professor of Islamic Education at Ahmadu Bello University Northern Nigeria and later Professor of Islamic Education and Dean of Arts at Bayero College, Nigeria. In 1976 he was appointed research professor at the Hajj Research Centre of King Abdul Aziz University in Saudi Arabia, stationed in London.

In 1978 he became director of the Islamic Cultural Centre (ICC) and Chief Imam of London Central Mosque in Regent's Park. He was elected chairman of the Imams and Mosques Council by the National Conference of Imams and Mosque Officials of the UK in 1984. Badawi subsequently held high office in many of the most important Islamic organisations in Britain and came to be considered possibly the "sanest and most moderate" Muslim voice in the country.

He was given an honorary knighthood in 2003 and took great pride in being a member of the Athenaeum.

He was an adviser to British financial institutions on such issues as Islamic mortgages. He was attending the fifth annual Islamic Finance Summit in London yesterday when he collapsed; he died shortly afterwards.

The Muslim College he founded was aimed at producing homegrown imams, which he felt would get round the problem of importing preachers who spoke little or no English and whose loyalties were sometimes a little suspect. Badawi is survived by his wife, a son and a daughter.

OBITUARY:
ZAKI BADAWI

The Guardian, January 25th 2006

Visionary Arab scholar who helped British Islam make peace with modernity

Zaki Badawi, who has died suddenly aged 84, was Britain's most influential Muslim. A brave, visionary figure, he identified the vulnerabilities of his community long before the Salman Rushdie affair, the emergence of Osama bin Laden and the wars in Afghanistan and Iraq exposed them to public view.

More importantly, he spent nearly 30 years almost singlehandedly creating British Islamic institutions and setting out arguments in their favour. Thus he laid the intellectual and bureaucratic foundations for that community to make peace with modernity, and live as a minority in a western society - a process now beginning to protect British Islam against hijack by the powerful forces of Middle East conflicts.

Islam lacks the hierarchies of the Christian churches, but Badawi ranked on matters of faith alongside the archbishop of Canterbury and the chief rabbi. As chairman of the council of imams and mosques and founding principal of the Muslim College, which trains imams for British mosques, he used his position to question constantly the assumptions of the prejudiced: namely that Islam is characterised by violence and primitive practices often oppressive of women, and that it is on a collision course with western values.

To the first charge, Badawi would quote the farewell sermon of the Prophet Muhammad at the foot of the Mount of Mercy: "God had made inviolable for you each other's blood and each other's property until you meet your Lord." He campaigned vigorously in favour of women's rights and, most particularly, against forced marriage and female circumcision: he considered the latter to be an African custom erroneously inserted into religious tradition, in some parts of the Islamic world.

As an enthusiastic leader of inter-faith dialogue, he highlighted Islam's history of flexibility and tolerance - particularly of Judaism - speaking of the common Abrahamic roots and Hellenistic heritage of Islam and Christianity. "Their ethical principles are not in conflict," he would say. "Past and even present conflicts between them originate in territorial ambitions and over the acquisition of resources."

At crucial moments of tension, Badawi used

his considerable learning and authority to steer British Islam (he coined the term) on a wise course. He immediately condemned the 9/11 atrocity as "a violation of Islamic law and ethics". When, in 1989, other Islamic figures threatened Salman Rushdie with death for his novel The Satanic Verses, Badawi called on Muslims to spurn the book but spare the man, and declared that he would not hesitate to offer the novelist sanctuary in his home. As the media highlighted fears that British Muslim soldiers would not fight in Iraq, he urged Muslims to obey orders and accurately predicted that there would be no problem of divided loyalty.

The Guardian | Wednesday January 25 2006 31

Obituaries

Zaki Badawi

Visionary Arab scholar who helped British Islam make peace with modernity

Badawi set up the Muslim College to train imams for the west Graham Turner

He is survived by his wife and two children.
Jack O'Sullivan

Mohamed Aboulkhair Zaki Badawi, scholar, born January 14 1922; died January 24 2006

Small, confident, occasionally curmudgeonly but always with a keen sense of humour, Badawi had a skill in rescuing his community from marginalisation that sprang from a lifetime's experience of the British empire. Born in Sharkia, Egypt, to a religious family that dedicated him to the study of religion, he agitated against the British presence as part of the fundamentalist Muslim Brotherhood, but eschewed its resort to violence.

He was educated at the University of Al-Azhar in Cairo, the Islamic world's Oxford, and later became a celebrated scholar and professor there. He went on to teach Islamic studies in Singapore and Malaya. While teaching for 12 years in Nigeria (1964-76), he established a reputation as a tolerant figure, hiding Christian Ibos in his home during the civil war, to save them from slaughter by Muslims who were convinced that their brethren had been killed.

During these three decades of travelling the world, from his graduation from Al-Azhar in 1947 until he settled in Britain in 1976, Badawi was already being drawn into British life. In 1951 he arrived to spend three years studying psychology at London University. There, he met a fellow student, Mavis, who had been born into a middle-class Buckinghamshire family. She could speak French to the Egyptian Islamicist with poor English. They soon married, and had a son, Faris, and a daughter, Laila.

But it was his appointment in 1978 as the first chief imam at Regent's Park mosque, in London, that convinced Badawi that his mission was to save British Islam from dangerous isolation. "I was horrified that none of the other imams could speak English," he recalled. "I was amazed that they didn't understand anything about other religions and were so unfamiliar with western culture."

His attempts to place Islam at the heart of British life were many and various. He liked to recall the claims that King John had promised to convert to Islam in return for Moroccan military support against his rebellious barons, and recalled a belief by some in the Muslim world that Queen Victoria had converted to Islam.

Badawi's hero was the Catholic leader, Cardinal Basil Hume. Before his death in 1999, Hume had led his community on the final steps to acceptance in Britain, so that now, for example, his successor can be found even preaching to the Queen at Windsor. "It was so clever," said Badawi, "how Hume inserted Catholicism into the establishment without compromise."

Likewise, Badawi enjoyed a close relationship with the Prince of Wales, whom he admired for his outspoken sympathy with Islam. Ironically, despite calling for high-ranking Muslims to be elevated to the House of Lords - an environment in which he would have thrived - he was never ennobled himself, although he was awarded an honorary knighthood in 2004 (having chosen to remain an Egyptian citizen).

A closeness to the establishment did at times lead to accusations that he was an Uncle Tom figure, too ready to adapt the tone of Islam to suit a western audience. He also ran the risk of isolation by making damning statements about the community he led - words from an Arab intellectual that an often poorly educated Asian community found hard to stomach. "I blame my community because they have the ability to remedy the thing I am asking them to do," he would say as he attacked dogmatic leadership. "For too long, we have had Muslim chemists or businessmen represent us in a religious function. Because they lack knowledge, they are often rigid, whereas a scholar can be more flexible."

But Badawi was more than a critic: like the late Michael Young, his indefatigable appetite for social innovation lasted well into his ninth decade. In 1984, he founded the council of imams and mosques in an attempt to bring scholarship and unity to the leadership of British Islam. Likewise, in 1986, he established the Muslim College, in west London, as a postgraduate seminary to train imams and religious leaders for the west. He also established and chaired the sharia council to resolve conflicts between Islamic law and civil law.

Alongside longstanding, and ultimately successful, work to make no-interest Islamic mortgages available, historians will find in Badawi's achievement a systematic approach to showing how Muslims can live at ease in a western liberal environment. For him, the mission was more than about Britain; his goal was to show how the gulf between east and west, ancient and modern, could be bridged peacefully and fruitfully.

He is survived by his wife and two children.

Jack O'Sullivan

Mohamed Aboulkhair Zaki Badawi, scholar, born January 14, 1922; died January 24, 2006

OBITUARY:
ZAKI BADAWI

The Independent, January 27th 2006

'Grand Mufti of Islam in Britain'

Zaki Badawi was a well-rounded Islamic scholar who never allowed circumstances to colour either his actions or edicts, an activist who knew how to pursue an agenda within a political network too sophisticated and complex for most of his co-religionists, and a believer who never compromised on what he thought was right.

THE INDEPENDENT FRIDAY 27 JANUARY 2006

1926 WEDNESDAY 27 JANUARY

Logie Baird demonstrates television
In an attic laboratory in Soho, London, John Logie Baird gave the first public demonstratio[n] – showing the image of two ventriloquist dummies – to 40 members of the Royal Institu[tion]

ZAKI BADAWI

'Grand Mufti of Islam in Britain'

Zaki Badawi was a well-rounded Islamic scholar who never allowed circumstances to colour either his actions or edicts, an activist who knew how to pursue an agenda within a political network too sophisticated and complex for most of his co-religionists, and a believer who never compromised on what he thought was right.

Badawi's contribution towards Islam in Britain was invaluable. It can be claimed that he invented both the terms "British Islam" and "Islamophobia". Urbane, passionate and wise, he was the father of Muslim engagement in Britain – forging inroads into mainstream society and making the so-called "Muslim case" long before it became fashionable.

More than anything, Badawi was a global Muslim: although born in Egypt, he spent most of his life in other countries and in the process touched the lives of people from West Africa to the Pacific Rim. But he held a soft spot in his heart for Britain. He loved the country, its institutions, its countryside, its dynamism and its "civilising potential". And for three decades he dedicated himself to building institutions that would not only consolidate and stabilise Islam in Britain, but also energise it. Always a teacher, he was one of the main advocates for faith-based schools that were inclusive, broad-minded and of excellent academic standards.

Badawi's imamship at the London Central Mosque in Regent's Park from 1978 was pioneering and exemplary. He was the first imam of a prominent mosque to invite leaders of other faith communities "for tea and theology – whatever they prefer" – as he fondly remembered. This pioneering initiative led to the emergence of an inter-faith movement to which Badawi was committed and dedicated all his life. Once he showed me a picture of him with a group of priests – Buddhist, Hindu, Muslim and Christian – explaining that it was the first inter-faith gathering he had organised, while teaching in Singapore in the early Fifties.

In 1997 Badawi established the Three Faiths Forum with Sir Sigmund Sternberg and the Rev Marcus Braybrooke. The idea of encouraging friendship, goodwill and understanding amongst "people of the book" appealed to the halal globetrotter who always envisioned himself as a bridge-maker of peace and understanding. Badawi was for many years until his death a leading member of the Tripoli-based World Islamic Call Society which shared his conviction of Muslim benevolence across the world. He was Vice-Chairman of the World Congress of Faiths and a founder director of the Forum Against Islamophobia and Racism (Fair).

Perhaps the most ambitious project Badawi initiated was the setting up in London in 1986 of the Muslim College, of which he remained Principal until his death. The Muslim College was not only a visionary but a pragmatic effort towards the construction of "British Islam". Long before it became an obsession of desperate civil servants faced with radical Islam, Badawi had realised the significance of a home-grown Islam in Britain – "free of the cancer of Muslim culture, neurosis and ignorance".

The story of Badawi's life is one of struggle, commitment, ambition and success. He was born in Sharkia, a small village outside Cairo, in 1922, to a traditional, pious Muslim family. He graduated from Al-Azhar University in Cairo, the foremost theological college in the Muslim world, with honours and was awarded the King Fuad First Prize for the best graduate of the year in 1945, then, between 1951 and 1954, he studied Psychology at University College, marrying a fellow student, Mavis. He earned a London University PhD in Modern Muslim Thought, then set off to teach in Malaysia, Singapore and Nigeria, finally settling in London in the mid-Seventies and becoming Chief Imam at Regent's Park Mosque and director of the Islamic Cultural Centre in 1978.

During the three decades he was in public life, Badawi dealt intimately with three prime ministers, three archbishops and two cardinals. The network he developed over the years included laymen and scholars, presidents and priests, politicians and academics. An animated conversationalist and generous host, Badawi never felt uncomfortable with dialogue or exchanging ideas and opinions with anyone.

A born leader, Badawi, however, had little time for the representational politics that proliferate in our times. He believed in himself and in the legitimacy of his opinions and had little time for "charlatans and jokers" – as he described people who made comments about Islam without the qualifications to do so. Of the Muslim leaders feted in the corridors of power in modern Britain he was the only "alim" – Islamic scholar. Essentially Badawi unofficially occupied the position of the "Grand Mufti of Islam in Britain" – a title which had become extinct in the first half of the last century. The title had been given to the Liverpudlian solicitor Abdullah Quilliam by the last Ottoman Caliph in the 19th century.

Disagreeing with Badawi was both a frustrating and futile exercise. He never personalised an argument or harboured malice just because you disagreed with him – you really had to work very hard at it to make an enemy of him. He loved the simple things of life: taking the train to work, a walk in the park and buying chestnuts at the wayside during cold winter days.

To the last, his love continued to be teaching. He made it a point never to miss his classes and hated to be late for an appointment. Unlike other dignitaries, he never minded how he travelled. If he believed in the journey he would take any sensible route there. Many fellow luminaries were shocked to see him in economy when travelling as he found first-class "wasteful and not really necessary".

His efforts to try and bring together religious leaders under the Council of Imams and Mosques never really took off because of the sectarianism and anarchy that exists within different communities. Although of Arab ancestry himself, he loved the Aziziye Mosque in Dalston, east London, where the majority of the congregation is of Turkish origin.

As British Islam enters what augurs to be difficult times, it will miss the wisdom, courage, passion and vision of its most vociferous proponent. However, they are many signs that Badawi's idea of an Islam based in tradition, yet not afraid of modernity and ready to adapt to the realities of a dynamic, plural Britain, has made deep roots.

It seems a long time since the days when Badawi was castigated by Muslim leaders because he talked to the authorities, invited "the other" to the mosque and called for caution in the mixing of culture and religion.

Fuad Nahdi

Mohamed Aboulkhair Zaki Badawi, cleric and Islamic scholar: born Sharkia, Egypt 14 January 1922; Director, Islamic Cultural Centre and Chief Imam, London Central Mosque, Regent's Park 1978-81; Principal, Muslim College 1986-2006; OBE (Hon) 1998, KBE (Hon) 2004; married (one son, one daughter); died London 24 January 2006.

Badawi: inter-faith 'tea and theology'

Badawi's contribution towards Islam in Britain was invaluable. It can be claimed that he invented both the terms "British Islam" and "Islamophobia". Urbane, passionate and wise, he was the father of Muslim engagement in Britain - forging inroads into mainstream society and making the so-called "Muslim case" long before it became fashionable.

More than anything, Badawi was a global Muslim: although born in Egypt, he spent most of his life in other countries and in the process touched the lives of people from West Africa to the Pacific Rim. But he held a soft spot in his heart for Britain. He loved the country, its institutions, its countryside, its dynamism and its "civilising potential". And for three decades he dedicated himself to building institutions that would not only consolidate and stabilise Islam in Britain, but also energise it. Always a teacher, he was one of the main advocates for faith-based schools that were inclusive, broad-minded and of excellent academic standards.

Badawi's imamship at the London Central Mosque in Regent's Park from 1978 was pioneering and exemplary. He was the first imam of a prominent mosque to invite leaders of other faith communities "for tea and theology - whatever they prefer" - as he fondly remembered. This pioneering initiative led to the emergence of an inter-faith movement to which Badawi was committed and dedicated all his life. Once he showed me a picture of him with a group of priests - Buddhist, Hindu, Muslim and Christian - explaining that it was the first inter-faith gathering he had organised, while teaching in Singapore in the early Fifties.

In 1997 Badawi established the Three Faiths Forum with Sir Sigmund Sternberg and the Rev Marcus Braybrooke. The idea of encouraging friendship, goodwill and understanding amongst "people of the book" appealed to the halal globetrotter who always envisioned himself as a bridge-maker of peace and understanding. Badawi was for many years until his death a leading member of the Tripoli-based World Islamic Call Society which shared his conviction of Muslim benevolence across the world. He was Vice-Chairman of the World Congress of Faiths and a founder director of the Forum Against Islamophobia and Racism (Fair).

Perhaps the most ambitious project Badawi initiated was the setting up in London in 1986 of the Muslim College, of which he remained Principal until his death. The Muslim College was not only a visionary but a pragmatic effort towards the construction of "British Islam". Long before it became an obsession of desperate civil servants faced with radical Islam, Badawi had realised the significance of a home-grown Islam in Britain - "free of the cancer of Muslim culture, neurosis and ignorance".

The story of Badawi's life is one of struggle, commitment, ambition and success. He was born in Sharkia, a small village outside Cairo, in 1922, to a traditional, pious Muslim family. He graduated from Al-Azhar University in Cairo, the foremost theological college in the Muslim world, with honours and was awarded the King Fuad First Prize for the best graduate of the year in 1945; then, between 1951 and 1954, he studied Psychology at University College, marrying a fellow student, Mavis. He earned a London University PhD in Modern Muslim Thought, then set off to teach in Malaysia, Singapore and Nigeria, finally settling in London in the mid-Seventies and becoming Chief Imam at Regent's Park Mosque and director of the Islamic Cultural Centre in 1978.

During the three decades he was in public life, Badawi dealt intimately with three prime ministers, three archbishops and two cardinals. The network he developed over the years included laymen and scholars, presidents and priests, politicians and academics. An animated conversationalist and generous host, Badawi never felt uncomfortable with dialogue or exchanging ideas and opinions with anyone.

A born leader, Badawi, however, had little time for the representational politics that proliferate in our times. He believed in himself and in the legitimacy of his opinions and had little time for "charlatans and jokers" - as he described people who made comments about Islam without the qualifications to do so. Of the Muslim leaders feted in the corridors of power in modern Britain he was the only "alim" - Islamic scholar. Essentially Badawi unofficially occupied the position of the "Grand Mufti of Islam in Britain" - a title which had become extinct in the first half of the last century. The title had been given to the Liverpudlian solicitor Abdullah Quilliam by the last Ottoman Caliph in the 19th century.

Disagreeing with Badawi was both a frustrating and futile exercise. He never personalised an argument or harboured malice just because you disagreed with him - you really had to work very hard at it to make an enemy of him. He loved the simple things of life: taking the train to work, a walk in the park and buying chestnuts at the wayside during cold winter days.

To the last, his love continued to be teaching. He made it a point never to miss his classes and hated to be late for an appointment. Unlike other dignitaries, he never minded how he travelled. If he believed in the journey he would take any sensible route there. Many fellow luminaries were shocked to see him in economy when travelling as he found first-class "wasteful and not really necessary".

His efforts to try and bring together religious leaders under the Council of Imams and Mosques never really took off because of the sectarianism and anarchy that exists within different communities. Although of Arab ancestry himself, he loved the Aziziye Mosque in Dalston, east London, where the majority of the congregation is of Turkish origin.

As British Islam enters what augurs to be difficult times, it will miss the wisdom, courage, passion and vision of its most vociferous proponent. However, they are many signs that Badawi's idea of an Islam based in tradition, yet not afraid of modernity and ready to adapt to the realities of a dynamic, plural Britain, has made deep roots.

It seems a long time since the days when Badawi was castigated by Muslim leaders because he talked to the authorities, invited "the other" to the mosque and called for caution in the mixing of culture and religion.

Fuad Nahdi

Mohamed Aboulkhair Zaki Badawi, cleric and Islamic scholar: born Sharkia, Egypt 14 January 1922; Director, Islamic Cultural Centre and Chief Imam, London Central Mosque, Regent's Park 1978-81; Principal, Muslim College 1986-2006; OBE (Hon) 1998, KBE (Hon) 2004; married (one son, one daughter); died London 24 January 2006.

Zaki Badawi was dismissed in 1981 by the Saudis as chief imam at the Central London Mosque in Regent's Park for refusing to toe the Wahhabi line - even though he was offered a vast sum of money by the Saudis to do so. He had always resented the profligacy of the Saudi princes, telling me in no uncertain terms what he thought should be done with some of them. Badawi had the nerve even to tell the late King Fahd of Saudi Arabia to his face that, "You will never be the leader of the world's Muslims." To which the King replied, "What an arrogant man..." How galling it must have been for the Saudis to see Badawi re-establish his authority in London as principal of the Muslim College.

One of Badawi's greatest disappointments was the betrayal of the Bosnian Muslims by the government of John Major in the early 1990's, on the breakup of Yugoslavia. Badawi repeatedly asked for a short sharp shock to be administered to the Serbs, by one or two RAF sorties over Belgrade, to stop them in their tracks. But the Major government told him it would be ineffective. Badawi was proved right in 1995 when NATO bombed Serb targets in Bosnia and brought the Serbs to the negotiating table. Badawi was well aware of the West's pre-disposed dislike for the Islamic ideal (in the sense that the prophet Muhammad was viewed as a false prophet who had brought in a competing religion). Accordingly, Badawi advised Alija Izetbegovic not to declare independence for Bosnia as no-one would come to their aid, when inevitably a furious Slobodan Milosevic of Serbia would attack. Izetbegovic thought the West would help his new country. Badawi knew better. The mass rape and killing of the Bosnian Muslims went on for four years.

And in March 2004, Badawi was badly let down by George Carey - the former Archbishop of Canterbury, when Lord Carey accused Islam of being the cause of most of the world's problems. Badawi told me that, "George's view of Islam depends on the last book he read." As George Carey had, in fact, just finished reading one particularly misguided work on the history of Islam. Forget the Crusades shall we? Forget also the more recent crimes of the Christian Orthodox Serbs and Catholic Croats in their slaughter of the Bosnian Muslims? Zaki Badawi told me he had met Pope John Paul II twice and the Pontiff had apologised to him for the part played by the Christian West in leaving the Bosnian Muslims to their fate. And who, not infrequently, supports the authoritarian regimes of the 'Islamic' world? The West.

Chapter 4

Muslim women's struggle to wear what they like

The Independent, 23rd June 2003

Yasmin Alibhai-Brown

Muslim women's struggle to wear what they like. In Iran and Iraq, Afghanistan and Pakistan, young women are rejecting the idea that they must live covered in shrouds and veils

The hejab is back in the news. In France, once more, the state is in bitter conflict with Muslim schoolgirls wearing the hejab. The government wants no religious symbols in the secular education system, and for some French Muslims this is an attack on their faith. Meanwhile in Iran and Iraq, Afghanistan and Pakistan, younger women are rejecting the idea that they must live and die covered in shrouds and veils.

I have to confess a prejudice. I feel uneasy when I see young women and girls wearing the hejab, usually grey, white, or black. I am not convinced that these are always free choices made after thought and study. The flaming, independent spirit inside me (a blessing and a curse) shrieks with indignation, though I do often hold my tongue because I have been lectured at by so many holier-than-thou Muslims who tell me that this is an order from Allah or that it is a mark of a proud identity fighting Islamophobia, or that it gives women countless freedoms denied to those of us who like to feel the wind in our hair.

They may be right but not as right as they claim. Such righteous and absolute conviction makes hejabis as perverse as those who rush to judge them as weak and oppressed. The hejab is a controversial issue, within Islam as much as outside it, and the most striking debates and disputes are arising in the country where modern, stark, authoritarian Islam first materialised - Iran.

It was here, after the 1979 revolution that toppled the US-friendly Shah, that Ayatollah Khomeini's theocracy imposed the hejab. Hatred of the monarchy was so intense that for ordinary Iranians anything was preferable. There was genuine popular support for Khomeini and his never-ending string of fatwas that, bit by bit, took away many of the fundamental liberties of women.

Men may have found this appealing, but in time many women did not. Soldiers monitored their clothes, watched out for any touch of make up or flash of ankle. Hundreds of women were imprisoned and beaten on the soles of their feet so they could not walk for months; some were hanged for transgressions of dress codes or for disallowed love affairs. A woman I admired enormously, the child psychiatrist Homa Darabi, set her veil alight and burnt herself to death in a square in Tehran in 1994. She was protesting against the imposition of the hejab and against other injunctions that had incarcerated Iranian women in the home, in their roles, in themselves.

This was at a time when Algerian women, especially university students, were being assassinated for not covering themselves properly. In Saudi Arabia today, women who are publicly beaten or beheaded are completely covered - they don't even have the right to show their tears, or look at the sky before their heads roll.

In Britain the hejab became an equally powerful symbol of the Islamic awakening which followed the Satanic Verses furore. Young women did, in fact, take the hejab to show pride in who they were. But in time this choice has turned into a supreme directive; while simultaneously fashionable alternatives are emerging with some daring women wearing brightly coloured turbans or designer scarves, logo and all.

Much blood has been shed around this "freedom", but British hejabis don't much talk about this because it distracts them from their certainties.

In Iran today young women, desperate to escape imposed "modesty", are wearing chic scarves in silk and chiffon, reds and greens and gold, tied so that slips of wayward curls escape. Their cloaks are tighter and a little shorter and the dress police are out once more venting their brutish force against such innocent pleasures.

The Koran has a lighter touch than these brutes, according to Dr Riffat Hassan, a US-based Muslim scholar. Believers, men and women, are told to behave with modesty and to be mindful of their dignity. Nowhere is there anything that says men can beat and kill women who refuse to be caged in the dullest of fabrics.

Dr Hassan has recently been attacked by a new zealot in Pakistan - Farhat Hashmi, a middle-class woman whose influence is spreading throughout Pakistan and Britain. Through her Islamic teaching centres, Hashmi pronounces that the hejab is too revealing, that Muslim women must cover their faces, too, and their arms and legs, so none of their female characteristics can be detected or imagined.

And now when you go to many Muslim enclaves in this country, this is what you see, girls whose faces cannot show smiles or fears, or love or delight.

My question is this: isn't it terribly unjust to degrade Muslim men in this way? Are we saying that they are so uncontrollably driven, so insanely preoccupied with sex, that the sight of a wrist is enough for them to go into spasm? If they were truly virtuous, which many are, you could walk naked virgins before them and they would concentrate on their prayers and not flinch.

As for respect - I am told hejabis are more respected than women who show their hair or legs, which I do. Sorry sisters, the greater feat is to win the respect of men and women without getting into costume. Is the Egyptian novelist Ahdaf Soueif, chairperson of this year's Orangeprize, not respected because she dresses in Western clothes? Last week the Albert Hall in London was filled with Pakistanis who had come to watch their pop stars, fashion designers and poets. It was a brilliant show, with the majority of women dressed to please, their faith unquestionably solid.

Yes, people of all backgrounds are worried about the coarse debauchery of Western societies, but the burqa and the hejab are not a solution to this pervasive social degradation. It is like locking up your daughter so she will not be killed by the increasing traffic on our roads.

As for body image, women in burqas and hejabs are as anxious as the rest of us. Last year researchers found that Iranian women living in Iran had a more pathological relationship with their bodies than Iranian women living in the United States. I went recently into the bookshop of the Regent's Park mosque. In between all the religious books and guidance for a pure life, I found anti-cellulite cream and lines of perfume. I was told that they were "Islamic" because they contained no alcohol. In some ways this is wonderful - that inside a mosque the beauty needs of women are catered for. And the women must know that the faith police cannot stop their intoxicating perfumes getting up the nostrils of men who are not cousins, brothers, fathers and husbands. In Afghanistan, too, beauty parlours carried on throughout the worst days of the Taliban.

You wonder, too, how many of these shrouded women have vitamin-D deficiencies, which can cause health problems such as rickets in children and osteomalacia in adults, because they cannot let the sun fall on their skins. You should see too - as I have - the scars and bruises and broken bones an efficient burqa can hide.

As my Iranian friend Layla says: "Muslim women need to stop fooling themselves. This hejab and burqa is not for religion, only for men to have power over them. Open your eyes I want to say to them." Me too.

y.alibhai-brown@independent.co.uk

French school bars girls for wearing headscarves

The Guardian, Thursday September 25th 2003

Two Muslim schoolgirls were facing expulsion from their state secondary school in the suburbs of Paris yesterday after they refused to remove their headscarves before lessons. Their case has inflamed the controversy over France's commitment to secularism.

Teenage sisters Alma and Lila Levy were sent home from their lycee yesterday morning as punishment for breaking a nationwide ban on all displays of religious faith in the schoolroom. Their highly-publicised exclusion gives new difficulties to the right-wing government as it battles to control a row over headscarves.

"We are being asked to decide between our religion and our education; we want both," Alma, 16, told local media, after the school decided to exclude her and her sister for two weeks. Over the next fortnight, a disciplinary committee will debate whether or not to expel the sisters permanently.

"The conviction of the young girls is so strong, it is not compatible with the secular principle," a school spokesman said.

The campaign for the right to wear headscarves has intensified in recent months, as the government pushes for more integration of France's five million Muslims into society.

Younger Muslims, who have grown up in the west, are the most ardent proponents of the headscarves and the conflict has surfaced with growing frequency in some of the country's militant suburbs.

French law dictates a strict separation of church and state and the celebration of secular values. The hardline interior minister, Nicolas Sarkozy, is a strong proponent of integration and earlier this year insisted Muslim women would have to go bare-headed when posing for identity cards.

Current legislation permits the wearing of headscarves in schools if it is not "aggressive or proselytising", but individual schools are left to decide how this should be enforced.

Prime Minister Jean-Pierre Raffarin said on Sunday that he favoured clearer legislation if it proved impossible otherwise to resolve the issue.

Describing himself as "opposed to the ostentatious expression of one's religious conviction", he said: "School is not the place for propaganda — neither religious nor political."

The government will wait until the end of 2003 for the recommendations of a commission set up by President Jacques Chirac in July to see how the secular principle may be enforced.

Attempts to compromise on how the sisters wear their headscarves have failed despite their readiness to wear coloured and patterned scarves (deemed less aggressive by the school). "We are being asked to wear a veil that lets our ear-lobes show, and that reveals our hair and our necks," said Alma, whose mother is Muslim and whose father is an atheist Jew. "We don't agree with this."

Many of their schoolfriends are sympathetic. "Nobody says anything to people who come wearing Satan T-shirts," one adolescent said.

● Germany's top court said yesterday a woman teacher could wear a Muslim headscarf in school. The federal constitutional court said authorities in Stuttgart were wrong to bar Afghan-born Fereshta Ludin from teaching over the issue.

Amelia Gentleman in Paris

French school bars girls for wearing headscarves

Amelia Gentleman in Paris

Two Muslim schoolgirls were facing expulsion from their state secondary school in the suburbs of Paris yesterday after they refused to remove their headscarves before lessons. Their case has inflamed the controversy over France's commitment to secularism.

Teenage sisters Alma and Lila Levy were sent home from their lycée yesterday morning as punishment for breaking a nationwide ban on all displays of religious faith in the schoolroom. Their highly-publicised exclusion gives new difficulties to the right-wing government as it battles to control a row over headscarves.

"We are being asked to decide between our religion and our education; we want both," Alma, 16, told local media, after the school decided to exclude her and her sister for two weeks. Over the next fortnight, a disciplinary committee will debate whether or not to expel the sisters permanently.

"The conviction of the young girls is so strong, it is not compatible with the secular principle," a school spokesman said.

The campaign for the right to wear headscarves has intensified in recent months, as the government pushes for more integration of France's five million Muslims into society.

Younger Muslims, who have grown up in the west, are the most ardent proponents of the headscarves and the conflict has surfaced with growing frequency in some of the country's militant suburbs.

French law dictates a strict separation of church and state and the celebration of secular values. The hardline interior minister, Nicolas Sarkozy, is a strong proponent of integration and earlier this year insisted Muslim women would have to go bare-headed when posing for identity cards.

Current legislation permits the wearing of headscarves in schools if it is not "aggressive or proselytising", but individual schools are left to decide how this should be enforced.

Prime Minister Jean-Pierre Raffarin said on Sunday that he favoured of clearer legislation if it proved impossible otherwise to resolve the issue. Describing himself as "opposed to the ostentatious expression of one's religious conviction", he said: "School is not the place for propaganda – neither religious nor political."

The government will wait until the end 2003 for the recommendations of a commission set up by President Jacques Chirac in July to see how the secular principle may be enforced.

Attempts to compromise on how the sisters wear their headscarves have failed despite their readiness to wear coloured and patterned scarves (deemed less aggressive by the school). "We are being asked to wear a veil that lets our ear lobes show, and that reveals our hair and our necks," said Alma, whose mother is Muslim and whose father is an atheist Jew. "We don't agree with this."

Many of their schoolfriends are sympathetic. "Nobody says anything to people who come wearing Satan T-shirts," one adolescent said.

● Germany's top court said yesterday a woman teacher could wear a Muslim headscarf in school. The federal constitutional court said authorities in Stuttgart were wrong to bar Afghan-born Fereshta Ludin from teaching over the issue.

Muslim girls face scarf ban at French schools

The Times, Friday December 12th 2003

President Chirac says wearing the hijab is seen as an aggressive act.

FRANCE is likely to ban Muslim girls from wearing head-scarves in schools after a state commission yesterday called for the prohibition of all conspicuous religious costumes and signs, including large crosses and Jewish skullcaps.

The commission also called for greater "respect for all religious options" and suggested that schools include Muslim and Jewish festivals in their holiday calendar.

The commission's advice, which is likely to form part of President Chirac's legislative proposals next week, attempts to resolve an impassioned conflict between champions of tolerance and opponents of a growing trend for Muslim girls to wear the hijab to school.

NEWS THE TIMES FRIDAY DECEMBER 12 2003

Muslim girls face scarf ban at French schools

President Chirac is ready to outlaw 'conspicuous' religious symbols, writes **Charles Bremner**

FRANCOIS LO PRESTI / AFP

Causing controversy: President Chirac says wearing the *hijab* is seen as an aggressive act

FRANCE is likely to ban Muslim girls from wearing head-scarves in schools after a state commission yesterday called for the prohibition of all conspicuous religious costumes and signs, including large crosses and Jewish skullcaps.

The commission also called for greater "respect for all religious options" and suggested that schools include Muslim and Jewish festivals in their holiday calendar.

The commission's advice, which is likely to form part of President Chirac's legislative proposals next week, attempts to resolve an impassioned conflict between champions of tolerance and opponents of a growing trend for Muslim girls to wear the *hijab* to school.

The commission also recommended moves to limit religious dress in the public services and to prohibit Muslims from refusing education and medical care on religious grounds.

Catholic bishops opposed the school ban but Jewish leaders welcomed it and Dalil Boubakeur, president of the French Muslim Council, said: "If there is a law, we will ask our girls to obey it."

The mainstream political parties of Right and Left favour a ban, although Nicolas Sarkozy, the hardline Interior Minister, broke government ranks by opposing a law, saying that it would further alienate Muslims.

The intellectual world is largely in favour, with women's rights campaigners in the lead, but anti-racist groups are largely opposed on the grounds that a ban would amount to discrimination and would further isolate Muslims.

Jean-Marie Le Pen, leader of the anti-immigrant National Front, denounced the proposed ban as a pro-Muslim move that would draw more immigrants to France.

The commission was instructed by M Chirac last spring to redefine France's tradition of secular institutions in an age of ethnic diversity.

France has six million Muslims, Europe's biggest Islamic community. These are mainly from former North African colonies.

M Chirac last week said that wearing the *hijab* was perceived as an aggressive act. The President's words reflected the sharp difference between France's traditional belief that the state has a duty to promote integration and equality in a muscular way and the view in Britain and elsewhere that accepts the co-existence of separate ethnic and religious communities.

The argument has simmered for years. It boiled up again with the emergence of a more militant Islam which has seen a rise in *hijab*-wearing.

Although only a handful of *hijab*-wearers have been excluded from schools, the issue has generated much heat among teachers, who are found on both sides of the argument.

The commission said the testimony of 140 witnesses left it alarmed by evidence of a breakdown in France's tradition of integration, tolerance and equality. Sections of the Muslim community were seeking to enforce segregation, with women refusing treatment by male doctors and some refusing to be taught by male or non-Muslim teachers.

It was also worried by growing anti-Semitism, mainly among disaffected Muslim youths.

Under the new law, large crosses, Muslim veils and the skullcaps of Jewish boys would be outlawed. Discreet signs such as small crosses, stars of David or little Korans, would be acceptable. The commission said: "All punishment will be proportional and imposed only after pupils have been invited to conform."

Private schools would not be affected by the law.

Universities would be encouraged to prevent students refusing teachers for reasons of gender or religion. Companies would be entitled to "regulate" the dress of workers who have contact with customers. Hospital patients would be barred from refusing care from a doctor or nurse on religious grounds.

A national school of Islam would be created; a Muslim chaplain-in-chief would be appointed to the armed forces; state canteens would be required to propose pork-free meals and municipal cemeteries would required to set aside burial grounds for Muslims.

BRITISH TOLERANCE

British headteachers have been advised against issuing bans on religious headwear (Glenn Owen writes). David Hart, general secretary of the National Association of Head Teachers, said his members were aware that such action could "inflame sensitivities", particularly in areas with high concentrations of Muslim pupils.

Britain has always accepted that schools could be run by the Catholic or Protestant churches, a principle extended to Muslim, Jewish, Greek and Sikh faiths which has encouraged tolerance towards religious dress.

The commission also recommended moves to limit religious dress in the public services and to prohibit Muslims from refusing education and medical care on religious grounds.

Catholic bishops opposed the school ban but Jewish leaders welcomed it and Dalil Boubakeur, president of the French Muslim Council, said: "If there is a law, we will ask our girls to obey it."

The mainstream political parties of Right and Left favour a ban, although Nicolas Sarkozy, the hardline Interior Minister, broke government ranks by opposing a law, saying that it would further alienate Muslims.

The intellectual world is largely in favour, with women's rights campaigners in the lead, but anti-racist groups are largely opposed on the grounds that a ban would amount to discrimination and would further isolate Muslims.

Jean-Marie Le Pen, leader of the anti-immigrant National Front, denounced the proposed ban as a pro-Muslim move that would draw more immigrants to France.

The commission was instructed by M Chirac last spring to redefine France's tradition of secular institutions in an age of ethnic diversity.

France has six million Muslims, Europe's biggest Islamic community. These are mainly from former North African colonies.

M Chirac last week said that wearing the hijab was perceived as an aggressive act. The President's words reflected the sharp difference between France's traditional belief that the state has a duty to promote integration and equality in a muscular way and the view in Britain and elsewhere that accepts the co-existence of separate ethnic and religious communities.

The argument has simmered for years. It boiled up again with the emergence of a more militant Islam which has seen a rise in hijab-wearing.

Although only a handful of hijab-wearers have been excluded from schools, the issue has generated much heat among teachers, who are found on both sides of the argument.

The commission said the testimony of 140 witnesses left it alarmed by evidence of a breakdown in France's tradition of integration, tolerance and equality. Sections of the Muslim community were seeking to enforce segregation, with women refusing treatment by male doctors and some refusing to be taught by male or non-Muslim teachers.

It was also worried by growing anti-Semitism, mainly among disaffected Muslim youths.

Under the new law, large crosses, Muslim veils and the skullcaps of Jewish boys would be outlawed. Discreet signs such as small crosses, stars of David or little Korans, would be acceptable. The commission said: "All punishment will be proportional and imposed only after pupils have been invited to conform."

Private schools would not be affected by the law.

Universities would be encouraged to prevent students refusing teachers for reasons of gender or religion. Companies would be entitled to "regulate" the dress of workers who have contact with customers. Hospital patients would be barred from refusing care from a doctor or nurse on religious grounds.

A national school of Islam would be created; a Muslim chaplain-in-chief would be appointed to the armed forces; state canteens would be required to propose pork-free meals and municipal cemeteries would [be] required to set aside burial grounds for Muslims.

BRITISH TOLERANCE

British headteachers have been advised against issuing bans on religious headwear (Glenn Owen writes). David Hart, general secretary of the National Association of Head Teachers, said his members were aware that such action could "inflame sensitivities", particularly in areas with high concentrations of Muslim pupils.

Britain has always accepted that schools could be run by the Catholic or Protestant churches, a principle extended to Muslim, Jewish, Greek and Sikh faiths which has encouraged tolerance towards religious dress.

Belgium next in line as Europe's veil ban spreads

The Times, Monday January 19th 2004

SCHOOL pupils and civil servants in Belgium could soon be banned from wearing Islamic headscarves as the emotive debate over the hijab spreads across Europe.

Inspired by French law, two Belgian senators drafted legislation to ban the veil and other overt religious symbols from state schools, causing outrage from Islamic groups.

Patrick Dewael, the Belgian Interior Minister, was denounced by members of his Government last week for declaring that he supports the ban, not just in schools but in all state institutions, including hospitals and government offices.

In Germany, the hijab is banned in schools in 7 out of its 16 states. The Bavarian Government insists that the ban was necessary because the scarf had become "a symbol of fundamentalism and extremism".

The two Belgian senators, Anne-Marie Lizin and Alain Destexhe, say that the ban is needed to combat what they say is Islamic sexism. "The veil amounts to oppression of the individual in the name of religion," Ms Lizin, a Socialist, said. Belgium has 350,000 Muslims, mainly of North

Belgium next in line as Europe's veil ban spreads

From Anthony Browne
in Brussels

SCHOOL pupils and civil servants in Belgium could soon be banned from wearing Islamic headscarves as the emotive debate over the *hijab* spreads across Europe.

Inspired by French law, two Belgian senators drafted legislation to ban the veil and other overt religious symbols from state schools, causing outrage from Islamic groups.

Patrick Dewael, the Belgian Interior Minister, was denounced by members of his Government last week for declaring that he supports the ban, not just in schools but in all state institutions, including hospitals and government offices.

In Germany, the *hijab* is banned in schools in 7 out of its 16 states. The Bavarian Government insists that the ban was necessary because the scarf had become "a symbol of fundamentalism and extremism".

The two Belgian senators, Anne-Marie Lizin and Alain Destexhe, say that the ban is needed to combat what they say is Islamic sexism. "The veil amounts to oppression of the individual in the name of religion," Ms Lizin, a Socialist, said. Belgium has 350,000 Muslims, mainly of North African and Turkish origin, in a population of ten million.

Mr Dewael, a Liberal Democrat, argued that the wearing of religious symbols "threatens principles such as the separation between the Church and the State".

Setting out his views in a lengthy document, he said that all civil servants, including teachers, judges and police officers, should be banned from wearing any overtly religious symbol at work and that the ban should also apply to state schools. As in France, the ban would apply not just to Islamic veils but to Jewish *yarmulkes* and the wearing of large crucifixes.

Explaining his thinking in the Belgian newspaper *De Morgan*, Mr Dewael wrote: "The Government should remain neutral ... so there should be no visible use of religious symbols or veils for police officers, judges, clerks or teachers in public schools. It is also clear that students in public schools should not wear veils or other religious symbols."

The proposed ban has split the Belgian coalition Government, however. Maria Arena, the Social Integration Minister, accused Mr Dewael of "electioneering" before this year's regional and European polls. "When high-ranking ministers make such radical and aggressive comments without taking the time to consult widely, the result is very dangerous for social cohesion," she said.

Opposition parties also denounced the proposed ban, apart from the anti-immigration Vlaams Blok party.

A ban on the *hijab* is already spreading piecemeal among Belgian schools and other state institutions, which have the legal right to set their own dresscodes. When the Athenée Royal High School in Brussels, which has a high number of immigrant pupils, introduced a ban recently, Francis Lees, the school's administrator, said: "We have changed our rules to forbid the wearing of headscarves because the situation was no longer tenable. Some pupils have since left the school, but we have been able to break out of our ghetto."

Islamic groups in Belgium have combined forces to condemn the attempt to copy the French ban. In a joint communiqué, 15 groups, including the Imam League and the Association of Parents of Muslim Children, argued that for many Muslim women wearing a veil was a "divine obligation".

The statement said that a ban on headscarves and veils "would deprive Muslim citizens of the pleasure of exercising their civic rights".

Supporters say that the veil is already banned in schools in Tunisia and Turkey, both Muslim countries.

Last week a Belgian court ruled that a Muslim woman was allowed to be photographed for her identity card wearing a veil, saying that she had the right to appear in the photograph as she usually does in real life.

African and Turkish origin, in a population of ten million.

Mr Dewael, a Liberal Democrat, argued that the wearing of religious symbols "threatens principles such as the separation between the Church and the State".

Setting out his views in a lengthy document, he said that all civil servants, including teachers, judges and police officers, should be banned from wearing any overtly religious symbol at work and that the ban should also apply to state schools. As in France, the ban would apply not just to Islamic veils but to Jewish yarmulkes and the wearing of large crucifixes.

Explaining his thinking in the Belgian newspaper *De Morgan*, Mr Dewael wrote: "The Government should remain neutral ... so there should be no visible use of religious symbols or veils for police officers, judges, clerks or teachers in public schools. It is also clear that students in public schools should not wear veils or other religious symbols."

The proposed ban has split the Belgian coalition Government, however. Maria Arena, the Social Integration Minister, accused Mr Dewael of "electioneering" before this year's regional and European polls. "When high-ranking ministers make such radical and aggressive comments without taking the time to consult widely, the result is very dangerous for social cohesion," she said.

Opposition parties also denounced the proposed ban, apart from the anti-immigration Vlaams Blok party.

A ban on the hijab is already spreading piecemeal among Belgian schools and other state institutions, which have the legal right to set their own dresscodes. When the Athenée Royal High School in Brussels, which has a high number of immigrant pupils, introduced a ban recently, Francis Lees, the school's administrator, said: "We have changed our rules to forbid the wearing of headscarves because the situation was no longer tenable. Some pupils have since left the school, but we have been able to break out of our ghetto."

Islamic groups in Belgium have combined forces to condemn the attempt to copy the French ban. In a joint communique, 15 groups, including the Imam League and the Association of Parents of Muslim Children, argued that for many Muslim women wearing a veil was a "divine obligation".

The statement said that a ban on headscarves and veils "would deprive Muslim citizens of the pleasure of exercising their civic rights".

Supporters say that the veil is already banned in schools in Tunisia and Turkey, both Muslim countries.

Last week a Belgian court ruled that a Muslim woman was allowed to be photographed for her identity card wearing a veil, saying that she had the right to appear in the photograph as she usually does in real life.

Why should we defend the veil?

Catherine Bennett, The Guardian 22nd January 2004

Shortly after the fall of the Taliban, two years ago, Cherie Blair held a press conference at Downing Street in which she demanded that the women of Afghanistan be granted their human rights: "For women to make a contribution they need opportunities, self-esteem and esteem in the eyes of their society." She deplored their subjugation under the Taliban regime, noting, in particular, how the burqa "symbolises the oppression of women". She circled her fingers round her eyes, like blinkers, to emphasise the point.

Now that the French dispute over veil-wearing in schools has travelled to Britain, it would be intriguing to have an update on Blair's views. Is the abbreviated drapery pinned to the heads of some Muslim schoolgirls entirely unrelated to the restrictive burqa? And if not, should we be smiling on this particular expression of cultural difference?

However modestly sized the hijab, many of us would recognise it - like a nun's wimple - as a clear nuisance and hindrance, and more importantly, as a prominent signifier of female subservience, enforced at the behest of men - not the Quran. Last year, in an essay titled Life in Blinkers published in Index on Censorship, one of the Arab world's leading poets, Adonis, declared: "Despite what the fundamentalists would have us believe, nowhere in the Quran or hadith is there a single, unequivocal passage that imposes the veil on Muslim women. Their view is based on a different reading of the text."

Earlier this week in the Guardian, Natasha Walter argued most persuasively that, even if lifelong cranial or bodily concealment is not something many Muslim women easily accept, we should none the less extend our support to those who embrace the veil: "If we believe in women's self-determination, then we must also respect those choices that are not our own."

The suggestion that the Muslim women we see veiled, or, in some parts of London, sailing along with only their faces or eyes peeping from yards of leg-tangling, windblown drapery, actually want to dress like this, is impossible to refute. Who knows? Maybe, inside all that dark material,

The Guardian 22.01.04 | 9

CatherineBennett

Why should we defend the veil?

they are brimming with self-esteem.

In newspaper articles, the point that headscarves are, contrary to decadent western propaganda, actively empowering, is generally made by some brainy young professional wearing a becoming lace-trimmed hijab. Fine. There must surely be more doubt about freedom of choice when the veil is worn by a child in school. As Adonis wrote, "When one sees girls as young as four years old wearing the veil in the streets of Paris, for example, can anyone seriously claim they are doing this voluntarily?"

Even if hijab wearing is a genuine choice, does that make it obligatory for us to respect it? Any more than hijab wearers respect women who wear shamefully little? What we would not ban, we do not have to condone. It is the choice of some women in Britain to force marriage on their unwilling daughters. Or genital mutilation. Both practices have, occasionally, been defended by western feminists putting multi-culturalism before human rights.

In her 1991 essay on clitoridectomy, for example, an American academic, Dallas Browne, asserted that "imposing our moral values on others is normally unjustifiable in a pluralistic, multicultural society". She proposed that women from the developing world, living in western countries, should be entitled to clitoridectomies in hospital: "If western women and men have the right to purely elective cosmetic surgery, then denying third world women access to elective surgery of their choice seems tantamount to legal paternalism and denial of their comparable right of self-determination." Assaults and offences we would never permit against our own girls, those treasured beneficiaries of freedoms laboriously acquired over centuries, may freely be committed on girls from more exotic communities, as if what they've never had, they won't miss.

As Walter said, "The whole trajectory of feminism in the west has been tied up with the freedom to uncover ourselves". In other parts of the world women risk prison, or beatings for the same freedom. Why should we show respect to people who would love to restate female invisibility in this country? Equally, why should men feel happy about the unsubtle insinuation of the veil: that they are helpless victims of lustful appetites, which may all too easily be awakened by the glimpse of female hair?

The wearing of a hijab, that ostensibly mild statement of cultural difference, is, Adonis argues, harmfully socially divisive: "It is, in fact, the symbol for a desire for separation: it means we refuse integration." Moreover, as he reminds us, such overt demonstrations of difference may have nothing to do with religion. An ostentatious cross is not, as we often notice with the behaviour of our own bishops, any guarantee of advanced beatitude. Or wisdom.

As the response to the French president's proposed prohibition on the hijab in schools has shown, this attempt to rid France's classrooms of all conspicuous signs of religious allegiance (including oversized crosses and skull-caps) has only led to more florid demonstrations of religious difference. Including here, where there is no intention of emulating the French ban— as there cannot be, not while state-funded faith schools are idiotically promoted by the government.

Last week's demonstration by ranks of hijab-wearing women in London will be followed, tomorrow, by an all-women seminar, organised by a group called Hizb ut-Tahrir, whose professed goal is to re-establish the Islamic Caliphate. The women will "discuss the French proposal". It seems pretty clear how the discussion is going to go: "Organisers hope that the seminar will encourage the audience to correctly respond to the French moves by challenging secularism and maintaining their Islamic identity".

And those of us who are rather keen on secularism, who do not have an Islamic, or any other kind of religious identity? Presumably we simply defer to this free expression of the correct choice.

France votes for hijab ban

The Times, Wednesday February 11th 2004

Paris: The French parliament voted yesterday by 494 to 36 to ban Muslim headscarves and other religious emblems in state schools, ensuring that the measure will be applied with the new school year in September (Charles Bremner writes). The ban, backed by the Socialist Opposition as well as President Chirac's centre-right majority, is aimed at keeping religion out of the classroom in a state system that jealously guards its secular foundation.

Jean-Pierre Raffarin, the Prime Minister, is also aiming to introduce legislation to restrict Muslim dress and practices in hospitals and other public services.

France votes for hijab ban

Paris: The French parliament voted yesterday by 494 to 36 to ban Muslim headscarves and other religious emblems in state schools, ensuring that the measure will be applied with the new school year in September (Charles Bremner writes). The ban, backed by the Socialist Opposition as well as President Chirac's centre-right majority, is aimed at keeping religion out of the classroom in a state system that jealously guards its secular foundation.

Jean-Pierre Raffarin, the Prime Minister, is also aiming to introduce legislation to restrict Muslim dress and practices in hospitals and other public services.
Leading article, page 19

Cleared in minutes

Daily Mail, Friday March 12th 2004

Ordeal ends for teacher accused of tearing off a girl's scarf

Daily Mail, Friday, March 12, 2004 Page 45

Cleared in minutes

By Beth Hale

Ordeal ends for teacher accused of tearing off a girl's scarf

Acquitted: Hazel Dick

'It has been slow torture'

The accuser: Selina Sabeel, now 16

A TEACHER with a 16-year unblemished record was cleared of assaulting a teenage pupil and insulting her religion yesterday.

A jury took just 50 minutes to acquit Hazel Dick, who burst into tears as her year long ordeal came to an end.

The trial was the second she had endured after the first was abandoned for legal reasons.

At Peterborough Crown Court yesterday a ban on naming the girl pupil who accused Miss Dick was lifted. Selina Sabeel had twice been excluded from school and is on a final warning for expulsion.

The charge was brought after Miss Dick, head of science at Bretton Woods Community School in Peterborough, asked Selina to change her hijab, the traditional Muslim headscarf.

Miss Dick, 43, wanted her to swop the decorative black garment for a plain black one edged in the school colours.

Selina, who was 15 at the time, accused her of pulling the scarf from her head, scratching her with a pin used to hold it in place.

She also claimed Miss Dick told her: 'Islam is all a big joke.'

Miss Dick was charged with religiously aggravated assault despite the support of headmaster John Gribble, parents and colleagues.

But the jury accepted her explanation that she had helped Selina remove the scarf because she was undressing in a corridor and felt this inappropriate.

Miss Dick, who is head of science at the 900-pupil school, said: 'I said to her that she did not have much respect for her religion because uniform formed part of her religion.'

'She said she did have respect for her religion. She was upset because of the comment and stormed off.'

The court heard Selina had been warned for 'persistent breach of school rules' and had used 'disgusting, degrading and foul language'.

Outside court yesterday Miss Dick's brother, Kenny Vaughan said the arrest and subsequent trial had been a 'traumatic and demanding time'.

He said the family had received messages of support from people of all faiths, including Muslims, adding: 'My sister is a religious woman who has always treated other religions with respect.'

Cambridge-educated Miss Dick used to help Muslim teenagers with extra A-level tuition at a local mosque.

Mr Gribble said: 'It can't be right that someone completely innocent should have suffered for a year. It's been slow torture.'

The National Union of Teachers said children who made false accusations against teachers should face 'action' to deter others from doing the same.

The charge of religiously aggravated assault has been brought just nine times since it was introduced in 2001. With such crimes the attack only has to be perceived as racially aggravated by the victim.

The Crown Prosecution Service said the case had been 'thoroughly and carefully reviewed' and it had been in the public interest to bring it to court.

Miss Dick is the latest teacher to be accused by pupils and then cleared.

In November Pam Mitchellhill was cleared of assault after being accused of slapping a six-year-old girl pupil at her school in Sandwell West Midlands. The girl denied she had been hit but the case still went to court.

In October, headmaster David Watkins was cleared of forcing a dead fish into a pupil's mouth at a school in Norwich.

It is not the first time the wearing of the hijab as part of school uniform has caused controversy.

Icknield High School in Luton banned girls from wearing the scarves, but governors lifted the ban after being warned it could breach the Race Relations Act.

By Beth Hale

Jurors clear teacher over Muslim girl's assault claim

The Daily Telegraph, Friday March 12th 2004

News

Jurors clear teacher over Muslim girl's assault claim

AN "OUTSTANDING" teacher was unanimously cleared by a jury yesterday of a religiously motivated assault on a Muslim pupil.

Hazel Dick, the head of science at a comprehensive in Peterborough, had the charge of religiously aggravated assault hanging over her for a year after a girl claimed that she had ripped off her headscarf. Yesterday, at the end of a three-day trial, it took just 50 minutes for a jury at Peterborough Crown Court to find her innocent. As the verdict was announced in one of the first cases of its kind since religious aggravation was introduced into law, friends, family and supporters of the Cambridge-educated teacher broke out in spontaneous applause in the public gallery as Mrs Dick wiped away tears.

Afterwards, her head teacher at Bretton Woods Community School said that the case illustrated the vulnerability of teachers to false accusations by pupils and said that the Government should consider the call by the NAS/UWT for teachers facing allegations of misconduct to remain anonymous.

Mrs Dick, 43, was charged after Selina Sabeel, 15, claimed that she had sustained a scratch on her chin when the teacher ripped her "hijab" scarf from her head.

The girl, who has an appalling disciplinary record and is currently on notice of expulsion after twice being excluded from school for misbehaviour, claimed that the teacher made insulting remarks about Islam during the incident.

Mrs Dick had consistently denied calling Islam "a big joke" and, after the verdict, Judge Nicholas Coleman told her: "I hope you can put this behind you. You go with the good wishes of the court."

Kenny Vaughan, 50, the teacher's brother, said outside court: "My sister is a religious woman and has always treated other religions with the highest respect.

"Over this hard period she has received a number of well wishes and prayers from Christians and Muslims. My sister would now like to be left alone to rebuild her life and get back to what she has always strived to do, which is to teach and develop young people." The incident in March last year began when Mrs Dick ordered the girl to remove a non-uniform headscarf and replace it with a school one. The girl claimed that Mrs Dick had told her that she had no respect for Islam and said that her religion "is all a big joke".

Miss Sabeel then said that she was scratched by a pin when the teacher ripped the scarf from her head. Mrs Dick, however, denied insulting the girl's religion or forcibly removing the scarf. "I said to her that she did not have much respect for her religion because uniform formed part of her religion," she had told the court. "She said she did have respect for her religion. She was upset and stormed off.

"I didn't do or say anything to insult her religion. I was surprised by her reaction. She was not hurt in any way when she left."

Mrs Dick said the girl later called her "a f****** bitch" after she had kept her in at lunchtime because she was late for a science lesson. The following afternoon, the teacher was made aware that the girl had accused her of assault.

John Gribble, the school's head teacher, who described Mrs Dick as an "outstanding" teacher, said afterwards: "The school is delighted to learn that the jury has acquitted Mrs Dick.

"Mrs Dick has a distinguished and unblemished record at the school and enjoys the trust and admiration of her colleagues and governors. The case raises serious issues concerning the vulnerability of staff. Just as appropriate rules must exist to ensure the protection of children, so too must there be a duty of care for staff.

"The campaign by the NAS/UWT for anonymity of staff who are subject to allegations of misconduct deserves serious consideration by government."

By David Sapsted

Fundamentalism

As defined in The Concise Encyclopaedia of Islam, Revised Edition, 2001 by Cyril Glassé

Fundamentalism. The term "Fundamentalism" is Western and misleading because many Muslims are quick to claim that Islam has always been fundamentalist and that the contemporary phenomenon by this name is simply a return to Islam as such. It is not, however, an Islam that would have been familiar to al-Ghazali or to Abu Hanifah, or even Ibn Taymiyyah whom many Fundamentalists regard as their model. The term used, until recently, in Arabic for the phenomenon was not Fundamentalism, but extremism (*mutatarifin*). Now it has been replaced by the more politically correct *Usuliyyah*, a literal translation of fundamentalism. It is characterized by absolutist application of *some* ideas which constitute Islam, and the total rejection of other ideas, which are no less Islam, and no less the Koranic words of revelation. It is marked by the inability to integrate ideas into coherent and stable wholes. Fundamentalism reduces religion to rules and laws and materialism, and ignores transcendence and spirituality.

Following the modern reformer Mawdudi most Fundamentalists insist in the veiling of all women. The custom arose in some parts of the Islamic world, not in all; in 'Abbasid Baghdad it was the reinstatement of a Persian usage. The classical Jurist Ibn Qutaybah (d. *276*/889) a leading traditionist of the *3rd*/9th century, opposed obligatory veiling saying that veiling was a special Koranic condition for the Prophet's wives only who were a focus of attention and, who unlike other women, were also not allowed to marry any one else after his death. (The "veiling" of the Prophet's wives in the Koran in all likelihood did not mean the wearing of a veil, but that audiences with them should be carried out with a separating curtain.)

Nor are apparently similar schools in the past exactly analogous to modern Fundamentalism. The rise of the Zahiri, or literalist school of law in the *3rd*/l0th century, rather than a rigidification was in some ways actually an escape, an alternative to a hardening of legalism in the Islamic world. It was in any case an organic development rather than a reaction to forces from without. Paradoxically, this school was often adopted by extremely liberal thinkers and Sufis seeking greater freedom of thought. Similarly the acceptance by many of predestinarianism in the *2nd*/8th century was a defense against oppression (as well as the logical consequence of certain metaphysical dogmas). Politics has often disguised itself behind a religious front in the Islamic world as elsewhere. Very often ambitious leaders created their power bases around religious affiliations: the ‘Abbasids and Safavids come to mind, as do the Sanusiyyah and Tijaniyyah, and the attempt of the Emir 'Abd al-Qadir of Algeria to build support through the Qadiriyyah. A common characteristic was to label those who did not belong to the movement as ungodly, or as unbelievers, in order to be able to attack them militarily, often not for conquest but simply for plunder, with a clear conscience, for war between Muslims is prohibited. This characteristic has not only continued down to present times, it has been exploited even more, down to the declaration of holy war in circumstances in which not only holy war is impossible under the legal conditions, Islam not being in danger, but any war in the first place from the religious point of view.

These earlier movements had by their nature a very high degree of religious content. The phenomenon of present day fundamentalism does not. Islam as religion, Islam as piety, has been replaced by Islam as ideology and as a kind

FREE WILL – FUNDAMENTALISM

then burn for 1468 years, which is very close to the length of the Sothic year (1460).

Free will, see MAKTŪB; QADARIYYAH.

Friday Prayer (Ar. *salāt al-jum'ah*). The special Friday midday prayer is performed in a congregational mosque, that is, a large mosque where worshipers come together who may well perform the other daily prayers in a smaller, local mosque. Here an Imam, or prayer leader competent to do so, delivers an exhortation (*khutbah*) usually lasting from fifteen minutes to a half hour.

After the *khutbah*, the worshipers end the assembly by performing a two-*raka'āt* prayer in place of the normal four-*raka'at Ẓuhr*, or noon prayer. Attendance at Friday prayers is insisted upon as not only meritorious but a duty. Commercial transactions between the moment the prayer is called to the time it is performed are forbidden, although business may be carried on during the rest of the day.

In Saudi Arabia where Sunday is not a holiday, Thursday and Friday are the equivalent of the two-day weekend found in the West. In other countries where European usage prevails, Saturday and Sunday are civil holidays while Friday remains the day of assembly. The observance of the special congregation takes about one hour.

Fundamentalism. The term "Fundamentalism" is Western and misleading because many Muslims are quick to claim that Islam has always been fundamentalist and that the contemporary phenomenon by this name is simply a return to Islam as such. It is not, however, an Islam that would have been familiar to al-Ghazālī or to Abū Ḥanifah, or even Ibn Taymiyyah whom many Fundamentalists regard as their model. The term used, until recently, in Arabic for the phenomenon was not Fundamentalism, but extremism (*mutaṭarifin*). Now it has been replaced by the more politically correct *Uṣuliyyah*, a literal translation of fundamentalism. It is characterized by absolutist application of *some* ideas which constitute Islam, and the total rejection of other ideas, which are no less Islam, and no less the Koranic words of revelation. It is marked by the inability to integrate ideas into coherent and stable wholes. Fundamentalism reduces religion to rules and laws and materialism, and ignores transcendence and spirituality.

Following the modern reformer Mawdudi most Fundamentalists insist in the veiling of all women. The custom arose in some parts of the Islamic world, not in all; in 'Abbāsid Baghdad it was the reinstatement of a Persian usage. The classical Jurist Ibn Qutaybah (d. *276*/889) a leading traditionist of the *3rd*/9th century, opposed obligatory veiling saying that veiling was a special Koranic condition for the Prophet's wives only who were a focus of attention and, who unlike other women, were also not allowed to marry any one else after his death. (The "veiling" of the Prophet's wives in the Koran in all likelihood did not mean the wearing of a veil, but that audiences with them should be carried out with a separating curtain.)

Nor are apparently similar schools in the past exactly analogous to modern Fundamentalism. The rise of the Ẓahiri, or literalist school of law in the *3rd*/10th century, rather than a rigidification was in some ways actually an escape, an alternative to a hardening of legalism in the Islamic world. It was in any case an organic development rather than a reaction to forces from without. Paradoxically, this school was often adopted by extremely liberal thinkers and Sufis seeking greater freedom of thought. Similarly the acceptance by many of predestinarianism in the *2nd*/8th century was a defense against oppression (as well as the logical consequence of certain metaphysical dogmas). Politics has often disguised itself behind a religious front in the Islamic world as elsewhere. Very often ambitious leaders created their power bases around religious affiliations: the 'Abbāsids and Ṣafavids come to mind, as do the Sanūsiyyah and Tijanīyyah, and the attempt of the Emir 'Abd al-Qādir of Algeria to build support through the Qādiriyyah. A common characteristic was to label those who did not belong to movement as ungodly, or as unbelievers, in order to be able to attack them militarily, often not for conquest but simply for plunder, with a clear conscience, for war between Muslims is prohibited. This characteristic has not only continued down to present times, it has been exploited even more, down to the declaration of holy war in circumstances in which not only holy war is impossible under the legal conditions, Islam not being in danger, but any war in the first place

149

of nationalism. Sometimes this has taken the form of grass roots democracy, but also as the rule by a class claiming religious authority. It has also taken the form of Islam seen as some kind of economic system, not readily definable, and ultimately whatever one wants it to be. It has taken root chiefly among the poor and uneducated as a utopianism without spirituality. Above all it seems to be a reaction to what are perceived as foreign systems, a reaction which has taken the form of an aggressive, sometimes totalitarian application of religious practices as blind rules. As a rejection of alien influences it can be seen as a defensive mechanism, in which, unfortunately, an awareness of the positive meaning of religion is often obscured.

What is perhaps distinctive about contemporary Islamic Fundamentalism is that it attempts to combine modernism, with its secular and materialist tendencies, with a religious conservatism in a vacuum, cut off from tradition and a matrix of organic process. Some modernist Fundamentalist movements have refused to observe Islamic laws on the grounds that they should not be expected to do so until the whole world does so! As the nature of modern Fundamentalism is contradictory, the precursors do not fall into an orderly group representing similar thinking. They in fact form a composite of the contradictory forces that make up Fundamentalism. Among them are the Indian modernist reformer Sayyid Ahmad Khan (*1232-1316*/1817-1898) who founded the Aligarh College and who saw Great Britain as a model; Jamal ad-Din al-Afghani (*1254-1314*/l838-1897) who tried to make himself the spokesman of different currents of his time for his own advancement; Muhammad Abduh (*1265-1323*/1849-1905) who attempted to make revisions in Islamic Law to meet modern conditions, such as the fatwah which permitted interest on capital; 'Ali 'Abd ar-Razzaq in Egypt who advocated the separation of religion and state as an original historic dogma of Islam; Rashid Rida who advanced the notion which now is an unquestioned premise of Fundamentalist political theory, the slogan of shura, or consultation i.e. democracy; Hasan al-Banna' in Egypt (d. *1368*/1949) the founder of the Muslim Brotherhood is another important figure. The Muslim Brotherhood has tried to overthrow what it considers un-Islamic regimes by force, including terrorism, from within; Muhammad Iqbal (*1290-1357*/l873-1938) in Pakistan, who combined certain aspects of modern European philosophy, entirely secular and humanistic in its world view, with Islam; Sayyid Abu'-l Ala Mawdudi (*1321-1399*/1903-1979), a highly influential Pakistani thinker who advocated authoritarian conservatism with modern dynamism. Combining the militancy of the Muslim Brotherhood and the legal legitimism of Mawdudi, Sayyid Qutb denounced believing Muslims as unbelievers if they did not agree with him. Qutb was executed in *1386*/1966 in Egypt by the Nasser regime. The absolute rejection of those who disagree is in the nature of Fundamentalism, the principle of consultation being reserved for adherents of the particular school. Groups derived from Qutb have been implicated in much violence in Egypt including the assassination of President Sadat in 1981, who himself, along with Nasser when they were "Free Officers", belonged to the Muslim Brotherhood at the beginning of his career. (Sadat, as any politician, looked to various groups for possible support, including Sufis; he belonged to the Shadhilis and even as Head of State he performed pilgrimages to the tomb of Imam Shadhili by the Red Sea.)

In Iran, Dr. 'Ali Shari'ati (d. *1397*/1917) was extremely popular among students for what was a combination of Leftist politics, Western Existentialism, and Iranian Ishraq (the two are fundamentally very similar) served up under the label of Islam. The revolution of Ayatollah Khomeini (d. *1409*/1989) for a time provided a banner for young Muslims in many countries, who, having often been fed a diet of revolutionary rhetoric blaming the West for the under-development of the Third World, rallied around what seemed to be revolution through Islam rather than through some alien ideology. The ultimate failure of the Iranian revolution to provide any real solutions, and the disastrous Iran-Iraq war have blunted enthusiasm for the promises put forward by Islamic Government.

The heteroclitic nature of modern Fundamentalism as reaction can be seen from this description of the Muslim Brotherhood by Hasan al-Banna': A Sunni ("orthodox") Salafiyyah movement [part of a general reform restoration movement that came into being almost one hundred years ago to what was perceived as the original Islam of the "pious ancestors"], a Sufi truth (i.e. "a mysticism"), a political organization, an athletic group, a cultural and educational union, an economic company, and a social idea. From this collection of unconnected and even contradictory appeals it can be seen that the guiding principle of Fundamentalism is the attempt to acquire power, sanctified with the sauce of holy righteousness, on the part of those who do not have power today. It is also the fusion of Islam with technological modernism.

Fundamentalism is a phenomenon which has marked all religions in modern times. Materialism and literalism, the rejection of tradition, utopianism and millenarism, the dawning of the age of the dominance of the disenfranchised and oppressed are its hallmarks. In the case of Islam it is as if the magic that neutralized what were originally destructive tendencies into a beneficent synthesis has evaporated and instead of a unity or one reality which guided men's thoughts there are now two which are at war with each other and with themselves. Religions come as rectifications to a state of error and dissolution. When they age, the original forces which had to be confined behind a kind of wall, like the Gog and Magog of the Koran, burst out anew to wreak the havoc of the ancient times. See HAMAS; HIZB ALLAH; KHOMEINI; MUSLIM BROTHERHOOD; PAHLAVI.

Photos taken from book entitled 'Holy Terror' by Amir Taheri.

Published by Sphere Books Ltd 1987

The army of 'twenty million'. A group of female soldiers of Allah march in a Tehran street. They form part of the nucleus of 'the army of twenty million' which Khomeini hopes to raise before the end of the decade in order to 'liberate the whole of Islam.' *(Frank Spooner Pictures}.*

The army of 'twenty million'. A group of female soldiers of Allah march in a Tehran street. They form part of the nucleus of 'the army of twenty million' which Khomeini hopes to raise before the end of the decade in order to 'liberate the whole of Islam' (*Frank Spooner Pictures*).

Women's day in Tehran. Armed women belonging to the Zaynab Commando Squads march through the streets of Tehran. They are not allowed to remove the chador even on the battlefield (*Gamma/Frank Spooner Pictures*).

Women's day in Tehran. Armed women belonging to the Zaynab Commando Squads march through the streets of Tehran. They are not allowed to remove the chador even on the battlefield. *(Gamma/Frank Spooner Pictures).*

Muslim dress ban thwarts extremists

The Times, June 16th 2004

HEAD TEACHERS welcomed a High Court decision that prevents a schoolgirl from wearing strict Islamic dress.

David Hart, general secretary of the National Association of Head Teachers, said the school in Luton was right to seek to protect other Muslim pupils from fundamentalists.

Mr Justice Bennett threw out a challenge by Shabina Begum, 15, against Denbigh High School's refusal to allow her to wear the jilbab, a dress that leaves only the hands and face exposed. The judge said that the uniform policy aided the proper running of a multifaith secular school.

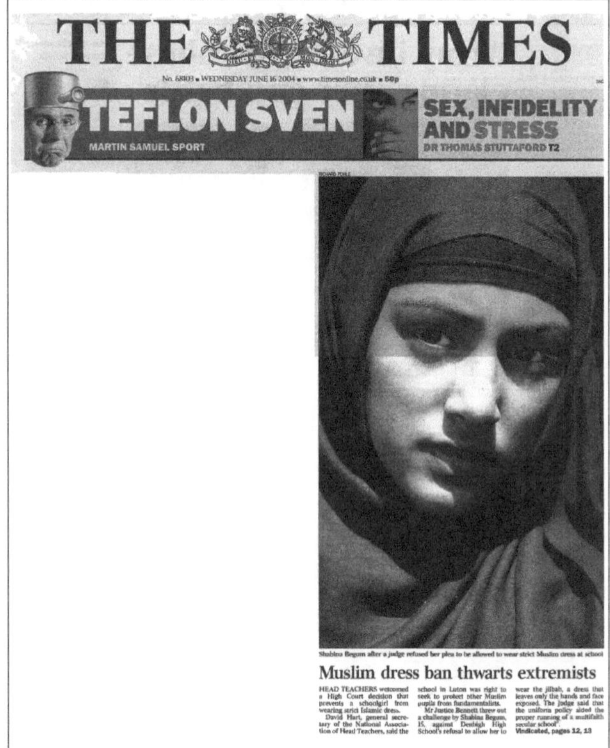

THE TIMES

No. 68103 ■ WEDNESDAY JUNE 16 2004 ■ www.timesonline.co.uk ■ 50p

TEFLON SVEN

MARTIN SAMUEL SPORT

SEX, INFIDELITY AND STRESS

DR THOMAS STUTTAFORD T2

Shabina Begum after a judge refused her plea to be allowed to wear strict Muslim dress at school

Muslim dress ban thwarts extremists

HEAD TEACHERS welcomed a High Court decision that prevents a schoolgirl from wearing strict Islamic dress.

David Hart, general secretary of the National Association of Head Teachers, said the school in Luton was right to seek to protect other Muslim pupils from fundamentalists.

Mr Justice Bennett threw out a challenge by Shabina Begum, 15, against Denbigh High School's refusal to allow her to wear the jilbab, a dress that leaves only the hands and face exposed. The judge said that the uniform policy aided the proper running of a multifaith secular school".

Vindicated, pages 12, 13

Judge backs school ban on girl who defied rules by wearing Islam dress

By Lewis Smith

A HEADTEACHER was right to bar a pupil from wearing Muslim dress that breached school uniform policy, a judge ruled yesterday.

Shabina Begum, 15, was sent home from school in September 2002 for wearing a jilbab, which covers all the body except hands and face.

She has since refused to go to lessons at Denbigh High School, Luton, and went to the High Court in London to try to get the decision reversed.

In his judgment, Mr Justice Bennett dismissed her demand, saying that to overturn the policy on uniforms risked creating the perception that Muslims were being given preferential treatment.

The school already allows girls to wear a headscarf with the shalwar kameez — loose trousers and tunic approved by local Muslim leaders.

Miss Begum, however, said the shalwar kameez did not conceal her arms and lower legs adequately and maintained that the school was violating her right to an education and her human right to freedom of religious expression.

Mr Justice Bennett said that by sticking to its rules on uniform the school was protecting pupils from unwelcome outside influences and contributing to "social cohesion and harmony".

Many girls at the school did not wish to wear a jilbab and would feel "pressure on them either from inside or outside the school" if it were adopted.

"The present school uniform policy aims to protect their rights and freedoms," he said. "Further, if the choice of two uniforms were permitted for Muslim female pupils it can be readily understood that other pupils of different or no faiths might well see that as favouring a particular religion."

He said the school had legitimately drawn up its policy on uniform, in consultation with Muslim leaders, to ensure the "proper running of a multicultural, multifaith, secular school".

The agreed uniform, the judge said, ensured that there was "no outward distinction" between Muslims, Hindus and Sikhs at the school. The judge said that the school, where 80 per cent of pupils are Muslim, had made its uniform policy clear to the girl when she joined and that she happily wore the uniform from 2000 until two years ago when a deepening of her religious belief led her to insist on the jilbab.

While accepting that Miss Begum was entitled to an education, he said that the right did not extend to "be educated at a particular school". He pointed out that there were other schools where she would be allowed to wear the jilbab.

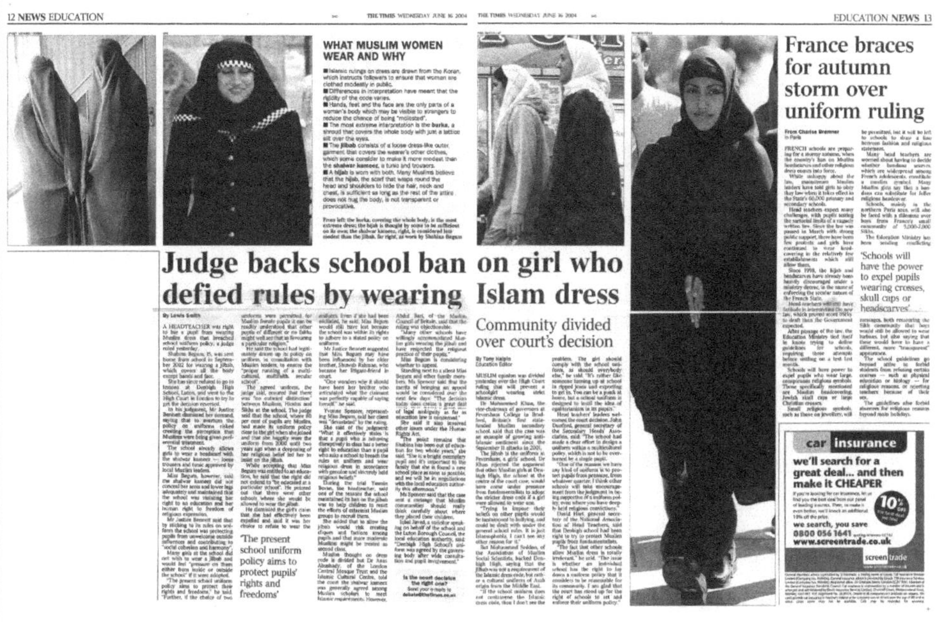

12 NEWS EDUCATION THE TIMES WEDNESDAY JUNE 16 2004

THE TIMES WEDNESDAY JUNE 16 2004 EDUCATION NEWS 13

WHAT MUSLIM WOMEN WEAR AND WHY

■ Islamic rulings on dress are drawn from the Koran, which instructs followers to ensure that women are clothed modestly in public.
■ Differences in interpretation have meant that the rigidity of the code varies.
■ Hands, feet and the face are the only parts of a woman's body which may be visible to strangers to reduce the chance of being "molested".
■ The most extreme interpretation is the **burka**, a shroud that covers the whole body with just a lattice slit over the eyes.
■ The **jilbab** consists of a loose dress-like outer garment that covers the wearer's other clothes, which some consider to make it more modest than the **shalwar kameez**, a tunic and trousers.
■ A **hijab** is worn with both. Many Muslims believe that the hijab, the scarf that wraps round the head and shoulders to hide the hair, neck and chest, is sufficient as long as the rest of the attire does not hug the body, is not transparent or provocative.

From left: the burka, covering the whole body, is the most extreme dress; the hijab is thought by some to be sufficient on its own; the shalwar kameez, right, is considered less modest than the jilbab, far right, as worn by Shabina Begum

Judge backs school ban on girl who defied rules by wearing Islam dress

By Lewis Smith

Community divided over court's decision

By Tony Halpin, Education Editor

'The present school uniform policy aims to protect pupils' rights and freedoms'

France braces for autumn storm over uniform ruling

From Charles Bremner in Paris

'Schools will have the power to expel pupils wearing crosses, skull caps or headscarves'

He dismissed the girl's claim that she had effectively been expelled and said it was her choice to refuse to wear the uniform. Even if she had been excluded, he said, Miss Begum would still have lost because the school was within its rights to adhere to a stated policy on uniforms.

Mr Justice Bennett suggested that Miss Begum may have been influenced by her older brother, Shuweb Rahman, who became her litigant-friend in court.

"One wonders why it should have been her brother who articulated what the claimant was perfectly capable of saying herself," he said.

Yvonne Spencer, representing Miss Begum, said her client was "devastated" by the ruling.

She said of the judgment: "What it effectively states is that a pupil who is behaving disruptively in class has a better right to education than a pupil who asks a school to breach the rules on uniform and wear religious dress in accordance with genuine and sincerely held religious beliefs."

During the trial Yasmin Bevan, the headteacher, said one of the reasons the school maintained its ban on the jilbab was to help children to resist the efforts of extremist Muslim groups to recruit them.

She added that to allow the jilbab would risk creating cliques and factions among pupils and that more moderate Muslims might be treated as second class.

Muslim thought on dress code is divided but Dr Anas Abushady, of the London Central Mosque Trust and the Islamic Cultural Centre, told the court the shalwar kameez was generally agreed among Muslim scholars to meet Islamic requirements. However, Abdul Bari, of the Muslim Council of Britain, said that the ruling was objectionable.

"Many other schools have willingly accommodated Muslim girls wearing the jilbab and have respected the religious practice of their pupils."

Miss Begum is considering whether to appeal.

Standing next to a silent Miss Begum and other family members, Ms Spencer said that the merits of bringing an appeal would be considered over the next few days: "The decision today does create a great deal of legal ambiguity as far as education law is concerned."

She said it also involved other issues under the Human Rights Act.

"The point remains that Shabina has been out of education for two whole years," she said. "She is a bright exemplary pupil and it's important to the family that she is found a new school place as soon as possible, and we will be in negotiations with the local education authority this afternoon."

Ms Spencer said that the case sent a message that Muslim communities should really think carefully about where they placed their children.

Iqbal Javed, a solicitor speaking on behalf of the school and the Luton Borough Council, the local education authority, said: "Denbigh High School's uniform was agreed by the governing body after wide consultation and pupil involvement."

Is it a human right to make girls wear Islamic dress?

Evening Standard, Wednesday June 16th 2004

THE story of Shabina Begum, the Muslim schoolgirl who has just lost a legal battle for the right to wear full Islamic dress in class, could not be more sensitive. Muslim groups have already branded Britain's education system Islamophobic and called for Muslim children to be offered their own faith schools.

The trouble is that what looks to one culture like modest religious dress appears suspiciously like oppression to another.

Years ago, I taught in a London school with a large number of Muslim girls. At the front of the class, there were 14-year-olds from Pakistani and Bangladeshi backgrounds who were as innocent and co-operative as British girls would have been in 1930.

In the back two rows, meanwhile, were white girls who managed to customise school uniform so it looked like something J-Lo would draw the line at, and whose idea of group discussion was cheery banter comparing their favourite flavour condom.

I could readily imagine the horror of any Muslim parent at their daughter being exposed to such values, or lack of them. There were days in front of those sheltered young women when I blushed myself at the depths to which my own liberal, God-less culture had sunk.

As a Westerner, I had a passionate sense of the advantages my society offered to women. It was hard not to get upset when my Muslim girls were barred from the pleasures of swimming because it would involve removing some of their clothes. Hard not to fret for them on a baking June day when they sat in the airless classroom in the designated modesty costume: roll-necks under tunics, which were worn over trousers.

One day, a girl was not allowed to come on a trip to Hampton Court because rumours had spread that the visit involved a large bed. Henry VIII's bed.

Evening Standard Wednesday, 16 June 2004 15

Allison Pearson

Is it a human right to make girls wear Islamic dress?

I PROTESTED that the bed was 500 years old and no longer in use, but to no avail. Such an impasse makes a mockery of multiculturalism. How could I, as a teacher, feel entirely positive about a culture that denies valuable experiences to its young women? On the other hand, how can Muslims entrust their precious children to a society where kids appear to have lost all respect — for their elders, for their teachers, even for their own bodies?

For two years, Shabina Begum happily wore trousers and a tunic, permitted by the rules of her Luton school. When she returned after the summer in 2002 wearing the jilbab, which covers the entire body except for the hands and face, she was told to go home and change.

The 15-year-old's lawyers argued that her human rights had been breached.

I suspect that the majority of Britons would wonder what kind of human right would put a teenager into a costume that marked her out so cruelly from her peers.

And Shabina Begum, let us not forget, is British.

Allison Pearson

Revealed: radicals who backed girl in dress fight

The Sunday Times, June 20th 2004

Nicholas Hellen

Social Affairs Editor

THE teenage girl who fought a two-year legal battle to wear full Islamic dress to school was influenced by an extremist Muslim splinter group.

Hizb ut-Tahrir (HuT), which is legal in Britain but banned in Germany and much of the Middle East, advised Shabina Begum, a 15-year-old orphan. Her case, which was funded by legal aid, was thrown out by the High Court last week.

Mainstream Muslim leaders reacted angrily to news of extremist involvement in the case. They fear it risks stirring up the sort of controversy sparked in France when the government banned the wearing of the hijab, or headscarf, in school.

Khalid Mahmood, Labour MP for Birmingham's Perry Bar constituency, said: "Most Muslims are happy with the existing dress code. I think they [HuT] are trying to pick a fight. The Home Office needs to look at some of their activities. At the moment they are very close to the edge."

Mahmood said HuT's role was particularly disturbing because of Begum's vulnerability. She was 13 when, in September 2002, she was sent home from Denbigh high school in Luton for wearing a jilbab, an ankle-length dress that leaves only the face and hands visible.

Begum, who was regarded as a promising pupil, was orphaned last April with the death of her mother. Her father had died in 1992. Her 21-year-old brother, Shuweb Rahman, who helped her bring the case, is an HuT supporter.

Although she still intends to sit seven GCSEs next year, she has not attended any classes for almost two years. Her teachers have sent her schoolwork and have taught her outside school hours on a small number of occasions.

Dr Imran Waheed, an HuT spokesman, confirmed that leading activists had encouraged Begum in the dispute. "Our members in Luton have consistently advised Shabina and her family to stand up for her right to an education and her right to observe the Islamic ordinances, including

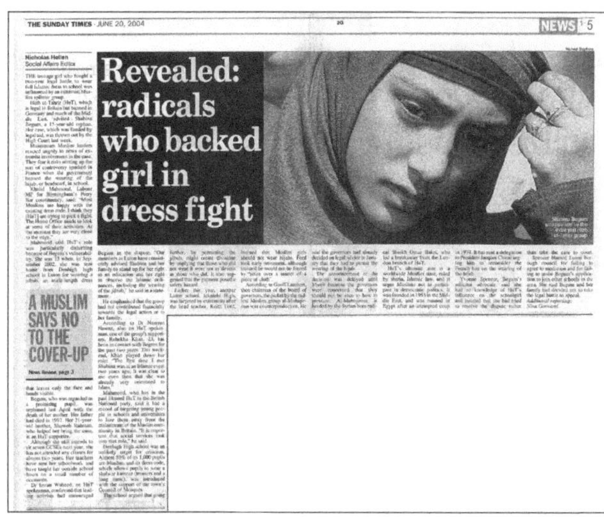
THE SUNDAY TIMES JUNE 20, 2004

NEWS 15

Revealed: radicals who backed girl in dress fight

A MUSLIM SAYS NO TO THE COVER-UP

the wearing of the jilbab," he said in a statement.

He emphasised that the group had not contributed financially towards the legal action or to her family.

According to Dr Nazreen Nawaz, also an HuT spokesman, one of the group's supporters, Rebekha Khan, 23, has been in contact with Begum for the past two years. This weekend, Khan played down her role: "The first time I met Shabina was at an Islamic event two years ago. It was clear to me even then that she was already very orientated to Islam."

Mahmood, who has in the past likened HuT to the British National party, said it had a record of targeting young people in schools and universities to lure them away from the mainstream of the Muslim community in Britain. "It is important that social services look into that role," he said.

Denbigh High school was an unlikely target for criticism. Almost 80% of its 1,000 pupils are Muslim, and its dress code, which allows pupils to wear a shalwar kameez (trousers and a long tunic), was introduced with the support of the town's Council of Mosques.

The school argued that going further, by permitting the jilbab, might create divisions by implying that those who did not wear it were not as devout as those who did. It also suggested that the garment posed a safety hazard.

Earlier this year, another Luton school, Icknield High, was targeted by extremists after the head teacher, Keith Ford, insisted that Muslim girls should not wear hijabs. Ford took early retirement, although insisted he would not be forced to "retire over a matter of a piece of cloth".

According to Geoff Lambert, then chairman of the board of Governors, the picket by the radical Muslim group al-Muhajiroun was counterproductive. He said the governors had already decided on legal advice in January that they had to permit the wearing of the hijab.

The announcement of the decision was delayed until March because the governors were concerned that they should not be seen to bow to pressure. Al-Muhajiroun is headed by the Syrian-born radical Sheikh Omar Bakri, who led a breakaway from the London branch of HuT.

HuT's ultimate aim is a worldwide Muslim state, ruled by sharia, Islamic law, and it urges Muslims not to participate in democratic politics. It was founded in 1953 in the Middle East, and was banned in Egypt after an attempted coup in 1974. It has sent a delegation to President Jacques Chirac urging him to reconsider the French ban on the wearing of the hijab.

Yvonne Spencer, Begum's solicitor advocate, said she had no knowledge of HuT's influence on the schoolgirl and insisted that she had tried to resolve the dispute rather than take the case to court.

Spencer blamed Luton borough council for failing to agree to mediation and failing to assist Begum's application to join other schools in the area. She said Begum and her family had decided not to take the legal battle to appeal.

Additional reporting: **Nina Goswami**

As a Muslim, I say no to the cover-up

The Sunday Times, June 20th 2004

Mona Bauwens is delighted that the judge last week threw out the case brought by Shabina Begum, who wanted to wear the jilbab to school

I am delighted that the Muslim schoolgirl Shabina Begum has lost her battle to wear the jilbab to school. As an Arab Muslim woman brought up in this country, I was angry that Shabina demanded to wear the strict head-to-toe gown to school because wearing the school's uniform was "eroding her human rights". To me, her demand was a flagrant abuse of the human rights this country has given her, and I feel strongly that Shabina should show more respect for life in Britain.

Shabina is a British subject. This is where her parents brought her from Bangladesh and where she gets all the benefits of being a British national; the NHS, education, sexual equality and so on. The school she attended for two years, Luton's Denbigh high school, devised a dress code with local Muslim clerics that was acceptable to the majority of the students. Girls have the option of wearing trousers, skirts or a shalwar kameez (trousers and tunic) with a scarf if they wish to cover their hair. The school didn't want its pupils to wear the jilbab because it worried that those who did might be regarded as "better Muslims" and because there was a simple safety risk of tripping over it.

Shabina, who was orphaned earlier this year following the death of her mother, wore a shalwar kameez to school for two years. But, abruptly, in September 2003, she changed her mind and demanded to cover up, branding the shalwar kameez "too revealing". The school would not allow her to attend wearing a jilbab. Shabina claimed this violated her right to an education and her human right of religious expression.

While I respect Shabina's interpretation of Islam, I am disturbed at the attempt to link choice of dress to human rights. I am worried because there seems to be a very strong revival in traditional Muslim women's dress in Britain. As a child growing up here, it was extremely rare to

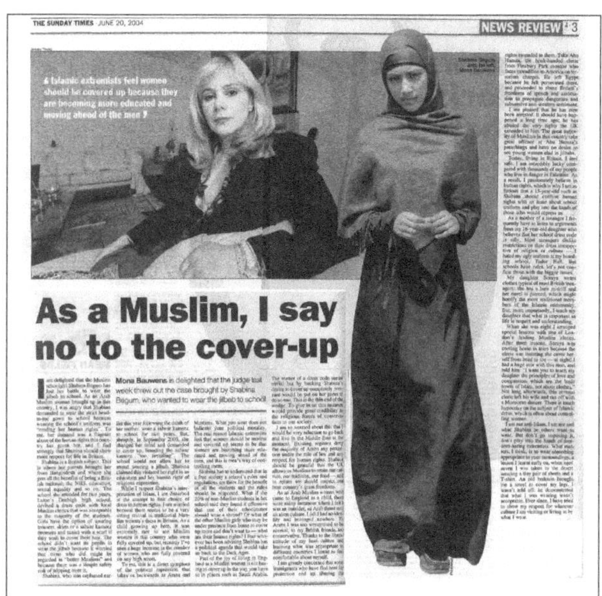
THE SUNDAY TIMES JUNE 20, 2004

NEWS REVIEW 3

'Islamic extremists feel women should be covered up because they are becoming more educated and moving ahead of the men'

As a Muslim, I say no to the cover-up

Mona Bauwens is delighted that the judge last week threw out the case brought by Shabina Begum, who wanted to wear the jilbab to school

see Muslim women in this country who were fully covered up, but recently I've seen a huge increase in the number of women who are fully covered on any high street.

To me, this is a direct symptom of the political repression that takes us backwards as Arabs and Muslims. What you wear does not indicate your political morality. The real reason Islamic extremists feel that women should be modest and covered up seems to be that women are becoming more educated and moving ahead of the men, and this is men's way of controlling them.

Shabina has to understand that in a free society a school's rules and regulations are there for the benefit of all the students and the rules should be respected. What if the 20% of non-Muslim students in her school said they found it offensive that one of their schoolmates should wear a shroud? Or what of the other Muslim girls who may be under pressure from home to cover up more and don't want to — what are their human rights? I fear whoever has been advising Shabina has a political agenda that would take us back to the Dark Ages.

Part of the joy of living in England as a Muslim woman is not having to cover up in the way you have to in places such as Saudi Arabia.

The matter of a dress code seems trivial but by backing Shabina's desire to cover up completely pressure would be put on her peers to do so too. This is the thin end of the wedge. To give in on this instance would provide great credibility to the religious forces of conservatism in our society.

I am so worried about this that I would be

very reluctant to go back and live in the Middle East at the moment. Existing regimes deny the majority of Arabs any protection under the rule of law and any respect for human rights. Shabina should be grateful that the UK allows us Muslims to retain our culture, our tradition, our food — and in return we should respect our host country's great freedoms.

As an Arab Muslim woman who came to England as a child, there were many instances where I felt I was an outsider, an Arab thrust into an alien culture. I felt I had no identity and belonged nowhere. To Arabs I was too westernised to be normal; to my British friends, too conservative. Thanks to the liberal attitude of my host culture and learning what was appropriate in different countries I learnt to feel comfortable about myself.

I am greatly concerned that some immigrants who have fled here for protection end up abusing the rights extended to them. Take Abu Hamza, the hook-handed cleric from Finsbury Park mosque who faces extradition to America on terrorism charges. He left Egypt because he felt persecuted there, and proceeded to abuse Britain's freedoms of speech and association to propagate dangerous and subversive anti-western sentiment.

I am pleased that he has now been arrested. It should have happened a long time ago; he has abused the very rights the UK extended to him. The great majority of Muslims in this country take great offence at Abu Hamza's preachings and have no desire to see young women clad in jilbabs.

Today, living in Britain, I feel safe. I am incredibly lucky compared with thousands of my people who live in danger in Palestine. As a result, I passionately believe in human rights, which is why I am so furious that a 15-year-old such as Shabina should confuse human rights with an issue about school uniform and play into the hands of those who would repress us. .."

As a mother of a teenager I frequently have to listen to arguments from my 16-year-old daughter who believes that her school dress code is silly. Most teenagers dislike restrictions on their dress irrespective of religion or culture — I hated my ugly uniform at my boarding school, Tudor Hall. But schools have rules, let's not confuse those with the bigger issues.

My daughter Soraya wears clothes typical of most British teenagers: she has a bare midriff and her navel is pierced, which might horrify the more traditional members of the Islamic community. But, more importantly, I teach my daughter that what is important in life is respect and understanding.

When she was eight I arranged special lessons with one of London's leading Muslim clerics. After three lessons, Soraya was coming home in tears because the cleric was insisting she cover her self from head to toe — at eight! I had a huge row with this man, and told him: "I want you to teach my daughter the principles of love and compassion, which are the basic tenets of Islam, not about clothes." Not long afterwards, this revered cleric left his wife and ran off with a Moroccan dancer. There is much hypocrisy on the subject of Islamic dress, which is often about controlling women.

I am not anti-Islam. I am not anti what Shabina or others want to wear. But don't go imposing it, don't play into the hands of freedom-hating extremists. What matters, I think, is to wear something appropriate to your surroundings, a lesson I learnt early on, when aged seven I was taken to the desert wearing a tiny pair of shorts and a T-shirt. An old bedouin brought me a towel to cover my legs. I wasn't told off: he demonstrated that what I was wearing wasn't acceptable. Ever since, I have tried to show my respect for whatever culture I am visiting or living in by what I wear.

Now I live in London and I more or less wear what I want, as do most women in London's sophisticated Arab community. I love fashion and wearing designer clothes — a very short skirt, maybe, or, a strapless bustier or décoletté cocktail dress — and I don't feel disrespectful in any way to my religion. I want it to stay that way.
Mona Bauwens

Mona Bauwens is correct in all she writes, except in the way she allows her daughter to dress and in the way she herself dresses. Even the most liberal of Muslim scholars would say that there is no way under the sun that Muslim women should dress like that.

Lifting the veil on women's suffering

The Mail on Sunday, June 20th 2004

Suzanne Moore

THERE is no uniform at my daughter's school but the pupils are not allowed to wear hoods and caps. It could indicate gang membership or act as a disguise.

After school the hoods are defiantly up, a statement of cool or intimidation depending on where you're coming from.

Is this an infringement of anyone's human right I wonder, that teenagers cannot observe their allegiance to a gang or a fashion?

For surely, if any of these kids were smart enough to claim they needed their hoods up for religious, rather than cultural, reasons we would all have to bow down our heads in reverence.

If clothes symbolise one's allegiance to a gang, what bigger gangs are there than the religious ones?

We now find ourselves in the peculiar situation where Muslim girls are going to court to argue for the right to be covered from head to toe while other girls are getting kicked out of school for wearing far too little.

The judge in the case of Shabina Begum, the 15-year-old Muslim girl who went to court because she wants to wear a jilbab, a loose garment that covers the entire body, dismissed her demand. Shabina has not been to school for two years, insisting that because of her religious beliefs the wearing of the hijab (headscarf) and the shalwar kameez (tunic and trousers) was not enough.

What helped convince me that the judge was right was listening to the view of Shabina's classmates, bright, sassy, Muslim girls who don't want to wear the jilbab or have their religious devotion assessed by what they wear.

Yet as a non-Muslim am I even entitled to an opinion on this? For we now live in such overheated times that we only have to put the word Islam in front of any other word for it to mean very bad things.

So we now have 'Islamo-facists', bad men who think and do very bad things, but to say so might mean you have a bad case of 'Islamophobia'.

As always, what we end up with is a total inability to separate culture from religion. While

June 20, 2004 The Mail on Sunday

29

Suzanne Moore

Lifting the veil on women's suffering

some Muslims see this ruling as objectionable, others find it entirely reasonable, pointing out the jilbab is not based on the teachings of the Koran but on the dress codes of the Arab world.

Most Muslim scholars agree that the shalwar kameez meets the requirements of modesty. Britain is properly laissez-faire on most such issues, much more so than France, although it is worth noting that Turkey manages a more secular education system than either country.

On Panorama last week, some Muslim women explained why they choose to veil themselves. They were articulate, thoughtful and challenging but still when I see a fully veiled woman it is almost impossible for me to think, 'Here is an honoured woman.' Quite the opposite.

I cannot see the female body as the sole repository of all desire and responsible for all impure thoughts, so no I wouldn't make a great Catholic either.

I've tried being liberal, respectful, even multicultural, down the years but I have stood in enough school playgrounds with enough women in jilbabs to know that they are not allowed to talk to the likes of me, and that their English will never improve as their sons speak for them.

I have been in maternity wings with women who have had dreadful complications at birth because they have been forbidden from attending antenatal appointments.

So yes I see that burkhas, jilbabs, whatever,

may shelter women from some kinds of male lust. But in the end they still suffer the consequences of it.

I don't doubt there are certain benefits to wearing a shroud - none of the 'does my bum look big in this?' dilemma - but surely any discussion of rights must include those of women who never get given any kind of choice.

We know who Shabina Begum is. But it's the women we literally can't see who I worry about.

At the other extreme, exhibitionism is frequently uppermost in the mind of the indigenous non-Muslim schoolgirl. Often, looking as sexy as possible is all that matters to them. Three newspaper articles on this point follow.

School bans all skirts

The Sunday Times, June 20th 2004

A MIXED state school has banned girls from wearing skirts because their hemlines were getting too short, *writes Sarah-Kate Templeton.*

The governors at Kesgrave high school near Ipswich, Suffolk, have ordered all female pupils to wear trousers because girls were turning up for lessons in skimpy miniskirts.

It is believed to be the first British school to ban skirts. Although many parents are sympathetic to the drive to regulate school uniforms, others claim that the move is draconian.

The Equal Opportunities Commission (EOC) even believes that the pupils may be able to challenge the ruling on the grounds that they are being denied the normal dress options available to women.

George Thomas, the school's head teacher, said the ban was necessary because the girls' attire had become impractical as well as immodest.

"There is a tendency for some of the girls to wear really short skirts," he said. "Some of them are Lycra skirts. Kesgrave has a huge percentage of pupils who cycle to school and short skirts are inappropriate for girls cycling to school.

"Nor are they suitable for an active curriculum. Rather than have teachers continually shout at the girls for wearing short skirts, we are switching to a new uniform."

The new dress code has attracted a mixed response from parents. The father of a 15-year-old girl said: "It's an extreme measure but I can see their point. When I see my daughter and some of the other girls come out of school at the end of the day, they do look a bit inappropriate.

THE SUNDAY TIMES

28 PAGES OF SPORT
Pat Cash's Wimbledon
SPECIAL PREVIEW
COOL CAT
I'm not a true woman

School bans all skirts

A MIXED state school has banned girls from wearing skirts because their hemlines were getting too short, *writes Sarah-Kate Templeton.*

The governors at Kesgrave high school near Ipswich, Suffolk, have ordered all female pupils to wear trousers because girls were turning up for lessons in skimpy miniskirts.

It is believed to be the first British school to ban skirts. Although many parents are sympathetic to the drive to regulate school uniforms, others claim that the move is draconian.

The Equal Opportunities Commission (EOC) even believes that the pupils may be able to challenge the ruling on the grounds that they are being denied the normal dress options available to women.

George Thomas, the school's head teacher, said the ban was necessary because the girls' attire had become impractical as well as immodest.

"There is a tendency for some of the girls to wear really short skirts," he said. "Some of

Continued on page 2

School skirt ban

Continued from page 1

them are Lycra skirts. Kesgrave has a huge percentage of pupils who cycle to school and short skirts are inappropriate for girls cycling to school.

"Nor are they suitable for an active curriculum. Rather than have teachers continually shout at the girls for wearing short skirts, we are switching to a new uniform."

The new dress code has attracted a mixed response from parents. The father of a 15-year-old girl said: "It's an extreme measure but I can see their point. When I see my daughter and some of the other girls come out of school at the end of the day, they do look a bit inappropriate.

"But one would think they could enforce some sort of regulation skirts rather than ban them completely."

Kesgrave, however, found that trying to regulate hemlines was impossible. Its policy was for girls to wear skirts just above the knee; but pupils were opting for much shorter skirts or, in some cases, very long ones worn by girls aiming for a "grunge" look.

The EOC said: "From a legal point of view the issue would be about whether the uniform was more restrictive for girls than for boys. If we look at business dress, it would be equally acceptable for women to wear a smart trouser suit or a dress.

"This [uniform change] could be restricting girls as they would have fewer options than the normal dress choices open to women."

Marcelle D'Argy Smith, the former editor of Cosmopolitan magazine, believes the school has made the right decision: "I am with the school on this one. Children are at school to learn and girls wearing skirts hardly covering their bottoms with skimpy underwear showing, just as the boys' testosterone levels are soaring, is not ideal."

"But one would think they could enforce some sort of regulation skirts rather than ban them completely."

Kesgrave, however, found that trying to regulate hemlines was impossible. Its policy was for girls to wear skirts just above the knee; but pupils were opting for much shorter skirts or, in some cases, very long ones worn by girls aiming for a "grunge" look.

The EOC said: "From a legal point of view the issue would be about whether the uniform was more restrictive for girls than for boys. If we look at business dress, it would be equally acceptable for women to wear a smart trouser suit or a dress.

"This [uniform change] could be restricting girls as they would have fewer options than the normal dress choices open to women."

Marcelle D'Argy Smith, the former editor of Cosmopolitan magazine, believes the school has made the right decision: "I am with the school on this one. Children are at school to learn and girls wearing skirts hardly covering their bottoms with skimpy underwear showing, just as the boys' testosterone levels are soaring, is not ideal."

Trousers only ...school bans skirts after girls refuse to cover up

The Mail on Sunday, 20th June 2004
By Richard Allen and Peter Zimonjic

June 20, 2004 The Mail on Sunday

Trousers only ...school bans skirts after girls refuse to cover up

By Richard Allen and Peter Zimonjic

Head forced to act as pupils insist on 'indecent' minis

A SECONDARY school has taken the extraordinary step of banning girls from wearing skirts because too many pupils wear them indecently short.

The school is thought to be the first in the country to ban skirts and will now allow girls to wear only trousers.

George Thomas, headteacher of Kesgrave High School near Ipswich, Suffolk, said: 'Some girls wear really short skirts, not helped by the fact that not many practical skirts are stocked by shops.

'Many of our pupils cycle to school and some of the things the girls wear are not suitable.

'Rather than have teachers continually shout at the girls for wearing short skirts, we will switch to a new uniform.'

From September, girls will have a choice of two styles of dark-blue trousers. And their traditional shirt and tie will be replaced by a light-blue polo shirt and navy sweatshirt.

But last night some parents said the ban was an over-reaction. One mother of a 13-year-old girl, who asked not to be named, said: 'It makes no sense to introduce rules on the type of trousers when they could do the same thing for skirts.'

The father of a 15-year-old girl said: 'It's an extreme measure but I can see their point. When I see my daughter and some of the other girls coming out of school, they do look a bit inappropriate. But surely they could enforce a regulation skirt rather than ban them.'

Chair of Kesgrave High School's governors, Margaret Young, said: 'Two years ago we sent out an edict saying that skirts had to be school-uniform length but some mothers said it was very difficult to enforce because of peer pressure.

'Shops don't stock practical skirts'

'Girls were rolling them up at the top to make them shorter or changing into a different skirt once they left the house. We decided we couldn't send them all home.

'The teachers were getting fed up with concentrating on uniforms when they could have been concentrating on other things.

'We did consult pretty widely. We've had very few criticisms and those have been more on the grounds of expense.'

The Equal Opportunities Commission website devotes a page to the trousers-for-girls debate, with details on what to do if a school bans trousers for girls – but nothing on what to do if skirts are banned.

A spokesman for the Commission said: 'I've never heard of such a case. We would advise schools to make sure that their uniform guidelines reflect common sense and the modern working wardrobe.'

A spokesman for the Secondary Heads Association said: 'It is still the case that some schools ban trousers for girls but this is a new one on me.

'In the Sixties, they used to make the girls kneel, and if the skirt didn't touch the ground they sent them home to get a longer one. I can't imagine girls taking kindly to wearing trousers in summer.'

Nick Seaton, chairman of the Campaign For Real Education, said: 'Students have to be taught to respect a dress code but this can be done without forcing them to wear trousers.'

National Association of Schoolmasters and Union of Women Teachers (NASUWT) spokeswoman Kathy Duggan said: 'As a mother and a primary school teacher, I think this is silly. But so long as our members are not expected to overburden themselves to enforce the policy, then the union would not have a problem with it.'

Last week, a 15-year-old girl's fight to wear full Islamic dress to school was thrown out by a High Court Judge. Shabina Begum wanted to wear a jilbab, a long dress that leaves only the face and hands visible.

Has the school overreacted – or should others be just as strict about uniform? Have your say on www.mailonsunday.co.uk

TABOO: tiny skirts are outlawed

A SECONDARY school has taken the extraordinary step of banning girls from wearing skirts because too many pupils wear them indecently short

The school is thought to be the first in the country to ban skirts and will now allow girls to wear only trousers.

George Thomas, headteacher of Kesgrave High School near Ipswich, Suffolk, said: 'Some girls wear really short skirts, not helped by the fact that not many practical skirts are stocked by shops.

'Many of our pupils cycle to school and some of the things the girls wear are not suitable.

'Rather than have teachers continually shout at the girls for wearing short skirts, we will switch to a new uniform.'

From September, girls will have a choice of two styles of dark-blue trousers. And their traditional shirt and tie will be replaced by a light-blue polo shirt and navy sweatshirt.

But last night some parents said the ban was an over-reaction. One mother of a 13-year-old girl, who asked not to be named, said: 'It makes no sense to introduce rules on the type of trousers when they could do the same thing for skirts.'

The father of a 15-year-old girl said: 'It's an extreme measure but I can see their point. When I see my daughter and some of the other girls coming out of school, they do look a bit inappropriate. But surely they could enforce a regulation skirt rather than ban them.'

Chair of Kesgrave High School's governors, Margaret Young, said: 'Two years ago we sent out an edict saying that skirts had to be school-uniform length but some mothers said it was very difficult to enforce because of peer pressure.

'Girls were rolling them up at the top to make them shorter or changing into a different skirt once they left the house. We decided we couldn't send them all home.

'The teachers were getting fed up with concentrating on uniforms when they could have been concentrating on other things.

We did consult pretty widely. We've had very few criticisms and those have been more on the grounds of expense.'

The Equal Opportunities Commission website devotes a page to the trousers-for-girls debate, with details on what to do if a school bans trousers for girls - but nothing on what to do if skirts are banned.

A spokesman for the Commission said: 'I've never heard of such a case. We would advise schools to make sure that their uniform guidelines reflect common sense and the modern working wardrobe.'

A spokesman for the Secondary Heads Association said: 'It is still the case that some schools ban trousers for girls but this is a new one on me.

'In the Sixties, they used to make the girls kneel, and if the skirt didn't touch the ground they sent them home to get a longer one. I can't imagine girls taking kindly to wearing trousers in summer.'

Nick Seaton, chairman of the Campaign For Real Education, said: 'Students have to be taught to respect a dress code but this can be done without forcing them to wear trousers.'

National Association of Schoolmasters and Union of Women Teachers (NASUWT) spokeswoman Kathy Duggan said: 'As a mother and a primary school teacher, I think this is silly. But so long as our members are not expected to overburden themselves to enforce the policy, then the union would not have a problem with it.

Last week, a 15-year-old girl's fight to wear full Islamic dress to school was thrown out by a High Court Judge. Shabina Begum wanted to wear a jilbab, a long dress that leaves only the face and hands visible.

Headmaster's ban on bellies and bottoms...

The Times, Wednesday October 13th 2004

From Richard Owen in Rome

ITALIANS are renowned for their sense of style. But the fashion for bare midriffs and low-slung jeans proved too much for the headmaster of one of the country's largest secondary schools and his efforts to make pupils cover up have caused uproar across the country.

Angelo Bernardini, 61, Headmaster of the 1,600-pupil Liceo Vitruvio Pollione at Avezzano, in the Abruzzo region, has tried to impose a new dress code to counter "vulgar and indecent exhibitions of bare flesh". Schools across Italy including some in Milan and Rome are considering similar rules or even an outright ban on the styles.

Signor Bernardini said displays of "navels, bare bottoms, thongs and underpants" were distracting pupils and "making the teachers' jobs almost impossible. In any case it is a matter of good taste".

He said that he had acted because parents had asked him to do so. "They told me their children wouldn't listen to them and they didn't know what else they could do to make them dress suitably."

Some teenagers bared their midriffs or wore

Headmaster's ban on bellies and bottoms hits a sensitive button in stylish Italy

From Richard Owen
in Rome

ITALIANS are renowned for their sense of style. But the fashion for bare midriffs and low-slung jeans proved too much for the headmaster of one of the country's largest secondary schools and his efforts to make pupils cover up have caused uproar across the country.

Angelo Bernardini, 61, Headmaster of the 1,600-pupil Liceo Vitruvio Pollione at Avezzano, in the Abruzzo region, has tried to impose a new dress code to counter "vulgar and indecent exhibitions of bare flesh". Schools across Italy including some in Milan and Rome are considering similar rules or even an outright ban on the styles.

Signor Bernardini said displays of "navels, bare bottoms, thongs and underpants" were distracting pupils and "making the teachers' jobs almost impossible. In any case it is a matter of good taste".

He said that he had acted because parents had asked him to do so. "They told me their children wouldn't listen to them and they didn't know what else they could do to make them dress suitably."

Some teenagers bared their midriffs or wore low-slung jeans with "natural grace", but not all had the figure to carry it off, Signor Bernardini said.

This led to "ribald comments, especially when you can see pubic hair sticking out or an excessively generous amount of bottom". He said mini-skirts used to be a problem, "but now both boys and girls wear trousers".

Signor Bernardini said that his patience had snapped during a school trip last year to Vienna. "We were standing in front of St Stephen's Cathedral and one of the boy's trousers fell down in front of my eyes," he told *Corriere della Sera*.

"Fortunately the boy had underpants on. But that is part of the problem — it seems to be the fashion to show your brand-name underpants off by wearing trousers on the hips."

Whereas previous attempts to persuade schoolchildren to "cover up" have been half-hearted, Signor Bernardini's forthright language prompted nationwide television and newspaper coverage. It also sparked a boycott by pupils, with children milling about and resisting the headmaster's attempts to usher them into the empty classrooms.

In a circular to staff and pupils entitled *From Burkas to Bare Bottoms*, Signor Bernardini noted that some mayors in northern Italy had tried to ban Muslim women from wearing face-covering veils because they could not be identified. Going to the opposite extreme and uncovering bare flesh was equally unacceptable, however.

"There are rules which govern what we wear in different situations," said the circular, which was read out by teachers in every class. "You don't go to the beach wearing an overcoat. You don't wear bikinis in the main town square. Dress should be in keeping with the kind of place you are in and the activities you carry out there. Certain ways of dressing risk overstepping the limits of good taste and cause embarrassment and disturbance in the life of the community."

Signor Bernardini, a classics teacher and headmaster at Avezzano for the past 15 years, said that he had merely sought to offer "sensible advice dispensed with humour". His motto was *castigat ridendo mores*, or "castigate bad habits with a smile". He regretted that Italian schoolchildren did not wear uniform, which was a "democratic and equal" form of dress. Instead, a law dating from 1925 — during the Fascist period — simply refers to a "moral obligation to dress in a manner consonant with a scholastic environment".

Most pupils at the school appeared unfazed by the row. Vanessa, 17, said that the headmaster was "probably right — you should wear normal, discreet clothes to school". Francesco, also 17 and a member of the school council, said that the council was going to see the headmaster to try to clear things up. "But we don't agree that low-waisted trousers are at the opposite end of the spectrum from the burka. The opposite of the burka is wearing no clothes at all."

Antonio Floris, the Mayor of Avezzano, said: "With all due respect to the headmaster, parents come to me more worried about the lack of school facilities than about what their children wear."

Signor Floris, a member of the far-right Alleanza Nazionale, said that he was "much more concerned about other habits", a reference to drug taking.

Antonio Marziale, head of the Association for the Rights of Minors, said that Signor Bernardini's ruling was "good sense. But frankly the decline of standards in our schools is far more important."

Flesh out of school: the Headmaster of Liceo Vitruvio Pollione in Italy wants to ban bare midriffs. He says that low-slung trousers are too distracting low-slung jeans with "natural grace", but not all had the figure to carry it off, Signer Bernardini said.

This led to "ribald comments, especially when you can see pubic hair sticking out or an excessively generous amount of bottom". He said mini-skirts used to be a problem, "but now both boys and girls wear trousers".

Signor Bernardini said that his patience had snapped during a school trip last year to Vienna. "We were standing in front of St Stephen's Cathedral and one of the boy's trousers fell down in front of my eyes," he told *Corriere della Sera.*

"Fortunately the boy had underpants on. But that is part of the problem — it seems to be the fashion to show your brand-name underpants off by wearing trousers on the hips."

Whereas previous attempts to persuade schoolchildren to "cover up" have been halfhearted, Signor Bernardini's forthright language prompted nationwide television and newspaper coverage. It also sparked a boycott by pupils, with children milling about and resisting the headmaster's attempts to usher them into the empty classrooms.

In a circular to staff and pupils entitled From Burkas to Bare Bottoms, Signor Bernardini noted that some mayors in northern Italy had tried to ban Muslim women from wearing face-covering veils because they could not be identified. Going to the opposite extreme and uncovering bare flesh was equally unacceptable, however.

"There are rules which govern what we wear in different situations," said the circular, which was read out by teachers in every class. "You don't go to the beach wearing an overcoat. You don't wear bikinis in the main town square. Dress should be in keeping with the kind of place you are in and the activities you carry out there. Certain ways of dressing risk overstepping the limits of good taste and cause embarrassment and disturbance in the life of the community."

Signor Bernardini, a classics teacher and headmaster at Avezzano for the past 15 years, said that he had merely sought to offer "sensible advice dispensed with humour". His motto was *castigat ridendo mores*, or "castigate bad habits with a smile". He regretted that Italian schoolchildren did not wear uniform, which was a "democratic and equal" form of dress. Instead, a law dating from 1925 — during the Fascist period — simply refers to a "moral obligation to dress in a manner consonant with a scholastic environment".

Most pupils at the school appeared unfazed by the row. Vanessa, 17, said that the headmaster was "probably right — you should wear normal, discreet clothes to school". Francesco, also 17 and a member of the school council, said that the council was going to see the headmaster to try to clear things up. "But we don't agree that low-waisted trousers are at the opposite end of the spectrum from the burka. The opposite of the burka is wearing no clothes at all."

Antonio Floris, the Mayor of Avezzano, said: "With all due respect to the headmaster, parents come to me more worried about the lack of school facilities than about what their children wear."

Signor Floris, a member of the far-right Alleanza Nazionale, said that he was "much more concerned about other habits", a reference to drug taking.

Antonio Marziale, head of the Association for the Rights of Minors, said that Signor Bernardini's ruling was "good sense. But frankly the decline of standards in our schools is far more important."

Why it's right to ban the hijab in schools

Evening Standard, Wednesday 1st September 2004

I AVOID France on holiday because of the overt racism I have experienced there. While Paris is a global city, mostly at ease with itself, my children and I have been treated with contempt in some of the loveliest parts of the French countryside because they think we are Arabs. They stare, shut shop doors in our faces, ignore greetings, mutter xenophobic comments and make us feel wholly unwelcome.

London is a tough and rude city too, but most black and Asian Britons no longer face such sustained bigotry. France has not done enough to protect immigrants and has been slow to ensure they get equal rights. Yet today I find myself on the side of the French state, as the country is held to ransom by Iraqi militants over France's ban on the Muslim headscarf, the hijab, in schools.

Two French journalists, taken hostage two weeks ago, have been paraded on TV, their helplessness and horror put on show in the most repulsive way. Muslim spokespeople have finally been moved to condemn this blackmail. About time, too. For months these leaders have been inciting a revolt against the hijab ban. The French did not communicate the reasons for the new law well: the tone was provocative. But it was right to insist that in a multiracial country, education institutions should be secular spaces.

Yet in the UK, Islamicist hardliners keep testing institutions and rules: the girl in Luton who refused to go to school unless they let her wear a full body cloak is just the latest case.

Millions of us Muslims do not agree with this provocation at all. We do not cover our heads; our mothers only do so when praying. But how they castigate us, the hijab devotees.

WHERE will this end? Already thousands are moving towards complete body-and-face concealment. Tiny girls now walk around, their bright eyes peering out of shrouds. Nowhere in our sacred texts does it say a woman must hide her face so she can't even smile at her babies in a park. This kind of covering is used in deserts simply to keep out sand during sand storms. It is suddenly an obligation. How do teachers know who is taking exams? How do the girls eat?

We make a social contract with the countries we have migrated to. If we seek equality, it must mean just that — not special privileges when it suits us. By aggressively exacting unacceptable concessions, Muslims are jeopardising their own lives and futures.

Yasmin Alibhai-Brown writes for The Independent

Why it's right to ban the hijab in schools

I AVOID France on holiday because of the overt racism I have experienced there. While Paris is a global city, mostly at ease with itself, my children and I have been treated with contempt in some of the loveliest parts of the French countryside because they think we are Arabs. They stare, shut shop doors in our faces, ignore greetings, mutter xenophobic comments and make us feel wholly unwelcome.

London is a tough and rude city too, but most black and Asian Britons no longer face such sustained bigotry. France has not done enough to protect immigrants and has been slow to ensure they get equal rights.

Yet today I find myself on the side of the French state, as the country is held to ransom by Iraqi militants over France's ban on the Muslim headscarf, the hijab, in schools.

Two French journalists, taken hostage two weeks ago, have been paraded on TV, their helplessness and horror put on show in the most repulsive way. Muslim spokespeople have finally been moved to condemn this blackmail. About time, too. For months these leaders have been inciting a revolt against the hijab ban. The French did not communicate the reasons for the new law well: the tone was provocative. But it was right to insist that in a multiracial country, education institutions should be secular spaces.

Yet in the UK, Islamicist hardliners keep testing institutions and rules: the girl in Luton who refused to go to school unless they let her wear a full body cloak is just the latest case.

Millions of us Muslims do not agree with this provocation at all. We do not cover our heads; our mothers only do so when praying. But how they castigate us, the hijab devotees.

WHERE will this end? Already thousands are moving towards complete body-and-face concealment. Tiny girls now walk around their bright eyes peering out of shrouds. Nowhere in our sacred texts does it say a woman must hide her face so she can't even smile at her babies in a park. This kind of covering is used in deserts simply to keep out sand during sand storms. It is suddenly an obligation. How do teachers know who is taking exams? How do the girls eat?

We make a social contract with the countries we have migrated to. If we seek equality, it must mean just that — not special privileges when it suits us. By aggressively exacting unacceptable concessions, Muslims are jeopardising their own lives and futures.

● *Yasmin Alibhai-Brown writes for The Independent*

Muslim pupils bow to scarf ban

The Times, Friday September 3rd 2004

From Charles Bremner and Marie Tourres in Paris

IN WARM sunshine, Nisba Mohamad, 18, yesterday walked into the Lycée Jacques Brel at La Courneuve, a northern Paris suburb, and reluctantly slipped the black hijab off her head and on to her shoulders.

"I feel very bad about taking it off. I feel as if I am going naked," said Ms Mohamad, who has been wearing the full Muslim head covering in public since she was 13.

A Muslim student puts on a headscarf as she leaves school in Lille after her first day under a new law banning religious dress

Muslim pupils bow to scarf ban

She had aimed to wear a bandana instead, but had discovered that this was out too.

Her gesture was repeated by hundreds of girls across France yesterday as a law against religious dress in state schools came into force with the new school year.

Ms Mohamad, who was one of several pupils to wear the hijab up to the school gate, said that she deplored the law and did not agree that it reinforced France's tradition of secularism, which keeps religion out of schools. "I find it very unfair. This is not about secularism. Secularism should be about freedom to practise your own religion," she said.

To the relief of teachers and the Government, fewer than ten pupils out of 12 million were reported to have disobeyed the law against religious dress and symbols.

Tensions over the ban were heavily muted by this week's crisis over two French journalists who are being held by Islamic extremists in Iraq.

In Strasbourg, two 17-year-olds left their school after being barred from class. In Lille, Lyons, Marseilles, the Paris region and other places, teachers kept the few scarf-wearing girls out of the classroom and spent the day trying to persuade them to comply.

Many girls were, however, asked to remove bandanas and other less religious headgear. Sikh boys, caught up in a law designed to curb Islamic fundamentalism, wore narrow headbands instead of turbans.

Muslim leaders have been urging girls to obey the law to avoid encouraging the kidnappers, who are demanding that the French ban be lifted in return for the lives of the captive journalists.

After four days of hectic French diplomacy and mediation by Muslim leaders, hope was rising last night that they might soon be released.

The Courneuve lycée, in a rundown area of immigrant housing estates and with about three quarters of its 1,200 pupils of Muslim background, was one of a dozen around France that was closely watched for incidents as pupils returned. The school made the news last year when it allowed 15 girls to wear head scarves, despite a seven-year-old education ministry rule against them. Head teachers had freedom to interpret the old rule.

While widely condemned abroad, the outright ban is backed by France's mainstream political parties, teachers' unions and about 80 per cent of the public, according to polls. Opponents, who include about half of France's five million Muslims, see it as discrimination.

On Wednesday, the Courneuve school received a morale-boosting visit from Francois Fillon, the Education Minister. He praised the sense of responsibility that France's Muslim leaders had shown during the kidnap crisis. "It was not their aim, but the kidnappers have managed to forge a sense of national cohesion that is almost without precedent," he said.

Emerging yesterday for a cigarette in the street, Paul Morin, the headmaster, said he was relieved that the first day had gone quietly. "I think the girls have understood, because there was no problem today. We did have one girl who decided not to come back this year."

One girl pupil, Ehleme, 17, said: "We are in France and you have to obey the law."

First girls expelled over headscarf ban

The Times, Thursday October 21st 2004

From Charles Bremner in Paris

FIVE Muslim girls have been expelled from school in eastern France in the first of what are expected to be a dozen similar actions this week arising from refusal to obey a ban on religious symbols and clothing in state schools.

Dounia and Khouloude, both 12-year-olds of Algerian origin, were told to leave their college (junior secondary school) at Mulhouse after refusing to remove their headcovering since the new law took effect in early September.

Two other girls were expelled by different schools in Mulhouse, and the fifth girl was banned by her school in Caen. The remaining cases are expected to be decided before half-term next week.

At Bobigny, in the northern Paris outskirts, three teenage Sikh boys have appealed to a local court to order their school to allow them to return to classrooms from which they have been excluded for refusing to remove their headcover.

France's small Sikh community of about 30,000 has been caught up in a law which was primarily aimed at countering rising Islamist radicalism in schools, reflected in the wearing of the hijab, denial of the Holocaust, the intimidation of non-practising Muslims and attacks on Jewish pupils. The boys took off their full turbans and wore a simpler cloth cover to hold their hair, but the school said this still breached the law. Similarly, the two Mulhouse girls had swapped their full headcover for bandanas, but the head teachers deemed these still to breach the law.

Francois Fillon, the Education Minister, said the introduction of the law had been a success because only 72 pupils in France were refusing to obey it. Teachers had succeeded in changing the minds of the great majority of 620 girls who turned up at their schools with headcovers at the start of the school year, he said. The ministry had earlier delayed action against the girls in order to avoid raising tension while kidnappers in Iraq continued to hold two French journalists.

The pair is still being held by Islamic militants whose original demand, when they seized them in August, was that France abandon the ban on headcovers.

The Government said yesterday it believed that the hostages were still alive and was continuing efforts to contact their captors.

Khouloude told *Le Monde*: "They have destroyed my life." Dounia said: "They put us in quarantine. They wouldn't let us into the playground ... What they want is for us to wear tight trousers like all the other girls in the school."

THE TIMES THURSDAY OCTOBER 21 2004 3AC — WORLD NEWS 45

First girls expelled over headscarf ban

From Charles Bremner in Paris

FIVE Muslim girls have been expelled from school in eastern France in the first of what are expected to be a dozen similar actions this week arising from refusal to obey a ban on religious symbols and clothing in state schools.

Dounia and Khouloude, both 12-year-olds of Algerian origin, were told to leave their college (junior secondary school) at Mulhouse after refusing to remove their headcovering since the new law took effect in early September.

Two other girls were expelled by different schools in Mulhouse, and the fifth girl was banned by her school in Caen. The remaining cases are expected to be decided before half-term next week.

At Bobigny, in the northern Paris outskirts, three teenage Sikh boys have appealed to a local court to order their school to allow them to return to classrooms from which they have been excluded for refusing to remove their headcover.

France's small Sikh community of about 30,000 has been caught up in a law which was primarily aimed at countering rising Islamist radicalism in schools, reflected in the wearing of the hijab, denial of the Holocaust, the intimidation of non-practising Muslims and attacks on Jewish pupils. The boys took off their full turbans and wore a simpler cloth cover to hold their hair, but the school said this still breached the law. Similarly, the two Mulhouse girls had swapped their full headcover for bandanas, but the head teachers deemed these still to breach the law.

François Fillon, the Education Minister, said the introduction of the law had been a success because only 72 pupils in France were refusing to obey it. Teachers had succeeded in changing the minds of the great majority of 620 girls who turned up at their schools with headcovers at the start of the school year, he said. The ministry had earlier delayed action against the girls in order to avoid raising tension while kidnappers in Iraq continued to hold two French journalists.

The pair is still being held by Islamic militants whose original demand, when they seized them in August, was that France abandon the ban on headcovers.

The Government said yesterday it believed that the hostages were still alive and was continuing efforts to contact their captors.

Khouloude told *Le Monde*: "They have destroyed my life." Dounia said: "They put us in quarantine. They wouldn't let us into the playground ... What they want is for us to wear tight trousers like all the other girls in the school."

DAREK SZUSTER / MAXPPP

Dounia and Khouloude, both 12, were expelled from school despite attempting to stay within the rules by wearing bandanas

Schoolgirl banned from wearing Muslim dress wins appeal

The Independent, Thursday 3rd March 2005

A MUSLIM schoolgirl has won her battle to wear traditional "head-to-toe" dress in the classroom. The Court of Appeal has decided that her school acted unlawfully in barring her.

Shabina Begum, 16, won her case against Denbigh High School in Luton after Lord Justice Brooke ruled yesterday that the school denied her right to manifest her religious beliefs.

Muslim leaders welcomed the ruling as a "landmark decision" that should lead to more tolerance of religious beliefs.

But community leaders in Luton warned that it could create problems for schools and insisted that the vast majority of Muslims would not want their daughters to wear a jilbab - a full-length gown which exposes only the face and hands.

The case could have important implications for multifaith schools across the country which could be forced to reassess the way they enforce their uniform policies.

Schools in Britain set their own uniform regulations. But Lord Justice Brooke called on the Government to give schools more guidance on how to comply with the Human Rights Act.

Shabina described the ruling as a victory for all Muslims who wished to "preserve their identity and values" in the face of "prejudice and bigotry". The school insisted that it had only lost on a technical breach of the Human Rights Act.

Shabina had worn a shalwar kameez (trousers and tunic) in accordance with the school's uniform policy until September 2002 when she informed teachers that she would in future only wear a jilbab.

The school, where nearly 80 per cent of pupils are Muslim, would not allow her to attend lessons until she wore approved clothing. It argued that its uniform policy had been agreed as acceptable with Islamic scholars and if she could no longer abide by it she should change schools.

Shabina took the school to court but her case was rejected by High Court judges last summer. The school had argued that allowing her to wear a jilbab would impact on the rights of other Muslim girl pupils who opposed allowing the jilbab as they felt that it would create a hierarchy of belief at the school.

The Court of Appeal agreed that the school had a right to set a school uniform policy but said it had failed to consider Shabina's rights under

6 HOME NEWS THE INDEPENDENT ★ Thursday 3 March 2005

Shabina Begum after the court ruled she could wear a jilbab at school *Toby Madden*

Schoolgirl banned from wearing Muslim dress wins appeal

BY SARAH CASSIDY
Education Correspondent

A MUSLIM schoolgirl has won her battle to wear traditional "head-to-toe" dress in the classroom. The Court of Appeal has decided that her school acted unlawfully in barring her.

Shabina Begum, 16, won her case against Denbigh High School in Luton after Lord Justice Brooke ruled yesterday that the school denied her right to manifest her religious beliefs.

Muslim leaders welcomed the ruling as a "landmark decision" that should lead to more tolerance of religious beliefs.

But community leaders in Luton warned that it could create problems for schools and insisted that the vast majority of Muslims would not want their daughters to wear a jilbab – a full-length gown which exposes only the face and hands.

The case could have important implications for multifaith schools across the country which could be forced to reassess the way they enforce their uniform policies.

Schools in Britain set their own uniform regulations. But Lord Justice Brooke called on the Government to give schools more guidance on how to comply with the Human Rights Act.

Shabina described the ruling as a victory for all Muslims who wished to "preserve their identity and values" in the face of "prejudice and bigotry". The school insisted that it had only lost on a technical breach of the Human Rights Act.

Shabina had worn a shalwar kameez (trousers and tunic) in accordance with the school's uniform policy until September 2002 when she informed teachers that she would in future only wear a jilbab.

The school, where nearly 80 per cent of pupils are Muslim, would not allow her to attend lessons until she wore approved clothing. It argued that its uniform policy had been agreed as acceptable with Islamic scholars and if she could no longer abide by it she should change schools.

Shabina took the school to court but her case was rejected by High Court judges last summer. The school had argued that allowing her to wear a jilbab would impact on the rights of other Muslim girl pupils who opposed allowing the jilbab as they felt that it would create a hierarchy of belief at the school.

The Court of Appeal agreed that the school had a right to set a school uniform policy but said it had failed to consider Shabina's rights under the Human Rights Act.

After the judgment, Shabina, who attends a school where the jilbab is allowed, condemned her treatment by Denbigh School. "[Their] decision to prevent my adherence to my religion ... was a consequence of an atmosphere created in Western societies post 9/11, in which Islam has been made a target for vilification in the name of the 'war on terror'," she said.

Iqbal Sacranie, secretary general of the Muslim Council of Britain, argued that schools should accommodate a wide spectrum of beliefs. "Those that choose to wear the jilbab and consider it to be part of the faith requirement for modest attire should be respected," he said.

But Yasin Rehman of the Luton Council of Mosques, which supported the school during the first court challenge, said: "There is no prescribed Islamic dress code. People of Islam, like other religions, say that you should dress modestly. How do you define that? This will create a lot of complications."

In a statement, Denbigh High School said it was proud of its multiracial policy. "The case was lost due to a small technical breach of the Human Rights Act. The judges accepted that the school is entitled to have a uniform policy and could see nothing wrong with it."

Luton Borough Council said schools would be advised to take pupils' religion into account when imposing uniform rules.

the Human Rights Act.

Alter the judgment, Shabina, who attends a school where the jilbab is allowed, condemned her treatment by Denbigh School. "[Their] decision to prevent my adherence to my religion ... was a consequence of an atmosphere created in Western societies post 9/11, in which Islam has been made a target for vilification in the name of the 'war on terror'," she said.

Iqbal Sacranie, secretary general of the Muslim Council of Britain, argued that schools should accommodate a wide spectrum of beliefs. "Those that choose to wear the jilbab and consider it to be part of the faith requirement for modest attire should be respected," he said.

But Yasin Rehman of the Luton Council of Mosques, which supported the school during the first court challenge, said; "There is no prescribed Islamic dress code. People of Islam, like other religions, say that you should dress modestly. How do you define that? This will create a lot of complications."

In a statement, Denbigh High School said it was proud of its multiracial policy. "The case was lost due to a small technical breach of the Human Rights Act. The judges accepted that the school is entitled to have a uniform policy and could see nothing wrong with it."

Luton Borough Council said schools would be advised to take pupils' religion into account when imposing uniform rules.

BY SARAH CASSIDY
Education Correspondent

Muslim girl had been denied right to manifest religion

The Independent, Thursday 8th March 2005

Regina (on the application of B) v Governors of Denbigh High School ([2005] EWCA Civ 199) Court of Appeal, Civil Division (Lord Justice Brooke, Lord Justice Mummery and Lord Justice Scott Baker) 2 March 2005

A MUSLIM schoolgirl who had not been allowed to attend school wearing a jilbab, a form of Muslim dress, because it did not conform with the school uniform, was granted declarations that she had been unlawfully excluded from school, that she had been unlawfully denied the right to manifest her religion, and that she had been unlawfully denied access to suitable and appropriate education.

The Court of Appeal allowed the claimant's appeal against the dissmisal of her application for judicial review of a decision not to allow her to attend school wearing a jilbab.

A Muslim girl of Bangladeshi origin (the claimant) was a pupil at a mixed-community school. The school's uniform requirements for girls were a school jumper, a white shirt, a tie, socks and shoes. Girls might wear a skirt, trousers or a shalwar kameeze. Except in hot weather the girls wore their school jumper under the kameeze. Girls were also permitted to wear headscarves. The claimant contended that, for a Muslim woman who had started to menstruate, the shalwar kameeze did not comply with the strict requirements of her religion. She insisted that she shoud be allowed to wear the jilbab, which was a form of dress worn by Muslim women which effectively concealed the shape of their arms and legs.

At the start of the school year in September 2002 the claimant attended the school dressed in a jilbab. She was told to go away and change into proper school uniform. She refused to attend school unless she was wearing the jilbab.

She applied for judicial review of the school's decision to refuse to allow her to attend school unless she was wearing proper uniform. Her application was dismissed, and she appealed.

Cherie Booth QC, Carolyn Hamilton and Eleni Mitrophanaus (the Children's Legal Centre), for the claimant; Simon Birks (R.J. Stevens, Luton) for the governors.

Lord Justice Brooke said that the school had undoubtedly excluded the claimant. She had been sent away for a disciplinary reason because she was not willing to comply with the discipline of wearing the prescribed school uniform, and she had been unable to return to the school for the same reason.

There was no issue as to the sincerity of the claimant's belief in the correctness of her view that she was obliged to wear the jilbab. It followed that her freedom to manifest her religion or belief in public was being limited, and under the European Convention on Human Rights it would be for the school, as an emanation of the state, to justify the limitation on her freedom created by the school's uniform code and by the way in which it had been enforced.

The position of the school was already distinctive in the sense that despite its policy of inclusiveness it permitted girls to wear a headscarf which was likely to identify them as Muslim.

Therefore, the central issue was the more subtle one of whether, given that Muslim girls could already be identified in that way, it was necessary in a democratic society to place a particular restriction on those Muslim girls at the school who sincerely believed that when they arrived at the age of puberty they should cover themselves more comprehensively than was permitted by the school-uniform policy. The school had approached the issues in the case from entirely the wrong direction, and had not given the claimant's beliefs the weight they deserved.

KATE O'HANLON
Barrister

The Independent Tuesday 8 March 2005

Muslim girl had been denied right to manifest religion

TUESDAY LAW REPORT

8 MARCH 2005

Regina (on the application of B) v Governors of Denbigh High School ([2005] EWCA Civ 199)

Court of Appeal, Civil Division (Lord Justice Brooke, Lord Justice Mummery and Lord Justice Scott Baker) 2 March 2005

A MUSLIM schoolgirl who had not been allowed to attend school wearing a jilbab, a form of Muslim dress, because it did not conform with the school uniform, was granted declarations that she had been unlawfully excluded from school, that she had been unlawfully denied the right to manifest her religion, and that she had been unlawfully denied access to suitable and appropriate education.

The Court of Appeal allowed the claimant's appeal against the dismissal of her application for judicial review of a decision not to allow her to attend school wearing a jilbab.

A Muslim girl of Bangladeshi origin (the claimant) was a pupil at a mixed-community school. The school's uniform requirements for girls were a school jumper, a white shirt, a tie, socks and shoes. Girls might wear a skirt, trousers or a shalwar kameeze. Except in hot weather the girls wore their school jumper under the kameeze. Girls were also permitted to wear headscarves.

The claimant contended that, for a Muslim woman who had started to menstruate, the shalwar kameeze did not comply with the strict requirements of her religion. She insisted that she should be allowed to wear the jilbab, which was a form of dress worn by Muslim women which effectively concealed the shape of their arms and legs.

At the start of the school year in September 2002 the claimant attended the school dressed in a jilbab. She was told to go away and change into proper school uniform. She refused to attend school unless she was wearing the jilbab.

She applied for judicial review of the school's decision to refuse to allow her to attend school unless she was wearing proper uniform. Her application was dismissed, and she appealed.

Cherie Booth QC, Carolyn Hamilton and Eleni Mitrophanous (the Children's Legal Centre) for the claimant; Simon Birks (R.J. Stevens, Luton) for the governors.

Lord Justice Brooke said that the school had undoubtedly excluded the claimant. She had been sent away for a disciplinary reason because she was not willing to comply with the discipline of wearing the prescribed school uniform, and she had been unable to return to the school for the same reason.

There was no issue as to the sincerity of the claimant's belief in the correctness of her view that she was obliged to wear the jilbab. It followed that her freedom to manifest her religion or belief in public was being limited, and under the European Convention on Human Rights it would be for the school, as an emanation of the state, to justify the limitation on her freedom created by the school's uniform code and by the way in which it had been enforced.

The position of the school was already distinctive in the sense that despite its policy of inclusiveness it permitted girls to wear a headscarf which was likely to identify them as Muslim.

Therefore, the central issue was the more subtle one of whether, given that Muslim girls could already be identified in that way, it was necessary in a democratic society to place a particular restriction on those Muslim girls at the school who sincerely believed that when they arrived at the age of puberty they should cover themselves more comprehensively than was permitted by the school-uniform policy. The school had approached the issues in the case from entirely the wrong direction, and had not given the claimant's beliefs the weight they deserved.

KATE O'HANLON, Barrister

The Queen on the application of Shabina Begum v. Headteacher and Governors of Denbigh High School

Court of Appeal judgment 2nd March 2005

Case No: C1/2004/1394
Neutral Citation Number: [2005] EWCA Civ 199
IN THE SUPREME COURT OF JUDICATURE
COURT OF APPEAL (CIVIL DIVISION)
ON APPEAL FROM THE ADMINISTRATIVE COURT
BENNETT J
[2004] EWHC 1389 (Admin)
Royal Courts of Justice
Strand, London, WC2A 2LL

Tuesday, 2 March 2005
Before :

LORD JUSTICE BROOKE
Vice-President of the Court of Appeal (Civil Division)
LORD JUSTICE MUMMERY
and
LORD JUSTICE SCOTT BAKER

- -

Between :

The Queen on the application of SB
Claimant/
Appellant
- and -
Headteacher and Governors of Denbigh High School Defendants/
Respondents

- -

(Transcript of the Handed Down Judgment of Smith Bernal Wordwave Limited, 190 Fleet Street London EC4A 2AG
Tel No: 020 7421 4040, Fax No: 020 7831 8838
Official Shorthand Writers to the Court)

- -

Cherie Booth QC, Carolyn Hamilton and Eleni Mitrophanous (instructed by the Children's Legal Centre) for the Appellant
Simon A Birks (instructed by Head of Legal Services, Luton BC) for the Respondents

- -

Judgment
As Approved by the Court

Lord Justice Brooke:

This is an appeal by SB against an order made by Bennett J in the Administrative Court on 1st June 2004 whereby he dismissed her application for judicial review of a decision of the Headteacher and Governors of Denbigh High School, Luton ("the School"), who had refused to allow her to attend the School if she was not willing to comply with their school uniform requirements. The same judge refused to grant her permission to apply for judicial review of the local education authority's actions in the matter, and she has not been granted permission to appeal against that refusal.

1. The School is a mixed community school for children between the ages of 11 and 16. Children at the school speak 40 different languages, and 21 different ethnic groups (and 10 different religious groups) are represented in the school population. In 1993 90% of the pupils were Muslim, but since that time the school's intake has become more diverse. 79% of the pupils now classify themselves as Muslim. About 71% are of Pakistani or Bangladeshi heritage.

2. The Headteacher, Yasmin Bevan, was born into a Bengali Muslim family. She grew up in India, Pakistan and Bangladesh before coming to this country. She has had a great deal of involvement with Bengali Muslim communities in this country and abroad, and she says that she understands the Islamic dress code and the practices adopted by Muslim women. She does not, however, purport to have a detailed knowledge of the theological issues which surfaced in this dispute.

3. She qualified as a teacher in 1977, and became headteacher at the school in 1991. In

those days its performance was well below the national average, and it was viewed negatively by the local community. Its performance is now well above average for schools with a similar intake, and it cannot accommodate all the pupils who wish to attend it. It has ranked tenth in the country for adding value to its pupils' prior attainment. It has won school achievement awards from the Department for Education and Science (DfES), and it featured in a video on ethnic minority achievement which the department produced.

4. For many years the School has taught pupils from a wide variety of ethnic origins, cultural backgrounds and religious factions. The School's policy has been to accommodate everyone so far as it reasonably can, whilst providing a suitable environment in which children may learn and live together in harmony. The headteacher believes that a school uniform forms an integral part of the school's drive for high standards and continuous improvement. In her view a clear school uniform policy promotes a positive ethos and sense of community identity, and ensures that students are dressed in a way that is safe, practical and appropriate for learning. It also prevents them from feeling disadvantaged because they cannot afford the latest designer items, and makes them less vulnerable to being teased because they are wearing the wrong clothes.

5. This case is concerned with the School's uniform requirements for girls. No real issue arises over the requirements for the school jumper (navy blue v-neck jumper with school logo), shirt (plain white cotton/polyester shirt, short or long sleeve with collar), tie, socks and shoes. Girls may wear a skirt, trousers or a shalwar kameeze, and there are specifications for each. For the shalwar kameeze the specification reads:

"Shalwar: tapered at the ankles, not baggy.

Kameeze: between knee and mid-calf length, not gathered or flared. Fabric must be cotton or poplin, not shiny, silky or crinkly."

6. The uniform requirements are accompanied by a sketch of the front and back views of a girl wearing a shalwar kameeze, with appropriate commentary. The kameeze is a sleeveless smock-like dress with a square neckline, so that the girl's collar and tie are visible. The shalwar consists of loose trousers which taper at the ankles. Except in hot weather the girls wear their school jumper under the kameeze.

7. Girls are also permitted to wear headscarves so long as they comply with three specific requirements. They must be lightweight and navy blue, and worn so that the collar and tie can be seen. They must also cover the head, be folded under the chin and taken round to the back of the neck, with their ends tucked in in conformance with health and safety requirements.

8. The claimant contends that for a Muslim woman who has started to menstruate the shalwar kameeze does not comply with the strict requirements of her religion. She insists that she should be allowed to wear the jilbab, which is a form of dress worn by Muslim women which effectively conceals the shape of their arms and legs. Very strong religious beliefs are close to the centre of this dispute.

9. For the purposes of this judgment I will adopt the spelling of the words "kameeze" and "jilbab" that was used by the parties to this litigation.

10. The shalwar kameeze had featured in the school uniform policies prior to 1993, but in that year a Working Party report led to changes being made to details of the school uniform, and permission being given to girls to wear headscarves for the first time.

11. The shalwar kameeze was seen as satisfying the religious requirement that Muslim girls should wear modest dress, and girls from different faith groups, such as Hindus and Sikhs, also wear it. Parents, staff and students were all consulted over the new design, and there was also consultation with the local mosques. The design had to take into account not only religious considerations, such as the need for modesty, but also health and safety considerations, and it had to be suitable for all school activities.

12. The School's uniform policy has always had the support of the School's governing body. A quarter of the present governors have held that office since at least 1991. Four of the six parent governors are Muslim, as are three of the

governors appointed by the local education authority. One of the community governors chairs the Luton Council of Mosques. In March 2004, shortly before the judge heard this case, the governors reaffirmed their unanimous support for the uniform policy.

13. The claimant's family came to England from Bangladesh. She has two older sisters and two older brothers. She was born in this country in September 1988. Her father died in 1992, and through most of the history of the dispute she was living at home with her mother (who did not speak English) and one sister and one brother: the others had moved out. Her mother died in 2004. One of her brothers is acting as her litigation friend in these proceedings.

14. She first attended the School in September 2000, and during her first two years there she wore the shalwar kameeze without complaint. As she grew older, however, she took an increasing interest in her religion, and she formed the view that the shalwar kameeze was not an acceptable form of dress for mature Muslim women in public places. In her brother's view the shalwar kameeze originated as a Pakistani cultural dress without any particular religious foundation, and she believed that the Islamic Shari'a required women over the age of 13 to cover their bodies completely, apart from their face and hands. The shalwar kameeze was not acceptable, because the white shirt (which at the School is covered by a jumper except in hot weather) revealed too much of the arms, and the skirt length (which at the School may extend to the mid-calf) should go down to the ankles.

15. At the start of the new school year in September 2002 she attended the School dressed in a jilbab. She was accompanied by her brother and another young man. They saw the assistant headteacher, Mr Moore, who told her to go away and change into proper school uniform. He felt that the young men were being unreasonable and threatening. The three then went away, with the young men saying that they were not prepared to compromise on this issue.

16. In his careful judgment ([2004] EWHC 1389 (Admin)) the judge set out in great detail the subsequent history of events. Sadly, the parties rapidly reached an impasse, with the claimant refusing to attend school unless she was allowed to wear the jilbab, and the School refusing to allow her to attend unless she was wearing the shalwar kameeze. What was sadder still was that the attempts to provide her with some form of education while the impasse lasted did not bear any very fruitful results, and she lost the better part of two years' schooling. In September 2004, following the hearing before the judge, she was accepted by a different local school which permitted her to wear the jilbab.

17. If the claimant succeeded in her claim that her rights under Article 9 of the European Convention on Human Rights ("ECHR") were violated, a court would have had to hear contested evidence in relation to her claim for damages about the reasons why she did not avail herself of the educational opportunities the School maintained that it made available to her. It would have had to decide whether an award of damages was appropriate, and if so, the amount. We were told after the hearing of the appeal, however, that she does not wish to pursue that claim. We are therefore concerned only with her application for a declaration. This raises three questions:

i) Was the claimant excluded from the school?

ii) If "Yes", was it because her rights under ECHR Article 9(1) were being limited?

iii) If "yes", were they being justifiably limited pursuant to Article 9(2)?

(I should note here that she also claims that her right to education under Article 2 of the First Protocol to the ECHR was violated in the course of this dispute).

18. The judge's answers to these three questions were:

i) No

ii) No (on the premise that the first answer had been "Yes").

iii) Yes (on the premise that the first two answers had been "Yes").

19. In recent years the topic of exclusion from a school has been the subject of a good deal of attention both in Acts of Parliament and departmental guidance. In this context "exclusion" means "exclusion on disciplinary grounds" (see section 64(4) of the Schools

Standards and Framework Act 1998 ("the 1998 Act") and section 52(10) of the Education Act 2002 ("the 2002 Act"). A headteacher may exclude a pupil from the school for a fixed period or permanently, and in the former case, any fixed periods of exclusion may not exceed more than 45 school days in any one school year (1998 Act. s 64(1) and (2); 2002 Act s 52 (1)). A pupil may not be excluded from a maintained school (whether by suspension, expulsion or otherwise) except by the headteacher in accordance with s 64 of the 1998 Act. Statute provides for rights to make representations, and for rights of appeal in the event of an exclusion.

20. DfES Circular 10/99 gives special guidance to schools in relation to exclusions. It included the following statements:

"6.4 Exclusion should not be used for breaching school uniform....

6.5 The law allows head teachers to exclude a pupil for up to 45 days in a school year. However, individual exclusions of more than a day or two make it more difficult for the pupil to reintegrate into the school....

6.8 The Government is committed to ensuring that by 2002 all pupils excluded for more than 15 school days at a time receive full-time and appropriate education whilst excluded."

21. DfES Guidance 0087/2003 states:

"22. If the head teacher is satisfied that, on the balance of probabilities, a pupil has committed a disciplinary offence and the pupil is being removed from the school site for that reason, formal exclusion is the only legal method of removal. Informal and unofficial exclusions are illegal regardless of whether they are done with the agreement of parents or carers.

21. Exclusion should not be used for:

(c) breaches of school uniform rules, except where these are persistent and in open defiance of such rules."

As soon as a pupil has been excluded for more than 15 days, the local education authority is responsible for ensuring that he/she receives suitable full-time education (DfES Circular 11/99 para 5.1).

22. Departmental guidance on school uniform (DfES circular 0264/2002) contains advice at a high level of generality which was superfluous at Denbigh High School. Thus it advises that schools must be sensitive to the needs of different cultures, races and religions, and contains the expectation that schools should accommodate these needs within a general uniform policy: "For example, allowing Muslim girls to wear appropriate dress and Sikh boys to wear traditional headdress." Para 11 of that guidance states:

"The Department does not consider it appropriate that any pupil should be disciplined for non-compliance with a school uniform policy which results from them having to adhere to a particular cultural, race or religious code."

23. The judge held on the evidence that the claimant had not been excluded. The School earnestly and sincerely wanted her to attend school and placed no impediment or obstacle in her way. All it did was to insist that when she came to school she was dressed in accordance with the School's uniform policy, as indeed she had been happy to do for two years prior to September 2002:

"The Claimant had a choice, either of returning to school wearing the school uniform or of refusing to wear the school uniform knowing that if she did so refuse the Defendant was unlikely to allow her to attend. She chose the latter. In my judgment it cannot be said the actions and stance of the school amounted to exclusion, either formal, informal, unofficial or in any way whatsoever."

24. I do not accept this analysis. The school undoubtedly did exclude the claimant. They told her, in effect: "Go away, and do not come back unless you are wearing proper school uniform." They sent her away for disciplinary reasons because she was not willing to comply with the discipline of wearing the prescribed school uniform, and she was unable to return to the school for the same reason. Education law does not allow a pupil of school age to continue in the limbo in which the claimant found herself. It was very soon clear that she was not willing to compromise her beliefs despite the best efforts of the educational welfare officers who visited her home and the teachers at the school who tried to persuade her to return. If the statutory procedures and departmental guidance had been

followed, the impasse would have been of very much shorter duration, and by one route or another her school career (at one school or another) would have been put back on track very much more quickly.

25. Was she excluded because her freedom to manifest her religion or beliefs under ECHR Article 9(1) was being limited? Article 9 provides, so far as is material:

"(1) Everyone has the right to freedom of thought, conscience and religion; this right includes freedom to change his religion or belief, and freedom….in public or private to manifest his religion or belief….

(2) Freedom to manifest one's religion or beliefs shall be subject only to such limitations as are prescribed by law and are necessary in a democratic society in the interests of public safety, for the protection of public order, health or morals or the protection of the rights and freedoms of others."

26. The importance of the values set out in Article 9(1) was articulated by the European Court of Human Rights in Kokkinakis v Greece, 25 May 1993, Series A No 160-A, p 17, at paras 31 and 32:

"31. As enshrined in Article 9, freedom of thought, conscience and religion is one of the foundations of a 'democratic society' within the meaning of the Convention. It is, in its religious dimension, one of the most vital elements that go to make up the identity of believers and their conception of life, but it is also a precious asset for atheists, agnostics, sceptics and the unconcerned. The pluralism indissociable from a democratic society, which has been dearly won over the centuries, depends on it.

While religious freedom is primarily a matter of individual conscience, it also implies, inter alia, freedom to 'manifest [one's] religion'. Bearing witness in words and deeds is bound up with the existence of religious convictions.

…

33. The fundamental nature of the rights guaranteed in Article 9 para 1…is also reflected in the wording of the paragraph providing for limitations on them. Unlike the second paragraphs of Articles 8, 10 and 11…which cover all the rights mentioned in the first paragraphs of those Articles, that of Article 9 refers only to 'freedom to manifest one's religion or belief'. In so doing, it recognises that in democratic societies, in which several religions co-exist within one and the same population, it may be necessary to place restrictions on this freedom in order to reconcile the interests of the various groups and ensure that everyone's beliefs are respected."

27. On this second issue the judge took note of the fact that the claimant had been content to wear the shalwar kameeze for her first two school years. He was willing to accept that her motives and beliefs in desiring the change were completely genuine, but he held that the School's Governing Body Complaints Committee, who eventually considered the matter in October and November 2003, were entitled to find that the school uniform policy satisfied all the requirements of the Islamic dress code.

28. He annexed a copy of the committee's decision to his judgment. After setting out the history of how the school's uniform policy had developed, the committee took into account the following matters when reaching its decision:

i) The current school uniform policy was concluded after consultation (which included local mosques) had found it to be acceptable;

ii) The policy was reviewed regularly, and this was the first complaint that had ever been made about its compatibility with the requirements of the Islamic dress code;

iii) Since the complaint had been made, the School had consulted various authoritative bodies and received the following advice:

a) The Islamic Cultural Centre in Regent's Park had confirmed that the shalwar kameeze constituted appropriate Islamic dress;

b) The Muslim Council of Britain had confirmed that the dress code prescribed by the School was in accordance with the tenets of Islam.

iv) The committee took note of the fact that the Imams of two local mosques had given the Claimant's solicitors different advice from the advice they had previously given to the School, but they could see no good reason for this change of mind;

v) The committee also took into account a written reply from the London Central Mosque Trust on these matters.

29. Against this background the committee made the following findings of fact about the requirements of the Islamic dress code for a young woman of menstruation age:

i) A Muslim woman's dress should be strictly modest in public;

ii) It should cover all her body with the exception of her face and hands;

iii) It should not be tight or revealing but must be loose and thick enough in order to maintain complete modesty in public.

The committee concluded:

"The committee decided that the shalwar kameeze of the design illustrated as part of the school uniform policy....satisfied all those requirements of the Islamic dress code. Whilst accepting that the jilbab such as [SB] wishes to wear constitutes proper Islamic dress for adult Muslim women in a public place, the evidence presented to the committee does not suggest that it is the only form of dress that meets these requirements. Indeed, the evidence in the form of the letter from the Islamic Cultural Centre....specifically refers to the fact that a wide variety of garments are found throughout the Muslim world that meet those requirements."

30. I now turn to consider the relevant evidence in rather greater detail.

31. There was no expert evidence before the court, still less any evidence that has been tested and explored in cross-examination. There were, however, letters and expressions of opinion from a number of well-informed sources, including the Imams of local mosques, whom the parties consulted during the course of this dispute. For anyone with a deep knowledge of the teachings of Islam, what follows is bound to appear superficial, but this superficiality necessarily flows from the nature of the limited evidential material that is before the court. For the purposes of this judgment, because the epithet "fundamentalist" has resonations which it would be inappropriate to carry into the discussion of the issues in this difficult case, I will refer to those Muslims who believe that it is mandatory for women to wear the jilbab as "very strict Muslims", and those Muslims whose South Asian culture has accustomed them to consider the shalwar kameeze to be appropriate dress for a woman as "liberal Muslims", while being conscious that experts may find these epithets equally inappropriate.

32. The main sources of the Muslim religion are the Holy Quran, which Muslims believe to represent the word of Allah, and Hadiths, or sayings of the Prophet Muhammad, on different topics. A secondary source of authority is a canon of practices and sayings that are ascribed to Muhammad. These are known as the Sunnah, and a combination of the Holy Quran, the Hadiths and the Sunnah provide the basis for the Islamic laws known as the Shari'a. Scholars differ about the authority of the Sunnah, and some of these differences are apparent in the present dispute. In this field familiar problems arise when early traditions pass down the generations by word of mouth, and there is much scholarly dispute about the authority and authenticity of the earliest surviving written texts.

33. All Muslims endeavour to follow the teachings in the Holy Quran, which include the following:

"And tell the believing women to lower their gaze and guard their sexuality, and to display of their adornment only what is apparent, and to draw their head-coverings over their bosoms...."

"O Prophet, tell your wives and daughters and the believing women to draw their outer garments around them when they go out or are among the men."

A Hadith of the Prophet states:

"Whenever a woman begins to menstruate, it is not right that anything should be seen except her face and hands."

So much is common ground. What I will describe as the mainstream modern view among Muslims in England today was expressed by Dr Anas Abushudy, the deputy director-general of the London Central Mosque Trust, and chairman of its Religious Affairs Department. He told the School that "looking around the Muslim world" there was an amazing variety of garments which met the requirements in these writings. The clothes worn by Muslim women differed from country to country, and sometimes in different regions in the same country. He did not see any anti-Islamic act in wearing a shalwar kameeze. The important thing was that the dress of Muslim women must be within the Islamic guidelines, and that whatever was worn should be a full and honest Islamic hijab (veil) which clearly reflected the wearer's identity.

34. He said that that there were many schools of thought on Islam, which differed sometimes in the interpretation of the sayings of Allah. What he described represented the general consensus of the vast majority of Muslim scholars.

35. A contrary view was expressed to the claimant's solicitors by Dr Ahmed Belouafi, of the Centre for Islamic Studies in Birmingham. He originally gave this brief response:

"[W]e can confirm that with respect to the dress code of the female in Islam is the fact that Hijab is the minimum required dress. The traditional dress, be it Pakistani or Egyptian...etc., that some females wore are not enough if they do not meet the required conditions of the dress code as laid down in the teaching of the Quran and the Sunnah of the Prophet."

36. In a follow-up letter he set out, with regard to "the issue of the dress code of a woman in Islam", certain rulings derived by Sheikh Al-Albani, a famous scholar and traditionalist, from various sources of Islamic jurisprudence:

i) The whole body except for the exempted parts [face and hands] should be covered;

ii) Any veil, which itself becomes an attraction, is to be avoided;

iii) Garments should not be semi-transparent;

iv) Dress should not be tight-fitting;

v) Garments should not be perfumed;

vi) The form of dress should not in any way resemble that of a man;

vii) It should not resemble that of non-believers;

viii) Garments should not reflect worldly honour.

37. Dr Belouafi said that these basic requirements must be observed in any garments that women wore under the Islamic dress code, and that it was clear that the shalwar kameeze shown to him by the claimant's solicitors did not comply. (Unfortunately he had been sent a photograph of a girl in a shalwar kameeze whose arms were not covered, whose kameeze stopped at the knees, and whose shalwar consisted of ordinary trousers, rather than loose trousers gathered at the ankle: it may be that the opinions of other people consulted by the claimant's advisers might have been different if they had seen the School's actual design).

38. Dr Belouafi annexed to his response a copy of an article drawn down from the Internet. Although it is entitled "Hijab in the Light of the Quran and Hadith", it is clear that Sheikh Al-Albani also drew from other early texts when he drew up his "eight rules of hijab".

39. Dr Abushudy, for his part, had told the School that because the interpretation of sayings sometimes differed, what he described as the Seven Conditions of Hijab were not totally accurate and therefore not valid for all.

40. These two differing viewpoints, one more liberal, the other more strict, recurred again and again in the opinions expressed by other consultees, and sometimes within the same organisation. For instance, within the Muslim Council of Britain (which was founded in 1997 and now has over 350 institutions affiliated to it) there was a striking difference of approach between the chair of its Social Affairs Committee and the Chair of its Mosque and Community Affairs Committee.

41. The former, when consulted by the Comparative Religion Centre, produced a list of about 20 guiding principles entitled "Dress Code for Woman in Islam". This code said that Islam was a very practical and pragmatic religion. It allowed flexibility within its prescribed tenets. "Follow the middle path" was the proper approach. The wardrobe of a young Muslim girl or woman could be as varied as one would like it to be. Modesty should be observed at all times. If the headdress did not cover the bosom it could be covered by a separate cloth, scarf or jacket, and trousers with long tops and shirts for school wear were absolutely fine. A Muslim schoolgirl's uniform did not have to be so long that there would be a risk of tripping over and causing accidents.

42. The latter, however, said that in order to fulfil the obligation prescribed by the Holy Quran a Muslim woman must wear an outer garment, such as a jilbab, that was loose-fitting and did not show her body or shape in public. He said that

the majority view of ulama (jurists) was that the shalwar kameeze would not be sufficient to fulfil the requirements of Shari'a, because the shape of the bodily parts was not hidden, although it was accepted culturally as the female dress of many South Asian Muslims. His own considered opinion, in the light of rulings of Shari'a, was that the shalwar kameeze did not fulfil the Islamic dress requirement in public.

43. This opinion was shared by the Muslim Welfare House in Seven Sisters Road, London, who gave advice along the lines of that given by Dr Belouafi. They said that descriptively these requirements could be translated as a headscarf to cover the head and an outer body garment similar to at least a three-quarter length coat. They added that the Pakistani clothing known as shalwar kameeze dress did not meet the requirement of an outer garment. There is no evidence that they were shown the School's design.

44. In December 2002 the Imams of two local mosques in Luton advised the School that the shalwar kameeze was the dress that fulfilled the requirements of Islamic dressing and that for a lady it was not an anti-Islamic dress. However, when they were each approached by the claimant's solicitors six months later they qualified this advice. The Imam of the Madinah mosque in Luton quoted not only from a translation of the Holy Quran which refers to the jilbab ("Jalbaab") but also from a commentary on the Quran in these terms:

"It is related from the son of Abbas…that the definition of Jalbaab is that it be a long cloak in which a woman be covered from head to toe."

(Commentary of Huwair in refce from Al Quran, vol 7, p 217)

45. After reciting advice similar to that given by Dr Belouafi he said that in his opinion the claimant was correct in relation to the rights she was demanding from the School.

46. The Imam of the Central Mosque in Luton, Professor Masood Akhtar Hazarvi, made a distinction between his earlier answer to the effect that the shalwar kameeze was not anti-Islamic and his new answer that it did not comply with the Islamic rules for the dress required of a mature Muslim lady in a public place (like a school). He was of the opinion that the claimant's jilbab was "a requirement from Islam".

47. This was clearly the professor's personal view as a theologian. He also happened to chair the Luton Council of Mosques, which was formed in April 2003 as an umbrella organisation representing about 36,000 local residents who embraced the Muslim faith. In that capacity he told the School in March 2004 that the council believed that the School's uniform policy was satisfactory for the majority of the Muslim community.

48. From all this evidence one can see clearly the two main schools of thought (I exclude, for instance, those who rely on the interpretation of other ancient texts for their belief that a woman's face should also be covered). The first, which represents mainstream opinion among South Asian Muslims, from whom most of this country's Muslim population are descended, is that a garment like the shalwar kameeze (coupled with a headscarf) complies sufficiently with Islamic dress requirements, and that there is no need to go any further. The other, which is a minority view among Muslims in this country, but is nevertheless sincerely held, is that the shalwar kameeze, even when it goes down to mid-calf, is not compliant, and that a garment like the jilbab, which disguises the shape of the wearer's arms and legs, is required. This minority view received respectable support among those who were consulted during the course of this dispute. It was no doubt what Professor Masood Hazarvi had in mind when he told the School that the Luton Council of Mosques believed that the School's uniform policy was satisfactory "for the majority of the Muslim community".

49. The sincerity of the claimant's belief in the correctness of the minority view was not in issue in these proceedings. She believed that her religion prohibited her from displaying as much of her body as would be visible if she was wearing the shalwar kameeze, particularly if she was not wearing the school jumper over it in hot weather. So far as the legitimacy of her belief is concerned, in Hasan and Chaush v Bulgaria (26th October 2000: Appln No. 30985/96) the European Court of Human Rights said (at para 78):

"[The court] recalls that, but for very

exceptional cases, the right to freedom of religion as guaranteed under the Convention excludes any discretion on the part of the State to determine whether religious beliefs or the means used to express such beliefs are legitimate."

It follows that her freedom to manifest her religion or belief in public was being limited, and as a matter of Convention law it would be for the School, as an emanation of the state, to justify the limitation on her freedom created by the School's uniform code and by the way in which it was enforced.

50. I turn now to the third question. For the purposes of this case, SB's freedom to manifest her religion or beliefs may only be subject to limitations that are prescribed by law and are necessary in a democratic society in the interests of public safety, for the protection of public morals, or for the protection of the rights and freedoms of others. There was no suggestion that the protection of public morals had any relevance, and a justification on health and safety grounds was dismissed by the judge and not resurrected on the appeal once evidence had showed that other schools (including the local school which the claimant now attends) had been able to accommodate girls wearing the jilbab without any serious concern being raised on that ground.

51. Three witness statements from the School addressed this issue. Mr Moore, the Assistant Headteacher, devoted most of his evidence to explaining why he was concerned to enforce the School's uniform policy, and the support that policy had received from those the School had consulted, both locally and nationally. His witness statement ends in these terms:

"Several staff have been approached by non-Muslim pupils saying that they are afraid of people wearing the jilbab, as they perceive this form of dress to be associated with extreme views. This makes them feel vulnerable. Whilst I would not consider it right to pander to the prejudices or fears of some pupils, I think it would be most unfortunate if some pupils were to be held in fear by others, or regarded as in some way separate, because of the clothes they wear.

Similarly this view has also been reflected by some Muslim girls who have indicated to staff that they do not wish to wear the jilbab, as this would identify them as belonging to extreme Muslim sects. They do not wish to be identified with such people.

In a recent pupil survey, not connected with wearing of the jilbab, there was a space for further comments. Many pupils indicated how much they liked Denbigh High School and the uniform in particular. One pupil suggested that the school introduce the jilbab. She did not suggest that she wanted to wear one. As she wears trousers to school and not the shalwar kameeze, I think it unlikely that she would wish to adopt the jilbab. There have been no other suggestions from pupils, parents, governors or teachers that we adopt the jilbab.

At the Appeal hearing the Claimant indicated that although she does not regard Muslims who wear the shalwar kameeze as bad people, she does think better Muslims wear the jilbab. I would not wish to see the introduction of two classes of Muslim, the inferior class that wears the shalwar kameeze and the better Muslim who wears the jilbab. In my view that would lead to real risk of pressure being brought upon Muslim girls to wear the jilbab or be regarded as religious inferiors. I would fear that this could lead to some girls feeling pressured into wearing the jilbab when they would prefer to wear the shalwar kameeze and might wish to avoid being classified with the kinds of people they believe wear the jilbab."

He ended by expressing a concern that if the school uniform was changed in the way the claimant suggested, this would lead to divisiveness within the school and would threaten the cohesion within the school.

52. Mr Connor, who has been the Deputy Headteacher since 1997, had six years' experience in the culturally diverse London Borough of Brent in the late 1980s. The earlier part of his statement was devoted to the concerns on health and safety grounds that are not now being pursued on this appeal. He then turned to explain that a major learning objective on the part of the curriculum concerned with citizenship was for pupils to work together positively and co-operatively in a community that fosters respect for all.

53. In this context he drew on his

experience of working in schools that incorporate wide diversity. He said there is the potential for pupils to identify themselves as distinct from other groups along cultural, religious or racial grounds, and for conflict to develop between such groups. He recalled an earlier incident in this school which had involved a very difficult and potentially dangerous situation of intransigent conflict between two groups of pupils who defined themselves along racial grounds. This was one of the reasons for a uniform policy that did not allow pupils to identify themselves obviously as belonging to a particular religion or race.

54. It was important in his experience to recognise that many adolescents require a lot of support to understand the importance of inclusion, equal opportunities, mutual respect and social cohesion, such as was fostered by the school's uniform policy. He attested to the same concerns among a number of girls at the school as Mr Moore had mentioned, and he believed that the school had a duty to protect these pupils from inappropriate peer pressures, or pressures from outside extremist groups. There had been an incident in February 2004 when some young men who represented an extremist Muslim group had picketed the school gates and distributed leaflets to the pupils which exhorted Muslims not to send their children to secular schools. A number of pupils understandably felt harassed by these activities.

55. At the end of his statement Mr Connor expressed a concern that any erosion of the uniform policy would make it more difficult for the school to recruit and retain staff. This was partly because he believed that the present clear policy contributed to the school's ethos of good behaviour and discipline. It was also partly because this was a secular school, and this was very important to many teachers who believe strongly that they do not wish to be associated with promoting a particular faith. If a new school uniform policy resulted in a significant proportion of pupils outwardly identifying themselves according to their faith, this could create the impression that this was a school which favoured that faith.

56. Mrs Bevan, the Headteacher, gave evidence similar to that given by Mr Moore and Mr Connor about the concerns expressed by children at the school, both Muslim and non-Muslim, and also by a number of parents. She said that she had been given the firm impression that a number of girls relied on the school to help them resist the pressures from the more extreme groups. She was afraid that if the school uniform were to be adapted to include the jilbab these girls would be deprived of proper protection and would feel abandoned by those upon whom they were relying to preserve their freedom to follow their own part of the Islamic tradition. She also referred to the picketing that had taken place "by groups of mainly young men who would appear to be from the more extreme Muslim traditions".

57. She said that all the requirements of the school uniform were well publicised before the claimant chose to attend the School. She was being treated in exactly the same way as all other pupils, a very high percentage of whom were Muslim, and since the requirements of the uniform policy were satisfactory to her for two years, and were also satisfactory to all the School's other pupils both past and present, she did not see how the School was discriminating against her.

58. The reasons given by the Chair of the Governors and by the Governors' Complaints Committee in the autumn of 2003 for rejecting SB's complaints did not add significantly to the reasons given by the School's senior staff. The Complaints Committee observed that they did not purport to have the legal knowledge to interpret complex legislation.

59. On the assumption (which he had rejected) that Article 9(1) was engaged in this case, the judge accepted the School's case that the limitations on the claimant's right to manifest her religion or beliefs were necessary for the protection of the rights and freedoms of others. His reasons can be summarised in this way:

i) The School is a multi-cultural, multi-faith secular school;

ii) The school uniform policy clearly promoted a positive ethos and a sense of communal identity;

iii) There was no outward distinction between Muslim, Hindu and Sikh female students, and the shalwar kameeze also satisfied the right of Muslim female students to manifest their religion;

iv) Any distinction between Muslim students who wore the jilbab and those who wore the shalwar kameeze was avoided;

v) The present policy protects the rights and freedoms of not an insignificant number of Muslim female pupils who do not wish to wear the jilbab and either do, or will feel pressure on them to do so from inside or outside the school;

vi) If the choice of two uniforms were permitted for Muslim female pupils, it could be readily understood that other pupils of different or no faiths might well see this as favouring a particular religion.

60. The judge concluded in these terms (at para 91):

"In my judgment the school uniform policy and its enforcement has, and continues to have, a legitimate aim and is proportionate. The legitimate aim was the proper running of a multi-cultural, multi-faith, secular school. The limitation was also proportionate to the legitimate aim pursued. The limitation was specifically devised with the advice of the Muslim community. Although it appears that there is a body of opinion within the Muslim faith that only the jilbab meets the requirements of its dress code there is also a body of opinion that the Shalwar Kameeze does as well. In my judgment, the adoption of the Shalwar Kameeze by the Defendant as the school uniform for Muslim (and other faiths) female pupils was and continues to be a reasoned, balanced, proportionate policy."

61. I turn now to set out my conclusions on this appeal. In my judgment, the limitation on the claimant's Article 9(1) freedom was one that was prescribed by law in the Convention sense. The governors were entitled by law to set a school uniform policy for the School. They published a clear, written policy which was available to all who might be affected by it, and the requirements of the ECHR for law that is both accessible and clear were satisfied in this respect. But was that limitation necessary?

62. The ECHR caselaw to which we were referred related to countries like Switzerland and Turkey which maintain a national policy of secular education in their state maintained schools. I did not derive any assistance from the cases we were shown which related to employment disputes.

63. In Dahlab v Switzerland (15th February 2001; Appln No 42393/98) the court declared inadmissible a complaint by a primary school teacher who had been prohibited from wearing an Islamic headscarf at her school. The court acknowledged the margin of appreciation afforded to the national authorities when determining whether this measure was "necessary in a democratic society", and explained its role in these terms (at p 11):

"The Court's task is to determine whether the measures taken at national level were justified in principle – that is, whether the reasons adduced to justify them appear 'relevant and sufficient' and are proportionate to the legitimate aim pursued… In order to rule on this latter point, the Court must weigh the requirements of the protection of the rights and liberties of others against the conduct of which the applicant stood accused. In exercising the supervisory jurisdiction, the court must look at the impugned judicial decisions against the background of the case as a whole..."

64. In that case the need to protect the principle of denominational neutrality in Swiss schools was treated as a very important factor which militated successfully against the applicant's case.

65. In Sahin v Turkey (29th June 2004; Appln No 44774/98) the applicant had been denied access to written examinations and to a lecture at the University of Istanbul because she was wearing an Islamic headscarf. This was prohibited not only by the rules of the university but also by the Constitution of Turkey, as interpreted in 1989 and 1991 by the Constitutional Court of Turkey. The European Court of Human Rights noted (in paragraphs 53 to 57) that attitudes towards wearing the Islamic headscarf in schools differed in different European countries. It accepted (at para 71) that the applicant was motivated by her desire to comply strictly with the duties imposed by the Islamic faith. It found (at para 81) that there was a basis for interference in Turkish law which was accessible and sufficiently precise in its views. The applicant conceded (at para 83) that in view of the importance of upholding the principle of secularism and ensuring the neutrality of

universities in Turkey, the interference could be regarded as compatible with the legitimate aims of protecting the rights and freedoms of others and of protecting public order. She vigorously disputed, however, the contention that the interference was necessary in a democratic society.

66. The Court first discussed the relevant principles and then applied them to the facts of this particular case. Although it made reference to the principle of gender equality, it placed most weight on the principle of secularism in Turkey. It said (at para 99)

"In a country like Turkey, where the great majority of the population belong to a particular religion, measures taken in universities to prevent certain fundamentalist religious movements from exerting pressure on students who do not practise that religion or on those who belong to another religion may be justified under Article 9(2) of the Convention."

67. It went on to say (at para 101) that where questions concerning the relationship between State and religion were at stake, on which opinion in a democratic society might reasonably differ widely, the role of the national decision-making body had to be given special importance. In such cases it was necessary to have regard to the fair balance that must be struck between the various interests at stake: the rights and freedoms of others, avoiding civil unrest, the demands of public order, and pluralism.

68. In applying these principles to the facts of the particular case the court said (at paras 104-6)

"104. It must first be observed that the interference was based, in particular, on two principles – secularism and equality – which reinforce and complement each other....

105. In its judgment of 7 March 1989, the Constitutional Court stated that secularism in Turkey was, among other things, the guarantor of democratic values, the principle that freedom of religion is inviolable – to the extent that it stems from individual conscience – and the principle that citizens are equal before the law....Secularism also protected the individual from external pressure. It added that restrictions could be placed on freedom to manifest one's religion in order to defend those values and principles.

106. This notion of secularism appears to the Court to be consistent with the values underpinning the Convention and it accepts that upholding that principle may be regarded as necessary for the protection of the democratic system in Turkey."

69. The court also noted (at para 107) the emphasis placed on the Turkish constitutional system on the protection of the rights of women. Gender equality – recognised by the European Court as one of the key principles underlying the Convention and a goal to be achieved by member States of the Council of Europe – had also been found by the Turkish Constitutional Court to be a principle implicit in the values underlying the Turkish constitution.

70. Matters the court took into account (at paras 108-109) when concluding that the national authorities in Turkey were entitled to prohibit the wearing of a Muslim headscarf in a university included:

i) The impact which wearing a headscarf, which is presented or perceived as a compulsory religious duty, might have on those who chose not to wear it;

ii) The fact that Turkey was a country where the majority of the population, while professing a strong attachment to the rights of women and a secular way of life, adhered to the Islamic faith;

iii) In such a context, imposing limitations on freedom in this sphere might be regarded as meeting a pressing social need by seeking to achieve those two legitimate aims, especially since the Muslim headscarf had taken on political significance in Turkey in recent years;

iv) The fact that there were extremist political movements in Turkey which might seek to impose on society as a whole their religious symbols and conception of a society founded on religious precepts: a Contracting State was permitted, in accordance with the ECHR provisions, to take a stance against such political movements, based on its historical experience.

71. Against this background the court

dismissed the applicant's complaint, saying (at para 110) that it was understandable in such a context where the values of pluralism, respect for the rights of others and, in particular, equality of men and women before the law, were being taught and applied in practice, that the relevant authorities would consider that it ran counter to the furtherance of such values to accept the wearing of religious insignia, including, as in the present case, that women students cover their heads with a headscarf while on university premises.

72. I have considered the case of Sahin in some detail for four main reasons. First, it is a recent judgment in which the European Court of Justice has set out carefully the structured way in which issues of this kind are to be considered under the Convention. Secondly, it shows that context is all-important: there are considerations to be applied in a state which professes the value of secularism in its Constitution which are not necessarily to be applied in the United Kingdom. Thirdly – and we did not receive any argument on this issue – there are clearly potential tensions between the rights and freedoms set out in a Convention agreed more than 50 years ago between Western European countries which on the whole adhered to Judaeo-Christian traditions, and some of the tenets of the Islamic faith that relate to the position of women in society. And fourthly, it is clear that a decision-maker is entitled to take into account worries like those expressed by the senior teaching staff of the School when it is deciding whether it is necessary to prohibit a person like the claimant from manifesting her religion or beliefs in public in the way in which she would wish.

73. The United Kingdom is very different from Turkey. It is not a secular state, and although the Human Rights Act is now part of our law we have no written Constitution. In England and Wales express provision is made for religious education and worship in schools in Chapter VI of the 1998 Act. Schools are under a duty to secure that religious education in schools is given to pupils, and that each pupil should take part in an act of collective worship every day, unless withdrawn by their parent. Sections 80(1)(a) and 101(1)(a) of the 2002 Act require the inclusion of religious education in the basic curriculum.

74. The position of the School is already distinctive in the sense that despite its policy of inclusiveness it permits girls to wear a headscarf which is likely to identify them as Muslim. The central issue is therefore the more subtle one of whether, given that Muslim girls can already be identified in this way, it is necessary in a democratic society to place a particular restriction on those Muslim girls at this school who sincerely believe that when they arrive at the age of puberty they should cover themselves more comprehensively than is permitted by the school uniform policy.

75. The decision-making structure should therefore go along the following lines:

1) Has the claimant established that she has a relevant Convention right which qualifies for protection under Article 9(1)?

2) Subject to any justification that is established under Article 9(2), has that Convention right been violated?

3) Was the interference with her Convention right prescribed by law in the Convention sense of that expression?

4) Did the interference have a legitimate arm?

5) What are the considerations that need to be balanced against each other when determining whether the interference was necessary in a democratic society for the purpose of achieving that aim?

6) Was the interference justified under Article 9(2)?

76. The School did not approach the matter in this way at all. Nobody who considered the issues on its behalf started from the premise that the claimant had a right which is recognised by English law, and that the onus lay on the School to justify its interference with that right. Instead, it started from the premise that its uniform policy was there to be obeyed: if the claimant did not like it, she could go to a different school.

77. The chair of the governors, whose decision is set out in full in paragraph 25 of Bennett J's judgment, adopted this line. He ended his decision dismissively by saying that it would not be appropriate "to make any further provisions for individuals' interpretations of religious codes." The Complaints Committee, too, was satisfied that the shalwar kameeze

constituted "appropriate Islamic dress" or was "in accordance with the tenets of Islam", and while it accepted that the jilbab constituted proper Islamic dress for adult Muslim women, it did not explore the reasons why the claimant sincerely believed that she must wear it. Indeed, the committee could see no good reason for the local mosques "apparently changing their minds", without appreciating that the two Imams had been addressing two quite different questions (see paras 45-48 above), namely whether the shalwar kameeze was or was not inappropriate for Muslim girls, and what in their view the teachings of Islam really required.

78. In my judgment, therefore, because it approached the issues in this case from an entirely wrong direction and did not attribute to the claimant's beliefs the weight they deserved, the School is not entitled to resist the declarations she seeks, namely:

i) That it unlawfully excluded her from school;
ii) That it unlawfully denied her the right to manifest her religion;
iii) That it unlawfully denied her access to suitable and appropriate education.

79. So far as this third matter is concerned, I am satisfied that the claimant is entitled to this declaration without the need for any inquiry into the rights and wrongs of what actually happened during the two years in which she was away from school when the School maintained that it was trying to send schoolwork to her at home. Any such expedient would have been inferior to a proper education, at best: compare A v Headteacher and Governors of Lord Grey School [2004] EWCA Civ 382 per Sedley LJ at [60].

80. The claimant no longer seeks a mandatory order that the School make swift arrangements for her return to school, and she also no longer seeks damages.

81. Nothing in this judgment should be taken as meaning that it would be impossible for the School to justify its stance if it were to reconsider its uniform policy in the light of this judgment and were to determine not to alter it in any significant respect. Matters which it (and other schools facing a similar question) would no doubt need to consider include these:

i) Whether the members of any further religious groups (other than very strict Muslims) might wish to be free to manifest their religion or beliefs by wearing clothing not currently permitted by the school's uniform policy, and the effect that a larger variety of different clothes being worn by students for religious reasons would have on the School's policy of inclusiveness;
ii) Whether it is appropriate to override the beliefs of very strict Muslims given that liberal Muslims have been permitted the dress code of their choice and the School's uniform policy is not entirely secular;
iii) Whether it is appropriate to take into account any, and if so which, of the concerns expressed by the School's three witnesses as good reasons for depriving a student like the claimant of her right to manifest her beliefs by the clothing she wears at school, and the weight which should be accorded to each of these concerns;
iv) Whether there is any way in which the School can do more to reconcile its wish to retain something resembling its current uniform policy with the beliefs of those like the claimant who consider that it exposes more of their bodies than they are permitted by their beliefs to show.

82. All this is for the future, and this case has achieved the result of ensuring that schools will set about deciding issues of this kind in the manner now required of them by the Human Rights Act. It may be thought desirable for the DfES to give schools further guidance in the light of this judgment: one is bound to sympathise with the teachers and governors of this school when they have had to try and understand quite complex and novel considerations of human rights law in the absence of authoritative written guidance. For the present, however, I would allow this appeal and grant the claimant the three declarations she seeks.

Lord Justice Mummery :

83. For the reasons given by Brooke and Scott Baker LJJ I agree that this appeal should be allowed. I only wish to add short comments on three points.

A. Justification

84. The claimant has succeeded in demonstrating that her right under Article 9(1) was engaged. She had the right to manifest her religion in the matter of dress at School. The effect of the School's stance on its uniform policy was that the claimant was unlawfully excluded from the School for not wearing the uniform, to which, for religious reasons, she objected. It was no answer for the School to say that she could have attended School if only she had chosen to wear the school uniform. Nor is it relevant to compare her position with that of an employee who is free to leave his employment and to find work with a different employer. (Ahmad v. UK (1981) 4 EHRR 126 and Stedman v. UK (1997) 23 EHRR CD 168 were cited on the position of employees asserting Article 9 rights). It is irrelevant to the engagement of Article 9 that the claimant could have changed to a school which accommodated her religious beliefs about dress. Education at the School or at another school was not a contractual choice. There was a statutory duty to provide education to the pupils. The School did not follow the proper statutory procedure for excluding her from education.

85. As the claimant has now moved to another school and will not be returning to the School, that is the end of the matter as far as she is concerned. She does not pursue a claim for damages. The case is about a point of principle. Declaratory relief is an adequate remedy. It should be emphasised, however, that, in general, the engagement of the right would not be the end of the matter. In fact, it would be the beginning of another stage. The next stage would be considerably more complex. The scope of the right and its exercise would be subject to the limitations in Article 9(2), which the School may seek to rely on to justify the school uniform policy. Freedom to manifest one's religion is subject, for example, to such limitations prescribed by law as "are necessary in a democratic society ...for.....the protection of the rights and freedoms of others."

86. The process of justification of a limitation on the right to manifest one's religion involves a careful and wise analysis in the very difficult and sensitive area of the relation of religion to various aspects of the life of the individual living in community with other individuals, who also possess rights and freedoms. The right to manifest one's religion under Article 9 is not necessarily a valid reason for overriding the social responsibilities of the individual holder of the right to others living in the community.

87. As is pointed out in the judgment of Brooke LJ (paragraph 82) it would still be possible for the School, on a structured reconsideration of the relevant issues, including the Article 9 right of a person in the position of the claimant, to justify its stance on the school uniform policy. If it could, there would be no breach of the Article 9(1) right.

B. The Role of the Court

88. In some quarters this decision may be seen as an instance of the court and/or the claimant overruling the Headteacher and the Governors of the School, undermining their authority on an internal school matter and interfering in the running of the School. That would be a misconception. The role of the court is confined to deciding whether the claimant was unlawfully excluded from the School and unlawfully denied her right to manifest her religion. The court has found that the relevant issues were, from a legal aspect, approached from the wrong direction. The result is that there was unlawful treatment of the claimant. As already explained, this does not mean that would be impossible for the School, if the matter were approached from the right direction, to justify the school uniform policy with regard to another pupil adopting the same position as the claimant.

C. Guidance

89. I agree with Brooke LJ on the need for teachers and governors to be given authoritative written guidance on the handling of human rights issues in schools. There are many issues that members of the staff, parents and pupils could raise under the Human Rights Act 1998 in respect of most of the Articles in the Convention. Headteachers and governors of all kinds of schools need help to cope with this additional burden. They need to be made aware of the impact of the 1998 Act on schools. They need clear, constructive and practical advice on how to anticipate and prepare for problems, how to spot them as and when they arise and how to deal

with them properly. It would be a great pity, if through lack of expert guidance, schools were to find themselves frequently in court having to use valuable time and resources, which would be better spent on improving the education of their pupils.

Lord Justice Scott Baker:

90. I agree with the judgment of Brooke L.J and the declarations that he proposes. In particular I wish to associate myself with his observations about the decision-making structure that should have been followed and should be followed in similar circumstances in future.

91. I have, however, considerable sympathy with the School and its governors in the predicament that they faced. They did not appreciate that they faced four square an issue that engaged Article 9 of the ECHR. It is perhaps understandable that a school that can rightly be proud of its contribution to the welfare of members of a multicultural society should have taken the line that it did, albeit one that on careful analysis has been shown to be erroneous in law.

92. Had the School approached the problem on the basis it should have done, that the claimant had a right under Article 9(1) to manifest her religion, it may very well have concluded that interference with that right was justified under Article 9(2) and that its uniform policy could thus have been maintained. Regrettably, however, it decided that because the shalwar kameeze was acceptable for the majority of Muslims the claimant should be required to toe the line.

93. As Brooke L.J. has pointed out, there are two different views in the Muslim community about the appropriate dress for women one, held by very strict Muslims, being that it is mandatory for women to wear the jilbab. The fact that this view is held by a minority, or even a small minority is in my judgment nothing to the point in considering the issue whether Article 9(1) is engaged. There is in my view force in the criticism that it is not for school authorities to pick and choose between religious beliefs or shades of religious belief.

94. The United Kingdom is not a secular state; there is no principle of denominational neutrality in our schools. Provision is made for religious education and worship in schools under Chapter VI of the School Standards and Framework Act 1998. Every shade of religious belief, if genuinely held, is entitled to due consideration under Article 9. What went wrong in this case was that the School failed to appreciate that by its action it was infringing the claimant's Article 9(1) right to manifest her religion. It should have gone on to consider whether a limitation of her right was justified under Article 9(2) in the light of the particular circumstances at the School. As it did not carry out this exercise it is not possible to conclude what the result would have been. The way matters progressed the claimant was excluded from the school without following the appropriate procedures and her Article 9(1) rights were violated in the process.

Looking at point 33 of the Court of Appeal judgement mention is made of a hadith of the Prophet:

"Whenever a woman begins to menstruate, it is not right that anything should be seen except her face and hands."

Dr. Zaki Badawi, former chief imam at the Central London Mosque, as I have previously mentioned, has gone on record to state that this very hadith of Al-Bayhaqi is acknowledged by Muslim scholars as *not* being of proven authenticity. This included Zaki Badawi's former colleague at the Central London Mosque, Dr S.M. Al-Darsh. Dr Darsh wrote a booklet called *Hijab or Naqab* (Publishers - Dar Al Dawa Bookshop, London) and on page 20 related the ancient scholar Ibn Kathir as saying of the above hadith, "This, however, is not based on a strong report."

So the Court of Appeal is wrong to state that, 'So much is common ground,' for all Muslims for this hadith. It is only 'common ground' for those that gave evidence in court and they had a particular agenda: to rely on a very weak hadith to promote their hijab-at-all-costs view.

Religion and school rules must both be respected

The Daily Telegraph, Thursday March 3rd 2005 - Leader column

Shabina Begum, 16, spouted a great deal of nonsense yesterday after the Appeal Court upheld her right to wear the full head-to-toe jilbab, in defiance of her former school's policy on uniform. Every word that this Muslim schoolgirl uttered smacked more of politics than of true religious feeling. The court's decision, she said, was a victory for all Muslims against prejudice and bigotry. "The decision of Denbigh High School to prevent my adherence to my religion cannot unfortunately be viewed merely as a local decision taken in isolation. Rather it was a consequence of an atmosphere that has been created in Western societies post-9/11, an atmosphere in which Islam has been made a target for vilification in the name of the 'war on terror'."

To portray Denbigh High School in Bedfordshire as a hotbed of bigotry and prejudice against Muslims would be outrageous and absurd. No fewer than 79 per cent of its 1,000 pupils are Muslims. Its head, Yasmin Bevan, was herself born into a Bengali Muslim family. The school rules allow pupils to wear the hijab head-dress and the trousers-and-tunic shalwar kameez. As the court acknowledged, one of Denbigh High's reasons for refusing to allow Miss Begum to wear the full jilbab was that other Muslim girls did not want to be put under pressure to wear it, while non-Muslim pupils were also afraid of its associations with extremism. Here was a school doing everything it thought best to allow all its pupils, from every background, to get on together. When Miss Begum confronted the school, accompanied by her brother and another young fnan whose behaviour the assistant head teacher found "unreasonable and threatening", it is pretty clear that she was out to make a fuss.

We cannot blame Lord Justice Brooke, however, for ruling in favour of this bloody-minded 16-year-old against the school. His job was simply to interpret the disastrous Human Rights Act as it applied to Miss Begum's case - the very Act now cited by this Government as its reason for having to take the power to put Britons under house arrest without trial. Nor, indeed, do we see anything wrong in principle with allowing pupils to wear the dress that their religious beliefs require - as long as their purpose in dressing differently is not simply to provoke ill-feeling or to stick two fingers up at the school authorities.

The sooner the Human Rights Act is repealed, the sooner British justice will be able to re-establish its contact with common sense. Meanwhile, we hope that as Miss Begum grows up, she will begin to realise how lucky she is to live in a tolerant society.

THE DAILY TELEGRAPH Thursday, March 3, 2005

The Daily Telegraph

Established 1855

Religion and school rules must both be respected

Shabina Begum, 16, spouted a great deal of nonsense yesterday after the Appeal Court upheld her right to wear the full head-to-toe jilbab, in defiance of her former school's policy on uniform. Every word that this Muslim schoolgirl uttered smacked more of politics than of true religious feeling. The court's decision, she said, was a victory for all Muslims against prejudice and bigotry. "The decision of Denbigh High School to prevent my adherence to my religion cannot unfortunately be viewed merely as a local decision taken in isolation. Rather it was a consequence of an atmosphere that has been created in Western societies post-9/11, an atmosphere in which Islam has been made a target for vilification in the name of the 'war on terror'."

To portray Denbigh High School in Bedfordshire as a hotbed of bigotry and prejudice against Muslims would be outrageous and absurd. No fewer than 79 per cent of its 1,000 pupils are Muslims. Its head, Yasmin Bevan, was herself born into a Bengali Muslim family. The school rules allow pupils to wear the hijab head-dress and the trousers-and-tunic shalwar kameez. As the court acknowledged, one of Denbigh High's reasons for refusing to allow Miss Begum to wear the full jilbab was that other Muslim girls did not want to be put under pressure to wear it, while non-Muslim pupils were also afraid of its associations with extremism. Here was a school doing everything it thought best to allow all its pupils, from every background, to get on together. When Miss Begum confronted the school, accompanied by her brother and another young man whose behaviour the assistant head teacher found "unreasonable and threatening", it is pretty clear that she was out to make a fuss.

We cannot blame Lord Justice Brooke, however, for ruling in favour of this bloody-minded 16-year-old against the school. His job was simply to interpret the disastrous Human Rights Act as it applied to Miss Begum's case – the very Act now cited by this Government as its reason for having to take the power to put Britons under house arrest without trial. Nor, indeed, do we see anything wrong in principle with allowing pupils to wear the dress that their religious beliefs require – as long as their purpose in dressing differently is not simply to provoke ill-feeling or to stick two fingers up at the school authorities.

The sooner the Human Rights Act is repealed, the sooner British justice will be able to re-establish its contact with common sense. Meanwhile, we hope that as Miss Begum grows up, she will begin to realise how lucky she is to live in a tolerant society.

Revealed: the brutal truth that hides inside the burqa

Evening Standard, 30th November 2005

By Yasmin Alibhai-Brown

LAST week when I was browsing in shops on Chiswick High Road, I became aware of a woman shadowing me, rather too close in that private space we all subconsciously carry around us. She was covered from head to toe in a black burqa. Tight white gloves covered her hands and her heels clicked. She wore perfume, or hair oil smelling of roses. At one point I nearly tripped over her foot and she said “sorry” softly.

I drove home, and 20 minutes later the doorbell rang. I opened the door to see the same woman standing there, her raven cloak billowing as a gust of wind blew up. Her eyes were light brown. She said nothing at first, then asked in perfect English if she could come in. I admit I felt panic rising. Because I write on controversial issues at this fraught time, death threats come my way and I have been advised by the police to be extremely careful about loitering strangers.

“Please," she said, "I know who you are and I must speak to you. I saw you in the shops and followed you. I must show you something."

"Who are you?" I asked, even more scared. She pleaded some more, told me her name, showed me her EU passport.

I let her in. She took off her burqa to reveal a sight I shall never forget. There before me was a woman so badly battered and beaten that she looked painted, in deep blue, purple and livid pink. The sides of her mouth were torn — "He put his fist in my mouth because I was screaming," she explained.

"My father and two brothers have forced me to wear the niqab (burqa) so no one can see what they've done. Many families do this. They beat up the women and girls because they want them to agree to marriages or just because the girls want a little more independence, to go to college and that. Then they make them wear the burqa to keep this violence a secret. They know the police are now getting wise to 'honour' killings and so they have this sheet to hide the proof."

Over the afternoon she sobbed and told me about the horrors of her life. She was 25, came from a lower-middle-class Pakistani background in Bolton and was a chemistry graduate. She wanted to be a teacher, but her brothers and father had resented her desire for independence and grown distrustful of her.

At least she was alive. She told me of a dead friend, killed, she claims, by family members who felt she had shamed them: "Someone told the family they had seen their daughter talking to a couple of men at the bus stop and that she was holding the hand of one of them. It was a lie. This gossip can kill us," she said. In her own case she says at first her father and brothers wanted to know if she, too, was as "bad" as her friend. Any contact or flirtation with a man they had not chosen for her was enough to merit an argument— and violence.

So they beat her, to get her to confess to things she hadn't done. Then they tried to get her

22 Wednesday, 30 November 2005 Evening Standard

Revealed: the brutal truth that hides inside the burqa

BY YASMIN ALIBHAI-BROWN

There has been a marked increase in the use of burqas in Britain — they are now a common sight on London streets. This is the next frontier for puritanical Muslims who believe females are dangerous seductresses who must be hidden from sight.

Women and girls as young as 12, they say, must cover up to avoid such provocation.

The pernicious ideology is propagated by misguided Muslim women who claim the burqa is an equaliser and a liberator. In a film that I made for Channel 4, I met an entire class of teenagers at a Muslim secondary school in Leicester who told me that negating their physical selves in public made them feel great.

I was shocked at the time by their mixture of modernity — they loved Madonna — and the restriction of the burqa which they said was voluntary. I think they were kidding themselves: a

whole class of burqa-clad girls suggests to me that there was strong parental pressure brought to bear.

I CONFESS now I respond to this garment with aversion. I find the hijab and the jilbab (the full body cloak) problematic too, because they again make women responsible for the sexual responses of men and they define femininity as a threat. But the burqa is much, much worse. It dehumanises half the human species. Why do women defend this retreat into shrouds?

When I try to speak to some of these shrouded women on the street, they stare back silently. In a kebab shop in Southall last week, a woman in a burqa sat there passively while her family ate — she couldn't put food into her own mouth. One mother told her young daughter in Urdu to walk away from me, a "kaffir" in her eyes.

Domestic violence is an evil found in all countries, classes and communities. Millions of female sufferers hide the abuse with concealing clothes and fabricated stories. But this total covering makes it completely impossible to detect, which is why "S" and other victims of family brutality are forced to wear it.

I now have 12 letters from young British Muslim women making allegations like these, all too terrified to go public. Several say that in some areas where hard-line Imams hold sway the hijab is seen as inviting because it focuses attention on the face. If the women refused to comply with wearing the burqa, they were beaten. Others write that their husbands insist on the covering because it is easier to conceal the brutality within the marriage. Mariyam writes: "He says he doesn't want his name spoilt — that his honour is important. If they see what he is doing to me, his name will be spoilt."

Not all woman in burqas are the walking wounded, but some are, and the tragedy is that it is impossible to pick up the signs. The usual network of concerned people — neighbours, colleagues, pupils, teachers, police or social workers — would need to be approached by the traumatised women and girls, as I was by "S".

Should the nation support *all* demands in the name of cultural or religious rights? In several schools now Muslim parents are refusing to let their girls swim, act or take part in PE, interference I personally find appalling. This is a society which prizes individual autonomy and the principle of equality between the sexes.

The burqa offends both of these principles, yet no politician or leader has dared to say so. Even more baffling is the meek acceptance of the burqa by British feminists, who must be repelled by the garment and its meanings. What are they afraid of? Afghan and Iranian women fight daily against the shroud and there is nothing "colonial" about raising ethical objections to this obvious symbol of oppression. The banning of the headscarf in France was divisive — yes. But it was also supported by many Muslims. The state was too arrogant and confrontational, but the policy was right.

A SECULAR public space gives all citizens civil rights and fundamental equalities and Muslim girls have not abandoned schools in droves as a result of the ban.

The Shabina Begum case should have been the moment to confront the challenge. This spring Shabina Begum took her school to the Appeal Court for refusing to let her "progress" from the hijab to the jilbab. She won the right. For many of us modernist Muslims this was a body blow, and today we fear the next push is well under way for British Muslim woman to wear the body cage of Afghan women under the Taliban.

Who said a mother had to hide her face from her babies in the park? Not the holy Koran, for sure. Its injunctions simply call for women to guard their private parts, to act with modesty. Scholars disagree about the jilbab and even the hijab. More than half the world's Muslim women do not cover their hair except when in mosque.

There are some who do choose the garment without coercion — the nun's option, you might say. I judge this differently. My experience of "S" and other women who have written to me in despair is that many are being forced or brainwashed into thinking their invisibility is what God wants. That is not a choice. The British state is based on liberal values — individuals can decide what they want to do as long as it doesn't cause harm to others.

But within this broad liberalism, there are still restrictions and denials for the sake of a greater good. Nudists cannot walk our streets with impunity and no religious cult can demand the legal right to multiple marriages. Why should the state then tolerate the burqa, which even in its own terms turns women into sexual objects to be packed away out of sight?

There is much anxious tiptoeing around the issue but it is one that affects us all.

Thousands of liberal Muslims would dearly like the state to take a stand on their behalf.

An increasingly common sight on London streets: but the burqa is at odds with British principles of individual automony and sexual equality

Even more baffling is the meek acceptance of the burqa by British feminists, who must be repelled by the garment and its meanings

to quit her teacher-training course. When she refused, they locked her in a bedroom and carried on abusing her; the youngest brother, in particular, was, she said, maddened with suspicion. A few days ago, she escaped, with her passport, and a friend drove her to London.

She was living with a friend's friend now, but she knew her family would find her and she was desperate to move on before they did.

I have a contact who runs a safe refuge in north-west London. I got "S" a place there and gave her some money, enough to live on for a few weeks. She has my number and I hope she calls if she needs to. As I dropped her off, she said she was feeling guilty that her escape would break her mother's heart. Where had her mother been in all of this? Equally powerless, it seemed. Her mother's heart, I said, should have broken to witness what was done to her daughter.

This incident shook me — and set me thinking again about the burqa and whether we, as a liberal country should accept it.

There has been a marked increase in the use of burqas in Britain — they are now a common sight on London streets. This is the next frontier for puritanical Muslims who believe females are dangerous seductresses who must be hidden from sight.

Women and girls as young as 12, they say, must cover up to avoid such provocation.

The pernicious ideology is propagated by misguided Muslim women who claim the burqa is an equaliser and a liberator. In a film that I made for Channel 4, I met an entire class of teenagers at a Muslim secondary school in Leicester who told me that negating their physical selves in public made them feel great.

I was shocked at the time by their mixture of modernity — they loved Madonna — and the restriction of the burqa which they said was voluntary. I think they were kidding themselves: a whole class of burqa-clad girls suggests to me that there was strong parental pressure brought to bear.

I CONFESS now I respond to this garment with aversion. I find the hijab and the jilbab (the full body cloak) problematic too, because they again make women responsible for the sexual responses of men and they define femininity as a threat. But the burqa is much, much worse. It dehumanises half the human species. Why do women defend this retreat into shrouds?

When I try to speak to some of these shrouded women on the street, they stare back silently. In a kebab shop in Southall last week, a woman in a burqa sat there passively while her family ate — she couldn't put food into her own mouth. One mother told her young daughter in Urdu to walk away from me, a "kaffir" in her eyes.

Domestic violence is an evil found in all countries, classes and communities. Millions of female sufferers hide the abuse with concealing clothes and fabricated stories. But this total covering makes it completely impossible to detect, which is why "S" and other victims of family brutality are forced to wear it.

I now have 12 letters from young British Muslim women making allegations like these, all too terrified to go public. Several say that in some areas where hard-line imams hold sway the hijab is seen as inviting because it focuses attention on the face. If the women refused to comply with wearing the burqa, they were beaten. Others write that their husbands insist on the covering because it is easier to conceal the brutality within the marriage. Mariyam writes: "He says he doesn't want his name spoilt — that his honour is important. If they see what he is doing to me, his name will be spoilt."

Not all woman in burqas are the walking wounded, but some are, and the tragedy is that it is impossible to pick up the signs. The usual network of concerned people — neighbours, colleagues, pupils, teachers, police or social workers — would need to be approached by the traumatised women and girls, as I was by "S".

Should the nation support *all* demands in the name of cultural or religious rights? In several schools now Muslim parents are refusing to let their girls swim, act or take part in PE, interference I personally find appalling. This is a society which prizes individual autonomy and the principle of equality between the sexes.

The burqa offends both of these principles, yet no politician or leader has dared to say so. Even more baffling is the meek acceptance of the burqa by British feminists, who must be repelled by the garment and its meanings. What are they afraid of? Afghan and Iranian women fight daily against the shroud and there is nothing "colonial" about raising ethical objections to this obvious symbol of oppression. The banning of the headscarf in France was divisive — yes. But it was also supported by many Muslims. The state was too arrogant and confrontational, but the policy was right.

A SECULAR public space gives all citizens civil rights and fundamental equalities and

Muslim girls have not abandoned schools in droves as a result of the ban.

The Shabina Begum case should have been the moment to confront the challenge. This spring Shabina Begum took her school to the Appeal Court for refusing to let her “progress” from the hijab to the jilbab. She won the right. For many of us modernist Muslims this was a body blow, and today we fear the next push is well under way for British Muslim woman to wear the body cage of Afghan women under the Taliban.

Who said a mother had to hide her face from her babies in the park? Not the holy Koran for sure. Its injunctions simply call for women to guard their private parts, to act with modesty. Scholars disagree about the jilbab and even the hijab. More than half the world's Muslim women do not cover their hair except when in mosque.

There are some who do choose the garment without coercion — the nun's option, you might say. I judge this differently. My experience of "S" and other women who have written to me in despair is that many are being forced or brainwashed into thinking their invisibility is what God wants. That is not a choice. The British state is based on liberal values — individuals can decide what they want to do as long as it doesn't cause harm to others.

But within this broad liberalism, there are still restrictions and denials for the sake of a greater good. Nudists cannot walk our streets with impunity, and no religious cult can demand the legal right to multiple marriages. Why should the state then tolerate the burqa, which even in its own terms turns women into sexual objects to be packed away out of sight?

There is much anxious tiptoeing around the issue but it is one that affects us all.

Thousands of liberal Muslims would dearly like the state to take a stand on their behalf. If it doesn't, it will betray vunerable British citizens and the nation's most cherished principles and encourage Islam to move back even faster into the dark ages, when we all need to face the future together.

House of Lords overturn Court of Appeal decision:

Uniform is no interference with religious freedom

HOUSE OF LORDS Regina (Shabina Begum) v Denbigh High School

Speeches March 22nd 2006
Times Law Report March 23rd 2006

A SCHOOL'S refusal to allow a pupil to attend unless she wore the prescribed uniform did not amount to an interference with her right to manifest her religion by wearing a garment which was in accordance with her strict religious beliefs.

The House of Lords allowed an appeal by the defendant Denbigh High School, Luton, from the Court of Appeal (Lord Justice Brooke, Lord Justice Mummery and Lord Justice Scott Baker) (*The Times* March 4, 2005; [2005] 1WLR 3372) allowing an appeal by the claimant, Shabina Begum, suing by her brother and litigation friend, Shuweb Rahman, from the refusal by Mr Justice Bennett (*The Times* June 18, 2004) of her application for judicial review of the school's refusal to admit her while wearing a jilbab.

Mr Richard McManus, QC, Mr Simon Birks and Mr Jonathan Auburn for the school; Ms Cherie Booth, QC, Ms Carolyn Hamilton and Ms Eleni Mitrophanous for Shabina Begum; Mr Jonathan Crow for the Secretary of State for Education and Skills, as intervener.

LORD BINGHAM said that Shabina, now aged 17, contended that the defendants excluded her from school, unjustifiably limited her right under article 9 the European Convention on Human Rights to manifest her religion or beliefs and violated her right under article 2 of the First Protocol to the Convention not to be denied education.

His Lordship emphasised that the case concerned a particular pupil and a particular school in a particular place at a particular time. It would be most inappropriate for their Lordships to be asked to rule whether any feature of Islamic dress should be permitted in UK schools.

Denbigh High School was a maintained secondary community school taking pupils of both sexes aged 11-16. It had a diverse intake with 21 different ethnic groups and 10 religious groupings represented. About 79 per cent of its pupils were now Muslim. It was not a faith school and was therefore open to children of all faiths or none.

The governing body of the school always contained a balanced representation of different sections of the school community. At the time of these proceedings four out of six parent governors were Muslim, the chairman of the Luton council of mosques was a governor and three of the local education authority governors were also Muslim.

The head teacher, Mrs Yasmin Bevan, was born into a Bengali Muslim family. She grew up in the Indian sub-continent and had had much involvement with Bengali Muslim communities here and abroad and was familiar with the ideas and practices governing the dress of Muslim women.

She believed that a school uniform played an integral part in promoting a positive sense of communal identity and avoiding manifest disparities of wealth and style. The school offered three uniform options. One was the shalwar kameeze: a combination of the kameeze, a sleeveless smock-like dress with a square neckline revealing the wearer's collar and tie, with the shalwar, loose trousers tapering at the ankles.

There was no suggestion by those consulted, including the imams of three local mosques, that the shalwar kameeze failed to satisfy Islamic requirements. The school went to some lengths to explain its dress code to prospective parents and pupils.

Shabina Begum was a Muslim. Her father died before she entered the school. She lived with her mother, who did not speak English and had since died, a sister, two years older, and a brother, five years older who was now her litigation friend.

The family lived outside the school's catchment area, but chose it for Shabina and her sister. They were told in clear terms of the school uniform policy.

For two years before September 2002

Shabina wore the shalwar kameeze happily and without complaint. It was also worn by her sister who continued to wear it without objection throughout her time at school.

On September 3, 2002, the first day of the autumn term, Shabina, then aged nearly 14, went to the school with her brother and another young man. They asked to speak to the head teacher, who was unavailable, and they spoke to the assistant head teacher, Mr Stuart Moore.

They insisted that Shabina be allowed to attend the school wearing the long coat-like garment known as a jilbab that she had on that day. They talked of human rights and legal proceedings.

Mr Moore felt that their approach was unreasonable and threatening. He told Shabina to go home, change and return wearing school uniform. He did not believe he was excluding her, which he had no authority to do, but did not allow her to enter the school dressed as she was.

The jilbab she said, was the only garment which met her religious requirements because it concealed, to a greater extent than the shalwar kameeze, the contours of the female body and was appropriate for maturing girls. Shabina then left with her brother and the other young man. The young men said they were not prepared to compromise over the issue.

After solicitors for the respondent had written to the school and the local education authority, the latter, in December 2002, sought independent advice on whether the school uniform offended the Islamic dress code. Two mosques in Luton, the London Central Mosque Trust and he Islamic Cultural Centre advised that it did not.

It was common ground that at all material times Shabina sincerely held the religious belief which she professed to hold. It was not the less a religious belief because her belief might have changed or because it was a belief shared by a small minority.

Thus it was accepted that article 1 was engaged. The main questions were whether Shabina's freedom to manifest her belief by her dress was subject to limitation or interference within the meaning of article 9.2 and if so, whether such limitation or interfence was justified.

The school went to great lengths to inform parents of its uniform policy. There were three schools in the area at which the wearing of the jilbab was permitted. Shabina's application for admission to one of them was unsuccessful because the school was full, and it was asserted in argument that the others were more distant.

But there was no evidence to show that there was any real difficultly in her attending them, as she has in fact done and could have done sooner than she had chosen. On the facts and applying jurisprudence of the European Court of Human Rights at Strasbourg, there was no interference with her rights to manifest her religious belief.

To be justified under article 9.2 a limitation or interference must be (a) prescribed by law and (b) necessary in a democratic society for a permissible purpose, that is, it must be directed to a legitimate purpose and must be proportionate in scope and effect.

The school was, in his Lordship's opinion, fully justified in acting as it did. It had taken immense pains to devise a uniform policy which respected Muslim beliefs but did so in an inclusive, unthreatening and uncompetitive way.

The school had enjoyed a period of harmony and success to which the uniform policy was thought to contribute. It still appeared that the rules were acceptable to mainstream Muslim opinion. It was feared that acceding to Shabina's request would or might have significant adverse repercussions.

It would be irresponsible of any court,

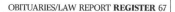

OBITUARIES/LAW REPORT **REGISTER** 67

LAW REPORT

Uniform is no interference with religious freedom

HOUSE OF LORDS
Published March 23, 2006
Regina (Shabina Begum) v Denbigh High School
Before Lord Bingham of Cornhill, Lord Nicholls of Birkenhead, Lord Hoffmann, Lord Scott of Foscote and Baroness Hale of Richmond
Speeches *March 22, 2006*

A SCHOOL'S refusal to allow a pupil to attend unless she wore the prescribed uniform did not amount to an interference with her right to manifest her religion by wearing a garment which was in accordance with her strict religious beliefs.

The House of Lords allowed an appeal by the defendant Denbigh High School, Luton, from the Court of Appeal (Lord Justice Brooke, Lord Justice Mummery and Lord Justice Scott Baker) (*The Times* March 4, 2005; [2005] 1 WLR 3372) allowing an appeal by the claimant, Shabina Begum, suing by her brother and litigation friend, Shuweb Rahman, from the refusal by Mr Justice Bennett (*The Times* June 18, 2004) of her application for judicial review of the school's refusal to admit her while wearing a jilbab.

Mr Richard McManus, QC, Mr Simon Birks and **Mr Jonathan Auburn** for the school; **Ms Cherie Booth, QC, Ms Carolyn Hamilton** and **Ms Eleni Mitrophanous** for Shabina Begum; **Mr Jonathan Crow** for the Secretary of State for Education and Skills, as intervener

LORD BINGHAM said that Shabina, now aged 17, contended that the defendants excluded her from school, unjustifiably limited her right under article 9 the European Convention on Human Rights to manifest her religion or beliefs and violated her right under article 2 of the First Protocol to the Convention not to be denied education.

His Lordship emphasised that the case concerned a particular pupil and a particular school in a particular place at a particular time. It would be most inappropriate for their Lordships to be asked to rule whether any feature of Islamic dress should be permitted in UK schools.

Denbigh High School was a maintained secondary community school taking pupils of both sexes aged 11-16. It had a diverse intake with 21 different ethnic groups and 10 religious groupings represented. About 79 per cent of its pupils were now Muslim. It was not a faith school and was therefore open to children of all faiths or none.

The governing body of the school always contained a balanced representation of different sections of the school community. At the time of these proceedings four out of six parent governors were Muslim, the chairman of the Luton council of mosques was a governor and three of the local education authority governors were also Muslim.

The head teacher, Mrs Yasmin Bevan, was born into a Bengali Muslim family. She grew up in the Indian sub-continent and had had much involvement with Bengali Muslim communities here and abroad and was familiar with the codes and practices governing the dress of Muslim women.

She believed that a school uniform played an integral part in promoting a positive sense of communal identity and avoiding manifest disparities of wealth and style.

The school offered three uniform options. One was the shalwar kameeze: a combination of the kameeze, a sleeveless smock-like dress with a square neckline revealing the wearer's collar and tie, with the shalwar, loose trousers tapering at the ankles.

There was no suggestion by those consulted, including the imams of the three local mosques, that the shalwar kameeze failed to satisfy Islamic requirements. The school went to some lengths to explain its dress code to prospective parents and pupils.

Shabina Begum was a Muslim. Her father died before she entered the school. She lived with her mother, who did not speak English and had since died, a sister, two years older, and a brother, five years older, who was now her litigation friend.

The family lived outside the school's catchment area, but chose it for Shabina and her sister. They were told in clear terms of the school's uniform policy.

For two years before September 2002 Shabina wore the shalwar kameeze happily and without complaint. It was also worn by her sister who continued to wear it without objection throughout her time at school.

On September 3, 2002, the first day of the autumn term, Shabina, then aged nearly 14, went to the school with her brother and another young man. They asked to speak to the head teacher, who was unavailable, and they spoke to the assistant head teacher, Mr Stuart Moore.

They insisted that Shabina be allowed to attend the school wearing the long coat-like garment known as a jilbab that she had on that day. They talked of human rights and legal proceedings.

Mr Moore felt that their approach was unreasonable and threatening. He told Shabina to go home, change and return wearing school uniform. He did not believe he was excluding her, which he had no authority to do, but did not allow her to enter the school dressed as she was.

The jilbab she said, was the only garment which met her religious requirements because it concealed, to a greater extent than the shalwar kameeze, the contours of the female body and was appropriate for maturing girls. Shabina then left with her brother and the other young man. The young men said they were not prepared to compromise over the issue.

After solicitors for the respondent had written to the school and the local education authority, the latter, in December 2002, sought independent advice on whether the school uniform offended the Islamic dress code. Two mosques in Luton, the London Central Mosque Trust and the Islamic Cultural Centre advised that it did not.

It was common ground that at all material times Shabina sincerely held the religious belief which she professed to hold. It was not the less a religious belief because her belief might have changed or because it was a belief shared by a small minority.

Thus it was accepted that article 9.1 was engaged. The main questions were whether Shabina's freedom to manifest her belief by her dress was subject to limitation or interference within the meaning of article 9.2 and if so, whether such limitation or interference was justified.

The school went to great lengths to inform parents of its uniform policy. There were three schools in the area at which the wearing of the jilbab was permitted. Shabina's application for admission to one of them was unsuccessful because the school was full, and it was asserted in argument that the others were more distant.

But there was no evidence to show that there was any real difficulty in her attending them, as she had in fact done and could have done sooner than she had chosen. On the facts and applying jurisprudence of the European Court of Human Rights at Strasbourg, there was no interference with her right to manifest her religious belief.

To be justified under article 9.2 a limitation or interference must be (a) prescribed by law and (b) necessary in a democratic society for a permissible purpose, that is, it must be directed to a legitimate purpose and must be proportionate in scope and effect.

The school was, in his Lordship's opinion, fully justified in acting as it did. It had taken immense pains to devise a uniform pol cy which respected Muslim beliefs but did so in an inclusive, unthreatenirg and uncompetitive way.

The school had enjoyed a period of harmony and success to which the uniform policy was thought to contribute. It still appeared that the rules were acceptable to mainstream Muslim opinion. It was feared that acceding to Shabina's request would or might have significant adverse repercussions.

It would be irresponsible of any court, lacking the experience, background and detailed knowledge of the head teacher, staff and governors to overrule their judgment on such a sensitive matter.

The power of decision had been given to them for the compelling reason that they were best placed to exercise it and there was no reason to disturb their decision.

As to article 2 of the First Protocol, the question was whether between September 3, 2002, and the date, some two years later, of Shabina's admission to another school, the defendants denied her access to the general level of educational provision available in this country.

In his Lordship's opinion they did not. The interruption was the result of her unwillingness to comply with a rule to which the school was entitled to adhere and of her failure to secure prompt admission to another school where her religious convictions could be accommodated.

It was also clear that the school did not intend to exclude Shabina in the statutory sense of that word nor believed that it was doing so. It was therefore entirely unsurprising that it did not invoke the statutory procedures.

LORD HOFFMANN, agreeing, said that article 9 did not require that one should be allowed to manifest one's religion at any time and place of one's own choosing. Common civility also had a place in religious life.

Shabina's discovery that her religion did not allow her to wear the uniform she had been wearing for the past two years created a problem for her.

She could have sought the help of the school and the local education authority in solving the problem. They would no doubt have advised her that if she was firm in her belief, she could change schools. That might not have been entirely convenient for her, particularly when her sister was remaining at Denbigh, but people sometimes had to suffer some inconvenience for their beliefs.

Instead, she and her brother decided that it was the school's problem. They sought confrontation and claimed that she had a right to attend the school of her own choosing in the clothes she chose to wear.

The jurisprudence of the European Court of Human Rights was clear that in such circumstances there was no infringement of article 9.

Lord Scott delivered a speech agreeing with Lord Bingham and Lord Hoffmann.

Lord Nicholls and Lady Hale agreed that any interference with Shabina's article 9.1 rights was justified under article 9.2.

Solicitors: Mr R. J. Stevens, Luton; Sharpe Pritchard; Treasury Solicitor.

lacking the experience, background and detailed knowledge of the head teacher, staff and governors to overrule their judgment on such a sensitive matter.

The power of decision had been given to them for the compelling reason that they were best placed to exercise it and there was no reason to disturb their decision.

As to article 2 of the First Protocol, the question was whether between September 3, 2002, and the date, some two years later, of Shabina's admission to another school, the defendants denied her access to the general level of educational provision available in this country.

In his Lordship's opinion they did not. The interruption was the result of her unwillingness to comply with a rule to which the school was entitled to adhere and of her failure to secure prompt admission to another school where her religious convictions could be accommodated.

It was also clear that the school did not intend to exclude Shabina in the statutory sense of that word nor believed that it was doing so. It was therefore entirely unsurprising that it did not invoke the statutory procedures.

LORD HOFFMANN, agreeing, said that article 9 did not require that one should be allowed to manifest one's religion at any time and place of one's own choosing. Common civility also had a place in religious life.

Shabina's discovery that her religion did not allow her to wear the uniform she had been wearing for the past two years created a problem for her.

She could have sought the help of the school and the local education authority in solving the problem. They would no doubt have advised her that if she was firm in her belief, she could change schools. That might not have been entirely convenient for her, particularly when her sister was remaining at Denbigh, but people sometimes had to suffer some inconvenience for their beliefs. Instead, she and her brother decided that it was the school's problem.

They sought confrontation and claimed that she had a right to attend the school of her own choosing - in the clothes she chose to wear.

The jurisprudence of the European Court of Human Rights was clear that in such circumstances there was no infringement of article 9.

Lord Scott delivered a speech agreeing with Lord Bingham and Lord Hoffman.

Lord Nicholls and Lady Hale agreed that any interference with Shabina's article 9.1 rights was justified under article 9.2.

Solicitors: Mr R.J. Stevens, Luton; Sharpe Pritchard; Treasury Solicitor

---

ARTICLE 9 of the European Convention on Human Rights

9.1. Everyone has the right to freedom of thought, conscience and religion; this right includes freedom to change his religion or belief, and freedom, either alone or in community with others and in public or private, to manifest his religion or belief, in worship, teaching, practice and observance.

9.2. Freedom to manifest one's religion or beliefs shall be subject only to such limitations as are prescribed by law and are necessary in a democratic society in the interests of public safety, for the protection of public order, health or morals, or the protection of the rights and freedoms of others.

Chapter 5

The Legacy of Mrs Ataturk

The Independent 1st July 2006

Eighty years ago, a best selling new biography reveals, Turkey's first lady, Latife Ataturk, helped liberate her countrywomen by urging them to cast off their veils. But as her key role in the secularisation of Turkey comes to light, the headscarf is once again stirring passionate debate in Anatolia.
Pelin Turgut *reports from Istanbul*

Turkey in the 21st century

Deep in the heart of Istanbul's bustling business capital, emerging from the crowd of sharply-dressed female executives, Emine Erdogan, the wife of Turkey's Prime Minister, takes centre stage. Quietly poised and softly spoken, she talks eloquently and passionately to her audience about the need to encourage more young girls to attend school. It is an issue she has made her own.

But there is something strikingly different about this particular champion of women's rights. Dressed in a smart beige suit, with a skirt that reaches to her ankles, Mrs Erdogan's earnest face is framed by a matching cream-coloured headscarf. The thrust of her talk is that Turkey's strict ban on head-scarves in schools violates gender equality because it means families keep their daughters at home rather than educate them. It has taken some getting used to for the Turks, this leading lady who covers her hair with pride. It is, after all, somewhat different from the turbulent 1920s, when the revolutionary leader Mustafa Kemal Ataturk was placing modern Turkey on the road to Western-style reform. At his side was a woman whose achievement, above all others, was to throw off her Islamic-style top-to-toe veil and urge her female counterparts to do the same.

Under strict secular laws dating back to Ataturk's reforms, the headscarf is banned from public places such as schools, state-run universities and even the president's palace. But Mrs Erdogan, famously, has yet to attend a reception at the palace – when invited, her husband goes alone, as indeed do many of his MPs for the same reason.

For decades, the principle of secularism, the separation of religion and the state, was the guiding force of the modern Turkish republic. Ataturk, with his sweeping reforms and visionary politics, raised his country from the ashes of the Ottoman Empire and recreated it as a modern, dynamic society that was still largely Muslim but embraced Western values. Getting Turkish women out of the kitchen and out from under the veil was central to Ataturk's modernising agenda and, for many Turks, his most enduring legacy.

But who was the real modernising force in Ataturk's campaign to build a modern Turkey? Previously unseen documents now reveal the crucial role played by another first lady - Latife

THE INDEPENDENT SATURDAY 1 JULY 2006 | EUROPE 27

Turkey in the 21st century

THE LEGACY OF MRS ATATURK

Eighty years ago, a bestselling new biography reveals, Turkey's first lady, Latife Ataturk, helped liberate her countrywomen by urging them to cast off their veils. But as her key role in the secularisation of Turkey comes to light, the headscarf is once again stirring passionate debate in Anatolia. **Pelin Turgut** reports from Istanbul

At a time when women were veiled from head to toe, Latife lobbied for laws that gave Turkish women rights few European countries had

Ussaki, Ataturk's wife - in liberating Turkish women.

A daring new biography, 25 years in the making, has finally been released in Turkey that challenges the cult of Ataturk and tells the true story of his marriage to the young suffragette who has, until now, remained a footnote in the history of both her husband and her country. Arguably, Latife's most important symbolic step was to shun Islamic attire, donning Western garb instead. She showed her face to the world with a defiance that simultaneously shocked and delighted onlookers.

The *New York Times* reported: "Her clothes are a pledge of reform. Her riding breeches indicate her intention of sweeping away harem conventions." Shortly after their wedding, Ataturk took her on a tour of Anatolia by train to show off his unveiled wife as a role model for modern Turkish women. "It's not just a honeymoon, it's a lesson in reform," one observer wrote.

Ironically, more than 80 years later, the way Turkey's prime ministerial spouse dresses is still a subject of national debate. While her husband, Prime Minister Recep Tayyip Erdogan, has been compared in some quarters with Ataturk thanks to his dogged pursuit of Turkish membership of the EU and, Emine Erdogan makes headlines for doing precisely the opposite of her 1920s counterpart. Instead of shunning the headscarf, she wears it with pride.

Official history portrays Latife as a rude, shrewish woman whose penchant for stomping downstairs to wrest her husband away from late-night drinking sessions and chastising him in public eventually wrecked their marriage. She is mentioned only in passing in the drama that was Ataturk's premiership.

Yet, bizarrely for someone considered apparently so insignificant, Latife's diaries and other papers were for years judged so potentially explosive that they were kept under lock and key in a sealed vault by the Turkish History Institution for 25 years. Her family subsequently refused to make the vault's contents public out of respect, they said, for Ataturk.

The author Ipek Calislar, who spent several years researching Latife's life, said: "The biography sheds light on the real Latife, her marriage, her ideas, in a way that official history hasn't. It also lays bare a different side of Mustafa Kemal - as a husband." The book is already a smash hit in Turkey, selling 20,000 copies in two weeks.

A veteran journalist, Calislar paints a detailed picture of a feisty young woman who played a far larger role in the radical reform and creation of the modern republic than has been previously thought. Educated abroad, multilingual, charming and confident, Latife fearlessly broke with tradition.

At a time when women were consigned to the home and veiled from head to toe outside it, she lobbied for laws, such as the right to vote, that gave Turkish women rights few European countries had at the time. Foreign correspondents wrote that she symbolised "the birth of a new Turkey".

She even sought to become an MP, but was snubbed by Ataturk. So forceful a character was she, Calislar suggests, that ultimately it was the couple's clash of wills that led to the breakdown of their marriage. After a heated argument one evening in 1925, Ataturk decided to divorce her - by decree - and sent her back to her parental home in Izmir. They never spoke again. Latife went on to live the life of a recluse. She never spoke in public, and died in 1975, thoroughly air-brushed out of Turkish history.

Not so her husband. No taboo is greater in Turkey than the inviolability surrounding Ataturk, whose name means literally Father of the Turks and figuratively carries equal significance. His picture stares down from every classroom wall in the country, every office, every shop. Banknotes carry his portrait, his statue is in every town and his sayings are regarded as sacrosanct. He may have died in 1938, but rather than fading into the background over the past seven decades, Ataturk has attained an almost mythical, omnipresent status that is rivalled by none.

Not surprisingly for a man with such godlike credentials, the details of Ataturk's personal life have always been strictly off-limits. Little is known of his existence outside the public arena; the very idea of delving into his romantic life is considered akin to sacrilege. This, coupled with the disappearance of Latife, his wife for a brief two-and-a-half years, from the collective national memory, has fuelled enormous interest in the new biography.

Mrs Erdogan's headscarf has now become the central issue in the debate over whether her husband should run for president next year. The presidency is largely ceremonial, but it is the post held by Ataturk and so comes with many symbolic strings attached. Secularists are incensed at the prospect of a veiled woman as first lady because they see it as an affront to the reforms that Ataturk strove to introduce.

"Turkey cannot have a president whose wife wears a headscarf," insists Deniz Baykal, leader of the main opposition People's Republican Party (CHP). To hardline secularists such as Mr Baykal, the headscarf is a symbol of "backwardness".

The female deputy leader of the CHP, Canan Aritman, recently wrote and made public a letter to Mrs Erdogan that said: "The way you dress while on trips abroad where you are representing the Republic of Turkey offends Turkish women. I respect your personal preference. But women in the modern Republic of Turkey have accepted a non-veiled, contemporary Western style of dress. If you must go on visits abroad with your husband, be like a contemporary Turkish woman. If you can't be that way then please stay at home."

All this outrage over a headscarf might seem bizarre to the outside world. But that small square of cloth has become the arena in which Turkey's secularists - who include the military and the courts - and the ruling, Islamic-rooted Justice and Development Party (AKP) do battle. Secularists argue that it has become a symbol of political Islam and is one step towards a secret agenda that seeks to convert Turkey to Islamic sharia law. Islamists, meanwhile, see the issue as a basic human right. Although the AKP came to power in 2002 by pledging to lift the ban on headscarves in universities and schools, it has not dared defy the military, for whom this is a cornerstone of Turkey's secular identity. The AKP had hoped that Turkey's European Union accession bid and attendant human-rights progress would help them ease restrictions but those hopes were dashed last year when the European Court of Human Rights ruled to uphold the ban and said that it was constitutional.

And the fact remains that Turkey's EU membership is looking increasingly unlikely. Only yesterday, the Finnish Prime Minister, Matti Vanhanen, said that the European Union could suspend entry talks with Turkey during his country's presidency if Ankara failed to meet the bloc's requirements. "There is always the possibility to stop the negotiations, I believe Turkey knows that."

The future, then, is uncertain, both for Mrs Erdogan and her husband's presidential ambitions, and for Turkey itself. More than four decades after Latife made a very public point of removing her veil, the tensions tugging at Turkey's soul are still embodied in the piece of fabric that a woman wears on her head.

Ermine Erdogan, wife of the Prime Minister of Turkey, is just another ill-informed hijabi Muslim trying to foist on her country's female population the idea that God instructed Muslim women to cover up from head to toe. The Turkish authorities must stand firm and continue their efforts to ban the headscarf wherever and whenever possible. Secularisation should not come into it. The headscarf, simply, is not required in Islam for daily use. It is only required when women are at prayer. The likes of Ermine Erdogan perpetuate the myth that Islam obligates women to cover themselves.

European Court of Human Rights judgements regarding the headscarf

29th June 2004 and 10th November 2005

330
29.6.2004

Press release issued by the Registrar

CHAMBER JUDGMENTS IN THE CASES OF

LEYLA SAHIN v. TURKEY AND ZEYNEP TEKIN v. TURKEY

The European Court of Human Rights has today notified in writing judgments[1] in the cases of Leyla Sahin v. Turkey (application no. 44774/98) and Zeynep Tekin v. Turkey (application no. 41556/98).

In the case of Leyla Sahin v. Turkey the Court held unanimously that there had been no violation of Article 9 of the European Convention on Human Rights (freedom of thought, conscience and religion); and no separate question arose under Articles 8 (right to respect for private and family life) and 10 (freedom of expression), Article 14 (prohibition of discrimination) taken together with Article 9 of the Convention, and Article 2 of Protocol No. 1 (right to education).

In the case of Zeynep Tekin v. Turkey, the Court decided unanimously to strike the case out of the list.

(The Leyla Sahin v. Turkey judgment is available in English and French; the Zeynep Tekin v. Turkey judgment is available only in French).

1. Principal facts

Leyla Sahin v. Turkey

The applicant, Leyla Sahin, is a Turkish national who was born in 1973. She has lived in Vienna since 1999, when she left Istanbul to pursue her medical studies at the Faculty of Medicine at Vienna University. She comes from a traditional family of practising Muslims and considers it her religious duty to wear the Islamic headscarf.

At the material time she was a fifth-year student at the faculty of medicine of the University of Istanbul. On 23 February 1998 the Vice-Chancellor of the University issued a circular directing that students with beards and students wearing the Islamic headscarf would be refused admission to lectures, courses and tutorials.

In March 1998 the applicant was denied access to a written examination on one of the subjects she was studying because was wearing the Islamic headscarf. Subsequently the university authorities refused on the same grounds to enrol her on a course, or to admit her to various lectures and a written examination.

The faculty also issued her with a warning for contravening the university's rules on dress and suspended her from the university for a term for taking part in an unauthorised assembly that had gathered to protest against them. All the disciplinary penalties imposed on the applicant were revoked under an amnesty law.

Zeynep Tekin v. Turkey

The applicant, Zeynep Tekin Pomer is a Turkish national who was born in 1975 and lives in Izmir.

At the material time she was a second-year student at nursing college at the University of Ege. The Higher-Education Authority issued a circular on 22 December 1988 requiring student nurses to wear special headwear when doing clinical training. In December 1993 the applicant was reprimanded for wearing the Islamic headscarf instead of the regulation headwear. She was subsequently caught wearing the Islamic headscarf on a number of occasions and on 23 December 1993 was suspended from the college for 15 days in accordance with the circular of 22 December 1988.

The applicant appealed against the disciplinary penalty to the administrative court. It dismissed her appeal on the grounds that the principle of secularism established by Article 2 of the Constitution prevailed. In a judgment of 16 October 1997 the Supreme Administrative Court upheld the lower court's judgment.

2. Procedure and composition of the Court

The applications were lodged with the European Commission of Human Rights on 2 March 1998 and transmitted to the Court on 1 November 1998. They were declared admissible on 2 July 2002. A public hearing was held in Strasbourg on 19 November 2002.

Judgment was given by a Chamber of seven judges, composed as follows:

Nicolas Bratza (British), President,
Matti Pellonpää (Finnish),
Antonio Pastor Ridruejo (Spanish),
Elisabeth Palm (Swedish),
Riza Türmen (Turkish),
Marc Fischbach (Luxemburger),
Josep Casadevall (Andorran), judges,

and also Michael O'Boyle, Section Registrar.

3. Summary of the judgment[2]

Complaints

In both cases the applicants complained under Article 9 of the Convention that they had been prohibited from wearing the Islamic headscarf at university. They also complained of an unjustified interference with their right to education, within the meaning of Article 2 of Protocol No. 1 to the Convention.

Miss Sahin further complained of a violation of Article 14, taken together with Article 9, arguing that the prohibition on wearing the Islamic headscarf obliged students to choose between education and religion and discriminated between believers and non-believers. Lastly, she relied on Articles 8 and 10.

Decision of the Court in the case of Leyla Sahin

Article 9 of the Convention

Without deciding whether it was always the case that Islamic headscarves were worn to fulfil a religious duty, the Court noted that Miss Sahin's decision was inspired by a religion or belief. Accordingly, it proceeded on the assumption that the regulations in issue, which placed restrictions of place and manner on the right to wear the Islamic headscarf in universities, constituted an interference with her right to manifest her religion.

There was a legal basis for that interference in Turkish law, as the case-law of the Constitutional Court made it clear that authorising students to "cover the neck and hair with a veil or headscarf for reasons of religious conviction" in universities was contrary to the Constitution. In addition, the Supreme Administrative Court had for many years taken the view that wearing the Islamic headscarf was not compatible with the fundamental principles of the Republic. Furthermore, it was beyond doubt that regulations on wearing the Islamic headscarf had existed well before the applicant had enrolled at the university. Students, particularly those who, like the applicant, were studying a health-related subject, were required to comply with rules on dress. In those circumstances, it would have been clear to Miss Sahin, from the moment she entered the University of Istanbul, that there were regulations on wearing the Islamic headscarf and, after the circular was published in 1998, that she was liable to be refused access to lectures if she continued to do so.

The Court found that the impugned measure primarily pursued the legitimate aims of protecting the rights and freedoms of others and of protecting public order.

As to the "necessity" of the interference, the Court observed that it was based on two principles – secularism and equality – which reinforced and complemented each other.

Under the Constitutional Court's case-law, secularism in Turkey was, among other things, the guarantor of: democratic values; the principle that freedom of religion was inviolable, to the extent that it stemmed from individual conscience; and, the principle that citizens were equal before the law. Restrictions could be placed on freedom to manifest one's religion in order to defend those values and principles. That notion of secularism appeared to the Court to be consistent with the values underpinning the Convention and it noted that upholding that principle could be regarded as necessary for the protection of the democratic system in Turkey. It further noted the emphasis placed in the Turkish constitutional system on the protection of the rights of women. Gender equality – recognised by the European Court as one of the key principles underlying the Convention and a goal to be achieved by member States of the Council of Europe – was also regarded by the Turkish Constitutional Court as a principle implicit in the values underlying the Constitution.

Like the Constitutional Court, the Court considered that, when examining the question of the Islamic headscarf in the Turkish context, there had to be borne in mind the impact which wearing such a symbol, which was presented or perceived as a compulsory religious duty, could have on those who chose not to wear it. The issues at stake included the protection of the "rights and freedoms of others" and the "maintenance of public order" in a country in which the majority of the population, while professing a strong attachment to the rights of women and a secular way of life, adhered to the Islamic faith. Imposing limitations on freedom to wear the Islamic headscarf could, therefore, be regarded as meeting a pressing social need by seeking to achieve those two legitimate aims, especially since that religious symbol had taken on political significance in Turkey in recent years. The Court did not lose sight of the fact that there were extremist political movements in Turkey which sought to impose on society as a whole their religious symbols and conception of a society founded on religious precepts. It considered that the regulations concerned were also intended to preserve pluralism in the university.

It was the principle of secularism which was the paramount consideration underlying the ban on the wearing of religious insignia in universities. It was understandable in such a context where the values of pluralism, respect for the rights of others and, in particular, equality between men and women, were being taught and applied in practice, that the relevant authorities would consider that it ran counter to the furtherance of such values to accept the wearing of religious insignia, including as in the case before the Court, that women students covered their heads with a headscarf while on university premises.

As to the manner in which the university authorities had applied the measures, the Court noted that it was undisputed that in Turkish universities, to the extent that they did not overstep the limits imposed by the organisational requirements of State education, practising Muslim students were free to perform the religious duties that were habitually part of Muslim observance. In addition, the resolution adopted by Istanbul University on 9 July 1998 had treated all forms of dress symbolising or manifesting a religion or faith on an equal footing in barring them from the university premises.

Irrespective of the case-law of the Turkish courts and the applicable rules, the fact that some universities might not have applied the rules rigorously – depending on the context and the special features of individual courses – did not mean that the rules were unjustified. Nor did it mean that the university authorities had waived their right to exercise the regulatory power they derived from statute, the rules governing the functioning of universities and the needs of individual courses. Likewise, whatever a university's policy on the wearing of religious symbols, its regulations and the individual measures taken to implement them were amenable to judicial review in the administrative courts.

The Court noted that by the time the circular was issued on 23 February 1998 there had already been a lengthy debate on whether students could wear the Islamic headscarf. When the issue had surfaced at Istanbul University in 1994 in relation to the medical courses, the university authorities had reminded the students of the applicable rules. Rather than barring students wearing the Islamic headscarf access to the university, the university authorities had sought throughout the decision-making process to adapt to the evolving situation through continued dialogue with those concerned, while at the same time ensuring that order was maintained on the premises.

In those circumstances and having regard in particular to the margin of appreciation left to the Contracting States, the Court found that the University of Istanbul's regulations imposing restrictions on the wearing of Islamic headscarves and the measures taken to implement them were justified in principle and proportionate to the aims pursued and, therefore, could be regarded as "necessary in a democratic society".

Articles 8 and 10, and Article 14 taken together with Article 9, of the Convention and Article 2 of Protocol No. 1

The Court found that no separate question arose under these provisions, as the relevant circumstances were the same as those it had examined in relation to Article 9, in respect of which it had found no violation.

Decision of the Court in the case of Zeynep Tekin

In a letter of 19 February 2003, the applicant informed the Court that she wished to withdraw her application, without offering any explanation. She did not reply to a letter from the Court requesting further information about the reasons for her decision and the Turkish Government did not comment on it.

The Court found that it was no longer justified to continue the examination of the application within the meaning of Article 37 of the Convention (striking out applications) and decided unanimously to strike the case out of the list.

***

The Court's judgments are accessible on its Internet site (http://www.echr.coe.int).

Registry of the European Court of Human Rights
F – 67075 Strasbourg Cedex
Press contacts: Roderick Liddell (telephone: +00 33 (0)3 88 41 24 92)
Emma Hellyer (telephone: +00 33 (0)3 90 21 42 15)
Stéphanie Klein (telephone: +00 33 (0)3 88 41 21 54)
Fax: +00 33 (0)3 88 41 27 91

The European Court of Human Rights was set up in Strasbourg by the Council of Europe Member States in 1959 to deal with alleged violations of the 1950 European Convention on Human Rights. Since 1 November 1998 it has sat as a full-time Court composed of an equal number of judges to that of the States party to the Convention. The Court examines the admissibility and merits of applications submitted to it. It sits in Chambers of 7 judges or, in exceptional cases, as a Grand Chamber of 17 judges. The Committee of Ministers of the Council of Europe supervises the execution of the Court's judgments. More detailed information about the Court and its activities can be found on its Internet site.

---

[1] Under Article 43 of the European Convention on Human Rights, within three months from the date of a Chamber judgment, any party to the case may, in exceptional cases, request that the case be referred to the 17-member Grand Chamber of the Court. In that event, a panel of five judges considers whether the case raises a serious question affecting the interpretation or application of the Convention or its protocols, or a serious issue of general importance, in which case the Grand Chamber will deliver a final judgment. If no such question or issue arises, the panel will reject the request, at which point the judgment becomes final. Otherwise Chamber judgments become final on the expiry of the three-month period or earlier if the parties declare that they do not intend to make a request to refer.

[2] This summary by the Registry does not bind the Court.

608
10.11.2005

Press release issued by the Registrar

GRAND CHAMBER JUDGMENT
LEYLA SAHIN v. TURKEY

The European Court of Human Rights has today delivered at a public hearing its Grand Chamber judgment [1] in the case of Leyla Sahin v. Turkey (application no. 44774/98).

The Court held:

by sixteen votes to one, that there had been no violation of Article 9 (freedom of thought, conscience and religion) of the European Convention on Human Rights;
by sixteen votes to one, that there had been no violation of Article 2 of Protocol No. 1 (right to education);
unanimously, that there had been no violation of Article 8 (right to respect for private and family life);
unanimously, that there had been no violation of Article 10 (freedom of expression);
unanimously, that there had been no violation of Article 14 (prohibition of discrimination).

(The judgment is available in English and French.)

1. Principal facts

The applicant, Leyla Sahin, is a Turkish national who was born in 1973. She has lived in Vienna since 1999, when she left Istanbul to pursue her medical studies at the Faculty of Medicine at Vienna University . She comes from a traditional family of practising Muslims and considers it her religious duty to wear the Islamic headscarf.

At the material time she was a fifth-year student at the faculty of medicine of Istanbul University . On 23 February 1998 the Vice-Chancellor of the University issued a circular directing that students with beards and students wearing the Islamic headscarf would be refused admission to lectures, courses and tutorials.

In March 1998 the applicant was refused access to a written examination on one of the subjects she was studying because was wearing the Islamic headscarf. Subsequently the university authorities refused on the same grounds to enrol her on a course, or to admit her to various lectures and a written examination.

The faculty also issued her with a warning for contravening the university's rules on dress and suspended her from the university for a semester for taking part in an unauthorised assembly that had gathered to protest against them. All the disciplinary penalties imposed on the applicant were revoked under an amnesty law.

2. Procedure and composition of the Court

The application was lodged with the European Commission on Human Rights on 21 July 1998 and transmitted to the Court on 1 November 1998 . It was declared admissible on 2 July 2002 . The Chamber held a hearing in public in Strasbourg on 19 November 2002 .

In its judgment of 29 June 2004 the Chamber held that there had been no violation of Article 9 and that no separate question arose under Articles 8 and 10, Article 14 taken together with Article 9, and Article 2 of Protocol No. 1 to the Convention.

On 27 September 2004 the applicant asked for the case to be referred to the Grand Chamber, in accordance with Article 43 [2] of the Convention. On 10 November 2004 a panel of the Grand Chamber accepted her request. The Grand Chamber held a hearing in public in Strasbourg on 18 May 2005 .

Judgment was given by the Grand Chamber of 17 judges, composed as follows:

Luzius Wildhaber (Swiss), President,
Christos Rozakis (Greek),
Jean-Paul Costa (French),
Boštjan M. Zupancic (Slovenian),
Riza Türmen (Turkish),
Françoise Tulkens (Belgian),
Corneliu Bîrsan (Romanian)
Karel Jungwiert (Czech),
Volodymyr Butkevych (Ukrainian),
Nina Vajic (Croatian),
Mindia Ugrekhelidze (Georgian),
Antonella Mularoni (San Marinese),
Javier Borrego Borrego (Spanish),
Elisabet Fura-Sandström (Swedish),
Alvina Gyulumyan (Armenian),
Egbert Myjer (Netherlands),
Sverre Erik Jebens (Norwegian), judges,

and also Lawrence Early, Deputy Grand Chamber Registrar.

3. Summary of the judgment

Complaints

The applicant complained under Article 9 that she had been prohibited from wearing the Islamic headscarf at university, of an unjustified interference with her right to education, within the meaning of Article 2 of Protocol No. 1 and of a violation of Article 14, taken together with Article 9, arguing that the prohibition on wearing the Islamic headscarf obliged students to choose between education and religion and discriminated between believers and non-believers. Lastly, she relied on Articles 8 and 10.

Decision of the Court

Article 9

Like the Chamber, the Grand Chamber proceeded on the assumption that the circular in issue, which placed restrictions of place and manner on the right to wear the Islamic headscarf in universities, constituted an interference with the applicant's right to manifest her religion.

As to whether the interference had been "prescribed by law", the Court noted that the circular had been issued by the Vice-Chancellor within the statutory framework set out in section 13 of Law no. 2547 and in accordance with the regulatory provisions that had been adopted earlier. According to the applicant, the circular was not compatible with transitional section 17 of that law, which did not proscribe the headscarf but instead provided that students were free to dress as they wished provided that their choice did not contravene the law.

The Court reiterated that, under its case-law, "law" was the provision in force as the competent courts had interpreted it. In that connection, it noted that the Constitutional Court had ruled that freedom of dress in institutions of higher education was not absolute. The Constitutional Court had held that authorising students to "cover the neck and hair with a veil or headscarf for reasons of religious conviction" in the universities was contrary to the Constitution. That decision of the Constitutional Court, which was both binding and accessible, as it had been published in the Official Gazette of 31 July 1991, supplemented the letter of transitional section 17 and followed the Constitutional Court's previous case-law. In addition, the Supreme Administrative Court had by then consistently held for a number of years that wearing the Islamic headscarf at university was not compatible with the fundamental principles of the Republic. Furthermore, regulations on wearing the Islamic headscarf had existed at Istanbul University since 1994 at the latest, well before the applicant enrolled there.

In these circumstances, the Court found that there was a legal basis for the interference in Turkish law and that it would have been clear to the applicant, from the moment she entered the university, that there were restrictions on wearing the Islamic headscarf and, from the date the circular was issued in 1998, that she was liable to be refused access to lectures and examinations if she continued to wear the headscarf.

The Court considered that the impugned interference primarily pursued the legitimate aims of protecting the rights and freedoms of others and of protecting public order.

As to whether the interference was necessary, the Court noted that it was based in particular on the principles of secularism and equality. According to the case-law of the Constitutional Court, secularism, as the guarantor of democratic values, was the meeting point of liberty and equality. The principle prevented the State from manifesting a preference for a particular religion or belief; it thereby guided the State in its role of impartial arbiter, and necessarily entailed freedom of religion and conscience. It also served to protect the individual not only against arbitrary interference by the State but from external pressure from extremist movements. The Constitutional Court added that freedom to manifest one's religion could be restricted in order to defend those values and principles.

Like the Chamber, the Grand Chamber considered that notion of secularism to be consistent with the values underpinning the Convention. Upholding that principle could be considered necessary to protect the democratic system in Turkey.

The Court also noted the emphasis placed in the Turkish constitutional system on the protection of the rights of women. Gender equality – recognised by the European Court as one of the key principles underlying the Convention and a goal to be achieved by member States of the Council of Europe – had also been found by the Turkish Constitutional Court to be a principle implicit in the values underlying the Constitution.

In addition, like the Constitutional Court, the Court considered that, when examining the question of the Islamic headscarf in the Turkish context, there had to be borne in mind the impact which wearing such a symbol, which was presented or perceived as a compulsory religious duty, may have on those who chose not to wear it. As had already been noted, the issues at stake included the protection of the "rights and freedoms of others" and the "maintenance of public order" in a country in which the majority of the population, while professing a strong attachment to the rights of women and a secular way of life, adhered to the Islamic faith. Imposing limitations on the freedom to wear the headscarf could, therefore, be regarded as meeting a pressing social need by seeking to achieve those two legitimate aims, especially since that religious symbol had taken on political significance in Turkey in recent years.

The Court did not lose sight of the fact that there were extremist political movements in Turkey which sought to impose on society as a whole their religious symbols and conception of a society founded on religious precepts.

Against that background, it was the principle of secularism which was the paramount consideration underlying the ban on the wearing of religious symbols in universities. In such a context, where the values of pluralism, respect for the rights of others and, in particular, equality before the law of men and women were being taught and applied in practice, it was understandable that the relevant authorities should consider it contrary to such values to allow religious attire, including, as in the case before the Court, the Islamic headscarf, to be worn on university premises.

As regards the conduct of the university authorities, the Court noted that it was common ground that practising Muslim students in Turkish universities were free, within the limits imposed by educational organisational constraints, to manifest their religion in accordance with habitual forms of Muslim observance. In addition, a resolution that had been adopted by Istanbul University on 9 July 1998 showed that various other forms of religious attire were also forbidden on the university premises .

When the issue of whether students should be allowed to wear the Islamic headscarf had surfaced at Istanbul University in 1994 in relation to the medical courses, the university authorities had reminded them of the relevant rules. Further, throughout the decision-making process that had culminated in the resolution of 9 July 1998 the university authorities had sought to adapt to the evolving situation in a way that would not bar access to the university to students wearing the Islamic headscarf, through continued dialogue with those concerned, while at the same time ensuring that order was maintained on the premises.

As to how compliance with the internal rules of the educational institutions should have been secured, it was not for the Court to substitute its view for that of the university authorities. Besides, having found that the regulations pursued a legitimate aim, it was not open to the Court to apply the criterion of proportionality in a way that would make the notion of an institution's "internal rules" devoid of purpose. Article 9 did not always guarantee the right to behave in a manner governed by a religious belief and did not confer on people who did so the right to disregard rules that had proved to be justified.

In those circumstances, and having regard to the Contracting States' margin of appreciation, the Court found that the interference in issue was justified in principle and proportionate to the aims pursued, and could therefore be considered to have been "necessary in a democratic society". It therefore found no violation of Article 9.

Article 2 of Protocol No. 1

Contrary to the decision of the Chamber on this complaint, the Grand Chamber was of the view that, having regard to the special circumstances of the case, the fundamental importance of the right to education and the position of the parties, the complaint under Article 2 of Protocol No. 1 could be considered as separate from the complaint under Article 9 and therefore warranted separate examination.

On the question of the applicability of Article 2 of Protocol No. 1, the Court reiterated that it was of crucial importance that the Convention was interpreted and applied in a manner which rendered its rights practical and effective, not theoretical and illusory. Moreover, the Convention was a living instrument which had to be interpreted in the light of present-day conditions. While the first sentence of Article 2 essentially established access to primary and secondary education, there was no watertight division separating higher education from other forms of education. In a number of recently adopted instruments, the Council of Europe had stressed the key role and importance of higher education in the promotion of human rights and fundamental freedoms and the strengthening of democracy. Consequently, it would be hard to imagine that institutions of higher education existing at a given time did not come within the scope of the first sentence of Article 2 of Protocol No 1. Although that Article did not impose a duty on the Contracting States to set up such institutions, any State that did so was under an obligation to afford an effective right of access to them. In a democratic society, the right to education, which was indispensable to the furtherance of human rights, played such a fundamental role that a restrictive interpretation of the first sentence of Article 2 of Protocol No. 1 would not be consistent with the aim or purpose of that provision.

Consequently, the Court considered that any institutions of higher education existing at a given time came within the scope of the first sentence of Article 2 of Protocol No. 1, since the right of access to such institutions was an inherent part of the right set out in that provision.

In the case before it, by analogy with its reasoning on the question of the existence of interference under Article 9, the Court accepted that the regulations on the basis of which the applicant had been refused access to various lectures and examinations for wearing the Islamic headscarf constituted a restriction on her right to education, notwithstanding the fact that she had had access to the university and been able to read the subject of her choice in accordance with the results she had achieved in the university entrance examination. As with Article 9, the restriction was foreseeable and pursued legitimate aims and the means used were proportionate.

The measures in question manifestly did not hinder the students in performing the duties imposed by the habitual forms of religious observance. Secondly, the decision-making process for applying the internal regulations satisfied, so far as was possible, the requirement to weigh up the various interests at stake. The university authorities judiciously sought a means whereby they could avoid having to turn away students wearing the headscarf and at the same time honour their obligation to protect the rights of others and the interests of the education system. Lastly, the process also appeared to have been accompanied by safeguards – the rule requiring conformity with statute and judicial review – that were apt to protect the students' interests.

Further, the applicant could reasonably have foreseen that she ran the risk of being refused access to lectures and examinations if, as subsequently happened, she continued to wear the Islamic headscarf after 23 February 1998.

In these circumstances, the ban on wearing the Islamic headscarf had not impaired the very essence of the applicant's right to education and, in the light of the Court's findings with respect to the other Articles relied on by the applicant. Neither did it conflict with other rights enshrined in the Convention or its Protocols. The Court therefore found that there had been no violation of Article 2 of Protocol No. 1.

Articles 8, 10 and 14

The Court did not find any violation of Articles 8 or 10, the arguments advanced by the applicant being a mere reformulation of her complaint under Article 9 and Article 2 of Protocol No. 1, in respect of which the Court had concluded that there had been no violation.

As regards the complaint under Article 14, the Court noted that the applicant had not provided detailed particulars in her pleadings before the Grand Chamber. Furthermore, as had already been noted, the regulations on the Islamic headscarf were not directed against the applicant's religious affiliation, but pursued, among other things, the legitimate aim of protecting order and the rights and freedoms of others and were manifestly intended to preserve the secular nature of educational institutions.

Consequently the Court held that there had been no violation of Articles 8, 10 or 14.

Judges Rozakis and Vajic expressed a joint concurring opinion and Judge Tulkens expressed a dissenting opinion. These opinions are annexed to the judgment.

***

The Court's judgments are accessible on its Internet site (http://www.echr.coe.int).

Registry of the European Court of Human Rights
F – 67075 Strasbourg Cedex
Press contacts: Roderick Liddell (telephone: +00 33 (0)3 88 41 24 92)
Emma Hellyer (telephone: +00 33 (0)3 90 21 42 15)
Stéphanie Klein (telephone: +00 33 (0)3 88 41 21 54)

Beverley Jacobs (telephone: +00 33 (0)3 90 21 54 21)
Fax: +00 33 (0)3 88 41 27 91

The European Court of Human Rights was set up in Strasbourg by the Council of Europe Member States in 1959 to deal with alleged violations of the 1950 European Convention on Human Rights. Since 1 November 1998 it has sat as a full-time Court composed of an equal number of judges to that of the States party to the Convention. The Court examines the admissibility and merits of applications submitted to it. It sits in Chambers of 7 judges or, in exceptional cases, as a Grand Chamber of 17 judges. The Committee of Ministers of the Council of Europe supervises the execution of the Court's judgments. More detailed information about the Court and its activities can be found on its Internet site.

[1] Grand Chamber judgments are final (Article 44 of the Convention).

[2] Under Article 43 of the European Convention on Human Rights, within three months from the date of a Chamber judgment, any party to the case may, in exceptional cases, request that the case be referred to the 17 member Grand Chamber of the Court. In that event, a panel of five judges considers whether the case raises a serious question affecting the interpretation or application of the Convention or its protocols, or a serious issue of general importance, in which case the Grand Chamber will deliver a final judgment. If no such question or issue arises, the panel will reject the request, at which point the judgment becomes final. Otherwise Chamber judgments become final on the expiry of the three-month period or earlier if the parties declare that they do not intend to make a request to refer.

[3] This summary by the Registry does not bind the Court.

Arab women

The Economist, June 19th 2004

Their time has come

Arab women are demanding their rights—at last

Even the Saudis - or rather, the small number of men who actually rule their troubled country - are giving ground in the struggle for women's rights. For sure, the recommendations handed this week to Crown Prince Abdullah at the end of an unprecedented round of "national dialogue" concentrating on the role of women were fairly tame (see page 27). In the reformers-versus-reactionaries litmus test of whether women should be allowed to drive cars (at present they cannot do so in the kingdom, nor can they travel unaccompanied, by whatever means of motion), the king was merely asked to "assign a body to study a public-transport system for women to facilitate mobility". No mention, of course, of the right to vote—but then that has been denied to men too, though local elections, on an apparently universal franchise, are supposed to be held in October. In sum, it is a tortoise's progress. But the very fact of the debate happening at all is remarkable—and hopeful.

It is not just in Saudi Arabia that more rights for women are being demanded but across the whole of the Arab and Muslim world. The pushy Americans have made women's rights part of their appeal for greater democracy in what they now officially call the "Broader Middle East", to include non-Arab Muslim countries such as Iran, Turkey and even Afghanistan. Many Arabs have cautioned the Americans against seeking to impose their own values on societies with such different traditions and beliefs. Many leading Muslims have accused the culturally imperious Americans of seeking to destroy Islam. The appeal for more democracy in the Muslim world issued by leaders of the eight biggest industrial countries was watered down for fear of giving offence. Yet, despite the Arabs' prickliness, the Americans have helped pep up a debate that is now bubbling fiercely in the Arab world, even though many Arab leaders, none of whom is directly elected by the people, are understandably wary of reforms that could lead to their own toppling. Never before have women's rights in the Arab world been so vigorously debated. That alone is cause to rejoice.

Don't blame the Koran

One of the great falsehoods deployed by the conservatives, nearly all of them men, is that the Koran, the word of God as imparted to Muhammad more than 13 centuries ago, decrees that women should remain in second place. The trouble in Saudi Arabia (and in Iran, just outside the Arab fold but still influential in parts of it, such as Iraq and Lebanon) is that conservatives, on whom—for reasons of history and realpolitik - the regime still relies, have grabbed a near-monopoly of religious authority, imposing an exceptionally narrow interpretation of Islam on the people, especially women. To take but one example, it is written that women should dress modestly, but nowhere is it stated that they should be covered from top to toe in black. Nor, for that matter, is it stated that women should be denied an equal say in decisions of state.

Saudi Arabia, it should be stressed, is exceptionally behindhand. Yet, compared with most of their western sisters, Arab women elsewhere still, on the whole, enjoy fewer rights. But they have generally been gaining ground apace. And there are now numerous examples in the Muslim (but not yet in the Arab) world where, without in any way disavowing Islam, women have actually headed governments: for instance in Bangladesh, Indonesia, Pakistan and

Arab women

Their time has come

Arab women are demanding their rights—at last

EVEN the Saudis—or rather, the small number of men who actually rule their troubled country—are giving ground in the struggle for women's rights. For sure, the recommendations handed this week to Crown Prince Abdullah at the end of an unprecedented round of "national dialogue" concentrating on the role of women were fairly tame (see page 27). In the reformers-versus-reactionaries litmus test of whether women should be allowed to drive cars (at present they cannot do so in the kingdom, nor can they travel unaccompanied, by whatever means of motion), the king was merely asked to "assign a body to study a public-transport system for women to facilitate mobility". No mention, of course, of the right to vote—but then that has been denied to men too, though local elections, on an apparently universal franchise, are supposed to be held in October. In sum, it is a tortoise's progress. But the very fact of the debate happening at all is remarkable—and hopeful.

It is not just in Saudi Arabia that more rights for women are being demanded but across the whole of the Arab and Muslim world. The pushy Americans have made women's rights part of their appeal for greater democracy in what they now officially call the "Broader Middle East", to include non-Arab Muslim countries such as Iran, Turkey and even Afghanistan. Many Arabs have cautioned the Americans against seeking to impose their own values on societies with such different traditions and beliefs. Many leading Muslims have accused the culturally imperious Americans of seeking to destroy Islam. The appeal for more democracy in the Muslim world issued by leaders of the eight biggest industrial countries was watered down for fear of giving offence. Yet, despite the Arabs' prickliness, the Americans have helped pep up a debate that is now bubbling fiercely in the Arab world, even though many Arab leaders, none of whom is directly elected by the people, are understandably wary of reforms that could lead to their own toppling. Never before have women's rights in the Arab world been so vigorously debated. That alone is cause to rejoice.

Don't blame the Koran

One of the great falsehoods deployed by the conservatives, nearly all of them men, is that the Koran, the word of God as imparted to Muhammad more than 13 centuries ago, decrees that women should remain in second place. The trouble in Saudi Arabia (and in Iran, just outside the Arab fold but still influential in parts of it, such as Iraq and Lebanon) is that conservatives, on whom—for reasons of history and realpolitik—the regime still relies, have grabbed a near-monopoly of religious authority, imposing an exceptionally narrow interpretation of Islam on the people, especially women. To take but one example, it is written that women should dress modestly, but nowhere is it stated that they should be covered from top to toe in black. Nor, for that matter, is it stated that women should be denied an equal say in decisions of state.

Saudi Arabia, it should be stressed, is exceptionally behindhand. Yet, compared with most of their western sisters, Arab women elsewhere still, on the whole, enjoy fewer rights. But »

14 Leaders The Economist June 19th 2004

› they have generally been gaining ground apace. And there are now numerous examples in the Muslim (but not yet in the Arab) world where, without in any way disavowing Islam, women have actually headed governments: for instance in Bangladesh, Indonesia, Pakistan and Turkey.

It cannot be denied that there are problems, for liberals and supporters of full female emancipation, with the application of *Sharia*, the body of laws deemed to derive from the Koran, in those countries where the judicial system is wholly or partly based on it. Laws of inheritance, the relative weight of evidence given in court by men and women, rights of divorce and of children's custody—these, if taken literally, all diminish women. But there is far more flexibility and fuzziness, even here, than the conservatives concede. *Sharia* is not an actual code nor is it clearly defined; it is merely a basis for a system inspired but not dictated by the Koran. It is certainly not incumbent on all good Muslims to insist that the government use *Sharia*—or indeed the Koran—as the sole source of law. And both are open to wide interpretation, as they should be, to meet the changing demands of modernity.

Christians hardly need reminding that for centuries they fought bloody wars over competing versions of their faith, and bodies such as the Catholic Inquisition testify to the cruelties that can flow, within any religion, from a dogmatic determination to impose a particular set of beliefs. Over the years, however, a separation of church and state has helped to nurture individual creativity alongside reasonable governance under temporal laws. A wider measure of separation of mosque and state would probably provide similar benefits, as it has done, for instance, in Turkey.

In the end, democracy, entailing a freedom of choice, is the prerequisite, for Muslims as much as anyone else, for creating a society that is both cohesive and fair. There is no reason why Muslim Arabs, women included, should not have the democratic freedom enjoyed by people of other faiths. It would, after all, liberate men too. ■

Turkey.

It cannot be denied that there are problems, for liberals and supporters of full female emancipation, with the application of *Sharia*, the body of laws deemed to derive from the Koran, in those countries where the judicial system is wholly or partly based on it. Laws of inheritance, the relative weight of evidence given in court by men and women, rights of divorce and of children's custody - these, if taken literally, all diminish women. But there is far more flexibility and fuzziness, even here, than the conservatives concede. *Sharia* is not an actual code nor is it clearly defined; it is merely a basis for a system inspired but not dictated by the Koran. It is certainly not incumbent on all good Muslims to insist that the government use *Sharia*—or indeed the Koran—as the sole source of law. And both are open to wide interpretation, as they should be, to meet the changing demands of modernity.

Christians hardly need reminding that for centuries they fought bloody wars over competing versions of their faith, and bodies such as the Catholic Inquisition testify to the cruelties that can flow, within any religion, from a dogmatic determination to impose a particular set of beliefs. Over the years, however, a separation of church and state has helped to nurture individual creativity alongside reasonable governance under temporal laws. A wider measure of separation of mosque and state would probably provide similar benefits, as it has done, for instance, in Turkey.

In the end, democracy, entailing a freedom of choice, is the prerequisite, for Muslims as much as anyone else, for creating a society that is both cohesive and fair. There is no reason why Muslim Arabs, women included, should not have the democratic freedom enjoyed by people of other faiths. It would, after all, liberate men too.

Special report - Arab women

The Economist, June 19th 2004

Out of the shadows, into the world

Slowly, but sometimes showily, the female half of the population is beginning to find a voice

IT WAS called a "national dialogue", but to western eyes it was a strange kind of conversation. From June 13th-15th, in Medina, Saudi Arabian women and men discussed how women's lives could be improved. The women, however, were invisible to the men, except on a television screen.

From kindergarten to university to the few professions they are permitted to pursue, as well as in restaurants and banks and in other public places, the female half of Saudi Arabia's population is kept strictly apart. Women are not allowed to drive a car, sail a boat or fly a plane, or to appear outdoors with hair, wrists or ankles exposed, or to travel without permission from a male guardian. A wife who angers her husband risks being "hanged"; that is, suspended in legal limbo, often penniless and trapped indoors, until such time as he deigns to grant a divorce. And then she will lose custody of her children. The 19 recommendations that went to Crown Prince Abdullah on June 15th would change matters somewhat, if they are ever enacted. Participants asked for special courts to deal with women's issues, more women's sections in existing courts, and a public-transport system for them. They wanted more education, more jobs and more voluntary organisations dealing with women's issues. Amid much vague good feeling, the phrase that recurred was "more awareness"—not just of women's rights, but of women as human beings.

Saudi Arabia certainly presents male chauvinism at its worst. Yet it is a mistake to imagine, as many westerners do, that Arab women as a whole suffer strictures as tight as their Saudi sisters'. It is equally incorrect to judge the donning of veils and headscarves—attire that is optional everywhere save in Saudi Arabia and non-Arab Iran—to be a sign of exclusion. For some it is simply a personal expression of religious devotion; for others, a means of escape from the tyranny of fashion.

It is even wrong to assume that life for the purdahed women of Saudi Arabia is necessarily hard. Boring, yes, and cluttered with minor annoyances, but also full of compensating richness. Many Saudi women take pride in the protectiveness, family-centredness and Muslim piety of their society—aspects that were stressed first in the list of recommendations.

Slowly but surely, too, the lot of Saudi women is improving, just as it has been for women in most Arab countries. Saudi girls were not even allowed to go to school until 1964. Now, some 55% of the kingdom's university students are female. Similar trends can be seen elsewhere. In Kuwait's and Qatar's national universities, women now make up fully 70% of the student body. Across the wider region, the average time girls have spent in school by the age of 15 has increased from a mere six months in 1960 to 4.5 years today. This may still be only three-quarters of the schooling that Arab boys get, but female education has improved faster in Arab countries than in any other region. Tunisia has narrowed the literacy gap between young men and women by 80% since 1970. Jordan has achieved full literacy for both sexes.

The Arab performance in improving women's health is also unmatched. Female life expectancy is up from 52 years in 1970 to more than 70 today. The number of children borne by the average Arab woman has fallen by half in the past 20 years, to a level scarcely higher than world norms. In Oman, fertility has plummeted from ten births per woman to fewer than four. A main reason for this is a dramatic rise in the age at which girls marry. A generation ago, three-quarters of Arab women were married by the time they were 20. That proportion has dropped by half. In large Arab cities, the high cost of housing, added to the need for women to pursue degrees or start careers, is prompting many to delay marriage into their 30's. Again, that is not much different from the rest of the world.

Houris and hijabs

Outsiders may think of Arab women as shrouded, closeted ghosts, but the images that come to Arab minds these days are likely to be quite different. Flick on a television in Muscat or Marrakesh, and you find punchy, highly competent and pretty female presenters. Competition between Lebanese television networks is so keen that their gorgeous weather-announcers, pantomiming, say, rain on the mountains, can be rather startling. More eye-opening still is the procession of video clips on the many highly popular satellite channels broadcasting round-the-clock Arabic pop music.

Special report Arab women

Out of the shadows, into the world

Emancipation in Beirut

Strapless *houris* (beauties), such as Lebanon's Nancy Ajram and Egypt's Ruby, croon and gyrate with scarcely less abandon than their western prototypes.

True, such imagery remains deeply controversial, and not just to feminists. In relatively open-minded Egypt, the state broadcasting monopoly has banned the more provocative female stars and has forbidden costumes that reveal belly buttons, saying they corrupt the country's youth. The saucy video clips are regularly blasted at Friday sermons in the mosques.

It is also true that provocatively clad starlets are hardly representative of Arab womanhood. Broadly speaking, the percentage of Arab women who wear some form of hijab, or veil, does seem to be inching upwards. Numbers vary hugely, however, from around 10-20% in Lebanon or Tunisia to perhaps 60% in Syria and Jordan, to 80% in Kuwait and Iraq. In rural Egypt, the near-universal adoption of the veil in recent years is as much a reflection of city fashions creeping into the countryside (where women traditionally worked in the fields unveiled) as of rising conservatism. The popularity of veils in Egyptian cities, meanwhile, is partly due to a rise in the number of women who leave home to work or study. In a sense, for traditional families the hijab is a sort of convenient half-way station to fuller freedom.

At the same time, the late-night club-culture of cities such as Cairo, Dubai and Beirut is thriving as never before. Even those women who shun the packed bars and discos may now venture into the cafes, once a male preserve. The sight of groups of women smoking waterpipes has become quite common. Such delights have helped attract a fast-growing number of tourists, especially Gulf Arabs, for whom the free mingling of sexes is itself a spectacle. Inevitably, these looser strictures have an influence back home.

Those other modern media, the internet and the mobile phone, increasingly reinforce such shifts in attitude. Hard as it may still be to meet members of the opposite sex openly, ever-growing numbers of young Arabs are chatting, flirting and even getting hitched over the ether. And that is the innocent side. This correspondent's wholly unscientific survey of internet cafes in several Saudi cities revealed that virtually all the websites recorded as "favourites" were blatantly pornographic.

Even the many Arabs who dismiss MTV and on-line dating as the preserve of gilded, westernised youth will admit that female role-models have changed a great deal. In all but three out of 22 countries in the Arab League, women have the right to vote and run for office. (Recall that the Swiss canton of Appenzell did not grant such rights until 1991). Arab women also work as ambassadors, government ministers, top business executives and even, in Bahrain, army officers. A fifth of Algeria's Supreme Court judges are women, and women hold 15% of the top judicial posts in Tunisia. Even in Saudi Arabia, Lubna Olayan heads the kingdom's leading private industrial group, and Thoraya Obeid runs the UN'S family-planning agency, though admittedly in New York.

The darker side

Yet Arab women should not rest complacent. It is for good reason that the UN's devastating, and much-quoted, Arab Human Development Report cites women's rights, along with education and governance, as the main challenge facing the region. Statistics cannot easily capture, for example, the fact that the very idea of an unmarried woman living alone remains taboo in all but a few Arab countries. Numbers do not adequately measure the harassment that "immodest" dress routinely attracts in most Arab cities, or the destructive social impact of habits such as female circumcision (still practised widely in Egypt and Sudan), polygamy (sanctioned by Islam, yet rare except in the wealthy Gulf states), or "honour killings" (sanctioned by tribal custom, not religion, and declining—but in Jordan, more than 20 women are still murdered by their own suspicious relatives every year).

The numbers can still be revealing, though. In Egypt, a recent study showed that among families with low levels of education, baby girls are twice as likely to die as baby boys. In Yemen, the illiteracy rate among young women (54%) is three times that of men. And as for those proud Saudi women who are now earning most of the kingdom's university degrees, their prospects of careers are dim. Barely 6% of the country's workforce is female. Across the Arab region as a whole, only a third of adult women have jobs, compared with three-quarters of women in East Asia.

Just as disturbingly, movement towards equality in some Arab countries has shunted into reverse. Such is the case of Iraq, a country that during the 1960's and 1970's was in the vanguard of progress. Saddam Hussein's two decades of war and sanctions crushed the life out of the country's once large and rich middle class. Their decline discredited social models, such as the nuclear family, which had begun to replace the old patriarchal clan system. The lot of most Iraqi women has worsened even more dramatically since the war. In the cities, women are simply afraid to go out alone. The rise of religious radicalism has prompted many to adopt the veil, out of fear as much as conviction.

Even in more peaceable Arab countries, the gains women have made are not fully secure. As far back as the 1950's, for example, secularist Tunisia granted women full equality, going so far as to contravene Islam and ban polygamy. With their rights to vote, divorce, work in any profession and so forth, Tunisian women remain the envy of Arab feminists elsewhere. Yet they themselves complain that male attitudes have not really changed. A Tunisian sociologist notes a trend by wealthy men to seek brides from poor villages, since city women are "too independent". And the incidence of wife-beating remains high.

Egypt was another Arab pioneer in women's rights. The first Arab feminist manifesto, "The Liberation of Woman", was published in Cairo in 1899. By the 1920's, society women were dropping their veils; by the 1960's, the country had more female doctors than many in the West. But progress stalled in the 1980's, when the parliament scotched a law that would have ensured nearly full sexual equality.

Discriminatory laws still hinder women's progress in many other countries. Algeria's 1984 family statutes give men an automatic right to divorce, with no legal obligation to their former spouse. In all but a few Arab countries, citizenship may only be passed on by the father of a child, not its mother. Similarly, custody of children customarily goes to the father, a fact that comes into tragic prominence every year in consulates across the region, when the foreign divorcees of Arab men discover that they may lose their children. And Islamic inheritance law grants female heirs only half the portion given to males.

Islam's importance

Outsiders commonly assume that Islam itself is the cause of sexual inequality in the Arab world. This is not strictly true. Earlier this year, for instance, Morocco adopted a progressive family status code which, among other things, grants both sexes equal rights to seek divorce and to argue before a judge for custody of children. It also places such tight conditions on polygamy as to render the practice virtually impossible. Yet the new law won backing not just from King Muhammad VI, who declared it to be "in perfect accordance with the spirit of our tolerant religion", but also from the country's main Islamist parties.

In Kuwait, too, religion is being used to push reform. Five years ago, Islamists in the country's parliament blocked a law that would have granted women the right to vote and run for office. The same law is being tabled again this year, but this time several Islamist MP's have defected to the liberals. One reason is a *fatwa* recently issued by a prominent cleric, which questions the reliability of the source who, 14 centuries ago, reported the Prophet Muhammad as saying "A nation commanded by woman will not prosper."

Aside from giving them the short stick on inheritance, and having their testimony in law considered half as weighty as men's, and letting husbands marry up to four wives, whom they may beat if they are disobedient, the Koran itself is not unkind to women. Centuries before Christian women in the West, Muslim women freely enjoyed full property rights. In many Arab societies, it has been customary to evade statutory inheritance laws by simply signing over property to female relations before your death.

The trouble, in places like Saudi Arabia, lies more in how the holy text—as well as the *hadiths*, or Prophet's sayings, that inform the *Sharia*—are interpreted. Such texts are often not so much interpreted, as twisted to fit pre-existing traditions. The ban on driving, for instance, is unique to Saudi Arabia. Yet even Saudi clerics are hard-put to find support for the rule in holy scripture. (And in any case, according to one survey, 29% of Saudi women say they already know how to drive.)

The extreme Saudi phobia regarding *ik-htilat*, or mixing of the sexes, also has no textual justification. And although the Koran mentions modesty in dress, how much is a matter of opinion. Most scholars agree that *hadiths* about fuller covering relate to the Prophet's own wives. Whether to follow their example should be a free choice, as indeed it is in most Muslim societies.

Some countries, such as non-Arab Tunisia, have simply bypassed such questions by imposing fully secular laws. For the time being, Arab public opinion is strongly opposed to this; the link to Islamic roots is seen as essential. Yet when it comes to women's rights, the evidence is that Arabs, even the men among them, acknowledge the need for improvement. In a 2002 survey of social attitudes carried out in seven Arab countries by Zogby International, 50% of respondents considered the improvement of women's rights a high priority (see chart on previous page). Significantly, the firmest support for change came from Saudi Arabia.

The reformers will eventually get their way. Saudi women are, in fact, already chalking up important gains. Last month they were granted the right to hold commercial licences, a significant advance considering that women own a quarter of the $100 billion deposited in Saudi banks, with little opportunity to make use of it. In 2001, they won the right to have their own identity cards (though a male guardian must apply for them). Saudi businesswomen spoke eloquently, to long applause, at a major conference in Jeddah earlier this year. Since January, Saudi state TV has employed female newscasters.

The kingdom's best-known TV personality also happens to be a woman. Rania al-Baz won further fame earlier this year when her husband beat her almost to death. Instead of staying silent, as her mother would have done, Mrs al-Baz invited photographers into her hospital room to show the world her broken face. She has now formed a group to combat the abuse of women in Saudi Arabia.

This feature by the Economist is very informative, but not completely fair when it describes the Koran as giving women, *'...the short stick on inheritance, and having their testimony in law considered half as weighty as men's, and letting husbands marry up to four wives, whom they may beat if they are disobedient...'* The detail and the historical background to these edicts has to be explained properly, which is beyond the scope of this book. However, the Economist should not be too self-righteous when one sees the massive exploitation of (very willing) women by men in the porn industry, the high divorce rates, record delinqency and abortion levels etc. etc. in the 'liberated' West.

Chapter 6

Muslims are right about Britain

The Spectator, 6th August 2005

John Hayes says Islamic moderates are correct to despise our decadent culture of gay rights and lager louts

Muslims are right about Britain

John Hayes says Islamic moderates are correct to despise our decadent culture of gay rights and lager louts

'This is the worst drought we've had for 50 years!'

John Hayes is Conservative MP for South Holland and The Deepings.

12 THE SPECTATOR 6 August 2005

Many moderate Muslims believe that much of Britain is decadent. They are right. Mr Blair says that the fanatics who want to blow us up despise us, but he won't admit that their decent co-religionists — who are the best hope of undermining the extremists at source — despair of us. They despair of the moral decline and the ugly brutishness that characterise much of urban Britain. They despair of the metropolitan mix of gay rights and lager louts. And they despair of the liberal establishment's unwillingness to face the facts and fight the battle for manners and morals.

They are not alone. The *Windrush* generation of Caribbeans came to Britain with the most traditional of values — proud Christians with dignity and a sense of duty — the kind of people so steeped in our history that they gave their children names like Winston, Milton and Gladstone. As vice-chairman of the British Caribbean Association, I recently had the chance to ask such people why so many young British blacks had got into trouble with the law. They unequivocally blamed the licence they encountered almost as soon as they arrived here, which made it so hard to inculcate their standards in the next generation.

The alienation felt by young blacks and Asians is not a result of any intolerance shown towards them, but of the endless tolerance of those who would allow everything and stand up for nothing. It is the excesses permitted by a culture spawned by the liberal Left that have produced a generation that feels rootless and hopeless. The young crave noble purposes as children need discipline; neither get much of them in modern Britain and the void is filled by disrespect, fecklessness, mindless nihilism or, worse, wicked militancy.

It is unreasonable to expect Muslim leaders to put right what's wrong in their communities if we are not going to be honest about what's wrong with ours.

Some of rural Britain (including the area in which I live and represent) still has strong communities. There, many of the old-fashioned values lost elsewhere prevail. Beyond these heartlands, much else is ailing. A sickening decadence has taken hold. People's sense of identity has been eroded as our traditions and the institutions that safeguard them have been derided for years. People's sense of history has been weakened by an education system that too often emphasises the themes in history rather than its chronology, and which indoctrinates a guilt-ridden interpretation of Britain's contribution to the world. People's sense of responsibility has been undermined by a commercial and media preoccupation with the immediate gratification of material needs, regardless of consequences — we want everything and we want it now, so we spend and borrow, cheat and hurt. People's self-regard has diminished as, robbed of any sense of worth beyond their capacity to consume and fornicate, they feel purposeless. We have forgotten that pleasure is a mere proxy for the true happiness which flows from commitment and the gentle acceptance that it is what we give, not what we take, that really matters.

The vulnerable are the chief victims of decadence. Children suffer when families break down. The old suffer as their needs are seen as inconvenient and their wisdom is no longer valued. For the rich, decadence is either a lifestyle choice or something you can buy your way out of. But for the less well off — stripped of the dignities which stem from a shared sense of belonging and pride — the horror of a greedy society in which they can't compete is stark. The civilised urban life that was available to my working-class parents is now the preserve of those whose wealth shields them from lawlessness and frees them from the inadequate public services that their less fortunate contemporaries are forced to endure.

Safely gated, the liberal elite do not merely turn a blind eye — though that would be bad enough. They voyeuristically feed the masses with Big Brother and legislate to allow 24-hour drunkenness. In answer to the desperate call for much-needed restraint, we hear from those with power only the shrill cry for ever more unbridled liberty.

Politicians who should know better fear debates about values, preferring to retreat to morally neutral, utilitarian politics, as uninspiring as it is unimaginative. It is the kind of discourse which leaves those who aspire to govern reduced — in the heat of a general election campaign — to debating how efficiently their respective parties can disinfect hospitals. Most Church leaders have also given up the fight. Many have convinced themselves that to be fashionable is to be relevant and that being relevant is more important than being right. Is it any wonder that the family-minded, morally upright moderate Muslims despair?

So, with little understanding of the past, little thought for the future, little respect for others and virtually no guidance from those appointed or elected to give it, many modern Britons — each with their wonderful, unique God-given potential — are condemned to be selfish, lonely creatures in a soulless society where little is worshipped beyond money and sex.

The roots of this brutal hedonism are in soulless liberalism. Against all the evidence, the liberal elite — who run much of Britain's politically correct new establishment — continue to preach their creed of freedom without duty, and rights without obligations. Pope John Paul II:— perhaps the greatest figure of our age — said 'only the freedom which submits to the truth leads the human person to his true good'. Freedom without purpose is the seed corn of social decay. It is through the constraints on self-interest and the restraint that good Muslims revere that we can rebuild civil society. The most fitting response to the terrorist outrages would be the kind of moral and cultural renaissance that would make Britons of all backgrounds feel more proud of their country.

John Hayes ***is Conservative MP for South Holland and The Deepings.***

Letters section:
The Spectator, 13th August 2005

Our 'decadent' society

From Brian Binley MP and others

Sir: As Conservative MPs elected at this year's general election we represent a new generation unencumbered by the political baggage of the past. In this spirit we enthusiastically endorse the rejection articulated by John Hayes ('Muslims are right about Britain', 6 August) of the liberal establishment's assumptions about our society. For too long politicians of the centre and centre-Left — including some who curiously wear the badge of Conservatism — have ignored the common-sense opinions of the hard-working, patriotic majority of Britons who retain their belief in traditional values. In a recent Centre for Social Justice pamphlet, Iain Duncan Smith suggests 'that it is noteworthy — even remarkable — that [what he calls] Britain's conservative majority has persisted in the face of a largely hostile broadcast media and hesitant Church leaders'.

Some liberals remain in denial, unwilling to face the decadent consequences of years of their ideas being put into practice. But whether it is lawlessness, family breakdown, the menace of drugs, binge-drinking, teenage pregnancies or merely the coarse brutishness which, as Mr Hayes suggests, has infested popular culture, the results of years of woolly-minded liberal thinking (with the licentiousness it has created) are plain to see. Conservatives can choose either to help prop up the failed ideas of the liberal elite, or answer the people's plea for certainty, order and decency. Choosing the latter is the key to success.

Brian Binley MP, Peter Bone MP, David Burrowes MP, Philip Davies MP, Robert Goodwill MP, Mark Harper MP

Our 'decadent' society

From Brian Binley MP and others

Sir: As Conservative MPs elected at this year's general election we represent a new generation unencumbered by the political baggage of the past. In this spirit we enthusiastically endorse the rejection articulated by John Hayes ('Muslims are right about Britain', 6 August) of the liberal establishment's assumptions about our society. For too long politicians of the centre and centre-Left — including some who curiously wear the badge of Conservatism — have ignored the common-sense opinions of the hard-working, patriotic majority of Britons who retain their belief in traditional values. In a recent Centre for Social Justice pamphlet, Iain Duncan Smith suggests that 'it is noteworthy — even remarkable — that [what he calls] Britain's conservative majority has persisted in the face of a largely hostile broadcast media and hesitant Church leaders'.

Some liberals remain in denial, unwilling to face the decadent consequences of years of their ideas being put into practice. But whether it is lawlessness, family breakdown, the menace of drugs, binge-drinking, teenage pregnancies or merely the coarse brutishness which, as Mr Hayes suggests, has infested popular culture, the results of years of woolly-minded liberal thinking (with the licentiousness it has created) are plain to see. Conservatives can choose either to help prop up the failed ideas of the liberal elite, or answer the people's plea for certainty, order and decency. Choosing the latter is the key to success.

Brian Binley MP, Peter Bone MP, David Burrowes MP, Philip Davies MP, Robert Goodwill MP, Mark Harper MP

Yes we DO need drastic measures - because Labour has engineered a collapse in morality

Daily Mail, Monday October 10th 2005
The Melanie Phillips column

THE disclosure that the Government is apparently drawing up sweeping powers to deal with anti social behaviour is likely to provoke relief, belly-laughs and outright hostility in equal measure.

According to weekend Press reports, Whitehall's 'respect' unit is preparing a set of radical proposals which will target 'nightmare neighbour' households, parents of out-of-control children and binge-drinkers. Feckless parents would face community penalties, and those in council houses would lose their homes if they failed to control their children's yobbish behaviour. The worst families would be moved to secure gated areas guarded by wardens and CCTV cameras where they would be confined under curfew.

And there was also a suggestion that children under ten — the age of criminal responsibility — might be subject to antisocial behaviour orders for the first time.

No sooner had these reports surfaced than the Government distanced itself from them, with Downing Street claiming that it 'did not recognise' such proposals.

Obscenities

This has all the hallmarks of the classic Government tactic of floating measures which are likely to be deeply contentious — not least within government, where there are reportedly tensions between the Home Secretary and the Prime Minister's 'respect czar' Louise Casey — in order to gauge public reaction while denying that the plan has any substance.

The fact is that measures such as these would be greeted with overwhelming relief by thousands of people whose lives are being wrecked on a daily basis by antisocial behaviour.

People are being terrorised not just by yobbish children and teenagers but by their disorderly parents. Those who have done no wrong are running a gauntlet of vandalism, litter and noise, and are forced to become prisoners inside their own homes for fear of the violence or obscenities that threaten them if they step outside.

Moreover, all the cards are stacked against them by a state which seems to privilege those who do wrong, rewarding miscreants with houses and benefits while being unable or unwilling to protect their victims through the criminal justice system.

The sheer scale of this breakdown in order indicates why these new proposals deserve a measure of scepticism. Whole swathes of the country have simply descended into anarchy, with feral children who have been abandoned to fatherlessness and parents whose response to any remonstration is to turn violent themselves.

Yes, we DO need drastic measures – because Labour has engineered a collapse in morality

THE Melanie Phillips COLUMN

Our once-civilised country has been turned into this social battleground because of a collapse of the disciplines that once governed people's behaviour. But this is a collapse which the Government itself has wilfully accelerated.

The single most important reason for this widespread disorder is the disintegration of the family. Yet the Government has promoted the society-busting myth that 'all lifestyles are equal'. It has actually encouraged lone parenthood by weighting welfare benefits towards unmarried parents — a critical incentive for those at the bottom of the financial scale.

It has made the chronic problem of teenage pregnancy even worse through sex education which projects sexual relations among the young as normal and effectively condones illegal sexual activity among under-age children.

Its professed aim to curb binge-drinking is absurd given the way it has presided over an explosion of drinking which it is now further exacerbating by allowing alcohol to be sold all night.

And its reclassification of cannabis as a less dangerous drug has fuelled a rise in drug-taking of all kinds, resulting in a corresponding eruption of criminal behaviour among users for whom these drugs destroy moral inhibitions against wrong-doing.

What we are experiencing in parts of our country is nothing less than social and moral meltdown. These proposed measures, however tough they might sound, merely amount to an incoherent attempt to deal with the symptoms by a government which is itself a serial offender.

Nihilistic

One also has to be sceptical about whether any of this will actually see the light of day. Last year, the Labour MP Frank Field introduced a Bill to strip antisocial households of welfare benefits. But his Bill was scuppered by John Prescott while Mr Blair stood mutely by.

The new package would require massive resources to fund all the resettlement and the policing involved. Who can be confident that these would be forthcoming? Isn't this just what we have heard so many times before — rhetorical fire-breathing by the Prime Minister while nothing actually gets done?

And if these measures were to be enacted, they would provide no more than a sticking plaster approach unless the Government abandoned its nihilistic approach to family life, drinking and drug-taking.

That said, we are where we are. Even if there were the political will to address the root causes of this disaster, that would take time. For thousands of law-abiding people, there is a social emergency that simply has to be dealt with right now.

As a matter of urgency, we have to end the situation where decent people are being held hostage by hooligans who are indulged by the state. We have to put power back into the hands of the law-abiding.

That means — as these proposals suggest — ending the lunatic practice of rewarding anti-social families. It does mean punishing parents who fail to control their children. It does mean taking away their houses, and it should mean taking away their welfare benefits.

This might seem unfeeling. But how much more unfeeling is it to allow decent people to live in daily terror and misery? Is it not better to withdraw the means by which people are able inflict the terror and misery and to teach them instead how to lead responsible lives?

In ultra-liberal Holland, after all, disruptive families are uprooted from their estate and re-housed in vandal-proof steel containers. Houses and benefits are the privileges of citizenship — and citizenship requires a duty to behave in ways that do not make other people's lives intolerable.

Blighted

Communities should be given back their power. They should be able to go to the police and get a delinquent removed instantly, not after months of judicial procedure.

The onus should be on the miscreant to argue why this should not happen, not on his victims to argue that it is necessary. After all, summary justice is meted out for parking offences; aren't public safety and the relief from intimidation more important?

Of course, this will be ferociously opposed by human rights lawyers and other comfortable folk in our governing class. But they don't have to live in these blighted communities. They merely create them.

After eight years in government, Mr Blair has precious little to show for his ambitious plans to heal the divisions in society. 'Tough on crime, tough on the causes of crime' was the inspired slogan that first brought him to power.

This latest package is his last desperate attempt to avoid the looming judgment of history that his legacy was instead to create large areas of Britain where the life of the law-abiding had turned into the seventh circle of hell.

Yes, tough measures such as these are probably now necessary. But they will have little impact unless Mr Blair reverses the whole direction of his Government, which has ruthlessly encouraged disorderly lifestyles on the grotesque grounds of 'anti-discrimination', 'self-esteem', 'social inclusion' and all the rest of the politically correct group-think of metropolitan trendydom.

As ever, the Prime Minister wills the socially desirable ends — but refuses to acknowledge the difficult means by which he must achieve them.

m.phillips@dailymail.co.uk

Chapter 7

Octoberfest 2006

Take off the veil, says Straw - to immediate anger from Muslims

The Guardian, 6th October 2006

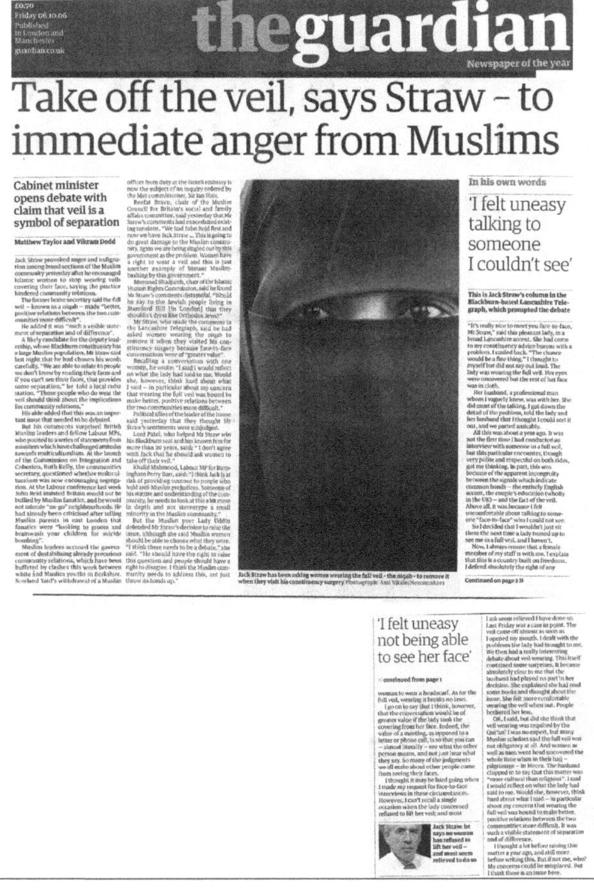

theguardian

Take off the veil, says Straw – to immediate anger from Muslims

Cabinet minister opens debate with claim that veil is a symbol of separation

Matthew Taylor and Vikram Dodd

In his own words

'I felt uneasy talking to someone I couldn't see'

'I felt uneasy not being able to see her face'

Cabinet minister opens debate with claim that veil is a symbol of separation

Jack Straw provoked anger and indignation among broad sections of the Muslim community yesterday after he encouraged Islamic women to stop wearing veils covering their face, saying the practice hindered community relations.

The former home secretary said the full veil - known as a niqab - made "better, positive relations between the two communities more difficult".

He added it was "such a visible statement of separation and of difference".

A likely candidate for the deputy leadership, whose Blackburn constituency has a large Muslim population, Mr Straw said last night that he had chosen his words carefully. "We are able to relate to people we don't know by reading their faces and if you can't see their faces, that provides some separation," he told a local radio station. "Those people who do wear the veil should think about the implications for community relations."

His aide added that this was an important issue that needed to be debated.

But his comments surprised British Muslim leaders and fellow Labour MPs, who pointed to a series of statements from ministers which have challenged attitudes towards multiculturalism. At the launch of the Commission on Integration and Cohesion, Ruth Kelly, the communities secretary, questioned whether multiculturalism was now encouraging segregation. At the Labour conference last week John Reid insisted Britain would not be bullied by Muslim fanatics, and he would not tolerate "no-go" neighbourhoods. He had already been criticised after telling Muslim parents in east London that fanatics were "looking to groom and brainwash your children for suicide bombing".

Muslim leaders accused the government of destabilising already precarious community relations, which have been buffeted by clashes this week between white and Muslim youths in Berkshire. Scotland Yard's withdrawal of a Muslim officer from duty at the Israeli embassy is now the subject of an inquiry ordered by the Met commissioner, Sir Ian Blair.

Reefat Bravu, chair of the Muslim Council for Britain's social and family affairs committee, said yesterday that Mr Straw's comments had exacerbated existing tensions. "We had John Reid first and now we have Jack Straw... This is going to do great damage to the Muslim community, again we are being singled out by this government as the problem. Women have a right to wear a veil and this is just another example of blatant Muslim-bashing by this government."

Mussoud Shadjareh, chair of the Islamic Human Rights Commission, said he found Mr Straw's comments distasteful. "Would he say to the Jewish people living in Stamford Hill [in London] that they shouldn't dress like Orthodox Jews?"

Mr Straw, who made the comments in the Lancashire Telegraph, said he had asked women wearing the niqab to remove it when they visited his Constituency surgery because face-to-face conversations were of "greater value".

Recalling a conversation with one women, he wrote: "I said I would reflect on what the lady had said to me. Would she, however, think hard about what I said — in particular about my concern that wearing the full veil was bound to make better, positive relations between the two communities more difficult."

Political allies of the leader of the house said yesterday that they thought Mr. Straw's sentiments were misjudged.

Lord Patel, who helped Mr Straw win his Blackburn seat and has known him for more than 20 years, said: "I don't agree with Jack that he should ask women to take off their veil."

Khalid Mahmood, Labour MP for Birmingham Perry Barr, said: "I think Jack is at risk of providing succour to people who hold anti-Muslim prejudices. Someone of his stature and understanding of the community, he needs to look at this a bit more in depth and not stereotype a small minority in the Muslim community."

But the Muslim peer Lady Uddin defended Mr Straw's decision to raise the issue, although she said Muslim women should be able to choose what they wore. "I think there needs to be a debate," she said. "He should have the right to raise this question and people should have a right to disagree. I think the Muslim community needs to address this, not just throw its hands up."

In his own words

'I felt uneasy talking to someone I couldn't see'

This is Jack Straw's column in the Blackburn-based Lancashire Telegraph, which prompted the debate

"It's really nice to meet you face-to-face, Mr Straw," said this pleasant lady, in a broad Lancashire accent. She had come to my constituency advice bureau with a problem. I smiled back. "The chance would be a fine thing," I thought to myself but did not say out loud. The lady was wearing the full veil. Her eyes were uncovered but the rest of her face was in cloth.

Her husband, a professional man whom I vaguely knew, was with her. She did most of the talking. I got down the detail of the problem, told the lady and her husband that I thought I could sort it out, and we parted amicably.

All this was about a year ago. It was not the first time I had conducted an interview with someone in a full veil, but this particular encounter, though very polite and respectful on both sides, got me thinking. In part, this was because of the apparent incongruity between the signals which indicate common bonds - the entirely English accent, the couple's education (wholly in the UK) - and the fact of the veil. Above all, it was because I felt uncomfortable about talking to someone "face-to-face" who I could not see.

So I decided that I wouldn't just sit there the next time a lady turned up to see me in a full veil, and I haven't.

Now, I always ensure that a female member of my staff is with me. I explain that this is a country built on freedoms. I defend absolutely the right of any woman to wear a headscarf. As for the full veil, wearing it breaks no laws.

I go on to say that I think, however, that the conversation would be of greater value if the lady took the covering from her face. Indeed, the value of a meeting, as opposed to a letter or phone call, is so that you can - almost literally - see what the other person means, and not just hear what they say. So many of the judgments we all make about other people come from seeing their faces.

I thought it may be hard going when I made my request for face-to-face interviews in these circumstances. However, I can't recall a single occasion when the lady concerned refused to lift her veil; and most I ask seem relieved I have done so. Last Friday was a case in point. The veil came off almost as soon as I opened my mouth. I dealt with the problems the lady had brought to me. We then had a really interesting debate about veil wearing. This itself contained some surprises. It became absolutely clear to me that the husband had played no part in her decision. She explained she had read some books and thought about the issue. She felt more comfortable wearing the veil when out. People bothered her less.

OK, I said, but did she think that veil wearing was required by the Qur'an? I was no expert, but many Muslim scholars said the full veil was not obligatory at all. And women as well as men went head uncovered the whole time when in their hajj — pilgrimage — in Mecca. The husband chipped in to say that this matter was "more cultural than religious". I said I would reflect on what the lady had said to me. Would she, however, think hard about what I said — in particular about my concern that wearing the full veil was bound to make better, positive relations between the two communities more difficult. It was such a visible statement of separation and of difference.

I thought a lot before raising this matter a year ago, and still more before writing this. But if not me, who? My concerns could be misplaced. But I think there is an issue here.

One glance took away my freedom

The Times, 7th October 2006

ANN TRENEMAN
BEHIND THE VEIL

EVERY time that I have worn a veil it has been for a man. The first man was my editor, and so obviously had to be obeyed. It was five years ago and, after seeing all those women in those billowing tents with eye-grills in Afghanistan, he asked me to wear one around Tunbridge Wells. I did feel a bit of a fraud but, other than that, I wasn't disgusted by it all: indeed, in many ways my new identity made me feel safer.

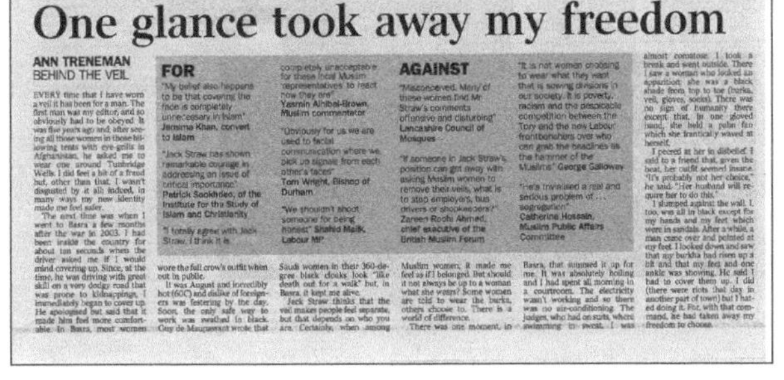

One glance took away my freedom

ANN TRENEMAN
BEHIND THE VEIL

FOR

"My belief also happens to be that covering the face is completely unnecessary in Islam" Jemima Khan, convert to Islam

"Jack Straw has shown remarkable courage in addressing an issue of critical importance" Patrick Sookhdeo, of the Institute for the Study of Islam and Christianity

"I totally agree with Jack Straw. I think it is completely unacceptable for these local Muslim representatives to react how they are" Yasmin Alibhai-Brown, Muslim commentator

"Obviously for us we are used to facial communication where we pick up signals from each other's faces" Tom Wright, Bishop of Durham

"We shouldn't shoot someone for being honest" Shahid Malik, Labour MP

AGAINST

"Misconceived. Many of these women find Mr Straw's comments offensive and disturbing" Lancashire Council of Mosques

"If someone in Jack Straw's position can get away with asking Muslim women to remove their veils, what is to stop employers, bus drivers or shopkeepers?" Zareen Roohi Ahmed, chief executive of the British Muslim Forum

"It is not women choosing to wear what they want that is sowing divisions in our society. It is poverty, racism and the despicable competition between the Tory and the new Labour frontbenchers over who can grab the headlines as the hammer of the Muslims" George Galloway

"He's trivialised a real and serious problem of ... segregation" Catherine Hossain, Muslim Public Affairs Committee

The next time was when I went to Basra a few months after the war in 2003. I had been inside the country for about ten seconds when the driver asked me if I would mind covering up. Since, at the time, he was driving with great skill on a very dodgy road that was prone to kidnappings, I immediately began to cover up. He apologised but said that it made him feel more comfortable. In Basra, most women wore the full crow's outfit when out in public.

It was August and incredibly hot (60C) and dislike of foreigners was festering by the day. Soon, the only safe way to work was swathed in black. Guy de Maupassant wrote that Saudi women in their 360-degree black cloaks look "like death out for a walk" but, in Basra, it kept me alive.

Jack Straw thinks that the veil makes people feel separate, but that depends on who you are. Certainly, when among Muslim women, it made me feel as if I belonged. But should it not always be up to a woman what she wears? Some women are told to wear the burka, others choose to. There is a world of difference. There was one moment, in Basra, that summed it up for me. It was absolutely boiling and I had spent all morning in a courtroom. The electricity wasn't working and so there was no air-conditioning. The judges, who had on suits, were swimming in sweat. I was almost comatose. I took a break and went outside. There I saw a woman who looked an apparition: she was a black shade from top to toe (burka, veil, gloves, socks). There was no sign of humanity there except that, in one gloved hand, she held a palm fan which she frantically waved at herself.

I peered at her in disbelief. I said to a friend that, given the heat, her outfit seemed insane. "It's probably not her choice," he said. "Her husband will require her to do this."

I slumped against the wall. I, too, was all in black except for my hands and my feet, which were in sandals. After a while, a man came over and pointed at my feet. I looked down and saw that my burkha had risen up a bit and that my feet and one ankle was showing. He said I had to cover them up. I did (there were riots that day in another part of town) but I hated doing it. For, with that command, he had taken away my freedom to choose.

I would prefer women not to wear the veil at all, says Straw

The Times, 7th October 2006

By Anthony Browne

Chief Political Correspondent

6 NEWS

THE TIMES SATURDAY OCTOBER 7 2006

I would prefer women not to wear the veil at all, says Straw

Islamic style is a blend of fashion and utility

Anger and headscarves on streets of Blackburn

JACK STRAW increased tensions with sections of Britain's Muslim community over use of the Islamic veil yesterday by declaring his opposition to women wearing them at all.

The Leader of the Commons faced anger from Muslim groups, but won backing from, among others, the Prime Minister, a bishop and a Muslim peer.

Mr Straw, the MP for Blackburn, where one in five of his constituents is Muslim toured broadcasting studios setting out his concerns that the growing use of veils that cover the face was damaging community relations. He had disclosed in a Lancashire newspaper that he had been asking constituents if they would mind removing the niqab covering their faces during meetings, so that he might see their facial expressions. He defended the right of Muslim women to wear a headscarf.

Yesterday, asked by BBC radio if he would in general prefer women not to wear veils, he said: “Yes. I'm not talking about being prescriptive but with all the caveats, yes, I would rather."

He insisted that he was opposed to the veil being banned by law, but said that it was a visible sign of difference that was "bound to make better, positive relations between the two communities more difficult.”

"Communities are bound together partly by informal, chance relations between strangers, people being able to acknowledge each other in the street or being able to pass the time of day," he said. That is made more difficult if "people are wearing a veil. That is just a fact of life."

The Prime Minister's official spokesman said yesterday that opposition to the veil was not government policy, but that Tony Blair "believes it is right that people should be able to have a discussion and express their personal views on issues such as this".

Ahmed Versi, the editor of *Muslim News*, said that it had become "open season to demonise Islam", adding: "Straw's action will exacerbate fragile community relations. It will also send signals to Muslim women to keep away from his surgery, leading to refusal to participate in the democratic process."

On Thursday Massoud Shadjareh, of the Islamic Human Rights Commission, accused, Mr Straw of discrimination.

But some Muslim representatives were more sympathetic, and there was support from other sources. Daud, Abdullah, of the Muslim Council of Britain, said: "This [veil] does cause some discomfort to non-Muslims. One can understand this." The Labour peer Baroness Uddin told *GMTV* yesterday that there was a need for debate, declaring: "It is about human rights on both sides — Jack’s right to say and the women’s right to wear what they please." The Right Rev Richard Chartres, the Bishop of London, said: "I can understand why he has said it."

Hazel Blears, the Labour Party chairwoman, said all sections of the community needed to discuss the Muslim veil and should not shirk the subject because of its sensitivity.

One minister told *The Times:* "Jack is pursuing a really important issue. He is not isolated. We need an honest debate: how much is it reasonable for Muslims to allow the State to adapt to their religion. We can't just say 'yes' to everything."

A telephone poll by the BBC also showed overwhelming public sympathy, with 93 per cent supporting his views.

Mr Straw, who has held Blackburn for Labour since 1979, did not wade into the debate accidentally. He started thinking about the issue about a year ago after a meeting with a constituent wearing a veil, at which he was disconcerted by his inability to see her facial expressions.

He said: "I had observed that, although it is still a tiny minority, more women were wearing the veil and picked up quite considerable concerns about this being a rather visible demonstration of separateness."

He has since been discussing the issue not just with Muslim women, but also with MPs and ministers, and raised it at a conference organised by the Muslim Council of Britain in June. "He is not out on a limb," a colleague said. "People understand it is an issue, and have been generally supportive."

But he was bound to provoke anger for wading into an issue that has become increasingly sensitive among Muslim groups. Islamic countries, namely Turkey and Tunisia, pioneered legal bans on the veil. France bans religious symbols, such as the Islamic veil, from state schools.

A Muslim woman has been left "extremely shocked and upset" after a man shouted racial abuse at her and snatched her veil as she waited at a bus stop, Merseyside Police said. The incident, in Liverpool, is being treated as a "hate crime". The woman, 49, from the Toxteth area, was waiting for a bus yesterday morning when the attack by the man, described as white and in his sixties, occurred.

Anger and headscarves on streets of Blackburn

By Carol Midgley

IT MIGHT just have seemed this way but every Muslim woman in Blackburn appeared to be wearing a veil yesterday. In greengrocers' shops, post offices, launderettes, everywhere you looked black headscarves seemed, quite conspicuously, to be the order of the day.

Could the Muslim women of Blackburn be making a mass two-fingered gesture to Jack Straw, a message of defiance that nobody, especially middle-aged white politicians, were going to tell them how to dress? It was a nice idea but, disappointingly, it proved not to be the case. In this area a great many abide by the Hanafi philosophy, which advocates the wearing of veils.

Many said that they always dressed this way and that Mr Straw was irrelevant. When asked about the rumpus he has caused by asking Muslim women who come to his constituency surgery to remove their veils, some just shook their heads and gestured as if swatting away a pesky fly.

There was little doubt, though, that Mr Straw's remarks, made through his column in a local newspaper, had left a lot of Muslims, male and female, feeling angry. Many would not talk and those that would were reluctant to give their names. One woman called her husband on her mobile telephone to ask whether she should speak to the press. He told her: "No."

At one point, as I stood in the streets of Brookhouse, near Mr Straw's constituency home, interviewing a 23-year-old woman in a burka, a car driven by a Muslim man pulled up. He wound down the window and shouted at my interviewee: "Don't talk to her. Ignore her. She's just being nosey." Happily, because she was articulate on the subject, she took no notice. "I think [Jack Straw] has got a point, but to expect women to take their veil off, I don't think it's fair," she said. "You can't tell people how to dress within their own culture. I have worn [a burka] since I left high school because it is what I am most comfortable with."

One woman phoned her local radio station to say that Mr Straw had once asked her to remove her veil at a meeting and she had refused.

Rukhsana Aslam, 20, was outraged by Mr Straw. "He cannot start asking women to remove their veils and scarves," she said. "I feel sinful for not wearing my veil all of the time in public."

Not all women were affronted by Mr Straw. In a newsagent's shop, Shazhad, 28, and Pravina, 53, (not their real names) both said that they chose not to wear burkas. Pravina said many women did it to please their husbands. "I don't think that's much of a life," she added. Shazhad said she thought it was "bad manners" to wear a burka in a one-to-one situation.

One thing that many seemed agreed on was that Mr Straw had used the issue to get himself on the front pages.

Why Muslim women should thank Straw

The veil is not a religious obligation - it is a symbol of the subjugation by men of their wives and daughters

The Times, 9th October 2006
Saira Khan

THE TIMES MONDAY OCTOBER 9 2006 COMMENT 21

Why Muslim women should thank Straw

The veil is not a religious obligation – it is a symbol of the subjugation by men of their wives and daughters

SAIRA KHAN

It is never right for a woman to shut herself off. And it is particularly wrong in Britain

MY PARENTS moved here from Kashmir in the 1960s. They brought with them their faith and their traditions. But they also arrived with an understanding that they were starting a new life in a country where Islam was not the main religion.

My mother has always worn traditional Kashmiri clothes — the *salwaar kameez*, a long tunic worn over trousers, and the *chador*, which is like a pashmina worn round the neck or over the hair. But no one in my immediate family—here or in Kashmir—covers their face with a *nikab* (veil). As a child I wore the *salwaar kameez* at home — and at school a typical English school uniform. My parents never felt that the uniform compromised my faith; the important thing was that I would fit in so that I could take advantage of all the opportunities school offered. I was the hockey team captain and took part in county athletics: how could I have done all of this wearing *salwaar kameez*, let alone a veil?

My mother has worked all her life and adapted her ways and dress at work. For ten years she operated heavy machinery and could not wear her *chador* because of the risk of it becoming caught in the machinery. Without making any fuss she removed her scarf at work and put it back on when she clocked out. My mother is still very much a traditional Muslim woman, but having lived in this country for 40 years she has learnt to embrace British culture — for example, she jogs in a tracksuit and swims in a normal swimming costume to help to alleviate her arthritis.

Some Muslims would criticise the way my mother and I dress. They believe that there is only one way to practise Islam and express your beliefs, forgetting that the Muslim faith is interpreted in different ways in different places and that there are distinct cultures and styles of dress in Muslim countries stretching from Morocco to Indonesia. But it is not a requirement of the Koran for women to wear the veil.

The growing number of women veiling their faces in Britain is a sign of radicalisation. I was disturbed when, after my first year at university in 1988, I discovered to my surprise that some of my fellow students had turned very religious and had taken to wearing the *jilbab* (a long, flowing gown covering all the body except hands and face), which they had never worn before and which was not the dress code of their mothers. They had joined the college's Islamic Society, which preached that women were not considered proper Muslims unless they adopted such strict dress codes. After that, I never really had anything in common with them.

It is an extreme practice. It is never right for a woman to hide behind a veil and shut herself off from people in the community. But it is particularly wrong in Britain, where it is alien to the mainstream culture for someone to walk around wearing a mask. The veil restricts women, it stops them achieving their full potential in all areas of their life and it stops them communicating. It sends out a clear message: "I do not want to be part of your society." Some Muslim women say that it is their choice to wear it; I don't agree. Why would any woman living in a tolerant country freely choose to wear such a restrictive garment? What these women are really saying is that they adopt the veil because they believe that they should have less freedom than men, and that if they did not wear the veil men would not be accountable for their uncontrollable urges — so women must cover-up so as not to tempt men. What kind of a message does that send to women?

But a lot of women are not free to choose. Girls as young as three or four are wearing the *hijab* to school — that is not a freely made choice. Girls under 16 should certainly not have to wear it to school. And behind the closed doors of some Muslim houses, women are told to wear the *hijab* and the veil. These are the girls that are hidden away, they are not allowed to go to universities, they have little choice in who they marry, in many cases they are kept down by the threat of violence.

So for women such as them it was absolutely right for Jack Straw to raise this issue. Nobody should feel threatened by his comments; after all, the debate about veils has been raging in the Islamic community for many years. To argue that non-Muslims have no right to discuss it merely reinforces the idea that Muslims are not part of a wider society. It also suggests, wrongly, that wearing the veil affects only Muslims. Non-Muslims have to deal with women wearing a veil, so why shouldn't their feelings be taken into consideration? I would find it impossible to deal with any veiled woman because it goes so deeply against my own values and basic human instincts. How can you develop any kind of a social relationship with someone who has shut themselves away from the rest of the world?

And if we can't have a debate about the veil without a vocal minority of Muslims crying "Islamophobia", how will we face other issues, such as domestic violence, forced marriages, sexual abuse and child abuse that are rife in the Muslim community? These are not uniquely Muslim problems but, unlike other communities, they are never openly debated. It is children and women who suffer as a result.

Many moderate Muslim women in Britain will welcome Mr Straw's comments. This is an opportunity for them to say: "I don't wear the veil but I am a Muslim." If I had been forced to wear a veil I would certainly not be writing this article — I would not have the friends I have, I would not have been able to run a marathon or become an aerobics teacher or set up a business.

This is my message to British Muslim women - if you want your daughters to take advantage of all the opportunities that Britain has to offer, do not encourage them to wear the veil. We must unite against the radical Muslim men who would love women to be hidden, unseen and unheard.

I was able to take advantage of what Britain has got to offer and I hope Mr Straw's comments will help more Muslim women to do the same. But my argument with those Muslims who would only be happy in a Talebanised society, who turn their face against integration, is this: "If you don't like living here and don't want to integrate, then what the hell are you doing here? Why don't you just go and live in an Islamic country?"

We don't yet live in an Islamic republic so I will say it - I find the veil offensive

The Independent, 9th October 2006
Yasmin Alibhai-Brown

We don't yet live in an Islamic republic, so I will say it – I find the veil offensive

YASMIN ALIBHAI-BROWN

A girl in a boob tube and a girl in a hijab are both symbols of unhealthy sexual objectification

Jack Straw's politics usually make me either furious or bilious. That fake sincerity, that oily handshake he extends to "ethnic minorities", his immoral support for the war in Iraq, and the unholy fiefdom he runs in Blackburn - the list is long. Suddenly the expedient appeaser has come out against the veil and I find myself agreeing with his every word. It is time to speak out against this objectionable garment and face down the Islamicists.

Straw has been denounced as Islamophobic by these ideologues who have reverted to what they do best, group blackmail. Just as reactionary have been the views of feminist white women who attack Straw for being aggressively prescriptive. As a man, they say, he has no business telling women what to wear. As an MP, I say, he has an obligation to express his concerns to his constituents. We don't yet live in an Islamic republic where men and women are forced to live on separate planets.

Millions of Muslims in Europe abhor these obscurantists for the way in which they have brain-washed young women to seek subjugation. It breaks our hearts. After all, caged creatures often prefer to stay in their cages even after they have been freed. I don't call that a choice.

A liberal nation has no obligation to extend its liberalism to condone the most illiberal practices, as long as it ensures genuine equal standards for all. Much of Europe still treats Muslims as undeserving inferiors, as underdogs. Muslims are victimised, feared, hated and excluded. Our own government has not tackled the racism or the disadvantages. Instead it blames us for failing to stop terrorism. The media lurches drunkenly between pandering to Muslim separatists and maligning us all as the aliens within. It is hard to be a Muslim today. And it becomes harder still when some choose deliberately to act and dress as aliens.

The young women in niqab who claim they have made the decision without coercion understand nothing about the sacred Islamic texts, the struggles for gender equality, the history or the unpleasantly sexual symbolism of what they claim is just one more lifestyle choice. "Oh, I won't have that green coat, think it is the black shroud for me. Suits me better, don't you think?"

Britons who support them are clueless about the silent march of Wahabism. I have been uncomfortable for years about the rapid spread of the hijab, too, because for Islamicist puritans it is the first staging post on a road map that leads to the burqa, where even the eyes are gauzed over. Some young hijab wearers say they feel wanton and must go "higher" to the niqab. So when does this country decide that it does not want citizens using their freedoms to build a satellite Saudi Arabia here?

We can't answer that question, because Islamicists say we are not allowed such national conversations. Straw isn't allowed because he is a white man; Parliament can't because there is no Muslim woman MP in it; I'm not allowed because I am a bad Muslim. Well, stuff that, I say. This, garment offends me, and here are my reasons why.

The sacred texts have no specific injunctions about covering the hair or face. The veil predates Islam and was common among the Assyrian royalty, Byzantine upper-class Christians, and Bedouins - men and women - when sandstorms blasted their faces. Women from the Prophet's family covered themselves, it is said, to prevent harassment from petitioners. The son of Umar, a companion to Prophet Mohamed, asked his wife to veil her face. She replied: "Since the almighty has put upon me the stamp of beauty, it is my wish that the public should view this beauty and recognise this Grace unto them." Nice one, lady, and my views exactly.

In the 10th century, veils were imposed

across the Middle East to diminish the status of women. Female chastity and "honour" became jealously guarded. The customs never spread far. You don't find the niqab in Bangladesh, Pakistan, Indonesia, Malaysia or Thailand. A witness account in Turkey in the 14th century noted that women's faces there were always visible. In 1899, a Muslim writer, Quasim Amin, wrote a treatise, "The Emancipation of Woman", in which he proved that the veil was not an inviolable part of revealed Islam. His ideas incensed conformist Muslim women, who attacked his gender, not his arguments, just as now. He inspired secularists like Ataturk in Turkey and the Shah of Iran who, too dictatorially, forbade the veil.

The Iranian revolution turned that into a cause, and the modern re-covering of women, voluntary and imposed, took off. In Iran, educated women who fail stringent veil tests are imprisoned by their theocratic oppressors. They are branded whores and beaten. It is happening in Iraq, Palestine and Algeria too. In Afghanistan, the Taliban are back pushing girls and women back into the home and full burqa. Instead of expressing solidarity with these females, sanctimonious British niqabis are siding with their foes.

Exiles from these regimes who fled to the West now find the evil has followed them. As Saba, a lawyer from Saudi Arabia, said to me: "The Koran does not ask us to bury ourselves. We must be modest. These fools who are taking niqab will one day suffocate like I did, but they will not be allowed to leave the coffin. They are choosing something they don't even understand."

The sexual signals of the hijab and niqab are even more suspect. These coverings are physical manifestations of the pernicious idea of women as carriers of Original Sin, whose faces or hair turn Muslim men into predators. In Denmark, a mufti said unveiled women asked for rape. As if to order, rape by Muslim men of white women is rising alarmingly. In truth, half-naked women and veiled women are both solely defined by sexuality. One group proffers it, the other withholds it. A young girl in a boob tube and a young girl in a hijab are both symbols of unhealthy sexual objectification. Western culture is wildly sexualised and lacking in restraint, but there are ways to avoid falling into that pit, and the veil is not one of them.

The niqab expunges the female Muslim presence from the landscape and hands the world over to men. It rejects human commonalities and even the membership of society itself. The women can observe their fellow citizens but remain unseen, like CCTV cameras. They dehumanise themselves and us.

There are practical issues too. I have seen appallingly beaten Muslim women forced into the niqab to keep their wounds hidden. Veiled women cannot swim in the sea, smile at their babies in parks, feel the sun on their skin.

Women can wear what they want in their homes and streets, but there are societal dress codes. Public and private institutions should have the right to ask citizens to show their faces to get goods and services. Hoodies and crash-helmet wearers already have to. Why should niqab wearers be exempt?

Niqab nonsense

The Daily Telegraph, 20th October 2006 - Leader column

The cult of victimhood has a new heroine. Aishah Azmi, the classroom assistant who insisted on wearing her *niqab* when in the presence of men (though not, apparently, when she was interviewed by a man for the job) has been awarded £1,100 for “injury to her feelings”.

Kirklees council had had the temerity to tell her to remove the veil when teaching because pupils said they found it hard to understand her. Mercifully, her claims of religious discrimination and harassement were thrown out. Yet that is unlikely to prevent Miss Azmi and her “supporters” proclaiming this as some sort of victory in an undeclared Holy War.

It is nothing of the sort. The wearing of a veil is a political and cultural statement, not a religious one, and the sooner this is more widely recognised, the less likely it will be that we have a repeat of this nonsense.

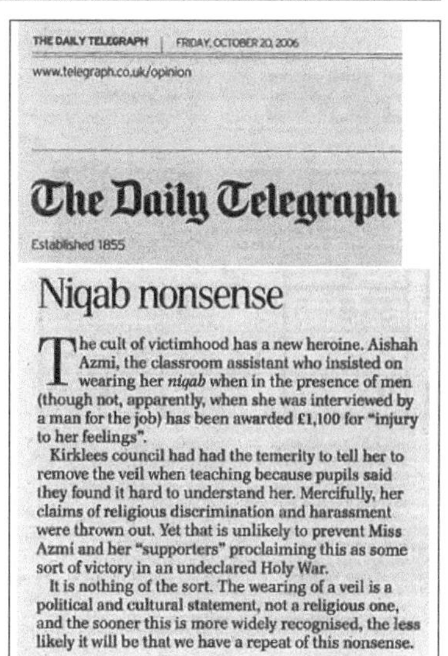

THE DAILY TELEGRAPH | FRIDAY, OCTOBER 20, 2006

www.telegraph.co.uk/opinion

The Daily Telegraph

Established 1855

Niqab nonsense

The cult of victimhood has a new heroine. Aishah Azmi, the classroom assistant who insisted on wearing her *niqab* when in the presence of men (though not, apparently, when she was interviewed by a man for the job) has been awarded £1,100 for "injury to her feelings".

Kirklees council had had the temerity to tell her to remove the veil when teaching because pupils said they found it hard to understand her. Mercifully, her claims of religious discrimination and harassment were thrown out. Yet that is unlikely to prevent Miss Azmi and her "supporters" proclaiming this as some sort of victory in an undeclared Holy War.

It is nothing of the sort. The wearing of a veil is a political and cultural statement, not a religious one, and the sooner this is more widely recognised, the less likely it will be that we have a repeat of this nonsense.

BAN IT!

Daily Express, 21st October 2006

By Paul Broster
and Padraic Flanagan

The veil is outlawed even by some Arab countries so why must we put up with it here?

PRESSURE was mounting last night for veils to be banned in Britain - just as they are in some Muslim countries.

And rebels plotting fresh court protests were given a blunt warning by lawmakers: "Carry on, and we will bar you."

The threat came amid a public outcry over the costs being racked up by teaching assistant Aishah Azmi as her lawyers, funded by taxpayers, continued their fight for her right to wear a veil in class. Daily Express readers responded in massive numbers to a poll on the crisis, with 99 per cent calling for the veil to be banned in schools, increasing pressure on the Government to act.

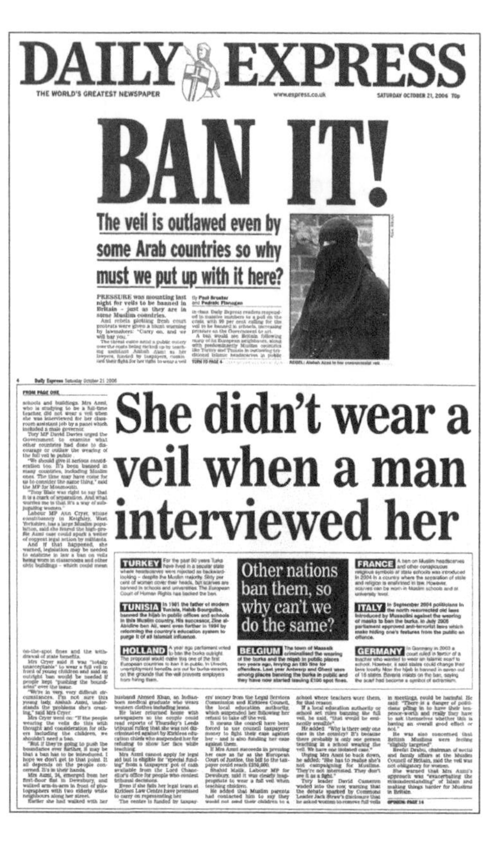

DAILY EXPRESS

THE WORLD'S GREATEST NEWSPAPER www.express.co.uk SATURDAY OCTOBER 21, 2006 70p

BAN IT!

The veil is outlawed even by some Arab countries so why must we put up with it here?

She didn't wear a veil when a man interviewed her

Other nations ban them, so why can't we do the same?

TURKEY For the past 80 years Turks have lived in a secular state where headscarves were rejected as backward-looking - despite the Muslim majority. Sixty per cent of women cover their heads, but scarves are banned in schools and universities. The European Court of Human Rights has backed the ban.

TUNISIA In 1981 the father of modern Tunisia, Habib Bourguiba, banned the hijab in public offices and schools in this Muslim country. His successor, Zine al-Abidine ben Ali, went even further in 1994 by reforming the country's education system to purge it of all Islamist influence.

HOLLAND A year ago parliament voted to ban the burka outright. The proposal would make this one of the first European countries to ban it in public. In Utrecht, unemployment benefits are cut for burka-wearers on the grounds that the veil prevents employers from hiring them.

BELGIUM The town of Maaseik criminalised the wearing of the burka and the niqab in public places two years ago, levying an £85 fine for offenders. Last year Antwerp and Ghent were among places banning the burka in public and they have now started issuing £100 spot fines.

FRANCE A ban on Muslim headscarves and other conspicuous religious symbols at state schools was introduced in 2004 in a country where the separation of state and religion is enshrined in law. However, scarves can be worn in Muslim schools and at university level.

ITALY In September 2004 politicians in the north resurrected old laws introduced by Mussolini against the wearing of masks to ban the burka. In July 2005 parliament approved anti-terrorist laws which make hiding one's features from the public an offence.

GERMANY In Germany in 2003 a court ruled in favour of a teacher who wanted to wear an Islamic scarf to school. However, it said states could change their laws locally. Now the hijab is banned in seven out of 16 states. Bavaria insists on the ban, saying the scarf had become a symbol of extremism.

A ban would see Britain following many of its European neighbours, along with predominantly Muslim countries like Turkey and Tunisia in outlawing traditional Islamic headscarves in public schools and buildings. Mrs Azmi, who is studying to be a full-time teacher, did not wear a veil when she was interviewed for her classroom assistant job by a panel which included a male governor.

Tory MP David Davies urged the Government to examine what other countries had done to discourage or outlaw the wearing of the full veil in public .

"We should give it serious consideration too. It's been banned in many countries, including Muslim ones. The time may have come for us to consider the same thing," said the MP for Monmouth.

"Tony Blair was right to say that it is a mark of separation. And what worries me is that it's a way of subjugating women."

Labour MP Ann Cryer, whose constituency in Keighley, West Yorkshire, has a large Muslim population, said she feared the high-profile Azmi case could spark a welter of copycat legal action by militants.

And if that happened, she warned, legislation may be needed to enshrine in law a ban on veils being worn in classrooms and other civic buildings - which could mean on-the-spot fines and the withdrawal of state benefits.

Mrs Cryer said it was "totally unacceptable" to wear a full veil in front of young children and said an outright ban would be needed if people kept "pushing the boundaries" over the issue.

"We're in very, very difficult circumstances. I'm not sure this young lady, Aishah Asmi, understands the problems she's creating," said Mrs Cryer.

Mrs Cryer went on: "If the people wearing the veils do this with thought and consideration for others including the children, we shouldn't need a ban.

"But if they're going to push the boundaries ever further, it may be that a ban has to be introduced. I hope we don't get to that point. It all depends on the people concerned. It's in their hands.

Mrs Azmi, 24, emerged from her first-floor flat in Dewsbury, and walked arm-in-arm in front of photographers with two elderly white neighbours along her street.

Earlier she had walked with her husband Ahmed Khan, an Indian-born medical graduate who wears western clothes including jeans.

He later returned home with newspapers so the couple could read reports of Thursday's Leeds tribunal ruling that she was not discriminated against by Kirklees education chiefs who suspended her for refusing to show her face while teaching.

Mrs Azmi cannot apply for legal aid but is eligible for "special funding" from a taxpayers pot of cash available from the Lord Chancellor's office for people who contest tribunal decisions.

Even if she fails, her legal team at Kirklees Law Centre have promised to carry on representing her.

The centre is funded by taxpayers' money from the Legal Services Commission and Kirklees Council, the local education authority, which suspended her following her refusal to take off the veil.

It means the council have been forced to use council taxpayers' money to fight their case against her - and is also funding her case against them.

If Mrs Azmi succeeds in pressing her case as far as the European Court of Justice, the bill to the taxpayer could reach £250,000.

Shahid Malik, Labour MP for Dewsbury, said it was clearly inappropriate to wear a full veil when teaching children.

He added that Muslim parents had contacted him to say they would not send their children to a school where teachers wore them, for that reason.

If a local education authority or school set rules banning the full veil, he said, "that would be eminently sensible".

He added: "Why is there only one case in the country? It's because there probably is only one person teaching in a school wearing the veil. We have one isolated case."

Urging Mrs Azmi to back down, he added: "She has to realise she's not campaigning for Muslims. They're not interested. They don't see it as a fight."

Tory leader David Cameron waded into the row, warning that the debate sparked by Commons Leader Jack Straw's disclosure that he asked women to remove full veils in meetings, could be harmful. He said: "There Is a danger of politicians piling in to have their ten-pence-worth and really they have to ask themselves whether this is having an overall good effect or not."

He was also concerned that British Muslims were feeling "slightly targeted."

Reefat Drabu, chairman of social and family affairs at the Muslim Council of Britain, said the veil was not obligatory for women.

She warned that Mrs Azmi's approach was "exacerbating the misunderstanding" of Islam and making things harder for Muslims in Britain.

Other nations ban them, so why can't we do the same?

TURKEY For the past 80 years Turks have lived in a secular state where headscarves were rejected as backward-looking - despite the Muslim majority. Sixty per cent of women cover their heads, but scarves are banned in schools and universities. The European Court of Human Rights has backed the ban.

TUNISIA In 1981 the father of modern Tunisia, Habib Bourguiba, banned the hijab in public offices and schools in this Muslim country. His successor, Zine al-Abidine ben Ali, went even further in 1994 by reforming the country's education system to purge it of all Islamist influence.

HOLLAND A year ago parliament voted to ban the burka outright. The proposal would make this one of the first European countries to ban it in public. In Utrecht unemployment benefits are cut for burka-wearers, on the grounds that the veil prevents employers from hiring them.

BELGUIM The town of Maaseik criminalised the wearing of the burka and the niqab in public places two years ago, levying an £85 fine for offenders. Last year Antwerp and Ghent were among places banning the burka in public and they have now started issuing £100 spot fines.

FRANCE A ban on Muslim headscarves and other conspicuous religious symbols at state schools was introduced in 2004 in a country where the separation of state and religion is enshrined in law. However, scarves can be worn in Muslim schools and at university level.

ITALY In September 2004 politicians in the north resurrected old laws introduced by Mussolini against the wearing of masks to ban the burka. In July 2005 parliament approved anti-terrorist laws which make hiding one's features from the public an offence.

GERMANY In Germany in 2003 a court ruled in favour of a teacher who wanted to wear an Islamic scarf to school. However, it said states could change their laws locally. Now the hijab is banned in seven out of 16 states. Bavaria insists on the ban, saying the scarf had become a symbol of extremism.

In the book *Sarajevo - A Biography* by Robert J. Donia (2006), on the section dealing with the social transformations in Bosnia after the second World War, the following extract from this work (pages 217 to 220) explains the vigorous efforts made by the Muslim establishment to effect the abandonment of the veil, which, with the assistance of government legislation eventually proved successful:

More than any other group, the Muslim women of Sarajevo suffered from traditional barriers to social advancement. Most spent the majority of their time sequestered in their homes, and while in public most wore a veil or a head-to-foot robe (feredža) that included a veil. Their traditional attire was an impediment to employment in many shops and factories. Muslim women had a low literacy rate and endemic health problems, and until 1945 they had not been allowed to vote. The Antifascist Women's Front took aim at each of these problems in the late 1940s....

The Antifascist Women's Front of Bosnia-Herzegovina launched a campaign at its second congress in 1947 to encourage women to abandon the veil. Removing the veil, in the words of the congress's resolution, began a "life without inequality and without enslavement of one person by another, a life in which there shall be no darkness and backwardness." As soon as the resolution was adopted, Šemsa Kadić, a delegate from Travnik, demonstratively removed her veil to the applause of the assembled delegates, and on her urging other Muslim women followed suit. The next three years the organization sponsored rallies and held meetings to encourage other Muslim women to shed their veils. The crusading women approached the effort with infectious revolutionary enthusiasm. Prominent male political leaders were enlisted to endorse the effort. Veils were ceremonially removed at rallies held in neighborhoods and enterprises, particularly in the tobacco and textile factories that employed large numbers of women.

The newly-designated Reis-ul-ulema, Ibrahim Fehić, led a group of progressive, progovernment Islamic leaders in endorsing the anti-veiling campaign. In his inaugural address on September 12, 1947, Fehić praised the achievements of the people's liberation war and denied rumors that the new Yugoslav constitution was at odds with Islamic law. "One valuable legacy of the liberation war of our peoples is the proclamation of women's equality," he proclaimed. "But unfortunately women cannot achieve the full expression of that equality, as they are inhibited by wearing the veil and gown." On November 1, 1947, the Sarajevo-based Supreme Islamic Council of Yugoslavia (Vrhovno islamsko starješinstvo FNRJ) endorsed the Reis's position and assured Muslims that "the veiling of women is not required by religious code. Muslim women, as regards religion, are free to walk about unveiled and tend to their affairs." The council urged Islamic leaders to "spread this message to the broadest levels of our peoples, to approach the topic without spite in a favorable manner without the use of force ... since harmony and brotherhood are most necessary to us." These religious leaders hoped that Muslim women would voluntarily give up wearing their veils and robes, thereby, avoiding government-imposed measures: "If possible, this problem [should] be solved by only Muslims as a purely Islamic matter."

Despite the best efforts of progovernment Islamic leaders, the campaign encountered staunch resistance, especially among women outside of Sarajevo and among Muslim men. Statistics compiled by the women's front showed that 95 percent of Sarajevo's Muslim women had abandoned the veil by late 1950, but fewer than 50 percent had done so in other towns of Bosnia-Herzegovina. Faced with widespread resistance to the unveiling campaign, the Bosnian Assembly resorted to compulsion to end the practice completely. Legislation banning the veil was introduced by Džemal Bijedić, who was later to become Yugoslavia's prime minister and emissary to nonaligned nations. Passed on September 28, 1950, the law declared a ban on wearing the veil, "with the goal of ending the centuries old symbol of inferiority and cultural backwardness of Muslim women." Violators were subject to fines and to prison sentences of up to three months. Veils soon disappeared in Sarajevo, and resistance to unveiling elsewhere in the republic was gradually overcome as well.

The second key to improving the status of women, particularly Muslim women, lay in education....

Because the traditional barriers to women's advancement were stubbornly held, educational parity probably could not have been achieved in the absence of the government's compulsory measures to end the veiling practice.

Chapter 8

Two articles now follow on the subject of the origins of the veiling of Christian women. It will be seen that the reasons for the old Christian practice have nothing to do with the reasons argued by the Muslim supporters of the headscarf in its various guises. In Christianity the veiling of the woman indicated God's decreed order of things: that the woman was under the authority of the man, although this was not meant to imply that woman was inferior to man.

The Christian Veiling

By Leland M. Haines

I. THE SCRIPTURAL BASIS

"Now, I praise you, brethren, that ye remember me in all things, and keep the ordinances, as I delivered them to you" (I Cor. 11:2)

Paul introduces his discussion on the Christian woman's veiling by praising the Corinthian Christians for their faithfulness in observing and practicing the "all things." These past instructions properly occurred when Paul was in Corinth "a year and six months, teaching the word of God among them" (Acts 18:1). In the discussion that follows, he will confirm what he had previously taught them; he is not introducing new doctrine.

Apparently Paul wrote to answer questions about the basis of the veiling. Undoubtedly most of the Corinthian church's sisters followed the correct practice of the veiling because of the opening remarks that they "remembered me in all things." This conclusion is also supported by this conciliatory opening that differs sharply from the next section's opening, where Paul wrote, "Now in this that I declare unto you I praise you not, that ye come together not for the better, but for the worse" (11:17).

Beginning with this conciliatory remark was an effective and proper method to introduce this subject because the Corinthians' faithfulness deserved praise. This set Paul's readers in a mood to learn more about the basis of the veiling.

The Greek word paradosis, translated ordinance in the King James Version and tradition in many new translations, is used in I Corinthians 11:2 and in II Thessalonians 2:15 and 3:6. In each case Paul was referring to oral and written traditions that represent Christian doctrine as well as practical areas of Christian living. These traditions are expressions of God's will; they are inspired by God and are to be kept. Paul wrote in II Thessalonians 2:15: "Hold the traditions which ye have been taught, whether by word, or our epistle." By "traditions" Paul no doubt meant the whole body of teachings -- doctrinal and practical -- he had transmitted to them either verbally, during his missionary visit, or by letter. In the same letter Paul wrote, "Withdraw yourselves from every brother that walketh disorderly, and not after the tradition which ye received of us" (3:6). This shows Paul believed his teachings held high importance. In the Corinthian passage before us, he again stress this importance: "keep the ordinances." What other reasons do we need to keep the ordinances "delivered" to us from Christ through the apostles (I Cor. 11:23)?

The term traditions is used also in Matthew 15:2, 3, 66; Mark 7:3, 5, 8, 9, 13; Galatians 1:14; Colossians 2:8; and I Peter 1:18. There "traditions" are man-made practices and teachings that nullify the Word of God and make it of no effect. They are "not after Christ" (Col. 2:8) and for this reason are condemned. This is not the type of tradition Paul is writing to the Corinthians about.

Concerning the word translated "tradition," H. S. Bender writes:

> The sense of this English word is hardly fair to the Greek for we include a derogatory implication in the concept. A tradition to us is something scarcely reliable, a partly vague mythological affair. But this is not the Greek at all. Paradosis is simply something "given out" or "given over" by one to another for keeping. From the hands of the teacher or preacher it might be either simple facts, narrative or descriptive, or doctrines or usages. Here it is doubtless meant to include the sum total of Paul's instruction. [1]

In summary, the main point we learn from Paul in 11:2 is that the veiling was among the traditions or ordinances he praised the Corinthians for keeping.

"But I would have you know, that the head of every man is Christ; and the head of woman is the man; and the head of Christ is God" (v. 3).

In v. 3 Paul gives the basis of the veiling ordinance. By the opening words, "I would have you know," he indicates he wants us to understand the principle of the divine order and to know God's plan for relationships within His family. The meaning behind this ordinance will be explained to the believers, as were all ordinances.

Before he declares the relationship of woman to man, Paul points to the relation man has to his Head, Christ. Man is not free to do as he pleases; he has a Head. Just as the human body is controlled by its head, man too is controlled by his Head, Christ.

Because Paul first stated that man is subject to a Head, women should not be surprised or feel inferior that "the head of woman is the man." Headship implies a leadership function and does not mean one person is inferior to another. Paul emphasized this twice in other epistles (Eph. 5:21-33; Col. 3:18-25).

The next statement, "the head of Christ is God," helps us understand the meaning of this relationship. The "headship" of man to woman is to reflect the headship of Christ to God. The order between God and Christ makes Christ no less God but shows that headship exists even on the divine level. Between God and Christ, God the Father takes the leadership and initiative roles.

We find an expression of this leadership role in Christ's experience in going to the cross. In Gethsemane Christ "went a little further, and fell on his face, and prayed, saying, O my Father, if it is possible let this cup pass from me: nevertheless not as I will, but as thou wilt" (Mt. 26:39). Christ the Son was submissive to the Father. The relation between man and woman is to be characterized by the woman voluntarily accepting man's leadership, so long as it does not violate the will of Christ. Woman should lovingly accept her place in the divine order and be as complete and joyous with man's headship as Christ is to God's headship. Just as Christ was highly exalted, the Christian woman will too be exated by her acceptance of the divine order.

In the divine order there is a unity in relationship in its gradual subordination: God - Christ - man - woman. The dependence and submission of the lower to the higher is one of lovingly yielding to the divinely appointed headship. This relation and trust, which is built upon love, will be carefully exercised in wisdom. It will also be directed toward the good of the next lower one. Thus the lower person should have no fear that he or she will be treated unfairly.

Peter also spoke of the proper relationship between man and woman. He wrote, "Likewise, ye wives, be in subjection to your own husbands" and "likewise, ye husbands, dwell with them according to knowledge, giving honor unto the wife, as unto the weaker vessel, and as being heirs together of the grace of life; that your prayers be not hindered" (I Pet. 3:1, 7). Thus we see this relationship was not just a Pauline teaching.

"Every man praying or prophesying, having his head covered dishonoureth his head. But every woman that prayeth or prophesieth with her head uncovered dishonoureth her head" (vv. 4-5a).

After explaining the divine order, Paul clearly states what is physically upon a man's or woman's head is important because it reflects the divine order. Men should pray or prophesy (speaking "to exhortation, edification, and comfort," 14:3) with their heads uncovered, and women should have their heads covered (KJV) or veiled (ASV, RSV). To do otherwise shows disregard of the divine order and thus brings dishonor to one's head.

The Greek word translated "covered" is katakalupto. It is a compound word of kata meaning "down" and kalupto meaning "to cover up." This covering that hangs down is perhaps best described by the English word "veil."

When man wears a special covering such as the Jewish Tallith (prayer cap), he is telling others that has abdicated his place in the divine order to accept a lesser position. This brings dishonor to his Head, Christ, because it shows man's disregard for Christ's lordship by not accepting the place and purpose that has been given to man in creation. Since Paul is writing about praying or prophesying, which are spiritual exercises, man should not wear any special type of head covering carrying a spiritual significance.

God has established the veiling as an emblem of servitude. Thus it would be contrary to the divine principle of headship for man to wear one. This meaning of the veiling originates with God and not with society. In many cultures the veiling still has this meaning, even among non-Christians. As Wenger points out, these cultural practices only confirm the divine will and are not the source of the veiling's meaning. [2] Just because God's will and a cultural practice agree, it should not lessen our acceptance that the practice originates in the will of God.

The woman's veiling symbolizes her voluntary acceptance of her place in the divine order. When she "prayeth or prophesieth" with her head unveiled, she brings dishonor to her head, man. This occurs because she is indicating that she has stepped out from under his authority or leadership and is challenging his position in the divine order. Not to wear the veiling implies freedom from submission to man. For a woman to be bareheaded is to tell the world that she stands on equal ground with man in leadership responsibilities.

When a woman is unveiled during prayer or prophesying, she not only dishonors her own head, man, but also Christ. Christ is dishonored by her disobedience to God's headship plan. All who adopt their own plans in preference to the revelation given in the inspired Word bring dishonor to Christ by rejecting His Word and lordship.

Paul uses the same terms “praying and prophesying” to describe both man's and woman's area of activities. Paul does not modify them, for instance, by writing of "praying and prophesying in the church." Wherever these activities occur, man is to be unveiled and woman veiled.

From v. 5 it might seem at first that Paul allows women to pray or prophesy wherever they wish so long as they are properly veiled. But this is not the case; other instructions govern where women may prophesy. Paul wrote in the same letter, "Let your women keep silence in the churches: for it is not permitted unto them to speak; but they are commanded to be under obedience, as also saith the law. And if they will learn anything, let them ask their husbands at home: for it is a shame for women to speak in the church" (I Cor. 14:34-35). In another letter Paul wrote similarly, "Let the women learn in silence with all subjection. But I suffer not a woman to teach, nor to usurp authority over the man, but to be silent" (I Tim. 2:11-12). These two statements show that women are not to prophesy in church meetings. This should help us understand where woman is to wear the veil. It is to be worn wherever these activities occur, not just in church meetings. Of course, the Christian woman would naturally be veiled in church meetings, even though she would not prophesy there, since she could silently pray there.

In summary, both men and women are to live within the divine order God has established. This is not degrading to either but uplifting, since it is the will of God. Both will experience joy by living within God's plan, and many problems will be prevented in the home and society. And man and woman will bear witness to their desire to live within the divine order and under the lordship of Christ as they faithfully observe this ordinance.

"For that is even all one as if she were shaven. For if the woman be not covered, let her also be shorn: but if it be a shame for a woman to be shorn or shaven, let her be covered" (vv. 5b-6).

Paul had just written, "But every woman that prayeth or prophesieth with her head uncovered dishonoureth her head." Next he said that if she rejects God's established veiling standard, she might just as well go the whole way and lose all her dignity through shaving her head, which would bring shame upon herself.

A woman has dignity when she accepts her place in God's established order. To pray or prophesy bareheaded causes her to lose this dignity and brings shame upon her. Bender stated: "Put to shame really means to disgrace - deprive of proper dignity and honor." [3] The shame she would bring upon herself is the same as if her head were "shaven." In other words, to be unveiled is as shameful an act as if she would cut off her hair and cleanly shave her head. What woman would not be ashamed of herself if she cut off her hair and shaved her head? Since no woman would want to appear with a shaven head, Paul says that she should be covered with a veiling.

Lenski writes:

Paul presents two alternatives regarding women to the Corinthians: either shorn or covered. Or, to carry it to its climax in both directions: either both covering and hair completely removed or a covering over the hair. The key to these alternatives is the conditional clause: "now if it is a shame for a women to have herself shorn or shaven." This condition of reality, which implies that it would certainly be a shame, expresses a universal feeling and conviction regarding women (with a corresponding conviction regarding men, v. 14). We may express it in this way: It is the intent of nature that women should wear long hair. Back of nature is the Creator. A beautiful head of hair is the natural crown which God has given to a woman. Made for man, she is to be attractive to him, and one of her great attractions is her beautiful hair. Hence to discard it is shameful for her. . . . This matter of being merely uncovered is in reality only an inconsistency. She stops halfway. She only compromises. Halfway positions and compromises are untenable. Hence, let her carry out the idea of its legitimate and logical conclusion: "let her also have herself shorn" . . . it cannot be denied that leaving the head uncovered is a grave step in the wrong direction, the outrageous nature of which appears fully when it is carried to its consistent limit by discarding also the hair, having it shorn, or by going to the absolute limit in the wrong direction, having all of it shaved off with a razor - then let the women do the complete and consistent thing in the right direction: "let her have herself covered." Then there will be no question in regard to shame or honor in regard to her position as a woman having a man as her head according to the Creator's design. [4]

"For a man indeed ought not to cover his head, forasmuch as he is the image and glory of God; but the woman is the glory of the man. For the man is not of the woman: but the woman of the man. Neither was the man created for the woman; but the woman for the man" (vv. 7-9).

Having established the principle of divine order, and having stated the importance of the veiling in both man's and woman's lives, Paul next gives several statements that support what he has just written. He could have let the matter stand on his apostolic authority alone, but through the guidance of the Holy Spirit he went on to further explain its basis.

The first of these statements points back to Creation. A man indeed ought not to cover his head since he heads the human race and has been created in the image and the glory of God. The Creation account tells us, "God said, Let us make man in our own image, after our likeness: and let them have dominion . . . over all the earth" (Gen. 1:26). Man was created first, and woman was created as a helpmate for him (2:18-23). Man's being in the "image of God," among other things, means he is to master and subdue the earth. He is the controlling one, but he is not left alone in his task; he has a helpmate, woman.

Thus man might be considered God's vice regent in this world, the one who is to govern God's kingdom in His absence. In this he exhibits the image and glory of the Creator. As part of this, man was given certain spiritual responsibilities, spoken of here as praying and prophesying. When these are exercised, man should clearly show his headship over the creation. Therefore he should exercise these responsibilities without any sign of subjection such as a prayer cap or veiling.

The woman, however, was fashioned to be man's helper. She is the glory of man inasmuch as she makes his exalted position in creation manifest. When she accepts his leadership, she acknowledges his rightful place in the divine order. When Paul wrote of "the glory of man," he was speaking principally of man's headship position. Paul was not speaking about a spiritual relation; therefore, he did not use the term image. "Image" would have been unsuitable because it could give the impression that the divine image is not present in woman.

"For this cause ought the woman to have power on her head because of the angels" (v. 10).

This is one of the difficult verses in the New Testament, and there has been much comment about it. The first part of the verse is clear. "For this cause" refers back to the preceding facts surrounding the creation of man and woman. Because of the creation events, the woman should have "power" on her head. It is generally agreed that the word "power" when interpreted in the context of these verses can only mean the veiling of the head. The term translated "power" in the King James Version would perhaps be better rendered "authority." The veiling becomes a symbol of this authority, i.e., "a symbol of authority" (NASB), "sign of authority" (NIV). This translation avoids any connection with the idea that the veiling conveys some magical power on the user.

The difficult part of this verse is the ending phrase, which gives another reason for the veil "because of the angels." There have been many suggestions as to what Paul meant here. To understand its meaning let us first look at these created beings, the angels. From the psalmist we learn that angels are special servants of God: "Bless the Lord, ye his angels, that excel in strength, that do his pleasure" (Ps. 103:20-21). They are special ministers of the Lord and carry out His will. They were created in a slightly higher position than man: "What is man, that thou art mindful of him? . . . Thou madest him a little lower than the angels" (Heb. 2:6-7; cf. v. 9).

The psalmist explains one of the angel's ministries: "For he shall give his angels charge over thee, to keep thee in all thy ways. They shall bear thee up in their hands, lest thou dash thy foot against a stone" (Ps. 91:11-12). This function is emphasized by the author of Hebrews; when speaking of angels he writes, "Are they not all ministering spirits, sent forth to minister for them who shall be heirs of salvation?" (Heb. 1:14). Part of this ministry involves being "guardians" over man (Mt. 18:10; Ac. 12:15), which makes them well aware of man's activities (I Cor. 4:9; I Tim. 5:21).

Understanding angels' ministries and their relation to believers, "because of angels" must imply that they are aware of a woman's attitude and whether she is in the proper order when praying and prophesying. Apparently she should not offend them by getting out of God's ordained order. Bender wrote, "From the context we are forced to the conclusion that Paul conceived of the angels as concerned in keeping the divine order of society intact and hence would be directly affected and concerned when a woman violated the order by appearing bareheaded. Let the women remember this when they contemplate such bold steps." [5]

As Shetler points out, the full significance of this phrase may not be understood by us, but it must be important for the Christian woman to wear the veiling because the angels are involved. [6]

"Nevertheless neither is the man without the woman, neither the woman without the man, in the Lord. For as the woman is of the man, even so is the man also by the woman; but all things of God" (vv. 11-12).

The preceding verses emphasize that the divine order calls for man to exercise a position of leadership and woman is to follow his leadership. Paul next cautions man that he should not interpret these principles in such a way that would mean the depreciation of woman. He opposes this on the grounds that both are dependent on each other in their spiritual lives as they are in their physical lives.

The relationship of man to woman is one of mutual dependence; they complement each other in their headship relationship. This means they exist together and neither one can stand alone. "In the Lord" can be understood more clearly if one looks at what Paul wrote about it elsewhere: "There is neither male or female: for ye are all one in Christ Jesus" (Gal. 3:28). There is no distinction when it comes to salvation and living the Christian life. Both have high value and are "one in Christ Jesus." The headship Paul discusses is about a difference in function of the two and not one of value. There is no superiority or inferiority of those in Christ. Although man and woman have distinctive and different responsibilities in the area of leadership, this must not become a competitive relationship. Rather, their relationship should be a complementary one.

Neither man nor woman can argue from nature her or his independence or try to lower the value of the other. The mere headship role of man or physical motherhood of woman should not become grounds for strife between the two. The origin of the woman and the fact that man is born of woman show that neither is independent of the other. When either begins to think too much of his importance, he should consider that "all things [are] of God." Both originate from God and whatever they are is not of themselves but because of their Creator's will and design.

If one keeps in mind Paul's meaning of headship, that it involves a functional difference and not a difference of value, there should be no danger that this teaching on divine order will be abused.

"Judge in yourselves; is it comely that a woman pray unto God uncovered? Doth not even nature itself teach you, that, if a man have long hair, it is a shame unto him? But if a woman have long hair, it is a glory to her; for her hair is given her for a covering" (vv. 13-15).

Paul next appeals to his readers' own common sense to show that it is proper that a woman pray veiled. Does not God teach through His creation that a woman's head should be covered?

Nature teaches us that it is proper for woman to have long hair and man to have short hair. Man's hair rarely grows with such beauty as woman's, indicating there is a difference between the two concerning the covering of their heads. If woman by nature has such long hair, it would be "womanish" for a man to have long hair, and thus shameful for him to have it. Long hair is womanly since it is a natural constitution of her sex.

Woman conforms to her nature when she keeps her hair long. Long hair is a natural symbol of her position in the divine order and one of the most beautiful assets she has: "It is a glory to her." When women cut their hair to be fashionable, they lose this natural, beautiful symbol. They act contrary to feminine nature as given by God.

Many have tried to lessen the force of this teaching by asking, "What is meant by long hair?" The answer to this question should be simple for the Christian woman. If she has a question about how long is long, she should let the Father determine the length of her hair. When He determines the length we can surely say she has long hair.

John, in his gospel, writes about Mary anointing Jesus' feet and wiping them with her long hair (John 12:3). This gives us a glimpse of the hair length of one of Jesus' disciples. It was long enough to wipe Jesus' feet.

Miller wrote:

When God says long hair is a glory to a woman and shorn hair is a shame for her, why should any heart that loves Him seek to get as far away as possible from that which He calls a glory and try to get as close as possible to that which He calls a shame? When God calls a thing a shame, then we had better continue to do so also, even though our current sub-Christian society may drift far from His standard of what is shameful or glorious. [7]

The Christian woman should arrange her long hair in such a way that is consistent with her veiling and not display her feminine glory before men to attract them. Paul uses the word glory, not to infer that the Christian woman's hair should be shown off, but in the sense that it is a special part of her feminine endowment. The Christian woman also should not forget other scriptural teachings that her adornment should be an inner beauty, not one of outward show "with broided hair" or "outward adorning of plaiting the hair" (I Tim. 2:8-9; I Pet. 3:3-5). These Scriptures show that fancy hair arrangements have no place in the Christian's life.

Paul writes about the woman's long hair that "her hair is given for a covering." It is a natural covering indicating that she should be veiled. Some persons have suggested that the hair is given her to be "the covering," the only one required. It is true that her long hair is a natural covering, but she is to add a second covering, the veil. Paul is using her long hair as an illustration to support the idea that a veiling is needed. This can be seen when one examines the Greek words translated "covering." Paul uses two different words. The word translated "covering" in v. 15 is peribolaion, which is different than katakalupto used in vv. 4, 5, 6, and 7. This suggests there is a difference in the hair covering and the veiling. Peribolaion indicates "something thrown around one, i.e., a mantle, veil, covering, vesture." [8] This suggests how the hair, the natural covering, should be worn.

Common sense reasoning indicates that the hair is not the veiling Paul wrote about earlier. Verse 6 reads, "If a woman be not covered, let her also be shorn." If her hair is the covering, and she be not covered, she would have her hair removed and it would make no sense to talk about letting her be shorn. To be shorn would involve cutting the hair off a second time!

That the hair is not the covering (veiling) can be seen in v. 4, where Paul wrote about man having his head covered. Having it covered while praying or prophesying would involve putting on hair during those times and removing it at other times. This hardly makes sense if the hair is the covering. Who would advocate that man is to take his hair off during prayer or while prophesying? Paul is not teaching that men should be bald.

"But if any man seems to be contentious, we have no such custom, neither the churches of God" (v. 16).

Paul closes his discussion on the divine order and the veiling by rebuking anyone who wishes to become contentious over the necessity of man's head being uncovered and woman's head being veiled. Those who remain deaf to the reasons given will have to be silenced by Paul's authority and general church practice: "We have no such custom, neither the church of God." All followed the practices Paul wrote of in this chapter. It was not just a local church practice at Corinth. It was a universal practice in the Church.

Men still universally pray and prophesy with uncovered heads in the churches. The teaching that woman should be veiled was also universally practiced until the twentieth century. This practice has a biblical basis and should be followed today by all Christian women.

II. A TEACHING FOR TODAY

At the beginning of I Corinthians, Paul appealed to the Corinthian Church in these words: "By the name of our Lord Jesus Christ, that ye all speak the same thing, and that there be no divisions among you; but that ye be perfectly joined together in the same mind and in the same judgment" (1:10). He wanted the Corinthians to agree and have no dissension; they all were to understand the truth and stand united behind it. It was reported to him that there was quarreling among them, but apparently this did not involve the teaching on the headship veiling, for he commended them "that ye remembered me in all things, and keep the ordinances, as I delivered them to you" (11:2). Paul's desire for unity was not just for the local church: he wanted unity throughout the Church. This unity existed in the Church on the veiling teaching. We know this from his comments at the end of his discussion. He disposed of those who wanted to be contentious about the veiling by appealing to the Church's united position on this teaching (I Cor. 11:6).

Today the situation is different. Even though the Protestant Church until the late 1800s and the Roman Catholic Church in general held to some aspects of this teaching until the 1970s, only a few churches remain faithful to this teaching today. Why has this change taken place? What reasons are given for rejecting a teaching so long held by the Church?

The reasons generally given against practicing the headship veiling teaching are that (1) it was a local and temporary practice, (2) it is a trivial matter, and (3) the hair is the covering.

The first reason is the one most frequently given. Erdman writes, "All will agree that most of the instruction which Paul gives concerns a custom of dress which was merely local and temporary." [9] This assertion is unacceptable for the following reasons:

1. Paul specifically stated in v. 16 that he and "the churches of God" observed these practices. This was not just a local dress custom, as Erdman states. It was taught throughout the Church. This conclusion is not based only on v. 16, but on other statements made in the letter. It is shown in Paul's statement to the Corinthians about why he sent Timothy to them. He sent him to "bring you into remembrance of my ways which be in Christ, as I teach every where in every church" (4:17). It is shown in his writing on marriage when he wrote, "So ordain I in all churches" (7:17). What Paul taught the Corinthian believers was taught in all the churches.

Church history also shows that this teaching was widely practiced. Clement (153-217) of Alexandria and Tertullian (145-220) of northern Africa spoke of the veiling. Clement included teaching on the subject in his book Instruction. This guide taught on the meaning of the Christian life. Tertullian mentioned the veiling in several of his writings and wrote a thesis entitled "On the Veiling of Virgins," which dealt with the question of the veil applying to unmarried sisters. This issue arose because Paul used the Greek term gynee for the term women. Some questioned if gynee included the unmarried, but they did not question the veiling in general. Today we accept gynee as meaning "any adult female [virgins are included]." [10] We have, therefore, very early evidence that Paul's teaching was followed not only in Corinth. The headship veiling was not just a local, temporary practice; it was universally practiced in the early Church. The writings of these early Church fathers also indicate their practice was different from that of the non-Christian society.

2. The bases for Paul's teachings are as binding today as they were two-thousand years ago. The relation within the divine order has not changed: it is still a disgrace for a woman to be shaven, the history of creation remains the same, the function of angels remains the same, and nature still shows that woman's long hair is a glorious aspect of her femininity. Since the bases of Paul's teaching all remain in effect today, why shouldn't Paul's conclusion that woman is to be veiled still be binding?

3. If the Corinthian women's hair and veiling was only a local and temporary issue, Paul used a completely different style of writing in this passage than he used elsewhere. When he taught that one's actions should be modified because of cultural considerations, he always explained these considerations. Examine, for instance, his teachings about meat and idols found in Romans 14 and in I Corinthians 8 and 10:14ff. He clearly taught what the Christian point of view was, and when and why cultural considerations should cause one to do otherwise.

4. Paul made no mention of the view of Corinthian society regarding prostitutes and the veiling in this passage. There is no evidence that their views influenced his writing. Lenski confirms this:

> As far as prostitutes are concerned, all the evidence that has been discovered proves that only a few of the very lowest types had shorn or shaven heads. As a class these women endeavored to make themselves as attractive as possible and did their utmost to beautify their hair. We cannot, therefore, accept the idea that is advanced by not a few of the best commentators that in our passage Paul refers to the practice of the prostitutes and intends to tell the Corinthian women that, if they pray or prophesy with uncovered heads, they act the part of a lewd woman. [11]

As Shetler has pointed out, one would have expected Paul to make the following type of statement if the Corinthian culture was influencing this teaching: "For the present time I would have you women to be veiled and you men remain unveiled, so that your new-found freedom in Christ be not misunderstood. I do not want you brethren at Corinth to disregard your Corinthian husband-wife mores, so that through this the outside public will stumble at what they consider impropriety." [12]

5. Christ permanently established several ordinances in His Church. They are baptism, communion, feet washing, the woman's veiling, the holy kiss, anointing with oil, and marriage. Although these ordinances may have some things in common with Jewish or other cultural practices, Christ made them symbols of specific Christian truths. They are intended to symbolize these truths and keep them alive among God's people. They are new instructions and represent God's will for the Church.

6. The teaching on communion found in 1 Corinthians 11:17-34 is almost universally observed in the Church. On what grounds is this teaching accepted and the teaching on the veiling, found in the first part of the same chapter, rejected? Who gives one authority to reject any part of God's Word? True Christians will accept the whole Bible as the revelation of God.

7. We can see the importance Paul placed on this teaching when we examine his view on the preaching of the gospel. When he explained why he baptized only a few at Corinth, he said that he did so because some might think he baptized in his own name (I Cor. 1:15). He did not want this to happen because, as he wrote, "Christ sent me not to baptize, but to preach the gospel" (v. 17). He would not have brought the veiling teaching to this church if it was not an important part of the gospel. His concern that the gospel be preached with clarity was too great to risk confusing the gospel with the veiling teaching if it

was not an important part of it.

In summary, we have strong evidence that the veiling was not just a local and temporary practice but a permanent one, to be followed in all churches throughout time.

The second argument against the practice of this teaching is that veiling is a trivial matter since only Paul wrote about it in one letter. This must be rejected because of the following reasons:

1. Paul's teaching in I Corinthians 11 is a part of God's Word. The Holy Spirit guided the New Testament writers: "All scripture is given by inspiration of God, and is profitable for doctrine, for reproof, for correction, for instruction in righteousness" (II Tim. 3:16). From this we can conclude that this portion of Scripture is profitable for all believers today.

Paul was an apostle of Jesus Christ. He was called by Christ to teach His will. Christ said, "[Paul] is a chosen vessel unto me; to bear my name before the Gentiles, and kings, and the children of Israel" (Ac. 9:15). Paul had authority to write for Christ, which is acknowledged in I Corinthians: "The things I write unto you are the commandments of the Lord" (14:37).

2. It should not be necessary for God to tell His children more than once what His will is. A born-again person will listen the first time; he does not need to be told again and again. He will act in simple obedience because he has repented and has been born again to become a disciple of Christ. The disciple will not try to get around God's Word by proposing confusing interpretations or by asking questions that need answering before a passage can be accepted. How many times must a Christian be told before he will act? Once should be enough.

Why can't this teaching be accepted when taught only once in the Scripture? Most Christians are willing to accept the commandment to baptize in the name of the Father, Son, and Holy Spirit when told only once. Why can't we accept this one?

3. God's commands are never trivial. They each represent a challenge to one's faith. When one disobeys, this shows lack of obedient faith.

4. The reason the headship veiling teaching is found only in I Corinthians is that the Holy Spirit guided only Paul to give an answer for a clearer understanding of this practice. We know, as mentioned above, it was taught and practiced in all the churches (I Cor. 4:17; 7:17; 11:16).

5. The veiling speaks to a very important issue: the relation of men and women. Many problems in the family and society are caused by the divine headship order being ignored. God established the veiling to keep alive the proper order between man and woman. If this teaching was followed, God's order for men and women in the Church would not be ignored. This is not a trivial teaching but an important, serious one.

The third reason given by some for the Christian woman not to be veiled is that her hair is given as the covering, and no additional veiling is required. This objection has already been answered in Part II of this study, but it will be reemphasized here.

1. Paul uses two different terms for the word translated "covering" in the King James Version. In v. 15 where it is connected with the hair, he uses peribolaion. In vv. 4, 5, 6, and 7 it is katakalupto. This shows there is a difference between the hair covering and the veiling.

2. Plain reasoning tells us the hair is not the covering Paul wrote of vv. 4, 5, 6, and 7. Verse 6 reads, "If a woman be not covered, let her also be shorn." If her hair is the covering and she be not covered, she would already have her hair removed. It would make no sense to write about letting her be shorn. This would involve removing the hair twice!

3. In v. 4 Paul writes about man having his head covered. If the hair was the covering, this would involve taking off the hair during prayer or prophesying and putting it back on at other times. This is an absurdity!

Common sense shows that the hair is not the covering or veiling Paul is writing about to the Corinthians; he is writing about the veiling.

The veiling is an important Bible teaching that should be accepted in the Church today as an ordinance. We have seen that Scripture clearly teaches its practice. And it has the earmarks of an ordinance. The generally accepted earmarks of an ordinance are (1) there are definite words of institution, (2) it was given by divine authority by an apostle chosen by Jesus Christ, and (3) it requires a literal act to be practiced that has a spiritual significance. The teaching on the Christian woman's veiling possesses all of these.

Paul's concern for unity in the Church involved the veiling teaching. Christians today should heed his appeal to "speak the same thing, and that there be no divisions among you" (I Corinthians 1:10). Let us pray that all Christians will come to a greater knowledge of God's plan to keep the divine headship principle alive in the Church through a faithful observance of this ordinance.

III. ITS PRACTICE

We have seen that God has established that men are to pray and prophesy with their heads uncovered and women are to be veiled when praying and prophesying. In Part II of this study it was shown that this teaching is for the Church today. The questions now to be discussed are "How is this teaching to be applied?" and "When and where is it to be practiced?"

The Scriptural Form

First, in applying this Scripture, one must realize that the veiling is a symbol of a biblical, spiritual truth. Therefore, one should expect its physical makeup to convey a spiritual meaning. Many have suggested that an ordinary hat is an adequate "covering." But this cannot be accepted since ordinary hats are not intended to be symbols of Christian truths and thus do not convey the spiritual principles of divine order taught in this passage.

When other New Testament ordinances are considered, one can see that a special form of the covering is required, one that is worn only to fulfill the requirements of this passage. Just as baptism is not simply getting wet with water or communion is not just eating bread or drinking, so the covering is not just a physical covering. When one does a physical activity that is the same as that done in observing an ordinance, he is not necessarily observing the ordinance. The activity must be done specifically to show the ordinance's spiritual truths. Thus the "covering" must be something that is worn only for the purpose of being a symbol of woman's subordination to man. It must be designated for the purpose of showing the divine order. A protective covering or a stylish hat do not meet this requirement.

It is appropriate that the form of the veiling be defined by the church. As with the other Christian ordinances and teachings, the exact form of the veiling is not given in the Bible. But the Church can find some general guidelines on the form of the veiling in Paul's teaching on it. In vv. 4 and 5 Paul uses the Greek term katakalupto. This word, as stated earlier in this study, is a compound one, composed of kata, meaning "down," and of kalalupto, meaning "to cover up." This "hanging down" covering is perhaps best described in English by the word "veiling." From this one would expect the veiling to adequately cover the head.

The term veiling has been used throughout this study. It is a better term than the term covering. Its use helps to avoid the confusion in some minds that the hair or a hat will serve the purpose in this passage. It also has more of a symbolic religious connotation.

We can also get indications on the form of the veiling from Paul's statement that the "hair is given as a covering" (I Cor. 11:15). The natural hair covering is used to show the need for a veiling. These two forms of the "covering," the one natural and the other artificial, should cover the same area. The Greek term peribolaion, translated covering in v. 15, indicates that the hair is "something thrown around one, i. e., a mantle, veil, covering." This suggests the hair should be put on the head. If the veiling is to cover the same area, the Church should specify a veiling form that adequately covers the woman's hair and head.

The form of the veiling has been defined differently by different churches in different parts of the world. Historically there have been two general forms of the veiling, a long veil that hangs down over the shoulders [13] and a close fitting "cap" type.

The Amish, Brethren in Christ, Church of

the Brethren, and Mennonites have historically had a thin white veiling that fitted closely to the head. I believe this is adequate. As Wenger wrote, "The American Mennonite Church sees no other satisfactory alternative than to retain the chaste and simple European veil as the most suitable application of the New Testament command for women to be veiled." [14] This veiling form has value because it has been the recognized veiling. But the change it has undergone in the last one hundred years needs to be reversed if it is to come closer to the biblical and early Church style. This change would require it to become larger, having very wide covering "strings" that hang down over the shoulders - in short, becoming a veiling.

I would think Christian women in these churches should want to accept this historical veiling. They should not make changes to forms that may be closer to their own liking, which in the end make their veiling symbols of disorder in the Church and of individuality instead of divine order. They should accept the Church's historical standard and not become contentious or rebellious over the details of the veiling form. We live in an age where everything is questioned, and each one does his own thing. But this is not the way Christians should act. They should "do all things without murmurings and disputing: that ye may be blameless and harmless, the sons of God, without rebuke, in the midst of a crooked and perverse nation, among whom ye shine as lights in the world" (Phil. 2:14).

The Scripture Times

The second area we would like to address concerns when and where the veiling is to be worn. Paul wrote that the woman should be veiled when she prays or prophesies (I Cor. 11:4, 5, 13). From this some conclude that the veiling should be worn only in the church worship services. But the wearing of the veiling should not be limited to church worship services.

As Lenski wrote,

It is quite essential to note no modifier is attached to the participles to denote a place where these activities were exercised. So we on our part should not introduce one, either the same one for both the man and the woman, for instance, "worshiping and prophesying in church," or different ones, for the man "in the church" and for the woman "at home." But omitting reference to a place, Paul says this: "Wherever and whenever it is proper and right for a man or for a woman to pray or to prophesy, the difference of sex should be marked as I indicate." [15]

The woman, as the man, is to be always in a prayerful spirit. Jesus taught that "man ought always to pray, and not faint" (Luke 18:1). This is emphasized in the epistles: "Pray without ceasing" (I Thess. 5:17) and "continuing instant in prayer" (Rom. 12:12). Prayer is to be a frequent activity and not one limited to church services. The veiling is not a "church veiling" but should be worn whenever the woman prays. The fact that this is to be a frequent activity suggests a continuous wearing of the veiling; otherwise, she would be constantly putting it on and taking it off.

Furthermore, doesn't the Christian woman prophesy more in her home and in other areas of everyday life than in public worship? According to the Scriptures, "the women [should] keep silence in the churches: for it is not permitted unto them to speak" (I Cor. 14:34), and "let the woman learn in silence with all subjection. But I suffer not a woman to teach, nor to usurp authority over the man, but to be silent" (I Tim. 2:11-12). The Christian woman should not prophesy in a public worship service.

We must not think, however, of prophesying as an event that occurs only in public worship services. In defining the term, Paul wrote, "He that prophesieth speaketh unto men to edification, and exhortation and comfort" (I Cor. 14:3). There is nothing in this definition that would limit it to public worship services.

Lenski's writings help clarify when and where this prophesying is to occur.

An issue has been made of the point that Paul speaks of a woman as prophesying as though it were a matter of course that she should prophesy just as she also prays, and just as the man, too, prays just as she also prays and prophesies. Paul is said to contradict himself when he forbids woman to prophesy in 14:34-36. The matter becomes clear when we observe that from 11:17 onward until the end of chapter 14 Paul deals with the gatherings of the congregation for public assemblies. The transition is clearly marked: "when ye come together," i.e., for public worship, v. 20. In these public assemblies Paul forbids the woman, not only to prophesy, but to speak at all (14:14-36) and assigns the reason for this prohibition just as he does in I Timothy 2:11, etc.

It is evident, then, that women, too, were granted the gift of prophecy even as some still have this gift, namely, the ability to present and to properly apply the Word of God by teaching others. And they are to exercise this valuable gift in the ample opportunities that offer themselves. So Paul writes, "praying and prophesying with reference to the women just as he does with reference to the men. The public assemblies of the congregation are, however, not among these opportunities - note . . .in the assemblies," 14:34. At other places and at other times women are free to exercise their gift of prophecy . . . The teaching ability of Christian women today has a wide range of opportunity without in least the introducing itself into public congregational assemblies. [16]

The veiling is a symbol that constantly reminds the woman of the importance of God's order. Although Paul speaks only of wearing the veiling during times of praying and prophesying, it cannot be concluded that these are the only times to wear it. It is not to be quickly put on when these activities occur and then quickly removed when they are over. The Christian woman should be willing to give her witness that she is aware of her place in God's order, not only during the public worship services, but at all times. That witness is clearly needed in our society today.

The principles of this passage are not drawn out of a public worship context but rather out of a creation context. Woman's naturally long hair was given in creation as a witness too. Since they complement each other, it will appear they should be worn at the same time. Since the natural hair covering is worn continuously, the veiling should also be.

A Consistent Witness

The headship veiling and long hair are inseparable. For Christian women to wear a veiling on top of cut hair is inconsistent. Both speak to the same principle of divine order and cannot be separated. One can hardly bear a positive witness to the principle of divine order by wearing a veiling and at the same time by having short hair, which witnesses against it.

Another area of concern is the wearing of hats. It would be inconsistent for a woman to wear a veiling patterned according to God's will and a fashionable hat that is patterned by a sinful society along non-Christian standards. Christian women should wear headgear that follows Christian principles and that can be consistently worn with the veiling.

A Christian woman who wears a veiling should also be consistent in the area of dress. The veiling should be worn along with simple and modest dress as taught in the Bible (I Tim. 2:9ff.; I Pet. 3:1ff.). Notice that these Scriptures speak both about dress and woman's submissiveness, that is, her place in God's order. The I Timothy passage speaks to the reasons woman is to be submissive, and in doing so it points to the same creation account Paul used in the I Corinthians 11 passage. The I Peter passage also speaks to an area Paul raised in I Corinthians 11, that of hairstyle. Woman is not to outwardly adorn herself with fancy "braiding of the hair."

In practicing the wearing of the veiling, it should go without saying that there must be concerns about attitudes related to the divine order. This ordinance, as all ordinances, is only a symbol of a Christian truth. Its practice has no intrinsic merit. For the veiling to be a blessing, the Christian woman who follows its practice must also live within the divine order. It is always a must to keep the significance of divine order and veiling together. The veiling symbol is to keep alive the proper relationship between man and woman. There can be no special blessing accommodating obedience to the veiling practice unless the submissive attitude to which the veiling speaks is alive and visibly present with the person. The blessing will come to the Christian woman who possesses the inner attitude that corresponds to the spiritual meaning of the veiling. The woman who wears the veiling and inwardly rebels and is "bossy" will find it of little value unless she allows it to bring about a change in attitude in her life.

In closing, we all know that too often twentieth-century mans disregards God's order. If ever in the history of mankind witness to God's divine order was needed, it is today. The

Christian woman can be an effective witness to society by wearing the headship veiling as a symbolic sign that she has accepted her rightful place in God's order and wishes to continue to do so. She should not fail to take advantage of this opportunity.

During the last one hundred years, there has been a dynamic shift in the relation of man and woman in society, and there is almost a complete disregard of the veiling practice in professed Christendom. No new biblical discoveries have brought about this change; it seems to be just a part of the general falling away that has occurred. The language of I Corinthians 11:2-16 is not hard to understand. Most Christians generally agree with what it teaches. Too many professing Christians just do not follow biblical teachings in everyday life. They consistently find easy ways to explain them away. This reflects the state of the Church today and its attitude toward the Word of God and the importance of "obedience of faith."

I believe many Christian women would be willing to wear the veiling as the symbol of their place in God's order, if there was a change in attitude toward the Word and the importance of discipleship and obedience was taught. Christian women need to hear a clear voice of certainty about Bible teachings in these days of uncertainty and skepticism. It is time for church leaders to change their wrong attitudes toward the Bible. This will result in a change in attitude toward the divine order and the veiling. These leaders are largely responsible for the failure of modern woman to accept her place in God's order and the general breakdown of the "Christian" home in America. Present-day Christianity has become a religion of convenience and American culture because the Church has taken a similar attitude toward other Bible teachings as it has toward I Corinthians 11:2-16.

Those Christians who follow the veiling teaching should be encouraged to remain faithful in their "obedience of faith" to Jesus Christ. Their witness to and acceptance of the divine order is needed in these last days. These should receive praise just as Paul praised the Corinthians: "I praise you, brethren, that ye remember me in all things, and keep the ordinances, as I delivered them to you" (I Cor. 11:2). They will surely receive a blessing for remaining faithful.

ENDNOTES

1 H. S. Bender, "An Exegesis of I Cor. 11:1-16," an unpublished manuscript in the Mennonite Historical Library, Goshen College, Goshen, Ind., p. 5.

2 J. C. Wenger, The Prayer Veiling in Scripture and History, Scottdale, Penna.: Herald Press, 1964, p. 9.

3 Bender, p. 7.

4 R. C. H. Lenski, Interpretations of I and II Corinthians, Columbus, Ohio: Wartburg Press, 1946, pp.339, 440.

5 Bender, p. 14.

6 Sanford G. Shetler, Paul's Letter to the Corinthians, 55. A.D., Harrisonburg, Va.: Christian Light, p. 93.

7 Paul M. Miller, The Prayer Veiling, Indiana-Michigan Mennonite Conference, 1953, p. 11.

8 James Strong, The Exhaustive Concordance of the Bible: . . . Greek Dictionary, New York: Abingdon, p. 57.

9 Charles Erdman, The First Epistle of Paul to the Corinthians, Philadelphia: Westminster Press, p. 97.

10 William F. Arndt and F. Wilbur Gingrich, A Greek-English Lexicon of the New Testament, Chicago: University of Chicago Press, 1979, p. 168.

11 Lenski, p. 439.

12 Shetler, p. 80.

13 See Andre Grabar, Early Christian Art, New York: Odyssey Press, 1968. pp. 58, 68, 100, 119, 120, 210, 211.

15 Lenski, pp. 436, 437.

16 Lenski, pp. 436, 437.

The Biblical Practice of Headcovering

Dr. Brian Allison

What does the Bible teach about headcovering? Should women wear a headcovering today in the Church, or was this practice peculiar to the early Church? Was the wearing of a headcovering simply an stopgap measure to address the cultural concern of prostitution? Should we not view a woman's hair as her headcovering? The questions can be multiplied. Have you asked questions similar to these? There is much confusion over this issue of headcovering, and discussion on it is often controversial. In this booklet, I want to present a Biblical exposition on this much misunderstood practice. Are you open to be instructed from the Scriptures or have you already made up your mind? If the Bible teaches the propriety of a Christian woman wearing a headcovering, will you obey and conform to that Scriptural practice? Do you believe that God's Word is authoritative and relevant for today?

The passage that teaches on headcovering is 1 Corinthians 11:2-16. It reads:

2 Now I praise you because you remember me in everything, and hold firmly to the traditions, just as I delivered them to you. 3 But I want you to understand that Christ is the head of every man, and the man is the head of a woman, and God is the head of Christ. 4 Every man who has something on his head while praying or prophesying, disgraces his head. 5 But every woman who has her head uncovered while praying or prophesying, disgraces her head; for she is one and the same with her whose head is shaved. 6 For if a woman does not cover the head, let her also have her hair cut off; but if it is disgraceful for a woman to have her hair cut off or her head shaved, let her cover her head. 7 For a man ought not to have his head covered, since he is the image and glory of God; but the woman is the glory of man. 8 For man does not originate from woman, but woman from man; 9 for indeed man was not created for the woman's sake, but woman for the man's sake. 10 Therefore the woman ought to have a symbol of authority on her head, because of the angels. 11 However, in the Lord, neither is woman independent of man, nor is man independent of woman. 12 For as the woman originates from the man, so also the man has his birth through the woman; and all things originate from God. 13 Judge for yourselves: is it proper for a woman to pray to God with head uncovered? 14 Does not even nature itself teach you that if a man has long hair, it is a dishonor to him, 15 but if a woman has long hair, it is a glory to her? For her hair is given to her for a covering. 16 But if one is inclined to be contentious, we have no other practice, nor have the churches of God.

Let us work progressively through this challenging passage.

The introductory statement to the argument

It is critically important to understand that the introductory statement to this argument on headcovering sets the context and stage for properly understanding the teaching that the apostle Paul gives--"Now I praise you because you remember me in everything, and hold firmly to the traditions, just as I delivered them to you" (11:2). We need to take note of the distinct language that the apostle uses. Often, when we deal with this question of headcovering, we fail to view it within its proper setting, and thus fail to acknowledge its true ethical character and import.

Paul first commends these Corinthian believers for obeying and carrying out what he had taught them, especially the traditions. They had generally accepted and acknowledged every authoritative apostolic teaching and instruction, and had both tenaciously adhered to, and complied with, all of them. Paul initially commends their obedience because, first, he would require the same response to the teaching which he was about to give (or rehearse?); and second, he would encourage them to evidence the same obedient attitude concerning headcovering. His praising them prepares for and anticipates a subsequent appeal to them. Again, this introductory statement is critically defining for understanding the importance and necessity of headcovering; for the logical conclusion, from appreciating the apostle's point here, is that headcovering constitutes part of the traditions; for having made reference to their obedience to the traditions, the apostle immediately addresses this matter.

The term which is translated 'traditions' (Gk. - paradosis) is used thirteen times in the New Testament; and it means teaching which has been passed on or handed down from one group to another, and which typically entails the idea of customary practice. It is teaching which has recognized and established historical and religious significance, relating to outward or visible conduct; and thus assumes the form of conventional propriety. Thus, the apostle affirms, with respect to headcovering, "But if anyone is inclined to be contentious, we have no other practice [Gk. - sunetheia; i.e., custom], nor have the churches of God" (11:16). This term 'traditions' is found in other Scripture passages. For instance, the Pharisees and scribes challenged Christ, "Why do your disciples transgress the tradition [paradosis] of the elders? For they do not wash their hands when they eat bread [a long-standing practice or custom]" (Matt 15:2; cf. Mk. 7:3-13). Needless to say, the 'traditions' were to be highly esteemed, and implied moral and religious obligation.

This term paradosis is used three times with respect to Christian teaching. Apart from its use in 1 Corinthians 11:2, the term is used in 2 Thessalonians 2:15, "So then, brethren, stand firm and hold to the traditions which you were taught, whether by word of mouth or by letter from us;" and again in this same epistle, 3:6, "Now we command you, brethren, in the name of our Lord Jesus Christ, that you keep aloof from every brother who leads an unruly life and not according to the tradition which you received from us." The apostle proceeds to specifically identify the tradition in view: "For you yourselves know how you ought to follow our example [lit. imitate us], because we did not act in an undisciplined manner among you, nor did we eat anyone's bread without paying for it, but with labor and hardship we kept working night and day so that we might not be a burden to any of you" (vv. 7,8). Notice that in referring to the 'tradition' here, the apostle identifies it in terms of visible practice or observable behaviour. It refers to ethically acceptable behaviour. It touches on appropriate moral and religious conduct. It is teaching that is to be demonstrated in how one lives. The proper and only response therefore to a Christian 'tradition' is obedience.

Accordingly, when Paul says in 1 Corinthians 11:2 that these believers held "firmly to the traditions," just as he had taught them, he has in mind teaching that involves a practical and observable demonstration of truth, entailing religious and historical value. The practice of headcovering, as mentioned, is identified as part of the 'traditions', and thus must be viewed as an ethical and religious practice, with recognized historical roots, to which obedience and conformity are required.

The foundational principle of the argument

One foundational principle governs and undergirds the apostle Paul's argument on headcovering--"But I want you to understand that Christ is the head of every man [Gk. - aner; 'male'], and the man is the head of a woman, and God is the head of Christ" (11:3). This foundational principle underlies and provides the impetus and support for the subsequent teaching. Before actually addressing this practical matter (and the confusion of these Corinthian believers) concerning headcovering, Paul first presents the truth which would guide and navigate his thinking. The practice of headcovering is not rooted in personal preference or culturally-occasioned exigencies, but rather in the Biblical teaching on the divinely-ordered authority structure. The wider context in which we are to understand this particular practice is the lines of authority which God ordained and instituted with the original creation, and reaffirmed (in light of the Christ-event) in the new creation of the Church.

God is the head or authority of Jesus Christ, the God-man, Who willingly subjected Himself to the will of the Father as the incarnate second person of the Trinity. Christ is the head or authority of the man (i.e., the male) who was the first of the sexes to be created. The man is the head or the authority of the woman who was created from man in order to be his helper. God has duly ordained an authority structure in order to ensure harmony and order. Authority requires submission.

Now, Paul is not primarily addressing the issue of the authority structure in the home, though the principle he is presenting applies to the home. Though the teaching definitely and specifically refers to the husband and wife relationship, the original Greek terms should not be understood as 'husband' and 'wife', but rather as 'male' and 'female', though the actual application of the subsequent teaching has in view primarily, not exclusively, husbands and wives. Again, the apostle is articulating the creational lines of authority (i.e., what is the God-ordained functional relationship between the sexes). Further, in viewing this male-female relationship creationally, it does not mean that we should view it pervasively; that is, every female is not practically subordinate to every male, and in every conceivable situation (i.e., a woman may be an employer, under whom are male employees).

So, Paul argues according to God's original design of creation. The creational order is clearly in his mind, and not simply individual relationships. This is obvious as we read further on in the passage when Paul refers to the actual creation of the male and female, which supports and further develops Paul's main thesis or foundational principle (see 11:8,9). Again, though this particular truth has specific relevance and application to a husband-wife relationship (particularly as the practice of headcovering is carried out in public worship), the specific context in which Paul applies the teaching is in the Church, not in the home, nor even in society at large. Paul's concern in writing this epistle is primarily the conduct and protocol required in the Church. It is clear that this practice of headcovering is a Church matter, rather than a universal or domestic one. First, the general context demands this understanding--chapters 10 to 14 of this Corinthian epistle specifically deals with Church practice and order. Second, Paul indicates in 11:16 that headcovering is a practice in "the churches." Third, Paul specifically states that the teaching concerning headcovering relates to the gathered Church. He states, "But in giving this instruction [about headcovering], I do not praise you, because you come together not for the better but for the worse" (11:17).

The issue or problem identified and addressed

Apparently, these Corinthian believers misunderstood the purpose and practice of headcovering. A. R. Fausset writes, "The Corinthian women, on the ground of the abolition of distinction of sex in Christ, claimed equality with men, and, overstepping propriety, came forward to pray and prophesy without the customary headcovering."1 Hence, having laid the foundational Biblical principle which would guide his logic and application, the apostle Paul now proceeds to identify and address the issue or problem concerning the propriety and legitimacy of headcovering. Who is to cover the head?--"Every man who has something on his head [lit. down the head; e.g., a veil or tallith] while praying or prophesying, disgraces his head. But every woman who has her head uncovered [i.e., nothing on the head; e.g., a veil] while praying or prophesying, disgraces her head; for she is one and the same with her whose head is shaved" (11:4,5). The apostle does not present the full rationale for who is or who is not to cover the head until after (see 11:7) he first states who is and who is not to cover the head, adding what it means if such a required practice is not carried out, depending upon the sex.

If a male has 'something' on his head while praying or prophesying, he then disgraces his head, that is, his ruling head or authority, namely, Christ (see v. 3); and if a female has her head uncovered (i.e., no veil, kerchief, etc.) while praying or prophesying, she disgraces her head, that is, her ruling head or authority, namely, the husband [or father, if unmarried]. Calvin writes, "Someone asks if Paul is speaking of married women only. It is true that some restrict what Paul teaches here to married women, because subjection to the authority of a husband does not apply in the case of virgins [or the unmarried]. But these people are only showing their ignorance; for Paul looks higher, viz. to the eternal law of God, which has made the female sex subject to the authority of [the male sex]."2

But ask yourself the question: Why would the man's natural head be disgraced if he were to pray or prophesy with his head covered? Admittedly, this teaching on headcovering initially seems arbitrary, but the teaching was received by Paul in the form of a command, a command which found its justification and significance in the creational order. Paul's teaching originated from direct revelation, he spoke morally-obligatory truth. For instance, Paul writes to this same Church, "If anyone thinks he is a prophet or spiritual, let him recognize that the things I write to you are the Lord's commandment [which, of course, included the 'traditions']. But if anyone does not recognize this, he is not recognized" (14:37,38).

The apostle further elaborates on this matter of the woman disgracing her spiritual head or authority, if her head is uncovered--"For she is one and the same with her whose head is shaved" (11:5b). An uncovered Christian woman is as scandalous and reproachful as a bald-headed woman (haircutting was an act of grief - Deut 21:12; or an act of infamy - Isa 7:20)--remember that a woman's hair is a God-given endowment which reveals and highlights her beauty (see 11:15). Of course, in making this bold statement, the apostle is assuming and accepting the correctness and necessity of headcovering for the woman. He is simply stating that which an uncovered Christian woman may be identified with.

Paul proceeds to argue in such a way that the Christian woman has no option but to have a covering or veil on her head. He argues, "For if a woman does not cover her head, let her also have her hair cut off; but if it is disgraceful for her to have her hair cut off or her head shaved, let her cover her head" (11:6). Notice the tight, irresistible logic. Do you recognize the syllogism (i.e., an argument consisting of two premises and a conclusion)?

Premise 1: Head not covered, then cut hair off

Premise 2: Cut hair or shaved head is a disgrace

Conclusion: Therefore you must have head covered
(for an uncovered head is a disgrace)

Therefore Christian women must have their heads covered with some material in the Church (i.e., in the public worship of the gathered assembly).

The practice of headcovering relates to public worship

Why do you think the apostle Paul only refers to the Church activities of praying and prophesying? Why doesn't it say, for instance, in verse 4, "Every man who has something on his head while praying and prophesying [or teaching, preaching, etc.]..."? The apostle is specifically addressing the legitimacy and propriety of women wearing a headcovering in the public worship; and according to early Church practice, the only two official verbal ministries in which women could participate in public worship were praying and prophesying. So, Paul makes reference simply to these two activities. If women were permitted to preach or teach in the public worship, then Paul, no doubt, would have applied this regulation of headcovering to these activities as well. According to the early Church practice, women were to keep silent in the context of preaching and teaching. They were not (and are not) permitted to engage in these verbal-didactic ministries in the gathered assembly. Thus, the apostle exhorts in this same epistle, "Let the women keep silent in the churches [when it comes to preaching and teaching in a mixed group]; for they are not permitted to speak, but let them subject themselves, just as the Law also says. And if they desire to learn anything [concerning what is preached or taught], let them ask their own husbands at home; for it is improper for a woman to speak [didactically in a mixed group] in church" (1 Cor. 14:34,35). Elsewhere we read, "Let a woman quietly receive instruction with entire submissiveness. But I do not allow a woman to teach or exercise authority over a man, but to remain quiet [with respect to officially teaching in the gathered church]" (1 Tim 2:11,12). Now, if someone wants to argue that this injunction of silence upon the woman is universal (i.e., she cannot open her mouth at all), then it must be concluded that women should not even sing (melodious talk) in public worship; but we read, "Speaking to one another in psalms and hymns and spiritual songs, singing and making melody with your heart to the Lord" (Eph. 5:19). This prohibition to women relates to the teaching-learning context of the gathered Church which consists of a mixed group, for women are not to have authority over men in this context.

So, in the early Church, the two verbal ministries in which a woman could engage (within the gathered church consisting of men and women) were praying and prophesying. Someone may criticize and argue that prophesying was teaching; but we need to understand the peculiar nature of prophesying. As I write elsewhere, "the Scripture distinguishes between the office of an elder [or pastor] and the office of a prophet(ess) (Eph. 4:11). The gift of teaching (typically associated with elders) and the gift of prophecy (associated with prophets or prophetesses) are essentially different (cf. Rom 12:6,7). Prophesying was the direct communication of divine revelation from God (see 1 Cor. 14:30,31). Therefore, the actual content of communication was (pre-)determined. The prophet or prophetess never spoke independently, but was directly "moved by the Holy Spirit" (2 Pet. 1:21). Personal freedom in actual communication of the truth was precluded. The analytical and reflective powers of the mind became virtually obsolete. So, for instance, the injunction for the early church was: "And let two or three prophets speak, and let the others pass judgment. But if a revelation is made to another who is seated, let the first keep silent" (1 Cor. 14:29,30). The elder or pastor [who exercises the gift of teaching], on the other hand, has a degree of personal freedom in actual communication, though the essential content must remain unalterable. He must harness and direct his analytical and reflective powers of the mind. Thus, the possibility of error or heresy continually looms.

"Furthermore, in accordance with the progressive revelation of God, this gift of prophecy was initially an extraordinary and temporary spiritual gift associated with the inauguration of the dispensation of the Spirit and the universal thrust of the Gospel. Both men and women were to participate in the initiation of the new era in fulfilment of Old Testament prophecy (Joel 2:28-32; cf. Acts 2:17-21). [On the day of Pentecost, both men and women prophesied within the gathered church (Acts 2:1-4)]. With the coming of the age of the Spirit and grace, there is spiritual egalitarianism. In Christ, "there is neither Jew nor Greek, there is neither slave nor free man, there is neither male nor female" (Gal. 3:28). There is equality in spiritual status and position before Christ, but diversity in functions and roles (Rm. 12:4ff; 1 Cor. 12:4ff.). So the appearance of the extraordinary spiritual gifts was a unique phenomenon which marked the commencement of the new spiritual age. Such gifts are not now a part of normative church practice and ministry" (Why Women Should Not Be Pastors, 9f.).

Further, some would criticize and argue that only men are to pray in the public worship, referring to 1 Timothy 2:8, "Therefore I want the men [Gk. - aner; i.e., male] in every place to pray, lifting up holy hands, without wrath and dissension." Yet, Paul is not excluding the women from praying at all, with this injunction, but is simply indicating his preference for, and providing encouragement to, men to take the lead in this holy practice, in keeping with their functional role as heads. The practice of the early Church certainly suggests the propriety and acceptability of women praying in the public worship. For instance, we read concerning the imprisonment of Peter, "So Peter was kept in the prison, but prayer for him was being made fervently by the church to God.... And when he realized this, he went to the house of Mary, the mother of John who was also called Mark, where many were gathered together and were praying" (Acts 12:5,12).

Now, the question is raised: Assuming that the practice of headcovering is Biblical and requisite, doesn't the passage teach that a woman need only wear a covering on her head if she is actually praying or prophesying? Not at all. Though the apostle focuses singularly on the verbal ministries of public worship, this regulation of headcovering has universal application within the context of the Church in which both men and women gather for the purpose of worship. Remember, Paul's main concern is conforming to, and respecting, the authority structure ordained at creation. The wearing of a headcovering, as we will see with verse 10 of this passage, symbolizes the fact that the woman is under the authority of the man.

The intimate correlation between the symbol and the truth

There is an intrinsic relationship between the symbolism associated with a Christian practice or custom and the spiritual truth which is communicated or conveyed through that practice or custom. Accordingly, the notion of an authority-submission relationship clearly means that one is 'over' or 'above' (functionally speaking) and one is 'under' or 'below'. There is a leader or head, and there is a follower or helper. The symbolism of wearing a headcovering merely and aptly communicates that the woman is 'under' the authority of the man, for the covering (which is a symbol of authority - 11:10) is 'over' her head. God wants the woman to show that she is 'under' the man's rule and protection. Man is not to have 'something' on his head, for as the natural head he is not creationally 'under' woman or the rest of the creation. Certainly, you see the appropriateness of the symbolism associated with this practice, and how it adequately captures the spiritual truth in view.

Similarly, baptism is the symbolic act of regeneration; but, again, there is an intimate, correlative connection between the symbolism of the act and the spiritual truth conveyed through that act. In the act of baptism, one is immersed in water and is 'washed', signifying a spiritual washing from sins, and the assumption of a new spiritual nature. Similarly, the Lord's Table communicates our communion and our participation in Christ, and with Christ and His people. We have spiritually partaken of His body and His blood, that is, we have an invested saving interest in His body and His blood; and we demonstrate that fact by ceremonially eating the bread (which symbolizes 'eating' His body) and ceremonially drinking from the cup (which symbolizes 'drinking' His blood). Again, the religious symbolism directly correlates with the spiritual truth to which the Christian practice or act points. The customs to which Christians must adhere are spiritual in nature. Accordingly, the practice of headcovering should be viewed as a spiritual practice which communicates divine truth, rather than as a male-imposed or chauvinistically-driven rite.

The rationale for the regulations concerning headcovering

Having identified the problem of the practice of headcovering (11:4-6), the apostle Paul then provides the rationale for why a man should not have his head covered and why a woman should. He argues, "For a man ought not to have his head covered since he is the image and glory of God; but the woman is the glory of man" (11:7). Both the man and the woman are made in the image of God (see Gen 1:26); but the matter of distinction and importance here concerns the notion of 'glory'. Paul apparently refers to the fact that man is the image of God to indicate that the orbit and ground for this teaching on authority (as already argued) is the original creation. Being created first, the man has the creational priority, he is the head; and creational priority entails functional authority.

Man is the glory of God in that he reflects and manifests the wonder, strength, and power of God, being the first, highest and greatest expression of God's creation. Man is the glory of God in that he is created to be God's chief representative; and as the glory of God, man is to assume headship or leadership over creation, even as God has headship over the whole universe. Now, woman is the glory of man in that she came from his 'strength' and now reflects him. So, Paul continues to teach, giving the reason why the woman is the glory of man, "For man does not originate from woman, but woman from man; for indeed man was not created for the woman's sake, but woman for the man's sake" (11:8,9). As God's representative or head, God was pleased to create for him, and give to him, a helper--someone who would perfectly and completely meet his needs and provide him with the necessary companionship and aid to subdue the whole creation. Woman was made for the benefit, not abuse, of man. Now, this fact does not mean that the woman is inferior to the man; she is not. Men and women are equal in worth and value, but different in roles and functions, according to the original design of God.

The necessity for the woman to wear a headcovering

The apostle Paul, having provided some rationale underlying the practice of headcovering, definitively concludes and emphatically states the necessity of the practice. He affirms, "Therefore, the woman ought to have a symbol of authority on her head, because of the angels" (11:10). Because the woman is the helper and the follower of the man, being under his authority, she must clearly demonstrate that truth through the wearing of a covering on her head, which symbolically conveys the fact that she is indeed under authority; as God intended from the beginning. Notice the note of moral obligation--"ought to have..." (i.e., it is necessary from God's point of view).

Accordingly, we ought not to understand this practice as merely cultural or relative to the Corinthian Church. Some critics contend that Paul was addressing a problem peculiar to the Corinthian Church, or contend that the rationale for women wearing a headcovering was to distinguish them from prostitutes who did not. So, the critics argue that the practice was either relativistic or cultural, and thus it does not have universal significance and application. No. Remember that this practice is part of the 'traditions', and thus has permanent, and not merely relative value. Further, Paul proceeds to teach that this practice has a universal application--it was observed in all the churches (11:16).

Moreover, the cultural argument carries no validity or weight, for Paul, as stressed, grounds his reasoning in the teaching of the original creation. It is not a cultural issue, but rather a creational one. You cannot argue honestly from the passage itself that this practice of headcovering is cultural. Another point against the cultural interpretation is that Paul argues for the necessity of headcovering "because of the angels." This direct reason for the necessity and propriety of headcovering immediately removes the rationale from the cultural realm and gives it universal value.

What does this phrase mean--"because of the angels." Some fact pertaining to the existence, activity, or behaviour of angels provides the reason for the observance of this practice. One reason believers should observe this practice 'because of the angels' is because the angels are being taught the wisdom of God through the Church; and this would be a very instructive and practical lesson for them as they witness the reversing of the effects of sin and the creation returning to its original state. So, Ephesians 3:10 reads, "In order that the manifest wisdom of God might now be made known through the church to the rulers and the authorities [i.e., angels] in the heavenly places;" again, "It is revealed to them that they were not serving themselves, but you, in these things which now have been announced to you through those who preached the gospel to you by the Holy Spirit sent from heaven--things into which angels long to look (1 Pet 1:12; see also 1 Cor 4:9). God is pleased to teach angels through the Church, even this matter of creational authority.

A second reason believers should observe this practice 'because of the angels' is so that they do not commit the same fatal and tragic act of the fallen angels who rejected being under authority. Rejection of authority results in disaster and judgement. Jude 6 reads, "And angels who did not keep their own domain, but abandoned their proper abode, He has kept in eternal bonds under darkness for the judgment of the great day;" again, "For if God did not spare angels when they sinned, but cast them into hell and committed them to pits of darkness, reserved for judgment" (2 Pet 2:4). The fall of the angels should serve as a helpful reminder and lesson for believers. Paul's concern is that the lines of authority be acknowledged and adhered to. Living within the constituted lines of authority results in safety and blessings. There is a need for submission to authority in order to guarantee order and decency.

Furthermore, the apostle seems to be working with a distinct parallelism here. The relationship that the angels sustain with God in the larger universe, women should sustain with man (the image and glory of God) in the physical world. Angels are the ministering spirits of God. Woman is the 'suitable' helper for man. As the angels should be in submission to God, as the universal head, particularly of the heavenly realm (of course, everyone should be in submission to God), so the woman should be in submission to the man, the natural head of the physical realm. The angels rebelled against God, resulting in confusion and chaos; the women are to be under the authority of men in order to guarantee order and decency. The angels veil their face and feet (showing submission and reverence) in the presence of God (Isa 6:2); and similarly women are to veil their heads in the presence of men. Fausset interestingly notes, "St. Paul [probably] had before his mind the root-connection between the Hebrew terms for 'veil' (Radid) and subjection (Radad)."3

Now, though man was created first and thus has the priority; and because the woman was made for the benefit of the man; the man should not be considered as superior in any way. A necessary interdependence exists between the man and the woman. The apostle states (possibly in anticipation of male gloating and abuse!), "However, in the Lord, neither is woman independent of man, nor is man independent of woman. For as the woman originates from the man, so also the man has his birth through the woman; and all things originate from God" (11:11,12). Man may have the creational priority, but he is not intrinsically better than the woman, nor can he exist or survive without her. A mutual dependence exists between the male and female. Each one needs the other. The mutual dependence is clearly seen in the fact that neither can come into existence apart from the presence and mediation of the other. Yet, the man and woman should remember that they both are dependent upon God, and find their existence and life in Him.

An appeal for acceptance of the practice

Having clearly stated the need for the practice, the apostle Paul now appeals to these believers to accept the teaching, and thus carry out the practice. These subsequent remarks are secondary considerations, and are not germane to his main argument. (This should be remembered when we come to v. 15 which deals with the fact that a woman's long hair is her covering). He exhorts, "Judge for yourselves: is it proper for a woman to pray to God with head uncovered?" (11:13). Though addressing the whole congregation, the apostle particularly refers to the role of the prophets who have the gift and ability to discern whether Paul's teaching and command (which is by way of revelation) is true or not. This activity of 'judging' is used technically, and refers to prophetic activity. Hence, we read in 1 Corinthians 14:29,30, "Let two or three prophets speak, and the others pass judgment. But if a revelation is made to another who is seated, let the first keep silent." If Paul is simply referring to a kind of general judgement, on what do we base such a judgement? Against what or according to what should the average believer judge the validity and propriety of this practice? We could only know this truth through revelation, which Paul has communicated and the prophets were able to confirm. Thus, Paul writes, "If anyone thinks he is a prophet or spiritual, let him recognize that the things which I write to you are the Lord's commandment" (1 Cor 14:37).

The apostle further appeals, "Does not even nature itself teach you that if a man has long hair, it is a dishonour to him, but if a woman has long hair, it is a glory to her? For her hair is given to her for a covering" (11:14,15). Paul suggests that instinctively we recognize that there is a difference in how man and woman should appear with respect to the physical head. We instinctively realize (generally speaking) that long hair on a man (remember long hair is considered well below the shoulders) is inappropriate; that it should, at least, be above the shoulders. God has put this natural sensibility within us, with a view toward acknowledging differences between the sexes. Paul is simply observing that the physical heads, by God's original design, sustain a difference, and thus it should not seem strange that there be a difference in how the physical heads are understood and treated within the Church context. Again, the practice of headcovering finds its roots in the original creation. The practice of headcovering echoes an essential aspect of the clear distinction between the natures of the man and the woman.

Now, someone may contest that a woman's covering is her hair. Obviously, that interpretation runs counter to, and is clearly contradicted by, all that has been argued to this point. Such an interpretation denies the clear logic and simple meaning of this passage. Some resort to this position, not because they are honestly constrained by the teaching of the passage, but because of self-justification or pride. It really is a question of obedience to God's Word. When it states that "her hair is given to her for a covering," the apostle uses a different word than in verse 4. The word he uses here is peribolaion, and means coat, shawl, or mantle. You, no doubt, can see the obvious point. The 'long hair' serves as a coat or shawl for the woman. It adorns her as an ornament. Its appearance contributes to her beauty and 'strength'; and, in this sense, a woman's long hair "is a glory to her" (11:15b). It accentuates her loveliness and attraction.

Notice, for instance, how ludicrous it would read, if we were to substitute 'hair' for 'covering'--"For if a woman does not cover her head [that is, have her hair], let her also have her hair cut off [but the hair would supposedly be already off!]; but if it is disgraceful for a woman to have her hair cut off or her head shaved, let her cover her head [that is, have her hair; the logic is tautological]" (11:6).

The concluding remark

Having addressed the issue of headcovering, providing the meaning, purpose, and rationale for such a practice, the apostle Paul concludes, "But if one is inclined to be contentious, we have no other practice, nor have the churches of God" (11:16). Apparently, there were upset believers over this issue. They were argumentative; but Paul was inflexible. For him, it was a matter of truth, regardless what was required. Many at Corinth were "arrogant" (see 1 Cor. 5:6, 19; 5:2), and they needed to be humble and obedient. Calvin writes, "A contentious man is one who takes a delight in stirring up quarrels, and gives no consideration at all to the place of truth. Included in this category are all those who destroy good and useful customs where there is no need to do so; who raise controversies about matters which are as clear as day; who will not listen to reason; who cannot endure anyone getting the better of them."4 Paul clearly declares that this particular practice was observed by all churches, without exception, and they too would have to observe it. Marvin Vincent comments, "The testimonies of Tertullian and Chrysostom show that these injunctions of Paul prevailed in the churches. In the sculptures of the catacombs the women have close-fitting head-dress, while the men have the hair short"5

Some critics argue that Paul is setting forth a principle, and not a practice; and so, practically speaking, the principle may be applied in our day in different ways (e.g. the wife wears a ring to indicate union and submission). In response, any honest treatment of the passage demands the acknowledgement that Paul is arguing for the practice, and not just the principle. Again, this practice was observed in all the churches; a practice which comprises part of the 'traditions'.

For many women, this practice initially may seem strange or unnecessary. Many may feel embarrassed to conform to the practice, feeling group pressure to abstain. Some will wrestle with pride. But the question is this: What does God require? It seems clear that the wearing of a headcovering by women is Biblical and required. It is a spiritual act, communicating spiritual truth. It is a command of the Lord, and thus the response should be one of obedience. This practice shows respect for the husband (see Eph. 5:33), and certainly brings honour and glory to God, which should be the goal of all that we do.

Christianity

As defined in The Concise Encyclopaedia of Islam, Revised Edition, 2001 by Cyril Glassé

Christianity. In theory, Islam accepts Christianity as a Divinely revealed religion. Christians in a state under Muslim rule cannot be compelled to become Muslims, their churches are not to be taken away from them, and they are entitled to civil protection. In former times non-Muslims were obliged to pay a special tax (see DHIMMI). It is legal for a Muslim man to marry a Christian woman (or a woman of any of the Divinely revealed religions).

The protection of adherents of other religions has been a legal principle in Islam from the beginning, and in most Muslim countries there have been large minorities of Christians and Jews, and lesser ones of other religions such as Hindus, Buddhists, animists, and others depending on the country.

In the Muslim view, the Christian doctrine of the Trinity and the Divine nature of Jesus, and other points of difference from Islam, are deviations from what they believe Jesus's true teachings to have been. Muslims assume that because the Koran says that Jesus was a Divine Messenger like the Prophet, his message could not have been different from the Prophet's; that is to say, that Jesus's message could not have been anything other than Islam as they know it. Despite this perspective, the historic attitude of Islam towards Christianity has been largely sympathetic. Under the Ottomans many churches received privileges which they later lost under secular Christian governments. The Koran says: "and thou wilt surely find the nearest of them in love to the believers are those who say 'We are Christians'; that, because some of them are priests and monks [those devoted entirely to God], and they wax not proud." (5:85) See BIBLE; JESUS; COPTS; MARONITES; NESTORIANS.

Chishti, Muīn ad-Dīn Muḥammad (*537-633*/1142-1236). A famous Sufi of India, venerated as a great Saint and buried in Ajmir. An important *tarīqah* is named after him, the Chishtiyyah Order.

Chivalry, *see* FUTUWWAH.

Christianity. In theory, Islam accepts Christianity as a Divinely revealed religion. Christians in a state under Muslim rule cannot be compelled to become Muslims, their churches are not to be taken away from them, and they are entitled to civil protection. In former times non-Muslims were obliged to pay a special tax (*see* DHIMMI). It is legal for a Muslim man to marry a Christian woman (or a woman of any of the Divinely revealed religions).

The protection of adherents of other religions has been a legal principle in Islam from the beginning, and in most Muslim countries there have been large minorities of Christians and Jews, and lesser ones of other religions such as Hindus, Buddhists, animists, and others depending on the country.

In the Muslim view, the Christian doctrine of the Trinity and the Divine nature of Jesus, and other points of difference from Islam, are deviations from what they believe Jesus's true teachings to have been. Muslims assume that because the Koran says that Jesus was a Divine Messenger like the Prophet, his message could not have been different from the Prophet's; that is to say, that Jesus's message could not have been anything other than Islam as they know it. Despite this perspective, the historic attitude of Islam towards Christianity has been largely sympathetic. Under the Ottomans many churches received privileges which they later lost under secular Christian governments. The Koran says: "and thou wilt surely find the nearest of them in love to the believers are those who say 'We are Christians'; that, because some of them are priests and monks [those devoted entirely to God], and they wax not proud." (5:85) *See* BIBLE; JESUS; COPTS; MARONITES; NESTORIANS.

Circumcision (Ar. *khitān* or *khitānah*). Albeit strongly adhered to, this is a custom rather than a legal obligation. In South East Asia it is called simply *Sunnah*, i.e. "custom". In Muslim countries it may be performed on boys when the child is seven or older. Circumcisions are then occasions for the sacrifice of a sheep or another animal in Africa or the Middle East, and for other festivities elsewhere. However, because of the expense of such celebrations, circumcision is sometimes simply not performed among the poor. Because it is *Sunnah*, but not a requirement of the *sharī'ah*, circumcision is not obligatory upon adult converts.

"Female circumcision", even as a purely symbolic act, a light excision of skin (*khifāḍ*), is not a practice recommended by religion; but it has been apparently tolerated as custom. Such a practice, while serving no purpose except as an imitation of male circumcision, normally did not go so far as to be a mutilation; usually it was harmless. There also exist, however, practices such as clitoridectomy, and/or removal of the labia: these are a grave violence against the person and are strictly forbidden in Islam. Such practices are found in some backward milieus and are due to gross ignorance; they have absolutely no religious basis, and, like all mutilations, are not sanctioned by Islamic law and legally prohibited in the United States.

Clothing, *see* 'ABĀ'; IHRĀM; TURBAN.

Coffin, Suspended, *see* FALLACIES and INACCURACIES about ISLAM.

Commander of the Faithful (Ar. *amīr al-mu'minīn*). A title of the Caliph (since 'Umar, the second Caliph) as military chief. It has also been used by some Kings. *See* CALIPH.

Commentaries on the Koran. Commentaries which are straightforward explanations by way of background information with some degree of interpretation are called *tafsīr*; allegorical and mystical exegesis is more strictly called *ta'wīl*. The latter as allegory (but not necessarily as mysticism) has often, rightly, been considered extremely suspect.

A standard commentary is that of 'Abd Allāh ibn Umar al-Baydāwi (d. *685*/1282), *Anwār at-Tanzīl wa Isrār at-Ta'wīl* ("The light of Revelation and the Secrets of Interpretation"). It was frequently used in traditional courses of study and includes some of the more dependable opinions taken from earlier commentaries. Another famous commentary, quoted by virtually all later commentators, is the *Tafsīr* of

Jesus

As defined in The Concise Encyclopaedia of Islam, Revised Edition, 2001 by Cyril Glassé

Jesus, Son of Mary (Ar. *'Isa ibn Maryam*). He holds a singularly exalted place in Islam. The Koran says that Jesus was born of a virgin (3:45-47); that he is a "Spirit from God" (*ruhun mina' Llah*), and the "Word of God" (*kalimatu-Llah*) (4:171). He is usually called "Jesus son of Mary" (*'Isa ibn Maryam*), and his titles include Messiah (*masih*), Prophet (*aabi*), Messenger of God (*rasul*) and "one of those brought nigh [to God]". According to the Koran he performed various symbolic miracles; he raised the dead, brought the revealed book of the Gospel (*Injil*), and called down as a sign from heaven a table laden with sustenance (5:112-114), which symbolizes the communion host of Christianity.

In Islam, on the authority of the Koran, Jesus has a mission as a rasul, a Prophet of the highest degree who brings a restatement of God's religion (3:46-60). It is said, too, that he did not die upon the cross: "They slew him not but it appeared so to them" (4:157). A crucifixion took place, but Jesus is alive in a principial state, outside the world and time: "But God took him up to Himself. God is ever Mighty, Wise" (4:158).

It is in fact the common belief among Muslims that the crucifixion was an illusion, or that someone else was substituted for Jesus. Although this bears a resemblance to the Docetist teachings regarding the event, the reasons for the idea are quite different. While popular belief cannot be held to account, the crucifixion as a pointless charade can hardly be to meet God's purpose, and two thousand years have not shown what God could have meant by such sleight of hand. Nor does the Koran warrant such a view. Rather, it is that the crucifixion of Jesus does not play a role in the Islamic perspective any more than does his superhuman origin, for salvation in Islam results from the recognition of the Absoluteness of God and not from a sacrificial mystery. Since Islam believes that Jesus will return at the end of time, his death was no more than apparent and did not, as in Christian belief, involve a resurrection after the event. In Islam it is the absolute, or higher, reality that takes precedence in the Koran over the appearances of this world, be they of life or of

JESUS, SON OF MARY

originally so called from *al-bayt al-muqaddas*, "the Holy House", that is, the Temple of Solomon). The holiest place in Islam after Mecca and Medina, Jerusalem is sometimes referred to as "the third *haram*". Its holiness for Muslims derives, in the first place, from its association with the Old Testament Prophets, who are also Prophets in Islam. The association with Jesus is no less important, and Jerusalem figures in popular accounts of apocalyptic events as seen by Islam.

However, the sacred nature of Jerusalem is confirmed for Muslims above all by the Night Journey, in which the Prophet Muhammad was brought by the angel Gabriel to the Dome of the Rock on the Temple Mount. From here they ascended together into the heavens (Koran 17:1). The Koran refers to Jerusalem as the *al-Masjid al-Aqsā*, or "the Furthest Mosque" (that is, the Temple of Solomon) "whose precincts We [God] have blessed" (Koran 17:1). The Dome of the Rock sanctuary now stands over the rock, and nearby is the mosque today called *al-Masjid al-Aqsā*. The Temple Mount is called *al-Haram ash-Sharif* ("the Noble Sanctuary").

Other Islamic monuments in Jerusalem include the Ashrafiyyah, Jawliyyah, As'ardiyah, Mālikiyyah, Tankiziyyah, and 'Uthmāniyyah *madrasahs*, the 'Umari and al-Ḥamrā' mosques, fountains (those of Qa'it Bey, Bāb an-Nadhir), *khāns* or hospices (of Muḥammad Ibn Zamin), and gates, palaces, and mausoleums.

Jerusalem's importance is such that when 'Abd Allāh ibn az-Zubayr was elected Caliph in defiance of the Umayyads and seized Mecca in 64/683, the Umayyads could proclaim that the pilgrimage was to be performed to Jerusalem, which they controlled, instead of Mecca.

The city first came under Muslim rule in 17/638 when the patriarch Sophronius surrendered it to the troops of Caliph 'Umar. The Caliph visited the city after the conquest and Sophronius accompanied him to the Temple mount to search for the *miḥrāb* (prayer niche) of David, of which 'Umar had heard the Prophet speak. The Temple mount had fallen into great disorder through neglect, and was covered with refuse. The Caliph ordered it cleaned and had a place of prayer built nearby.

The Turkish Caliphs paid a great deal of attention to the city, adding more edifices to its ancient heritage. The present walls were built by Sulayman the Magnificent. *See* al-AQṢĀ'; DOME of the ROCK; NIGHT JOURNEY; SOLOMON.

Jesus, Son of Mary (Ar. *'Īsā ibn Maryam*). He holds a singularly exalted place in Islam. The Koran says that Jesus was born of a virgin (3:45-47); that he is a "Spirit from God" (*rūḥun mina' Llāh*), and the "Word of God" (*kalimatu-Llāh*) (4:171). He is usually called "Jesus son of Mary" (*'Īsā ibn Maryam*), and his titles include Messiah (*masīḥ*), Prophet (*nabī*), Messenger of God (*rasūl*) and "one of those brought nigh [to God]". According to the Koran he performed various symbolic miracles; he raised the dead, brought the revealed book of the Gospel (*Injīl*), and called down as a sign from heaven a table laden with sustenance (5:112-114), which symbolizes the communion host of Christianity.

In Islam, on the authority of the Koran, Jesus has a mission as a *rasūl*, a Prophet of the highest degree who brings a restatement of God's religion (3:46-60). It is said, too, that he did not die upon the cross: "They slew him not but it appeared so to them" (4:157). A crucifixion took place, but Jesus is alive in a principial state, outside the world and time: "But God took him up to Himself. God is ever Mighty, Wise" (4:158).

It is in fact the common belief among Muslims that the crucifixion was an illusion, or that someone else was substituted for Jesus. Although this bears a resemblance to the Docetist teachings regarding the event, the reasons for the idea are quite different. While popular belief cannot be held to account, the crucifixion as a pointless charade can hardly be meet to God's purpose, and two thousand years have not shown what God could have meant by such sleight of hand. Nor does the Koran warrant such a view. Rather, it is that the crucifixion of Jesus does not play a role in the Islamic perspective any more than does his superhuman origin, for salvation in Islam results from the recognition of the Absoluteness of God and not from a sacrificial mystery. Since Islam believes that Jesus will return at the end of time, his death was no more than apparent and did not, as in Christian belief, involve a resurrection after the event. In Islam it is the absolute, or higher, reality that takes precedence in the Koran over the appearances of this world, be they of life or of death. It is this verse about the state of martyrs which holds the key to understanding "They slew him not": "Say not of those who are slain in God's way that they are dead; they are living but you

239

death. It is this verse about the state of martyrs which holds the key to understanding "They slew him not": "Say not of those who are slain in God's way that they are dead; they are living but you perceive not" (2:154). Or: "Think not of those who are slain in the way of God that they are dead. Nay! they are living. With their Lord they have provision" (3:169).

According to various Hadlth, Jesus will return before the Day of Judgement, and destroy the Anti-Christ (*ad-dajjal*) who, towards the end of time, presents an inverted version of spirituality, misleading mankind in a final and fatal delusion. Then Jesus, it is said, will bring the cycle of Adamic manifestation to an end, and inaugurate another, in what is, in effect, the Second Coming.

There are certain Hadith which say that Jesus and Mary did not cry out when they were born; all other children do because, according to the symbolic interpretation, they are touched by the devil in coming into this world. In the words of the Prophet Muhammad, Jesus and Mary were the only beings in history to be born in such a state of sinlessness.

Although the position of Jesus in Islam is

extraordinary in a number of ways, even for a Prophet, that Islam should concede any idea of his divinity or admit that he is the Son of God is entirely precluded. This, or any trinitarian idea of God, or any suggestion that Jesus is somehow an hypostasis of God, is rejected by Islam.

Many Muslims think that the Christian trinity includes Mary, and certain Christian sects in ancient Arabia actually held such a belief. However, the trinitarian concept, in any form, is necessarily alien to Islam, because the principle which saves in Islam is precisely the recognition of the Divine Unity, the all-embracing Reality of the Absolute.

Because the Koran says that all God's Prophets have brought only the one religion of Islam, it is impossible for most Muslims to conceive that the religion brought by Jesus could, in reality, have been anything other than the Islam of the Muslim believer, the Islam of the "Five Pillars". That there is an Islam beyond form which is the religion of each Divine messenger as he faces God, or that a formless Islam is the essence of each religion, are necessarily esoteric concepts. That Christianity as it exists is based upon the doctrine that Jesus is a Divine incarnation, and that his crucifixion and resurrection have redeemed the sins of mankind and saved those who believe in him, can only be explained in the mind of the Muslim as some extraordinary historical error of interpretation or understanding.

It would perhaps seem therefore that Jesus as he is viewed in Islam, and despite the extraordinary attributes credited to him by the Koran, would actually have a role and a nature that could be interpreted into the Islamic universe only with great difficulty. Such, however, is not the case, because Christianity, like Judaism, is specifically mentioned as a revealed religion and Islamic legislation gives it a protected status. It is the nature of Jesus as a Prophet among the other Prophets of the Old Testament which is decisive for Muslims, and the disturbing elements of Christianity as it actually exists are simply set aside, placed outside of Islam, and in practice pose no great enigma, being seen as a kind of archaic survival which God in the Koran has chosen to tolerate. If this seems puzzling to Christians, they must remember that their rejection of the Prophethood of Muhammad is an equally incredible act for Muslims. Ultimately, it is perhaps only with the fulfillment of the role that God has assigned in prophecy to Jesus at the end of time, when the world and history are swallowed up by the purely miraculous, that the different cadences of the great religions will resolve themselves into one. See BIBLE; DAJJAL; MARY.

Chapter 9

Perverse Interpretations

To illustrate just how disasterous the contributions of so called 'established' Islamic theologians can be due to their perverse interpretations, we now look at the issues of abortion and female circumcision.

Dealing with abortion first, we refer to the entry for abortion in The Concise Encyclopaedia of Islam, Revised Edition, 2001, by Cyril Glassé.

Abortion. This is acceptable in Islam, according to most theologians, as long as the foetus is not fully formed; a state which is said to occur 120 days after conception, as described by the fourth hadith of Nawawi which summarizes the states of foetal development:

Verily the creation of each one of you is brought together in his mother's belly for forty days in the form of a seed (nutfah), then he is a clot of blood ('alaqah) for a like period, then a morsel of flesh for a like period (mudhghah), then there is sent to him the angel who blows the breath of life into him.

The breath of life is the ensoulment which was the critical issue for medieval theologians. To call the foetus a human being before this point would have been the same as to equate a possibility with an actuality, or to equate non-existence with existence. It is against this that Aristotle's law of non-contradiction, the first law of reality is set. Or as the theologian Sa'd ad-Din at-Taftazani (d. *175*/791) insisted: possibility is not a thing. The Hanafis permitted abortion until the fourth month and many Shafi'is and Hanbalis did also. The Malikis make abortion before the fourth month discouraged (*makruh*) but most did not make it prohibited (*haram*) until after the fourth month.

The doctrine of ensoulment after 120 days was held by the Catholic Church as well, but in the 19th century was de-emphasized as inopportune precisely because it was recognized it would be used to justify abortion. The idea is consistent with the traditional view, expressed as early as Aristotle, that the soul attaches itself to the foetus out of the unseen at a precise moment around 120 days after conception, and that only with the soul attached has the foetus become a human being. Abortions performed before the term of 120 days are therefore acceptable; others would prolong the term still further. In any case, no objections are raised to abortions performed after this moment if their aim is to safeguard the health or safety of the mother. There is an increase in vociferous anti-abortion polemics in the Islamic world, just as in the Christian world, because Fundamentalism corresponds to a rebirth of Mu'tazilite-like or dualist tendencies that can be seen in all religions at the present time. See BIRTH CONTROL.

ABLUTIONS – ABORTION

of squares which make up a larger square (the figure is related to a "magic square"). The letters are then transposed from one square to another in the diagram according to a certain algorithm or procedure which results in an arithmetical operation of multiplication or division. The square is also used for divination since the letters, while signifying numbers, also produce words. In another approach, the substitution of numbers for letters and then other letters of the same numerical value is a method of mystical exegesis known as the *'Ilm al-Ḥurūf*, similar to the Hebrew Gematria. (*See* 'ILM al-ḤURŪF.)

Abjad order rather than alphabetical order is used when the letters are used as ordinals. That is, a, b, c, d, as ordinals would in Arabic be *alif, ba', jim, dal* (instead of *alif, ba', ta', tha'*, which is Arabic alphabetical order today).

The *abjad* values are:

1	2	3	4	5	6	7	8
ا	ب	ج	د	ه	و	ز	ح
9	10	20	30	40	50	60	70
ط	ي	ك	ل	م	ن	س	ع
80	90	100	200	300	400	500	600
ف	ص	ق	ر	ش	ت	ث	خ
700	800	900	1000				
ذ	ض	ظ	غ				

The mnemonic formula is:

أبجد هوز حطي كلمن
سعفص قرشت ثخذ ضظغ

Ablutions. There are three kinds of ablution which symbolically restore the believer to a state of equilibrium or purity and, for the purposes of ritual, do so effectively.

The first is *ghusl* ("greater ablution"). This involves a ritual washing of the whole body, which removes the impurities (called *junub* or *janābah*) that are the consequences of: sexual intercourse; intromission; ejaculation with or without coitus; menstruation; childbirth; major bloodletting; and contact with a corpse. The performance of *ghusl* also accompanies conversion to Islam and the putting on of *iḥrām* (consecration for pilgrimage). One must also be in a state of *ghusl* before one can enter a mosque or an area purified for prayer (*see* PURIFICATION), or touch an Arabic Koran.

The second kind of ablution is the *wuḍū'* ("lesser ablution") which removes the impurities which are called *aḥdāth*. These include impurities in the state of the individual caused by: the bodily functions, breaking wind, touching a dog, minor bleeding (but not as small as insect bites), and by loss of consciousness or an interval of sleep. It is the *wuḍū'*, a brief washing of the hands, face, and feet, which is performed before the canonic prayer (*salāt*), but only if the state conferred by *ghusl* has not been lost.

The third kind of ablution is *tayammum* where – through lack of, or legitimate aversion to, water – a substitute of sand, earth, or unfashioned stone, is used in the place of water in a single, special ritual which replaces either the *wuḍū'*, or *wuḍū'* and *ghusl* together. For descriptions, see GHUSL; WUḌŪ'; TAYAMMUM.

Abortion. This is acceptable in Islam, according to most theologians, as long as the foetus is not fully formed; a state which is said to occur 120 days after conception, as described by the fourth ḥadīth of Nawâwī which summarizes the states of foetal development:

Verily the creation of each one of you is brought together in his mother's belly for forty days in the form of a seed (*nutfah*), then he is a clot of blood (*'alaqah*) for a like period, then a morsel of flesh for a like period (*mudhghah*), then there is sent to him the angel who blows the breath of life into him.

The breath of life is the ensoulment which was the critical issue for medieval theologians. To call the foetus a human being before this point would have been the same as to equate a possibility with an actuality, or to equate non-existence with existence. It is against this that Aristotle's law of non-contradiction, the first law of reality is set. Or as the theologian Sa'd ad-Dīn at-Taftāzānī (d. *175*/791) insisted: possibility is not a thing. The Ḥanafīs permitted abortion until the fourth month and many Shâfi'is and Ḥanbalīs did also. The Mālikīs make abortion before the fourth month discouraged (*makrūh*) but most did not make it prohibited (*ḥarām*) until after the fourth month.

The doctrine of ensoulment after 120 days was held by the Catholic Church as well, but in the 19th century was de-emphasized as inopportune precisely because it was recognized it would be used to justify abortion. The idea is consistent with the traditional view, expressed as early as Aristotle, that the soul attaches itself to the

20

Stacey International, the publishers of *The Concise Encyclopaedia of Islam* were, in 2003, advised that CYRIL GLASSÉ'S declaration that Abortion "is acceptable in Islam" was completely wrong and they in turn notified Mr Glassé, about this communication. But Cyril Glassé's declaration was made with some historical precedent as for centuries a minority of Muslim scholars have indeed used or interpreted Nawawi's hadith to infer that abortion up to 120 days is acceptable. But this interpretation is totally unjustified and very tenuous at best.

Dr. Zaki Badawi has stated that the above hadith of Nawawi must not be used as an argument to justify abortion; indeed some time ago Dr. Badawi wrote to the Pro-Life Alliance Party of Great Britain to state the correct Islamic position on abortion: Abortion is not permitted from the moment sperm unites with egg. Only if the mother's life is in danger can abortion be considered. Dr. Badawi has also stated that this hadith of Nawawi is not meant to literally mean that the soul goes into the foetus only after 120 days and that in any case no justification should be inferred from, nor should any connection be made with, this hadith and the right to have an abortion.

Below is an extract from a newsletter from the Association of Lawyers for the Defence of the Unborn which deals precisely with the true Islamic position.

The Association of Lawyers for the Defence of the Unborn
40 Bedford Street, London WC2E 9EN

Winter 1999/2000 Number 84

News and Comment

Miscellany

During the past few weeks we have received letters and proposed contributions from several different quarters giving views and ideas about abortion and related topics as seen from the perspective of various cultures. Believing that our readers might be interested in these contributions we are including them in this Newsletter. All of the contributions are quite short and do not pretend to be anything other than a brief insight into the subject. They represent the views of their respective authors, and if they contain any errors then they are the errors of those authors. We are, however extremely grateful to each of these authors for taking the trouble to write to us.

We begin with the following commentary upon the Islamic view of abortion sent to us by an Islamic member of ALDU.

The killing of babies through abortion is prohibited in Islam.

All human life is sacred in Islam, from conception through to natural death. Only God (ALLAH), The Creator of all, can create life or ordain that it be taken away. The moment of death has been fixed in advance by God.

Our bodies belong to The Creator, and neither men nor women have the right to treat them as they wish. This includes all or part of our bodies, and anything else arising from conception.

Suicide, euthanasia (assisted suicide or 'mercy killing') and abortion are all forbidden in Islam.

There is nothing in the Holy Qu'ran or in the sayings (Sunnah) of the prophet Muhammad (peace be upon him) which allows abortion. On the contrary, there are verses in the Holy book Al-Qu'ran which are clearly against the killing of any baby or child, male or female, by any means:

In the name of Allah, The Most Compassionate, The Most Merciful, 'Do not kill or take human life which God has declared to be sacred', (Chapter 6, verse 151).

'Do not kill your children for fear of poverty: it is we who shall provide sustenance for them as well as you. Killing them is currently a great sin' (Chapter 17, verse 31).

'Whoever kills a human being (a soul), unless it be for murder or corruption on earth, it is as though he had killed all mankind, and whoever saves a life it is as though he had saved the life of all of mankind' (Chapter 5 verse 31).

Muslim women are decribed in Al-Qu'ran as (amongst other things) those who ***'do not kill their children'***, (Chapter 60, verse 12).

In Islam we are asked to marry, conceive and maintain conception full term to produce children. Thus in an Islamic society every conception is legitimate and every pregnancy is desired: nothing is called an 'unwanted pregnancy'. Every child is regarded as a gift from Allah.

Many verses in Al-Qu'ran describe beautifully and scientifically all the different stages of development and growth of a baby, producing great admiration for The Creator, the best of designers.

Ibn Taymiyah, one of Islam's great scholars, said ***'it is the consensus of all fuqaha* **[renowned Muslim scholars]** *that abortion is prohibited'.***

Not only that, Islamic law prescribed clear punishment for anyone performing or assisting in abortion:

'Al-Gurrah (blood money) is payable if the baby is aborted dead. (At current rates this would be about 5000 Saudi Riyals).

Full diyyah (about 100,000 Riyals) is payable if the baby is aborted alive.

Every day in Britain, some 500 innocent babies are killed through abortion, Muslims, watch out for abortion under: ***'Reproductive Health', 'Reproductive Rights' 'Control of Fertility' 'Population Control' and even 'Human Rights'*** (especially in United Nations documents). We respect womanhood and family life: beware of pro-abortionists who use the words ***'Women's Rights'*** and ***'Family Planning'*** to promote abortion!

Muslims should work closely with pro-life organisations, Christians and others, to stop the killing of the innocent babies at any place or at any time (A MUSLIM DUTY).

This is the development of the baby (fetus) in the last Holy Book Al-Qu'ran (Islamic Embryology):-

'Man We did create from a quintessence (of clay), then We placed him/her as a drop (nutfah) in a place of rest firmly fixed, then We made the drop into a leech-like clot (alaqah) which clings; then We made the clot into a lump of flesh (mudgah); then We made out of the lump bones and clothed the bones with flesh (muscles): then We developed out of it another creature....so blessed be Allah the best to create.' (Al-Qu'ran Chapter 23, verses 12-14).

The Association of Lawyers for the Defence of the Unborn

Winter 1999/2000 Newsletter

Copy of original article describing the the true Islamic position on the matter of abortion.

The Association of Lawyers for the Defence of the Unborn

40 BEDFORD STREET, LONDON, WC2E 9EN

Chairman: R. M. HAIG, LL.B., 35 Parkway, Wilmslow, Cheshire, SK9 1LS
Vice Chairman: C. G. P. LAKEMAN, B.A., Dip. Dt. Fr. (Paris – XI),
2 Longfield Lodge, La Route du Petit Clos, St. Helier, Jersey, JE2 3FX
Hon. Membership Secretary: T. E. WARD, LL.B., The Chestnuts, Coddenham Road, Needham Market, Ipswich, IP6 8NU
Hon. Treasurer: T. G. A. BOWLES, M.A. (Cantab.), 40 Bedford Street, London, WC2E 9EN

Winter 1999/2000 **News and Comment** **Number 84**

Miscellany

During the past few weeks we have received letters and proposed contributions from several different quarters giving views and ideas about abortion and related topics as seen from the perspective of various cultures. Believing that our readers might be interested in these contributions we are including them in this Newsletter. All of the contributions are quite short and do not pretend to be anything other than a brief insight into the subject. They represent the views of their respective authors, and if they contain any errors then they are the errors of those authors. We are, however, extremely grateful to each of these authors for taking the trouble to write to us.

We begin with the following commentary upon the Islamic view of abortion sent to us by an Islamic member of ALDU.

The killing of babies through abortion is prohibited in Islam

All human life is sacred in Islam, from conception through to natural death. Only God (ALLAH), The Creator of all, can create life or ordain that it be taken away. The moment of death has been fixed in advance by God.

Our bodies belong to The Creator, and neither men nor women have the right to treat them as they wish. This includes all or part of our bodies, and anything else arising from conception.

Suicide, euthanasia (assisted suicide or 'mercy killing') and abortion are all forbidden in Islam.

There is nothing in the Holy Qu'ran or in the sayings (Sunnah) of the prophet Muhammed (peace be upon him) which allows abortion. On the contrary, there are verses in the Holy Book Al-Qu'ran which are clearly against the killing of any baby or child, male or female, by any means :

> *In the name of Allah, The Most Compassionate, The Most Merciful, 'Do not kill or take human life which God has declared to be sacred'*, (Chapter 6, verse 151).

> *'Do not kill your children for fear of poverty : it is we who shall provide sustenance for them as well as you. Killing them is certainly a great sin'.* (Chapter 17, verse 31).

> *'Whoever kills a human being (a soul), unless it be for murder or corruption on earth, it is as though he had killed all mankind, and whoever saves a life it is as though he had saved the life of all mankind'.* (Chapter 5, verse 31).

Muslim women are described in Al-Qu'ran as (amongst other things) those who *'do not kill their children'*, (Chapter 60, verse 12).

In Islam we are asked to marry, conceive and maintain conception full term to produce children. Thus in an Islamic society every conception is legitimate and every pregnancy is desired : nothing is called an 'unwanted pregnancy'. Every child is regarded as a gift from Allah.

Many verses in Al-Qu'ran describe beautifully and scientifically all the different stages of development and growth of a baby, producing great admiration for The Creator, the best of designers.

Ibn Taymiyah, one of Islam's great scholars, said: *'it is the consensus of all fuqaha* [renowned Muslim scholars] *that abortion is prohibited'*.

Not only that, Islamic law prescribed clear punishments for anyone performing or assisting in abortion :

'Al-Gurrah (blood money) is payable if the baby is aborted dead. (At current rates this would be about 5,000 Saudi Riyals).

Full diyyah (about 100,000 Riyals) is payable if the baby is aborted alive.'

Every day in Britain, some 500 innocent babies are killed through abortion. Muslims, watch out for abortion under : *'Reproductive Health', 'Reproductive Rights', 'Control of Fertility', 'Population Control'* and even *'Human Rights'* (especially in United Nations documents). We respect womanhood and family life : beware of pro-abortionists who use the words *'Women's Rights'* and *'Family Planning'* to promote abortion !

Muslims should work closely with pro-life organisations, Christians and others, to stop the killing of the innocent babies at any place or at any time (A MUSLIM DUTY).

This is the development of the baby (fetus) in the last Holy Book Al-Qu'ran (Islamic Embryology) :-

> *'Man We did create from a quintessence (of clay), then We placed him/her as a drop (nutfah) in a place of rest firmly fixed, then We made the drop into a leech-like clot (alaqah) which clings ; then we made the clot into a lump of flesh (mudgah) ; then We made out of the lump bones and clothed the bones with flesh (muscles) ; then We developed out of it another creature . . . so blessed be Allah, the best to create'.* (Al-Qu'ran Chapter 23, verses 12-14).

With regard to female circumcision this is just another obsession with curtailing femininity in some parts of the Muslim world.

Again, quoting from Jan Goodwin's *Price of Honour* on pages 334 and 335 of Chapter 13, entitled *Egypt : the Mother of the World:*

A major campaign of Saadawi's organization before the government closed it was to halt female circumcision. "The majority of rural Egyptian women are still circumcised. Here they remove only the clitoris; they do not do the much more extensive procedure, but even so, there are many problems. Infection, bleeding, damage to the urinary tract, sepsis, even death. Later, it may cause pain during coitus, and psychological damage. In the villages it is performed on girls just before puberty, by untrained village midwives using any kind of knife or razor, without painkillers, and in unsanitary conditions. In the middle and upper classes, it may be carried out by a doctor. The reasons given for clitoridectomies in Egypt are 'cleanliness,' and 'so that girls will not run after men.'" In many societies, it is also believed that if the baby's head touches the clitoris during delivery, the infant will die.

Female circumcision is frequently described as an "age-old Muslim ritual," when in fact it predates Islam and is even believed to be pre-Judaic. There is no mention of it in the Koran, and only a brief mention in the authentic *hadiths*, which states: "A woman used to perform circumcision in Medina. The Prophet said to her: 'Do not cut severely, as that is better for a woman and more desirable for a husband." But because of this still debated *hadith*, some scholars of the Shafi school of Islam, found mostly in East Africa, consider female circumcision obligatory. The Hanafi and most other schools maintain it is merely recommended, not essential. In the nineteenth century, women in the United States and Europe were sometimes circumcised because it was believed to relieve epilepsy, hysteria, and insanity.

Today, an estimated one hundred million women have undergone the sexual mutilation. It is performed in many African countries, including Sudan, Somalia, Ethiopia, Kenya, and Chad. It is also a tradition among Muslims in Malaysia and Indonesia, and in a number of countries in the Middle East, including Egypt, the UAE, and parts of rural Saudi Arabia. Coptic Christians in Egypt and animist tribes in Africa as well as Muslims, undergo the ritual.

More than 90 percent of Sudanese women undergo the most severe form of circumcision, known as "pharaonic," or infibulation, at the age of seven or eight, which removes all of the clitoris, the labia minora, and the labia majora. The sides are then sutured together, often with thorns, and only a small matchstick-diameter opening is left for urine and menstrual flow. The girl's legs are tied together and liquids are heavily rationed until the incision is healed. During this primitive yet major surgery, it is not uncommon for girls, who are held down by female relatives, to die from shock or hemorrhaging. The vagina, urethra, bladder, and rectal area may also be damaged, and massive keloid scarring can obstruct walking for life.

After marriage, women who have been infibulated must be forcibly penetrated. "This may take up to forty days, and when men are impatient, a knife is used," recounted Sudanese women at a conference that I attended several years ago in Cairo on the "Development of Women in the Islamic World." They also told of special honeymoon centers built outside communities so that the "screams of the brides will not be heard." At this time also, the risks of infection and hemorrhaging are high.

During childbirth, the scar tissue must be cut and the opening enlarged, otherwise mother and child may die. In the mid-eighties, American *Nursing* magazine began advising medical practitioners in the United States how to treat such patients, since the influx of women from countries where circumcision is standard meant that U.S. health-care providers were now seeing them in hospitals here. And if such cases are not handled correctly, major complications can ensue. The tradition of female circumcision in many countries is so strong that circumcised women even in the United States usually request reinfibulation after each delivery.

Jan Goodwin quotes a particular hadith which is in fact from Abu Da'ud (born 817 and died 888 A.D.) a noted collector of hadith, who himself said that this particular hadith on female circumcision was poor in authenticity. But to be clear, this hadith, according to the majority of Muslim scholars *today* is definitely *not* authentic and the practice of female circumcision has been roundly condemned by them as barbaric. But this vile operation is now so established in some areas, in reliance on the ingrained fraudulent rulings of past scholars (including some at Al-Azhar) - and eased by centuries of cultural practice - that it continues to flourish. Imposed on defenceless, often submissive, girls.

I come now to one more widespread and perverse attitude problem: that of inbreeding springing from the inability even to trust or mix with 'outsider' Muslims. The British press exposed the practice amongst British Asians but it *also* occurs to a significant extent in the Middle East. And it has strong links to the isolationist mechanism of the headscarf. Three articles follow :

Minister warns over in-breeding in Asians

The Daily Telegraph, February 11th 2008

By James Kirkup
Political Correspondent

Minister warns over in-breeding in Asians

By James Kirkup
Political Correspondent

ARRANGED marriages between British Asians raise the risk of in-breeding and birth defects, a Government minister has said.

Phil Woolas, a junior environment minister, came under fire from Muslim groups already concerned about the public reaction to the Archbishop of Canterbury's remarks about sharia law.

Mr Woolas, the Labour MP for Oldham East and Saddleworth, said that marriages between first cousins are a factor in birth defects and inherited conditions.

He said: "Part of the risk, I am told by the health service, is first-cousin marriages. If you are supportive of the Asian community then you have a duty to raise this issue."

The Muslim Public Affairs Committee, a campaign group, suggested the minister was demonising British Muslims.

An MPAC spokesman last night accused Mr Woolas of "flirting with Islamaphobia" and said: "Gordon Brown should either back him or sack him. We should be told what the Government thinks about this."

Downing Street and the Department for the Environment last night refused to comment on Mr Woolas' remarks, but the minister received public support from Geoff Hoon, the Labour chief whip.

Mr Hoon said that it was right to discuss the issue of congenital defects and intermarriage.

"It is important that we look at that in terms of scientific expertise and the extent to which it is actually causing problems," he said.

"I am confident that what he has said will have been said with sensitivity and with proper regard to his Muslim constituents and Muslims right across the United Kingdom."

Arranged marriages are common among several British Asian groups, but intermarriage of relatives is a particular characteristic of people of Pakistani origin.

It is estimated that more than 55 per cent of British Pakistanis are married to first cousins, resulting in an increasing rate of genetic defects and high rates of infant mortality. Figures show that British Pakistani children account for as many as one third of birth defects despite making up only three per cent of all UK births.

The likelihood of unrelated couples having the same variant genes that cause recessive disorders are estimated to be 100-1. Between first cousins, the odds increase to as much as one in eight.

In Bradford, more than three quarters of all Pakistani marriages are believed to be between first cousins. In 2005, the city's Royal Infirmary Hospital said it had identified more than 140 different recessive disorders among local children, compared with the usual 20-30.

A study by two Indian doctors published in *Neurology Asia*, a medical journal, last year found a "significantly higher rate" of epilepsy among the children of parents who were blood relatives.

The issue of birth-defects and cousin marriage was first raised in parliament two years ago by Ann Cryer, the Labour MP for Keighley in West Yorkshire.

Yesterday, she said marriage between cousins was "to do with a medieval culture where you keep wealth within the family".

She said: "If you go into a paediatric ward in Bradford or Keighley you will find more than half of the kids there are from the Asian community. Since Asians only represent 20-30 per cent of the population, you can see that they are over-represented."

Storm over Muslim cousin marriages

Daily Mail, February 11th 2008

By Jane Merrick
Political Correspondent

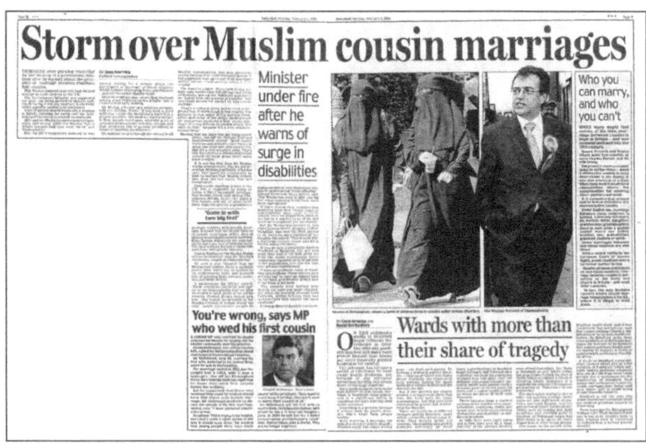
Storm over Muslim cousin marriages

Minister under fire after he warns of surge in disabilities

Who you can marry, and who you can't

You're wrong, says MP who wed his first cousin

Wards with more than their share of tragedy

Minister under fire after he warns of surge in disabilities

DEMANDS were growing yesterday for the sacking of a government minister after he warned about the problems of marriage between Pakistani first cousins.

Phil Woolas claimed that this had caused a surge in birth defects in the UK.

The Environment Minister also suggested the issue was being ignored by Muslim leaders, declaring it was the 'elephant in the room' which urgently needed to be addressed. It set off another heated debate about Muslims in Britain, following the outcry over the Archbishop of Canterbury's remarks on sharia law.

MPs said Mr Woolas's comments were insensitive and wrong, while the Muslim Public Affairs Council said they were 'racist' and 'Islamaphobic'. But the MP's supporters insisted he was merely calling for a debate about the prevalance of marriage of blood relations within families originating from rural Pakistan - and not the entire Muslim world.

Medical evidence also shows that marriage among blood relations carries a higher risk of children with birth defects.

Mr Woolas, a former race relations minister, told the Sunday Times: 'If you have a child with your cousin the likelihood is there'll be a genetic problem. The issue we need to debate is first-cousin marriages, whereby a lot of arranged marriages are with first cousins, and that produces lots of genetic problems in terms of disability [in children].'

He insisted the practice did not extend to all Muslim communities, but was prevalent among families from rural Pakistan. Research has suggested that up to half of all marriages within these communities involve first cousins.

The minister added: 'If you talk to any primary care worker they will tell you that levels of disability among the Pakistani population are higher than the general population. And everybody knows it's caused by first-cousin marriage.'

'That's a cultural thing rather than a religious thing. It is not illegal in this country. The problem is that many of the parents themselves and many of the public spokespeople are themselves products of first-cousin marriages. It's very difficult for people to say, "You can't do that" because it's a very sensitive, human thing.'

Warning that the issue was not being talked about, the MP for Oldham East and Saddleworth added: 'Most health workers and primary care trusts in areas like mine are very aware of it. But it's a very sensitive issue. That's why it's not even a debate and people outside of these areas don't really know it exists.'

It is not the first time Mr Woolas, whose constituency has an above-average Muslim population of 8.5 per cent, has upset the community. In 2006 he warned that Muslim women who wear the veil cause 'fear and resentment'.

First-cousin marriage is legal in the UK, but is regarded by many as taboo. A BBC2 Newsnight investigation in 2005 found that among Pakistanis in Britain, 55 percent marry a first cousin, and are 13 times more likely than the general population to produce children with genetic disorders. It found that one in ten children of cousin marriages either dies in infancy or develops a serious disability. While British Pakistanis are responsible for just 3 per cent of all births in the UK, they account for one in three children born with genetic illnesses.

Asghar Bukhari of the Muslim Public Affairs Committee said Mr Woolas's comments 'verged on Islamophobia'.

He said it was 'bizarre' that Mr Woolas had spoken about a sensitive health issue which has no relation to his environment brief, and accused him of ignoring links between pollution and birth defects.

A spokesman for MPAC added: 'These comments are racist and typical of the Islamaphobia that we have witnessed in large parts of the media recently. Gordon Brown should sack him.' But Inayat Bunglawala of the Muslim Council of Britain would say only: 'Islam encourages people to marry outside of their immediate families to avoid having "weak offspring".' Liberal Democrat Chris Huhne said: 'Phil Woolas has gone in with two big feet when tiptoeing would have been more appropriate.'

'If there is now clear evidence that marrying your first cousin leads to unacceptably high risks of birth defects, then we should look again at the law as it applies to all of us, and not seek to single out one community.'

But Mr Woolas was backed by Ann Cryer, Labour MP for Keighley in West Yorkshire, who said the NHS needed to do more to warn parents of the dangers. She added: 'This is to do with a medieval culture where you keep wealth within the family.'

'If you go into a paediatric ward in Bradford or Keighley you will find more than half of the kids there are from the Asian community. Since Asians only represent 20 to 30 per cent of the population, you can see that they are over-represented.'

'I have encountered cases of blindness and deafness. There was one poor girl who had to have an oxygen tank on her back and breathe from a hole in the front of her neck.'

'The parents were warned they should not have any more children. But when the husband returned from Pakistan, within months they had another child with exactly the same condition.'

Downing Street refused to comment.

You're wrong, says MP who wed his first cousin

A LABOUR MP who married his cousin criticised Mr Woolas for singling out the Muslim community over the practice.

Khalid Mahmood, one of four Muslim MPs, called for better education about marriages between blood relatives. Mr Mahmood, now 46, married his first wife, believed to be named Rifat, when he was in his twenties.

The marriage ended in 1992, but the couple had a child, who is now a teenager. The MP for Birmingham Perry Barr told the Mail last night that he knew they were first cousins before the wedding.

But he suggested that those who believed they could be related should have DNA blood tests before marriage. Mr Mahmood declined to discuss the details of his first marriage, saying only: 'I have personal experience of this.'

He added: 'Phil Is trying to be helpful, but I don't think it came across in the way it should have done.' He insisted that young people were 'very much aware' of the problems. They want to move away from that, they don't want to marry their cousins at all.'

Mr Mahmood left his first wife to marry bank clerk Naseem Akhtar, with whom he has a 13-year-old daughter, Zara. In 2004 he left her for a failed Conservative parliamentary candidate, Elaina Cohen, who is Jewish. They are no longer together.

Wards with more than their share of tragedy

By Chris Brooke and David Derbyshire

ON THE children's wards in Bradford Royal Infirmary the evidence is clear. Day after day, paediatricians deal with many more genetic illnesses than almost any other inner-city general hospital in the country.

The infirmary has become a centre of excellence for such tragic health problems, not because of any specialist research or funding, but simply down to the huge caseload.

Many medical experts believe the high number of first-cousin marriages in Bradford's Asian population is a significant factor in explaining the city's worrying child health problems.

Inbreeding is a problem because it whittles away the genetic diversity which helps keep people healthy.

Most worrying, it increases the risks of a recessive genetic disorder. Children inherit two copies of every gene - one from each parent. To develop a recessive genetic disorder, a child must inherit two faulty genes. Normally the chances of both parents having the same faulty gene variant is small and the diseases are rare.

But if the parents are closely related, it is much more likely that they will both have the same mutated gene. And that puts their children at far greater risk of inheriting the disorder.

There are hundreds of different recessive genetic disorders - some which cause life-threatening illness. They include sickle cell anaemia, haemophilia and growth hormone deficiency. Dr Peter Corry, a paediatrician at Bradford Royal Infirmary, said 'informal data collection' amongst his colleagues revealed they had dealt with 140 different autosomal recessive disorders (where both parents carry a mutated gene) in recent years. Dr Corry said a typical health authority would see about 20 to 30 such disorders.

There has also been a marked increase in the number of neurode-generative conditions (brain and spinal cord deterioration causing dysfunction and disability) in children in Bradford.

In 1986 there were eight cases and in 2005 there were 45. A 'large majority' of the affected children were of Pakistani origin. The 'Born in Bradford' project, which began last year, hopes to track the lives of 10,000 babies to explain a clutch of worrying health statistics in a deprived city with the UK's highest proportion of Pakistanis in the population.

The city's infant mortality rate is twice the national average, while there are also high levels of diabetes and heart disease. And the prevalence of infant childhood disability, such as hearing and sight problems, and cerebral palsy in children of Pakistani origin has been found to be up to ten times higher than in other ethnic groups.

One report on the launch of the Bradford health study said it was 'suspected' but not proven that first-cousin marriage played a 'significant role' in the grim health statistics. In Bradford more than three quarters of all Pakistani marriages are believed to be between first cousins and many health studies appear to support a trend of serious health problems in this ethnic group.

A study by Bradford social services showed about five in 1,000 children of Pakistani origin suffered hearing problems compared with one in 1,000 from other racial groups. But a spokesman for the Association of Bradford Deaf Asians said he believed cousin-to-cousin marriages were being used as a 'blame tool' to avoid doing proper scientific research.

Bradford is not the only city where doctors are concerned about the medical problems caused by inbreeding.

Three years ago the Birmingham Primary Care Trust estimated that one in ten of all children born to first cousins died in childhood or suffered from a serious genetic disorder.

Who you can marry, and who you can't

WHILE many might feel uneasy at the idea, marriage between cousins is legal in Britain - and was common until well into the 20th century.

Queen Victoria and Prince Albert were first cousins, as were Charles Darwin and his wife Emma.

The practice made economic sense in earlier times - when it allowed the wealthy to keep their riches in the family, it was also practical at a time when many lived in small rural communities where the opportunities for meeting future partners was small.

It is estimated that around half of British Pakistanis are married to first cousins.

Under English law, marriage between close relatives is banned. A man may not marry his mother, sister, daughter, grandmother, granddaughter, neice or aunt, while a woman cannot marry her father, brother, son, grandfather, grandson, nephew or uncle.

Some marriages between non-blood relatives are also illegal.

Until a recent ruling by the European Court of Human Rights, a man could not marry his former mother-in-law.

Despite all these restrictions on non-blood relatives, marriage between cousins is permitted by the State and Church in Britain - and most other countries.

In fact, the only Western country where cousin marriage remains taboo is the U.S., where it is illegal in most states.

It is one of the great taboos of multi-cultural Britain – and one of the most heart-breaking: children born with cruel genetic defects because their parents are cousins

Daily Mail, February 16th 2008
Special Report by Sue Reid

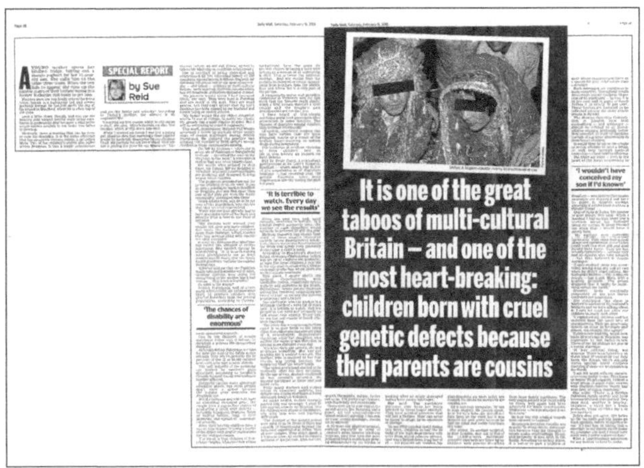
SPECIAL REPORT
by Sue Reid

It is one of the great taboos of multi-cultural Britain – and one of the most heart-breaking: children born with cruel genetic defects because their parents are cousins

'It is terrible to watch. Every day we see the results'

'The chances of disability are enormous'

'I wouldn't have conceived my son if I'd known'

A YOUNG mother opens her kitchen fridge, taking out a mango yoghurt for her 11-year-old son. She calls him to the table three times. When the boy fails to appear, she runs up the narrow stairs of their terrace house in a former Yorkshire mill town to get him. Minutes later, the boy finally enters the living room. Imran is a handsome lad and seems perfectly normal. He has just spent the day at his school in Bradford, where he is often top of the class.

Look a little closer, though, and you can see hearing aids tucked behind each of his ears. Imran is profoundly deaf because a vital nerve which carries sounds to his brain has failed to develop.

Medically, there is nothing that can be done to cure his disability. It is the same affliction that has struck his teenage cousin, a girl called Myra. Two of the children's uncles also suffer severe deafness. Is this a tragic coincidence and are the family just unlucky? According to Imran's mother, the answer is an emphatic 'No'.

'I married my first cousin, which is why Imran is deaf,' she says. 'Myra's parents are also first cousins, which is why she is also deaf.'

'When I started my family I was just a young girl. I had no idea that marrying a close relative would be medically dangerous for any children I had. My parents did not know either. Now our son is paying the price for our ignorance.' The mother (whom we will call Zuhra) agreed to talk to the Mail only on condition of anonymity. She is terrified of being identified and condemned by her extended family of 100 members, spread across Northern England, for speaking out about one of the most controversial — and taboo — subjects in multi-cultural Britain: inter-marriage between cousins which has left hundreds of children damaged or dead. 'My parents would think I had betrayed them,' she says. 'They were born in Pakistan and are stuck in the past. They are good people, but they can't accept that my son's deafness has been caused by my husband and myself being so closely related.'

'My father would like my oldest daughter, who is 18 and at college, to marry her cousin. He already has a male relative in mind. But I will do everything to avoid it happening.'

This week Government Minister Phil Woolas provoked a furore by warning of the health risks of cousin marriages among British Pakistanis. He claimed the practice was sending the number of birth defects among children in these communities soaring.

The MP for Oldham — where one in seven are of Pakistani or Bangladeshi heritage — described the issue as the 'elephant in the room': a contentious matter that was never talked about. His words were echoed by Ann Cryer, the Labour MP for Keighley in Yorkshire, who says cousin marriages are medieval and designed to keep wealth within families.

'The problems provoked are not fair to the children or to the NHS. If you go into a paediatric ward in Bradford or Keighley, you will find more than half of the kids are from the Asian community,' continued Mrs Cryer.

'Since Asians form only 20 to 30 per cent of the population, you can see that they are over-represented.'

'There was one poor girl who had to have an oxygen tank on her back and breathe from a hole in the front of her neck.'

'Her parents were warned they should not have any more children. But when the husband returned again from Pakistan, within months they had another child with exactly the same condition.'

It is not the first time that Mrs Cryer has raised the dangers of cousin marriages. She caused uproar by commenting: 'It is heartbreaking when grandparents are so keen cousins should marry that the family health problems continue throughout generations.'

'A doctor told me that one Pakistani family believed it was the will of Allah, because doctors were doing the wrong thing or the mother was a bad woman... this is not acceptable.'

So what is the reality?

British Pakistanis, half of whom marry a first cousin, are 13 times more likely to produce children with genetic disorders than the general population, according to Government-sponsored research.

One in ten children of cousin marriages either dies in infancy or develops a serious life-threatening disability.

Although British Pakistanis account for three per cent of the births in this country, they are responsible for 33 per cent of the 15 to 20,000 children born each year with genetic defects.

The vast majority of the problems are caused by recessive gene disorders, according to London's Genetic Interest Group which advises families affected.

Everyone carries some abnormal recessive genes, but most people don't have a defect because the normal gene overrules the abnormal one.

But if a husband and wife *both* have an abnormal recessive gene, the couple have a one-in-four chance of producing a child with defects — including blindness, deafness, heart or kidney failure, lung or liver problems, and a myriad of neurological ailments.

Even their healthy children have a one-in-four chance of being a carrier of the defect with drastic implications for the next generation.

The result is that children of first-cousin couples, whatever their ethnic background, have the same six per cent chance of having a baby with defects as a woman of 41 conceiving a child. This is twice the national average. And few realise that the problem includes other ethnic communities from southern Asia, the Middle East and Africa. Yet it is only part of the picture.

A community nurse and genetics counsellor in Yorkshire told me this week that the 'trouble really starts' when a first cousin marries a first cousin and the couple's own grandparents are cousins, too.

'I have heard of first-cousin marriages going back generation after generation in some families. The chances of disability among children then increase enormously.'

Of course, unrelated couples can also have babies that are born damaged, maybe as a result of the mother binge-drinking or taking drugs during pregnancy.

The incidence of mothers choosing to have children late in life is also having an impact on birth defects.

But Dr Peter Corry, a consultant paediatrician at St Luke's Hospital, Bradford — where nearly one in five of the population is of Pakistani heritage — has revealed that 140 genetic disorders have been diagnosed in the city during the past few years. Some are very rare and, until recently, unknown in Britain. In a typical health authority area, the number of such disorders would normally be between 25 and 30 a year.

Medical research has shown that many of these genetic disorders include neuro-degenerative conditions, where the proper functioning of the brain and spinal cord gradually decline after a child is born.

According to Bradford's District Infant Mortality Commission (which was set up to examine the problem), at least five more children a year die in the city than in areas with a similar economic profile but where there are no first-cousin marriages.

This week, I spoke about the medical consequences with paediatric nurses, community health workers and midwives in the North, Birmingham (where genetic disorders among the Pakistani community are twice as high as among the general population) and London.

One staff sister who has worked in a Midlands children's ward for 13 years said: 'It is terrible to watch. Very few people in the NHS are prepared to talk about this openly. Every day, we see the sad results of blood relatives marrying.'

'The other day, a very young mother came in to give birth to her third child. Her eldest boy has already died of a neurological degenerative condition while her daughter, who suffers the same brain disorder, is getting more disabled every day.'

'When the baby girl arrived, she had problems breathing. She was not reacting like a normal newborn. The mother, who is married to her first cousin, was crying because she suspected what the future holds.'

'The eldest son's head started to be unsteady after his first birthday. By the age of two, doctors confirmed he was mentally retarded. He became paralysed at three and just faded away.'

While many doctors and nurses refuse to comment publicly, the debate over cousin marriages is being discussed freely on websites.

An Asian health worker recently posted this sad message: 'I went to two special schools on Monday. One for children with physical disabilities; one with kids who had learning difficulties.'

'The children at the second school were aged 13 to 19. None of them was capable of functioning beyond the behaviour expected of an infant. They all wore nappies. They didn't speak, a few grunts aside. All needed inordinate amounts of special care, from doctors, speech therapists, nurses, tutors and so on. The parents are drained, both financially and emotionally.'

'There were six 16-year-olds at the second school, five Pakistani and a Tamil. All had consanguineous [blood-related] ancestry. I can rest my case: cousin marriages should not be allowed.'

A 42-year-old physiotherapist, working regularly in three of London's most famous teaching hospitals, says that even the most dedicated health workers are growing disheartened by the burden of looking after so many damaged babies from cousin marriages.

She said: 'The paediatric intensive care beds are being blocked by these tragic children. They have medical problems that will last a lifetime. Most can never be cured by drugs, by an operation or therapy.'

'In one NHS hospital that I visited this week, children in half the 20 beds of the high-dependency unit were from blood-relative unions. One was a British-born Iraqi boy of 16 — his parents are cousins, his grandparents on both sides are cousins. No doubt his ancestors are cousins, too.'

'He is mentally incapable. He lies in huge nappies. He cannot speak, he is fed by a tube. He should not have been on the ward, but it was deemed the best place because he had the mind and bodily functions of a baby.'

She added: 'In another hospital, in East London, four out of five of the £l,850-a-week paediatric intensive care beds are taken up by children with genetic disorders from inter-family marriages. The only young patient who could really be made well again had been admitted for more conventional treatment — he was knocked down by a lorry.'

So how has this medical tragedy been allowed to happen?

Marriages between cousins are popular in many ethnic communities because they are thought to create stable relationships. Money and property is also kept in the family. According to society elders, it is better to pick a nephew or niece whose character you know as a spouse for your child rather than a stranger.

Such marriages are traditional in many countries. Throughout South Asia cousin unions comprise 23 per cent of all marriages — in Iraq it is 50 per cent and in parts of Saudi Arabia it is nearly 60 per cent. These figures are believed to be reflected among the same ethnic groups in Britain.

The Human Genetics Commission in London says that counselling — and screening — should be offered to all blood-relative couples, preferably before they conceive, in order to establish the risk of a genetic abnormality in their future children.

It would then be up to the couple to decide whether to have a family, or seek help through medical technology to have healthy offspring.

But there are some — even at the heart of the Asian community in Bradford — who believe that cousin marriages are outdated and have no place in modern society, especially if a child faces death or a chronic illness.

One of those is Zuhra, the mother of deaf Imran. She said: 'When I married, I had no idea there was a problem about my husband being my cousin. It never crossed my mind that I would have a poorly baby.'

'My parents were culturally backward. They came from a rural village and moved here so my father could work in a wool mill and send money back home. They are not cousins themselves — because they had no cousins who were suitable — but they believed in cousin marriages.'

'I only realised there was something wrong with my son at two when he didn't start talking. My husband's brother — who is also my cousin — has a girl, Myra, with a hearing problem. The penny dropped that it might be something within the family.'

Genetic tests eventually conducted on her and Imran confirmed her suspicions.

She continued: 'My sister is married to another of my husband's brothers and we were talking about it. I said we must not allow our children to marry each other.'

'I explained my children and her children have the same sets of grandparents. They are genetically almost as close as brothers and sisters, not cousins. She agreed.'

Zuhra's own wedding, which took place 20 years ago in Yorkshire, was organised by her father-in-law. Three of her six siblings are also in a cousin marriage.

'It was cultural thing, not religious. There is no insistence on these kind of unions in our holy book, the Koran, which actually warns against blood relatives marrying if there are weaknesses in the family.'

'I am not angry with my parents, or even my father-in-law. They knew no better. To get support, I joined a small group of other Asian women with disabled children. Nearly half were born of cousin marriages.'

She adds: 'There is a British Pakistani family nearby who have intermarried and intermarried. Two sons died, another is hearing-impaired, a third has a brain problem. Their mothers say it is just bad luck.'

Zuhra does not agree. She tidies up the tea table and lets Imran go back upstairs, before whispering to me: 'If I had had an inkling that a marriage to my cousin would make my youngest son deaf, I would have made sure I never conceived him.'

What a heartbreaking admission for any mother to have to make.

Finally, some Muslims - without any definitive support from the Quran - regard music, *per se*, as immoral.

Muslim pupils kept out of music lessons

By Laura Clark
Education Correspondent
Daily Mail, 2nd July 2010

MUSLIM pupils are being withdrawn from music lessons because some families believe learning an instrument is anti-Islamic.

The move comes despite the subject being a compulsory part of the national curriculum.

While parents have legal rights to withdraw children from religious and sex education classes, no automatic right exists to pull them out of lessons such as music.

One education expert said up to half of Muslim pupils were withdrawn from music lessons during Ramadan.

And the Muslim Council of Britain said music lessons were likely to be unacceptable to around ten per cent of the Muslim population in Britain.

However, in certain branches of Islam - such as Sufism, which is dominant in Pakistan and India - devotional music and singing is actually central to the religion.

A BBC investigation found that in one London primary school, 20 pupils were removed from rehearsals for a Christmas musical and one five-year-old girl remains permanently withdrawn from mainstream music classes.

Under some interpretations of Islam, music is considered 'haram', or forbidden.

Certain scholars point to passages of the Koran and other sacred texts that appear to condemn musical instruments, because of the corrupting effect they can have on the mind and body. But the meaning of these passages is often disputed, and other scholars say music is permissible.

At Herbert Morrison Primary in Lambeth, 29 per cent of children come from mainly Somalian Muslim families. Headmistress Eileen Ross said some parents 'don't want children to play musical instruments and they don't have music in their homes'.

One girl remains permanently withdrawn from the school's music curriculum, which consists of a government-backed project to learn instruments such as the violin. 'There's been about 18 or 22 children withdrawn from certain sessions, out of music class, but at the moment I just have one child who is withdrawn continually,' Mrs Ross told the BBC. 'It's not part of their belief, they feel it detracts from their faith.'

Ofsted and education experts raised concerns at the findings.

The Open University's Dr Diana Harris, an expert on music education and Muslims, said she had visited schools where half of the pupils were withdrawn from music lessons by parents during Ramadan.

'Most of them really didn't know why they were withdrawing their children,' she said. 'The majority of them were doing it because they had just learned it wasn't acceptable.'

A spokesman for Ofsted said: 'Music is an important part of any child or young person's education.'

Daily Mail, Friday, July 2, 2010

Muslim pupils kept out of music lessons

MUSLIM pupils are being withdrawn from music lessons because some families believe learning an instrument is anti-Islamic.

The move comes despite the subject being a compulsory part of the national curriculum.

While parents have legal rights to withdraw children from religious and sex education classes, no automatic right exists to pull them out of lessons such as music.

One education expert said up to half of Muslim pupils were withdrawn from music lessons during Ramadan.

And the Muslim Council of Britain said music lessons were likely to be unacceptable to around ten per cent of the Muslim population in Britain.

By **Laura Clark**
Education Correspondent

However, in certain branches of Islam – such as Sufism, which is dominant in Pakistan and India – devotional music and singing is actually central to the religion.

A BBC investigation found that in one London primary school, 20 pupils were removed from rehearsals for a Christmas musical and one five-year-old girl remains permanently withdrawn from mainstream music classes.

Under some interpretations of Islam, music is considered 'haram', or forbidden.

Certan scholars point to passages of the Koran and other sacred texts that appear to condemn musical instruments, because of the corrupting effect they can have on the mind and body. But the meaning of these passages is often disputed, and other scholars say music is permissible.

At Herbert Morrison Primary in Lambeth, 29 per cent of children come from mainly Somalian Muslim families. Headmistress Eileen Ross said some parents 'don't want children to play musical instruments and they don't have music in their homes'.

'Significant concerns'

One girl remains permanently withdrawn from the school's music curriculum, which consists of a government-backed project to learn instruments such as the violin. 'There's been about 18 or 22 children withdrawn from certain sessions, out of music class, but at the moment I just have one child who is withdrawn continually,' Mrs Ross told the BBC. 'It's not part of their belief, they feel it detracts from their faith.'

Ofsted and education experts raised concerns at the findings.

The Open University's Dr Diana Harris, an expert on music education and Muslims, said she had visited schools where half of the pupils were withdrawn from music lessons by parents during Ramadan.

'Most of them really didn't know why they were withdrawing their children,' she said. 'The majority of them were doing it because they had just learned it wasn't acceptable.'

A spokesman for Ofsted said: 'Music is an important part of any child or young person's education.'

Chapter 10

HIJABI ROBOTS

The Quran does not require the headscarf

As Muslim women, we actually ask you not to wear the hijab in the name of interfaith solidarity

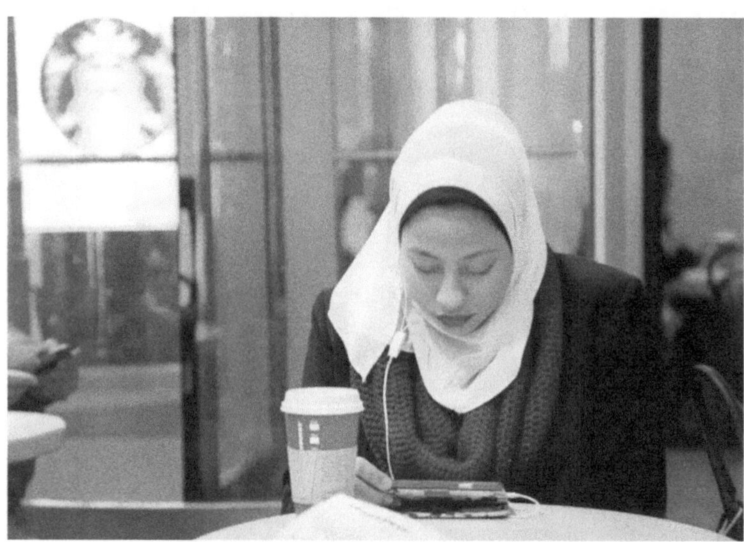

A woman pays attention to her iPhone while seated in a Starbucks coffee shop on Dec. 16 in New York. (Mark Lennihan/AP)

By Asra Q. Nomani and Hala Arafa The Washington Post. 21 Dec 2015

Last week, three female religious leaders — a Jewish rabbi, an Episcopal vicar and a Unitarian reverend — and a male imam, or Muslim prayer leader, walked into the sacred space in front of the ornately-tiled minbar, or pulpit, at the Khadeeja Islamic Center in West Valley City, Utah. The women were smiling widely, their hair covered with swaths of bright scarves, to support "Wear a Hijab" day.

The Salt Lake Tribune published a photo of fresh-faced teenage girls, who were not Muslim, in the audience at the mosque, their hair covered with long scarves. KSL TV later reported: "The hijab — or headscarf — is a symbol of modesty and dignity. When Muslim women wear headscarves, they are readily identified as followers of Islam."

For us, as mainstream Muslim women, born in Egypt and India, the spectacle at the mosque was a painful reminder of the well-financed effort by conservative Muslims to dominate modern Muslim societies. This modern-day movement spreads an ideology of political Islam, called "Islamism," enlisting well-intentioned interfaith do-gooders and the media into promoting the idea that "hijab" is a virtual "sixth pillar" of Islam, after the traditional "five pillars" of the shahada (or proclamation of faith), prayer, fasting, charity and pilgrimage.

We reject this interpretation that the "hijab" is merely a symbol of modesty and dignity adopted by faithful female followers of Islam.

This modern-day movement, codified by Iran, Saudi Arabia, Taliban Afghanistan and the Islamic State, has erroneously made the Arabic word hijab synonymous with "headscarf." This conflation of hijab with the secular word headscarf is misleading. "Hijab" literally means "curtain" in Arabic. It also means "hiding," "obstructing" and "isolating" someone or something. It is never used in the Koran to mean headscarf.

In colloquial Arabic, the word for "headscarf" is tarha. In classical Arabic, "head" is al-ra'as and cover is gheta'a. No matter what formula you use, "hijab" never means headscarf. The media must stop spreading this misleading interpretation.

Born in the 1960s into conservative but open-minded families (Hala in Egypt and Asra in India), we grew up without an edict that we had to cover our hair. But, starting in the 1980s, following the 1979 Iranian revolution of the minority Shiite sect and the rise of well-funded Saudi clerics from the majority Sunni sect, we have been bullied in an attempt to get us to cover our hair from men and boys. Women and girls, who are sometimes called "enforce-hers" and "Muslim mean girls," take it a step further by even making fun of women whom they perceive as wearing the hijab inappropriately, referring to "hijabis" in skinny jeans as "ho-jabis," using the indelicate term for "whores."

But in interpretations from the 7th century to today, theologians, from the late Moroccan scholar Fatima Mernissi to UCLA's Khaled Abou El Fadl, and Harvard's Leila Ahmed, Egypt's Zaki Badawi, Iraq's Abdullah al Judai and Pakistan's Javaid Ghamidi, have clearly established that Muslim women are not required to cover their hair.

Challenging the hijab

To us, the "hijab" is a symbol of an interpretation of Islam we reject that believes that women are a sexual distraction to men, who are weak, and thus must not be tempted by the sight of our hair. We don't buy it. This ideology promotes a social attitude that absolves men of sexually harassing women and puts the onus on the victim to protect herself by covering up.

The new Muslim Reform Movement, a global network of leaders, advocating for human rights, peace and secular governance, supports the right of Muslim women to wear — or not wear — the headscarf.

Unfortunately, the idea of "hijab" as a mandatory headscarf is promulgated by naïve efforts such as "World Hijab Day," started in 2013 by Nazma Khan, the Bangladeshi American owner of a Brooklyn-based headscarf company, and Ahlul Bayt, a Shiite-proselytizing TV station, that the University of Calgary, in southwest Canada, promotes as a resource for its participation in "World Hijab Day." The TV station argues that wearing a "hijab" is necessary for women to avoid "unwanted attention." World Hijab Day, Ahlul Bayt and the University of Calgary didn't respond to requests for comment.

In its "resources," Ahluly Bayt includes a link to the notion that "the woman is awrah," or forbidden, an idea that leads to the confinement, subordination, silencing and subjugation of women's voices and presence in public society. It also includes an article, "The top 10 excuses of Muslim women who don't wear hijab and their obvious weaknesses," with the argument, "Get on the train of repentance, my sister, before it passes by your station."

The rush to cover women's hair has reached a fever pitch with ultraconservative Muslim websites and organizations pushing this interpretation, such as VirtualMosque.com and Al-Islam.org, which even published a feature, "Hijab Jokes," mocking Muslim women who don't cover their hair "Islamically."

Last week, high school girls at Vernon Hills High School, outside Chicago, wore headscarves for an activity, "Walk a Mile in Her Hijab," sponsored by the school's conservative Muslim Students Association. It disturbed us to see the image of the girls in scarves.

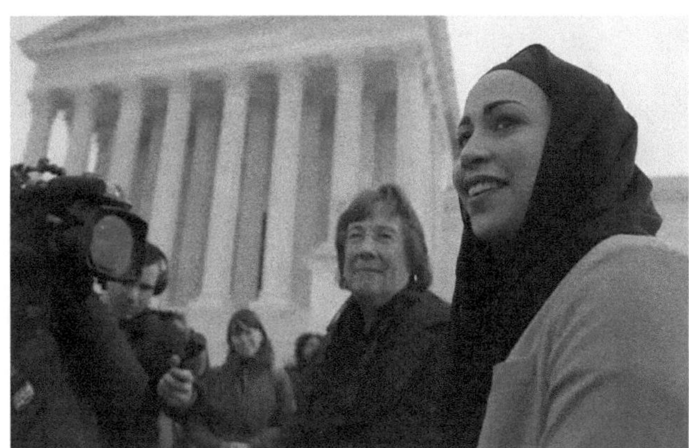

Muslim woman Samantha Elauf (R), who was denied a sales job at an Abercrombie Kids store in Tulsa in 2008, stands with U.S. Equal Employment Opportunity Commission (EEOC) lead attorney Barbara Seely (C) at the U.S. Supreme Court. REUTERS/Jim Bourg

Furthermore, Muslim special-interest groups are feeding articles about "Muslim women in hijab" under siege. Staff members at the Council on American-Islamic Relations, which has pressed legal and PR complaints against U.S. companies that have barred employees from wearing hijabs on the job, has even called their organization "the hijab legal defense fund."

Today, in the 21st century, most mosques around the world, including in the United States, deny us, as Muslim women, our Islamic right to pray without a headscarf, discriminating against us by refusing us entry if we don't cover our hair. Like the Catholic Church after the Vatican II reforms of 1965 removed a requirement that women enter churches with heads covers, mosques should become headscarf-optional, if they truly want to make their places of worship "women-friendly."

Fortunately, we have those courageous enough to challenge these edicts. In early May 2014, an Iranian journalist, Masih Alinejad, started a brave new campaign, #MyStealthyFreedom, to protest laws requiring women to wear hijabs that Iran's theocracy put in place after it won control in 1979. The campaign's slogan: "The right for individual Iranian women to choose whether they want hijab."

Important interpretations of the Koran

The mandate that women cover their hair relies on misinterpretations of Koranic verses.

In Arabic dictionaries, hijab refers to a "barrier," not necessarily between men and women, but also between two men. Hijab appears in a Koranic verse (33:53), during the fifth year of the prophet Muhammad's migration, or hijra, to Medina, when some wedding guests overstayed their welcome at the prophet's home. It established some rules of etiquette for speaking to the wives of prophet Muhammad: "And when ye ask of them anything, ask it of them from behind a hijab. This is purer for your hearts and for their hearts." Thus, hijab meant a partition.

The word hijab, or a derivative, appears only eight times in the Koran as an "obstacle" or "wall of separation" (7:46), a "curtain" (33:53), "hidden" (38:32), just a "wall of separation" (41:5, 42:52, 17:45), "hiding" (19:14) and "prevented" or "denied access to God" (83:15).

In the Koran, the word hijab never connotes any act of piety. Rather, it carries the negative connotation of being an actual or metaphorical obstacle separating the "non-believers" in a dark place, noting "our hearts are under hijab (41:5)," for example, a wall of separation between those in heaven and those in hell (7:46) or "Surely, they will be mahjaboon from seeing their Lord that day (83:15)." Mahjaboon is a derivate verb from hijab. The Saudi Koran translates it as "veiled." Actually, in this usage, it means, "denied access."

The most cited verse to defend the headscarf (33:59) states, "Oh, Prophet tell thy wives and thy daughters and the believer women to draw their jilbab close around them; this will be better so that they be recognized and not harmed and God is the most forgiving, most merciful." According to Arabic dictionaries, jilbab means "long, overflowing gown" which was the traditional dress at the time. The verse does not instruct them to add a new garment but rather adjust an existing one. It also does not mean headscarf.

Disturbingly, the government of Saudi Arabia twists its translation of the verse to impose face veils on women, allowing them even to see with just "one eye." The government's translation reads: "O Prophet! Tell your wives and your daughters and the women of the believers to draw their cloaks (veils) all over their bodies (i.e. screen themselves completely except the eyes or one eye to see the way). That will be better, that they should be known (as free respectable women) so as not to be annoyed, and God is most forgiving, most merciful."

Looked at in context, Islamic historians say this verse was revealed in the city of Medina, where the prophet Muhammad fled to escape persecution in Mecca, and was revealed to protect women from rampant sexual aggression they faced on the streets of Medina, where men often sexually harassed women, particularly slaves. Today, we have criminal codes that make such crimes illegal; countries that don't have such laws need to pass them, rather than punishing women for the violent acts of others.

Another verse (24:31) is also widely used to justify a headscarf, stating, "... and tell the believing women to lower their gaze and guard their chastity, and do not reveal their adornment except what is already shown; and draw their khemar over their neck. . . ."

In old Arabic poetry, the khemar was a fancy silk scarf worn by affluent women. It was fixed on the middle of the head and thrown over their back, as a means of seducing men and flaunting their wealth. This verse was revealed at a time, too, when women faced harassment when they used open-air toilets. The verse also instructs how to wear an existing traditional garment. It doesn't impose a new one.

Reclaiming our religion

In 1919, Egyptian women marched on the streets demanding the right to vote; they took off their veils, imported as a cultural tradition from the Ottoman Empire, not a religious edict. The veil then became a relic of the past.

Asra Nomani talks to audience members in 2009 after Doha Debate in which she argued for the right of Muslim women to marry anyone they choose. (Photo courtesy of the Doha Debates)

Later, Egyptian President Gamal Abdel-Nasser said in a speech in the early 1960s that, when he sought reconciliation with members of the Muslim Brotherhood group for attempting to assassinate him in 1954, the Supreme Leader of the Brotherhood gave him a list of demands, including, "imposing hijab on Egyptian women." The audience members didn't understand what the word hijab meant. When Nasser explained that the Brotherhood wanted Egyptian women to wear a headscarf, the audience members burst out laughing.

As women who grew up in modern Muslim families with theologians, we are trying to reclaim our religion from the prongs of a strict interpretation. Like in our youth, we are witnessing attempts to make this strict ideology the one and only accepted face of Islam. We have seen what the resurgence of political Islam has done to our regions of origin and to our adoptive country.

As Americans, we believe in freedom of religion. But we need to clarify to those in universities, the media and discussion forums that in exploring the "hijab," they are not exploring Islam, but rather the ideology of political Islam as practiced by the mullahs, or clerics, of Iran and Saudi Arabia, the Taliban in Afghanistan and the Islamic State.

In the name of "interfaith," these well-intentioned Americans are getting duped by the agenda of Muslims who argue that a woman's honor lies in her "chastity" and unwittingly pushing a platform to put a hijab on every woman.

Please do this instead: Do not wear a headscarf in "solidarity" with the ideology that most silences us, equating our bodies with "honor." Stand with us instead with moral courage against the ideology of Islamism that demands we cover our hair.

Asra Q. Nomani is a former Wall Street Journal reporter and the author of "Standing Alone: An American Woman's Struggle for the Soul of Islam." She is a co-founder of the Muslim Reform Movement, a new initiative of Muslims and their allies, advocating peace, human rights and secular governance. She can be reached at asra@asranomani.com. Hala Arafa is a retired journalist who worked for 25 years at the International Bureau of Broadcasting as a program review analyst. She was a news editor at the Arabic branch of the Voice of America.

The So-Called 'Islamic' Headscarf Helps Destroy Muslim Hopes *'17 June 2019*

It is eight years now since the failure of the Arab Spring in Egypt. Hosni Mubarak was ousted of course, but the main objective was not achieved: the emergence for the first time of a healthy democracy based on decency and the ethic of 'love thy neighbour' - one compatible with the basic virtues and principles of Islam. The rapidly deposed elected president, Mohammed Morsi, of the Muslim Brotherhood died today in court in Cairo. Poor man. He didn't deserve that.

Held in captivity for years by a vengeful President Sisi of the Egyptian Army. No mercy there. Trumped up charges. God, obviously, did not protect Mr Morsi. Now Morsi will see the reality of what happens after death.

The failure of the Arab Spring meant that once again it all went wrong for the Egyptians. God did not help them and God continues to ignore them. They pray, they fast in Ramadan, they do the pilgrimage to Mecca, they have faith, they strive. And they leave Egypt if they can - to a better life elsewhere in 'infidel' lands. God is not helping them at all. We wonder why.

In the 1950's and 60's the Muslim Brotherhood had a very popular leader called Sayyid Qutb who President Nasser executed in 1966 for subversion. One of the first things that Qutb asked of Gamal Abdel Nasser, when he returned to Egypt from his life-changing stay in America, was that he impose the headscarf on Muslim women in Egypt. Nasser, rightly, refused. All that seemed to matter to Qutb was that Muslim women did not look like floozies. No hair must be shown: only loose women show their hair. Qutb was convicted of plotting to kill Nasser and paid the ultimate price.

One essential element of the Muslim Brotherhood's ideology was the mistaken belief that God instructs Muslim women to cover their hair because showing it will inflame the passions of men and create possible immediate disorder. Of course, the fact that every day Western women, who never cover their hair, are left alone to go about their business seems to be lost on these Muslims. The Brotherhood believe that the hair of a woman is a 'charm' like her breasts: a sexual appendage in other words. It does not say anywhere in the Holy Quran that a woman must cover her hair. It says hide 'your charms'. The Brotherhood consider the hair of a woman - her crowning glory - a charm that must be hidden. The Brotherhood's close spiritual associates, the Salafis, go further: they believe that the face of every woman is a charm too. So the face of every Salafi woman is covered in a niqab. They go round all day looking like letter boxes or bank robbers or as if they are shrouded in funeral wear ready for burial. The Salafi women wear gloves to stop men looking at those sleek, sexy hands. Many of them flatter themselves: they would not be looked at twice in the street even if they showed their hair. These fanatics cannot get it into their heads that dressing in garments up to the neck and down below the knee, as happened in Victorian times, is enough to conform with the Islamic ideal of modesty. They cannot understand that to many people going round all one 's life never being able to show one's hair (or face) in public is seen as completely abnormal. A sign of instability. The men in authority have persuaded these pitiful women that God will punish them severely if they do not cover up. The religious teachers at Al Azhar, the highest Islamic teaching institution in the Muslim world, who subscribe to this view of head covering once also firmly believed (as do many of them still) that it was God 's will to circumcise women: remove the clitoris and labia to reduce sexual pleasure. Female genital mutilation (FGM) is still widely practiced in Egypt today. So this utterly perverse interpretation of the need to 'remove sin' from a woman is one of the beliefs of those same men who think the headscarf is a mandatory requirement in Islam. In 1970's Egypt few wore the headscarf. Over the centuries it went in and out of fashion. The Wahhabi fanatics of Saudi Arabia enforce the wearing of the headscarf on Saudi women. These same people think that music in all its' forms is a sin. That democracy is against God's law. That celebrating birthdays is a sin. That for women to shake the hand of a man is a sin because it can lead to fornication. Interpretations of Islam like these put non-Muslims off Islam altogether. They put off moderate Muslims in Egypt as well. That is why the Arab Spring failed: those millions of Egyptians whose protests helped overthrow Hosni Mubarak did not trust the Freedom and Justice Party of President Morsi and his Muslim Brotherhood to properly interpret the rules of Islam to fit in with the sort of democracy that they so dearly craved. Tensions and mistrust ensued. Those opposed to the Brotherhood and its affiliate, the Freedom and Justice Party, came onto the streets in their hundreds of thousands and begged the Army to rid the country of President Morsi. The Egyptian military took their chance to re-establish their authoritarian stranglehold on society and, in the name of law and order, stage a coup. The hapless President Morsi was deposed in 2013 and spent the rest of his life in solitary confinement. Some reward eh for a lifetime's service to Allah.

The cult of the headscarf has helped ruin a country's path to democracy. These so called Muslims of the hijab and niqab deliberately misinterpret the Holy Quran to suit their misplaced impressions of God's will. The headscarf revolution in the 1980's brought Egypt nothing but misery.

Younger members of the Muslim Brotherhood protested that the Brotherhood was now in favor of democracy. That indeed the headscarf may not be mandated by Allah after all. That FGM was in fact a perversion. That the old guard was in decline. Too late! The moderates in Egypt did not believe them. They did not trust them. They revolted against Morsi and took to the streets until the army intervened.

These same 'Islamist' idiots now infect the United Kingdom and the rest of Europe. 'Islam is the Solution' they say. Yes, but not your brand thank you. If you hijabis don't want men to approach you in the street then wear a badge saying 'F*** off!' or 'I'm a devout Muslim' or 'Leave me alone'. Don't besmirch the religion of Islam by perpetuating the myth that God instructs Muslim women to cover their hair and faces. No wonder God has, it seems, abandoned the Muslims!'

Islamic State and The Headscarf

Shamima Begum of Islamic State originates from East London

Home Secretary Sajid Javid does not want her back in the U.K. Shamima Begum is certainly a brainwashed simpleton - ignorant of the founding values of Islam. And she used her life to aid the most perverted ideology the Muslim world has ever known in what was initially a fight against the murderous tyrant, Bashar Al-Assad of Syria. Assad ironically, was, in his younger days, a trainee eye surgeon in London - it's plain to see that U.K democracy had absolutely no effect on his administrative arrangements back home in Damascus.

The Alawite dictator is no Muslim: his secretive faith believes in transmigration of the soul - a form of reincarnation, which is repugnant to the three Abrahamic faiths. So I.S have had a fatal, ruinous contribution to the cause of justice in the Islamic world. Ms Begum has lost three of her children. She has suffered and should be allowed back to the U.K to face justice and give further explanation as to the background to her association with Islamic State. She can explain her starting point - that it all began with the wearing of the headscarf - then the burqa. This attire is regarded as an absolute necessity by I.S. God will punish you in hellfire if you do not cover up.

Your hair is a sexual appendage. For your entire life you can never show your hair in public. We will force you to cover up and if you don't we will beat you and even kill you. For you have disobeyed God in a fundamental way. In many parts of the Muslim world honor killings occur if girls do not cover up. Or at the least threats and beatings and abuse. Not just physical abuse but psychological abuse. Ostracism and bullying.

All this is a recent phenomenon: in the 1970's few in the Middle East wore the headscarf. After the Iranian revolution and the Saudi drive for Wahabbi Islam it all changed: it was a grave sin to show one's hair. You were a quasi-whore if you did. All this is part of the I.S ideology. They kill to perpetuate this myth. And where is the Islamic world at the moment? Sorry, the so-called Islamic world. Nowhere. Ruled by unelected dictatorships, unaccountable to the people. Failing in every way. The Prophet Muhammad would be appalled if he were alive today.'

Shamima Begum

The Fanatics Have Even Infected Wales

Hijabi zealots poison our schools with their perverted version of Islam.

Sir Zaki Badawi, former senior imam at the Central London Mosque in Regent's Park and later of the Muslim College has said that the hijab and niqab have no place in Islam. Badawi was educated at Islam's highest seat of learning, Al Azhar in Cairo. This misinformed hijabi clone, Shutha of Cathays High School in Cardiff, must not be allowed to perpetuate the Saudi inspired myth that the headscarf is a part of God's instruction. They rely on a weak/forged Hadith. Nowhere in the Quran does it say the hair must be covered. Pupils like Shutha must be disabused of their ignorance. The BBC facilitates this hijabi perversion by giving oxygen to these Asian fools. Parroting their parents sociophobic rants. Shutha must be engaged directly in debate as to her disgraceful misrepresentation of Islam.

Schoolgirl Shutha (pictured) from Cathays High School in Cardiff. Note the black headscarf, in line with Islamic State (I.S) instruction. The thin end of the wedge: have the British learnt nothing?

Pervert Sahar Al-Faifi of the Muslim Council of Wales. A Muslim attention seeker who perverts the founding values of Islam. Given oxygen by the BBC. She must be shown up to be the nutter she in fact is. She is an apologist for Islamic State. A Salafi fanatic. Shun her. Ridicule her. Do not let her corrupt other impressionable, gullible Muslim youth. The niqab has no part in Islam. This bank robber, pillar box (and if our Prime Minister Boris Johnson can say this then we, as enlightened Muslims, can say it too) must be sent back to where she (spiritually) belongs...and we don't mean Rochdale; we mean Afghanistan.

From page 78 of report from the Nixon Center: 'Bearers of Global Jihad? Immigration and National Security after 9/11' by Robert Leiken (2004).

Page 78: "Statutes designed to promote religious toleration ironically appear to have sanctioned the current level of hate speech often found in British mosques today. According to Zaki Badawi, the dean of the Muslim College in London, the majority of imams in the U.K are imported from tribal regions of South Asia (Pakistan, Afghanistan and Bangladesh). They do not know English or England and their training, usually consisting of mastery of the Quran in a religious school or madrassa is funded by Saudi Arabia.

British immigration guidelines allow a community which cannot find "a minister of religion" in the country to import one from abroad. Their cultural background makes them particularly susceptible to fundamentalist interpretations of Islam. In England Islamist sects openly recruited for the Taliban, reportedly enjoying most success in villages and small towns. The infection is not contained within British shores. Once admitted to a European country, individuals may freely enter other EU countries. German officials complain that radical imams from Britain minister in German mosques. They suspect them of carrying messages for Al Quaeda".

Hijabi Clones

Here we have photos taken in 2019 of Indonesian tourists in a U.K High Street. Grandfather, grandmother, mother and son

Note the old lady still finds it necessary to cover up to hide her 'charms'. Exposing her hair will, she believes, inflame the passions of men tempting them to harass her and lead them both into sin. So she dresses as if she is on her way to her own funeral, enshrouded in her 'Islamic' attire. She is oblivious to the public around her where the indigenous ladies walk around freely, hair flowing, without the slightest sign of harassment or public disorder in their wake.

The other lady is a raving beauty. We can all agree on that can we not? Without her headscarf on we are sure that men would be falling over themselves to attract her attention. So we'll excuse her from any outright condemnation. In truth it is the fat, ugly ladies who we have to wonder at - in their self-delusion vis a vis members of the opposite sex. Love at first sight eh! Hijabi robots, hijabi clones, following a perversion of Islam.

Children Forced to Wear Headscarf in Iran

I was forced to wear a hijab. It wasn't liberating.

GETTY IMAGES

Why World Hijab Day is an insult to girls like me

Soutiam Goodarzi, The Spectator, 16 February 2019

It was World Hijab Day earlier this month. You probably missed it, but you can imagine the idea: 'global citizens' of all faiths and backgrounds were asked to cover their heads for a day 'in solidarity with Muslim women worldwide'. It is done in 'recognition of millions of Muslim women who choose to wear the hijab and live a life of modesty'.

Wearing a hijab is not such an abstract cause for me: I used to wear one a few years ago when I was at school in Iran. And in the spirit of solidarity, I'd like to tell you a bit more about the world I left behind when I moved to Britain in 2011 when I was nine years old.

I was six when I was first made to wear the hijab to school. When I was eight, I was forced to wear the hijab while walking around Arak, my hometown in north–western Iran. I did so in fear of the 'modesty' police, who patrolled the streets looking for anyone who dared to remove their hijab.

For one year we had a nice teacher who on rare occasions allowed us to take our hijabs off in class, provided the door was closed, the windows shut and the blinds completely pulled. Why? There was a male janitor who used to sweep the playground, and Allah forbade that he should lay his eyes on an underage girl's hair. She could go to hell for that.

My teachers deemed it appropriate to

shove their hands into my hijab and push my hair back to prevent a single strand of hair being on show. The intrusion didn't stop there. Each week, we had physical checks of our hair and nails — and also, in case we were tempted to try jewellery, our ears, chests and wrists. Wearing large hairclips wasn't allowed, despite the fact that they were hidden by our hijabs. To this day I haven't figured out why a flower-shaped clip is provocative. Underneath the hijab, our hair had to be either short or in a firm ponytail, so that the style of hair didn't accentuate certain areas of the fabric.

Schoolteachers weren't the only ones keeping a close eye on us. Iran's modesty police were a constant and stressful presence in our lives. I'd learned, out of habit, to avoid them as much as possible, though that certainly became difficult when they didn't want to avoid you. They used to park tactically in the road where the hair and makeup salons were ready to arrest anyone who they deemed 'immodest'. They even arrested someone I know who was at the airport about to board a flight to Australia, because her manteau (a loose jacket that is mandatory in Iran for modesty reasons) was 'too short'. And no, this wasn't another era: it was just a few years ago.

I was taught that the hijab was intended to keep a girl pure and away from the eyes of men. This is why the hijab represents a form of victim-blaming. The premise is that men are expected to act like predators, and that girls should feel they are to blame should anything untoward happen.

If the janitor were to think impure thoughts about one of the girls in my class, that would have been her fault. If a married man thinks about a woman inappropriately, it is deemed to be her fault. Then again, he could always take her as his second wife (a practice still common in Iran).

Some argue that the hijab is liberating for women. Having come from the inside, I can tell you: the hijab, and the kind of rule I lived under, isn't about feminism. It isn't an empowering rejection of being judged by your appearance. It is a form of submission: the chaining up of women to the mullahs who promulgate this nonsense. For women who have been forced to wear a hijab, World Hijab Day is an insult. It's an open attempt to portray oppressors as victims, and to overlook the feelings of women who have been taught to believe throughout their lives that they are second-class beings.

I have found my life in Britain to be a liberation, but it staggers me to see so much nonsense spoken about the hijab and the regime I escaped. There are brave women imprisoned in Iran for various infractions of the modesty code; there are women who have been treated appallingly for wearing a hijab that is too loose or transparent. More recently, there have been women punished for not wearing a hijab. And yet the hijab is now celebrated in the West. 'It's OK to be modest,' say the hijab's apologists. Well of course, but there is nothing modest about brushing over the suffering of the women and girls of Saudi Arabia and Iran.

I have tended to keep quiet about the fact that I used to wear a hijab. I was so wounded by the horrors of Islam that I wanted to pretend it never existed. But in Britain I realise I now have a voice, and that I am not a second-class citizen who should be scared of talking out of turn. I have also realised that I don't deserve to be scolded by religious women for ditching the hijab. In Britain, it is acceptable to be a free woman. You don't have to obey the restrictive demands of your father, husband or government.

I have changed a lot since I was six. I'm now 16, and while I can't say I have better hair, I have something even better: freedom. I now try to see World Hijab Day as a day to celebrate being free of the hijab. Women like me who have escaped the veil can use this day to rejoice in our newfound liberty.

Chapter 11

SAUDI MADNESS

From Chapter 15 'Women' in Ed Husain's book 'The House of Islam - A Global History' published by Bloomsbury Publishing in 2018 & 2019:

At a secondary school in Mecca, Saudi Arabia, one hot spring day in 2002, the girls had taken off their oppressive black abayas and headscarves as usual. Saudi men wear flowing white robes that reflect back the searing desert heat, but women and girls must wear black, the most uncomfortable colours for the climate. Islam sets no colour code for women's dress, but black was the traditional women's costume in the Najd region of central Arabia, from which the Al Saud tribe came, conquered the holy cities of Islam, and established its rule across the whole of what is now Saudi Arabia. Mecca was part of the colourful, urbane Hijaz region, but the puritan Najdis disliked its cosmopolitan ways. Colourful Hijazi clothing was banned in 1932, and now even these teenage girls were legally required to wear black. At least inside their all-girls school, with its all-female staff, they could take off their hijab and relax.

But on that day, 22 March 2002, a fire broke out in their school. The girls made a rush for the exit only to be met with resistance at the gates and forced by the Mutawwa'a, the Saudi religious police, back into the blazing building. They were not allowed out because they were not wearing headscarves and abayas. Fireman arrived at the site but were prevented from entering the building because there were teenage girls present with their hair uncovered. When parents arrived, the Mutawwa'a used their police powers forcibly to stop them getting in to rescue their children. Fifteen girls burned to death.

Their lives could have been saved, but Saudi Salafi Islam prioritised the rules on women's dress over the sanctity of human life. And this happened in Mecca, the home and heart of Islam. The first key principle of the sharia, first of the five Maqasid - preservation of life - had been abandoned. Pedantry of the literalist rule trumped the reason for the law.

The Saudi Salafi clerical classes, obsessed with covering up and concealing women, go so far as to argue that the aurah ('private parts') of a woman include her voice. Since a woman's voice can be seductive, that too is aurah. Once such a view is tolerated and accepted, there is no stopping it. It snowballs. Salafi clerics have argued that even a woman's name is aurah, and should not be mentioned in public. Most men in Saudi Arabia and the Gulf today will not speak the names of their wives, sisters or daughters. They refer to them, instead, as hurmah, or honour.'

Chapter 12

Zaki Badawi

The Reformers of Egypt, - A Critique of Al-Afghani, 'Adbuh and Ridha

Muhammad Aboulkhir Zaki Badawi was born in Egypt in 1922. After maktab where he memorised the Qur'an. Zaki Badawi took the degrees of Al-Azhar. He then took B.A, (hons) in psychology and Ph.D from the University of London. he then returned to Al-Azhar as a teacher,

From Al-Azhar, Zaki Badawi went to teach at the Muslim College of Malaya, then joined the University of Singapore and later the University of Singapore and later the University of Malaya in Kuala Lumpur. In 1964 he moved to Nigeria. There until 1976, he was Professor of Islamic Studies at Abdullahi Bayero College, Ahmadu Bello University, Kano.

He joined the Haji's Research Centre at King Abdul Aziz University in 1977 as Professor of Islamic Studies. Then a Director at the Islamic Cultural Centre and the London Central Mosque.

Preface

SINCE these chapters were written some years ago, many significant works bearing on the subject have been published. But I found little reason to alter my presentation or analysis. The most important addition to our knowledge concerns the early life of Jamal al-Din Al-Afghani (1) whose Iranian origin has now been firmly and perhaps finally established. But I had little interest in Al-Afghani's biography. There is no doubt that the portrait of Al-Afghani based on factual documents is a most valuable contribution but need not make us change our view of him or adduce to him less honourable motives or regard him as a political trickster without loyalty to anything except agitation and disorder. We must attempt to understand his dilemma. A born Shi'i who has the vision of uniting the fragmented Ummah has the choice of proclaiming his call in his stark Shi'i colours only to be cruelly dismissed by the narrow minded Sunnis of the thirteenth century A.H. Alternatively, he could declare his conversion to Sunnism as a prelude to his call for unity but if the Sunnis believed his conversion to be genuine, his call to unity with the Shi'is would be bound to arouse their suspicion. You do not seek such recognition for the creed you have just discarded. Further, it would not be logical to expect the Shi'is to answer his call to unity when he had just defected from their ranks. The only course open to Al-Afghani was the one he took in claiming to have been born a Sunni. What he did in this matter given his aims and aspirations is not abhorrent to Muslim Law or ethics.

My standpoint in writing these chapters was (and still is) that Islam is the true and final revelation of Allah. It is the straight path, but it is a broad path with many parallel lanes all springing from the same source and leading to the same destination. This view of Islam is derived from the Prophet who advised his companions to be tolerant and not opt for the difficult and rigid rules thinking them to be more pious for being more painful(2). This allowed for the absorption and assimilation of many diverse cultures and civilizations by Islam. The end result was the greatest of all civilizations, the civilization of Islam. This view of Islamic civilization might appear as a large claim. The fruits of modern science and technology appear to make life so much more comfortable and work so much less arduous. This leads some to argue that we live and experience the 'greatest of all civilizations.'

But we must compare civilizations in all their manifestations and not only in one or two limited aspects. If the aim of human organisation is the achievement of happiness, then Islam will be found as having provided for contentment without passivity, for reliance on Allah without destroying human initiative or undervaluing human action. A happy civilization is a great civilization. Power, wealth and skill can be instruments of happiness and can be tools of misery. Let those who admire modern technology be content with the destruction it has brought upon man and his environment. Let those who appreciate the high standard of physical health brought about by modern medicine lament the low standard of mental health perpetrated by the pressures of industrialization.

Modern man might have been able to conquer the moon and probe at the planets but he has not been able to conquer his own doubts about himself, his place in the world, his ethical values and even the value of his life itself. The empty temples of the discarded gods of the "civilized world" have been replaced by vulgar shrines where physical pleasure and material wealth are held supreme. Fear of ultimate retribution is minimal and hope for final salvation has given way to despair. Is it any wonder then that the most powerful civilization is also one of the most unhappy? No, I stick to my claim that Islam's is the greatest civilization. Should Islam absorb and assimilate the modern civilization, the result would be a civilization with power restrained by ethical values, and wealth justly distributed by religious law and pleasure circumscribed by moral standards. This is the obvious role of Islam in the next phase of history and this, also, is the challenge that confronts the Muslims as they approach the end of the Fourteenth Century of the Hijra.

I pray to Allah to guide mankind into the sirat al-mustaqeem - Ameen!

ZB

(1) See for instance the important publications of Professor Nikki Kiddi

(2) The Prophet is reported as having said "The Religion (of Islam) is the easy not the difficult way."

Introduction

MODERN Muslim thought emerged as a reaction to the impact of the west upon Muslim society. The west forced its way into the Dar Al-Islam, interfering in its affairs and reshaping its destiny. The initial reaction of the Muslims consisted of fortifying themselves with western weaponry. It soon, however, became clear that a modern army presupposed a modern society. The age of the savage fighter descending upon the civilized world to ravage and plunder was over. Military power became one of the dimensions of the degree of modernity.

The influence of the west stemmed from the example of the victor whose culture and system of values carry the prestige of the overlord. But even more important than the western example was modernity. The accumulation of knowledge has become institutionalized. Research laboratories and universities are driven by an unsatiated curiosity to discover and invent. It no longer responds solely to human needs. It invents them. But modernity having grown in the western environment has been stamped with its own characteristic colour. There was naturally confusion in the minds of the Muslims as to what constituted progress and what was specifically western. The distinction between the west and modernity, and consequently westernization and modernization, became blurred. The westernizers took it for granted that to be modern the Muslim community must be western. The way to progress was assumed to be one way - the western way.

As the confrontation between the west and the Muslim world was one between enemies of long historical standing, and as the Muslims faced modernity not gradually and piecemeal but in a highly developed form, their reaction was somewhat uncertain. Even more unsettling for Muslims was the continuous development arising from modernity allowing for little time to adjust and react. The experience of the Muslims in relation to Hellenism was hardly helpful in solving the new crisis. The problem caused by the impact of Hellenistic thought arose during a period of strength and independence. It confronted the Muslims with a static set of principles to incorporate, and it allowed the Muslims to accept or reject them. All these aspects were absent in its confrontation with modernity. Muslim society of the 12 - 13th (eighteenth and nineteenth) centuries was weak and decadent. More importantly, it was not allowed to ignore such a powerful force (modernity) which impinged on the physical as well as on the intellectual and social environment of man. Adjustment to modernity thus took sometimes the form of accepting or adopting western solutions before formulating specifically Muslim solutions stemming from Muslim culture and taking into account the Muslim system of values.

It was against the background of westernization that the reform school emerged. Its main aim was to provide solutions to allay Muslim conscience and permit Muslims to adopt and partake in western scientific development. It was in a sense a resistance to European cultural penetration, and in another it was a yielding to what was considered science and technology. The distinction between the two aspects was never completely clear and the reformers sometimes accepted western cultural values on the assumption that they constituted modernity. Yet it was this particular problem which aroused the strongest controversy in the Muslim world. Those who opposed change called every departure from the old tradition westernization, that is imitation of the hated enemy, the infidel west. Those who supported change called every aspect of it modernization, however irrelevant the particular innovation might be to the needs of man in the scientific and technological age. The problem arising from this controversy touched upon theology, ethics, law and education. And because of the encroachment of the west on the political setup of the Muslim society, the political issues became also involved.

Modernity grew out of the environment dominated by the nation-state, by ideas of liberalism, individuality and limitations of the power of the authorities. The Muslims were quick to notice that and, like their western contemporaries, to consider such institutions as parliament and all the trappings of western political systems as in themselves the necessary dimensions of an advanced society.

The first Egyptian Muslim to perceive the importance of these institutions was Rifa'a Al-Tahtawi who regarded them as good, though not contained in the Shari'a. It is important to note that Tahtawi was hardly a supporter of democracy. His advocacy of the French institutions of parliament and constitution, etc. did not stem from any idea of limiting the powers of the executive. A generation later these institutions were made by the reformists a part of the Islamic political system, and ever since some Muslim writers and apologists have come to equate _Shura_ with parliament, and _Bay'ah_ with election. Thus western institutions were interalized within the theoretical structure of the Islamic reform movement in Egypt.

Islamic reform was only one of many reactions that emanated from the _Ummah_ in response to the challenge of European civilization. There were at least four other distinctive reactions ranging from extreme conservatism to extreme westernism. Perhaps it might help determine the place of the reform school if an outline of the other reactions is given:

1. The conservative reaction favours the _status quo_ of the Muslims and abhors change in whatever form and under whatever banner. The upholders of this view are those scholars who accept the works of some authors (generally belonging to the 8 - 9th century A.H.) as the final and unquestionable authority on Islam. Any deviation from their stated opinion is regarded as a deviation from Islam itself.

The _Ummah_, the conservatives declare, should not be drawn away from the true path by the false Christian civilization or the enticing arguments of those misguided Muslims who claim for themselves the right and ability to present other ideas about Islam. The door of _ijtihad_, they contend, is firmly closed because on the one hand no one is any more qualified for it and on the other there is no need for it.The authoritative books in use contain all the satisfactory answers to all the _valid_ questions.

Central to this outlook is the view that modern civilization is false and transient. It will go away in its own accord so why tamper with the eternal message of Islam for the sake of the unreal and ghost-like civilization.

Thus, in the field of ideas and emotional commitment, they think and argue and feel as if the world around them had remained static since their chosen author had finally concluded the last paragraph of his work. In real life, however, they live and act like all of their contemporaries.

Included in this category (the conservatives) are some - though not all - Sufi leaders whose doctrine rejects this world and advocates withdrawal from it into the eternal reality. To withdraw from the unpleasantness of this world rather than seek to change it is tantamount to accepting or at least tolerating it as it is, i.e. conserving it.

2. The westernizing reaction is on the other extreme. It is for the total acceptance of western culture along with the adoption of science and technology. This view is best expressed in the words of Taha Husain: "Let us adopt western civilization in its totality and all its aspects, the good with the bad and the bitter with the sweet". Fundamental to this outlook is the conviction that "progress" rather than religion is what matters. Religion is, therefore, relegated to the limited sphere of relation between man the individual and his chosen deity. Thus Islam, in this view, is equated with all other religions and doctrines as one of manifold forms of belief systems which may exist but need not significantly influence the march to "civilization".

3. Close to this viewpoint but somewhat different from it is that of the Muslim secularists. They subscribe to the goal of the modernists _viz_ that the legitimate aspiration of the _Ummah_ is that of civilization and progress. They differ, however, in claiming that their view is based not on the intrinsic value of "civilization and progress" but on Islam itself. When the secularist Ali Abdul-Razik proclaimed that the Caliphate was a secular not a religious institution and that the political, judicial and economic activities of the Muslims should be guided by their wordly interests unfettered by religious consideration, he was applauded by every westernizer. But he went further and bestowed on his opinion the authority of Islam itself.

He thus introduced an interpretation of Islamic history and doctrines at variance with the accepted view and proceeded to proclaim that every one was wrong - presumably including the Companions - in believing that Islam aimed at further than the uplift or man's spiritual life and moral values. As for the mundane aspects of society, he stated, they were too trivial to be of concern to Allah's revelation.

Neither the westernizer nor the secularists succeeded in gaining much ground within the ranks of the Ummah. Their ideas were rejected but their programme was, however, implemented. The Muslim communities - with few exceptions - live at present under secular governments administering imported "civilized" systems of law and forming a part of a European-dominated economic system. The disparity between the ideal of the Ummah and its actual could not be more glaring or more agonising. To bridge this gap the revivalists came on the scene.

4. The revivalist or revolutionary reaction proclaims that the ills of the Ummah cannot be remedied except by reference back to Islam in its purity as represented by Al-Qur'an and the Prophetic Traditions. It might be argued that revivalism should not be categorised as a modern reaction to a contemporary challenge since Muslim history is punctuated by revivalist movements emerging as a result of internal factors rather than external threats.

While not denying that the dynamic nature of Islam brings forth from time to time movements of revival to check the drift of the Ummah from the straight path, there is no doubting the fact that the modern revivalists focused most of their effort on exorcising the pernicious influence of modern civilization. The reader can test this claim by glancing at the works of some of the modern revivalists such as Hassan al-Banna of Egypt, Maududi of Pakistan, Muhammad Nassir of Indonesia and Burhanussin Al-Hilmi of Malaya.

The revivalists aim at re-establishing Islam in its totality through persuasion, if possible, or force, if necessary. Hence the emphasis on the duty of jihad and the repeated allusions to the early days of Islam with all the sacrifices and struggles that preceded the final triumph. In contrast with the reformists, the westernizers and the secularists, the revivalists are a mass movement, confident in the Divine source of its belief and certain of the final victory of its Faith.

Although the revivalists sought to stem the tide of westernization, and naturally incurred the hostility of the westernizer and the secularists, they have not in the process gained the confidence or the support of the conservatives. In fact the struggle between the conservatives and the revivalists was often more bitter and deadly than with any other group. The reason can be found in the fact that they both seek to control the masses.

In the circumstances of the Ummah divided as it is into nation-states, the political leadership in nearly all of them remains for the moment in the hands of westernizers of whatever variety. The revivalists are generally ignored as long as they are few and unsuccessful but once they assume the leadership of the masses, the secular authorities bring to bear upon them the might of the westernized state.

The reformists, though they are as Ridha described them the party of the few, are of great significance in modern Muslim thought. They represent a form of synthesis of various trends within the Ummah and their influence is much greater than their number warrants.

The westernizer and secularists sometimes claim to be the natural heirs of the reformists while some revivalists such as Hassan Al-Banna was in certain respects a continuation of Ridha, the reformist.

It must, however, be pointed out that these categories are points on a continuum stretching from extreme conservatism to extreme westernism. The place of a thinker on this continuum is determined by his views on a majority of the important issues. Few, if any, hold the same attitude on all issues and it is therefore possible for one and the same person to be conservative with regard to a particular question while being almost a westernizer in relation to another and still a reformist in connection with yet another question. This observation must be born in mind when assessing the views of the reformists in particular. By the nature of their stand they seem the least consistent as the middle course is the most elusive.

In the following pages we will deal with the views of three major leaders of the Reform School in Egypt. Jamal Al-Din Al-Afghani, Muhammad 'Abduh and Rashid Ridha. The first was the Socrates of the movement. He wrote little but inspired a great deal. It is difficult to be certain with regard to the early contributions of 'Abduh, what emanated from Al-Afghani and what was exclusively'Abduh's. The relationship between 'Abduh and Ridha is even more complex especially when it is realised that Ridha sometimes read into'Abduh's thought what was entirely his own.

Readings

(1) H.G.S. Hodsson: "Modernity and the Islamic Heritage", Islamic Studies, Vol.I no.2, p.115

(2) Modernization and Westernization are used as synonyms in many works. See for instance: I. Abu Lughd: Arab Rediscovery of Europe (Princeton 1963) p.3 ff.

(3) Rifa'i Tahtawi: "Takhlis Al-Ibriz ila Tarikh Baziz" (Cairo n.d.) p.96

(4) Leon Zolondek: "Al Tahtawi and Political Freedom" Muslim World, Vol.LIV

(5) Taha Husain "Mustaqbah Al-Thqafa fi Misre" (Cairo 1939)

Chapter 1

JAMAL AL-DIN AL-AFGHANI

THE epithet of the "Awakener of the East" with which Rashid Ridha often prefaces the name of Al-Afghani is probably an exaggeration. He, however, was not alone in attributing to Al-Afghani a major role in the disturbed reaction of the Muslim world to European expansion in the last quarter of the nineteenth century.(1) That he influenced or associated himself with all the important developments in countries as widely separated as India and Egypt, the Sudan and Iran is well known. He was able through political activities, skilful propaganda and an unusual understanding of European expansionist designs to assume such a position vis-a-vis Europe that most colonial powers watched him with apprehension and some even sought an understanding with him.(2) It is nevertheless important that we should bear in mind that the movement of ideas with which Al-Afghani's name is so closely associated had its genesis in Muslim countries well before he appeared on the scene. Had he never existed, someone would most certainly have come forward to play the role. It was merely the formulation of the problem and the forceful articulation of the solutions that bore the stamp of his powerful personality. He was a born leader. His genius manifested itself not so much in the sphere of ideas as in the correct analysis of a situation and identifying himself with the most plausible and acceptable trend.

Important though he is for the historian of Muslim thought and Muslim revolutionary movements, his life remains full of obscurities. Many gaps are still to be filled, and most of our information about him was supplied by himself. Corroborating evidence for his information had not always been available. He remains historically a shadowy figure. Politically and intellectually he is a vivid force.(3)

Al-Afghani first visited Egypt in about 1869 where he stayed for some forty days on his way to Istanbul. Though he was then, according to his own account a political refugee, he was announced as a man of great learning from Afghanistan.(4)

After a short stay in Istanbul, he was expelled in consequence of a dispute between him and the Shaikh Al-Islam. It appeared that Al-Afghani treated prophecy in a way that provoked the animosity of religious officials. There seem also to have been other personal reasons.(5)

Riadh Pasha, the Chief Minister of Egypt, invited Al-Afghani to stay in Egypt; and without specifying any duties for him he granted him ten thousand piastres a month. No doubt Riadh Pasha, like many of the progressive Turks in Istanbul, was greatly impressed by Al-Afghani and must have assumed that the presence of such a great teacher would be of cultural value to Egypt. Al-Afghani fulfilled this promise, for he gathered around him many students, government officials and intellectuals of various calibre and instilled his ideas into them. He further held regular courses in philosophy, logic and higher theology in his own residence for a number of admiring students. He also encouraged his students to disseminate his ideas through the press and he was at least partially responsible for the appearance of a newspaper of opinion which became his mouthpiece.(6)
But this was not the limit of Al-Afghani's activities. His restless personality, sharp intelligence and violent temperament were not wholly suited to the contemplative tasks of the scholar. The deterioration of government under Isma'il, the growth

of European influence and the collapse of Egypt's economy combined to create for the first time in the history of modern Egypt a public opinion against the government. The traditional attitude which makes obedience to the ruler a manifestation of obedience to Allah no longer held in Egypt. Everyone was trying to find a way to salvation. Isma'il was now completely without friends. But more important than the destiny of the ruler was the destiny of the system itself. Muhammad 'Ali's greatly centralized government was now failing and an alternative was being desperately sought. There was a strong current of opinion that Isma'il's failures resulted from absolute power and that the remedy would be to limit the powers of the ruler. As many of the leading intellectuals and politicians in Egypt at that time were French educated, the French model of constitutional government proved to them very attractive. These 'constitutionalists'(7) under the leadership of Sharif Pasha had their faces firmly turned towards Europe, or more specifically France.

They operated under the misapprehension that Europe's progress was due to the form of its government. Seldom, if ever, did they suspect that governmental institutions reflected social forces within the society. Al-Afghani appeared to have been among the few who were fully aware of this fact.(8)

As events grew more confusing and dangerous, Al-Afghani suspended his regular lessons presumably to devote his time to political intrigue.(9) At this stage he conducted a campaign through the press and public speeches to expose Isma'il and demolish whatever little prestige his government still had.(10)

It is significant that neither Al-Afghani nor his students spoke as Muslims. His writings and those of his chief disciple reflect nationalist and sometimes racialist rather than specifically Muslim inspiration.

He further betrayed a hatred for Britain that was to characterize most of his activities. In his opinion Great Britain constituted the gravest menace to Islam and in combatting her ambitions he was willing to enlist the support of France, Russia or any other force available.(12)

His main preoccupation was external defence, but he realised that it could best be achieved through internal reform. External threat, he reasoned, was brought about by European superior techniques. "The Oriental Question" he said to Makhzumi "would never have existed had the Ottomans matched the West in the field of civilization and coupled its material conquests with scientific power."(13)

The visible military threat from the West figures very largely in Egyptian horizons. Al-Afghani was very conscious of the dangers inherent in the situation in the late 1870s, and like many others thought reforms were necessary, but he was uncertain as to the specific nature of these reforms. In his conversations with Makhzumi he recalled how he expressed his doubts about the value of a legislative assembly unless it emerged from the people themselves. "An assembly brought forth at the behest of a king, prince or a foreign power.... its authority will be illusory and dependent on the will of its creator."(14) He nevertheless advised Tawfiq that he should "hasten to make the nation participate in government ...and should order an election to choose representatives to legislate." This Al-Afghani suggested "would be a strength to the throne and give permanence to your authority."(15)

This confusion between advocating a particular system of government and doubting its suitability for the Orientals' may have been a reflection of Al-Afghani's own inability to reconcile constitutional government with the precepts of Islam. It may on the other hand indicate certain authoritarian tendencies on his part, for his famous article on absolute government calls not for a representative, democratic government but for an enlightened dictatorship.(16)

The positive contents of Al-Afghani's politics are always ill-defined. Although he regarded the republican form of government (al-Hukumat al-Jumhuriyyah) as the highest(17), he was still willing to support an enlightened dictator.(18) He, however, brought to Egyptian politics two fundamental concepts; the first is that rulership was not the privilege of a particular race and was not unconditional(19); the second was that a ruler's retention of power is contingent in his performing his duties.(20) In the quietistic and submissive Egyptian society these ideas were extremely revolutionary, and if a few years after Al-Afghani's departure from Egypt an Egyptian fellah could stand in front of the Khedive and say "We are born free"(21), it was in no small measure due to Al-Afghani's revolutionary agitation.(22) Al-Afghani extended his views into international politics and was perhaps the first Oriental in modern times to reject the idea of European supremacy. Fundamental to his activities and agitation was his conviction that the imperial system was of a temporary duration.(23) It was for this reason among others that he attacked Sir Ahmad Khan so severely(24) and expressed his astonishment at the failure of 'Abduh to expel the British from Egypt after he returned from exile.(25)

The biographers may differ about many things concerning Al-Afghani, but one thing they all agree upon is that he unswervingly opposed British colonialism. His booklet on the relation between the British and Afghanistan(26) expressed his views with vehemence. Al 'Urwat Al Wuthqa was another and more violent expression of his enmity towards British colonialism. In a sense his hatred for the colonial system constituted the motive force in his life.(27) He decried European expansion as immoral and unjust because of the violence that was its basis. "The English", he said to Makhzumi, "deny the wealth of India to the Indians. They take it as their own simply because the Indians are weaker than themselves."(28) Because he regarded Europe of the nineteenth century as unjust he declined to describe it as civilized. "All the scientific gains and whatever good these (western) nations' civilization, if weighed against the wars and sufferings they cause, these scientific gains would undoubtedly prove to be too little and the wars and sufferings too great. Such a progress, civilization and science in this fashion and with these results are undiluted ignorance, sheer barbarism and total savagery. Man in this respect is lower than animal."(29) This strong indictment however is not carried to the point of complete pacifism. Like the good theologian he was, he found war objectionable only if it was unjust or unnecessarily cruel.

In other words he was moved not by humanitarian sentiments but by religious dogma. In his view there was a fundamental distinction between Muslim and European expansion both in manner and purpose; the latter lacked the humane and gentle attitude towards adversaries of the former. Further, European conquests were motivated by greed and sustained by oppression and deceit. In contrast Muslim drive against their neighbours was to free the peoples from tyranny and to allow them an unhampered access to the message of Allah.(30)

His activities must have attracted the secret services of the colonial powers. Statesmen and thinkers took note of his ideas as he grew in importance through the newspapers he helped to create.(31) There is no doubt that he attempted an understanding with the various colonial powers on issues of importance to Islam. The report suggesting that he offered himself for the British Secret Service must, however, be regarded with extreme scepticism.(32)

If his political standing against the British is clear and unequivocal, his religious conviction has been doubted by many scholars. His contemporaries among the conservative ulemas accused him of heresy.(33) But as the nature of orthodoxy changed and liberal ideas penetrated deeply into the Muslim society Al-Afghani became more acceptable, indeed he proved a hero. Doubts about his conviction nevertheless remained supported by a few Muslims and many Orientalists.(34)

Suspicions concerning Al-Afghani's convictions stemmed from various reasons. His enemies in Istanbul, namely Hassan Effendi the Shaikh Al Islam, accused him in 1869/70 of heresy concerning his exposition of prophecy. 'Abduh considered the views of Al-Afghani on this issue to be in accordance with orthodoxy. The Prophet was the spirit which completed the happiness of man in society.(35) A.M.Goichon contradicts this view in suggesting that Al-Afghani deviated from orthodoxy in emphasising the utilitarian function of prophecy.(36)

Elie Kedouri(37) bases his arguments largely on circumstantial evidence and guilt by association. His contribution to the discussion is his emphasis on the general trend in Muslim elite circles of speaking to the masses with different tongues and different symbols and on the fact that despotic rule in the Orient did not permit for freedom of expression. N.R.Keddie goes further(38) in calling upon the Persian environment which she supposed to form the background of Al-Afghani with its traditional scepticism among the intellectuals to throw further doubt on Al-Afghani. In another work(39) she promised to show that Al-Afghani's "Al-Radd Ala Al Dahriyyin" "Refutation of the Materialists" has in fact a double meaning and could be read and understood differently by the elite and the mass of the people.

Amidst all these accusations one point had to be accounted for, namely the unbounded energy and enthusiasm of Al-Afghani for the cause he claimed as his own. A.Hourani holding the opposite viewpoint observes(40) that Al-Afghani "not only believed that Islam was as true or false as other religions, but that it was the one true, complete and perfect religion" Such a belief appears essential as a motive force for Al-Afghani's life and work. It is difficult to explain his activities in terms of purely political ambition. There are so many things and many episodes in his life that could not be accounted for in this fashion.(41) Doubts stemming from his statements, however, cannot be disregarded simply as false interpretation, nor can these statements be twisted to accord with his other and more acceptable ones, except at the expense of either language or common sense.(42)

It appears that insincerity cannot be an adequate explanation for Al-Afghani's work nor can the near sainthood, conferred upon him by Rashid Ridha, explain fully the inconsistencies in Al-Afghani's life and statements. In the view of this writer, Al-Afghani was consistent with regard to one over-riding emotion and loyalty. He conceived of himself as a member of a community with Islam as the base of its culture and facing the same destiny as the rest of the 'Orient'. In this sense Al-Afghani did not have to have a strong belief in Islam as a religion, nor necessarily address the public with regard to his real beliefs. This is not to accuse him of insincerity, for it is my view that he was completely and utterly sincere. He was cast in the role of the Muslim Oriental by nineteenth century Europe with all the implications of cultural backwardness and racial inferiority. Not surprisingly, he clashed over these two issues with Renan, the first European thinker to give intellectual formulation to prevailing prejudices.(43) The effect of Europe experienced at first hand by Al-Afghani was to strengthen his attachment to the Umma and probably shake his faith still further. His overt statements were motivated by the first tendency whereas his private and restricted utterances or writings may have represented the second. His article in Abu Naddara and Al-Basir(44) together with Al Urwat Al Wuthqa manifested the former whereas his rejoinder to Renan was not meant for the general public. There is no reason for us to surmise as regards this. In a recently uncovered letter written by 'Abduh to Al-Afghani, 'Abduh says "We were informed before the arrival of your letter about what was published in "Le Journal des Debats" by yourself in defence of Islam (and what a defence!) in reply to Monsieur Renan. We thought it one of those religious triflings (sic) which would find acceptance on the part of the believers. We urged one of those religious ones to translate it. But the issues of "Le Journal des Debats" were not (Praise be to Allah) available to us till the arrival of your letter. We perused the two issues translated to us by Hassan Effendi Bayham. We consequently dissuaded our first friend from translating it and we used in this respect a promise to give him the Arabic origin of the article which we told him would be coming and then published, and therefore no reason for translation. Thus what we feared was avoided."(45) This significant letter which was either suppressed by Rashid Ridha or more likely was kept from him by 'Abduh confirms our interpretation of Al-Afghani's attitude. It continues as follows "We are at present following your straight path (the head of religion is cut off only with the sword of religion) if you therefore saw us you would see ascetics continuously worshipping, bending and prostrating, never disobeying God in what He orders them and doing what they ordered. "Without hope life would be unbearable." Thus confirms the suggestion that both Al-Afghani and 'Abduh may have been less conformists than many of their admirers would like, but we need not accept the views of their detractors who depict them as more charlatans motivated purely by political ambitions. There is no doubt in my mind that both Al-Afghani and 'Abduh believed in the superiority of Islamic culture and Islamic religion over all other religions. It must be noted that both 'Abduh and Al-Afghani stressed the cultural side of Islam at the expense of the purely theological.

Far more important than the actuality of his belief is the image he built for himself, or was built for him throughout the Muslim world. Whether he was a Sunni Afghan or a Shi'i Persian or a scpetic, his influence remains powerful and as the colonial era declines his views become vindicated. The Muslim nations who would like to document their real or imagined resistance to the encroachment of Europe may seek consciously or unconsciously to inflate the image of Al-Afghani and to magnify his contribution.(46) It is significant that in recent years several biographies of him have been published in the Arabic language, and that many editions of his most famous works, namely Al 'Urwat Al Wuthqa and Al Radd 'ala al Dahriyyin have also appeared. His reputation, which was largely posthumous(47), continues to grow, stifling all criticism and calling for less than a scholarly study of his life work.(48)

The name of Al-Afghani is closely associated with the Pan-Islamic Movement which flourished in the last quarter of the nineteenth century and the early years of the twentieth century. There is no doubt that Al-Afghani, at least when he was in Europe, was working for the unity of the Muslim world under the Caliph.(49)

He was, however, enough of a realist to appreciate the difficulty of Muslims coming under one rule. He therefore suggested that the Muslims need not be united in one single state but could achieve such a unity as essential for their defence. In other words, Al-Afghani suggested unity in foreign policy and defence.(50) 'Abduh's denial of Pan-Islamism being a policy of Al-Afghani belong to a different period and as shown below aimed at pacifying the anger of militant Europe. Unity in itself was not the aim of Al-Afghani. It was a means to an end, namely to the realization of Islam's position in the world vis-a-vis its major enemy the Christian West.(51)

But to deal with Europe necessitated the learning of the secret of its power andadopting the instruments of its military strength. Thus Al-Afghani was calling not only for the discarding of internal disputes but also of the barriers which kept the Muslims unable or unwilling to partake in science and technology. These two proposals have far reaching consequences. In the first place, the insistence of unity meant either the discarding or the radical re-interpretation of Muslim history. Al-Afghani chose to re-interpret Muslim history and to attribute differences between the Shi'a and the Sunni to the machinations of kings.(52) But this was to say the least an over-simplification, yet Al-Afghani was bent on achieving unity between the Shah and the Caliph and he formulated an outline of an agreement between them upon which it appears that he was invited to Istanbul.(53)

To re-interpret the history of a religion is to re-interpret the religion itself, and Al-Afghani was led into the position of advocating a new Ijtihad and the discarding of the authority of the established scholars. Their opinion he contended is not binding upon us. The aim of the new Ijtihad is to arrive at the true Islam, the Islam which is not corrupted by harmful ideas and practices. Thus Al-Afghani while adopting the call of the Wahhabis "Let us go back to the Qur'an and the Tradition" twisted it into "Let us modernize our society to compete on equal terms with the West." In other words he agreed with the Wahhabis in decrying the innovations of the Middle Ages but he did not decry innovations as such for it was one of his major aims to renovate Muslim society.

In advocating a new Ijtihad, Al-Afghani hit at the base of nineteenth century Islam and the general concept of Muslims of themselves. He could no longer accept the position current in his time of fatalism and the inevitable deterioration of mankind. He rejected most firmly the concept of man as a feather in the wind and insisted that he is capable of influencing events and deciding his destiny.(54) He also advocated the idea that man can strive for perfection and claimed that Islam provides him with the social system best suited to help him achieve this task.(55)

But if Islam was the religion best suited to progress why should the Muslims be less progressive than their contemporaries? Al-Afghani found the answer in analysing Muslim history. He discerned that causes of Muslim decline as being the corruption and alterations introduced by the Sufis, the Zindiqs, the Sophists and those who fabricated the sayings of the Prophet. Through all these the concept of Islam as a fatalistic, backward-looking religion without social responsibility and with a strong objection to activity and ambition was developed.(56)

Al-Afghani regarded Islam as the essential basis for the progress of Muslims. It was vital therefore that Islam itself should present not only neutrality towards progress but a positive encouragement of it. For this purpose the presentation of Islam must be in terms of civilization rather than theology. Similarly the attack on the religion of Islam must be regarded as an attack aimed at the very existence of the Umma. He saw a conspiracy against the Umma not only in the attacks of missionaries and priests but also in the pro-Western modernism of Ahmad Khan.(57) He observes that those Muslims who renounce Islam, unlike the anti-religious Europeans, lose their allegiance to their countries and to their nation, thus making it easier for the foreigner to dominate them.(58)

The call for a new Ijtihad and for striving towards perfection meant that the community must discard its lethargy and take part in the struggle for progress. A Muslim Reformation was in his view necessary for achieving this.(59) He often mentioned Luther and attributed to his movement the success of Europe and felt that a similar Reformation would rejuvenate Islam and set the Umma on the road to progress.(60)

Beyond these broad principles Al-Afghani seldom ventured. He avoided discussing detailed programmes, whether because of his intellectual limitations(61) or because the task he set for himself demanded evoking the emotional response for the general principles as a prelude to the more reasoned attitude for the detailed programme (62) is difficult to ascertain.

Al-Afghani wanted to reform Islam not to modernise it.(63) He proposed to the Umma that it should base its progress on its own religion and its own Qur'an.(64) If he rejected imitating the ancient Muslim scholars, he was as firm in rejecting imitating the modern European.(65) He was contemptuous of those who adopt the customs of other nations, and regarded them as a menace to the security of the nation.(66) This was his final Pan-Islamic phase. In his early career in Egypt, as has already been observed, he spoke in terms of nationalism and according to Rashid Ridha formed a nationalist party and addressed the masses of Egyptians as 'Amhouri reported alluding to race rather than religion.(67) Al-Afghani like 'Abduh believed that the use of religion as the basis for reform and progress was essential even inevitable in the Muslim society. If religion is the base upon which reform is to be built, it follows inevitably that the adoption of new measures and new ideas must accord with the basic principles of Islam. In other words, Islam rather than any other social system must be the measure against which reform is to be valued. This amongst other things was an important distinction between him and Sir Sayyid Ahmad Khan.(68)

His dispute with Ahmad Khan coming so soon after Al-Afghani's expulsion from Egypt and his 'conversion' to Pan-Islamism was prompted by the political implications of Khan's programme. Al-Afghani, however, went beyond the limits of intelligent discussion and accused Ahmad Khan, without as it appears reading any of his works, of heresy as well as treason. In the work which was written in reply to a question about Ahmad Khan's ideas, Al-Afghani chose to discuss the ideas of all the 'materialists' from Ancient Greek to nineteenth century philosophers but without reference to the ideas of Ahmad Khan. In Al Urwat Al Wuthqa his references to Ahmad Khan are both erroneous and venomous.(69) It is true that Ahmad Khan's ideas may lead to the "dethronement of God"(70) but, as Al-Afghani knows, religious ideas are not measured by their implications, only by their direct statements. Al-Ghazali in his most restrictive phase did not brand either the Mu'tazila or the Philosophers as Kafirs for their adherence to the principles of causality.(71)

The function of religion as Al-Afghar saw was to instil in the human soul the basis of human society and civilization and the motive force to drive "the peoples and tribes towards progress to the limits of perfection."(72) Religion he suggests instils in the human soul the conviction that man is the noblest creature and that one's nation is the noblest of nations and that mankind came into this world to achieve perfection to prepare him for ascendance into a world more noble and embracing than this.(73) He felt that these beliefs influence moral behaviour towards adherence to the accepted norms of society and towards honesty and truthfulness. He declares these to be essential to the survival of society and without which social conflict would be inevitable. He therefore sees materialism as a direct threat to the well-being of human society and is careful in his 'historical survey' of materialism to show its close association with decline and decadence.(74) He attributes to the belief in the Day of Judgement and in a transcendental being the power to control human behaviour without wh vice would be rife. He concludes his book with a section to prove that Islam was the greatest religion and that it contained all these aspects which ensure the complete happiness of nations.(75) He believes these aspects to be the freedom of the mind from superstitions and the belief in oneself to be capable of reaching the highest degree of human perfection except that of prophethood, and that reason should be the basis of belief without imitation but through proper evidence. He quotes Guizot's "Histoire de la civilisation en Europe" as supporting the idea that European civilization came about largely through the efforts of those with independent minds who claimed the right to question the basis of belief in Christianity and rejected the authority of religious officials. Al-Afghani also considered as a basis of civilization the existence of a section of the population to guide the nation in the fields of knowledge and behaviour and another to educate and lead it to the ideal behaviour.(76)

In Al-Afghani's view the ideal state cannot be realised in this world except through Islam.(77) He promised to write an essay proving this point. It was an unfulfilled promise just as his promise to write a theological (rather than sociological) refutation of the materialists was unfulfilled.(78) What significance is there for the failure of Al-Afghani to write these two essays? Is it because of lack of conviction or because, as observed earlier, of intellectual limitation?

In the realm of politics Al-Afghani was consistent in his opposition to British imperialism. He also decried absolute rule prevalent in the Muslim countries of his time; but he was no constitutionalist.(79) His inspiration appears to vacillate between liberal ideas common in the Francophile circles of Egypt and the traditional concepts of the ideal Muslim government. Whether this vacillation was due, as Ahmad Amin suggests, to his historical development(80) or to a lack of clarity in his positive programme is difficult to ascertain though this writer is inclined to the second view.

He rejected as Ahmad Khan did the nineteenth century Islam and insisted that people must free themselves from Taqlid, (blind imitation). To the suggestion that the door of Ijtihad was closed, he replied "What does it mean? On the basis of what authority was it closed and which Imam said that no-one after me should think independently in matters of religion or should derive guidance from the Quran the authentic Tradition, deduction through analogy in accordance with modern science and the needs of the age and its contingencies?"(81)

He declared that "Religion should not contradict scientific facts. If it appeared to do so then it must be re-interpreted." He decried the ignorant and rigid ulemas of his day whose attitude led to the accusation that the Quran contradicts the established scientific facts but the Quran is innocent of what they say and the Quran must be regarded as too noble to contradict scientific facts especially with regard to general principles."(82) He even went further and claimed that the Quran contains references to scientific discoveries which can only be seen once human knowledge arrives at them.(83) Perhaps this claim was the origin of the trend towards scientific exegesis of the Quran as Tantawi Jawhari attempted later.

But the rebellion against traditional Islam disguised as an attack on blind imitation has as a conscious aim the breaking up of the exclusiveness of Muslim society to allow for greater unity among Muslims and co-operation with non-Muslims for their common interest. Al-Afghani therefore advocated the unity of Sunni and Shi'i Muslims and also the unity of all Orientals vis-a-vis Europe. This was the phase after his expulsion from Egypt characterised by his efforts in Al Urwat Al Wuthqa and also his writings in India.(84) He regarded religion per se especially the three Semitic religions (Judaism, Christianity and Islam) as not a dividing factor. It becomes so only through the professionals with their vested interests.(85)

If he sought to break the exclusiveness of Muslim society and open up its boundaries to new influences and new alliances, he was not calling for less than a transformation of the mentality of the people of his day and the change in the social system to allow for greater flexibility and movement within the society from one class to another and of the society from one stage of development to another. It is this principle of movement, action and development which characterises Al-Afghani's thought and life. He objected most strongly to the lethargy of nineteenth century Muslims and refuted its theological foundation and portrayed Islam as synonymous with action.(86)

Al-Afghani's basic aim was resistance to Europe. His most important means was the awakening of the Muslims from slumbers of superstition and ignorance to partake in modern civilization, especially science and technology. The battle against Europe consumed most of his time and effort at the expense of preparing the Muslim educationally and socially. The teacher in him gave way to the politician or in the words of Rashid Ridha, Al-Afghani "was a theologian overcome by politics."(87) It led him into a tacit alliance with the French (he did not refer to their colonial conquests) who allowed him to use Paris as the headquarters of his secret society and the home of his publication. Its suspension within eighteen months must be attributed to the British either cutting off its financial resources in India and Egypt or else to their success in persuading the French to stop its publication.(88) His departure to Russia and long sojourn there was probably connected with the growing interest of the Czar in India and the approaches to its borders through Afghanistan. His appearance later in Western Europe and meetings with the Shah and travels to Persia and his expulsion from there are episodes reflecting his fluctuating fortunes. Though he might have been regarded by the rulers of his day as a man of exceptional ability he was too much of a revolutionary to adjust to the system of his day. His objection to the Khedive, the Shah or the Sultan must have been much more than he cared to admit. He never succeeded in keeping an office for long. He always attempted to speak to the public over the heads of the rulers.

One point, however, must strike his biographers: that is his relation with the ulema of his day. In his Egyptian period he appeared to be contemptuous of them and incurred their enmity especially the most conservative. In India, however, he allied himself with the conservatives, giving their case a modern twist. But in Europe he regarded the ulema as the pivot of his grand design. If Islam is to be the vehicle of rejuvenation and the weapon of resistance then its knights, the ulema, must be treated with care and during this period the ulema were called upon to lead the people with their knowledge into battle against the invaders and against religious corruption. His call evoked little immediate action in Sunni circles. Among the Shi'ites, however, especially with reference to the tobacco incident, his agitation got immediate and positive response.(89) Although his stay in Persia during his active period was short, his influence remained immensely powerful and his followers not only murdered the Shah but were instrumental in propagating his ideas which were not without influence in the 1905 Revolution. Was this because Al-Afghani was more able to speak to the Shi'i than to the Sunnis? Was it because his conduct and ideas conformed more with a Shi'i background than that of a Sunni 'alim of the nineteenth century, or was it because Al-Afghani's activities in the area of Perso-Afghanistan were those of the politician whereas his activities in the Sunni world brought him into competition with its ulema?(90)

Though many aspects of Sir Sayyid Khan's programme were acceptable to him, he objected to the political assumptions that lay behind it and may have suspected the theological foundations of the naturists.(91)

He fully deserves the statement by Professor W.C. Smith: "A very great deal of subsequent Islamic development is adumbrated in his personality and career. In fact, there is very little in twentieth-century Islam not foreshadowed in Al-Afghani."(92)

His legacy of resistance was carried later by the many nationalist leaders in Egypt and elsewhere. His programme for reform was elaborated by his disciple 'Abduh and carried by Rashid Ridha into wider and more detailed fields.

Chapter 2

MUHAMMAD 'ABDUH

AL-AFGHANI'S most important student was the Egyptian Azharite Muhammad 'Abduh. Like his teacher 'Abduh perceived his task as attempting to bring the Muslim society forward into the modern world. Also like his master he appreciated the role of education, the importance of social organisation and the need to understand Islam in terms relevant to the conditions of the day. However, 'Abduh played a role that made him much more than a student of Al-Afghani.

After his exile from Egypt he joined Al-Afghani in 1882 in Paris where they published the periodical Al Urwat Al Wuthqa for the specific purpose of frustrating British policies in the Muslim world through uniting Islam against them. The political and religious views contained in this publication emanated from Al-Afghani(1) but it is certain that 'Abduh declared his disillusionment with political activities and was critical of Al-Afghani's preoccupation with them.(2) It is important to appreciate the true relationship between Al-Afghani and 'Abduh. Al-Afghani, a man of unbounded energy, unlimited ambitions, and above all a man untied to family or country, was naturally free to indulge in political intrigues that took him into many parts of the globe and made of him a fugitive. His anchor was in his ideal of Muslim unity and his sometimes unrealistic optimism filled him with hope of achieving what all contemporary observers knew to be impossible. But Al-Afghani the revolutionary thrived on being always in opposition. His colourful, romantic personality, his message of hope, the role of the scholar fighter in which he cast himself attracted Muslims greatly to him. 'Abduh's fame, derived no doubt through the activities of Rashid Ridha, was one of the windfalls of his association of Al-Afghani. Ridha declares openly that his attraction to 'Abduh was simply because he was the best available substitute for Al-Afghani.(3) Whenever he compares 'Abduh with Al-Afghani it is invariably to the disadvantage of the former.(4)

'Abduh, a peasant in origin, a family man and a practical and unadventurous person was ready to co-operate with the authorities. Extremism was never one of his traits except under the influence of Al-Afghani. He had all the peasant's attachment to the land of his origin and all the family man's desire for security. While he was a student and a colleague of Al-Afghani he was completely influenced by him. Indeed for a considerable period after the exile of Al-Afghani from Egypt in 1879 until the Urabi rebellion, Al-Afghani's influence was still powerful in 'Abduh's writings; yet 'Abduh exhibits the civil servant's care not to offend superiors.(5) When arrested after the British victory over Urabi in 1882 his defence was that he obeyed orders from his superiors throughout his work. Broadly, his English lawyer at the trial in Cairo found 'Abduh's claim completely confirmed.(6) It is this part of his character, his strong desire to associate himself with power that was both his greatest asset and most damaging weakness. He was able to be an associate of Al-Afghani, the revolutionary, and a supporter of Riadh Pasha, the gradualist reformer.

Once Riadh fell from power he found it easy to switch his allegiance to the revolutionary army officers, reversing all his arguments for gradualism and patience.(7) His quarrels with the army officers appear to have been motivated more by regard for the susceptibilities of the rulers than by the unfeasibility or otherwise of their programme. Once he was allowed back in Egypt he immediately made approaches to the real power in the country, namely Cromer. In a letter he wrote to Cromer on his arrival he openly offers his co-operation to combat 'fanaticism' and propagate the benefits of the Cromer regime through education.(8) He hoped that Cromer would help him obtain the principalship of Dar-Al-Ulum. What grounds must 'Abduh the ex-chief editor of the most violent anti-British periodical have had to make him hope that a British colonial administrator would entrust him with an influential educational office? It has been suggested that 'Abduh might have had to undertake not to interfere in politics before he was allowed to return to Egypt(9) but it is a strange way to interpret such an undertaking as meaning co-operation or even justification of the Cromer regime. No sooner was he in Egypt than it became known that he was popular with the British. His ability alone could not explain his meteoric rise in the judicial system.(10) Ability under the colonial system and especially under Cromer was the last criterion for advancement of Egyptians.(11) His fortune was assured and the nationalists never tired of accusing him of sacrificing everything for love of power. His reputed courage in standing up to Khedive Abbas in a trivial matter concerning Al Azhar is illusory. He as well as everybody else in Egypt was aware that Abbas was impotent vis-a-vis the protection of Cromer.(12) 'Abduh's co-operation with the British and the acceptance of their position in Egypt was, however, an act of practical politics. He never attempted to sanction it by the Shari'a. This is the most fundamental difference between his politics and those of Sir Sayyid Ahmad Khan in India. 'Abduh was too good a theologian to permit himself to misrepresent the Qur'an.(13)

'Abduh was more fortunate than his teacher in leaving many works, but he was never able to confine himself to academic tasks. He took a hand in most of the reform movements taking place in the country, be it in the fields of literature, politics, theology, position of women or education. His biographers, taking their line from Rashid Ridah, devote chapters to his activities outside the purely academic pursuits. Adams(14) was certainly justified in devoting a good deal of attention to these activities as manifestations of 'Abduh's basic principles for, despite his writings, 'Abduh's ideas are best approached by the student through both his reform activities and his writings.

The major events in the life of 'Abduh which have influenced his thought fall into two main categories: the personal, that is those events which take place in one's life and decisively affect it but with little if any wider significance; the second category denotes those developments, political, economic and cultural which engulf one's environment and probably affect the whole world.

Under the first category we may mention the influence of the Sufi Shaikh Darwish who left a profound impression upon 'Abduh's thought and character. Ever since that chance meeting between them and the subsequent interest in which the Shaikh took in 'Abduh, 'Abduh remained for the rest of his life closer to the position of the Sufis than to that of the jurists. Reformism as we know is tinged by strong antipathy towards the Sufi orders but 'Abduh like his teacher Al-Afghani gave public support to Sufism in its orthodox manifestations. It was due to his Sufi tendencies that 'Abduh retained a great deal of tolerance and freedom of mind that were unusual amongst his contemporary jurists. When he later joined Al Azhar and became prominent in its affairs, it was natural for him to join with the more liberal Sufi party against the more rigid jurists within the university.(15)

The second such event may be his meeting with Al-Afghani. It is perhaps difficult to decide whether Al-Afghani, an international phenomenon himself, could be listed under the strictly personal category, but his influence on 'Abduh had the distinct flavour and importance to justify considering it as an event in itself separate from the general impact of Al-Afghani on Egypt or the world of Islam. The relationship between Al-Afghani and 'Abduh appeared to have acquired the character of that of the Shaikh and the Murid in the Sufi order. In his early articles written under Al-Afghani's influence the name of Al-Afghani is always preceded and followed with adjectives that could seldom be found outside Sufi literature.(16) In a particular letter he wrote to Al-Afghani after the former's exile to Beirut, he addresses him in the following terms: "I wish I knew what to write to you - you know what is in my soul as I know what is in yours, you fashioned me with your hands, and you emanated into my matter its perfect form... Through you we know ourselves and also through you we know you, and through you we know everything else."(17) In his preface to this particular letter Rashid Ridha expresses astonishment that 'Abduh should use the language and symbol of pantheism which he always combatted; and also at his admission in the body of the letter of his subservience to Al-Afghani, a position that runs contrary to his cherished claim of independence in thought and action. To this writer this letter probably expressed the true nature of the relationship between Al-Afghani and 'Abduh until the collapse of Al Urwat and the return of 'Abduh to Egypt.'Abduh's tacit acceptance of the British position in Egypt and his open collaboration with Cromer could not be reconciled with continuous adherence to Al-Afghani's uncompromising antagonism to Britain and his unqualified call for continuous struggle against the invader. Though as we shall see 'Abduh described his position as leaving politics to others and concentrating on religious and language reform,(18) his decision to abandon politics was a political act, it is true he did not go as far as Ahmad Khan in India, but to all practical purposes he was of equal value to the British.

'Abduh's emancipation from Al-Afghani's influence began, according to'Abduh's story, in Paris where he claimed to have questioned the wisdom of political agitation and preferred concentration on education and writing.(19) This writer suspects that 'Abduh's claim was probably a hindsight. The real difficulty in the relationship between the teacher and the student might have begun when 'Abduh fearing the consequences in Egypt, sought to hide the fact of his continuing connections with Al-Afghani by refraining from signing a letter to him.(20) The tempestuous Al-Afghani accused him of cowardice, and in consequence the correspondence between the two did not continue. No doubt 'Abduh, finding the gains of collaboration with the British as visible as the possible hardship that would result from antagonising them, thought it wise not to continue his relationship with Al-Afghani. Characteristically, however, he justified his behaviour towards his teacher by a major principle claiming for himself to have recognised all alone the futility of Al-Afghani's course of action. Such claims must be regarded with scepticism.(21) The ghost of Al-Afghani continued to haunt 'Abduh's behaviour with regard to his famous letter to de Guerville(22) criticising Cromer's educational policy in Egypt and his conversation with Blunt can only be explained in terms of the conflict between Al-Afghani's militancy and 'Abduh's quiescence.(23)

The major events that shaped 'Abduh's character and thought consisted of those developments which brought aggressive Europe into the heart of Muslim lands and with it its virile culture and technologically oriented civilization. Like Al-Afghani, he was conscious of Europe as a political force to be resisted and a social ideal to be imitated. In the later years of his life after he had abandoned the political struggle his whole effort was devoted to interpreting Islam in terms of modernity. His efforts in this respect, more courageous than successful(24), brought him fame and following particularly amongst the small section of the Muslim population who had been exposed to western education. In this field, like any other, 'Abduh expanded and deepened Al-Afghani's ideas. In discussing 'Abduh's thought like those of the major thinkers in modern Islam it is proposed that four main topics will be discussed, namely: politics, theology, education and legal reform. Though other headings may have claim to be considered, it is my opinion that a clear picture of 'Abduh's position could be obtained from discussing his views on these four issues, and that in consequence it would be possible to predict his position on any other topic. This will be followed by an assessment of 'Abduh as a thinker and of his impact on Egyptian and Muslim thought.

Politics

'Abduh's political thought was a reflection of the circumstances of his environment. In his early days he, like Al-Afghani, concentrated on the politics of Egypt and for many years after Al-Afghani's departure he continued this interest in his capacity as the editor of the official magazine Al Waqa'i al Misriyya. He looked upon the problems of Egypt in terms of national interest transcending religious and racial boundaries. He conceived, again like Al-Afghani, world politics as a struggle between an aggressive West and a victim East. To him this struggle was but a chapter in a long drama in which the two actors for ever antagonistic win or lose in accordance with the conditions and implements at their disposal. In an article he published in Al Ahram in December 1876 he says, "This antagonism (between East and West) is hereditary and worthy of consideration but as power has become Western centred and the East has grown defenceless the West marched in attack and the East could offer no resistance." He continued in the vein of Al-Afghani, "What made the East reach this low ebb was nothing but disunity to the extent that some people derive pleasure from having other Orientals beset with misfortune through enemy conquest." He then goes on to say "They do this instead of discarding in these times all religious fanaticism and sectarian differences(25) for the defence of their homeland and its protection from invasion of their enemies. Those enemies wish only to expand their domain at our expense, we Orientals, and to be able to enslave us so that they may enrich themselves and use us as a shield to protect their countries and their men." And then he significantly declares, "You Orientals are the children of one country and the partners in its good and ill and everything else. If one of you is fortunate, his fortune will be a fortune for the others."(26)

As events developed in Egypt leading to the downfall of Isma'il and the growth of Anglo-French control and the expulsion of Al-Afghani, 'Abduh who was recalled from his village. where he had been confined by the order of the Khedive to edit the official journal, found himself in a strong position to influence events through the use of his pen. His political articles at this period show two distinct and contradictory trends. Throughout the ministry of Riadh Pasha he subscribed most faithfully to the cautious, gradual approach of the Prime Minister. In three articles entitled "Khata 'Al-'Ugala'" "The Error of the Wise" he criticised the hotheads who wished constitutional government to be implemented at once and he supported the long-term reforms followed by Riadh. He continued, however, to speak as a nationalist who regards the authority of the state to be underlined by political and geographical boundaries rather than religious allegiance.

In an article published in November 1881 dealing with political life, he suggested that the idea of 'watan' country is the best unifying factor. He defined it as meaning in the political sense "Your place to which you belong and in which you have rights and towards which your duties are known and in which you have security for yourself and yours and for your property." He further pointed out that loyalty to the 'watan' was based on three things. First, that it is the place of residence in which food, shelter, family and children exist; secondly, that it is the place of rights and duties upon which political life revolves and thirdly, it is the place to which the person belongs and from which the individual derives glory or shame. This article(27) was published after the fall of Riadh Pasha and its whole tone was to show 'Abduh's conversion to the views of the revolutionaries. In it he declares, "Some people were attempting to deprive those of duties and rights in Egypt of their nationalist title and to tarnish them with the colour of ignorance and humiliation; but events proved, despite them, that we exist in the national sense and that we have a public opinion." In December the same year, he wrote about 'Shura' (consultation) in which he attempted to justify the victory of the 'Urabists in forcing the Khedive to call a national assembly by suggesting that the new system was the modern equivalent of early Islamic tradition.(28) It must be noted here that whereas Tahtawi in a previous generation suggested that constitutional institutions did not conflict with Islamic tradition, 'Abduh has gone far to claim not merely lack of conflict but complete identity. The consultation or 'Shura' of the past was to be the consultative assembly of the present. His concept of 'watan' was borrowed completely from European writers.(29) As there is no such concept in Muslim political thought the whole idea rested uneasily in his thinking. His attempt to relate constitutional advancement to Islam was perhaps motivated by his own need to relate developments to well-founded traditional beliefs whenever possible. The concept of 'watan' runs counter to the universal community 'Umma' so basic to Islam. It could only be justified in terms of utility, that is to say as the only possible way for combatting enemy threats. The judicial mind could easily accept the necessities of defence, the imperative need to unite the inhabitants of the country and the importance of recruiting non-Muslim inhabitants of Egypt with their superior skills and ability in the defence against Europe as sufficient reasons for propagating nationalism. Utility and necessity are well established principles of Muslim law but it would defeat 'Abduh's purpose if he were to state that his talk of 'watan' was only a matter of temporary convenience. His hatred of the Turks reported by Blunt(30) need not have been motivated by patriotism. The idea of a ruling class, race or family though present in Muslim thought could not be used to justify Turkish rule. And in any case the prolonged disappearance of the Quraish and the Arabs in the ruling circle of the Empire has converted many Muslim theologians, chief among them Al-Afghani and 'Abduh, to a near Khariji position.(31) The secure loyalty which 'Abduh advocated at this stage was therefore dictated by the climate of opinion amongst the many French educated constitutionalists. However, 'Urabi himself and the whole nation as well as the British regarded developments in Egypt, especially when the British sent their troops against her, as a fight between the Cross and the Crescent. It is important, however, to point out that the betrayal of Egyptian resistance came not from the non-Muslim minorities but from the Muslim ruling classes and the Muslim Bedouin Arabs.

The occupation of Egypt and the exile of 'Abduh ended for him and his master the nationalist phase of their political thought. In Paris in 1883 they both issued Al Urwat Al Wuthqa, whose positive aim was to unite all Muslims under the Caliphate and to attempt to analyse the factors that led to the decline and fall of Muslims and to charter for them the way to regaining their position.(32) Although Al Urwat Al Wuthqa declares its interest in the defence of Orientals in general and Muslims in particular,(33) the periodical was written in Muslim symbols utilising Muslim beliefs and ideas and drawing for inspiration on Muslim history. It was thus a periodical for Muslims. The catastrophe of Egypt in its view was a catastrophe that injured the hearts of Muslims everywhere.(34) 'Watan' as a bond was now superseded by religion. "The religious bond between them (the Muslims) is stronger than those of race and language."(35)

Underlining the editorial of Al Urwat is an attempt to lay the theoretical foundations for an esprit de corps based on a new concept of Islam.(36) Though Al Urwat avoided as much as possible any direct confrontation with the ulemas, it nevertheless continued to emphasise Al-Afghani's and 'Abduh's concept of religion being vindicated in its social manifestations rather than in theological arguments. This ilhad (disbelief) was treated as a social disease and an interpretation of Islam in terms of European culture in the fashion of Sir Sayyid Ahmad Khan was regarded as treason to the unity of the Umma. Behind the emotional overtone of its articles, reformism was ushered in. Al Urwat diagnosed Muslim political failures as resulting from all-too-powerful rulers who are followed by their nations without question.(37) It was, therefore, logical for Al Urwat to call upon Muslim nations to control despotic rulers and their removal if proved necessary.(38) Like all nationalist ideologies, Muslim nationalism as propagated by Al Urwat was justified in terms of history, selectively presented.(39) Al Urwat also attempted to activate the lethargy of Muslim communities by arguing against its theoretical foundation and by minimising the obstacles and the powers of the enemies.(40)

It is important to note that Al Urwat attempted to differentiate between religion and the causes of power. It regarded Islam as a religion following the same laws as other religions in its social setting. It also considered that the laws of nations are applicable also to Muslims whose Sunni beliefs sought to portray them as the exception to the rule. The Muslims were therefore told that it is not enough to be Muslims and they must also partake with energy and drive in the competition for power and success.(41) The Umma was addressed in the most flattering terms and was told that its concensus was sanctioned by God.(42) Its unity therefore was vital not simply for the defeat of its enemies but for its very salvation.

After the failure of Al Urwat and the return of 'Abduh from exile, he was to disown the idea of unity. Shattered, defeated and frightened, Muslims had to defend themselves against accusations of intolerance by intolerant Europe. While politicians in Britain and elsewhere were conceiving the struggle openly and expressly as a religious one,(43) the mere talk of Muslims' will to defend themselves was labelled fanaticism. To organise and execute actions against Muslims was civilization. If Europe was ever secular in its political attitudes, the Europe that looked with hatred at the Ottoman Empire on its deathbed was fired by the spirit of the Crusades. 'Abduh like many other leading figures in occupied Egypt feared that the spread of Pan-Islamic sentiment and manifestations may bring the wrath of Europe on a defenceless Muslim community.(44)

In his biography of Al-Afghani, he attempted to dissociate him from Pan-Islamism. He deliberately confused the aim with the method. That Al-Afghani aimed at Muslim unity is indisputable. In fact his whole career would be meaningless without it. Al-Afghani, however, sought to reach this aim by reforming the political institutions in one country sufficiently to permit the development and progress of such a country which would then become the base for operation. 'Abduh's famous statement suggests that Al-Afghani's "political aim to which he devoted his thoughts and for which he endeavoured all his life and as a result suffered a great deal was the revival of a Muslim state and guiding it to attend to its affairs so that it might become one of the powerful nations and through her Islam would regain its importance and glory. Implied in this was the humiliation of Britain in Muslim countries and the ejection of its shadow from Muslim communities."(45) It is obvious even from this statement with its reference to Muslim glory and importance that the final aim of Al-Afghani was Muslim unity through which alone the glory of Islam would be manifest. In his rejoinder to Hanotaux, 'Abduh rejects Pan-Islamism not on the ground of being invalid but of being impratical.(46) At no time in his career had he conceived Islam without the Caliphate. His return to Egypt however with its implied acceptance of British supremacy over Muslims was tolerated by the use of two devices. The first was that politics were outside his main sphere of activities and that political institutions are like trees that take a long time and careful nursing to grow. The second was that through education and cultural revival the Muslim community would eventually emancipate itself. 'Abduh raised this into a political creed and paraded this naive concept as a brilliant political approach to subject Muslims. In Tunisia and Algeria he counselled the Muslims to avoid political resistance to France and to concentrate their efforts on education.(47) The colonial powers gave prominence to the first part of his advice. The Muslims emphasised the second.(48) It is doubtful, however, that anyone took 'Abduh seriously in this respect. At best he was naive, at worst he was insincere. Very few Muslims thought it possible that 'Abduh would lack the understanding of the true nature of colonialism. In this connection, Mustafa Kamil following Al-Afghani points out that colonial powers have the habit of perpetuating themselves in their position and if a system of education was seen to lead to their eventual expulsion they would naturally resist it.(49) As Rashid Ridha pointed out,(50) 'Abduh's political pacifism was no more successful with the European powers than Al-Afghani's militance. It, however, had the disadvantage of taxing the emotions of Muslims and stretching to breaking point Muslim political theory in accepting in effect the secularization of Muslim politics.

The suspicion that 'Abduh evoked in the minds of his contemporaries especially in matters political may have prevented him from developing a political theory more in accordance with the prevailing situation. It was left to the traditional ulemas to formulate ideas tacitly accepting non-Muslim rule.(51) In an essay by Shaikh Muhammad Bakheet, evidence was purported to have been found for the legitimacy of a non-Muslim Caliph. Strong opposition to the idea came from Rashid Ridha who in the course of his review of the essay lamented that whereas the writer could get away with such an unorthodox idea 'Abduh would have run into very serious trouble with the ulemas had he merely hinted at it.

'Abduh's withdrawal from politics was simply a withdrawal from nationalist politics. The political intriguer in him, his deeply set enmity towards the Muhammad Ali family, and the Turkish ruling class brought him into conflict with Abbas II.

The quarrel was motivated, according to 'Abduh, by Abbas' cupidity and 'Abduh's refusal to allow him to take possession of the Waqf's money.(52) But it is doubtful that this was the real reason.(53) 'Abduh, like many who suffered in the aftermath of the 'Urabi revolt, carried their hatred against the Turkish aristocracy in Egypt to the extent of supporting the British. Further, the nationalist movement as epitomised by Mustafa Kamil had at that time little positive content. The choice offered appeared to be between the tyranny of Abbas and the autocracy of Cromer. 'Abduh had very little reason to hesitate as to whom he should choose.

In the age of nationalism triumphant, collaboration with the enemy is a black mark that must be erased then it must be explained away in a manner that would make it appear more like resistance than collaboration. Writing about 'Abduh in 1957, Professor M. Al-Bahay aplogises for 'Abduh's relations with Cromer as being a mere measure of convenience providing'Abduh with the necessary protection against the wrath of the Khedive thus allowing him to continue his mission of educational and legal reform.(54) As Professor Al-Bahay has classified 'Abduh as a struggler against Western expansion, he felt a particular distaste to equating him in his more genial period with Ahmad Khan of India.(55) Like Rashid Ridha before him he fell back on the 'Abduh of the pre-exile period to provide him with proofs of his opposition to colonialism. In the view of this writer such an attempt on the part of Professor Al-Bahay is motivated more by affection than by hard historical facts. On at least one occasion Al Manar called for collaboration with the British as the best possible allies for Islam.(56) No doubt Rashid Ridha then was reflecting 'Abduh's views.

The attack on Muhammad 'Ali - the ideal Muslim ruler in the eyes of Al-Afghani - by Muhammad 'Abduh in Al Manar of 1904 was perhaps motivated less by historical analysis than by his old hatred of that family, antagonism to Abbas, and sense of guilt at his collaboration with the British. 'Ali Yusuf in his obituary of 'Abduh says that in his later years he became convinced that he had been God sent to reform Islam.(57) Such illusions of grandeur emerge in a person of his intelligence and ability from insoluble conflict of loyalties, the loyalty to the Umma and Islam as he conceived it and the necessity of collaboration with the British with all its implications.

Like Al-Afghani, 'Abduh opposed autocratic government and subscribed to the idea that a legitimate authority was conditioned by the just application of the law.(58) That rebellion against unjust rulers was legitimate so long as it does not bring greater disasters in its wake.(59) In other words, the potential rebel must weigh carefully his chances of success before embarking on the act of rebellion. He must do so not merely to save his neck but also to save his soul. For it seems as a logical consequence of this view that failure in a noble endeavour is more sinful than not endeavouring at all. Perhaps 'Abduh was not thinking on these lines. He may have had in mind to express the importance of careful weighing of the consequences of rebellion so that legitimate rebellion may not become a licence. Otherwise the whole fabric of political life would disintegrate and anarchy prevail.

The Caliph in 'Abduh's concept was bound by law deprived of absolute powers, obliged to consult with Muslims, but further he was a civil and not a religious leader. In his reply to criticisms of Islam he states that the common criticism of Muslim political institutions among Christians, that Islam supports the identity of religious and political authority was unfounded.(60) He reasons that the Caliph was simply the political head of the community, he was not its Pope. He did not have the power or the position of the chief priest, nor did he have the exclusive right of interpreting the Will of God. 'Abduh felt, therefore, that Occidentals were unjust to Islam.(61) There is in point of fact a certain justification for 'Abduh's position. Western scholars apply to their studies of Islam principles derived from their own society. The separation between State and Church in the West was simply at least originally a separation between institutions, a definition of functions.(62) It was not intended for abandoning Christianity.

The suggestion of separating Islam from politics would be tantamount to abandoning Islam itself as there is no separate institution equivalent to the Church for the Muslim religion. To deprive the Muslim community of the support of the political arm of their society to the tenets of their religion is to abolish the religion itself.

As we noted earlier, 'Abduh was willing to incorporate into the body politics of Islam western institutions. In so doing he opened the way for political development within the Muslim community without the need for heart searching. Political reform, he contended, is in accordance with the true spirit of Islam. The early Muslims employed institutions suitable to their time and conditions; but Islam as a timeless religion must permit of various forms to fulfil the true aims of its principles.(63)

Theology

'Abduh's fame rests on his attempt to prove that Islam and modernity are compatible. This position, which he took over from Al-Afghani, was expanded and deepened. The claim when it was first voiced by Al-Afghani had two important social functions. On the one hand it appeased the Western educated and set their conscience at rest by allowing them to be loyal to both the culture in which they were born and the culture into which they were educated. On the other hand it allayed the fears of the traditionalists who were puzzled by the success of Europe and the failure of Muslims by telling them that Islam could also lead to a similar or even better success than that of Europe. Before Al-Afghani, in as much as the ulemas viewed modernity as incompatible with their religion, they condemned the former and concentrated on the negative side of life subscribing to the most bizarre aspects of decadent Sufism. For this reason both 'Abduh and Al-Afghani voiced strong opposition to prevailing Sufi ideas just as they did to prevailing legal and theological conceptions.

It is important for us to discern three distinct periods that characterised 'Abduh's thought. Under the influence of Shaikh Darwish and most probably in accordance with his own taste and inclination his thought was immersed in Sufi ideas. His first work 'The resalat al-Waridat' was an effort in this vein. It was in the tradition of the medieval Sufis. Its ideas though not departing from acceptable orthodoxy emphasised those elements that were common in Sufi writing. He later abandoned this position so much so that in the second edition of Vol.II of his biography, Rashid Ridha thought it better not to include 'Resalat al-Waridat' amongst his works. In his comments(64) Rashid Ridha says that 'Abduh had changed his position from that of 'Al-Waridat' and that it no longer represented his ideas. It must be pointed out, however, that though 'Abduh was writing as a Sufi using the symbols and the language of the Sufis, the ghost of Al-Afghani and his rationalist ideas were not hard to see.(65) Al-Afghani's rationalism however drew 'Abduh almost completely out of his Sufi slumber and his next effort was a commentary on the "Sharhe al Jalal al Diwani ala al Aqa'id Al-Adhudhiyyah." In this, he showed greater inclination towards philosophy and manifested a liberal attitude towards Muslim disputes.(66)

The third stage in 'Abduh's development is what is commonly known as the stage of Salafiyyat.(67) During this stage he drew inspiration from the fundamentalist reform school of Hanbali jurists, in particular Ibn Taimiya and Ibn al-Qayyim and their school. It is this particular stage which Rashid Ridha seeks to advance as the most genuinely representative of 'Abduh's thought. To this phase also belongs his most important contributions, namely the "Resalet Al-Tawhid" and the "Tafsir al-Qur'an" known as "ta/sir Al-Manar."

'Abduh thus travelled from Sufism through rational liberalism to Salafism. It is important to bear in mind that elements of these three trends are always present in his writing.(68) These three stages characterise emphases rather than conversion. This may appear as an oversimplification but it is important to note that though 'Abduh attempted to revive Muslim philosophy, he had always shown distaste for philosophical encroachment on the domain of religion.(69) 'Abduh consistently showed preference for revelation interpreted by reason, and reason limited in its search for truth by the precepts of revelation. At no time did he rate reason to be above revelation.(70)

Taking the liberal stage in 'Abduh's thought we note in his non-theological writings a concern for mundane affairs, a preoccupation with the vexed question of East and West, a striving to reach a definite identity for his people as a nation tied together with the bond of patriotism "wataniyyah"; an identity that tolerate religious differences. That 'Abduh should subscribe to religious and sectarian tolerance is therefore not strange. But what makes sectarian tolerance more significant is that unlike ordinary nationalists who advocate tolerance because of lack of certainty, 'Abduh suggests that various Muslim sects are equally true and equally acceptable. He quotes with approval the apocryphal tradition which states "The Umma will be divided into seventy-three divisions all of which will go to heaven except one." Concerned as he and Al-Afghani were about uniting oriental and particularly Muslim forces in the face of Europe, he tended to minimise theological differences as Al-Afghani attempted before. But whereas Al-Afghani attributed the extent of the schism between Sunni and Shi'i to the political machinations of rulers, 'Abduh sought to reconcile the various sects through theological manipulation. This phase contributed very little to theological thought as 'Abduh was preoccupied with the political problems of Egypt. His exile concluded this stage of his development and the period of Al 'Urwat al Wuthqa may be considered as a period of transition from the liberal attitude to the Salafi trend of thought. Circumstances were the major factor in these developments.

Probably his most important theological work is the 'Resalat al Tawhid'. It was originally given as a series of lectures in the Madrassah al Sullaniyyah in Beirut in 1303 Hijra. 'Abduh was then in exile after the failure of the 'Urabi rebellion and the collapse of Al 'Urwat al Wuthqa. His other theological works include his reply to Hanotaux and his rejoinder to the onslaught on Islam by Farah Antoun of Al Jami'ah magazine published later under the titles "Al Islam wal Nasraniyyah Ma'a al 'Ilm wa al Madaniyyah" and "Al Islam wa Al-Radd Ala Muntaqidesh" (Islam and Christianity in relation to Science and Civilization) and Islam and the answer to its critics respectively. This last work was by its very nature an apologetic work. Another effort were the articles in Al-'Urwat al Wuthqa which predates these two.(71)

The concept of religion emerging from Al-'Urwat is one that calls for intense activity, full human participation based on the freedom of will and the concept of moral responsibility. It perceived Islam not simply as a theology but as a civilization. Its apologia for it utilised in the first place its past success and in the second its texts devoid of medieval interpretation; on the other hand it sought in the negative sense to apologise for the failure of Muslims and the success of non-Muslims by linking wordly success to wordly factors, adding however that Islam among religions provides the fittest background for the emergence of the strongest and the most complete civilization. Al 'Urwat therefore accepts the criticism levelled by westerners but directs them against Muslim society rather than the faith of Islam. This logic leads to the call that "the remedy is by returning to the principles of religion, the upholding of its laws as it was in the beginning."(72)

'Abduh's later writing simply expanded and enriched these ideas. His reply to Hanotaux for instance is based on an expanded version of the arguments of Al 'Urwat. Hanotaux, who was then a Cabinet Minister in France, wrote an article in the newspaper "Le Journal" dealing with the problem of France's relationship with its Muslim subjects. After a short review of the expansion of Islam and then the growth of European power, Hanotaux pointed out that there were two basic opinions or trends in dealing with Muslims under European rule; one view was extremely antaganostic to Islam considering it as a disease and calling for the most vicious action against it including the extermination of one-fifth of the Muslim population and the enslavement of the rest of them in labour camps, and also the destruction of the Ka'aba and the exhibition of the remains of Muhammad in the Louvre. This was contrasted by another which saw in Islam a faith superior to Christianity. In between these two extremes there was another one that regarded Islam as a bridge between paganism and Christianity. The upholders of these last two points of view supported giving aid and assistance to Islam either as a faith superior to Christianity or as a road to it. That these views were observable aspects of European thought admits no dispute. What brought 'Abduh into conflict with Hanotaux was the latter's assessment or analysis of the causes for the emergence of these views. Hanotaux thought that though Islam and Christianity shared a common origin in Semitic and Hellenistic cultures, Islam represented more the Semitic mentality with its contempt for man and glorification of the deity; whereas Christianity reflected Aryan humanism that raises man's dignity to that of God. "The Trinity" says Hanotaux "in which man and God unite gives man more dignity, more central position than the transcendental concepts of Semites which creates a huge gap between an all-powerful God and an all-dependent man."

This racist concept of culture and religion goes back to Ernest Renan who reiterated the idea in "Le Journal de Debats" in 1883. Al-Afghani refuted the concept itself but it is difficult even in the most learned circles to overcome well-set prejudices, particularly those concerning nations who are visibly weaker. 'Abduh found no difficulty in refuting the theory that the Trinity was superior to transcendentalism. But Hanotaux linked the concept of the Trinity to the idea of free will and Muslim transcendentalism to fatalism and predetermination. It was not difficult for 'Abduh to point out the historical error in this view. Christianity no more than Islamar, Judaism solved with any finality the problem of all-knowing God and the morally responsible man. Like any other faith, Christianity had its fatalists and it is only due to ignorance that Hanotaux did not see the irrelevance of the Trinity to this problem.

The link between Aryanism and humanism on the one hand and the Semites and monotheism on the other was another historical error that 'Abduh was able to correct. Monotheism, he states, was a Hebrew rather than a generally Semitic idea. The Egyptians, the Arabs, the Phoenicians and the Aramaics were all polytheists, following a faith which is nearer to Monsieur Hanotaux's heart than monotheism. Human dignity on the other hand is not impaired in Semitic society. It is in the Hindu-Aryan religion. "Would Monsieur Hanotaux" asks 'Abduh "consider the caste system, the product of an Aryan race, a manifestation of human dignity?" As regards fatalism and the concept of predetermination 'Abduh lays the blame for its appearance in Muslim society on the Aryan converts to Islam, especially the Persians and the Romans (meaning Byzantines). "They (the Persians and the Romans) donned the garb of Islam and carried to it their (older) disputes and hypocrisy. And they introduced the innovation of theological argument and disobeyed Allah and the Prophets who forbade any discussion of Qadar. They deceived the Muslims with their sweet talk and false words until they succeeded in destroying their unity." 'Abduh goes farther to suggest that Hanotaux's ranking of religion was wrong. He contended that the higher the civilization of a community the greater the intellectual capacity of the individual the closer they become to the belief in a transcendent God. He cites to Hanotaux the rebellion of the great philosophers against Greek mythology, suggesting that Hanotaux seems to venerate the common Athenian at the expense of a Pythagoras, a Socrates, a Plato or an Aristotle. Anthropomorphism was fit for people of low mentality who perceived the world and the things around them in the way they perceive themselves or those who attribute divinity to any extraordinary person. The genius and the hero were divine. There is still a third type who is addicted to anthropomorphism and that is the people who depend on mediators between them and God and who perceive God through the image of their king surrounded by the same entourage and officials through whom one's pleas must go to reach Him. These priests enslave the people and control their thoughts and imagination.

These are the harmful effects of idolatory and its like, which could not be denied.(73) 'Abduh put great emphasis on strict monotheism. "In its essence," Muhammad 'Abduh tells us, "true religion is the recognition of a single God who is sole master of the universe. It must consequently be monotheist. It is precisely the case of Islam which has come to call humanity to tawhid, to pure monotheism and to the highest expression of tanzih."(74)

His strict monotheism, however, does not draw him into the arguments pursued by the Mu'tazilites and the Muslim philosophers. He prefers to ignore discussions such as the problem of God's attributes. He says "As to whether the attributes are an addition to him, and the attribute of speaking differs from knowledge of the contents of revealed books, and that hearing and seeing are different from knowing the objects heard and seen, and similar problems which divided thinkers and in which opinions differed, it is not permissible to indulge in, for our human reason cannot reach it and the usage of authoritative texts as proof indicates mental weakness and a religious deception for as we know language is not confined to primary usage. Further language does not bear directly on things as they are. These are philosophical ideas which if they did not lead the best of them astray have never guided any into conviction. We, therefore, must be limited to what our reason can handle and to ask God's forgiveness for those who believed in God and in what His Messengers brought and who nevertheless indulged in discussing these problems."(75) This last quotation represents the latest stage in 'Abduh's development, namely his adherence to Salafi principles and his anxiety to avoid disputes. The technique which he follows throughout the Resalet is simple. The disputes amongst thinkers of generations ago were mostly irrelevant or were caused by a misuse of the language. Irrelevant disputes such as the case of God's attributes, were brought in through the adoption of foreign ideas as the Mu'tazilites did when they "thought it pious to support religion by the utilization of (Greek) science without differentiation between what was really a fact and with what was only the result of imagination."(76) 'Abduh goes even further and decries the usage of philosophy and the application of its methods to theological problems. To this he attributes the demise of philosophy in Muslim society.(77) Its sphere he feels should be confined to those aspects of the physical world that could be useful, such as the advancement of industry or improve human organisation.(78) He voices his position unequivocally, "Our belief is that Islam is a religion of unity in conviction and not diversity in principles. Reason is amongst its strongest supporters and revelation is one of its strongest bases. Beyond this are delusions from Satan and whims of rulers. The Qur'an is a witness on everyone's actions and is the judge of its correctness or error."(79) This is a far cry from the call of young 'Abduh to study theological and modern sciences which he wrote while still a student of Al Azhar and Al-Afghani.(80) 'Abduh appears to subscribe to the views of his mentors Al-Ghazali and Ibn Taimiya who, though different in their outlook, were one in their extreme opposition to philosophy.(81) 'Abduh found it plausible or perhaps convenient to burden Greek thought with a large share of the dispute amongst Muslims. It was therefore natural that he should seek to ban it as harmful to Islam.

There is of course the added factor that despite its sophistication philosophy did not give any satisfactory answer to the question it undertook to solve. Man and especially religious man must fall back on revelation to guide him through the metaphysical maze. Unsatisfactory as this position might appear to the historians of ideas, one must bear in mind that 'Abduh's primary preoccupation was not with providing sophisticated answers to insoluble problems. Rather, he tried to put these problems in what he felt their proper perspective. In doing so he wished to achieve two objectives, the first was to narrow the sphere of doctrinal compulsion, that is to say to limit the number of doctrines to which Muslims must adhere thus leaving a wide area in which opinion may differ. He, however, advised against wasting effort in attempting to solve the insoluble. The second was to free Islam from a heritage that had become an anachronism. The Perso-Greek elements which dominated traditional Islam was incongruous with modernity and as the emergence of Galilean thought in the West undermined the supreme position of Aristotle 'Abduh strove to substitute modernity for Greek philosophy.

There was, however, a major difficulty in this procedure. The success which the Muslim philosophers achieved in reaching a compromise between Hellenism and Islam could not be repeated by 'Abduh as he was both limited in ability(82) and in understanding the true nature of science.(83) The early philosophers appreciated the spirit of Hellenism and were capable of projecting Islam into the universal Hellenistic structure which has previously affected both Christianity and Judaism. They did not perhaps possess precise knowledge as to the contribution of each individual philosopher and this sometimes led to certain difficulties.(84) But what was important was not the ability to pin down the exact ideas of each and every individual. The spirit of Hellenism itself modified by Semitic faith filtered through and was successfully adapted to its new environment by Muslim thinkers. 'Abduh was not so knowledgeable about the West nor was he acquainted to any sufficient degree with science or modern philosophy. His formula was simple: Modernity is based on reason, Islam must therefore be shown not to contradict reason thus we may prove that Islam is compatible with modernity.(85) As a programme this is very limited and 'Abduh more often than not went beyond this dictum to show agreement between detailed scientific theories or discoveries with Muslim revelation. The Qur'an contains certain things that might not be easily acceptable to the scientifically minded such as information pertaining to the world of jinn, and angels. It even contains apparent astronomical fallacies. 'Abduh would interpret these contents so as to agree with modern discoveries. The jinns in this way become the microbes and the story concerning astronomy could be stated to have been addressing simple people at their level of understanding.(86)

Two aspects of modern thought seem to have fascinated him enormously; the one was the theory of evolution which he sought to make compatible with the story of Genesis in the Qur'an and which he employed to prove that Muhammad was the seal of the Prophets.(87). The second is the concept of the scientific law as a formulation of a relationship between cause and effect. 'Abduh was greatly concerned to show that Islam does not reject the principle of causality. He was therefore bent on limiting the region of the miraculous and also on resurrecting the Mu'tazalites' view of the world in preference to the Asha'arite Sunnis who appeared to deny any automatic relationship between cause and effect. For this reason 'Abduh was sceptical of the Karamats,(88) (miracles performed by saints).

He used the simple formula of relying on the texts of the Qur'an and the Sunna without getting deeper into their implications. These ideas could hardly be deemed borrowed from the West. Their origin is firmly oriental and Muslim; yet what forced 'Abduh to make the choice was among other things the impact of western ideas as he understood them.

In his approach to prophecy 'Abduh introduced two new ideas: the first is the evolutionary nature of prophecy referred to above and the second is his emphasis of the moral, social and legal functions of prophets. He lays emphasis on the limits of the prophet's functions. It is not, he makes clear, within their sphere to teach arts or industries or sciences as the Prophet says: "You are better acquainted with the matters of industry and artisanship." This particular idea as we shall see was developed further by his students and by the secularists in their search for a legitimate way of limiting the authority of religion in the life of man.

The emphasis of the social functions of the prophets must bring forth the question of whether they were ever successful. If the prophets and if religion were concerned with making life happier, more successful and more responsible, is it not strange that the Muslims are the least happy, successful and responsible? 'Abduh realises the inevitability of such a question and resorts, as did Al-Afghani, to disclaiming any responsibility on the part of Islam for the failure of Muslims. He continues to attribute success when it occurs in a religious community to its faith and failure to its own action of excess in religiosity or neglect of religion.(89)

'Abduh considers the message of the prophets to be complementary to reason. It cannot possible contradict it, and it cannot supersede it. "How" he asks "could the place of reason be denied when the proofs of revelation must be sifted and evaluated by it."(90) But once reason arrives at the conclusion that the claimant to the prophecy is truthful, reason must accept all the information given by him. It must do so even if the nature of some of which are beyond it. In other words revelation can be accepted if it is above reason but not if it is in contradiction with reason.(91) If revelation appears to contradict itself or reason, we must not accept this apparent contradiction, then we have the choice either of interpreting revelation so as to arrive at a consistent meaning or else to spare ourselves the effort and simply rely on Allah. 'Abduh thus resurrects with full force the old principle specifying the relationship between reason and revelation.

His view of religion has certain interesting aspects. He says, for instance, "Religion is nearer to being an instinctive, intuitive drive than a conscious one. It is one of the most powerful of human forces. It is thus affected in the same way as other human forces."(92) 'Abduh thus puts Islam on a par with any other faith insofar as it affects human behaviour.

Fundamental to the idea of prophecy in Islam is the doctrine of its conclusion by Muhammad. Theologians have stated that God willed that His communication through revelation with man should end by a specific prophet at a specific time. That any further claim to prophethood must be regarded as false. The doctrine is supported by numerous verses from the Qur'an and reports of the Tradition. 'Abduh sought to give a sociological rationale to this doctrine. He suggests that revelation varied in accordance with human development, that when man was still in the stage of childhood "It was not wise to address them with high sentiments or reasonable evidence but it would be a sign of mercy to deal with them as a father deals with his young son. He approaches him only through his senses. Thus early religions used powerful commandments and frightening deterrents and demanded complete obedience even in matters beyond their comprehension, though it is clear to us."(93) The employment of miracles belongs to this stage, in 'Abduh's view, since they aim at overcoming opposition by subduing the emotions. Judaism represents this step in human development. Christianity on the other hand is regarded as belonging to a higher stage when perception has gone beyond crude sense perception.(94) It utilized sentiment, emphasised love. Its rituals reflected a tendency to turn away from the world and to Him Most High. It denied man any rights to possess wealth or to demand redress.

The third and highest stage is that of Islam. Here, the world has reached the final stage of development where his own power becomes a major factor in its direction. Hence its message was to be the final one, a religion which addresses man's reason as well as his sentiments and emotions to guide him into happiness in this world and the next. Islam says 'Abduh, answers all points of dispute proving that the religion of Allah in all generations is one and the same.(95)

The superiority of Islam as a faith does not extend to the fortunes of Muslims in other spheres of life. For generations Muslim scholars influenced by condemnations of the Jews in the Qur'an(96) were under the impression that misfortune in this world as well as success resulted from adherence to one particular faith or another. 'Abduh sought to dissociate social and economic conditions from those of religion. Insofar as society is concerned, its fortunes are determined by its own behaviour. Individuals do not necessarily suffer the consequences of their misguided actions in this world. The individual pious may suffer misery and unhappiness and poverty in the same way as tyrants and transgressors may enjoy the joys of this world. This, however, is not the case with nations for the law of Allah is unbreakable.(97) It is the Sunnat of Allah that the fortune of people is changed when they themselves change.(98) The spirit which is the basis of progress is contained in all divine religions. No people will suffer so long as they follow this spirit and none will experience happiness, glory, power and comfort without it.(99)

We must therefore accept the claims of the Prophet and believe in his message as contained in the unequivocal texts of the Qur'an and the undisputed Traditions, that is the Tradition transmitted by a sufficient number of people as to exclude the possibility of lying and, on the negative side, we must not add to this belief derived through less certain means.(100) 'Abduh makes it clear that it is essential for Muslims to accept the Qur'an and the practical Sunnah.(101) We must not, however, regard this as an abandonment of the Tradition. 'Abduh was voicing the essentials which constituted Islam and about which there was no dispute. It is, however, another stage to reject the Tradition as a source of Islam. He makes it clear that whoever rejects a thing which he adjudges to have come from the Prophets either through his words or his approval, such a person would have rejected the mission of the Prophet and cease to be a Muslim, and similarly with a person who neglects to acquaint himself with the essentials of the faith.(102) He does not bind the Muslim hand and foot by the texts of the Qur'an or the Tradition. In fact he states categorically that so long as the basic beliefs are kept any interpretation does not exclude the person from being a Muslim. He was aware that many aspects of religion were tailored for the common people rather than the philosophically minded minority, and provided that such a minority upholds the conviction in the existence of Allah, the belief in his Messengers, the hereafter and the respect of the Words of the Prophets, any interpretation of revelation to the satisfaction of their highly developed imagination is not barred. It should, however, not be followed by the common people.(103)

The Moral Law

Among the questions that stirred earlier Muslims was the one of the Moral Law, namely whether actions in themselves can be adjudged virtuous or evil and whether human reason is capable of discovering this unaided. This problem appeared in Mu'tazalite thinking as a consequence of their concept of the deity. Having conceived of God as the source of good they limited His actions to what accords to His nature. They also felt that evil to be punishable must be caused by man. To the Sunnis this view appeared closer to the old Persian belief in two forces, one for good and one for evil. The spirit of Islam they believed attributes everything to the creator. Goodness and badness in an action are relative aspects and could not be applicable to Allah. To punish the pious and reward the sinner is unjust only in our minds. Who are we to judge the owner of everything and the creator of everything? A judgement of this nature subjects Allah to the law of man. This Sunni view means in effect that the moral law is not an objective one nor could it be arrived at through the pursuit of human reason alone. What is good is what Allah informs us through the prophets is good. Similarly, what is bad is what Allah names bad. Reason must accept the dictates of revelation. To the Mu'tazalites such an argument would end up by making man no different from a feather in the wind thus destroying the very basis of moral and religious responsibility. Punishment and reward as promised by Allah necessitate freedom of action on the part of man and an inherent value in his actions. Implied in this is man's ability to discover for himself these values. Revelation would simply confirm what reason has already arrived at. The concept of God is thus at the heart of the argument. Is He the absolute and unquestioned ruler or is He some sort of constitutional monarch who like his subjects must adhere to the law?(104)

In his attempt to solve the problem of the moral law, 'Abduh following earlier Muslim scholars(105) treated it as a part of the general question of value.(106) Thus he uses the term beautiful to mean also good, and ugly denoting also evil. This procedure makes it possible to start from the concrete and move up to the abstract, so 'Abduh begins with the beautiful stating that "We find in ourselves the ability to distinguish between the beautiful and the ugly."(107) He observes that this applies to all sense modalities and that without having to go into the definition of beauty and ugliness it is not "a subject of dispute, that it is a characteristic of man and some animals to distinguish between the two."(108) He therefore concludes that "things in themselves have beauty and ugliness."(109)

Abstract ideas have also beauty and ugliness though not as easily perceptible as with concrete objects. It is in his view connected with perfection and the lack of it, so the "perfection of the abstract such as the absolute and the spirit and the human qualities has a beauty which the souls of those who know it feel." (110) In contrast, lack of perfection has ugliness which can similarly be perceived. No-one can dispute the ugliness of a lack of intellectual ability and similar shortcomings. That is why those who suffer from these shortcomings exert their utmost to hide them.

'Abduh concedes that sensory judgement can be modified by experience; thus things which may appear at first encounter ugly could become beautiful through their consequences or their association with what is beautiful. Thus a bitter medicine may be judged on the basis of its curative potency; just as a sweet food may be judged in accordance with its harmful consequence.

From things 'Abduh moves to actions and feels that they share existence with things and therefore should share the same classification into beautiful and ugly. He has three categories of actions:

1. actions beautiful in themselves like military parades, gymnastic or music; or ugly in themselves like the movements of the mob in a crisis and the sound of lamentation of women;
2. actions judged according to their consequences so every action which might cause pleasure or ward off pain is beautiful, while the opposite is ugly;

These two categories 'Abduh finds common to man and higher mammals The difference between them is only a matter of degree.

3. the actions which have to be judged on their delayed consequences. In other words the actions which will have to be considered not on the crude hedonic principle but on the principle of utility. Thus actions are beautiful if they are useful and ugly if they are harmful. This category is characteristic of man.(111)

'Abduh considers this to be axiomat[ic]. He, following the Muslim philosophe[rs] believes that man would arrive through the use of his reason to whether an action is moral or immoral. Since this depends on a quality in the actions in themselve[s] he brands those who oppose this vie[w] as depriving themselves of their reason.(112) He suggests that an ethical system based on reason alon[e] is possible although it is not with[in] the capacity of the common people t[o] discover it.(113)

He sees moral judgement to be influenced by man's memory, imagination and thinking. Since individual differences are only too evident with regard to these faculties differences as regards the specific judgment on actions as moral or immoral correspondingly differs. Therefore the human reason alone cannot achieve happiness in this world except with regard to a few individuals. Hence the need for guidance and this guidance is provided by the Prophet.

Through this psychological analysis 'Abduh was able to give strong support to the Mu'tazalite point of view(114) and, through his sociological observations of the endless differences as to what is good and what is bad, he approaches the position of the Ash'arites. The idea that the elite can arrive at the highest religious and ethical concepts is acceptable to most schools of Muslim thought.

Education

Al-Afghani's school set great store on education. In numerous places Al-Urwat emphasises the important role of education and as referred to above the Ulemas, whose most important function is teaching, occupied a pivotal place in Al-Afghani's scheme of things. Like him 'Abduh pinned his hopes for the survival of Islam and progress of the community on the improvement of its education. As is the nature with 'Abduh's life, three distinct periods can be distinguished each representing a dominant view in education: his pre-exile period ending in 1882, his activities during his exile which ended with his return in 1889 and the period after his return until his death.

In his early days under the influence of Al-Afghani, he recognised most clearly the shortcomings of Al Azhar education. In an article written in 1877(115) he called for the introduction of modern sciences together with the local sciences into Al Azhar university, and describes the strength of prejudice against them in Al Azhar and popular circles. He related the story, which was almost certainly his, of a student who ran into trouble with his father on account of indulging in these disciplines and how he had to swear that he would waste no time on them. He decried Al Azhar's failure to study these disciplines, some of which were being read in most Muslim mosques even in the capital of the Caliph himself. He relates that Al-Ghazali and others considered the study of logic and similar disciplines obligatory for the defence of Islam, and he felt that "In these days where peoples of many religions meet, it is clear that what our forefathers handed down and what our relatives informed us if not supported by evidence will be attacked by heretics and unbelievers."(116) He goes on to say "If this is our position in relation to disciplines which grew in Muslim environments for the last thousand years and which was inherited by us, what I wonder will be our position in relation to the new and useful sciences which are essential to our life in this age and which is our defence against aggression and humiliation and which is farther the basis of our happiness, wealth and strength. These sciences we must acquire and we must strive towards their mastery."(117) He argues the case for modern sciences in the classical legal fashion. "There is", he says, "no religion without a state and no state without authority and no authority without strength and no strength without wealth. The state does not possess trade or industry. Its wealth is the wealth of the people and the people's wealth is not possible without the spread of these sciences amongst them so that they may know the ways for acquiring wealth."(118) In the vein of Al-Afghani he calls upon the Ulemas to advise the people on this score and he apologises for them not having done so previously by claiming that "They did not pay attention to its necessity...Had they paid such attention and scrutinized the matter as it is, they would have worked hard to guide the people in this direction and they would have filled the mosques with speakers and preachers to urge the public to acquire what is essential for the protection of their faith."(119) These were the sparks of an enthusiastic young student who felt strongly about his belief and who was aware from first hand experience of the tremendous opposition and difficulty. Later, as an editor of the official journal Al-Waqai' Al-Misriyyah, he concerned himself with education and campaigned against educational policy during the 1880s to the extent that the then Minister of Education complained to the Prime Minister who in his turn stood by 'Abduh. He requested the Minister to take 'Abduh's criticisms seriously, and to assist in this respect an educational committee with 'Abduh as a member was instituted. Although the majority of members were Europeans, 'Abduh managed to obtain approval for the proposal that the Ministry be given the right to supervise foreign schools in the country. The question of the schools was important as they were regarded by Muslim opinion as less educational in nature and more as religious propaganda centres. 'Abduh's success in this direction was, however, nullified by the coming of the British.(120)

'Abduh was aware of the importance of education in matters of cultural influences and was critical of parents who allowed their children to be educated in missionary schools. In a somewhat amusing incident he and Al-Afghani once waded through the muddy streets of Alexandria for the sole purpose of re-converting a Muslim youth who under the influence of the missionaries in his school had become Christian.(121) Both were disturbed at the lack of concern in this respect of authorities in Egypt. 'Abduh expressed his view on foreign schools in no uncertain terms in an article published in August 1881 dealing with the influence of education in matters of religion and faith. He points out the obvious fact that "The missionary schools were not established for the purpose of profit but for the sole object of spreading knowledge and lighting the candle of civilization, or so they say, such as the Frere schools of American and English origin and others. Assuming that we accept what they say regarding their intentions in establishing these schools, it is a fact that the heads of these schools belong to one sect of Christianity or another. Headmasters are not obliged to issue special religious books to each student in accordance with his particular religion...and do not feel it their duty to employ religious teachers of a different denomination. They naturally specify religious books in accordance with their own outlook. This is the reason that all books in these schools fit in with the religious and sectarian beliefs of the headmaster. The Protestants use Protestant books, and the Catholics use Catholic books and so on and so forth. The students despite their religious differences are made to read one and the same type of book which accords with the particular beliefs of the founder of the school. If the students are exposed for a long time to the education in a Protestant school, for instance, there is no doubt that their beliefs will gradually change from Coptic, Catholic or Islamic faith to Protestant religion. This is also true in the case of the Catholic schools or the Muslim Maktabs such as the Qur'anic maktabs or the school of Al Azhar."(122) He consequently calls upon parents to refrain from sending their young children to schools established for the propagation of a different denomination or religion.

Muslim revivalism owes a great deal to the activities of the missionaries, which for the most part were crude, arrogant and ignorant. This caused Muslims to resent them and suspect everything European.(123) As European influence grew in Egypt so did the arrogance and irresponsibility of the missionaries. The fate of most missionary establishments in Egypt in the era of colonial withdrawal need not stimulate any pity or sorrow. The historical process necessitates the destruction of an educational system which was regarded as having derived its existence, its raison d'etre from European military superiority and from the desire to soften local resistance to European supremacy respectively.

'Abduh's opposition to the missionaries was in no way an

opposition to western science and technology. The essence of his reform is to introduce them into Muslim life. He was, however, opposed to imitation of western institutions without any reference to the cultural milieu of the Muslims. Like Al-Afghani, he distrusted the westernizers and he lumped them together with the conservatives under the derogatory nomenclature of Muqallidun (imitators).

The westernizers in Egypt were adopting western education, western sciences and even a western medium of teaching, namely French. 'Abduh in a strong article in Al-Waqai', December 1880, exclaims at the decision of the Ministry to use a foreign medium even in a school meant for popular education. He reminds his readers that "Evening schools in civilized countries teach sciences through the medium of the colloquial language, refraining as much as possible from the use of technical terms which might be difficult to understand." He then sarcastically asks "Is it possible that we have become more advanced than these civilized countries and that our evening schools have become of a higher level than theirs?" He draws attention to the fact that the student population in these schools consisted largely of foreigners and points out that the language of primary education, particularly in the evening schools must be the language of the country; thus the ignorant and the lazy would have no excuse in not joining them.

'Abduh comments with scorn on a directive by the Ministry of Education threatening punishment for various shortcomings in the teaching profression. He reminds the Ministry that "Decrees and high pronouncements without something tangible coming out of them have no place."(124) He calls upon the Ministry to see that simplified books in the Arabic language are written and made available to the students. (125)

In the opinion of 'Abduh the purpose of education is "To bring up minds and souls and to raise them to the point where the person becomes capable of achieving full happiness or as much of it as possible in his life and after death." 'Abduh rejects the mechanical view of schools and educational institutions as merely factories producing skilled robots. His view is that the school and the whole system of education must help a person mentally and spiritually. "We mean by the education of the mind" he says "bringing it out of simplicity and emptiness of knowledge and away from false concepts and bad ideas so that it acquires correct concepts and information. From this the mind becomes capable of distinguishing between good and bad, harmful and useful. This must reach the point of becoming a SAJYYAH (second nature)." This he regards as the first pillar of education. The second, however, is to do with the spirit. "We mean by the education of the souls the creation of qualities and good manners in the soul and training her in them and keeping her away from bad qualities so that the person grows up in accordance with the rules of human society and accustomed to them."(126)

'Abduh recognises that the two pillars are essential for education to have any significance or use. To him this fact is axiomatic. 'Abduh it must be realised was not a friend of free thought. He might have chided his opponents as imitators either of the classical writers or of western ideas, but he did not for that reason give free rein to the individual to find his own way. When appointed as the editor of the official magazine he became the ex officio censor of literature and books. He advocated a stern supervision of what the people were allowed to read. Once more he took himself to be the measure of all things. He used his authority to prevent the circulation of books which he considered to be corrupting or a waste of time. It is, however, significant that while objecting to the traditional epics of Egyptian society he commended certain French novels that were serialised in the Egyptian press of the time.(127) In another context he chides those advocating freedom in personal behaviour pointing out that the consequence of their so-called freedom of opinion was the destruction of religion and the release of the basest desires. This so-called freedom was not, he observed, based on any consistency of ideas for "I have met a person who though denying that God existed went on to ask about the significance of Muhammad's ascension to heaven, while others deny prophecy and at the same time believe in Satan and things of this nature." (128)

'Abduh's authoritarian vein runs through his ideas whether political, educational or religious. The freedom of the mind, as he advocated it, was one of a very limited nature as his attitude to the public was one of strong paternalistic flavour.(129)

After his exile from Egypt his interests in education became concentrated on religious education. Like Al-Afghani he saw a nefarious conspiracy behind any movement of westernization in the Muslim world. He subscribed to Al-Afghani's views of Ahmad Khan and his ideas, especially his advocacy of co-operation with the British. In Al-Urwat, Ahmad Khan was branded as a British agent to ruin Muslim beliefs and weaken their zeal for their religion.(130) Inasmuch as Al-Urwat concerned itself with the problem of education which was only by the way and incidental to its main concern, namely politics, it advocated a rise of the Ulemas to their duty of informing the public as to the principles of their religion and creating a climate under which the Muslims can in unity acquire knowledge of science and technology to match and even beat Europe. At the same time, Muslims were expected to live up to the ethical principles of their religion which in a sense meant a greater social conscience.(131) Naturally Al-Urwat was concerned with education only in the most general sense, that of influencing public opinion towards a particular direction, namely Muslim unity and resistance to western aggression. Al-Afghani, however, had certain ideas about education and he voiced them in this fashion: "Educational disciplines are aimed at the preservation of the virtues of the soul and remedying them if the soul falls short or goes astray, in the same way as medicine is aimed at the preservation of bodily health. The practical sages who concern themselves with education and guidance and the clarification of the distinction between bad and good and the transformation of the souls from imperfection to perfection are in this way similar to the physicians."(132)

After the collapse of Al-Urwat and 'Abduh's return to Beirut and the invitation to teach in Al Madrassah Al Sultaniyyah, 'Abduh became more and more concerned with education in the specific sense. In a speech he gave to the school he states that "The science which we feel in need of is thought of by some people to be technology and other means of mastering agriculture and trade. This is false, for if we look at what we complain of, we find something deeper than the mere lack of technology and similar disciplines. If technology was mastered by us we would find ourselves unable to keep it on. Though opportunities for benefitting ourselves come our way, they soon go and that is because of something within ourselves. We complain of lack of ambition, laziness, disunity, disregard of obvious interest. Technology cannot offer us remedies to such complaints. What we need to learn, therefore, is something beyond such a discipline, that is the discipline which touches upon the soul and this is the science of human life..."(133) In his view, "The science which will revive the souls is the science of disciplining the soul. Such a discipline exists only in religion, therefore what we lack is extensive knowledge of the ethics of religion and what we need in accordance with our feelings is to have a true understanding of religion."(134)

During his stay in Syria he submitted two proposals for the reform of religious education. The first was for the Shaikh Al Islam in Istanbul and the second was to the Governor of Beirut. His suggestion was that the improvement in education would be a protection for the Caliphate. He shuns nationalism, public interest "and similar high sounding words" in favour of religion as a motive force for stimulating Muslims towards the desired aim. He describes Muslims as having suffered from ignorance to the point that they are indistinguishable from animals. This he felt was because of religious weakness which he suggested "Opened the door to the foreign devils to reach the hearts of many Muslims and to sway them to fall in with their conspiracies and to listen to their tempting words." (135) He oberves that there is no place in the Muslim world without a school for the Americans, Jesuits, the Freres and other religious organisations. He mourns the fact that Muslims no longer objected to sending their children to these schools because their graduates have a better chance of earning a living, either because of their education or their knowledge of a foreign language. He warns that these schools are a danger to Islam and to the whole concept of Osmanism. He deals with the Muslim Maktabs and Madrassahs and points out that whatever religious education is claimed to exist there, it is far too inadequate and too formalistic to have any effect on the character of the Muslim student. He links the general distaste for military service to this ignorance of religion and weakness in conviction.

For his proposal he divides his Muslims into three groups or classes: the first is the general public consisting of the artisan, tradesman and agricultural people, the second is the government servants whether civil or military or judicial, the third is the Ulema class whose concern is the guidance and education of the people. He stresses that these divisions are not meant to be permanent. Anyone may if he acquires the necessary qualifications be admitted to the higher class.(136)

His specific educational programme for the general public would be the three Rs and a simple book on Muslim theology containing all the agreed aprinciples among the Sunnis "Refraining from any reference to disputes between Muslim sects and supporting them with easily understood proofs....verses of the Qur'an and authentic Traditions should be used in evidence." It is clear that he aimed at reducing the differences as much as possible between Muslims, an aim which has influenced his action and thought throughout his life. To emphasise this he suggests that such a general book should contain some references "To the disputes between us and the Christians and making clear the faults of their beliefs so that their (students) minds would be ready to defend Islam against the allegations of Christian missionaries."(137)

For the inspiration of the public he advises the teaching of a brief account of the Sirah and the history of early Islam and the days of Muslim glory followed by a brief history of the Osmani Caliphs.

'Abduh, like Al-Afghani, was well aware of the role of history as an instrument of public policy. Nothing can give a nation an inspiration more than a reference to a past glory, real or imagined.

Modern nationalism relies on a great many myths of past achievements. Muslim history, however, can, if selectively presented, offer such an inspiration and 'Abduh was simply advising such a course.

For the second class he offers similar but more intensive courses. The study of history at this stage must emphasise the purely religious side and it must be calculated to incite Muslims to regain the lost lands of Islam.

The third class, unlike the first two, must learn in Arabic and must read an intensive course in the various Muslim disciplines. It is noticeable that again he suggests that the study of history must be aimed at proving that the cause of Muslim contemporary difficulties was only religious ignorance.

He makes it clear that the aim of his programme is to establish the position of religion so deep in the heart of the students that it directs their every action, thus uniting them materially and spiritually in the service of Islam and "the support of the great protector of Islam and the defender of its land, the Amir al Mu'minin."(138)

'Abduh appears to use the same technique of persuasion, namely identifying the aims of his programme with those of the power-that-be at whatever time and place they happen to be. 'Abduh calls further for the training of a number of this last class to become preachers. This particular idea he claimed to have had in his mind for a long time. It may have inspired his student, Rashid Ridha, into establishing a school for preachers.

His memorandum to the Governor of Beirut is more a report on the actual situation of the Muslims in the area than a programme. He points out the fact that the Muslim Sunni is the citizen upon whom the Ottoman state must rely and whose education must thus be its primary concern to make him an effective instrument. Other groups such as the Christians, the Druze, the Shi'ites, the Nusayriyyah have for one reason or another felt disenchanted with Ottoman power. Behind this disenchantment there is always a foreign agent utilizing missionary techniques to create dissension. He thus invites the Governor to introduce proper education for these various groups to ensure their loyalty.

'Abduh returned to Egypt in 1889 greatly mellowed and resigned to live with an Egypt ruled by the British.

Characteristically he sought a position of power, namely a teaching post or even the principalship of Dar Al Ulum. Without many qualms or hesitation he sent a note to Cromer containing his views on education and putting suggestions to show that his views accorded with the aims of Cromer in Egypt, especially in reaching a position where Egyptian Muslims would feel no religious objection to British rule. He points out that because of political rivalry amongst European powers the incitement of Egyptians to rebel against the British was ceaseless, and he points out that religion has the greatest influence on the minds of Egyptian Muslims, and those bent on creating dissension in the country need only say that the ruler of your country "is not of your religion and you are enjoined to hate him and to use every opportunity to overthrow his power."(139)

To ensure Egyptian co-operation and compliance he suggests a system of education taking its basis from Islam. There is no reason to suspect that Islam by its very nature need stand in the way of co-operation between Muslims and non-Muslims. "The true religion of Islam is not against friendship and it does not war against love, nor does it forbid

Muslims taking advantage of the actions of those of other religions with whom they have common interests."(140) He points out that only through religion could any system of education succeed in Egypt. Purely secular education must fail. "The best evidence on the failure of the system of education which is called literary education (meaning secular) is the effect of such a system from the time of Muhammad 'Ali to this day. Its products became worse despite their greater knowledge but since their general knowledge and demeanour were not based on the principles of their religion it left no effect on their souls." (141) 'Abduh's criticism of secular education was undoubtedly sound. It has brought great hardship and dislocation to those exposed to it without safeguards. The duality of education system in Muslim countries was the direct result of this concept of secularization. Its consequences, social and educational, were so damaging that now it has become the trend throughout the emergent countries to merge the two streams into one, that is to create an honourable and meaningful place for the native culture in the largely western system. 'Abduh was certainly aware of the harmful effects of educational dualism. In his letter to Cromer. 'Abduh suggested the unification of education in Egypt through the development of Dar Al Ulum so that it could in future replace Al-Azhar.(142) He observes that education under Muhammad 'Ali had failed to achieve much in the way of training or character building. Muhammad 'Ali's aim, 'Abduh asserts, was not true education but simply the training of some children in disciplines such as engineering, medicine and translation so that they would be able to fill the necessary posts in the system of government which he created. "As for education based on sound ethical grounds, it has never occurred to him nor to those who run his schools."(143) After a gap of neglect between Muhammad 'Ali and Isma'il, schools flourished again; but Isma'il's aim was simply to give Egypt a westernized veneer so that "It might be said that he has in his government something similar to that of European governments."(144)

Foreign schools being representative of a different culture were seen by 'Abduh as more harmful than useful. The conflict between such a school and the Muslim home was inevitable as it was necessarily confusing for the child. 'Abduh touches on a sensitive nerve by reminding Cromer that these schools "caused Muslims to shy away from the heads of these schools and the nations from which they originated. Their history in this country is well known. They are harmful to friendship, against good relations despite the claims of those who run them. As a system of education it cannot supplant the national schools in its different forms."(145)

He describes the state of Al-Azhar, its spiritual and educational degeneration, and calls for urgent though gradual reform. He points out that there is no need to fear the antagonism of its Ulemas as Isma'il did when he attempted to introduce technical education. "The situation has transformed" he assures Cromer "and reform has become easier in Al-Azhar than in any other public institution in Egypt. Any Chief Minister can effect such reform almost effortlessly, and whatever the Chief Minister feels unable to do, the writer of this document undertakes to effect if charged to do so."(146) He, however, makes one point very clear, that the reform of Al-Azhar depends on the reform of the government school system. If this reform is effected, no-one, 'Abduh felt sure, would choose Al-Azhar and the unification of the education system becomes a reality. In his reference to the primary government Maktabs, 'Abduh suggests, among other things, that the history of Egypt should be studied with reference to "what the country has suffered in the past and the comfort which it has now reached."(147) He further suggests the teaching of civic duties so that the "student may learn to submit and follow every official in whatever directive might come from him."(148)

In his reference to the preparatory and higher education institutes he points out that education in its proper sense does not exist in them and suggests the introduction of religious and moral education to ensure that the graduates if not employed by the government will find other work without disenchantment with the regime.

His final comment is even more revealing. He seeks to tempt Cromer to his views by reminding him that education is the instrument of the government in directing its subjects and in pointing out that his suggestions would be more beneficial than Ahmad Khan's in India and would not stimulate such suspicion as Khan's did. In his last paragraph he says "I repeat that whoever sows will reap the best fruit and the value of this project will go beyond, into other, countries and will be beneficial to the originator. In a short while its fitness will be evident to the person in power (meaning Cromer) and to those ruled by him. He will be able to decide on those who have benefitted by this reform in the spirit of friendship and understanding and not on the basis of fear and terror. In this way he would have created for himself a new people to help him in the hour of need and support him in times of trouble and back him in any difficulty. It will erase from the minds of the people any attachment to others. Obstacles created by blind (jahili) fanaticism will disappear from his way together with unwise fanaticism dressed up as concern about religion. In my view opposition to this project constitutes an opposition to his power."(149)

As a final exposition of 'Abduh's educational ideas we may profitably refer to his practical application of these theories. 'Abduh after a long interval was able (probably with the help of Cromer) to persuade the Khedive of the need of reform in Al-Azhar. A committee was therefore formed with 'Abduh as a member. He was firmly convinced that the reform of Al-Azhar would be of great benefit to Islam. The conservatism of its Ulemas was recognised by 'Abduh as the greatest obstacle. His enthusiasm for reform and hope for a speedy transformation appeared to have been dampened by the advice of others. Rashid Ridha reports him as saying "If the conditions of Al-Azhar are improved before I die I shall go full of happiness. Indeed I shall feel like a king."(150) He saw the problem of Al-Azhar in simple terms; either it should reform or it should completely collapse. And though he very often linked the destiny of Islam with that of Al-Azhar he thought that the disappearance of Al-Azhar need not cause despair for Islamic reform. He appeared at this stage to have convinced himself that he had joined the government solely for the purpose of reforming Al-Azhar. It was therefore natural that he should say to Rashid Ridha again that if reform proved impossible in Al-Azhar "I shall resign my government post and choose a number of suitable persons and educate them in the Sufi method as I have been so that they may succeed me in the service of Islam. Then I shall write a book to expose Al-Azhar, the ethics of its people, their mental capacity and the degree of their knowledge together with their influence. I shall then publish the book in Arabic and a European language so that Muslims and non-Muslims will become aware of the true nature of this place."(151) One must note in this outburst elements of frustration leading to an exaggeration of his own position and abilities. Were the behavioural manifestations of this feeling responsible (at least partly) for what 'Ali Yusuf referred to as 'Abduh's thinking of himself as the God-sent reformer of Islam?

The activities of the Committee of Al-Azhar were recorded in a booklet written by 'Abduh's friend and collaborator, Abd Al-Karim Salman, who was also a member of the Committee.(152) The efforts of the Committee were frustrated by outside factors. It was probably a misfortune that the reform of Al-Azhar was so cleverly identified with 'Abduh who was prominent in the Cromer party. Al-Azhar therefore became one of the areas of conflict between the Khedive and Cromer. 'Abduh became a central figure in this dispute. Since any success in reforming Al-Azhar at that time would have been a victory for 'Abduh (and Cromer), the policy of the Khedive (and the nationalists) was directed at supporting the conservative wing of the Ulemas. 'Abduh in his turn was too ambitious to solve the problem by withdrawing from the scene and thus allowing the advancement of his policies but not his person to take place.

However a number of administrative reforms were adopted, but what was much more important, namely the academic reform, was almost totally rejected.

It would be erroneous to think that the majority of the Ulemas were not well aware of the value of academic reform or that they believed that modern sciences "wreck the basis of religion and corrupt the conviction of the Muslims."(153) As Rashid Ridha observed many of them sent their children to be educated in the modern disciplines in the government schools.

In the face of the strong conservative opposition to reform Cromer was content to stand neutral.

He prevented the Khedive from gaining a full victory by dismissing 'Abduh.(154) But he would not support 'Abduh in any positive way to reform Al-Azhar, probably because he thought that the case for Islam in the modern world was a hopeless one.(155)

'Abduh always regarded himself as a teacher. His concern with education was therefore closer to his heart than any other cause. He appeared to have read some western works on education and he translated from the French Spencer's Essay on Education.(156) There is, however, little echo of these ideas in 'Abduh's programme, probably because 'Abduh learnt French late in life and also the situation he faced within Al-Azhar demanded immediate practical reform at a level that demanded hardly any deep theoretical formulations.

'Abduh wished to end the duality of education and ensure the relevance of the school to the home and cultural environment. His aims in this respect would have the complete support of modern educationalists.

Legal Reform

Islam is the religion of the law. Any reform must by necessity use the law as its instrument and most obvious manifestation. The school of Al-Afghani attacked first and foremost the authority of those writers in the era of decadence whose books were studies throughout the Muslim world as the final arbiters in matters of law. True, jurists have always allowed for necessary social change to be accommodated within the system, thus reducing the tension between the ideal and the actual. The history of Islam in its legal aspect is a story of adjustment between the decrees of God and the needs of man. The impact of modernity, however, imposed such a radical transformation in Muslim society that piecemeal adjustment was no longer adequate.(157) The Ulemas whom Al-Afghani reported as declaring Islam to be incompatible with modern science were in fact stating the true assessment of the situation.(158)

Traditional Islam as it was then had no place for modernity. The school of Al-Afghani never disputed this assessment. It simply attempted to introduce a new Islam unsaddled by medieval thought, thus allowing for greater accommodation with modernity.

"Let us go back to the Qur'an and the authentic Tradition" was the cry of every movement for change in Islam. The school of Al-Afghani, however, gave it a new twist. It claimed not only that Islam was compatible with modernity but that it creates the best environment for modern civilization.

Egypt, under the impact of Europe, adopted a number of institutions, political economic and educational which were unknown in the Middle Ages when the books of law were written. They were introduced so rapidly and under Muhammed 'Ali without any consultation with religious authorities(159) that they became an accepted feature of Egyptian life.

Al-Afghani sought to bridge the gap between s system of law and an actuality that it no longer reflected. His device was simply to reject Taqlid (blind imitation) and to advocate Ijtihad (independent thinking) in matters of law. He was well aware of the function of (Ijma') the general consensus of the Ulemas, the leaders of the community or the community as a whole as a Muslim device to legitimize change.(160) But Al-Afghani and his school did not want to be hampered by an Ijma' that in their view was useless, even dangerous.(161)

The new institutions in Egypt were on the whole transplanted into the community and did not spring from it. The fact that the Ulemas did not feel any urgency for the legitimization of these institutions is an indication of how far they represented an emotional problem to the Muslims of the day. To the Ulemas the whole issue of Modernization became an insoluble problem.

This was perhaps one of the reasons that Al-Afghani and his students were suspected as enemies of Islam seeking to violate its precepts for the benefit of non-Muslims. Since Al-Afghani did not offer any specific programme beyond the call for a new Ijtihad, and since he later consumed his energy in the service of Muslim political unity, his name was hardly tarnished on this score. It fell to 'Abduh and later Rashid Ridha to put more definite solutions to the problems of the day.

Europe at that time was in the grip of a bourgeois revolution and to 'Abduh, Islam was to be interpreted in a way to effect the greatest congruity with bourgeois ideas. There is, however, a certain degree of restraint that must be exercised by the Muslim jurist, for on the one hand the Qur'an must be accepted as the absolute and final authority in matters legal, on the other the schools of law with their established institutions could not be dismissed out of hand. 'Abduh's legal reform, however, consisted primarily of resurrecting an old principle and giving it respectability. This principle was in effect what the Muslim jurists used to call Talfiq, that is following more than one school of thought in the performance of one or more actions. As the differences between schools sharpened it bordered on the heretical to deviate from one's own school to any other. 'Abduh realising the great advantage in flexibility which would accrue through the adoption of the more liberal policy suggested the use of all schools of thought and the works of all the Ulemas as a source from which to select the most suitable legislation for any current problem. In essence therefore what 'Abduh was calling for was the abandonment of specific Taqlid in favour of a general one. Throughout his career he never deviated from the established schools of law.(162).Sometimes he addressed questions sent to him on a point of law to the leaders of the various schools of law in Al-Azhar to ascertain their opinions before issuing his own.(163) The controversies that some of his judgements cause arose from his own personal position and his political role and rarely from a purely legal dispute.(164) His judgement in the Transvaal Fatwa was attested to by even the most conservative amongst the Ulemas. He could count amongst his supporters many jurists with traditional inclinations such as the leader of the conservative faction in Morocco, who however attacked 'Abduh for doctrinal rather than legal opinion.(165)

The point of departure in his legal thinking is that Islam is the religion of nature (Al Fitra) and the religion of the future. The Islam he was talking about was that of the Qur'an the great Prophet as derived from his life and Tradition and from the life of his righteous successors and the learned amongst his Companions. (166) He saw modern civilization to be leading towards Islam. Was this a true conviction on his part or was it a simple rationalisation for his infatuation with Europe and its civilization? (He often repeated that he visited Europe to regain his spiritual strength).(167) The obvious contradiction between Islam and modern society sprang according to him from the rigidity of the Muslims. This rigidity in the precepts of the Shari'a caused difficulties which made the people neglect it.

"In the days of true Islam the Shari'a was tolerant to the point of encompassing the whole world. Today it is so narrow even for its own people that they are forced to adopt other laws and to seek the protection of their rights outside it. Even the learned pious take their disputes to laws other than its own."(168)

The neglect of the Shari'a was further attributed by him to ignorance. He observed that only very few knew anything about it. In consequence it had lost its hold on the mind of the general public because of their inability to apply its precepts to their lives and "the most important barrier in the way of its application is the inability to understand its laws because of the difficult language used and because of the diversity of opinions."(169) Unlike many apologists, 'Abduh did not think that differences of opinion amongst Muslim jurists was a source of mercy. He conceived Muslim law as one based on the original sources and allowing for no schools. His opinion of the schools and their founders was that they were not binding on any Muslim. "The words of the Imam Mujtahid, that is the founder of a school, should not be elevated to the rank of religion. This is against Islam itself and those who do it commit what Allah warned against. They would have followed in the steps of the people of the Book about whom the Qur'an says "They took the learned and the monks to be their Gods in place of God."(170) He regarded the Shari'a to consist of two major parts. One part consists of clearly stated laws which every Muslim must know and abide by. These laws are all clearly stated in the Holy Book and explained in detail in the Prophetic Tradition, and have been transmitted from one generation of Muslims to another through practice. They are indisputable laws agreed to by everyone (that is supported by Ijma'). No room, regarding them, for individual independent thought. The second part consists of rules not derived from clear-cut texts nor supported by concensus and, therefore, a subject for independent thought. This type does not concern general rules of rituals or prohibitions, but it touches upon details of these aspects of religion and also upon the relationship between individuals (mu'amalat).(171) He advises that Muslims, if learned, should seek the evidence for each ruling, taking guidance only from the works of the early scholars. Their action, however, must accord with their own personal judgement. Laymen should consult with a person whom they can trust in matters of this nature. In this connection, 'Abduh quotes Malik as saying that all rituals must accord with the text without attempt at any interpretation. Mu'amalat on the other hand where there is no clear text should hinge on the interest of the public. According to this position the Muslim jurist is given a greater freedom than the traditionalists accorded him. Consequently Muslim society is accorded the same degree of liberty to develop its own laws in accordance with the principle of utility. In practice, however, 'Abduh never digressed from the beaten track of earlier scholars, and his advice to the authorities regarding the reform of the Shari'a courts was that the judge in these courts should not be tied to one school of thought but should be allowed to use his own opinion in applying the most suitable ruling without restriction to a particular school. He further, in contrast with his contemporaries, clearly states that wholesale prohibitions - common in those days of everything European - are not based on Muslim law. The early scholars such as Shafi'i and Abu Yusuf and the learned among the Companions of the Prophet never adjudged anything to be prohibited unless it was so clearly stated in the Holy Book that it needed no further explanation.(172)

In combatting the narrow views of Muslim law, 'Abduh resorted to the old scholars to support his more liberal views. He was able through the device of <u>Talfiq</u> on the one hand and the consideration of public interest on the other to justify some of the new institutions which his contemporaries initially ignored. In the economic sphere he legalized shareholding and the taking of interest on savings in the post office.(173) Among his Muslim contemporaries he was one of the first to recognise the problem of a plural society which was imposed upon the largely 'closed' Muslim society. Although 'Abduh's political and other quarrels contributed a great deal to linking his name in many Muslim circles with extreme liberalism, the truth of the matter is that 'Abduh was up against a traditional society that derived security and certainty from its long social isolation and its established habits. Once this isolation ended the habits derived from it became pointless or even harmful. The Ulemas were not, however, ready to discard them. On the contrary, they declared them inviolate. The Transvaal Fatwa for instance resulted from the new situation in which Muslims had to come into contact on a much wider basis than previously with non-Muslims, a situation which had not taken place since the earliest times of Islam. 'Abduh found for the legitimization of greater intercourse between Muslims and other societies: he was bound to do so not only because it was inevitable, but also because he regarded the interest of Muslims to be precisely in the continuation and growth of contact with others.

'Abduh contributed to the reform of the Shari'a courts. His proposals, particularly those bearing on the administrative side, were urgently needed and adopted. His theoretical position, namely giving equal authority to all schools of law, was much slower in establishing itself. Jurists, however, found themselves under the pressure of modern society, driven into defending Muslim law by the use of all schools, even the less recognised ones. This device, as shall be pointed out later, became a standard in the literature of Shari'a apologetics.

Naturally 'Abduh wished the maze of Egyptian justice in its numerous law systems and diversities of thought to be absorbed in one system of law, the Shari'a. He was, however, aware that with the power in the hands of a non-Muslim country, Britain, such a hope was well nigh impossible. He therefore secretly struggled (according to him) to protect the Shari'a courts, against what he thought to be Cromer's secret intention to abolish them,(174) through the appointment of two civil judges to the High Shari'a Court. Although he saw clearly the defects of Al-Azhar and the shortcomings of the courts of the time, he insisted on the continuation of the link bwteeen Al-Azhar and these judicial institutions. Only when he failed in his efforts to reform Al-Azhar did he turn to the idea of establishing an alternative institution. He would not have the "School of Law" as a substitute. His suspicion of the western oriented institutions remained powerful. He put forward a project for the establishment of a school for Shari'a law (Madrassat Al-Qada' Al Shar'i) insisting that though it could be linked to Al-Azhar as he wished, it must remain under the authority of the Mufit. (175) He died before the project was to materialise. When it was established later, the school performed its function for a number of years but under the pressure of Al-Azhar, whose leadership later agreed to the introduction of a number of reforms, the school was abolished in favour of an institute within Al-Azhar.

'Abduh's legal reforms, at least in their practical application, depended on the adoption of his reforms by Al-Azhar. As that one failed for the reasons mentioned above his legal reforms outside the administrative ones materialised only gradually, largely because of the transformation of Egyptian society. Undoubtedly 'Abduh paved the way for the liberal minded to follow, but one is bound to wonder whether his methods and his personality did not constitute a greater obstacle in the way of reform than need be.

Early in his career, 'Abduh viewed the law as reflecting the mentality of the people, their customs and traditions. It is natural, therefore, that it should differ from place to place and from one period of time to another. He was aware that laws do not change people but "only reflect the faculties which members of the community have acquired through its common practices and customs."(176) He makes it clearer by stating that the laws are not the instrument "which educate nations and improve their condition. Laws everywhere in the world are made only for the abnormal and the mistakes and faults. The laws which reform the people are those of education based on religion for every nation."(177) During this period he was speaking of the law in general terms. It was during his liberal nationalist phase. He, however, continued to hold these views and reconciled them with the doctrine of the finality of the Shari'a. He says "The Islamic Shari'a is universal and eternal. A corollary of this is that the Shari'a suits the interests of humanity at every time and in any place whatever the nature of the civilization. A Shari'a of such a nature, its specific items cannot be limited because it deals with the affairs of the people wherever they are."(178) He stresses the changing nature of the detailed items of the Shari'a in contrast to the permanent nature of its general principles.

Contrasting his views on the role of customs in relation to the Shari'a with his views on the role of reason in the discovery of ethical principles(179) one is bound to see a contradiction of a serious nature. In discussing man's ability to discover unaided by revelation the moral law which accords with the nature of the actions, 'Abduh appeared to subscribe to the rationalist ethics of Descartes.(180) Custom and convention are not regarded as reliable sources in the rationalist system. As is known, the Shari'a is not only a legal system but also an ethical one. It appears therefore that 'Abduh appeals to reason when discussing the theory of value and to custom and convention when considering the actualities of life. He thus subscribes to absolutism in theory and relativism in practice.

'Abduh's Impact on Egyptian and Muslim Thought

No Egyptian in modern times has been so highly regarded as 'Abduh, both in Egyptian and foreign circles.(181) It is important in assessing his contribution to the development of Egyptian and Muslim thought to see him in the proper perspective. He emerged in an Egypt faltering under the impact of European cultural influences. He was fortunate in meeting the indomitable Al-Afghani who introduced him to western culture and instilled in him ideas of liberty and political reform. Like all major Muslim thinkers, Sufism is the foundation of his ethical life and outlook. The rebellion against the orders and the revulsion of their doctrine, characteristics of modernism in general, was not against Sufism per se but against the corruption and decadence of its institutions in the nineteenth century.(182) He always recognised the Sufis as the incomparable teachers of ethic. He considered their decline to be the major cause for the decline of Islam.(183) He blamed the jurists for the plight of Sufism. It was under the jurists' pressure that the Sufis resorted to symbolism which obscured their true principles. This led to the ignorance of the true nature of Sufism and the decline of Islam. The jurists were no substitute for the Sufis. They lacked Tasawwuf "which is the true religion". In consequence they were ignorant of the politics and general conditions of their day. For this reason they were unable to implement the rules of the Shari'a.(184) He points out that the jurists unlike the Sufis were a tool in the hands of the political arm of the state. As such they were regarded with contempt by the rulers upon whom they were unable to exert any influence. He suggested as a remedy the abandonment of ideas of the era of decline in favour of the old masters. Again it was the same call: 'Let's go back to true Sufism in the days of its inception.'(185)

The effect of his attitude to the Sufis, however, was more destructive than constructive. The trend towards modernity in Muslim society militates against the Sufi orders, but 'Abduh and the Salafis offered an added and more powerful argument against them, an argument based upon religion. The decline in Sufi prestige and influence had immense consequences for Egypt. As shall be pointed out later, the emergence of religious societies or even political parties was at least in part caused by this decline. The function performed by the Sufi orders both in the social life of the individual and in his emotional and religious activities were left without a substitute. The sense of belongingness, the social cohesion, the emotional satisfaction, the depth of religious feelings and experience, and above all the sense of security derived from the concept of an ordered and paternalistic society had its foundation disturbed or even destroyed.

'Abduh's major failure derives from his lack of adequate response to the Muslim community. In his thought he addressed the West more than he did his fellow Muslims. He appeared to many of his contemporaries, and to some of the generation after, more as a follower of Europe than as an exponent of Islam.(186)

If 'Abduh's contribution to the weakening of the Sufi orders(187) can be considered significant, his influence upon legal thinking was limited for in the first place his sweeping proposals evoked suspicion that his limited and restrained application of them did not mitigate. We have observed earlier that he remained always within the framework of the schools of law. At no time could any competent jurist find faults with his judgements. Perhaps at the practical level he was able to recognise the fact that the stage of development in Muslim society at that time did not warrant the sweeping reforms that he suggested.(188) On the other hand, his failure to put his principles into actual practice may be an indication of his fear of the consequences. He, however, had a forceful ally, namely modernity. And it is not surprising that his supporters were drawn mainly from those exposed to western culture.

The party of 'Abduh, as Rashid Ridha called them or the Girondists of Egypt, as Cromer chose to name them, were a group of friends most of whom were deeply immersed in western ideas. They gathered around 'Abduh probably because they found with him a satisfaction which the conservatives could not provide and a sense of identity which the western masters were clearly incapable of giving. This party of 'Abduh was in reality more western than Muslim. The activities of Lufti Ali-Sayyid, the chief theoretician of the party, and his contributions only goes to prove this. The impact of the ideas he advocated on the Egyptian masses was negligible. Lufti Ali-Sayyid, despite the grand title of "The Teacher of the Generation" was always regarded more as a translator of Aristotle than as a leader of political or social thought.(189)

As a good number of the party of 'Abduh grew into the party of the West a cleavage appeared amongst his alleged disciples. His chief student and disciple Rashid Ridha grew disenchanted with the group that in 1907 he had regarded as the Hope of Egypt.(190)

'Abduh's compromise between modernity and Islam could be seen therefore to have at least in the social sense failed. The western wing of his supposed friends became more western, while the Muslim wing became in a manner of speaking more Muslim.

The emergence of Sa'd Zaghlul after the First War was regarded by Rashid Ridha as a victory for 'Abduh, and is so assessed by various other writers.(191) But it is important for us to realise that the militant nationalist in Zaghlul leads back directly to Al-Afghani rather than to 'Abduh.(192) In a sense Zaghlul took the position of Mustafa Kamil, the arch opponent of 'Abduh, and inherited his tremendous popular support. Like all good ambitious politicians Zaghlul identified himself with the most popular trend. He was aware like many nationalists the world over that oppressive rule was no longer feasible in the colonies and that he could with impunity challenge British power. The victory of the Wafd in popular terms and its success in forcing a British retreat cannot possibly be related to the passive and co-operative policies of 'Abduh. On the other hand the party's secular nationalist programme owes more to the westernizers than to 'Abduh's strict Muslim principles (in his last phase).

In the educational field 'Abduh's proposals were outdated by the rapid development of Egypt. His failure in Al-Azhar created in that institution a hardened reaction against reform. It was not until 1928 that a member of his school was brought into the office of Rector of that institution. His resignation a short time afterwards was the best indication of the strength and depth of the opposition to 'Abduh and his ideas.(193)

The slow development of Al-Azhar reflected the actual developments of Muslim society in Egypt. Despite the trappings of a western style government, the Egyptian village remained under a medieval authoritarian rule. Western type schools, being always city centred, left the village almost untouched. It is a fact that Al-Azhar, though situated in the town, drew the bulk of its students and exercised the greatest influence in the rural areas. The transformation of Al-Azhar presupposes the transformation of the Egyptian village, a fact that 'Abduh and his students never recognised and in consequence their influence was limited.

Probably the most important contribution of 'Abduh was that he offered to some western educated a road to Islam which the conservatives were unable to do. In so doing he may have delayed the movement of complete secularisation which was inherent in westernization. On the other hand, the immense literature about religion which appeared through his activities enriched Egyptian thought and helped to bring into focus a number of vexed social questions.(194)

The problem of the position of the Muslim woman, her inevitable progress towards emancipation, was given sanction by 'Abduh himself on various occasions.(195) But it was a member of his circle, Qassim Amin, in his famous book "Tahrir al-Mar'ah" (The Emancipation of Women) who attacked Muslim treatment of women as being in violation of Islam itself. The violent reaction that this book evoked was indicative of the state of society at the time. It was the first specific proposal in a matter of social and legal import that the circle of 'Abduh put forward. Both Rashid Ridha and Lufti Al-Sayyid inform us that 'Abduh witnessed the development of the ideas of the book.(196)

The gradual emancipation of the Egyptian woman, however, did not result from the arguments of Qassim Amin. It took place as a consequence of the growth of modern economic and cultural institutions despite the opposition of the main stream of 'Abdists.(197)

Even Qassim Amin himself shows the intensity of the conflict between Islam and western concepts. His first book sought to prove that the freedom of the woman was the intention of the Shari'a; his second "Al Mar'ah Al jadidah" ignored the Shari'a altogether and drew its concepts from the West.(198)

The critics of 'Abduh were obviously apprehensive of such a development. They clearly regarded 'Abduh as the Trojan Horse of westernization.

Despite the alienation of the two wings of 'Abduh's friends both sides held him in veneration and reverence; but as events in Egypt moved and the cleavage sharpened the confusion about the true nature of 'Abduh's thought and ideas became more acute. (199) Rashid Ridha and the Manarists were led into a fundamentalist position so close to the position of Ibn Taimiya that they found common cause with the Wahabbis.(200)

It is true that 'Abduh never criticised the Wahabbis except with regard to their excessive enthusiasm in supporting their ideas.(201) Their fanaticism rather than their theological position constituted for 'Abduh their main shortcoming but the care that 'Abduh had always taken in making his ideas less precise and less committed than might be, together with his mode of life and almost certainly enlightened though unwritten views contributed to the liberal image that has always been painted of him in westernized circles.(202)

In the field of literature and the development of the Arabic language, 'Abduh together with the other students of Al-Afghani was responsible for the literary movement that emerged in the closing years of the last century and the early years of this. 'Abduh, following a cue from Al-Afghani and conscious of the importance of the classical age as a source of inspiration and as a guide in the difficult circumstances of the Muslim world, was instrumental in reproducing the old classical words in various fields; but like many other things in the life of 'Abduh the young plant which he nursed was taken over by the westernizers and brought up to be a vastly different one from what he intended, if indeed his intentions could be ascertained. The Arabic that in the time of Al-Jaberticould not convey the idea of a republic(203) was made by this school and the following generation an adequate vehicle for western as well as eastern ideas. Thus Arabic freed from the shackles of medieval formalism and modes of thought developed into a meaningful activity reflecting and influencing the ideas of the modern Arab and the modern Muslim.

His role in the 'Urabi rebellion is not yet clear. His early equivocation and later enthusiasm did not endear him to either party.(204) His writing about the affair may have been motivated by factors other than the desire to proclaim the truth.(205) One must hesitate in agreeing with

Cromer's assessment of him as "one of the leading spirits of the movement."(206) The ideas that were influential then and the writers who were prestigious belonged to various sources and schools of thought.(207) His studied reasonableness and his comparative lack of emotion must have deprived his articles of much influence, especially those dealing with political problems. Only where he referred to the Ministry of Education did he show that aggressiveness characteristic of Al-Afghani's style.(208) Doubtless this contributed to the favourable reaction of the administration.

During his work with Al-Afghani he forcefully put their ideas in the periodical Al-'Urwat, which to this day remains one of the most influential periodicals in the history of modern Islam.(209) It was his image as the collaborator of Al-Afghani that his apologists resort to when defending his later co-operation with Cromer.(210) The latter period of his life was, however, the period of maturity in thought and greater concentration on academic work. It was also the period during which he aroused the greatest suspicion with regard to his political and religious views.

Probably his most famous contribution during the age of maturity was his Tafsir which is characterised by its concern for the practical, social problems and the attempt to arrive at the simplest and most direct meaning of the revelation. (211) Exegesists ever since have found it necessary to relate the Qur'an to the problems of everyday life.

'Abduh attempted to play the role of the political leader without its qualifications and sought to fulfil the function of a religious reformer but without adequate tools. The result was a thought marred by eclectic tendencies and preoccupation with the practical consequences of his ideas.(212) Despite this the name of 'Abduh grew in prestige as time went on. No doubt the reason for this was mainly Rashid Ridha and Al Manar.(213) 'Abduh the man may have been noticed by the historians of modern Islam as an important if not great figure, but 'Abduh the myth is a compelling and considerable force. Al Manar spread his name throughout the Muslim world and Rashid Ridha as his public relations officer explained away his faults and magnified his virtues. The imitators of Al Manar followed it into calling 'Abduh Al Ustaz Al Imam and holding him as an undisputed authority. One must wonder whether the various commemorative functions for 'Abduh would have been held had it not been for the moving spirit of Rashid Ridha. In a society of which 'Abduh himself lamented its incapacity to honour its great men it is surprising that so much honour has been bestowed upon him.

Outside Egypt, in India and Malaysia, Tunisia and Algeria, 'Abduh's name and more so the ideas associated with it exerted great influence on modern developments. The Muhammadiyyah (214) of Indonesia was inspired by his interpretation of Islam.

Muhammad 'Abduh as a Thinker

In his autobiography, 'Abduh states his objective as being two important matters, "the first is to liberate the minds from the chains of imitation, to understand religion in accordance with the ways of the Salaf before the appearance of disputes, and the return to its primary sources to acquire religious knowledge, and to consider religion as one of the controls over human reason which God has meant for guiding it away from error so that the will of Allah in preserving mankind may be fulfilled, therefore religion is a friend of science and a stimulus towards research into the secrets of the world, calling for the respect of the established facts....In this matter I deviated from the two great groups who constitute the Umma, the students of religion and the students of modern disciplines. The second was the reform of the style of the Arabic language ...."(215)

The intellectual task that 'Abduh set for himself is thus specified; to simplify Islam through the return to its early stages and thus allow for a place beside it for science and modern knowledge. The first, namely simplification, is a task that is much more difficult than is at first sight realised. It means more than shedding off of ideas and solutions to questions. It meant in reality the rejection of some of the questions themselves. (216) 'Abduh's criteria for a valid question were that it had practical implications and that it was derived directly from the sources and not emerged from pure speculation. Thus the rationalist was on this score an anti-rationalist. Historically as we have observed 'Abduh moved from Sufism through rationalism to the attitude of the Salafia school.

There was no consistent principle underlying his thought. He formed no philosophical system.(217) But his ideas were eclectic in nature with greater inclincation if no public objection took place to the views of the Mu'tazilah.(218)

He adopted the puritanical and fundamentalistic views of Ibn Taimiya, and also took over the ethical values of Ghazali. Further he attempted to incorporate and fuse into religious knowledge some aspects of modern science as he was able to understand it.(219)

The mixture aroused more suspicion than confidence in 'Abduh's intentions and even his sincerity. (220)

In the assessment of A. Hourani, 'Abduh effected a balance between Islam and modernity.(221) But one wonders whether this balance was not more illusory than real. In 'Abduh's view the conflict between religion and science arose from the rigidity of the religious officials, indeed rigidity which afflicted all spheres of the Muslim community. But he felt that once this rigidity disappears, and it must disappear, then they will find the Qur'an waiting for them "preparing the means of salvation and supporting them through it with a holy spirit and taking them into the sources of science."(222)

Does 'Abduh, therefore, consider religious truth to be also dynamic and unstable as that of science? Hardly, he could scarcely subscribe to such a view and Osman Amin errs in assessing 'Abduh as equating religion with science in this respect.(223) Indeed, at every level religion must assert absolutism, or be relegated to the position of mere speculation. Further, religion even if it permits the modification of certain inessential aspects by science it cannot possibly allow any tempering with its basic principles. 'Abduh was certainly aware that there are certain irreducible elements in Islam. He, however, appeared to think they they did not contradict science.

The final view of Islam emerging from 'Abduh's thought is imprecise, not so much because 'Abduh abhorred Taqlid as A. Hourani suggests(224) but more likely because his ideas were more in the nature of a programme of action and were not as easily implemented as he thought.

The tension between modernity and Islam was thus obscured and not resolved. Even during his lifetime members of his circle disputed most violently on matters of social policy.(225) The scientific dynamic attitude was not, through his system, projected on religion. On the contrary the rigid and final attitude of religion was conferred upon science.(226)

The circle of 'Abduh shared a negative attitude to nineteenth century Islam and a belief in the permanent truth of their faith and its suitability regardless of time and place to be the basis for human progress and happiness. Beyond this general attitude, they differed widely in hue between the conservative Manfaluti to the progressive and liberal Qassim Amin, between the fundamentalist Rashid Ridha and 'the scientific Tantawi Jawhari.'(227)

Underlying 'Abduh's programme was the elimination of disunity within the Umma and alleviating the spiritual crisis contingent on its failure to apply fully the law of Islam. Modern conditions having brought about foreign institutions in economic, educational, political and social matters drew the Umma gradually but irresistibly away from traditional and Shari'a precepts. His proposal for unity was to go back to Islam as it was before the disputes. But neither he nor Al-Afghani succeeded in uniting the Umma. On the contrary, they added to its factions a new one. However, the Salafis helped to allay the anguish of the community with regard to its failure to implement the law of God. The principle of utility in Muslim legislation was given a new force by'Abduh as he declares "If a ruling has become the cause of harm, which it did not cause before, we must change it in accordance with the prevailing conditions."(228) 'Abduh was not alone in voicing these views. He was even less adventurous than his counterpart in India.(229) But as we have noted earlier, a discrepancy between theory and practice is always present in his system. 'Abduh's achievement therefore consists of a method, albeit imprecise, rather than a complete interpretation of Islam. The ambiguity of his ideas served as a cover against criticism. 'Abduh was after all, as Rashid Ridha aptly suggested, a politician who had strayed into religion.(230)

Chapter 3

MUHAMMAD RASHID RIDHA

AL-AFGHANI was the inspirer of the Salafiyyah school. 'Abduh was its brains; but Rashid Ridha was its spokesman.(1) He was born in Syria, educated in the traditional manner of the ulema and was accorded the Certificate of 'Alim in 1897.(2) His teacher was one Shaikh Hussain Al-Jisr, a Syrian theologian of distinction. Though the Shaikh was certainly a traditionalist, his book "Al Resalat Al Hamidiyyah" in the defence of Islam indicates according to Hurgronje a change in the attitude of Muslims towards western opinion on Islam. It is a mark of his breadth of mind that he discussed Darwinism and suggested that if it proved true it need not contradict the Qur'an.(3) There is no doubt that such a teacher must have prepared the minds of his students to the ideas of the more progressive thinkers such as Al-Afghani and others.

Rashid Ridha indicates that he fell under the influence of Ghazali through his book "Ihiya 'Ulum Al Din" (The revival of the religious sciences) which led him into taking up some Sufi practices such as refraining from good food, sleeping on the ground and he even attempted to tolerate dirtiness in body and clothes but was unable to do so.(4) In his short notes about his life intended for publication with his book "Al-Manar wa Al-Azhar" he relates the many strange experiences he had.(5) During this period he joined the Naqshahbandi Order.(6)

The second book to influence his life was "Al Urwat Al Wuthqa" which changed his outlook completely. Before reading it his concern was with his salvation through the right belief and rituals. If his thoughts had ever gone beyond his personal salvation into the more mundane aspects of social life it was concentrated on local reforms, but when he read "Al Urwat Al Wuthqa" all this was changed. A universal outlook replaced the parochial and the affairs of Islam in general took the place of individual salvation.(7) One effect of his Sufi phase was that he refrained from learning Turkish and French when he had the opportunity in the national school, because he believed then that "There is no religious use in their study."(8)

After reading Al Urwat he started looking for the writings of Al-Afghani and 'Abduh, and all the writings about them. He also became a partisan of the two leaders to such an extent that no one could attack them in front of him. In 1893 he wrote a letter to Al-Afghani requesting to be accepted as a student. The letter contained such praise of Al-Afghani that he proudly showed it to many of his visitors, Ridha apologised for not joing Al-Afghani immediately because he believed "Constantinople, large as it is, even the Ottoman kingdom in its width has no place for the Sayyid because oriental kingdoms have become like a sick fool who refused medicine simply because it was medicine."(9)

His intention of joing Al-Afghani was frustrated by the latter's death in 1897, upon which Ridha decided to join 'Abduh. He met 'Abduh in Tripoli in Syria after the latter's return from Europe, and met him a second time in the same place when 'Abduh came on his summer holiday. On this occasion he stayed with him all the time from early morning to bedtime.(10) He later travelled to Egypt to join him. At their first meeting they spoke about the hope for Islamic reform, the reform of Al-Azhar and politics, of which 'Abduh expressed his distaste. They also mentioned certain aspects of saint worship which 'Abduh decried.

After this, and before the publication of Al-Manar, Rashid Ridha frequented 'Abduh's house to discuss with him various reform problems taking care to write down a summary of their discussion. He found that they did not differ "Except with regard to a few questions which ended after discussion in agreement, such as the question of 'Bab and Baha'."(11)

It is important to realise that Ridha before his immigration to Egypt had written a book with the title of "Al Hakmat Al Shar'iyyah" which seems to have impressed many contemporaries by its style and independence of opinion. Among the questions he discussed in the book were, significantly, the harm of the Mahdist outlook which makes Muslims pin their hopes for reform on an outside force, the threat of foreign domination and the question of dress from the point of view of religion, society, ethics and politics.(12) There is little doubt that Rashid Ridha before coming to Egypt was already an accomplished scholar and that the influence of 'Abduh upon him was more of a confirmation than an initiation.

As Ridha intended from the beginning to publish a paper in Egypt he consulted 'Abduh about it. 'Abduh, after a discussion, agreed to the idea and suggested that the paper should not be partisan nor indulge in arguments with other papers and should be independent of the so-called great personalities.

Although 'Abduh agreed with the contents of Al-Manar when it came into being, he was critical of the bluntness of its arguments, the difficulty of its language which put it beyond the scope of the ordinary reader and its involvement in Ottoman politics. It is a measure of 'Abduh's control over the paper that Rashid Ridha states in the preface to the twelfth volume "We sometimes wished to indulge in it (politics) but Al-Ustaz Al-Imam used to stop us. We did not get what we wanted until after Allah had called him."(13)

For four years Al-Manar struggled with a very small circulation and only in the fifth year did it become widely read.(14) The aim of Al-Manar was to continue the work of Al-'Urwat Al Wuthqa in fields other than the 'Egyptian' political field. It aimed at social, religious, political and economic reforms and to prove that Islam as a religion was not incompatible with contemporary conditions and that the Shari'a was still a practical instrument for modern government. On the negative side it aimed at purifying Islam from prevailing superstitions and combatting fatalism, narrow partisanship as regards the schools of law, saint worship and the harmful innovations of the Sufi orders. It aimed also at advocating tolerance and understanding between the various sects, the promotion of public education, the reform of school books and methods of teaching, the encouragement of science and arts and to stimulate the Muslim nations into competing with other nations in matters essential to their progress.(15)

Al-Manar republished a number of articles by Al-Afghani and 'Abduh from Al-Urwat and elsewhere which accorded with its policy. From the third year onwards it started publishing the famous Tafsir Al-Manar, the encyclopedic work of reformism. In the same year it also started a section for Fatwas, or legal opinion, to advise its readers on questions of shari'a or doctrines. There is no doubt that this last section was utilised by Ridha to disseminate his ideas of legal reform.(16)

For thirty seven years Al-Manar was involved in the affairs of the Muslim world, political, religious and social so much that it has become a record of the development of Islam in a crucial period of its history.

Many Muslims in areas as separate as Morocco and Indonesia read it regularly and correspond with it. It could not refrain from expressing opinions on problems such as the Tijanis in the Maghrib or the Alawis in Indonesia. Although during the life of 'Abduh it turned after a short period from a diagnosis of Muslim ills to putting suggestions to the authorities to effect reform, it found itself having to remind Muslims that mere suggestion without the active participation of the public was futile. In its discussions, style and subject matter it was a journal for a special section of the Muslim community: those who are learned or greatly interested in religious questions.

Most of Ridha's works were serialised in Al-Manar. The bulk of the contributions in the magazine were the product of his own pen.

His relationship with 'Abduh brought him benefits as well as powerful enemies. Among those enemies was Abbas II, whose pathetic efforts to silence him culminated in an address to Al-Azhar ulema in which he suggested that Ridha might just go home.(17)

He also earned the undying hatred of the conservative Azharites, and lacking that western veneer which made 'Abduh so attractive to many western educated he was unable to communicate adequately with them. His isolation which grew more and more acute was due to these intellectual differences. He belonged neither to Al-Azhar's circles nor to their opponents the westernizers.

A further reason for his isolation must be found in the fact that unlike 'Abduh who was content to leave vague principles alone and to accept what sometimes is contradictory positions, Ridha's personality, his training and strict adherence to the school of Ibn Taimiya drove him into attempting to give precise and definite statements of his position. In matters of religion, nothing calls for enmities more than the attempt to give unequivocal pronouncements on questions that by their very nature must be allowed to remain ambiguous.

At no time did Ridha think or suspect that he was deviating from 'Abduh. He was simply expounding and explaining the views of the master, or so he thought.(18)

Still a further cause for his isolation stems from the general development of Egyptian and Muslim society. In the decades following 'Abduh's death the flood gates of western ideas were opened wide and the upheavals of economic crisis, the Great War and the suddenly discovered ideals of the West as expressed in the Wilsonian principles. The establishment in Egypt in 1908 of a university on western lines to become intentionally or otherwise a centre for European ideas, made education at the higher level no longer (if indeed it had ever been since Muhammad Ali) the monopoly of Al-Azhar. The new university did not only reject the basic assumptions of Al-Azhar, but it challenged the very right of its existence. Rashid Ridha regarded it as the hotbed of heresies.(19)

At the social and political level Ridha acted as a foreigner. He attacked the Ottoman Empire and France when the nationalists pinned their hopes on them to dislodge the British out of Egypt. Belonging as he did to the group that befriended Cromer he was lumped together by the nationalists with the Syrian Christian journalists of Al Muqatam as 'intruders' (Dukhala'). Ridha resented this very greatly and lamented the sort of nationalism which equates an "Arab and a descendant of the Prophet with a heathen Mongolian or Chinese."(20) He decried the nationalism of the nationalist party declaring it against Islam.(21)

A still further though perhaps less obvious cause for Ridha's isolation was the fact of being a Sayyid. Despite Ridha's objection to the Alawiyyah claim to the supremacy of the descendants ot the Prophet, he retained as shall be pointed out their basic attitude and envisaged a privileged position for them within the framework of the democratic principles which are"prevalent nowadays."(22)

Despite his stay in Egypt for nearly forty years Rashid Ridha never managed to work his way into the ranks of Egyptian society. Unlike the Tunisian Shaikh Muhammad Al-Khadr Hussain who was able to obtain the post as the first editor of the official Al-Azhar magazine and some thirty years later to be appointed the Rector of Al-Azhar, Ridha maintained a contemptuous attitude towards the whole institution and its products. It seems as if 'Abduh's retreat from Al-Azhar was taken by Ridha as a permanent declaration of war. There is no better evidence for his failure to be absorbed within Egyptian institutions than that his friend and fellow disciple of 'Abduh, Mustafa Al-Maraghi, thought it prudent when he became Rector of Al-Azhar in 1928 only to consult with Ridha about the reforms in that institution without offering him any post in it.(23)

Near the close of his life Ridha became involved in a dispute with one of the traditional ulema and took the chance to heap contempt on the entire institution exempting only the few who like him were imbibed by Salafi tradition.(24)

Rashid Ridha's Legal Reform

The school of Al-Afghani and 'Abduh was concerned at the disparity between Muslim ideal and Muslim reality. At the centre of its aims is the bridging of the gap between the two. In no area of Muslim life was this disparity more manifest than in the field of law. As European influence, cultural and otherwise, grew in strength, European laws were adopted by Muslims, either under the pressure of the Western powers or through the voluntary imposition of the westernizing rulers. In Egypt, Isma'il used the pretext of non-co-operation on the part of the ulema in codifying Muslim law to borrow French codes wholesale.(25)

Of course there were areas of the legal system which were borrowed directly from European laws. These areas bore directly on the commercial and certain aspects of international law.(26) No doubt this encourages Muslim rulers to borrow further from the same sources and in certain ways may have softened the resistance to such a procedure.

The purpose and ambition of Al-Afghani and his disciples was to re-establish the Shari'a as the exclusive source of law in Muslim countries. Al-Afghani could simply voice such an opinion in general terms while 'Abduh may be drawn into giving more details of such proposals; but it was left to Rashid Ridha to argue the case.

Ridha starts from the doctrine that "There is nothing in our religion which is incompatible with the current civilization, especially those aspects regarded as useful by all civilized nations, except with regard to a few questions of usury (Riba) and I am ready to sanction (from the point of view of the Shari'a) everything that the experience of the Europeans before us shows to be needed for the progress of the state in terms of the true Islam. But I must not confine myself to a school of law, only the Qur'an and the authentic Tradition." (27) This statement formulates the problem though it was meant to describe the solution. What is the criterion upon which a practice is judged essential to progress? This is left unsaid.

But the statement gives reassurance to the ruling classes, the educated section of the community and to those who wish Muslims to partake in the modern progress that Islam as Ridha perceives it need not be antagonistic to their cherished aim.

The task which Ridha set for himself proved difficult and as those who followed him came to realise, much more revolutionary than he thought.

Ridha, like 'Abduh and Al-Afghani, emphasised the need for a continuous Ijtihad, but unlike them he was less tolerant of differences. With his extensive knowledge of the Tradition he was able to discount as untrue the famous Hadith "Differences amongst my umma is a source of mercy."(28) His overriding concern was to show that Islam, the religion of unity, could not possibly commend differences especially the type of differences which causes antagonism.(29)

He was aware, however, that differences of opinion were natural and must be permitted. The differences in legal matters to which he objected were those which raised the status of the Madzhab to that of religion itself. "The fanatic partisans of the Madzhabs (schools of law) refuse to make differences of opinion a source of mercy. Each one of them insists on the necessity of imitating his own Madzhab without a licence for its followers to imitate any other, even when it is needed or necessary."(30) Ridha contrasts this type of partisanship which divided Muslims over human opinions with the attitude of the pious forefathers (Salaf Saleh) who tolerated no disunity amongst Muslims on the strength of individual views.(31) He further points out that as regards the schools of law, their founders never claimed such authority for their independent opinions. The degeneration of the Muslims in the following generations, thinks Ridha, was shown most markedly in the blind imitation that led them into a position of near Kufre (unbelief).(32)

Rashid Ridha differentiates between three categories: doctrines, rituals and rules governing human relationships (mu'amalat). It is only this third category which permits of human effort. "Doctrines and rituals have been perfected in detail. They are not subject to addition or reduction. Whoever adds or reduces them is changing Islam and bringing forth a new religion."(33) Thus Rashid Ridha specifies the law proper as the subject of any possible reform or change. The basis of this reform is the interest of the Umma in accordance with the age. This, however, is not to give the Umma a free rein for Islam has "determined the principles of the obligation of virtue such as justice, equality and the prohibition of aggression, deceit and treachery and specified certain punishments for certain crimes and instituted the principle of consultation." The Umma, through the "Ulu Al 'Amr from amongst the ulemas and rulers who must be people of knowledge and social dignity ('Adalah)" is empowered to make decisions on matters of detail. They must decide through consultation "what is the best for the Umma in accordance with the times."(34)

He repeats the same idea in his introduction to Al-Tawfi's treatise on "Maslaha" (public interest) to which he gives precedence over the text.(35)

Rashid's statement on this occasion appears more liberal than any made by him on any other. There, he suggests that "Mu'amalat (social interaction) revolve in the view of the Shari'a on the principle of preventing harm and protecting or effecting what is useful."(36) He appears to place the principle of utility high above all other principles of jurisprudence. This may have happened under the influence of Al Tawfi. On other occasions Ridha branded as Kafirs Muslims who attempted to implement precisely this idea.(37) It is not surprising, therefore, to find that Rashid Ridha never allowed himself to go that far when it came to specific application.

He describes his position as falling in between two groups, the conservative ulema who follow blindly the works of medieval jurists. The other group are those who advise the abandonment of the Shari'a in favour of western laws.

His group are the moderates who hold that it is possible to revive Islam and to renew its true guidance through following the Qur'an, the authentic Tradition and the guidance of the Al Salaf Al saleh (the pious forefathers). The works of the leaders of the various schools of law are to be taken not as binding but simply as helpful in formulating our own opinions. They also believe that it was possible to reach a compromise between Islam and the best in modern civilization as the second group wishes. They even believe that religion and civilization are "two friends who always agree and never differ."(38)

Rashid Ridha was aware of the inherent danger in the twin call of his party to a new Ijtihad and strict adherence to the Salaf Saleh. He noted that some people have bestowed upon themselves the dignity of Mujtahids and interpreted the Qur'an without due consideration to its language or to the context. Since they were motivated by the desire to show identity between Islam and modern civilization they found it convenient to dismiss the Tradition altogether so as not to be encumbered by it. On the other side of the fence there were those who called themselves Traditionalists and adhered to the apparent meaning of every word reputed to have come from the Prophet. Being ignorant of the nature and the sciences of the Tradition they made no distinction between the categories of Sanads (chain of narrators) nor did they know the differences between what is authentic and what is false. Nevertheless, they branded any doubter of their position as a Kaffir (unbeliever) or a Fasiq (heretic).(39)

Rashid Ridha thus felt it essential to specify his programme and the principles upon which it is based. He declares that his moderate reformist party regards the Qur'an to be the word of Allah and to be binding on every Muslim and that every expression which bears only one meaning must be so accepted and complied with. On the other hand, if it is capable of different interpretations then it is subject to the efforts of interpretations by qualified people.(40) This is the first principle. We must note here that by insisting that:
(a) the clear and unambiguous verses must not be tampered with; and
(b) that ambiguous verses must be left to the trained people to interpret and explain, Ridha was pointing out the objections, or some of them, to the ultra modernists who without any training twisted the meaning even of the unambiguous texts.

The second principle is the acceptance of the Tradition of the Prophet in general terms for its rejection would entail with it the very rejection of the Qur'an itself and of Islam.(41) This, however, does not mean that every single Tradition must be accepted. A Tradition related by a single chain (Hadith Ahad), for instance, is only binding on the person who accepts it as authentic but it need not be made a general rule to which the Umma must adhere.(42)

The third principle is that of the Ijma' (concensus of opinion). In the view of Rashid Ridha only the Ijma' of the first epoch, providing its subject was unquestionably known to the Companions of the Prophet (Ma'lum bi al Dharurah), is binding on everyone. It was through such an Ijma' that the details of Muslim rituals and many aspects of the Shari'a reached us. Hence it would be tantamount to rejecting most aspects of Islam not to rely on their Ijma'. The individual Ijtihad of the Guided Caliphs, their judgements and political decisions are not to be regarded as part of the religion but simply as a pointer to what a Muslim government should do.(43)

Rashid Ridha, it must be noted, wishes to minimise the requirement for a Muslim so as to allow greater freedom for reform on the one hand, and on the other to keep an open mind with regard to questions of differences between Muslims. He used to say that "We should support each other in what we agree upon and tolerate each other on what we differ."(44)

Theoretically, Rashid Ridha frees himself greatly of Fiqh and of Tradition since he rejects the authority of the former altogether and suggests regarding the latter that it is only binding in a limited sphere. In practice, however, Ridha's programme demands a greater research in and reliance on Tradition and also a re-evaluation of the works of earlier scholars, for though they are not regarded as authorities, they are still regarded as guides. The new Ijtihad of Ridha's was thus tantamount to a revival of the

Traditional school of law with a few trimmings to fit modern conditions.(45)

While reiterating the principle that Islam is the most complete system under which man's perfection in faith and life can be realised, Rashid Ridha emphasises that matters outside the strict religious sphere are left entirely to the efforts of man.

He draws a distinction between Muhammad the Prophet and Muhammad in his wordly functions. In what Muhammad communicates as revelation his authority is absolute; on the other hand his political, military or wordly decisions not based on revelation are the product of human judgement and are, therefore, subject to error.(46)

Although Ridha took the sphere of doctrine and rituals outside the human endeavour, he was well aware that numerous modifications and innovations in the field of worship and a great deal of complexity and sophistication in the basic beliefs of Islam took place. Ridha, following 'Abduh, considered these aspects to be a source of disunity and a serious deviation from Islam itself. It is not, contends Ridha, for Muslims to use their own opinion to decide for the community what is religiously prohibited and what is permitted. Obedience to the people in authority is confined to wordly not religious matters. (47) Innovation in the affairs of man so long as they do not violate any of the basic aims of the Shari'a are not subject to any prohibition, indeed they may be regarded as obligatory.(48)

Regarding mu'amalat (social interaction), Rashid Ridha recognises that from the point of view of the evidence purported to bear on them, they are classified into five categories. The first comprises those aspects with specific texts which cannot be doubted either as to their applicability or authenticity.

The second are those aspects coming under a general rule either directly or by implication and were considered so by the First Generation. These two categories are outside the sphere of Ijtihad.

The third category is that with uncertain evidence such as a Hadith and was a subject of dispute between the Companions and the learned; this is the field of human effort and it is naturally a subject of dispute amongst the learned in all ages. Under this category comes the rulings on certain aspects of cleanliness (Tahara) which were subjects of differences amongst the Salaf. Similarly, the rules arrived at by some of the learned through the use of their own deductive methods from the texts of the Qur'an and the Sunna. These rules should not be regarded as general and no one should be obliged to follow them blindly.

Questions relevant to public affairs such as the rulings of judicial or political nature should be examined by the people of authority (Ulu Al Amr) whose opinion becomes binding.

The fourth category are questions of customs or public behaviour, such as the manner of eating, drinking, etc. The Hadiths bearing on them are not regarded as enjoining the Muslims to follow a specific behaviour. It is, however, better, so Rashid Ridha suggests, that Muslims should follow their rulings in the interest of unity, providing this does no violence to public or private interest.

The fifth category are those matters not dealt with by the Prophet(Shari'). No one has the authority to oblige or prohibit on religious grounds a Muslim from doing anything under this category.(49)

As Ridha supports the reliance on both the texts and the human evaluation in accordance with the principle of utility he subscribed to the middle position with regard to the use of

Qias. He rejects the views of Ahl Al-Ra'y, who use it excessively, and the Ahl Al-Zahir who oppose it totally.(50)

Ijma' is also examined by him. He observes that it has often been used by the opponents of reformism to discredit its proponents and to depict them as enemies of the Umma and of the faith. It was therefore natural that the concept should be examined by every reformer.

As a great many practices, religious, social and economic are venerated in Muslim society on the strength of Ijma', the reformer who seeks to change them must look into their basis.

Ridha, following early Hanbalis, points out that there are two types of Ijma': one which is manifested by positive agreement amongst those concerned; the other is what is called tacit agreement where those concerned were not reported to have objected to a particular practice or ruling that took place in their day. Ridha rejects the second category as an invalid instrument. He suggests that the absence of objection is difficult to prove since the absence of a report of opposition does not necessarily preclude it having happened. What remains, therefore, is the first category, and even this is subject to certain reservations. In the first place it must not violate a religious text such as the Qur'an or an authentic Tradition and in the second, it must include all those who should express an opinion on the matter. He notes that with the exception of the period of the Companions it is impossible to effect any such concensus. Even if it occurred in another generation, it would have the authority of a revelation only in relation to that generation. In other words, whereas the concensus of others stands only for as long as no other concensus cancels it.

Ridha thus throws very strong doubt on the very existence of Ijma' in a historical and viable sense except in a few cases where it acts as a supplementary evidence to the Qur'an and/or the Tradition. The Ijma' of later generations, if it could ever be proved to have taken place, is not binding on the generations after them.(51)

By looking afresh at the aspects of Muslim law with the aim of formulating a law more in line with the modern age, Ridha was able to modify a number of important questions such as the freedom of belief, the question of interest and the insurance in the Muslim state. It is significant, however, that he employed not the dynamic principle of utility but the traditional concept of discovering the intention of the Shari'a.

In the era of liberty and freedom of thought epitomised in the eyes of many educated Muslims by western liberalism, the question of apostacy in Islam looked very much like a blot on a faith whose apologists portray it as the religion of freedom. Jurists are unanimous that a Muslim renouncing Islam is punished by death. The practices of early Muslims in fighting the apostates and the Traditions specifying death for those changing their religion are cited as evidence for this rule. Ridha, however, saw this as an unfounded Ijma'. He rejected the Tradition outright as contradicting a general principle in the Qur'an, namely the Verse 256 Sura 2 which states "No compulsion in religion". Rashid Ridha also cites Tradition reporting the Prophet in other cases as having opposed compelling some Arabs who chose Judaism to become Muslims. He explains that the Wars of Apostacy (Hurub Al-Riddah) which were waged by the Companions as being political in nature, caused not by the simple act of renouncing Islam but by becoming a military and social threat to the community.(52)

On the questions of interest and insurance policies, Ridha decries those jurists who are quick to restrict the financial activities of Muslims thus leaving these affairs in the hands of non-Muslims and threatening the economic interests of the community. He sees nothing wrong with taking up a life insurance policy.(53) He also decries the jurists' misuse of Qias to extend the area of prohibition on taking interest on capital and suggests that the taking of interest on monies left in the bank or postal office does not come under the prohibited Riba.(54)

Although Ridha cites with evident support the views of Al-Tawfi and Al-Shatibi on the use of public interest as a basis for legislation preceding in importance every other basis including the Qur'an,(55) he in practice does not go beyond the texts. This is more evident with questions of social structure such as the position of the woman in society, the structure of the family and such questions as co-education. Regarding the position of the woman in society, Ridha published a book called "Nida' Ila Al Jins Al Latif" (A Call to the Fair Sex). His intention in this book was to clarify the position of the Muslim woman from the point of view of the Shari'a. He was anxious to show that the Muslim woman is given more rights and privileges than the woman of civilized societies. In his opinion this is not contradicted by the fact that in Islam a woman must always have a legal guardian "to give her all she needs to be an honoured virgin, a virtuous wife, a careful mother and a respected grandmother."(56) In a public discussion with a university female student, Rashid Ridha strongly supported the usual social restrictions on the Muslim woman and later branded the girl who wished for greater freedom to mix with the opposite sex as an apostate.(57) On this issue, Ridha retained and glorified the conservative position throughout his life, with the one exception that he thought women were eligible to political rights just as men. He does not, however, explain fully his statement on the subject.(58)

He also vehemently rejected any modification of the Shari'a penal law. The thief, he maintained, must be punished in accordance with divine law. No doubt Ridha, despite his liberalism or even radicalism in principles, could not bring himself to violate the basic texts of the Qur'an.(59)

The failure of Ridha to carry out his programme of reform has been attributed by M. Kerr(60) to two reasons. The first concerns the moral prestige of the Shari'a in the traditional society where its modification would come up against social convictions. The second is derived from a conflict in Ridha's own attitudes as both a reformer seeking change and an apologist seeking to prove the Shari'a to be self-sufficient. There might still be another reason, namely the absence of a model upon which to fashion a programme of reform. Early in his career the west, some of whose policies he was ready to accept, was his model. Only certain minor questions such as Riba were, according to him, all that separated the law of Islam from the civilization of the West. As Europe's prestige declined especially after the First World War, confusion set in. The reformists were thrown back into the certainty of the established system in preference to stepping into unchartered land.

Ijtihad in the Shari'a, Ridha declares, is the only foundation for a Muslim renaissance.(61) His effort in this respect may be regarded as falling short of setting Islam on the way to progress.

Rashid Ridha's Theology

Like 'Abduh, Ridha was essentially a jurist and like him he was averse to theological discussions of the type that caused disunity in the Umma, solved no problem, bore no relation to practical life and complicated the simple faith of Islam. The question that attracted him most urgently was the prevailing practices concerning saints(Awliya). He echoed the Wahhabis in their attacks on saint worship. His attacks brought a great deal of opposition from the conservative writers who accused Rashid Ridha of over-zealousness and disrupting the unity of the Umma. It was this question among others that divided him from the conservative wing of Al-Azhar ulemas and it was his partiality to the Wahhabis which brought about his famous dispute with Al-Azhar magazine (Nur Al Islam).(62)

For centuries the preoccupation of Muslim theologians like Muslim jurists had been the assurance of Muslim conscience that life as it is lived by Muslims was both legitimate in the eyes of the Shari'a and correct from the point of view of doctrine. They sought to reduce the tension inherent in the disparity between the actual and the ideal, as well as the social conflict arising from the existence of powerful factions by narrowing the gap between opposed poles.(63) Ridha contended that saint reverence to the extent of performing certain rituals regarded as legitimate and calling upon them as mediators between man and God makes the Muslims on a par with the jahilis. The power of his arguments was not missed by the ulema; but whereas his concern was with the purification of Islam, theirs was with the pacification of the minds and hearts of Muslims. It was better in the view of the ulema to show a general practice as consistent with Islam than to alienate the whole Umma by condemnation.

Ridha regarded the efforts of early theologians which were still studied in Muslim institutions as irrelevant both to the problems of the time and to strengthening the conviction in Muslim hearts. These works were written for apologetic purposes not for expounding the doctrines. Further, their arguments were directed at opinions prevailing in their day and age. The modern age is no longer concerned with these opinions and indeed new ideas which need to be dealt with have emerged. There is, therefore, a strong need for a purified Kalam (theology), a Kalam which is divested of irrelevancies, simplified and directed at current problems.(64)

Apart from his numerous articles on questions of doctrine, he published his book "Al Wahy Al Muhamadi" in the defence of Islam. This book he regarded as an improvement on 'Abduh's "Resalat Al Tawhid".(65) His aim in writing it was to call upon the non-Muslim world to accept Islam. He is convinced that modern civilization with its hypocrisy and misery and disputations leads nowhere, and that in the end there is no remedy to this situation except in the guidance of Islam, the religion of brotherhood, justice, mercy and peace.(66) He cites 'Abduh as saying "The civilized nations of the West will suffer from the troubles of their civilization and its political decadence to such an extent that they will be forced to seek an outlet; that outlet will be found only in Islam. The Islam of the Qur'an and the Sunna and not that of the theologians and the jurists."(67)

The book involves discussions of questions such as the need for religion which Ridha following Al-Afghani considers fundamental.(68) To Rashid Ridha, Islam is the only religion that could possibly be accepted by the civilized West. What bars Europe from adopting Islam, in his view, are the Churches and their propaganda against Islam, the European politicians who have inherited from the Church the same antipathy, and thirdly the Muslims themselves. Their pitiful condition, the decadence of their governments and nations, their utter ignorance of their religion and their wordly interests deter others from sharing with such backward people a belief which is held responsible for their ills. He agrees with Al-Afghani that this was the greatest obstacle between Europe and Islam.(69)

The book also deals with the problem of revelation (Wahy), prophecy and the need for it side by side with reason and acquired knowledge. The chapter dealing with these problems was added only from the second edition perhaps because it was necessary as an introduction to the major issue of proving the prophethood of Muhammad. His method of supporting the prophecy of Muhammad is not the traditional one of enumerating real or imagined miracles but, according to his views, the scientific and logical procedure. He considers miracles and other types of extraordinary happenings as more likely to deter people from accepting Islam.(70)

The second major problem with which the book deals is the Qur'an itself. He deals with it as a miracle and as a factor in the social and religious transformation of Muslims. He suggests that the aims of the Qur'an in social and political reform are achieved by the unity of mankind in the religion of the Shari'a, the religious brotherhood, nationality, language and judicial law.(71)

Although the book is apologetic in nature, it does not follow the usual trend of complete falsification of history. He strongly disapproves of those who seek to attribute to Islam aspects of modern civilization in the face of historical evidence. He thus points out that slavery was legalized in Islam, but freeing the slaves was the final goal of the faith.(72) His views on war are that Islam is basically peaceful, unless aggressed upon or the efforts of its missionaries are obstructed. Although legitimizing war, Islam greatly humanized it both in its application and its aim. The idea of Jihad therefore is modified into a simple method of defence for even in victory the Muslims according to Ridha are not permitted to compel the people of the Book to adopt Islam.(73)

Rashid Ridha's concept of causality deviates, or so he believes, from the general trend in the Ash'ari school. Like Al-Afghani and 'Abduh, he accepts without question that such a relationship exists and he rejects the traditional view that denies it.(74) In his opinion, Al-Ghazali also subscribed to the same views. He recalls his emancipation from the Ash'ari outlook before adopting the position of the Hanbalis. He says "At the beginning of our study of Kalam we used to see in the (Ash'ari) books the views of the Hanbalis reported, and from this we used to think that they were fundamentalists taken up by the letter of the Revelation without truly understanding it. They did not appear to have known the facts of science or to have related them to the religious texts. In our view the Ash'ari books alone were the source of religion and the path to certainty. Then we had a look at the books of the Hanbalis, and to our surprise we found them the true guide to the ideal path of the Salaf." He continues in this vein to describe the difference between the Hanbalis and the Ash'arites as that between "He who walks the straight path and he who swims into a stormy sea buffetted by the waves of philosophical doubt."(75)

The use of science and logic in place of miracles in religious arguments, the acceptance of the law of causality and the opposition to the practices connected with saints, drove Ridha logically into denying the possibility of miracles after the Prophet. He might also have been prompted by the desire to nullify the claims to sainthood; the basis of which among the common people is the Karamats performed by the saints.

He derived this from 'Abduh's own concept of the evolution of man and religion. In 'Abduh's view Islam, unlike Judaism and Christianity, addressed human minds without attempting to overwhelm them emotionally through miracles. Although 'Abduh never goes so far with his conclusions, it is a logical step. His position can lead to the view that the age of miracles has ended as man has matured and the Prophets have been sent. 'Abduh, while accepting the possibility of Karamats, saw no reason for a Muslim to accept every or any particular claim. Rashid Ridha went further to claim that Muhammad ended the age of miracles (Karamats) as well as prophethood.(76)

It was his conviction that in the age of science the less miraculous is the more acceptable, and he thought that had the Qur'an not contained reports of miracles it would have found ready acceptance from many "open minded Europeans."(77) It must not be concluded, however, from this position that Rashid Ridha subscribed to a rationalist interpretation of Islam within the limits of the texts. His denial of Karamats, apart from its importance in his argument against saint practices, was essentially apologetic. The main purpose of which was to show the 'scientific' nature of Islam. It did not bar him from accepting such beliefs as the evil eye for instance.(78) As there were traditions supporting this belief and as it did not appear to Ridha to contradict any of his main principles and more importantly as it was part and parcel of his cultural background he accepted it without a discussion. The rationalism of Rashid Ridha is therefore a rationalism limited by a specific aim to a specific sphere.

Rashid Ridha's Views on Education

The Salafi school, especially 'Abduh and Ridha, regarded education as the main instrument of social change. Rashid Ridha subscribed to the views of Al-Afghani and 'Abduh regarding the adoption of science and technology and like them he stressed the importance of religion in the educational system. He was critical of the Egyptian educational system which aimed at "preparing youth for the services of the government instead of aiming at training in itself." He was also critical of the school curricula for its lack of proper care with regard to religious education.(79)

Rashid Ridha, like 'Abduh, concerned himself less with education in general and more with religious education. Although Al-Manar had from its early days a special section for education and carried the translation of Jean-Jacques Rosseau's "Emil", Ridha's positive contribution to educational thought is best represented by the syllabus he designed for his school, the school for "propagation and guidance" (Madrassat Al Da'wah Wa Al Irshad).

The idea for this school may have been inspired by 'Abduh who claimed to have suggested something on this line to Al-Afghani when they were in Paris. The school was aimed at training two classes of people: the murshids (guides) who would work within the Muslim community to guide it into the right path and to combat religious deviation,(80) the second type is that of the du'ah (the propagators) who would carry the mission to the non-Muslims.(81)

Although the two types go over basically the same courses the emphasis differs in accordance with the functions of each. The murshids were to be more concerned about guiding the already convinced to the proper religious behaviour and conviction, whereas the du'ah were to be concerned with the defence of Islam against non-Muslims and against the heterodox factions. It is important to note that Rashid Ridha felt it essential that his students should study the actual situation of Muslims and not simply the ideal in the Muslim texts. He, for instance, feels that the study of Tasawwuf should include a social study of the Tariqas, their differences, influence and the factors assisting or hindering their spread. This study, he suggested, should be done side by side with comparison between the ideology of the Tariqas and the teachings of the Prophet.(82)

He includes in his programme international law and the laws governing companies, trade unions and similar organisations, and was not averse to using European authors.(83) Beside the religious subjects, he introduced psychology, sociology, biology, introductory mathematics, hygiene, geography and economics.(84) He also suggested perhaps for the first time in Egypt a proper study of the Bible and the history of the Church.(85)

The school was rightly described as "a college in which all the disciplines normally taught in colleges are catered for, in addition to religious education and more attention to the Islamic sciences."(86)

The student body consisted of young men (aged between twenty and twenty-five) belonging to various Muslim nations. Although the school had to close down at the beginning of the First World War, it could count amongst its graduates such luminaries as Sayyid Amin Al Husaini, the Grand Mufti of Jerusalem, Shaikh Yusuf Yassin, the prominent Saudi official, in addition to other leaders of thought in India, Malaysia and even Egypt.(87)

The education of women in the opinion of Rashid Ridha is essential. He, however, considers that the function of the woman in society is different from that of the man and therefore her education must also be different. He subscribes, as has been noted earlier, to the segregation of the sexes and objects most strongly to the movement for co-education in Egypt.(88)

Rashid Ridha's Political Thought

The West provided twin challenges to Egyptian society. On the one hand it shook the foundations of its stability and forced it into a re-examination of its basic assumptions. On the other it compelled it to adopt many institutions which did not grow within its own environment.

The Al-Afghani-'Abduh school was brought into existence in answer to this challenge. Believing as they did that western progress and might sprang from its political and social organisation, they sought to reconstruct Muslim ideals in a way to permit the internalization of western forms. What they specifically aimed at was a Muslim society which enjoyed all the advantages of the West. 'Abduh and Al-Afghani advanced as a central principle that Islam and modernity can both form the necessary synthesis for the dynamic and strong Muslim society which they hoped to construct. In Islam that society would find its identity, the cement to its unity and the motive force for its achievement, whereas modernity would provide the instruments of power. Both 'Abduh and Al-Afghani rejected any suggestion of contradiction between the two elements, Islam and modernity. The history of antipathy between religion and science in the European environment was regarded by both as provincial in nature. Islam, they both contended, was different from Christianity in precisely those points where it clashes with modernity. Since modernity was presumed to have its basis in reason it was the preoccupation of the school to prove the rationalism of Islam.

The political liberalism of the West, and particularly French constitutionalism,(89) exercised a great deal of attraction to Muslims in the nineteenth century. Both 'Abduh and Al-Afghani were at some stage advocates of some sort of republican regime. Neither, however, put forward precise formulations. Both men simply appealed to the past, claiming not only its perfection but also its identity with the reforms they now propose. They died before the disappearance of the Ottoman Caliphate. The practical considerations of its existence on the one hand and the external threat to the Umma on the other forced Al-Afghani to take the Abdul Hamid II as his ally. As for 'Abduh, after 1889 his pen if not his tongue kept largely silent on the matter.(90)

Rashid Ridha, however, died much later (1935) than his two intellectual forerunners. He thus witnessed the upheavals leading to, and consequent on, the First World War. Being a Syrian with direct experience of Turkish tyranny and probably less emotional involvement in the Egyptian dilemma than a native Egyptian, he was able to chart a course for himself unhampered by strict loyalty to the Sultan or fanatical concern with British occupation of Egypt. He was consequently accused whether justly or otherwise of being a party to many conspiracies against the Sultan and of co-operation with the British enemies.(91)

In Egypt under the British, Turkey and the Caliph were regarded together with France as the counterpoise for Britain. The Nationalist Party of Mustafa Kamil sought all along to exploit the ambiguous position of British power in Egypt and the unreal suzerainty of the Sultan of Turkey over Egypt to weaken British influence in the country. An attack on the Caliph therefore was seen in nationalist circles as a betrayal of the national cause. Both 'Abduh and Rashid Ridha suffered under the suspicion of disloyalty to the supreme head and most projects they sponsored were met with strong resistance since they were seen as the instruments of British machinations.(92)

The upheavels consequent upon the defeat of Turkey in the First World War and the imminent end of the Ottoman Caliphate brought the whole question of the Imamate into focus.

In India, the Muslim leader Abou Al-Kalam Azad published a series of articles on the Caliphate from the point of view of Islam in his magazine Al-Hilal, which was translated and published in Al-Manar Volumes XXII and XXIII. Among other things, Abou Al-Kalam was calling all Muslims to support the Istanbul Caliph. Azad defended the legitimacy of the Ottoman Caliphate declaring that, though the Sultan was not of Quraish, he was the legitimate Caliph because the Quraishi condition was a violation of the egalitarianism of the Qur'an. Rashid Ridha, who annotated the articles, strongly opposed this view. To him the legitimate Caliph must be a Quraishi one, which in effect meant a Sayyid. (93) His pride as a Sayyid and his belief in the role that the Sayyids could play in leading Muslim society made him put various suggestions at various times to various authorities or persons to have a Sayyids' university so that the Muslim world might have an educated elite as its leaders.

Rashid Ridha found adequate evidence from the authentic Tradition for this particular attitude, but living as he was in Egypt in the midst of a social and political transformation he was aware that claims based primarily on descent were no longer feasible in the "democratic age".(94)

Leaving aside his various activities in the political field both in Egypt, Syria and the Ottoman Empire,(95) his most important contribution to political thought was contained in his book "Al Khilafa Wal Imama Al Uzma" (The Caliphate and the Great Imamate). (96) Before its publication in book form it was serialised in Al-Manar Volumes XXIII and XXIV (1922-23). "The question of Caliphate and the Sultanate" he wrote, "is a source of trouble in Muslim society just as monarchy is a subject of trouble to all other nations. This question was dormant but recent events in these days brought it back to life. The Turks have abolished the state of the Ottomans and built from its remains a republican state in a new form. One of the basic principles of this state is that no individual, whether named Caliph or Sultan, will hold sway in the new government. They also separated religion from the state completely. They nevertheless named one of the former ruling family a Sultan and declared him a spiritual Caliph to all the Muslims.(97)

These events, Rashid Ridha contends, made it imperative for him to explain the rules of the Shari'a in detail regarding the whole question, and to discuss "the place of the Caliphate as a system of government among other systems and its history and what should be done in this day and age."(98)

His contribution to the debate consists of three major parts. The first deals with the theories and ideas of earlier scholars such as Mawardi and Taftazani. (99) The second part consists of a historical exposition from the point of view of Rashid Ridha of the operation of the Caliphate in history. The third consists of his advice to the Muslim community, especially the Turks, concerning the restoration of the true Caliphate. In the analysis that follows our interest will naturally concentrate on Ridha's own ideas, both as regarding the history of the Caliphate and his suggestions concerning its restoration.

Rashid Ridha approaches this problem in the manner not of the political scientist but of the theologian. The ideal period of the Caliphate is that of the four rightly guided Caliphs. These are the Caliphs who followed strictly the Sunna of the Prophet, and because of this the religion of Islam spread and its power grew. The institution of Caliphate, Rashid Ridha believes, was a new experience in human history. Prior to the coming of the Prophet Muhammad people suffered under the tyranny of their rulers. Except in a few and far between occasions, injustice, severity and deprivation was the lot of the ruled. But the Prophet "came with the message bringing wordly reform and religious guidance." One of the basic principles of this guidance was that he established for mankind a middle way religion, a just law and a consultative state; made their affairs the subject of consultation amongst them and abolished the autocracy of kings, their selfishness and conceit. He decreed that the head of their state, the symbol of their unity whose responsibility is to make the organisation and justice uniform in the nation, be chosen by election. The electors are the leaders of opinion, respectability (adalah) and knowledge who are trusted by the nation and he made the head of state responsible to them and equal in the eyes of the law to the lowest man in the land. He enjoined them to obey the head of the state in what is known to be truth and justice and forbade them to obey him in what is sinful, transgression or unjust. He placed the motive force in performing all this in our religion to ensure compliance both in secret and in public for the "true obedience is to Allah alone."(100) Rashid Ridha was not simply reporting the law in its ideal sense but he was suggesting that it was actually complied with and followed, that the system as depicted in the above passage was meant to be universal as Islam is.

He was aware that with the exception of the first Caliph the other three were assassinated, a situation that could not possibly be considered ideal; but he found a ready explanation in attributing blameworthy developments to foreign elements. The murder of 'Umar "did not result from envy or hatred on the part of the Muslims, not from the ambition of a possible successor but from the secret society of Majus who killed him in revenge for the conquest of their country."(101) The murder of 'Uthman was no less easy to explain but this time it was not the Persians alone who engineered the conspiracy, a Jew by the name of Abd Allah Ibn Saba' propagated some destructive doctrines amongst Muslims which ended in the rebellion against 'Uthman. The murder of 'Ali and the first civil war were only consequences of these foreign activities. Here, therefore, is an ideal society and an ideal government and an ideal faith which were divested of their deserved success by the encroachment of the foreign elements.

Mu'awiyah completed the process when he captured government by force of arms and established a monarchy. He failed to follow the path of the Rashidun and the guidance of the Qur'an and the Sunna of the Prophet. If it had not been for this failure, the Caliphate would not have attracted those slaves of pleasure and fame for "There is no bodily pleasure in the office of Caliphate nor is there an autocratic authority."(102)

He attributes this trend to the expansion of Muslim domain, the accumulation of many enemies to Islam from amongst the leaders of religions or nations that were conquered by Islam. Added to this external factor, Rashid Ridha identifies an internal one present in non-Arabs who adopted Islam and also those Arabs, other than the early Muslims, whose adherence to Islam was not strong as they have not understood it completely. "The difficulty in communication made it easy for the Sab'is and the Majus to spread disorder for Islam and the Arabs. It made it also easier for

Mu'awiyah to build up an army to fight the true Imam and to make the Caliphate a monarchy."(103)

For Rashid Ridha the struggle was between two ethical systems: the just (Islamic) one and the unjust which sprang from quarters bent on enmity to Islam. Those members of the Muslim community who were incapable of understanding the faith and who therefore did not experience the moral compulsion to follow its tenets were a ready prey for the enemy.

Ridha continues his moralistic analysis of the historical development of the Umma, attributing all its ills to foreign influences. The final decline of the Abbasids, for instance, is attributed by him to the flattery of the Turkish soldiers who, being unfamiliar with Islam and foreign to the egalitarian sentiments of the Arabs, treated the Caliphs like Gods and in the process divested them of all the vestiges of power.(104)

At this stage, he contends, it was impossible to sustain a system of government in accordance with the Rashidun tradition, or the way of the Umayyads, or early Abbasids who, as he now suggests, combined "wordly glory with religious interests."(105) By the time it was possible to effect the form that the Muslim government should take, the power of religion itself had declined and with it the whole civilization of Islam. In consequence, the Muslims "were not as successful as were the Franks (Europeans) in abolishing the autocracy of kings."(106)

But how could the Europeans without the benefit of the true religion outstrip the Muslims? Ridha assures us that there are elements of true Christianity in the West which sustains its civilization.(107) These elements were, however, soon disappearing heralding the decline of Europe. The Muslims, on the other hand, have broken God's covenant and therefore have been punished.(108)

Ridha emphasises the religious foundation of the political system of the Umma and discounts 'Asabiyyah as the basis of Muslim government in early times. This is in contradiction to Ibn Khaldun's analysis of the rise to power and its later loss by Quraish. Perhaps in the whole work nothing demonstrates the limitations of Rashid Ridha better than his discussion of Ibn Khaldun's theory. He is obviously appalled at such a mundane explanation which reduced the charismatic community to the same level as other human communities. Rashid Ridha, who in other contexts accepts the 'laws of society' as he conceives them to be neutral with regard to religion, insists in this context that Islam has made the Arabs different so that they lost their 'Asabiyyah and consequently were defeated by the Persians.(109) Such an interpretation of history hardly accords with the evidence.

His proposals, which were addressed to the Turks, advised them to call in a representative assembly elected freely by the people to take over from the military authorities. As for the question of the Caliphate, he suggested that it should be left to the Muslim peoples and the independent and semi-independent Muslim governments. He appeals to the Turks to save the world from "Muslim ignorance and European materialism"(110) by establishing the divine law and the Caliphate of Islam.

Like 'Abduh, Ridha regards the Caliph as the head of the community in the temporal as well as the religious sense. His spiritual power, however, encompassed all Muslims including those who do not come under his rule.(111)

The large majority of Muslims agree that the establishment of the Caliphate is obligatory on the Umma. Most authorities before Rashid Ridha were content to enumerate as evidence the practices of the Companions and the fact that it was regarded as essential to the proper performance of Muslim duties. Rashid Ridha, as is his habit, resorts to the Tradition for further evidence.(112)

But who shall establish the Caliph? Rashid Ridha following the Sunni position makes it the function of the "Ahl Al Hal Wa Al 'Aqd" (the people who are able to loosen and bind). But who are these people? Do they have to agree unanimously or would a majority suffice? Leaving aside the niceties of majority versus unanimity within this authoritative group, we must concentrate our attention on finding who they are, how they are formed, the basis of their authority and the limits of their power. Rashid Ridha, quoting from 'Abduh, deals with this question more extensively in the Tafsir of the verse calling on Muslims to obey "Allah, his Messenger and Ulu Al-Amr". He defines the Ulu Al-Amr in this fashion "Ulu Al-Amr in every community, county or tribe are known. They are those whom the people trust in the affairs of wordly and religious nature because they believe them to be better informed and more sincere in their advice."((113) He suggests that they were with the Prophet wherever he went but they dispersed after the conquests of various regions in the Muslim Empire. He also states that when the Muslims wanted to install a new Caliph they sent to the generals and leaders of the people in the various countries to obtain their allegiance (Bay'a).

There is no adequate definition in all this. We are not told clearly who these authoritative people are, or how they emerged and operated in history. One must suspect that the concept of Ulu Al-Amr is a question of dogma rather than history. They appear to have disappeared or at least to have been deprived of their rightful position by the emergence of the Umayyads. The Abbasids did nothing to restore their position, nor did the Turks in the successor states. All these governments were not based in the opinion of Rashid on obedience to Allah, his Messenger and Ulu Al-Amr. Rashid Ridha, however, seeks to help by giving a definition of the Ulu Al-Amr in his day and age. He says that "They are the leaders of the ulema, the chiefs of the armed forces, the judges and the big merchants, agriculturalists and those concerned with public affairs, the directors of societies and companies, the leaders of political parties, the important writers, doctors and lawyers, providing they are trusted by the nation in its affairs."(114) Rashid Ridha, feeling that his definition was inadequate as it does not give any clear claim to membership to any person of the categories he mentions, resorts to the simple, if not simple-minded, device of suggesting that these leaders of opinion are known in every country and it would be easy for the head of the govenment to identify them and to gather them for the purpose of consultation.(115) He thus falls back on the moralist concept of the good ruler who will call in the Ulu Al-Amr simply because of his moral excellence.

This obscure group with obscure basis in society and equally obscure powers vis-a-vis the executive was, however, treated by Rashid Ridha as the final authority in the affairs of the Muslims. Their advice must be sought by the Caliph and it is they who should establish the Caliphate and dismiss the Caliph if he fails in his duties. These authoritative people are not legislators in the strict sense, they are simply Mujtahids bound by the Shari'a itself.

The role of the general public in the classical theory of the Caliphate, which is followed closely by Rashid Ridha, was to say the least indirect if not completely negative. It is true that the Ulu Al-Amr were defined as those who are able to command the following of the Umma. But the means for this are not clearly stated. The army commanders surely are seldom followed for other reasons than the military force behind them. The ulema, the lawyers, the merchants and all the other categories must in the end rely on the same basis. The history of Islam itself shows that the armed forces superceded all other authorities and institutions. Rashid Ridha was aware of this fact, but his adherence to the classical theory in its totality prevented him from offering any proper remedies beyond the hope that the generals will be such pious men that their authority and power will not be used illegally.

This confusion regarding the Ulu Al-Amr bedevils all Ridha's efforts in formulating a consistent and tangible theory. His grafting of some western institutions such as a house of representatives (to which reference will be made presently) helps to increase the confusion; for unlike the legislature in European societies, the house of assembly in Rashid Ridha's concept does not legislate but simply seeks to discover the law of God. There are, of course, parallels, although on a limited scale, in European societies. The House of Commons in Britain does not often go against the tenets of the Church in social matters such as marriage and divorce. But this is so because of deference to public opinion and not because the House by the very nature of its establishment is limited by these religious laws. Whatever the state of public opinion might be in a Muslim society, Rashid Ridha would not wish the Ulu Al-Amr to follow unless it conforms with the tenets of Muslim law. The supposed representatives of the poeple are therefore a committee of Muslim jurists engaged in classical Shari'a discussion. They are not to divide for voting. Any difference must be referred to the specialists for advice. Since the concern is for the truth rather than the trend of opinion of the people, majority vote is irrelevant. (116)

The leaders of opinion whose categories he mentions presuppose a free society. They cannot, as he admits, emerge or function under conditions of autocratic rule whether by foreign or native administration. Dictatorship of whatever variety deprives the nation of its natural leaders either through corruption or removal by force.(117)

He observes that the Egyptians and Turks are striving to form parliaments. He declares these parliaments to be "in essence the same as the Ahl Al-Hal Wa Al-'Aqd in Islam, except that Islam requires them to be people of knowledge and moral excellence which neither the Europeans nor their imitators demand."(118) Once more he does not feel inclined to subscribe to the concept of a general suffrage as the westernizers were advocating. Inherent in the whole concept is the limitation imposed on the political behaviour of the religious society by the fact of it being religious. The person or persons to be elected as representatives of the Muslim community must first pass the test of religious knowledge and conformity to religious morals. (119) This is inevitable, just as in the case of certain states where an elected member must not violate the political principles of the state. The identity of the state and religion in Muslim political theory makes the position completely logical and arguments against it are in essence arguments against the concept of this identity.

Since the historical development of the last few centuries deprived the Umma of its proper leaders, and since without them no normal political life is possible, what is then the course of action? Rashid Ridha asks himself this question "Is there anyone in the Muslim countries of the Ahl Al-Hal Wa Al-Aqd who is able to undertake this cause (the Caliphate) and if there is not anybody with actual influence, are there some who are potentially influential? And if so, is it not possible for the Muslims to establish a system to make this potential influence an actual one?" He answers this positively admitting that the task is hard but it required a strong advocate. He pins his hopes on the moderate reformist Islamic Party, namely his own. The party he conceives as the one standing in the middle of two extremes: the rigid imitators of the fiqh' books and the equally slavish imitators of western ideas. This moderate party of his "combined independence in understanding Islam and the rules of the Shari'a and the essence of European civilization.

This party is the only one able to abolish disunity within the Umma on the questions of what is to be done to revive the Caliphate."(120)

Rashid Ridha was not oblivious of the fact of the strong penetration of European ideas such as nationalism with all its implications of secularism into the deepest areas of Muslim thought. He was one of the earliest thinkers to recognise the dangers of nationalism although he may have supported its final goal of freedom from colonial domination. Various nationalisms emerging in the Muslim world acted on the unity of Islam seeking to replace its universal ideology by a parochial one. The dismembering of the Umma in this fashion would militate against the revival of the Caliphate, for in the eyes of Rashid Ridha only one Caliphate was possible and legitimate.(121)

The obstacles in the face of reviving the true Caliphate were not only in the absence of the Ahl Al-Hal Wa Al-'Aqd but also in the absence of candidates for the high office who could meet the stiff conditions formulated by traditional theory. Among these conditions they mention such knowledge of Islam as to permit for independent thought (Ijtihad) and apart from personal excellence, moral and physical courage, genealogical purity must also obtain. The candidate must belong to the tribe of Quraish.(122) Rashid Ridha was insistent on the Quraishi condition not, he wishes to assure us, because of any consideration except compliance with the authentic Tradition and the concensus of the Companions. He branded Abu Al-Kalam Azad's egalitarian ideas as violating these Traditions, although Azad utilized precisely the same technique as did Ridha regarding the question of apostacy. As the candidates from Quraish who meet all the conditions were obviously few and thus limiting the choice of the Umma, Rashid Ridha hit on the idea of establishing a school for the candidates to the Caliphate.(123) Rashid Ridha was incapable of understanding the egalitarian nature of the forces of nationalism and the need to give an equally egalitarian interpretation to Islam. The claim of Quraish, however, justified in religious texts and Muslim past history could no longer be taken seriously in the modern world. Indeed, if anything the restricted concept of the Imamate prevalent among the Shi'a may be more logical than the halfway house position of the Sunnis. Rashid Ridha himself subscribed to this idea, but on the grounds of the certainty of the descent of the Hashemis.

Rashid Ridha having decided that the Caliphate must be Arab and must have as its occupant a Mujtahid, he went on to the local conclusion of declaring Arabic a national language for all Muslims. He was, however, equivocal about it. He says "It is not our intention to call upon all the non-Arab Muslims to learn Arabic. We simply remind the reformist party of what is known to most of its members that is the strong connection between the office of the Caliph and the Arabic language." He further claims that "It is impossible for the Muslims to be acquainted with each other and to be united to the best degree possible without Arabic."(124)

The end of Rashid Ridha's proposals was to resurrect the Arab Caliphate. His motives were a combination of the attraction of early Islam in its Arab purity, a revulsion from innovations and decadence associated with the coming of the non-Arabs and their machinations. The veneer of European institutions appeared to cause more confusion in Ridha's political concepts than clarification.(125) He suffers, like the early jurists, from great reliance on persons not institutions.

The central difficulty in the classical theory of the Caliphate stems from the lack of specific description of those powers of the Umma relating to the choice of the Caliph. Ridha does not givr any clarification of the problem. The terms Ahl Al-Hal Wa Al-'Aqd (those who are able to loosen and bind), the Ulu Al-Amr (those in authority), the Ahl Al-Shura (those who are to be consulted by the ruler), the Ahl Al-Ijma' (those who are legally authoritative and whose consensus is binding), were never accorded clear social definitions through which they could be identified. The Jam'a or Ummah (the community of believers) was not given free choice of its supposed members of parliament. Ridha,following 'Abduh, insisted that election to parliament must be free from compulsion, that the nation must select its Ahl Al-Hal Wa Al-'Aqd without interference from the executive. Such a sentiment deserves our respect and sympathy, particularly since the experience of Egypt under Isma'il showed how ineffectual the consultative committee were vis-a-vis the pressure of the ruler. This, however, is not extended to allowing the common people to learn from their mistakes, Ridha insists that the Ummah should be free to choose providing that it chooses the right people. If it failed to do so, it would be automatically disqualified. (126) Yet Ridha does not give the public any means of identifying the leaders it must choose. He uses circular definitions that are most unhelpful and sometimes suggests that they are known to everybody, and the ruler if he so wishes could consult them.(127) It is, therefore, essential to realise that the western terms used by Rashid Ridha are not necessarily employed in the same way as in the western context.

Perhaps the best assessment of his efforts in political thought is that of Emile Tyan, who commenting on H. Laoust's translation of "Al Khilafa" under the title "Le califat dans la doctrine de Rasid Rida" by declaring that Ridha could hardly be credited with having a special doctrine on this matter. "All the personal efforts of this author, animated by a very intense religious and apologetic spirit led him to propose certain adaptations in order to make possible the restoration of the Caliphate in modern Muslim states."(128) A similar view is expressed by Louis Gardet who credits Rashid Ridha with having recast Western assumptions in a Muslim fashion.(129)

We must, however, realise that despite Ridha's wish and hope to restore the Caliphate, he, unlike Al Mawardi, was less preoccupied with the legitimization and regularization of the institutions in being, and more with outlining the ideal political organisation.(130)

There is an important point in Ridha's exposition of the Islamic political system, namely the question of minorities. He advises the non-Muslims in Muslim domains to trust their future to a Caliphal government, which would give them autonomy, in preference to a secular one, which would deprive them of it. Further, the Muslim government is tied with the moral law of Islam which does not bind the civilian politicians.(131) There is nothing in all this about the participation in government by non-Muslims; but in 1909 Ridha wrote in support of the regime of the Society of Unity and Progress that "consultation between Muslims and non-Muslims and sharing each others opinions is not prohibited. It may even be obligatory."(132) He therefore saw no reason to question the membership of non-Muslims in the parliament, especially when they are not dominant in number over the Muslims.

Rashid Ridha's Impact on Egyptian and Muslim Thought

Al-Manar, Rashid Ridha's main contribution to modern Muslim journalism, was by far the most successful of its kind and the most influential. It was due in large measure to the personality of Rashid Ridha and his extensive contacts throughout the Muslim world that it was read in Java as well as in Morocco and that its influence was felt in Zanzibar and Mombasa as in Muslim Russia. Correspondents from all over the world kept in contact with him and he sent complimentary copies of Al-Manar to various Muslim organisations and leaders. He utilized the journal to project the personality of 'Abduh as the leader of a reform party throughout the Muslim world.(133) It is a measure of Rashid Ridha's success that 'Abduh's name became known throughout the lands of Islam.

After the death of 'Abduh, Rashid Ridha assumed the leadership of the Salafi movement. Through Al-Manar, Rashid Ridha's leadership was not in dispute; but even if it had not existed, Ridha's powerful personality, extensive learning and his success in maintaining and exploiting contacts would have brought him the leadership of the Manarists.

Events in Egypt and the Muslim world isolated him somewhat from the main stream of Muslim thought. The task that he and 'Abduh set for themselves was difficult. It was more so for Rashid Ridha who was hardly touched by European culture. The pace of westernization in Egypt attracted the bulk of 'Al Imam's Party' while the hostility of the conservatives to Rashid Ridha was intensified after the death of his teacher and protector. Rashid Ridha's ventures into Egyptian and Turkish politics brought him few friends. The rise of nationalism in Egypt isolated him still further for he objected to the movement naturally as a Syrian, but more so as a Muslim. He saw the nationalism of Egypt and other Muslim countries as a foreign incursion leading to the fragmentation of the Umma and the further weakening of Islam.(134) Though in the long run this may in fact have been true, the nationalism of Egypt, or at least the nationalism of the Mustafa Kamil party, was vastly different in the sense that it had a place in it for Islam. As Rashid Ridha well knew the party was regarded as a Muslim party,(135) but it was Rashid Ridha's need or his conviction to keep friendly or as friendly as possible with the British administration that brought him the enmity of the party even when the effective leadership passed over to the religiously oriented Abd Al-Aziz Jawish.

His idealization of 'Abduh and Al-Afghani hampered to some degree any objective study of either. He treated their lives and works almost as he treated religious texts. The reader could not help sometimes being overwhelmed by the personalities of two men who at his hands were turned into less of historical figures and more of legends.

He saw in front of his eyes what the conservatives had warned of all along, namely the growth of westernization in Egypt and faced the accusation that 'Abduh and himself were responsible for its growth. His defence that westernization predated the reformist party was essentially true, but irrelevant to the substance of the accusation. There is no doubt that the Salafi party weakened the authority of the traditional ulema and that 'Abduh in his later life allied himself with those who were more oriented towards Europe and who later proved to be much closer to the westernizers. Thus, Rashid Ridha gained 'Abduh's enemies and lost most of his friends.

Undercurrents were moving steadily in opposite directions from the secularization of Egyptian life. The virtual disappearance of the Nationalist Party and the domination of the strongly nationalistic Wafd of Egyptian politics created a gap between the nation and its leaders. This gap was hidden behind the smoke of emotion aroused in the heady years after the First War and the turbulence of the early twenties. As the dust settled down and Egypt began to fall into the pattern of political musical chairs, which lasted until 1952,(136) the gap between the political leaders and their western ideas on the one hand and the common people inspired by Islamic ideas and tradition was growing wider. Within this gap stepped Rashid Ridha and many of his friends. At this level he was willing to co-operate with the reactionary ulemas of Al-Azhar. It was not by accident that religious societies such as the Young Men's Muslim Association,(137) and the Muslim Brotherhood made their first appearance during this period and both had certain connections with Rashid Ridha. In spite of his quarrel with Al-Azhar he moved perceptibly towards reconciliation providing in all circumstances that no-one should do violence to any of his principal beliefs.

In the field of thought proper his tremendous energy and powerful pen which were previously preoccupied with the ulemas became more and more involved in arguments with the other extreme of the trilogy. The middle position which Rashid Ridha sought to occupy dictates that the greatest resistance must be directed at the side which exerts the greatest pull. At the turn of the century it was the ulema of Al-Azhar who held sway but within twenty years the picture had completely changed and the westernizers represented the greatest danger. If Rashid Ridha's advice to the ulema was liberalism, his advice to the westernizers was restraint. He led the attacks on Ali Abd Al-Raziq for his now famous book on the Caliphate (138), and was delighted when the authorities of Al-Azhar punished the author with severity. He was also in the forefront of the critics of Taha Hussain's theory on pre-Islamic poetry and found himself in this respect at variance with Lutfi Al-Sayyid, who early in the century was regarded by him as a prominent member of 'Al Imam's Party'. Both Abd Al-Raziq and Taha Hussain were phenomena of an Egypt exposed to a greater degree of westernization than Ridha would have liked.

The arguments against these writers were conducted by ulema not always with identical views as those of Ridha. But the authorities and not the writers in the end decided how the argument should be settled. Both Abd Al-Raziq and Taha Hussain lost their posts and the latter was forced to alter the offending section of his book. But neither was argued completely out of court; they both became symbols of a secularist and liberal ideology. The opposition to them took the form of traditionalism. In this issue there did not appear to be a middle course.

The early followers of 'Abduh from the western educated were quickly disappearing. Their whole educational system and the changed conditions of Egypt reduced the religious argument from a position of importance in educated circles replacing it with questions of politics and nationalist appeal. Religion was gradually relegated to a secondary place as a mere individual relationship between the citizen and the deity he elects to worship. The Umma appeared to have chosen the security of unity with non-Muslims in Egypt in preference to the romantic affiliation with Muslims outside. It was Al-Azhar and institutions built around it such as Dar Al Ulum that put a certain degree of restraint. Al-Azhar did not stand against nationalism but it did not subscribe to isolationism. It must have been strange for Rashid Ridha to realise that only within Al-Azhar and the circles of the Nationalist Party would he find his allies. The changes imposed on the curricula of Al-Azhar and the growth of knowledge amongst its younger ulema prepared a climate of opinion to make it more open to new ideas. Rashid Ridha on the other hand was perceptibly retreating from the adventurous position of the early years of the century. The grounds for co-operation were thus present, but Ridha had a merciless pen and a tendency to criticise immoderately. This did not endear him to the Azharites of his day. In the event, therefore, 'Abduh was gradually being accepted while Rashid Ridha was being simply ignored. Ridha's heirs were to be found later within the circles of the Muslim Brothers, the Young Men's Muslim Association and similar organisations.

The growth of these movements in Egypt was a reaction to extreme westernization. It was such a powerful reaction that avowed westernizers such as Haykal, Taha Hussain and Tawfik Al-Hakim had to respond by modifying their position of extreme secularism and speaking or writing in more glowing tones about Islam.((139) How much of this reaction could be attributed at least in part to Rashid Ridha is difficult to ascertain. His persistence and tenacity, his unlimited self-confidence and evident contempt for westernizers, however high their position in society or government, must have contributed to stimulating that reaction. Further, Rashid Ridha's stand on classical Islam and his conviction that it could withstand all arguments against it must be regarded as one of the foundations of the movements later to become so powerful in Egyptian society.

Outside Egypt Rashid Ridha, like Muhammad 'Abduh, was held in greater esteem. Many imitators of Al-Manar emerged in many parts of the Muslim world, and in Malaya in particular a group of Malay Arabs translated selected articles from it and published them in the journal "Al-Imam". The magazine was also widely read and imitated in Sumatra, and it influenced the Muhammadiyyah movement in Java. The convulsion of the Muslim world in the decades after his death brought into focus his ideas and those of his earlier masters.

Rashid Ridha as a Thinker

Compared with Al-Afghani and 'Abduh, Rashid Ridha was the least acquainted with western thought.(140) He learnt no foreign language and his knowledge of western ideas were of second or even third-hand nature. But of the three he was perhaps the best trained, and certainly the most knowledgeable in the field of Tradition. His mind could not tolerate ambiguity and, unlike 'Abduh, he could not stand happily with two contradictory ideas pretending that both could be held without difficulty. He lacked 'Abduh's polish and sophistication and had to contend with more acute problems than he did. His facade of liberalism or tolerance within the Umma in the interest of unity did not prevent him from lashing out at any opponent if he felt incensed. Although he agreed with the theoretical position of 'Abduh, he applied it much more strictly and therefore much more narrowly. The role of reason in his view was to rebel against the authority of the traditional ulema and their masters on the one hand, and against blind westernization on the other. In relation to revelation, however, the position of reason in Rashid Ridha's system appeared less free than in 'Abduh's. While 'Abduh may suggest that the story of Adam and Hawa' is allegorical referring to the stages of man's development, Ridha refrains from tampering with revelation in this way.(141)

Like 'Abduh, Rashid Ridha was more concerned with the didactic rather than the philosophical. In fact he measures the efforts of the early scholars from precisely this point of view. Although he may use the word philosopher to prefix the name of Al-Afghani or 'Abduh, this is no indication of his appreciation of Muslim philosophy. Hostility to philosophy and Sufism is inherent in the school of Ibn Taimiya of which Rashid Ridha was an exponent. (In over thirty years of publication Al-Manar has published not one considerable work by a Muslim philosopher). Philosophical complexities were rejected out of hand as a deviation from revelation and as didactically harmful. Islam in the view of Rashid Ridha did not need a new philosophy as much as it needed a simple exposition to make it within reach of the average person.

His attitude to science was vastly different from his attitude towards philosophy. Here the impressive achievements of the scientists have conferred an aura on the sciences as disciplines and also on scientific theories that no philosopher could aspire to. The school of Al-Afghani was primarily concerned at interpreting Islam in scientifically accepted terms and it appears that all of them have raised the status of theory to the level of fact. It was probably this particular attitude which prompted both 'Abduh and Rashid Ridha to seek to reduce the miraculous elements in the Qur'an to a minimum. Although Rashid Ridha might support 'Abduh's position on some of these questions he would be more inclined to subscribe to the old Salafi doctrine of accepting the texts with the proviso of 'Bila Kaif'.(142)

In 'Abduh's system public morality was partially freed from its religious basis and Rashid Ridha, while theoretically approving 'Abduh's position, retreated from it in practice.

This difference may be attributed to Ridha's greater knowledge of the Tradition and less acquaintance with other cultures. He, however, maintained that differences in matters of details or indeed in a question of doctrine should be tolerated within the Muslim community in the interest of unity. This attitude was dictated by the wider social and political considerations rather than the strictly intellectual appreciation of opposite views.(143)

Rashid Ridha was a revivalist preoccupied with the preaching of the doctrines of Islam in a simple and more acceptable form. Like all theologians, he conceived the role of reason to be the elaboration and elucidation of revelation. Like the jurists he regarded his task as discovering from the texts the appropriate rules for a pious life. In his system, philosophy has no role and science as an undeniable fact helps in the process of interpreting hidden meanings of the Qur'an and the Tradition. Though he owes his thought to Ghazali and Ibn Taimiya, he subordinates the former to the latter and sees Al Ghazali, as he does all the figures he admires, to have ended his life as a Salafi.(144)

Reform, as seen by Al-Afghani and more so by 'Abduh, consisted of balancing two elements, the irreducible and unchanging aspects of Islam and the need to change in other aspects to meet modern conditions.(145) The equilibrium between the two elements was upset in favour of the former by Ridha and if later leaders such as Al-Banna attacked the West and rejected it as a model this must be regarded as at least partially inspired by this trend.

Al-Afghani, Muhammad 'Abduh and Rashid Ridha

The journey of reformist Islam covering over half a century shows the stages of its growth and development. Al-Afghani injected a sense of urgency and a liberal ideology, while 'Abduh sought to demonstrate the congruity of Islam and modernity. The first was content with general proposals. The second formulated a more detailed proposal but found it essential to limit the role of human thought to the simple activity of removing apparent contradiction within revelation or between a revelation and what was regarded as science. Internal consistency was thus achieved sometimes at the expense of external realities. Rashid Ridha demonstrated still further this departure from reality, and together with greater internal coherence. The basic question of the relevance of Islam to Egyptian society both as a legal system and religious outlook was touched only in apologetic fashion. Despite liberalism in legal matters none of the leaders of reformist Islam was willing to allow fundamental alteration of the law. On the theological plane their most significant contributions appeared in arguments with European orientalists.(146) Rashid Ridha's lamentation that many Muslims read with delight the powerful rejoinder of 'Abduh to Hanotaux without concern about its contents(147) may have stemmed from the actual irrelevance of the whole affair to the true needs of Muslim society.

The reformist school, like the conservative ulema, was overtaken by developments in Egyptian and modern society. Both grew more and more irrelevant to its basic spiritual and social problems. Nevertheless the appeal of Islam remains powerful and the social, political and economic transformation had to be legitimized in the eyes of Islam to be acceptable with a clear conscience by the ordinary Muslim. This task of piecemeal admittance of change lacks cohesion or systematic examination of the facts and in consequence the ulema have taken a back seat in these matters resorting as their conservative predecessors did to issuing Fatwas in accordance with the wishes of the political power.

The task of the ulema has ceased to be the discovery of the revealed law and has become more openly and frankly the support of "the necessary changes" In short, the reformist Muslim thinker of our day can no longer offer the lead. He must simply follow. This was inherent though not immediately obvious in the reformist approach. Rashid Ridha, as previously noted, once suggested that all the necessary laws of modern civilization could be accommodated within the framework of the Shari'a with the exception of a few rules concerning Riba.

Reformist Islam consequently was incapable of leadership. The way was left wide open to another reaction to the impact of modernity, the revolutionary reaction. Where intellectual argument is not a satisfying exercise, forceful action is bound to be. This type of reaction does not call for the few to charter the way, but for the many to make one.

NOTES AND REFERENCES

Chapter 1

1. E.G. Browne, "The Persian Revolution of 1905-1909"(Cambridge 1910) portrays Al-Afghani as a hero of the revolution; and B. Michel and Shaikh Moustafha Abdal Razik, "Cheikh Mohammed Abdou, Rissalat al-Tawhid Expose de la Religion Musulmane" (Paris 1925) say in the introduction p.23 "Wherever he went he left behind a turbulent revolution. It is no exaggeration to state that all the nationalist liberation movements and the movements against European designs which we have witnessed in the East go back directly to his agitation." W.S. Blunt, "Secret History of the English Occupation of Egypt" (New York 1922) describes him as "The true originator of the liberal religious reform." p.76

2. Muhammad Al-Makhzumi, "Khatirat Jamal Al Din Al-Afghani" (Beirut 1931) reports Al-Afghani as saying that Lord Salisbury offered him the throne of the Sudan in exchange for his co-operation in its conquest, but Al-Afghani refused. See p.54

3. Elie Kedourie, "Nouvelle lumiere sur Afghani et 'Abduh", Orient, no.30, 1964, pp.37-55 and no.31, 1964, pp.83-104, argues that the reputation of both Al-Afghani and 'Abduh was posthumous and questions a great many of Al-Afghani's claims.

4. Muhammad Rashid Ridha, "Tarikh Al Ustaz Al Imam Al Shaikh Muhammad 'Abduh", vol.I (Cairo 1st ed. 1931) p.25

5. Ibid., p.30

6. Tarikh vol.II p.45 and Ibrahim 'Abduh, "A'laam Al-Sahafa Al-Arabiyya" (Cairo 1948, 2nd ed.) p.117

7. Cf. Nadav Safran "Egypt in Search of Political Community" (London 1961) pp.47 ff. and Mahmoud Al Khafif "Ahmad 'Urabi" (Cairo 1947) pp.26-27

8. Khatirat p.35

9. Tarikh vol.II 2nd ed. (Cairo 1344 A.H.) p.7. 'Abduh mentions in an article published in about the second half of 1879 that Al-Afghani "resumed teaching after an interval of more than one year."

10. Tarikh vol.I pp.46-47. 'Amhouri reports the increased activities of Al-Afghani in the political field in 1878 through the use of his pen and those of his friends, and that he "began to mix with the mass of the people" to arouse them against the government. Quotation from p.47

11. Al-Afghani's contribution to the magazine 'Misr' about absolute government 'al-hukumat al-istibdadiyyah' (republished in Al Manar vol.III pp.577-582 and 601-607) and also his article on the 'True Cause for the Happiness of Man' (Al-'illat al-Hagigiyyat li Sa'adat al Insan) republished in Al Manar vol.XXIII pp.37-45 contained nothing which indicated allegiance to a specific religion. Also the contributions of his disciple 'Abduh collected in Rashid Ridha's Tarikh vol.II(2nd ed.) pp.2-48 hardly refers to religion as such, except in one article pp.37-45 calling upon the ulemas to allow the study of modern sciences. In a particular article 'Abduh, no doubt under the influence of Al-Afghani, decries religious differences in favour of unity for the defence of the motherland, p.35

12. Tarikh vol.I p.41. Adib Ishaq reports that Al-Afghani "harboured a great hatred for the English state." He also reports him as having met with the French Consul General (c.1879) no doubt to enlist his support.

13. Khatirat pp.223-224

14. Ibid., p.35

15. Ibid., p.46

16. Al Manar vol.III pp.606-607

17. Ibid., p.577

18. Khatirat p.90

19. Al Manar vol.XXIII p.39 and Tarikh vol.I p.47. He called on Egyptians to stand as Egyptians distinct from all other Muslims, Turkish or Arabs.

20. Blunt "Secret History" pp.95 and 101 refers to a conspiracy by Al-Afghani to assassinate Isma'il in 1879, and Tarikh vol.II (2nd ed.) pp.335-336

21. Mahmoud Al-Khafif op.cit., p.82 describes the scene when 'Urabi confronted the Khedive with these words.

22. C.f. Shakib Arslan "Hadhir al-'alam al-Islami" (Cairo 1352 A.H.) vol.II p.292

23. Tarikh vol.i p.6 introduction reports Al-Afghani as saying to a Tartar student of his "Son, you will perform the funeral prayer on Czardom and you will attend the funeral of British power in India."

24. Al 'Urwat Al Wuthqa (Cairo 1957) p.96 Al-Afghani accused Ahmad Khan of aiming at helping the British through corrupting Muslim beliefs. Quoted by M. Al-Bahay "Modern Islamic Thought and its Relation With Western Colonialism" (Cairo 1957) p.15

25. Khatirat p.245

26. Al-Afghani "Al Bayan fi Tarikh al Inkelize wa al Afghan" "The clear account of the history of the English and Afghanistan." (Alexandria 1878)

27. C.f. Osman Amin "Introduction to Al Radd a'la al Dahriyyin" (Cairo and Baghdad) 2nd ed. p.8

28. Khatirat p.349

29. Ibid., p.149

30. Ibid., p.154 ff.

31. Al Manar vol.XXIII p.37 fn. Rashid Ridha says that the articles published by Al-Afghani in the newspaper Misr had "an influence in the British nation to the extent that their newspapers rebutted his arguments and he replied in a way that raised his prestige and this was the first reason for his name to be known in Europe." Italics are mine.

32. Elie Kedourie op.cit. no.31 p.93 where he quotes the Indian C.I.D. memorandum which claims that Al-Afghani offered his services to the British Government and his offer was declined. Surely, if he were willing to do so, he could have done so at a later date and with considerable rewards.

33. Rashid Ridha, Al Manar vol.II p.245 says that the conservative ulemas were critical of Al-Afghani on three counts: his knowledge of philosophy, his violation of certain customs which were considered part of the religion and the fact that he was surrounded by many irreligious persons.

34. Perhaps the earliest suspicion of Al-Afghani's conviction based on his statement was that of Mustafa Abd Al-Raziq, Al Manar vol.XXIV p.311. Abd Al-Raziq is there reported to have suspected his convictions since his rejoinder to Renan defended the Arabs strongly and Islam in a somewhat lukewarm fashion. Reference was made also to the paragraph where Al-Afghani accepts the contradiction between religion and philosophy. It is the same paragraph which S.G. Haim uses as a central argument for suspecting Al-Afghani's conviction. S.G. Haim "Arab Nationalism" An Anthology (Los Angeles 1962) p.11

35. Tarikh vol.I p.31

36. A.M. Goichon. "Refutation des Materialistes" her translation of Al-Afghani's Al-Radd Ala Al Dahriyyin (Paris 1942) Introduction p.41 n.2

37. Op.cit. p.50 et passim

38. "Religion and Irreligion in Iranian Nationalism" Comparative Studies in Society and History vol.IV pp.265-295. Quoted by Elie Kedourie op.cit. no.30 pp.38-39

39. "Symbol and Sincerity in Islam" Studia Islamica vol.XIX p.34 n.2

40. Op.cit. pp.122-123

41. Al Manar vol.XXXIII pp.232-233 reports Al-Afghani and 'Abduh wading through the mud at Alexandria to rescue a Muslim youth who had been converted to Christianity by the missionaries. Al-Afghani, remarking on the unconcern shown by Egyptian authorities about the matter, said to 'Abduh "It seems we are the only Muslims in this country."

42. See for instance Al Manar vol.XXIV p.312 where Rashid Ridha suggests th that Al-Afghani's article rejoinder to Renan was incorrectly translated.

43. E. Renan "Histoire generale et systeme compare des langues semitiques" (Paris 1883) vol.I 6th ed. pp.4-5 as quoted by Ibrahim Madkour "Fi al-Falsafat al-Islamiyyuh" (Cairo 1947) p.10

44. Republished in Al Manar vol. XVI pp.44-47

45. Iraj Afshar and Asghar Mahdavi "Documents Inedits Concernant Seyyed Jamal al Din Afghani", Publications de l'Universite de Teheran, no.841, 1963, plate 65. Italics are mine. This letter is not included in Ridha's Tarikh vol.II which contains 'Abduh's works.

46. C.f. J. Jomier, Encyclopaedia of Islam, New ed. p.419

47. C.f. Shakib Arslan "Hadhir al-'Alam al-Islami" vol.II p.301

48. See Mahmoud Abu Rayyah "Jamal Al-Din Al-Afghani" (Cairo no date) p.156 where the author chides the translators (Sadiq Nash'at and Abd Al Nadim Hasanain) or Mirza Lutfallah Khan's "Jamal Al-Din Al-Asadabadi al Ma'ruf bi Al-Afghani" (Cairo 1957) for publishing this book and ends by saying "He will remain forever an Afghan, even if they gave us a thousand pieces of evidence."

49. Tarikh vol.I p.33 quotes 'Abduh as saying that Al-Afghani was instructed by Al 'Urwat Al Wuthqa Secret Society to publish a journal "calling upon Muslims to unite under the banner of the Islamic Caliphate."

50. Ibid., p.307

51. Lothrop Stoddard as quoted by Ahmad Amin in "Zu'ama' al-islah." Cairo 1948 p.105 says that Al-Afghani regarded the West as influenced by the spirit of the Crusades and was bent on destroying the Muslim renaissance.

52. C.f. Ahmad Amin op.cit. p.113

53. J.M. Landau, "Afghani's Pan-Islamic Project" Islamic Culture vol.XXVI no.3 p.50

54. C.f. Al-Afghani 'Al Qada wal Qadar' Cairo no date pp.10-11. It is a reprint from Al Urwat al-Wuthqa which also appears in Tarikh vol.II 2nd ed. p.259

55. Al-Afghani "Al Radd 'ala al Dahriyyin" 2nd ed. Cairo and Baghdad 1955 p.87

56. Al-Afghani Al Urwat al-Wuthqa Cairo 1957 pp.70-71

57. Al Urwat al-Wuthqa pp.472-475

58. Loc.cit. and p.96

59. Tarikh vol.I pp.82-83 and Abd Al-Qadir Al Maghribi "Jamal al-Din Al-Afghani" (Cairo 1948) pp.95 ff.

60. Tarikh vol.I loc.cit.

61. C.f. H.A.R. Gibb "Modern Trends in Islam" (Chicago 1950) 2nd ed. p.29

62. C.f. Abd Al-Qadir al-Maghribi op.cit. pp.77 ff.

63. The term reform as used here means placing a greater emphasis on continuity vis-a-vis change. Modernization reverses this formula. Thus the Salafiyyat School is reformist, whereas Ahmad Khan and the Secularists are modernists.

64. Tarikh vol.I p.82

65. Tarikh vol.II pp.232-3

66. Op.cit. loc.cit.

67. Tarikh vol.I pp.46-47 and Zu'ama al Islah pp.72-73

68. C.f. Aziz Ahmad, "'Ahmad Khan, Al-Afghani and Muslim India" Studia Islamica vol.XIII pp.55-78 especially pp.56-63

69. These references are quoted by Muhammed Al-Bahay op.cit. pp.11-17

70. C.f. Bashir Ahmad Dar, 'Religious Thought of Sayyid Ahmad Khan' Lahore 1957 p.204 quoting Sayyid Muhammad 'Ali.

71. See Al-Ghazali "Tahafut al-Falasifah" translated by Sabith Ahmad Kamili (Lahore 1958) p.249

72. Al Radd p.28

73. Ibid., loc.cit.

74. Ibid., pp.47-64

75. Ibid., pp.77-88

76. Ibid., p.86

77. Ibid., p.87

78. See ibid., p.25 and p.87

79. A. Hourani, op.cit. p.116

80. Zu'ama' Al Islah p.113

81. Ibid., loc.cit.

82. Ibid., p.114 also Khatirat p.161

83. Khatirat p.162

84. See for instance his article quoted by Aziz Ahmad op.cit. p.59

85. Zu'ama Al-Islah p.113

86. Al Radd p.80

87. Tarikh vol.I Introduction p. n (nun)

88. Al-Afghani's suggestion reported in Tarikh vol.I p.33 is highly doubted. He there gives as the reason for suspending the paper, that it no longer reached its public in Egypt and India.

89. Tarikh vol.I pp.56-62 contains the letter to Mirza Hassan al-Shirazi calling upon him to oppose the Shah giving the concession to the British Tobacco Company.

90. According to Al-Afghani he held 'political offices' in both Persia and Afghanistan. In Egypt he was a teacher though with no specific duties. While in Turkey according to him he was offered the office of Shaikh al-Islam.

91. C.f. Aziz Ahmad op.cit. p.59 and his "Studies in Islamic Culture" Clarendon Press, 1964, p.56

92. W.C. Smith "Islam in Modern History" (Princeton 1957) p.48

Chapter 2

1. Tarikh vol.I p.289

2. Ibid., p.894

3. C.f. Tarikh vol.I p.998 also Shakib Arslan 'Rashid Ridha aw ikha' arba'ina Sanatan (Damascus 1937) pp.127-8

4. Tarikh vol.I p.974. 'Abduh is there described as more submissive to authority.

5. Tarikh vol.I p.974 ff.

6. As quoted in Tarikh vol.I p.226

7. Tarikh vol.II 2nd ed. compare his articles on pp.119 and 123 and 127 with his articles on pp.194 and 197.

8. Ibid., p.538

9. Ahmad Amin op.cit. p.310

10. His rapid advancement was attributed by some of his contemporary ulemas to his "masonic" affiliation c.f. Al Manar vol.VIII p.403

11. Lutfi al-Sayyid "Qessat Hayati" (Cairo 1962) pp.58-9

12. N. Safran op.cit. p.273 n.2 holds the opposite view.

13. For the views of Ahmad Khan as compared with Al-Afghani see Aziz Ahmad Studia Islamica vol.XIII pp.57-78 and the same article in a slightly modified form in "Studies in Islamic Culture in the Indian Environment" by the same author. (London 1964), especially pp.55-66

14. C. Adams "Islam and Modernism in Egypt" Arabic translation by Abbas Mahmoud (Cairo 1935) pp.30-168

15. C.f. Mustafa Abd Al-Raziq his article on 'Abduh in Al Manar vol. XXIII p.524

16. Tarikh vol.II pp. 7 & 46

17. Ibid., p.599

18. Tarikh vol.I p.12

19. Ibid., p.894

20. The incident is reported in Tarikh vol.I pp.896-897

21. See for instance his article published after his return from Paris to Beirut in August 1885 concerning the Indian Question in which he echoes the political views of Al Urwat Al Wuthqa. Tarikh vol.II pp.374-379

22. de Guerville, "La Nouvelle Egypte" (Paris 1905) pp.201-208. A part-translation appears in Osman Amin, "Ra'id al Fikr al Misri" (Cairo 1955) pp.251-3

23. Rashid Ridha defends 'Abduh's position. See Al Manar vol.XI pp.109 ff

24. C.f. J. Schacht in the Shorter Encyclopaedia of Islam, Eds. H.A.R. Gibb and J.H. Kramers, p.407

25. These ideas were widespread in the circle of Al-Afghani at the time. See for instance Abd Allah al-Nadim, "Sulafat al-Nadim", Cairo 1901, vol.I pp.99-120

26. Tarikh vol.II p.35

27. Ibid., pp.194-196

28. Tarikh vol.II p.199

29. He quotes La Bruyere by name. Ibid., p.194

30. Blunt, "The Secret History"p.191

31. As stated earlier, both legitimized rebellion. Further, neither advocated a Quraishi Khilafat. For the Kharijite view see Shorter Encyclopaedia of Islam p.248 article by G. Levi della Vida.

32. Tarikh vol.II p.221

33. Tarikh vol.I p.289

34. Ibid., p.219

35. P.J. Vatikiotis, "Muhammad 'Abduh and the Quest for a Muslim Humanism", Arabica vol.IV p.58 points out that both Al-Afghani and 'Abduh subscribed to the ideas they published. He rightly rejects Goldziher's portrayal which in effect would make 'Abduh a mere secretary to Al-Afghani. (E.I. 1st ed. vol.III p.678). Vatikiotis, however, falls into the same error by accepting 'Abduh's claim to have been against the political agitation and the advocacy of Pan-Islamism (while still writing in support of them).

36. C.f. P.J. Vatikiotis op.cit. p.59

37. Tarikh vol.II pp.288-9

38. Ibid., pp.335-336

39. Ibid., pp.237-249

40. Tarikh vol.II p.259 ff. and p.337 ff.

41. Ibid., p.227 ff.and p.325 ff.

42. Al Urwat al Wuthqa pp.145-6. It is noticeable that the term Ijma' used here by Al-Afghani (and 'Abduh) differs from Al-Afghani's concept as related by Al Maghribi op.cit. p.60, Al-Bahay op.cit. pp.71-2 suggests that perhaps Al-Afghani in Al Urwat was acting more in the fashion of a popular leader than of a thinker.

43. See Ahmad Amin "Yawm Al Islam" Cairo 1952, p.112 reports Gladstone as saying "The Qur'an must be eliminated".

44. See for instance Ahmad Lutfi al-Sayyid "Qessat Hayati" (Cairo 1962) pp.69-70 says "Europe need not fear this naive idea...it will not cause any worry to the European colonial power." Also R. Ridha in Al Manar vol.XIV pp.845-846

45. Tarikh vol.I p.34

46. 'Abduh "Al Islam Din Al-'Ilm Wa Al-Madaniyyah" T. Tanahi ed. (Cairo no date) p.84. The book is roughly a new edition with some additions of "Al Islam Wa Al Nasraniyya Ma'a Al 'Ilm Wa Al-Madaniyyah and "Al-Islam Wa Al-Radd Ala Muntagideeh"

47. Tarikh vol.I p.873 and Ali Merad "L'enseignement politique de Muhammad 'Abduh aux Algeriens (1903)" Orient no.28 pp.75-123 especially 121-2

48. The growth of the educational societies such as the Muhammadiyyah in Indonesia and the similar organisations in the Maghrib disguised their politics behind educational activities.

49. Abdal Rahman al Rafi'i "Mustafa Kamil" (Cairo 1939) reports Mustafa Kamil calling this policy the policy of doubletalk.

50. Tarikh vol.I p.977

51. Shaikh Muhammad Bakheet published two pamphlets in 1906 in which this occurs. See Ridha's review of them in Al Manar vol.IX p.153

52. Tarikh vol.I pp.571-2

53. As evidence for this view we note 'Abduh's criticism of Al-Afghani for his excessive honesty. Tarikh vol.I p.896. He says that Al-Afghani should have attempted to satisfy Abu-al-Huda's cupidity and love for glory to blunt his opposition to reform. Surely he would have been prepared not to stand in Abbas's way had he not realised the futility of such a concession.

54. Al-Bahay op.cit. p.150

55. C.f. Zu'ama al Islah pp.311-315. Bernard Lewis "The Middle East and the West" (London 1963) p.104 accepts Al-Bahay's position with regard to the cultural and intellectual influences where he also regards 'Abduh as opposing the Western onslaught in these fields.

56. Vol.V (1902) pp.545-550

57. Quoted by Ridha in Al Manar vol.XI p.98

58. "Al Islam Din Al 'Ilm Wa Al Madaniyyah" p.100 and Al Manar vol.V p.451

59. Al Islam pp.100-101, Al Manar vol.V loc.cit.

60. Al Islam p.101 and Al Manar vol.V p.452

61. Al Islam loc.cit.

62. Guido de Ruggiero "The History of European Liberalism", translated by R.G. Collingwood (Boston 1961). Second printing pp.403-406

63. Tarikh vol.II p.200

64. Tarikh vol.II p. L introduction

65. Tarikh vol.II 1st ed. p.9. 'Abduh says in the introduction to Al Waridat that the truth was clarified for him through "the perfect sage and the personification of Truth our master Sayyid Jamal al-Din Al-Afghani."

66. Orthodox commentators have since shown distate for 'Abduh's liberal attitude towards the various sects. He was strongly criticised for his inclination towards philosophy and tolerance of heresy by Sulaiman Dunia in his "al-Shaikh Muhammad 'Abduh bain al-falasifa wa'l Kalamiyyin" (2 vols Cairo 1958) which is an edition of 'Abduh's commentary. In the introduction, Dunia criticises 'Abduh's tolerance towards heresies. 'Abduh's own student and admirer Rashid Ridha criticised him for precisely the same position in vol.XXII Al Manar pp.736-7. Dunia's views correspond very much with those of Rashid Ridha as to suggest that he might have been aware of Ridha's criticisms.

67. Al Manar op.cit. loc.cit. Ridha says, "He ('Abduh) was one of those deeply immersed in philosophy and mysticism but Allah guided him because of his sincerity to Salaf Mazhab."

68. Although this writer sees little justification in the approach taken by Osman Amin in numerous works to the study of 'Abduh which lacks the developmental method, there is a sense of continuity in 'Abduh's thought. For instance, evidence of liberalism in his Sufi period may be noted in Al Waridat's introduction where he describes himself as having discarded the garb of the sects. Tarikh vol.II 1st ed. p.9. And also in his support for free will in the same work where he disguises his views in this fashion, "Allah is the doer when man is, and man is the doer where Allah is", ibid., p.25

69. Resalat Al-Tawhid p.19 Osman Amin "Ra'id Al Fikr al-Misri" (Cairo 1955) p.62 ff. objects to this view and suggests that Rashid Ridha misrepresented 'Abduh's ideas which in turn led Max Horton to think little of 'Abduh as a philosopher. I find Amin's views more rhetorical than constructive. He states that Muhammad 'Abduh wanted to separate "theology on the one hand from the commonly known philosophy on the other, or if you wish the imperfect knowledge of both philosophy and religion."!

70. Resalat pp.7-8

71. It is not clear how many contributors to Al-'Urwat there were. G. Zaidan reports that Ibrahim Al Mwailhi contributed to it. 'Bunat al Nahdat al'Arabiyyah' a shortened version of his Mashahir al-Sharq, (Cairo no date) p.175. Also it is reported that the Jewish Egyptian Nationalist, James Sanua, took a hand in it. See Gendzier I.L. "James Sanua, and Egyptian Nationalism" M.E.J. vol.XV no.1 p.27. Al-Afghani did contribute to Sanua's own paper Abu Naddara in Paris. See Al Manar vol.XXVI pp.44-5.

72. Tarikh vol.II p.235

73. Summarised from Al Islam Din Al 'Ilm wa Madaniyyah pp.51-66

74. Osman Amin "Muhammad 'Abduh's Apologetic for the Muslim Faith" Minbar Al-Islam vol.II no.1 p.19

75. Resalat al Tawhid the 17th ed. (Cairo 1935) p.52

76. Ibid., p.15

77. Ibid., p.20

78. Ibid., p.19

79. Ibid., p.23

80. Tarikh vol.II pp.37-45

81. See B.D. McDonald "Al Ghazali" E.I. Short p.112 and Moh. bin Cheneb "Ibn Taimiya" p.162

82. Al Manar vol.XXIII p.139. In his obituary of Abdul Karim Salman, Rashid Ridha makes it clear that he was superior to his colleague 'Abduh as regards ability and that 'Abduh's contribution was the result of hard work rather than innate intelligence. This from Rashid Ridha must be taken very seriously.

83. C.f. Nadav Safran op.cit. p.68 ff.

84. As in the case of Al-Farabi with regard to the apocryphal theology of Aristotle.

85. C.f. Al Manar vol.VII p.292. 'Abduh says "There are two books: one created which is the universe, and one revealed which is the Qur'an and only through reason are we guided by this book to understand that one."

86. C.f. Al Manar vol.XXXII p.758 and Tafsir Al Manar vol.I p.252 Cautious 'Abduh puts these views as mere possibilities.

87. Resalat al Tawhid pp.166-80

88. He dismisses the popular outlook on this matter as the view of those who "think that karamats....have become a type of profession in which Walis compete." Ibid., p.205

89. 'Abduh 'Tafsir Juz 'Amma' 3rd ed. (Cairo 1922) p.90 describes the work of prophets as "a reminder to the forgetful as to what Allah has instilled in his own nature."

90. Resalat p.129

91. Ibid., loc.cit.

92. Ibid., p.128

93. Resalat pp.166-67

94. Ibid., p.167

95. Resalat p.169

96. See Surah 3 Verse 112 and in other Surahs

97. Surah 63 Verse 63. "This is the law of Allah as manifested in the fortunes of those before you and the law of Allah shall never alter."

98. Surah 13 Verse 13. "Allah does not change the conditions of people until they change themselves."

99. Resalat pp.176-78

100. Ibid., p.200-1

101. Ibid., p.202

102. Ibid., loc.cit.

103. Ibid., loc.cit.

104. For a discussion of this problem see Ahmad Amin "Dhuha Al Islam" vol.III p.47 ff. also Goldziher "La loi et le dogme" Arabic trans. pp.106-7

105. Resalat p.66

106. C.f. "Al Iji al-Mawaqif" (Istanbul 1286 A.H.) pp.529-535 also Al Shahrastani "Nihayat al Iqdam" A. Guillaume trans.(Oxford 1934) pp.370-396

107. Resalat p.66

108. Ibid., loc.cit.

109. Ibid., loc.cit.

110. Ibid., loc.cit.

111. Ibid., p.69

112. Ibid., pp.71-2

113. Ibid., p.73

114. R. Caspar "Un aspect de la pensée musulmane modern: le renouveau du Mu'tazilism", Mélanges de l'Institut Dominicain d'Études Orientales du Caire, vol.IV pp.141-201 examines the relation between 'Abduh and the Mu'tazilites and labels him a neo-Mu'tazilite.

115. Tarikh vol.II p.37 ff.

116. Tarikh vol.II p.40

117. Ibid., loc.cit.

118. Ibid., p.43

119. Tarikh vol.II p.44

120. Tarikh vol.I p.145

121. Al Manar vol.XXIII pp.232-3

122. Tarikh vol.II pp.166-7

123. Ibid., p.451

124. Tarikh vol.II p.77

125. Ibid., p.76

126. Ibid., p.80

127. Ibid., p.156

128. Ibid., p.130

129. Ibid., p.156 he wrote strongly against the publication of books on magic and traditional epics and advised those who wished to read to read history instead or translations of European novels! See also his articles on "Errors of the Wise" pp.119-132

130. Ibid., p.256

131. Ibid., pp.215-341 especially pp.268-275

132. Ibid., p.5

133. Ibid., pp.352-353

134. Ibid., p.353

135. Ibid., p.507

136. Ibid., p.511

137. Ibid., p.512 This is meant to strengthen the in-group feeling by arousing a degree of antipathy towards the out-group.

138. Ibid., p.517

139. Ibid., p.536

140. Ibid., p.537

141. Ibid., p.537

142. Ibid., p.548

143. Ibid., p.539

144. Ibid., loc.cit.

145. Ibid., p.541

146. Tarikh vol.II p.542. Perhaps this letter was behind the choice of 'Abduh to sit on the Al-Azhar Committee.

147. Ibid., p.545

148. Ibid., loc.cit.

149. Ibid., p.551

150. Tarikh vol.I p.425

151. Tarikh vol.I p.426

152. The booklet is published in toto in Tarikh vol.I pp.430-492.

153. Al Manar vol.VIII pp.234-237. These sentences occur in a letter from Rashid Ridha to Muhsin Al Mulk of India.

154. Tarikh vol.I p.501

155. For the views of Cromer on Islam, which were exceptionally antagonistic, see R.T. Tignor "Lord Cromer on Islam" The Muslim World vol.III pp.223-233

156. Tarikh vol.I p.1034

157. Joseph Schacht "The Law" in "Unity and Variety in Muslim Civilization" G.E. von Grunebaum, editor (Chicago 1955) p.82 says "The impact of European ideas in the Islamic world in the present century, however, has brought about effects of a vastly different, unprecedented and irrevocable kind."

158. Zu'ama al Islah p.114

159. Muhammad 'Ali weakened the political as well as the social position of the ulemas by dividing them and depriving them of their leader, 'Umar Makram. See A. Al-Rafi'i "'Asr Muhammad 'Ali" (Cairo 1930) pp.71-95. Compare his position with that of Selim III and Mahmoud II of Turkey. See U. Heyd "The Ottoman Ulemas and Westernization" in "Studies in Islamic History and Civilization" (Jerusalem 1961) Editor U. Heyd, p.69 ff. The co-operation of the Ulemas in Turkey was important for the introduction of reform.

160. M. Al Bahay op.cit. pp.71-2

161. The essence of the school's attack on Taqlid is an attack on an established Ijma'. See I. Goldziher comments on the Wahabbis in "La Loi et Le Dogme en Islam" Ara.trans. by Muhammad Yusuf Musa et al. 2nd ed. (Cairo 1959) p.269. Also the view of Rashid Ridha concerning Ijma'. See his "Yusr al Islam" (Cairo 1928) p.3

162. Tarikh vol.I p.689 The Transvaal Fatwa was given in reply to a question sent to 'Abduh by an Indian living in that country asking as to whether an animal slaughtered by a Christian would be Halal for a Muslim to eat. 'Abduh answered in the affirmative. His enemies accused him of deviating from Muslim law. Ridha comments on the Transvaal Fatwa saying that "It is supported by the Qur'an, the Sunna and the practice of the Salaf and Khalaf and their words."Charles Adams op.cit. p.76 (Arabic translation) described his fatwas as representing a spirit of independence. This must be qualified by the statement above.

163. Tarikh vol.I p.647

164. Ibid., p.710 ff.

165. Ibid., p.716 and 'Abdul Hafiz al Fasi "Riyad al-Janna aw al mudhish al mutrib" (Fez, A.H. 1350) pp.48-50.

166. Ibid., p.939

167. Al Manar vol.VIII p.416 and Adams op.cit. pp.64-5

168. Al Islam p.138

169. Ibid., p.138

170. Tarikh vol.I p.940

171. Ibid., p.940

172. Ibid., p.941

173. Ibid., p.560

174. Ibid., p.612 fn. 1

175. Ibid., p.557

176. Tarikh vol.II p.163

177. Ibid., p.469

178. Tarikh vol.I p.614

179. Resalat pp.72-3

180. C.f. Osman Amin op.cit. pp.115-6

181. See for instance Osman Amin, "Muhammad 'Abduh" (Cairo 1945). Also by the same author "Ra'id al Fikr al Misri" (Cairo 1955) and numerous other articles by him. Also Muhammad Al Bahay "Muhammad 'Abduh, Erziehungsmethode zum national-bewusstsein" (Hamburg 1936) and his "Modern Muslim Thought". See also J. Schacht "Muhammad 'Abduh" in the Encyclopaedia of Islam. Also Charles Adams "Islam and Modernism in Modern Egypt" pp.20-168 (Arabic trans.)

182. See for instance quotations by Martin Lings in "A Moslem Saint of the Twentieth Century" (London 1961) p.110 where 'Abduh is quoted as saying that "The Sufis are concerned with the cure of hearts and purification from all that obstructs the inward eye." And also "I do not deny, my brother, the existence of many intruders among the Sufis - only too many - who deserve censure, and if you had concentrated on these, no one could have blamed you."

183. Tarikh vol.I pp.928-9 also Tafsir vol.II p.165

184. Tarikh vol.I p.928. H.A.R. Gibb utilises this view in his "An Interpretation of Islamic History" The Muslim World vol.XLV pp.129-133

185. Ibid., p.929

186. See the comment on him by the distinguished conservative Al-Dijwi in Al Manar vol.XXXIII p.678 quoted from Nur Al Islam. There he regrets 'Abduh's tendency to imitate every European idea before it was proved by conclusive evidence.

187. His "Waridat", however, had a positive contribution in influencing Shaikh Ahmad Al-'Alawi. See M. Lings op.cit. p.132 fn. 1

188. His theoretical adoption of the Maliki principle basing legislation concerning mundane matters on utility could not be upheld completely. My contention as to his limited influence is contradicted by several who attribute every development on the law of the Arab or Muslim world to 'Abduh. See for instance N.J. Coulson "A History of Islamic Law" Islamic Surveys no.2 (Edinburgh 1964) pp.210-1 where the writer suggests that reforms in Tunisian and Syrian personal law were based on the views of 'Abduh.

189. See Ahmad "The Intellectual Origins of Egyptian Nationalism" p.91 where he says Al-Jaridah was never a popular paper.

190. Al Manar vol.X p.15

191. Al Manar vol.XXVIII p.588 ff. Charles Adams op.cit. pp.218-221 (Arabic. trans.) Also Osman Amin "Ra'id" pp.209-11

192. C.f. Ahmad Amin "Zu'ama" p.108

193. Shaikh Mustafa Al-Maraghi, Rector of Al Azhar 1928-29 and 1935-45. The reforms introduced under the rectorship of another student of 'Abduh, Shaikh Al-Zawahiri, 1930-35, were inspired more by the example of the University than by 'Abduh. Osman Amin "Ra'id" pp. 212-214 cites Zawahiri as the representative of what he called 'Abduh's religious school. Rashid Ridha would have objected to this as Zawahiri was accused of equivocation in support of 'Abduh. See Al Manar vol.VIII p.114 and "Al Manar Wa Al-Azhar"(Cairo 1935) records a quarrel between Ridha and Al Azhar under Shaikh Zawahiri.

194. C.f. H.A.R. Gibb "Studies on the Civilization of Islam" (London 1962) p.225, Section 13, "Studies in Contemporary Arabic Literature"

195. See for instance his support for monogamy in Tafsir vol.IV pp.348-9

196. See Al Manar vol.XXXI p.352, also Lutfi Al-Sayyid "Qessat Hayati" (Cairo 1962) p.37. Ridha says that 'Abduh saw this book before its publication and corrected the Arabic, but not his second book. Could this account also for the difference between the two books? Rashid Ridha was noticeably unenthusiastic about the view of Qassim Amin and apologised for him by suggesting that he wanted less than he advocated, but demanded more to stimulate his readers who were at the extreme end of conservatism to move into a position of moderation. Had Qassim Amin belonged to a different group Ridha would not have been so mild. Al Manar vol.IV pp.31-32

197. See Rashid Ridha below

198. C.f. A. Hourani op.cit. p.168. The two books appeared in 1899 and 1901 respectively.

199. Osman Amin for instance in "Ra'id" p.222 accuses Ridha of deviating from the path of 'Abduh with regard to Ridha's opposition to Taha Husain and 'Ali Abd Al-Raziq.

200. C.f. H. Laoust "Essai sur les doctrines sociales et politiques d'Ibn Taimiya" (Cairo 1939) p.562

201. Tarikh vol.II pp.388-9

202. Tarikh vol.I p.890. 'Abduh is said to have been careful about voicing his opinions and did not write or say all that he believed.

203. See I. Abu-Lughod "Arab Rediscovery of Europe" (Princeton 1963)p.21

204. A.M. Broadly "How We Defended 'Urabi and His Friends" (London 1884) p.227 reports 'Urabi as saying that 'Abduh's head was more fit for a hat than a turban. Added to this is the bad relationship between 'Abduh and the spokesman of the revolutionary followers of Al-Afghani, Adib Ishaq. See "Documents Inedits" frame no.63. Also Tarikh vol.II p.601. The names were omitted by Rashid Ridha.

205. C.f. M.Al Khafif op.cit. p.555. At a meeting between 'Urabi and 'Abduh, arranged by Blunt, 'Urabi accused 'Abduh of writing with the purpose of pleasing the Khedive.

206. Modern Egypt vol.II p.179

207. To name a few, Abd Allah Al-Nadim,a brilliant speaker and journalist and the orator of the Rebellion, and Adib Ishaq the gifted writer and journalist and the official spokesman of the Constitutionalists. Both in their ways were much more respected than 'Abduh.

208. Tarikh vol.II p.69 ff. especially p.71

209. Charles Adams op.cit. p.11 (Arabic trans.)

210. See for instance M. Al Bahay op.cit. p.150

211. For discussion of the Tafsir see I. Goldziher "Richtungen der Islamischen Koranauslegung" (Leiden 1920) Arabic trans. Al Najjar pp.348 ff. Also J.M.S. Baljon "Modern Muslim Koran Interpretation (1880-1960)" (Leiden 1961) passim, and A.M. Shehatah "Manhaj Al Imam Muhammad 'Abduh fi Tafsir Al Qur'an Al Karim" (Cairo 1963) and J. Jomier "Le Commentaire Coranique du Manar" (Paris 1954).

212. Osman Amin op.cit. p.55 fn. 2 describes this tendency as PRAGMATIC HUMANISM and equates 'Abduh with the leaders of pragmatism such as William James and F.K.S. Schiller. This trend, however, was inspired by Ibn Taimiya rather than by an acquaintance with modern thought.

213. Tarikh vol.I pp.587-8 Ridha states that he had selected 'Abduh for the leadership of the Umma and was determined to build him up for that position.

214. On the activities of the Muhammadiyyah see "Indonesiche Documentatie" vol.III no.XIX p.720 (The Hague 1952). The report gives the numerical strength of the movement as 159,000 and 2,000 schools under its control.

215. Tarikh vol.I p.11

216. As for instance the questions on the attributes of God. See Resalat p.52 where he dismisses the question of whether the attribute should be regarded as separate or identical with the Godhead as being beyond human reason.

217. C.f. Osman Amin "Ra'id" pp.61-2

218. When Shanqiti objected to 'Abduh's Mu'tazilite views in regarding the Qur'an as being created not eternal, 'Abduh had it removed in the second and subsequent editions of the Resalat. See Tarikh vol.I p.963

219. As for instance his evolutionist interpretation of prophecy and religion. He utilizes evolutionist theory in many places of the Tafsir. See Adams op.cit. p.130 ff.

220. 'Abduh was suspected by Cromer "Modern Egypt" vol.II p.181 as being agnostic. His friend, W.S. Blunt, quoted by Thomas J. Assad in "3 Victorian Travellers" (London 1964) pp.98-9 saw him as having no faith in Islam. Many of his contemporary ulemas have also doubted his faith. See also Margoliouth's review of Adams' "Islam and Modernism" in the International Review of Missions vol.XXII pp.421-2

221. Op.cit. p.161 ff. especially p.163

222. Al Islam p.148

223. Ra'id p.61

224. Op.cit. p.163

225. The dispute between Manfaluti and Qassim Amin reported by H.A.R. Gibb op.cit. p.265 is an example of this. It reflects an attitude to social policy on the part of some of 'Abduh's friends lacking in dynamism which is concomitant with the scientific attitude.

226. C.f. N.Safran op.cit. p.69

227. See Charles Adams op.cit. pp.238-9

228. Tafsir Al Manar vol.IV p.350

229. Bashir Ahmad Dar op.cit. p.272 ff.

230. Tarikh vol.I Introduction p.nun. Blunt holds a similar view as shown by his remark to Harold Spender of the "Daily Chronicle" that "'Abduh was like Cardinal Manning, trading religion for politics. He was so clever that he forced the Khedive and Lord Cromer to appoint him head of the ulema in Egypt." Tarikh vol.III p.181

Chapter 3

1. Tarikh vol.I p.1013 states that 'Abduh found followings to himself in Tunisia and Algeria who knew him only through Al Manar.

2. Al Manar XXVIII p.65 also Adams op.cit. p.169

3. Adams op.cit. pp.169-70

4. Al Manar vol.XXXIII p.354

5. Ibid,, pp.357-372. No doubt he was prompted into publishing these aspects, previously unknown in his life, as a sort of self-defence against accusations by the traditionalists of heresy.

6. Op.cit. p.354

7. Tarikh Vol.I p.85 and Adams op.cit. p.171

8. Tarikh vol.I p.84

9. Ibid., pp.85-87 contains the letter and commentary. The quotation is from p.82

10. Ibid., pp.996-7

11. Ibid., p.1000

12. Ibid., p.1001

13. Ibid., p.1022

14. Al Manar vol.I 2nd ed. p.4 and Adams op.cit. p.172

15. Al Manar vol.I 2nd ed. pp.11 and 12

16. Goldziher as quoted by Adams op.cit. p.173

17. Tarikh vol.I p.514

18. Perhaps 'Abduh was himself responsible for this delusion by invariably approving what Ridha wrote in his name. Ibid., p.1018

19. See for instance Al Manar vol.XXVII p.622 where he quotes an unnamed Jew stating that the University represented anti-religious trends. Similar views are also held by a more recent writer, namely Dr Al Bahay op.cit. p.101

20. Al Manar vol.VIII p.478. Also Adams op.cit. p.176

21. Al Manar vol.VIII p.478

22. Al Manar vol.XXXII p.317

23. Al Manar vol.XXXIII p.534. Rashid Ridha mentions that Maraghi asked him to write a report on the advisability of an Azhar magazine, which he did. He was not, however, invited to hold any official post.

24. See Ridha "Al Manar wa Al- Azhar" (Cairo 1353 A.H.) serialised in Al Manar vols. XXXI and XXXII

25. Tarikh vol.I pp.620-1 relates the story that Isma'il requested Rifa'a Al-Tahtawi to persuade the ulema to codify the Shari'a law but he refused. (Isma'il in reality did not need any such codification as Muslim law had already been codified in the famous Majalah and was being applied in Ottoman domains).

26. C.f. J.N.D. Anderson "The Shari'a and Civil Law" The Islamic Quarterly vol.I p.29

27. Al Manar vol.XII p.239

28. Al Manar vol.XIV p.343

29. Rashid Ridha, the introduction to "Al Mughni" by Al Muwaffaq (Cairo 1925) p.15

30. Al Mughni p.16

31. Al Manar vol.XIV p.344

32. Al Mughni p.18

33. Al Manar vol.IV p.210

34. Ibid., loc.cit.

35. Al Manar vol.IX p.745. The treatise proper runs to p.770.

36. Ibid., loc.cit.

37. Al Manar vol.XXX p.704 ff. Ridha argues against M. Azmi who claimed that some of the ulema considered that Maslaha superceded even unambiguous texts. Ridha rejects both the contents of the claim and that any of the ulema supported it. As we know Al Tawfi put Maslaha above the texts. (See Mustafa Zaid "Al Maslaha Fi Al Tashri' Al Islami" (Cairo 1954) pp.63-4. Early in the century (1909) Ridha approvingly published Al Tawfi's treatise and appeared to support the same view in his "Muhawarat al Muslih Wa Al Muqallid" Al Manar vol.IV. This was in the heyday of liberalism. His position appears to have changed somewhat in the twenties and thirties where the emphasis on the authority of the texts and the restriction on Maslaha as an independent operative concept has become marked. This may be a reaction to the excesses of the modernists and westernizers. This line of analysis, however, will not be pursued further since Ridha failed to reflect these two phases in his rulings on specific issues.

38. Ridha "Yusr Al Islam" (Cairo 1928) Introduction pp. b, g and h

39. Ibid., Introduction p. z, a, y and e

40. Ibid., p.3

41. Ibid., loc.cit.

42. Ibid., loc.cit.

43. Ibid., loc.cit.

44. Al Manar Vol.XXIX p.424

45. His book "Muhawarat al Muslih Wa Al Muqallid" relies heavily on Ibn Al-Qayyim the Hanbali scholar as he himself admits in the introduction (Al Manar vol.IX p.823) whereas his "Yusr Al Islam" is a collection of opinions largely drawn from the same school.

46. Yusr Al Islam pp.17 -18

47. Ibid., p.79

48. Ibid., loc.cit. Rashid Ridha gives the authority to Ulu Al Amr in wordly affairs. Obedience to them is conditioned by them not contradicting the law.

49. Ibid., pp.78-79

50. Ibid., pp.37-75. He quotes approvingly from Ibn Al Qayyim.

51. Al Manar vol.XIV p.23

52. Al Manar vol.X p.287 ff. and vol.XXIII p.187 ff. and in various places in Tafsir Al Manar. See Jomier "Le commentaire" p.290

53. Al Manar vol.XXVII p.346 also vol.VII pp.384-388 and vol.VIII p.588

54. Al Manar vol.VII p.28

55. Yusr Al Islam pp.72-73

56. Nida' Ila Al-jins Al-Latif (Cairo 1351 A.H.) p.121

57. Al Manar vol.XXX p.610 fn.

58. "Al Wahy Al Muhamadi" 3rd ed. p.283

59. Al Manar vol.XXX p.780

60. M.Kerr "Rashid Ridha and Legal Reforms" The Muslim World vol.I p.180

61. Al Manar XXIV p.111

62. Al Manar vols.XXXI and XXXII carry the arguments between Ridha and Al Dijwi. The articles were later published in the separate book "Al Manar Wa Al-Azhar".

63. The effort of Al Ghazali in reconciling Sufism and orthodoxy may be cited as an example. See H.A.R. Gibb "An Interpretation of Islamic History" The Muslim World vol.XIV pp.129-130.

64. See for instance Al Manar vol.VIII p.620 where he says "The people have no longer any need for most of the theories contained in Ash'arite books."

65. Al Wahy Al Muhamadi 3rd ed. p.360

66. Ibid., pp.8 and 9

67. Ibid., p.10

68. Ibid., p.17 ff.

69. Ibid., pp.19 and 20

70. Ibid., p.62. The Qur'an is, however, exempt from this generalisation as it does not as a miraculous book tax the scientific mind in the same way as, say, the miracle of the break-up of the moon.

71. Ibid., p.255 ff.

72. Ibid., p.289 ff.

73. Al Manar vol.XXIII p.189

74. On Al Ghazali see Al Manar vol.V pp.762-768 and on the Ash'ari see vol.IX pp.109-110. There Rashid Ridha attributes this view to the later followers of Ash'ari and not to him. Under the influence of nineteenth century rationalism, Muslim reformists and modernists accepted the principle of causality without looking deeper into its implications. (The probable exception is Ahmad Khan). 'Abduh and Rashid Ridha did not appreciate fully the difficulty of the Ash'arites. For discussion of the problem of causality in Muslim thought see Majid Fakhry "Islamic Occasionalism" (London 1958) pp.56 ff. et passim.

75. Al Manar vol.VIII p.620

76. Al-Wahy p.199. The idea put forward previously by Dr M.T. Sidqi in Al Manar vol.XII p.120

77. Ibid., p.62

78. Ibid., p.201

79. Al Manar vol.I p.274 and Adams op.cit. p.186

80. Al Manar vol.XIV pp.809-810

81. Ibid., p.810

82. Ibid., p.809

83. Ibid., p.813

84. Ibid., pp.812-816

85. Ibid., p.811

86. Ibid., pp.786 and 801 and Adams op.cit. p.188. These ideas were not without influence on the reform of Al Azhar.

87. Al Manar vol.XXXV. The obituary of Rashid Ridhá by his cousin Sayyid Abd Al-Rahman 'Asim p.486.

88. Al Manar vol.XXX p.115 ff.

89. Guido de Ruggiero, op.cit. p.93 ff. and p.158 ff.

90. Tarikh vol.I p.915. Ridha says that he and 'Abduh aimed at Arab independence but without foreign interference or enmity with the Turks.

91. The suspicions surrounding Rashid Ridha reached far and wide. See for instance the recently uncovered letter from Abu Al Kalam Azad to Ridha accusing him of supporting the decentralization party and thus betraying his previously announced support for the Caliphate. A. Al-Nimr "Mawlana Azad Wal Khilafa" Majallat Al Azhar vol. XXXV Oct.1963 p.307

92. See for instance the arguments between Rashid Ridha and the Nationalist Party, notably A. Jawish concerning the "Madrassat Al Da'wah" Al Manar vol.XIV pp.40 and 121 ff.

93. See his comments Al Manar vol.XXIII p.695

94. See for instance Al Manar vol.XXXIII pp.317-8 where he suggests an elaborate Sayyid university to train specialists in all the sciences and arts "religious and worldly and the skills upon which civilization is based in this age." He ends thus "Only then will the Umma know that the Sayyids are her masters and leaders." He puts a similar suggestion in his writing on "Al Khilafat" where he advises the creation of a mujtahid school to prepare Quraishis to hold the office of Caliph. Al Manar vol.XXIV pp.110-111.

95. He took part in the "Decentralization Party" and may have participated in conspiracies against the Ottomans. After the war he played a prominent part in Syrian politics which he records in Al Manar vols. XXII and XXIII under the title "The Syrian Journey" and also "The European Journey". Abd Al-Muta'l Al-Saidi in his "Al Mujaddidun Fi'l Islam Min'al Qarn Al Awwal Ila'l Rabi Ashar" (Cairo no date) pp.542-3 reports Rashid Ridha as supporting King Fuad's claim to the Caliphate. This would have implemented the ideas of W.S. Blunt who aimed at creating an Arab Caliphate under the aegis of the British. Since Blunt's ideas expounded in his "The Future of Islam" (London 1882) were derived from 'Abduh's (see A. Hourani op.cit. p.155) it is conceivable that Al Sa'idi's report is correct. This need not reflect on Ridha. In the desperate situation after the fall of the Caliphate, Ridha might have felt that its continuation even on such a basis was better than its complete disappearance. The relationship between Sharif Hussain and Ridha is also a source of confusion. There is no doubt that Ridha supported Hussain's original moves until it became evident that the British had defaulted in their promises.

96. (Cairo 1341 A.H.) Translated into French by H. Laoust under the title "Le califat dans la doctrine de Rashid Ridha" (Beirut 1938). References are made to the Al Manar serialisation.

97. Al Manar vol.XXIII p.729

98. Ibid., loc.cit.

99. Ibid., pp.730-752

100. Al Manar vol.XXIV p.352

101. Ibid., p.353

102. Ibid., loc.cit.

103. Ibid., p.353

104. Al Manar vol.XXIV p.354. Ridha reports the encounter between 'Abhud Al-Dawlah the Turk and the Abbasid Caliph Al-Ta'i'. The Turk, while showing all veneration and respect, divested the Caliph of all his authority. This Rashid Ridha appears to suggest was done voluntarily by the Caliph. Had the Caliph had a better moral fibre, Rashid Ridha appears to imply, then he would have retained the powers of his office.

105. Ibid., p.355

106. Ibid., loc.cit.

107. Ibid., p.646

108. Ibid., pp.460-461

109. Ibid., p.353

110. Ibid., p.373

111. Ibid., p.198

112. Al Manar vol.XXIII p.731 where he quotes the Tradition "whoever dies not having given Bay'a dies a Jahiliyya death."

113. Al Manar vol.XIV p.9

114. Ibid., p.13

115. Tafsir vol.V p.190

116. Ibid., pp.190-1. These views are attributed to 'Abduh. Rashid Ridha also subscribed to them.

117. Al Manar vol.XIV pp.59-60

118. Al Manar vol.XXIV p.59

119. Tafsir vol.V p.190

120. Al Manar vol.XXIV pp.61-2

121. Ibid., p.48 ff.

122. Al Manar vol.XXIII pp.738-744

123. Al Manar vol.XXIV p.110

124. Ibid., p.119

125. C.f. Malcolm Kerr "Arab Radical Notions of Democracy" in Middle Eastern Affairs No.3, St Antony's Papers no.16 p.15

126. Tafsir vol.V p.200 and Al Manar vol.XIV p.14

127. Tafsir vol.V p.199. These views are 'Abduh's but Ridha subscribes to them also.

128. Emile Tyan "Institutions du droit public musulman" vol.II: Sultanat et califat (Paris 1956) p.264 fn.2

129. Louis Gardet "La cite musulmane: vie sociale et politique" (Paris 1954) p.352

130. For an evaluation of Al Mawardi's theory see Gibb "Studies on the Civilization of Islam" (london 1962) pp.151-164 especially pp.162-3

131. Al Manar vol.XXIV pp.259-261

132. Al Manar vol.XII pp.608-9

133. Al Manar vol.XXIV p.62

134. Al Manar vol.XIV pp.197-200

135. Ibid., p.199

136. During this period the conflict between Egypt and Britain was manifested in a triangular power struggle: the British, the Palace and the Wafd.

137. See G. Kampffmeyer in H.A.R. Gibb "Whither Islam?" Ch.3 (London 1932). Also Al Manar vol.XXVIII p.788 ff. Ridha says he thought of inaugurating one during the War but the military authorities refused permission.

138. Al-Manar vol.XXVI pp.100-104

139. N.Safran op.cit. pp.165-180

140. S. Arslan says "Although he (Ridha) may not be the equal of 'Abduh and Afghani in the logical sciences ('Ulum 'Aqliyyah) he outstripped them both in the volume of writing." "Rashid Ridha Aw Ikha' Arba'ina Sanatan" (Damascus 1937) p.255.

141. C.f. Tafsir vol.I p.284

142. See reference to this in Al Manar vol.XXXIII pp.529-530.

143. See for instance his bitter dispute with the Shi'is. Al Manar vol.IX pp.424 ff.

144. _Al Manar_ vol.IX p.20

145. C.f. R.A. Hourani, Introduction to J.M. Ahmed, op.cit.p.X

146. Al-Afghani versus Renan, 'Abduh versus Hanotaux and Renan, Rashid Ridha versus Dermingham, even Al-Afghani's _"Al Radd"_ etc. may be regarded as a discussion of European ideas.

147. _Tarikh_ vol.I p.799

Conclusion

It can be seen how far removed in crucial areas certain Muslim groupings are from the common sense, middle of the road observance of Islam that the Quran prescribes. Muslims are sometimes plagued by a warped mentality towards, and twisted interpretation of, their Islamic heritage. In spite of this, and broadly speaking, at the grass roots level Islam will always be in good health in the sense that its individual adherents believe passionately in the basic message of the Quran. But if that message is to succeed in the way it was meant to for proper organisation of the masses today there must be put in place assorted structures allowing the citizens of Muslim countries a say in effective governance of their lives, through meaningful institutions. In other words, there must be Islamic democracy - along with the mindset for it (which will need time to develop and mature) - which naturally includes protection for minorities. Nowhere in the so- called Islamic world does there exist this democratic consultation process in the genuine sense of the term. Dictatorship, corruption, incompetence, mis- management, over-population, poverty and ignorance are the abiding influences of the day. Looking to the Middle East, for the present, the region is doomed. The celebrated author Saïd K. Aburish in his book, *A Brutal Friendship - The West and the Arab Elite* (published by Indigo in 1998), ably demonstrates the history behind the current impasse. Muhammad Asad in his work, *The Principles of State and Government in Islam* (first published in 1961 by University of California Press with a new edition in 1980 published by Dar al-Andalus Limited, Gibraltar) gives the best guidance available as to how to begin giving the 'Islamic' countries an honorable code of laws (sharia) and hope for efficient self-government.

It is not therefore, necessarily, the proper thing to do to look to the 'Islamic' world for guidance on Islam or how it should be practiced. This is why Zaki Badawi was so keen to put into effect a 'British Islam.'

At the end of the Second World War the British were, of course, kicked out of India which was followed in 1947 by partition and independence for India and Pakistan. The Muslim state of Pakistan had been created. Nonetheless Asians soon came to the United Kingdom in large numbers, happy to embrace the opportunities offered here. They had rejected their former homelands. The new arrivals brought with them, though, their cultural backwardness and in the case of the Muslim migrants religious practices they thought, wrongly, were Islamic. These same cultural and religious practices, in no small measure, are still with us in Britain today (along with a new wave of zealotry). The Asians, for the time being, can hardly be admired as a yardstick for the Islamic ideal. Only after (as Zaki Badawi thought) a couple of generations, when Indian and Pakistani cultural baggage has been jettisoned, will things improve. When that time arrives, the Muslims will be better equipped to challenge the decadent ways that liberal Britain has so obviously been infected with.

Omar Hussein Ibrahim